Modern European Criticism and Theory

D1344444

Also available:

Modern British and Irish Criticism and Theory
Modern North American Criticism and Theory

Modern European Criticism and Theory

A Critical Guide

Edited by Julian Wolfreys

Edinburgh University Press

First published as part of *The Edinburgh Encyclopaedia
of Modern Criticism and Theory* in 2002

Edinburgh University Press Ltd
22 George Square, Edinburgh

Typeset in Ehrhardt by
Hewer Text UK Ltd, Edinburgh, and
printed and bound in Great Britain by
Antony Rowe Ltd, Chippenham, Wilts

A CIP record for this book is available from the British Library

ISBN-10 0 7486 2449 X (paperback)
ISBN-13 978 0 7486 2449 2

Contents

Preface

Modern European Criticism and Theory offers the reader a comprehensive critical overview of the widespread and profound contest of ideas within European 'thought', focusing primarily on the major voices in poetics, philosophy, linguistics and psychoanalysis, as well as those in what have become in the twentieth century literary and cultural studies from the Enlightenment to the present day. Examining how conceptions of subjectivity, identity and gender have been interrogated, over fifty essays critically assess the ways in which we think, see and act in the world, as well as the ways in which we represent such thought psychologically, politically, and philosophically and culturally.

Focusing on a broad range of singular critical voices, and to a great degree attending to the major conceptual interrogations, reorientations and, subsequently, movements and transitions in thought that have taken place as a result of the irreversible effects occasioned by those particular voices, the present volume offers successive narratives of transformation and translation. Charting various radical interventions in thinking concerning fundamental philosophical, political and poetic issues related to matters of being, meaning and identity, the essays provide themselves an intervention in and a continuation of that radical tradition. The narrative that unfolds from the essays of this volume and their interwoven yet discontinuous threads amounts to the unravelling of a cultural, historical and epistemological tapestry by which the most fundamental matters of ontology and the poetics and politics of being have come to be perceived. Whether presenting itself in terms that are primarily linguistic, psychoanalytic, political or philosophical, the historical narrative of critical discourse in and across Europe and its subsequent translation into the practices and discourses of modern criticism and theory, so-called, reveals itself here as one of continuous upheavals, shifts and processes of decentring contest. What is at stake in such contest, tension and conflict are the very grounds of thinking about thinking, in historically and culturally grounded and material ways concerning how the human subject can speak of its specificity, its experience and its singular encounters with all that inform and articulate its subjectivity.

While foregrounding the practice and theory of literary and cultural criticism in many of its historically specific guises, the present volume also provides extensive critical coverage of the related contextual discourses that inform those issues, and out of which criticism has developed in the guises that it now assumes. What the reader will therefore come to understand is that criticism cannot be thought separately from the many forms and traditions of thought, whether scientific or poetic, political or rhetorical, semantic or epistemological, which have been sustained in so diverse and fruitful a fashion as this collection suggests. The essays of this collection recognize the interanimation between discourses and cultures of thinking, and so explore matters of hybridity, translation and border crossings between discourses and cultures, between disciplines and forms of analysis and investigation. There is, in European thought, no one identity, no one articulation that seamlessly and homogeneously gathers together in undifferentiated form a discourse that could, itself, be described as European; and yet it is perhaps the very resistance to such ontological homogeneity and *in-difference* that is a strikingly 'European' feature of that which goes by the name of critical thinking, as these essays intimate.

Each of the essays thus chart and trace processes of translation and transformation, of hospitality to the other as well as attempted assimilations of that very alterity. In welcoming the other into one's home, across the threshold, boundary or border as a gesture of hospitality and welcome, there are also signs, if not of hostility, then of a hermeneutics of suspicion. Intrinsic to this welcome, inextricably tied up with any such act, is a desire to render the foreign, the other, that which is different, less strange or threatening perhaps. Hospitality assumes both tolerance and neutralization, and it seeks to maintain a degree of mastery through taking in just enough of the other into its system, immunizing itself if you will, in order to allow it to carry on with business as usual. What goes here by the name of 'European' thinking, or 'European' critical discourse, is shown by the critics who have contributed to this volume to be both negotiations of the very kind just outlined and yet, simultaneously, on the part of many of the critics, poets, writers and philosophers of whom they speak, a rigorous critique, and, occasionally, a 'deconstruction' of the very grounds on which the accommodation of difference and otherness takes place.

Such incorporations are not without consequences, without the rise of contest and conflict; and also, not inconsequent to the encounters are the misreadings and mispercep-tions, the avoidances, the non-reception, and even occasionally the hostilities that provide some of the more visible punctuations within the history of criticism and what we misname theory. The articles in the present volume chart and reflect on the accommodations and resistances, the tolerances and intolerances. In this, each article concerns itself not only with the formalist contours and epistemological parameters of a particular discourse, it also acknowledges the cultural, historical and ideological specificities of the emergence and transformation of criticism. The reader of this collection will not – *not necessarily* – learn how to read like, say, Paul Ricoeur or Luce Irigaray, Julia Kristeva or Michel Foucault (though each of the critics chosen to write about their subjects have been selected for their recognized ability to be faithful to the contours of the other's thought in its translation for the purposes of the present volume). The reader will, however, come to recognize *how* such thinkers have made it possible to open oneself to the most generous of accommodations while, at the same time, questioning what arrives so as to maintain its spirit, while effecting radical change.

Together and individually, the essays offer to the reader a view of the extent to which the discourses of philosophy, poetics, politics, aesthetics, linguistics and psychoanalysis have become part of the densely imbricated textures of critical practice. Furthermore, while remaining aware of the importance of the various contexts within and out of which criticism has grown, the essays herein also concern themselves with the equally important issue of cross-fertilization between the various academic and intellectual cultures under consideration. *Modern European Criticism and Theory* thus provides the reader with a comprehension of the key issues with the intention of demonstrating that those issues and the fields into which they are woven are marked by, even as they themselves re-mark, an unending and vital process of hybridization – of methodologies, disciplines, discourses and interests. In this, when taken together the essays comprising the present volume can be seen to question implicitly the very condition of the practice and theory of criticism itself or indeed, any propadeutic separation of notions of theory and practice.

In presenting the various facets of critical activity, there have been omissions, doubtless. This is true of the shaping of any narrative. Even so, it is hoped that the overall contours of critical thinking and discourse in Europe are not misrepresented, and that, concomitantly, the dominant hegemonies and cultures of thought in their particular historical and cultural moments are neither distorted nor in some other manner misrepresented (beyond, that is, any inescapable and inevitable translation process). It has to be said that if there is no such thing as a pure discourse, self-sufficient and closed off from influences, confluences and even contaminations, there is also no such thing as a finite determination, context or group of contexts. One obviously cannot speak of either purely national, conceptual, or universal determinations; equally one cannot ascribe to critical thinking a finite or unchanging condition. The very definition of literary criticism implicit here is of an identity always in crisis, and always accommodated as such in its mutability. Intellectual cultures, like literary genres, have moments of historical ascendance, ideological transformation, and hegemonic dominance. Appearing to lose that dominance, going 'out of fashion' as is sometimes perceived in the more journalistic of interpretations, traces, influences, remain, continuing to be transformed, and so to effect the cultures of criticism in which the reader is presently situated. It is with such issues, such processes and cultures of transformation and translation that *Modern European Criticism and Theory* is purposely involved.

Julian Wolfreys

1. René Descartes (1596–1650) and Baruch Spinoza (1632–1677): Beginnings

In his 1949 essay, 'The Mirror Stage' (1966), Jacques Lacan, attempting to take his distance from existentialism, divided philosophy into two camps: those that took the *Cogito* as their starting point and those that did not (this statement was repeated many times after, including by some of France's most important thinkers, among them Foucault and Canguilhem). With such a statement, Lacan located the origins of French or even European philosophy not in Husserl, Hegel or even Kant, but in the conflictual field of seventeenth-century philosophy, specifically in the opposing doctrines of René Descartes and Baruch Spinoza. This may come as a surprise to the Anglo-American reader for whom the only conflict associated with the seventeenth-century is that between rationalism and empiricism and for whom Spinoza is a secondary or even tertiary figure, a minor Cartesian only recently admitted into the canon of philosophers deemed worthy of scholarly attention. Further, while Descartes's *Meditations* is well-known even outside the field of philosophy, his name is primarily associated with his proof of God's existence and, through Locke, the doctrine of innate ideas, neither of which are particularly relevant to the concerns of modern French philosophy and theory. How then are we to understand the sense in which the conflict between these two philosophers (assuming that their relation is one of conflict) constitutes a 'beginning'?

There is no question of identifying a French or even continental reading, or readings, of Descartes and Spinoza which would then become the correct interpretation in counterposition to the Anglo-American. Nor is it a question of simply multiplying readings as if, without any true relation to their object, they can never be any other than projections of the culture or historical moment in which they emerge. Instead, we will argue that specific historical moments impose on philosophical texts a historically determined (and therefore identifiable) grid that in turn determines what in a text is visible or invisible, what is compelling and what devoid of interest. There are thus no readings independent of texts and no texts independent of reading. Both the text and its history are equally real, equally material; both must be explained.

Let us begin with Descartes: what did twentieth-century French philosophy select from Descartes and what determined this selection? The fact that Lacan could use a declension of a Latin verb, *cogito* ('I think'), as a noun, suggests very clearly the importance of the first two Meditations. In a very important sense (and Lacan himself, among others, would later have occasion to comment on this), the first two sections of the *Meditations* were abstracted from the text as a whole and even more importantly from the chain of arguments in which they were simply a preliminary step, the nature of which would be modified in the course of the demonstration. Indeed, the meticulous reconstruction of Descartes's 'order of reasons' by Martial Guéroult in a famous commentary many times the length of the *Meditations* themselves, showed beyond any doubt the impressionistic sketchy quality of such readings. The fact remains, however, that the reduction of the *Meditations*, or even Cartesian philosophy as a whole, to 'the Cogito' was not simply 'false', that is without any relation to the text, and it remains to be seen to what extent such a reading was authorized by the *Meditations* themselves.

One might simply read the first paragraph of the *Meditations* to discover what made Descartes so controversial in his own time and so much a contemporary of the twentieth century: the ubiquity of the first person pronoun 'I'. A work devoted to the establishment of the 'first philosophy', that is to the construction of an adequate foundation for philosophical and scientific inquiry, would customarily have avoided reference to the individuality of the philosopher, his fears, hopes and feelings, for fear of being dismissed as outside the universal. Indeed, a tradition dating from Aristotle, and which includes medieval Christian, Jewish and Islamic philosophy, regarded rationality or truth as necessarily collective in nature, residing in the totality of an ever present archive of authoritative works. An individual, in order to escape the particularity of individual existence, had to accede to and participate in this archive to formulate universally valid propositions. Descartes shocked his contemporaries by declaring the necessity of precisely the opposite course, that is of 'demolishing completely' and rejecting as false everything contained in this archive. Instead of referring to a tradition of inquiries and findings, he would begin his reasoning from a position of absolute certainty, not simply the position agreed upon by a majority as valid or true, but a position that could not be doubted.

What is perhaps even more significant is not merely that Descartes regarded it necessary for him as an individual (and it must be as an individual, since the mere existence of other minds – how does he know that the people he sees are not automatons? – and, at the extreme, anything outside of himself must be regarded as illusory until proven otherwise) to cast off all prior knowledge and learning, but that such an action was even possible. 'I am here quite alone,' he announces at the outset of the *Meditations*, a kind of Robinson Crusoe in philosophy, but who, unlike the hapless sailor, has by an act of will removed himself to an island far from others where he can reconstruct a world of knowledge from zero, sure of the foundations that he himself has built. Here it is necessary to step outside the *Meditations* and refer to a later work, *The Passions of the Soul* (1646), that explains in detail what is presupposed in the *Meditations*, namely the ability of the soul (*l'âme* or *mens*) to free itself from the world that envelopes it. Such a freedom is not easily won: 'my habitual opinions keep coming back, and, despite my wishes, they capture my belief which is, as it were, bound over to them as a result of long occupation and the law of custom' (*Meditations*, 15). In this way, the milieu or context of the philosopher is conceived of as external to him, to be accepted or rejected in part or as a totality by a mind endowed with the proper strength of will. Indeed, there is an ethical and even political dimension to the act by which one frees oneself from comfortable illusions and displays the fortitude necessary to endure the absolute solitude that is the necessary, if temporary, consequence of systematic doubt. This is what might be called the heroic moment in Cartesian philosophy: at least it would be regarded as such by philosophers as important to twentieth-century thought as Husserl and Sartre.

He will undertake to destroy the very foundations that support him, risking, as his critic Pascal noted, falling into an abyss in his attempt to find that one certain point from which adequate knowledge can be constructed and without which all hope of distinguishing truth from falsehood is lost. First, the evidence of the senses: although sometimes faulty, do they not present some indubitable truths? In a passage that occasioned a lively debate between two of France's most important philosophers (Derrida and Foucault), Descartes argues that it would appear 'quite impossible' to doubt 'that I am here, sitting by the fire, wearing a winter dressing-gown, holding this piece of paper in my hands' (*Meditations*, 13). Impossible, unless he entertains the idea that he is one of those madmen who believe that they are kings even as they languish in a dungeon. While such a notion might appear far-fetched, does not everyone, sane and mad alike, experience as real what upon awakening is revealed only to have been a dream? Are we not compelled then to doubt all that we glean from the senses? Fortunately (or so it appears for a brief moment), the subtraction of that which is derived from the senses leaves an important body of truths remaining. Surely, two and two equal four whether I am sane or mad, awake or asleep, just as a square necessarily has four sides? Here, Descartes will call upon God to sustain him in his doubt: if there is an omnipotent God, may it not be possible that He has only made it appear to our philosophical pilgrim that there is an earth, sun, sky, extended things, shapes, lines and places when in fact there are none? And if God in his infinite goodness could not be capable of such deception, is it not equally possible to entertain the idea of an evil genius, as powerful as God, but as evil as He is good? He now finds himself in the midst of a boundless, bottomless sea. Or so he fears: in fact, as is well known, doubt presupposes something that doubts. If I doubt, or think, I must exist. I may not have a body, there may not be an external world, but I nevertheless exist as a thinking thing. Descartes has not only established the priority of the individual over the collective, but of the mind over the body.

There is nothing as revolutionary in Cartesian philosophy as the notion that the knowledge of the soul must precede not only a knowledge of other bodies, but even our own body. From now on, we cannot know anything without accounting for how we know it: how do we know that we know? A study of the physical world must therefore begin with an inquiry into the soul, specifically into how it forms clear and distinct, i.e. adequate, ideas. As we have seen, the soul can know itself only by experiencing its independence from extended substance, Descartes's term for the material world; it must understand itself as a substance essentially free from space and time, and from the determinations proper to physical existence. The universe is thus comprised of two substances, the *res cogitans* and the *res extensa*, thinking substance and extended substance or thought and matter. While Descartes's ecclesiastical adversaries charged him with having thus rendered spirit (and God) irrelevant to the physical world, he argued that this freedom allowed for the possibility of the mind's mastery over itself and the bodily impulses to which it was subject.

These positions proved decisive for European philosophy. No longer was it possible to know the world without first understanding the mind that knows, which thus might appear as either the condition of or impediment to knowledge. As Guéroult has argued, some of the major currents in the subsequent history of philosophy are defined by their response to this problem. Kant argued that we cannot know the things in themselves independently of the mind that knows them; instead we must remain content with the world as it appears to us, the phenomenal world. Husserl's phenomenology 'solved' this problem by means of a 'bracketing' (*epoche*) of the world independent of our knowledge and experience, and positing an original agreement between the world as it is and the world as it appears to us. Further, the idea of a self, the 'I' of the 'I think' (*cogito*), finally separate from the world and free, as spiritual substance (*res cogitans*), from merely material determinations and able thus to direct itself, was central to the development of existentialism, especially that of Sartre.

As one of France's most important Spinoza scholars has argued, from the point of view of the perspective just outlined, Spinoza can be seen as Descartes's other, opposing his philosophy point for point. Unlike Descartes, Spinoza begins his major work, the *Ethics*, not with the I that thinks, but, on the contrary, with a set of propositions designed to prove that thought and extension or spirit and matter cannot be separate substances. The topic of Part I is, significantly, not the individual or even man, but God. Spinoza's arguments, nominally devoted to a proof of God's perfection, struck nearly all his contemporaries as a thinly disguised atheism. Drawing on theological controversies, many of which had their origins in medieval and early modern Judaism (Spinoza was born into the Sephardic community in Amsterdam, was educated in its institutions and was finally excommunicated for heresy in 1656), he argued that the notion of God as spirit, prior to matter, creating the material world and endowing it with meaning, was incompatible with the idea of God's greatness. How could spirit 'create' matter out of itself (especially if matter was regarded as inferior to spirit)? How, indeed, could there have been a moment of creation if God were truly omnipresent and all-powerful, that is a moment prior to which a part of God did not exist? How could what is eternally perfect have been lacking? Referring to a distinction between the actual and the possible, as if the latter were a kind of pre-existence, did nothing to solve the problem. The eternal and infinite has no origin, no beginning; all that can exists does: thus, 'whatever is, is in God and nothing can be or be conceived without God' (*Ethics* I, 15), just as God has no existence prior to or outside of creation. God is, according to Spinoza, an immanent cause, entirely coincident with what exists, his will nothing other than the necessity that governs nature as a whole. At the beginning of Part IV, Spinoza would go so far as to use the phrase that made him infamous: 'God, or nature', (*Ethics* IV, Preface), treating the two terms as interchangeable. It is not difficult to see how Spinoza's numerous critics regarded him as having made God disappear into creation, essence into existence and spirit into matter.

As if this were not enough to earn the enmity of theologians from all faiths, Spinoza, in the Appendix to Part I, seeks to explain the causes of the faulty conception of God that is so common and indeed so powerful that it will likely hinder the comprehension of his argument. People insist on regarding God as a transcendent cause, a cause that existed before the world and which brought the world into being to fulfil a pre-existing purpose. Such an idea is common precisely because it constitutes a projection of human experience on God (or Nature): we tend to imagine God in our own image. Spinoza, however, does not stop at the idea that the nearly universal conception of God is nothing more than an idol of human creation that reflects not the divine but the image of its creator. What philosophers in the latter half of the twentieth century have found so provocative in Spinoza's work is the argument that this projected belief in human beings as creators whose actions are undertaken with an end in view is itself false, an illusion heavy with consequences not simply for philosophy but for political and social life as well. We believe we are the causes of our actions and words, Spinoza argues, only because we are conscious of our desires to do or say something, but ignorant of the causes of our desires. We so need to feel that we are masters of ourselves in the face of a world consisting of an infinite concatenation of causes and effects whose course is indifferent to us, our welfare and happiness, that we imagine ourselves in our supposed freedom and transcendence to be the mirror of our creator who thus functions as the guarantor of our delusions of freedom and self-mastery.

Spinoza takes up these problems in detail in Part III of the *Ethics*, where he begins by denouncing the notion that the human world transcends nature, a spiritual realm of freedom in opposition to the necessity that governs the material world. It is this conception above all that prevents us from understanding our emotions which for Spinoza are governed by the same necessity as nature. Anger, hatred and jealousy, like rain and wind, are no less necessary for being inconvenient. The most common form of the notion that the human is outside of nature is our idea of the relation of body and mind. Spinoza's theory is often referred to as parallelism: mind and body are absolutely parallel and whatever happens in or to one also happens in or to the other. Parallelism, however, is not only a term Spinoza never uses, it also fails to convey the fundamental nature of his rejection of any separation of mind and body. For him they are the same: in the same way that he can write God or Nature, he might have said spirit or matter, mind or body. In a certain sense mind disappears into body and thought into action. We believe that the mind, at least during waking hours, directs the body. We believe that when the body undertakes an action, say writing a book, painting a painting or even something as simple as extending our hand to another person, it realizes an intention that existed outside of and prior to that action. For Spinoza, this is an illusion: nobody knows what the body can do solely determined by other bodies. In fact, he suggests, our bodies are moved by other bodies (and he is very interested in the forms of corporeal social organization, such as rituals and ceremonies both secular and religious), while we imagine, much like a dreamer who believes he is talking when in fact he is silent, that we cause an action over which in fact we have no control.

The political consequences of such a positions are serious. Because mind and body are one, whatever increases or decreases the power of the body to act, simultaneously increases or decreases the power of the mind to think. In this way Spinoza, anticipating Foucault, asks us to investigate the social histories of bodies. As for Foucault, the human body is not the atom of society, a fixed and stable point of origin, but is always an aggregate itself made up of smaller bodies and capable of becoming part of a larger body (a couple, a group, a mass, a society) that is no less real because it is an aggregate. It no longer makes sense to ask whether a people have consented to their ruler (which would thus render his rule, no matter how oppressive, legitimate) or a worker to his employer (which no matter how exacting and constraining the labour would then be a legally and morally binding contract). Instead we must begin by asking whether a given relation renders bodies powerful or weak; does it increase their pleasure or pain? In this way all the justifications of domination and exploitation become untenable. In fact, Spinoza refuses every notion of disembodied right (he argues that right equals power), asking only what people have the power to do with or without legal right. Once we cease to see politics in terms of right and law, and instead focus on power, the individual can no longer be the unit of analysis. The chief political force in any society, democratic or despotic, is what Spinoza calls in his last work the multitude or the masses whose support or at least tolerance is the condition of any regime. It is easy to understand why, beginning in 1968, so many of the great commentators on Spinoza have been connected to one variety or another of marxism.

God or nature, mind or body, right or power: Spinoza's anti-transcendentalism according to which that which is expressed disappears into its expression can only extend to that subtle matter, language. To explore this thesis, Spinoza turned his attention to the model of all texts, the Bible. He begins his discussion with a proposition that has proved oblique to many readers: the method of interpreting nature and scripture is the same. We may understand his meaning by returning to the view of nature that he rejects in the *Ethics*. For the superstitious, nature is a mere expression or reflection of something beyond it, something more real or more true: God, the Forms, etc. According to this model, one does not look at nature itself but beyond it to the ends for which it was created or the meaning that it in attenuated form expresses. Nature, from this perspective, is not primary but secondary; the operation of knowledge would be a reduction or a dispelling of nature as if it were the impediment to its own truth. In opposition, Spinoza posits the irreducibility or materiality of nature.

What does this mean for the understanding of scripture? Theologians have for centuries attributed to scripture a hidden depth, of which the literal text is but a mask. Spinoza argues that the meanings that they claim to have found hidden in its interior have in fact been added to the text. They treat scripture not as a text at all but rather as a pretext for the meanings that they will substitute for it. All their approaches amount to a denial of the text in its materiality, its irreducibility; by exhorting us to look beyond it they prevent us from knowing it. The first step in arriving at an adequate knowledge of scripture, then, is to describe its surface very carefully, even to the point of examining punctuation without assuming either coherence or sense. It may well be that certain passages literally do not make sense or are not written in the dialect or language; there may be obvious gaps and ellipses in the text. It may be the case that the text asserts as truth statements that contradict each other. Such a careful description is impossible for readers who begin by assuming the text's perfection and coherence. Their task will be different: not to describe and explain the heterogeneity, contradiction and absence of meaning that is to be found but to explain it away as mere appearance concealing the essence of the text.

Spinoza will treat it as a material, historical artefact. What are the languages of which it is comprised, from what historical period do they date, how many identifiable parts are there to scripture and who assembled them and under what conditions? If its statements are contradictory, can the contradiction be explained historically (texts written in different periods under different circumstances)? But Spinoza does not stop with these already provocative questions: it is not enough to establish the text once and for all and to explain it historically. The history of scripture is not over: it continues to produce new and different effects in new historical situations; it can even cease to mean anything at all and congeal into an indecipherable mass of paper and ink. Of course, if we follow Spinoza's reasoning to the letter, his method is not restricted to the text of scripture. On the contrary, because he rejects the most common postulates of the unity of any text, namely the notions that works originate in and express the intention of an author or that works reflect something more real than themselves which confers upon them their coherence and meaning, his critique extends to the way we read literary, philosophical and political texts as well.

We can see then that, despite certain similarities in language and some common reference points, Descartes and Spinoza stand in stark opposition: on the one hand, a philosophy of the Cogito (not just thought or even consciousness, but also the 'I' as origin of knowledge), positing the primacy of spirit over matter, of soul over body, at the extreme, a political as well as epistemological individualism; on the other, a materialism so thoroughgoing that spirit in all its forms has disappeared into matter, that the human individual is always part of larger individuals and right and law are immanent in power.

This conflict, although several centuries old, has never been more actual than now at the conclusion of the twentieth-century as the conflict to have passed through the crucible of our time unchanged: indeed, it is so intertwined with our thoughts and efforts that it is difficult to imagine a time when we will have passed beyond it.

Warren Montag

Further reading and works cited

Balibar, E. *Spinoza and Politics*. London, 1998.
Descartes, R. *The Philosophical Writings of Descartes, Volume II*. Cambridge, 1984.
Guéroult, M. *Descartes' Philosophy Interpreted According to the Order of Reasons*, Vols 1–2. Minneapolis, MN, 1984
Husserl, E. *Cartesian Meditations: An Introduction to Phenomenology*. The Hague, 1960.
Lacan, J. *Ecrits*. Paris, 1966.
Montag, W. *Bodies, Masses, Power: Spinoza and his Contemporaries*. London, 1999.
Spinoza, B. *The Collected Works of Spinoza*, Vols 1 and 2. Princeton, NJ, 1985.
—. *Tractatus Theologico-Politicus*. New York, 1991.
— and Stolze, T. (eds) *The New Spinoza*. Minneapolis, MN, 1997.

2. Immanuel Kant (1724–1804) and Georg Wilhelm Friedrich Hegel (1770–1831)

Few thinkers have cast shadows as long on the terrain of postwar literary criticism and theory as Immanuel Kant and G. W. F. Hegel who separately and together open, exemplify and in some respects close the period of European thought known as the Enlightenment. The figures and the work of Kant and Hegel have directly and indirectly been the material from which disciplines and approaches from psychoanalytic to phenomenological criticism, political philosophy to deconstruction have built their characteristic protocols. The vexed history of their influence, waxing and waning, punctuated with 'returns to ...' and disavowals of one or the other, makes up in some respects the history of modern literary theory itself.

This is a broad claim, and not self-evidently true. Literary criticism has only recently become explicitly concerned with examining its philosophical presuppositions, in ways that differ markedly from one country to another – and which may, indeed, be coming to a close as the period of 'high theory' wanes. For the greater part of the twentieth century the study of literature, even in settings traditionally more friendly to speculative thought than the US or England, found little of profit in taking stock of its procedures more or less systematically. Nor for that matter is it clear how Kant or Hegel's work might further that stocktaking, once it is under way. Kant has little to say about literature, and Hegel's interpretations of literary works have had an influence often more local than disciplinary (with the signal exception of Hegel's profound reshaping of the theory of tragedy, achieved in part through Bradley's renderings of the *Lectures on Aesthetics*). Very little of the practical work of literary criticism and interpretation has stood or fallen on the great questions posed and answered by German idealism.

As soon as 'criticism' gives way to 'literary theory', however, matters change dramatically. The shift from criticism to theory may in principle occur any time that one writes about texts. As a disciplinary matter, however, establishing the analytical bases of the study of literature only becomes a pressing matter in the immediate postwar period, when changes in material and political circumstances focus attention on the humanistic studies as a profession, and increasingly require of these studies different (economic, social, political) justifications. The forms that these legitimation procedures take are again quite distinct, depending on which cultural and educational tradition is at issue. Not only do the values that 'literature' and 'philosophical inquiry' hold in much of Europe (where the disciplinary border between literature and philosophy has for different reasons been fairly porous) differ from their value in the US (where until recently it has not), so do the social and economic roles played in the US and Europe by the universities where such inquiry most often takes place, though their disciplinary distinctions and pedagogical rationale derive complexly from the Encyclopaedist classificatory practices that are the indirect object of inquiry in Kant, and obviously at issue in the project of Hegel's *Encyclopaedia of the Human Sciences*. Further twisting matters, local critical traditions – whether Leavisite practical criticism, the forms of *explication de texte* in the French and Belgian *lycée* after the First World War, or the techniques of close reading developed and popularized in the US – construe and transform quite differently the various legacies of Enlightenment thought. And these, of course, become more widely available with the population displacements provoked by the Second World War, when exiled thinkers like Adorno, Wellek, Brecht, Arendt, de Man and others sought in various ways to rethink continental cultural traditions under the Cold War's light. Finally, the emergence of the thought of Kant and Hegel in central roles in the project of devising a theory of literature has much to do with the contested cultural value that the idealist tradition assumes in Europe in relation to the war itself. For the 'Enlightenment' defined and exemplified through the Weimar period the ideals of cultural literacy that the European wars so profoundly shook. Philosophical idealism embodies 'after' Verdun and 'after' Auschwitz a cultural fantasy in bitter contrast to the realities of two world wars, and is assessed, lionized or rejected in the postwar period in light of this lived contrast.

But the cultural value assumed at this time in Europe and in the United States by idealism's greatest exemplars is not expressed solely in debates over whether various strands of Enlightenment thought give rise to ideologies that lead to war, or whether a different or identical aspect provides the model for a rational public sphere that European political culture abandoned with the rise of fascism. A scattered number of counter-normative approaches to the idealist tradition are proposed in philosophical, political and literary journals immediately before and during the war and these lay the foundation for the reconsideration of Kant and Hegel's legacy that has marked continental philosophy and literary theory in the past thirty years. These counter-normative readings do not come together into anything resembling a coherent approach to the legacies of German idealism, but in retrospect their influential stress on the discontinuities of the Kantian analytics, or on the contingencies of the dialectic, seems to flow largely from their efforts to understand more precisely the place of the aesthetic in the critical and in the Encyclopaedic projects.

For Kant and Hegel, it emerges, reserve for aesthetic questions most broadly, and for literary ones particularly, a place at the defining edge of the discipline of philosophy. At issue are not only judgements concerning the content of this or that work but also judgements that embed a certain fictionality, indeed a kind of literariness, in propositions having no explicitly aesthetic content. In each case – differently, to be sure, but with considerable and fruitful continuities – the care with which the aesthetic judgement is philosophically confined by supplementary tactics suggests the dangerous stresses its necessary presence places on the understanding: necessary both because reflecting the particularity of the sensorium and because concerned with the characteristics of phenomena that distinguish them from concepts on the one hand and from ideas on the other; confined because the 'reflection of particularity' on the subjective side and the 'concern with the distinguishing character of phenomena' on the objective side have no bounds given *a priori* in either the subject or the object, and if unconfined through one heuristic or another can thus practically consume the faculty of judgement. The resulting, complex interaction between the 'necessary function' and the 'confinement' of aesthetic judgements is played out on the question that these judgements confront before all others, and indeed which gives rise to them in the first instance: the question of the relation between the form of presentation (*stellen*) of representations to thought, and their sensible characteristics – between phenomenality and perception.

The indeterminability of aesthetic judgements contrasts markedly with the seeming historical or conceptual teleology of the *Phenomenology of Spirit* or of the three *Critiques*. Just as markedly does it contrast with the largely unexamined historicism that characterized literary studies of the prewar period, and with the purported scientificity of models of intrinsic aesthetic and cultural analysis (predominantly structuralist in inspiration) that come to prominence after the war – defined by Vincent Descombes as the historicist or culturalist positivism of European thought. The appeal of aesthetic judgements is thus easy to understand. Enlisted as models of unconfined human freedom and of human pleasure at a time when the defining metanarratives of western elite culture are in crisis, they seem at once utopian and indispensable to increasingly heterogenous societies. In keeping with this fantasy of culture's social role, for much of the past quarter-century 'literature' was understood to be the aesthetic domain that most clearly staged the question of the relation between the indeterminability of aesthetic judgement and the seeming necessity of establishing determining, foundational premises for ethical judgements – staged it allegorically, referred to it fictionally, treated it thematically. During these years, and until different forms of materialist criticism (new and old historicism, cultural studies) achieved hegemony, the 'theory' of literature occupied itself broadly with formalizing that question and its various provisional answers (psychoanalytic, culturalist, philosophical, or more traditionally 'literary'). At the close of the twentieth century and in the wake of various formalisms, of 'high theory' and of different historicisms, literary criticism and theory has assumed as the programme of cultural studies the task of re-examining the historical and conceptual legacies of the idealist construction of aesthetic judgement set definingly in the Romantic reception of Kant and Hegel's work.

Kant and the doctrine of relative autonomy

'Two things fill the mind with ever new and increasing admiration and awe', Kant concludes his *Critique of Practical Reason*, 'the oftener and more steadily we reflect on them: the starry heavens above me and the moral law within me. I do not merely conjecture them

... I see them before me, and I associate them directly with the consciousness of my own existence.' This poetical observation sets out the broad architecture of Kant's *critical* philosophy – a term understood to cover the works dating roughly from 1774 to the end of his career. The domain, limits and characteristics of judgements concerning 'the place I occupy in the external world of sense' are the subject treated in the 1781 *Critique of Pure Reason*. Judgements concerning the moral law are the province of the *Critique of Practical Reason* (1788), *Metaphysics of Morals* (1797) and *Groundwork of the Metaphysics of Morals* (1785). The human mind, Kant argues, constitutes for itself the conditions of perception and sense *before* it has any experience of this or that object – hence to make judgements concerning our 'experience' or (to use a particularly Kantian word) our 'intuition' of the 'external world of sense' is in fact to address phenomena, 'objects conforming to our mode of representation' and regulated by this mode of representation, rather than 'things by themselves' or 'in themselves' (1998 B: xviii). The critique of metaphysics built on this is devastating: the boundaries Kant sets to speculative reason are the circumstance of the self-regarding subject rather than the 'external world' of things by themselves. To confuse one with the other is to 'destroy' the 'necessary practical use of pure reason', its *moral* use. For in the domain of *moral* judgement, Kant goes on to explain, the negative task undertaken in the *Critique of Pure Reason* yields a profound, *positive* result with respect to what in the *Critique of Practical Reason* he terms the 'only idea of speculative reason whose possibility we know a priori' (5): the idea of freedom. Our 'ignorance with regard to things by themselves', it turns out, restricts our capacity to understand or to know freedom 'by itself', but not, crucially, to '*think* freedom' (1998 B: xxvii). And the idea of 'freedom' is in this sense privileged not only as the *content* of thought or as the object of speculative reason (we think about the phenomenon of freedom, unable to know freedom by itself), but also as the *form* taken a priori by speculative thought in general and as its functional effect.

Kant's efforts to coordinate the domains of fundamental epistemology and of ethics, of knowledge and of desire, understanding and reason, require of him two related, controversial strategies, with profound methodological as well as thematic consequences. Both come under direct attack in the course of the twentieth century and provide the ground for some of the most far-reaching philosophical and literary-critical debates of the past quarter-century. The first concerns the role assigned in the critique of metaphysics to the notion and characteristics of the subject. The second concerns the subordination of aesthetic judgement to reason and understanding, and its simultaneous elevation to a necessary, analytic moment in the transition from epistemological to moral judgements.

Kant's subjects

Kant's critical system is indeed concerned with the status of human agents and of rational human acts, though he does not make such acts coextensive with human subjectivity or its origin. Instead, the Kantian critique of metaphysics turns upon the notion that acts (physical acts as well as certain acts of thought) originate in 'a transcendental ground of the unity of our consciousness in the synthesis of the manifold of all our intuitions' (1998, A:104). On this understanding, Kant's formulation consolidates an argument for the primacy of self-consciousness made sketchily, and with important flaws, as early as Descartes's *Meditations* – correcting and extending it to the domain of practical reason. Corresponding to the 'transcendental ground of unity' in the acting subject is the principle of the will's autonomy with regard to that act – the postulate that one's duty to moral law is coherent and compelling only if one subjects oneself 'only to laws given by oneself but still universal', laws in which one can have no *particular* interest, and which are in this sense *unconditionally* compelling (*Groundwork*, 40). To give oneself such laws requires crucially, Kant suggests, the intervention of the faculty of the imagination: every decision is submitted to the imaginary test of its *outcome* and of a notional universality (one acts 'as if' the grounds for deciding to act held universally, and 'as if' the outcome of the act were immediately and exhaustively present to thought). The representation of 'outcome' and 'universality' must be radically non-empirical (otherwise every decision would be an interested, hence a conditioned one, and never in Kant's sense a 'free' decision) – presented 'as if' they provided determining grounds for this or that decision, but also 'as if' entirely counter-factual. The immediate consequence of this imaginary test is the de-instrumentalization of human agents: every subject as such is presumed definitionally to be able freely and rationally to test his or her judgements in this way – to be autonomous – and cannot in consequence be construed as the means for another subject's judgements, only (in an abstract sense) as an end.

Different and differently influential treatments of political philosophy and of philosophical ethics flow from the notions of duty and *responsibility* that this foundational description of the imaginary autonomy of the will establishes. The debt to Kant is explicit in some cases, implicit in others. The coordination of the concepts of 'rational community', 'transparent communication' and 'public-sphere interest' in the work of Jürgen Habermas, the influential terms in which the North American ethicist John Rawls describes the hypothetical 'veil of ignorance' necessary to produce just judgements in social environments (1971), the emphasis placed by philosophers like Ronald Dworkin (1977) or Alisdair MacIntyre (1981) on rights-based analyses of legal standing, all suggest the scope of the contemporary return to Kant.

Where Habermas, Rawls, Dworkin and the late Foucault may be imagined to represent a return to a (qualified) Kantian foundationalism, engagement with Kant's critical philosophy has as often sought to provide non-foundational accounts. On the continent Nietzsche (refracted through readings of Freud, Marx and particularly of the work of Martin Heidegger) remained the primary philosophical point of reference, particularly in France and Germany. Heidegger's engagement with Kant is constant and fruitful. For Heidegger, the emergence of the notion of the subject is associated with the epochal forgetting of the authentic relation to Being that obtained before the Cartesian, and more properly Kantian, consolidation of the 'age of the world-picture' – an 'age' (though it is also a philosophical tactic, and a style of writing) that subordinates ontological questions (concerned with the nature of Being) to epistemological ones. What Kant describes as 'the objects' conforming to our mode of representation' Heidegger associates with the aligned distinctions between the apparent and the essential, between, as he puts it in *Being and Time*, the 'outside of me [*Aussenwelt*]' and the 'in me [*in mir*]' (Heidegger 1962, 204–5), between an object's phenomenality, or appearing-for-one, and its noumenality, or being-in-itself. This evasion, he argues, finds its modern crystallization in the emergence of the category of the *subiectus* (Heidegger 1962, 317–22); in the *Critique of Pure Reason* it is tied to the complex status accorded the coming-into-images (*Verbildlichung*) of the transcendental schemata. These, Heidegger argues in *Kant and the Problem of Metaphysics*, are images (*Bilder*) in a special sense: they are *both* removed from the empirical realm (of conditionality), *and* revealed to constitute the finitude of the 'I' as its being-in-time (thus making the pre-conditionality of time a non-empirical predicate of the 'I'). This means, however, that it is no longer possible (as both the *Critique of Practical Reason* and the *Critique of Judgement* propose) to construe the Being of beings under the aspect of the unconditionality of the subject's freedom to *understand* imaginative schemata for grasping the world. Rather, it becomes necessary to pose the question of the Being of beings – and of the emergence of the subject, as well as its autonomy – within the constraint of the *limited* freedom 'I' have to fashion those schemata.

Heidegger's anti-foundationalist re-historicization of the problem of representation and his recasting of conditionality (as Being-in-time) as 'my' pre-subjective condition prove decisive in the continental reception of Kant's critique of metaphysics. The influence is clearest in the general field of ethics, though Derrida's far-reaching influence in literary studies is in fact unthinkable without reference to the works he devotes, precisely, to Heidegger's encounter with Kant. The critique of foundational autonomy is pursued exactingly in the work of Emmanuel Levinas, of Gilles Deleuze and of T. W. Adorno.

Heidegger's encounter with Kant's work does not uniquely shape its postwar reception, of course. In the course of the 1950s and early 1960s the Kantian notion of the autonomy of the subject came under considerable pressure from psychoanalytically inflected work as well. The theorization of 'unconscious' causality dating to Freud's *The Interpretation of Dreams* had dramatically shifted the analytic distinction between 'conditioned' and 'unconditioned' decisions from its Kantian alignment with propositions concerning *empirical* judgements on the one hand and *a priori* intuitions on the other, to a fundamentally empirical frame in which every 'unconditioned' proposition or decision reveals itself to be merely an as-yet-unanalysed but always 'conditioned' proposition or decision. This psychic pre-conditioning, however, could quickly take an oppressively orthodox shape: the Oedipal scenario, archetypal psychoanalysis, even the description of infantile object-relations became not only institutionally but conceptually fixed, assuming in the work of postwar critics and psychoanalysts (in Klein, Winnicott, Erikson and others) the foundational role granted a priori, properly transcendent concepts in Kant. This re-transcendentalization of the psychoanalytic critique of idealism provoked its own powerful reaction. In Jacques Lacan's rendering, and beginning with the epoch-making essay from 1949 on 'The Mirror-Stage as Formative of the I as Revealed in Psychoanalytic Experience' (1966), the pre-conditionality of the human subject is the mark of its primary facticity, a mark of the original non-identity between the little man and the world of objects in which he finds himself cast. And this pre-conditionality of the subject, Lacan strikingly suggests in his 1958–9 Seminar and again in his 1963 *Critique* essay, 'Kant with Sade', (1966) is itself unconditioned: it is the source and form of *desire*, and the *duty* to follow these desires has a form exactly homologous to the Kantian duty to acquiesce to the autonomy of the imperatives of conscience. Gilles Deleuze, writing with Félix Guattari, mounted a devastating attack on the re-transcendentalization of the Oedipal scenario in the institutions and languages of psychoanalysis with *Anti-Oedipus* (1972), a work whose understanding of the resolutely Kantian roots of Oedipalization was to be brought out by two prominent followers, Klaus Theweleit (1977) and Peter Sloterdijk, whose *Critique of Cynical Reason* (1983) turns Deleuze's observation in *Nietzsche and Philosophy* that the Kantian critique of metaphysics finally safeguards the supersensible into a description of the pathology of futility that afflicts the legacy of the enlightenment, able to understand its disenfranchisement, to profit from that diagnosis, but unable to do anything to change it.

The distinction between 'foundationalist' and 'non-foundationalist' responses to Kant's work is rough at best, however. The interrupted arc of Michel Foucault's career provides the remarkable example of a thinker perched between disciplines whose ostensible movement from a philosophical historiography highly critical of the hypostatization of the 'humanist' notion of the subject to an autonomous ethics of 'care' in the final writing can be indexed against his encounters with Kant's work – but whose critique of foundationalism in no way follows the same path. Foucault's 1961 *thèse complémentaire* for the *doctorat ès lettres* was an annotated edition of Kant's *Anthropology from a pragmatic point of view*; his most probing early critiques of 'humanist' theses took direct or indirect aim at the de-historicization of the notion of autonomy and of the category of the subject that Foucault found at work in the Critical project. But Foucault's late pieces, 'The Subject and Power' (1983), 'Kant on Enlightenment and Revolution' (1986) and the posthumously published 'What is Enlightenment?' (1984) (a title borrowed from Kant) seem to qualify this critique of Kant's anthropological bent, in some measure assigning his own earlier positions to what he rather sharply calls the 'facile confusions between humanism and Enlightenment'. In a defining set of exchanges with Habermas, Foucault advocates reconstructing a notion of the Enlightenment on non-transcendental but on practical or *performative* bases, 'conceiving [Enlightenment] as an attitude, an ethos, a philosophical life in which the critique of what we are is at one and the same time the historical analysis of the limits that are imposed on us and an experiment with the possibility of going beyond them' (50). But Foucault's 'return' to Kant is only ostensible, for in crucial ways he never 'leaves' Kant at all: even at his most resolutely Heideggerian Foucault never abandons the highly Kantian notion that reason has an intrinsic, if historicized, relation to 'ethos' and to 'experiment'. Where Foucault differs from Kant – and from Habermas and Sloterdijk's versions of Kant – is in his understanding of the status and domain of that relation: it is not *aesthetics*, as in Kant's work, that provides the crucial hinge between reason and ethics, but what could be called (as in Nietzsche) *dynamics*, the critique of the forms in which power is materially exercised.

Sublime aesthetics

With the signal exceptions of its absorption by Benedetto Croce and its treatment in Cassirer's 1918 *Kant's Life and Thought*, Kant's aesthetic theory remained very much on the sidelines in philosophical circles during the first years of the twentieth century. The works in which it is explored – the precritical *Observations on the Feeling of the Beautiful and Sublime* (1763) and the *Critique of Judgement* of 1790 – are to this day treated by Anglo-American philosophers and by literary critics in the neo-positivist tradition with hardly any patience. In his critical period Kant becomes both surprisingly unclear and, as if by way of compensation, almost excessively scholastic in his treatment of the aesthetic. As to a perceived lack of clarity, the *Critique of Judgement*'s exposition of the immediate pleasure afforded reflective intuition by the beautiful (in art as well as nature) strategically muddies the two senses of 'taste' – the highly subjective expression of particular pleasure and the societal approval granted this or that work or natural object – so as to make the notorious particularity of judgements of taste into a general and teachable principle. This principle, however, is founded in peculiarly unanalysable terms that Kant uses nowhere else: there is, he finds, no 'method' for teaching the 'taste' for or the means of producing beautiful art, only a *modus* or 'manner'; nonetheless, the true propaedeutic for the foundation of taste 'is the development [*die Entwickelung*] of moral ideas and the culture of moral feeling', though the capacity to envision and understand, hence rationally to develop, such moral ideas depends upon the faculty of judgement that derives in part from the foundation of taste.

The work's purported 'technicality' notwithstanding, it is Cassirer's rendering of Kant's aesthetics that prevails in literary-critical circles of the postwar period – a reading stressing the crucial place in the architecture of the three *Critiques* that the aesthetical judgement occupies, and stressing, too, what High Romanticism from Goethe and Schiller to Coleridge would find most compelling in Kant's aesthetic project: the relation between the purposiveness of the aesthetic judgement and the *organicity* of natural objects. For Cassirer, Kant's muddiness concerning the status of taste captures a broader ambivalence present already in the *Critique of Pure Reason* on the subject of aesthetic judgements generally. The empirical function of aesthetics, concerned with *evaluating* the 'material' of representations can be bracketed or ignored, or set aside as a 'vain endeavour' (1998, A 20), or considered merely preliminary: aesthetic propositions set aside the question of ver- idification, and take the form 'these characteristics of the phenomenon *qua* phenomenon please or displease' – but the nature of this 'pleasing' or 'displeasing' is of interest only inasmuch as it represents the 'pleasure' at the discovery in relation to phenomena of a pure concept of the understanding. Important as the faculty of judgement may be in providing hypothetical representations of the outcome or possible universality of acts (on the moral side), or in providing *a posteriori* judgements concerning 'the matter of phenomena' (rather than their form, which in a particularly Aristotelian moment Kant proposes 'is ready for them in the mind': 1998, A 18), it is the consideration of the 'transcendental aesthetic' – the region of judgements concerning the *a priori*, pure form of all sensuous intuitions, and the domain of the 'pleasures' associated with the disclosure of those intuitions – that emerges as fundamental in providing what Kant calls the 'means of combining the two parts of philosophy [the theoretical and the practical] into a whole'. In the *Critique of Judgement* Kant seeks to achieve this combination by drawing an analogy between the 'purposiveness [*Zweckmäßigkeit*]' of nature and the 'purposiveness' of aesthetic objects. This 'purposiveness' is formal and transcendental, in the sense that we recognize from the First Critique – it requires no empirical concept of the body (object, etc.) of which it is predicated. Judgements about aesthetic objects work analogously (this work is beautiful, not for the purpose it concretely serves, but inasmuch as the work allows us to intuit in it an abstract purposiveness that no concrete purpose quite exhausts), and by means of this analogy Kant locates the capacity to produce art, to make propositions concerning the artistic object, and to experience pleasure at the intuition of abstract purposiveness, on the same level as the faculty of producing propositions concerning sensibilia and to make judgements concerning our desires (to accomplish this or that), the transcendental sense of purposiveness in the aesthetical judgement as pertains to nature (and by analogy art) becoming associated with the idea of freedom in the moral scheme. In building this analogy Kant finds it useful to return to the pre-Critical distinction between the beautiful and the sublime. The sidelining of the sublime, he continues, has to do in particular with its uselessness in the construction of the 'teleological judgement' forming the bridge between aesthetic and moral judgement, as 'in the sublime there is nothing at all that leads to particular objective principles and forms of nature corresponding to them'. 'We must seek', he concludes, 'a ground external to ourselves for the beautiful in nature, but seek it for the sublime merely in ourselves' (23).

Kant's influence, and particularly his treatment of the feeling of the *beautiful*, is felt acutely in the privilege that early formalist and new critical approaches granted what William Wimsatt called the poem's 'concrete universality', 'the principle by which the critic can try to keep ... rhetorical analysis of poetry together with evaluation, technique together with worth'. This principle, Wimsatt proposes, should be understood by analogy to Kant's 'telling how the imagination constructs the 'aesthetical normal Idea': 'It is the image for the whole race', he continues, citing from the *Critique of Judgement*, 'which floats among all the variously different intuitions of individuals, which nature takes as archetype in her productions of individuals of the same species, but which seems not to be fully reached in any individual case' (1954, 71–2). The organic relation between 'archetype' and 'individual' becomes the mainstay, not just of Wimsatt's explicitly Kantian conception of criticism, but of a protocol of reading concerned to find how the aesthetic work achieves a formal 'unity' between the pleasure that 'irrelevant concreteness' affords precisely as such, and the 'more than usual relevance' of concrete images to the logic of the work of art. In these particular verbal icons the archetype shines through universally, symbolically, supported philosophically on either side by the strong Kantian bolsters of purposiveness and aesthetic irrelevance, exemplified in the poetical and programmatic work of Coleridge and Schiller, and expressed characteristically by means of the synecdochal symbol.

Absent from the explicitly aesthetic formulation and with a rather different, anthropological-linguistic genealogy, this dynamic arrangement of 'concrete' and 'universal' provided in the late 1950s and early 1960s a philosophy for the human sciences in the shape of structuralism. Covertly indebted to Cassirer's understanding of the 'unity of the rule' in Kant, structuralism in the human sciences, and in literary criticism in particular, there are hypothesized the existence of structural rules governing the production and reception of disparate cultural phenomena. Between the two levels – the 'phenomena' of culture, the deep rules of structure – a methodical, indeed a methodological, path can be drawn, involving procedures taken most often from the field of synchronic linguistics, or, as in the fundamental work of Claude Lévi-Strauss, of social anthropology. The reception of Propp's *Morphology of the Folk Tale*, the work of Jakobson, Todorov, Girard and the European narratological school of the late 1960s and early 1970s, certain uses of Lacan and Althusser's work in the early to middle 1960s – all flow from the conceptualization of the regulative transcendental that Cassirer takes from the Critical project. In its aims and procedures structuralism, like New Criticism, appears to mount a strong attack on some of the most cherished legacies of the Enlightenment, the notion of a transcendent and originary 'human essence', isomorphous or not with the 'subject', being ostensibly incompatible with the existence and regulative dimension of abstract and non-human structures. What remains, to use Paul Ricoeur's characterization in 1963 of the work of Lévi-Strauss, is a 'Kantianism without a transcendental subject', 'structure' having assumed the functional position occupied by the 'subject' in the three *Critiques*.

The end of the structuralist moment in Europe, and of the New Critical moment in the United States, might then reasonably be associated with the exhaustion of the romantic response to idealist aesthetics, and the emergence of what is roughly called poststructural philosophy and literary theory with an explicit critique of the regulative transcendental. In a crucial chapter devoted to Kant, Jean-Paul Sartre's *What is Literature?* (1947) had outlined already the consequences of merely replacing the 'transcendental subject' with an aesthetic counterpart – 'form' or 'structure' or 'purposiveness'. Sartre's thinking, as influentially anti-foundational in its way as Heidegger's contemporaneous reading of Kant's ontology proved, bears two constructions. On the one hand, the resolute 'disinterestedness' of the aesthetic judgement proves to be conditioned already the moment one enters a relation to the aesthetic object. On the other hand, the 'task' under whose aspect the work of art presents itself bears a concrete relation to the world of the work's production and reception: literature, Sartre suggests, engages the reader in battles – battles that *What is Literature?* is at pains to make clear are quite literal ones. Each construction of Sartre's phrase might be understood to correspond to a type of critique of the romantic-formalist response to Kant, the first based on an intrinsic questioning of the transcendentalization of the rules of 'structure' or 'form' in the place of the Kantian subject, the second to a properly historicizing questioning of the founding terms of transcendental aesthetics. Curiously, both avenues of critique – often pursued in the same argument – emerge centrally with the reconsideration of Kant's 'mere appendix to the aesthetical judging of purposiveness', the aesthetic category of the *sublime*.

The notion of the sublime is sparsely attended to in literary studies in the US before the advent of philosophically inflected forms of criticism, in some measure because it is hard to square the concept, even in its uninflected form, with Wimsatt's notion that literary criticism should proceed by analogy to the construction of 'the "aesthetical normal Idea"' to bring 'rhetorical analysis of poetry together with evaluation, technique together with worth'. Hard upon the ground-breaking 1966 conference devoted to 'The Languages of Criticism and the Sciences of Man', however, philosophical and literary interest in the *Critique of Judgement* increased, both in the US, in England and particularly in France. A number of heterodox interpretations of Kant, in line with the double-edged critique sketched in Sartre's early essay, appeared in the middle to late 1970s, including in the United States a number of topical works treating the theme of the sublime in Keats, Blake and others – the essays of Harold Bloom and the more psychoanalytically inflected work of Thomas Weiskel and Neil Hertz being of particular significance. In France, and coinciding with a retreat from the rather overwhelming Hegelianism of French academic circles since the late 1930s, the middle to late 1970s saw the beginning of a remarkable effort to rethink the place of aesthetic judgement in Kant's critical philosophy. Jacques Derrida's *Truth in Painting* included an extended treatment of the notion of *magnitude* in the *Critique*. And there were others, equally influential (though lack of space does not permit going into detail). By the time that the colloquium on 'judgement' was held at Cerisy-la-Salle (1982) the marginalization of Kant's work on aesthetics and Kant's own discomforts with the category of the sublime were accepted, in France and among literary critics elsewhere interested in French intellectual culture, as symptomatic of a productive incoherence in the *Critique of Judgement* – a term initially set aside as leading 'merely' into ourselves rather than toward a supersensible analogue to natural purposiveness, but yielding what would become for Kant an increasingly disturbing instance of the presentation to thought of the radically unpresentable.

The *Critique of Judgement* describes the experience of the sublime as one of blockage and release, echoing on a conceptual level the physiological account of the experiences of the beautiful and the sublime found in Burke. For Kant, however, the 'pain' and 'pleasure' associated with aesthetic experience have nothing to do with the 'efficient causes' of these sensations – 'an unnatural tension and certain violent emotions of the nerves' in one case, the relaxation of that 'unnatural tension' in the other, as Burke famously puts it. Rather, the blockage described in the *Critique of Judgement* affects the faculty of reason, checked by the immeasurable gulf between its capacity to 'measure' an image that presents itself sensibly to thought, and the actual object of thought. What follows this 'painful' experience is the imaginative reconstitution of reason under the aspect of self-admiration.

But is this 'blockage' effectively overcome in Kant? Not entirely, as Lyotard, Bourdieu,

Derrida, Hertz and others show. Just where the critical project poses the means for making the transcendent analogy between epistemology and ethics, the group of philosophers and literary critics writing in the wake of the structural project finds a colossal 'monster', a 'habitus' or a 'differend' that blocks again the re-emergence of the rational, autonomous subject toward which the *Critique of Judgement* seems destined. Each of these terms – the 'colossal', the 'differend', the 'habitus' – might be seen to reflect the dramatic breach that the notion of the sublime opens in the transcendental aesthetic: the presentation of the 'independence of absolute totality' in nature occurs both as an ostensive, direct *representation* and as an *analogy*. This duplicity embeds the empirical (the analogy is driven by the sensible content of the presentation) within the transcendental, dramatically undercutting the association of aesthetics with the ideology of timeless 'taste', and opening the *Critique of Judgement* to radical re-historicizations in the Sartrean line, Pierre Bourdieu's *Distinction* (1979) and later *Logic of Practice* (1980) providing among the most compelling examples.

The Kantian aesthetic that emerged on the continent in the 1970s and early 1980s found its most striking echo in the USA in the work of literary theorists already reacting against the perceived organicism of New Criticism, and to the formalism of structuralist and narratological criticism. Deconstructive critical approaches in particular – indebted to Derrida's work, though inflected in the main by a more deliberately rhetorical language drawn from the work of Northrop Frye, J. Hillis Miller, Harold Bloom or Paul de Man – on occasion explicitly embraced a programmatic 'impersonality', as an early essay by de Man puts it, drawn partly from the work of Maurice Blanchot, but most consequentially from the politico-philosophical critique of Kantian humanism. The years from 1979 to the late 1980s saw the publication of a number of important literary-critical treatments of the *Critique of Judgement* and of the *Critique of Practical Reason*, ranging from the nuanced pragmatism of Barbara Herrnstein Smith's analysis of Kant's notion of 'taste' (1988), to approaches to the 'ethics of reading' that sought to develop non-foundational accounts of the relation between aesthetical and ethical judgements by means of the concept of 'affirmative deconstruction' (Miller, Brodsky, Caruth), to essays seeking to articulate the de-anthropologization of the Kantian aesthetic scheme with a non-positivist account of material change (Paul de Man's 'Kant's Materialism' and 'Phenomenality and Materiality in Kant').

Hegel: the 'outsides' of dialectical thought

The 'return to Hegel' that begins in earnest in France in the 1930s, and which had already taken root in Germany and Italy, amounts, suggests Althusser, to a selective and deliberate 'resurrection' of themes that serve the bourgeoisie's 'desperate efforts' to consolidate its endangered class position and privileges (1997b, 243, 256–7). Published anonymously and redacted only a few months after he attended Gyorgy Lukács' lecture on 'New Problems in Hegelian Research' at the Sorbonne, Althusser's article on 'The Return to Hegel' excited considerable interest, particularly among thinkers on the political Left like Emile Bottigelli and Henri Lefebvre. The article – along with Althusser's review (1947) of Alexandre Kojève's *Introduction to the Reading of Hegel* (1947) – marked the beginning of a vigorous public assault on the understanding of Hegel that dominated in France and Germany until the mid-1960s, the 'anthropological' or 'humanist' Hegelianism of Jean Wahl, of Kojève and of Althusser's teacher Jean Hyppolite.

For Althusser, writing at the beginning of the Cold War, the debate over Hegel's reception was clearly a matter of consequence – and of some personal urgency as well, as he himself had only two years earlier contributed to the 'Great Return' he strikingly condemns a *diplôme d'études supérieures* on the subject of 'The Notion of "Content" in the Thought of G. W. F. Hegel'. The stakes were surely high in part for the reasons that Althusser gives. The 'return to Hegel' ostensibly took Kantianism as its target, but its *means* of attacking idealism set in place an approach to Hegel, and in particular a means of understanding the mechanism of the dialectic, whose sources, as Kojève had made clear, lay in Heidegger's work rather than in Marx's. The result, Althusser suggests in 'The Notion of "Content" ', is that under the cover of a critique of idealism Hegelianism had been falsely returned to a Kantian, transcendental frame. We owe to Hegel, he proposes, what Kant could not allow himself to think: 'the recognition that the *a priori* is *a posteriori*', and the correlative necessity of 'thinking the reality of a transcendental empirical ... the *a-prioricity* of the *a posteriori*'. Had Kant been able to understand correctly the nature of his own categories – which are 'found' or wrought from the table of judgements – he 'would have been constrained to conceive of history', he would have seen like Hegel that 'totality is the reconciliation of Substance and Subject, coinciding in absolute truth', or, to put it in the slightly starker terms in which Althusser reviews Kojève and Hyppolite's works, Kant would have been constrained to conceive of history along the fundamentally Marxist lines suggested by the contradictory notion of the 'transcendental empirical'.

The Hegelian System – so often accused of excessive 'formalism', of 'totalitarianism' – does indeed turn on the great themes that Althusser's words sketch here: the 'reality' or irreality of the empirical, the 'reconciliation [*Aufhebung*, often translated as "sublation" or "subreption"]' of Substance and Subject, the history of consciousness as the coming-into-being of 'absolute truth' in that 'reconciliation', the role of 'contradiction' in the mechanics of the dialectic. The roots of 'anthropological' Hegelianism lie in Hegel's earliest work, rediscovered and circulated in the first decades of the twentieth century – the so-called Berne years, reflecting the critical influence of the mysticism of Jacob Böhme, and before the mature exchanges in Frankfurt and Jena with the poet Friedrich Hölderlin that so changed Hegel's view of Kant. Hegel, who in early correspondence with Schelling had imagined himself 'completing' Kant's philosophy, 'applying' it and 'popularizing' it, found himself increasingly turning away from the most important doctrines of the Kantian circle at the university town of Jena. For Hölderlin, and increasingly for Hegel also, the immediate positing function of the aesthetic amounted to a fantasy, effectively playing down what in the *Logic* Hegel would come to call the 'identity of Being and Nothing' by making this 'nothing' merely a predicate of the Self. The challenge then became to find a way to retain *both* the autonomy of the Subject *and* the radical externality of Substance with respect to Subjectivity, without resorting to the noumenal 'in- or by-itself-ness' of each to explain their relation.

The publication of the *Phenomenology of Spirit* in 1807 was Hegel's first step in providing such an account, a work still bearing considerable traces of the Jena conflation of Fichtean 'absolute Self' with the empirical figure of the Romantic artist, but also profoundly novel in its approach to the task of philosophical scrutiny: 'the true birthplace and secret' of Hegel's System, in Marx's words. The principal means for accomplishing the 'reconciliation' of Substance and Subject in the *Phenomenology of Spirit* is the complex shuttling motion of the dialectic, a term designating at once a logical and a phenomenological procedure, and hence not easily defined. The work, in fact, might as easily be called an *example* of dialectical thought and an *injunction* to perform such thought, as an exposition of its premises and results: every 'moment' of the argument of the *Phenomenology of Spirit* presents itself as a complete cycle of assertion, negation and elimination or elevation (*Aufhebung*), the 'elevated' or reconciled term manifesting, at a greater level of generality, a contradiction that again gets the cycle under way, the entire, repetitive – or, better, cyclical – set of iterations becoming itself the movement, form and content of consciousness as it sets itself before itself as an object of reflection. To whom, though, does the argument 'present itself'? Who is the 'I' that the *Phenomenology of Spirit* addresses? Here we find Hegel at his most daring: the 'experience' abstractly described in the pages of the *Phenomenology of Spirit* slowly reveals itself to be that of the work's reader, who understands the argument's moments by 'performing' them, and understands them to *be* the performance of the movement that it describes. Each 'moment' in the *Phenomenology of Spirit*, then, presents itself to its reader 'first' immediately, appearing as the immediate shining or appearance (*Erscheinung*) of the truth of a phenomenon – for instance, the 'truth' of sense-certainty with which the work opens, or of the richness of particular experience; the 'truth' of the relation that obtains definitionally between the master and the slave; and so on. But this immediate appearing, Hegel proposes, bears 'truth' only in the most impoverished sense, as it excludes every reflection: the 'immediate' truth of sense certainty, or of the apparent relation between the master and the slave, or of the superiority of 'abstract' to 'concrete' thought (or vice versa), in fact conveys no knowledge other than the merely ostensive, and adds nothing to what was already the sate of affairs – that here and now I am confronted with an object other than myself. But take account, Hegel proceeds, of the peculiar structure of the terms in which this apparently tautologous form of ostension operates – *this* object *here* and *now*, for *me* – and there arises, this time *mediated* by that very taking-account and by the conditions of utterance of the ostensive statement, an entirely different scheme. Every term at issue, Hegel writes, in the 'initial', 'empirical' moment when thought takes account of the experience of the senses, bears not only upon 'my' concrete experience, but on the general possibility of being-experienced of the phenomenon, and on the *abstractness* of the subject experiencing: the 'here' and 'now' of 'my' experience of 'this' object *both* locate and particularize the experience, *and* make it comprehensible beyond that particularism, as 'I' can serve to indicate now one, now another grammatical person, and 'here' and 'now' shift in this or that circumstance. The embedding of this generality within 'my' most private experience of the object brings 'me' before myself as an object, as 'nothing' (from the subjective point of view), or as a member of the logical class of 'concrete universals' – an externalization that makes manifest, or represents, what was already a constitutive division, denying me an immediate knowledge of myself ('I' know 'I' am no longer 'I') but making available to me, as my truth, the *experience* of my consciousness of that failed immediacy.

The break with Fichte's rendering of Kant is sharp, but the *Phenomenology of Spirit* proceeds beyond this first, epistemological moment along a path that Hegel will follow unswervingly for the rest of his career. If 'my' particular experience presents itself to me as also necessarily a general one, then the realm of 'my' relation to and consciousness of the world and myself presents itself also as proper to a class, 'my' historical circumstance as proper to the *condition* of historicity, and the particular shape taken for me by the failure of 'my' immediate *knowledge* of myself as the subject of my own thoughts and deeds as a general form of negation proper to the structure of historicity itself. The second moment in the *Phenomenology of Spirit* extends the initial account of the dialectic of sense-certainty to the sphere of social relations, transferring the dialectical elevation of 'my' weakness as mediate subject to an exceptionally influential description of the Slave's ascendancy over the Master. The synthetical notion of 'work' advanced at this level passes from the realm of ethical substance to the doctrines of State and Religion that seek to formalize and legislate that realm, and concludes at the level of greatest generality with the famous, lyrical description of the 'goal' of the 'slow-moving succession of Spirits [Geister, also "minds"]' that constitutes the 'conscious, self-mediating process' of History: totality, the mediately identical-with-itself, 'Absolute Knowing, or Spirit that knows itself as Spirit'.

Crucially, Hegel imagines this 'extension' of the first, epistemological moment into the realm of ethical substance, and then the 'slow-moving' and 'self-mediating' procession of consciousness up the scale of generalities, under the aspect of necessity (Notwendigkeit): once 'my' thought is under way (and to the extent that Hegel imagines 'thought' to be the manifestation of contradiction for itself, 'thought' has always already begun), then the moment 'I' come before myself as the experience of the consciousness of my mediacy, the terms of 'my' thought are necessarily 'cancelled' and 'elevated [aufgehoben]' to the more general level at which 'I' enter into relation with others in the sphere of my work, that is to the level of social labour. Once at that level (and as Hegel makes much clearer in the sections on 'Taking possession of a Thing [Sache]' in the Elements of the Philosophy of Right), the definition of work as the transformation of matter for use entails understanding all matter as matter-to-be-appropriated and laboured-over, or as potentially 'my' property. Because this 'my' suffers the familiar and contradictory particular universalism that Hegel's pronouns manifest at the 'first', epistemological level, 'my' work opens necessarily onto the spheres of law and of religion, the domains, Hegel argues in the Elements of the Philosophy of Right, where the contradiction intrinsic to a matter that is both particularly 'for me', generally 'for all' and intrinsically 'for itself' must be negotiated. The notion of necessity that the Phenomenology of Spirit employs thus furnishes Hegel with a powerful historical heuristic as well, concrete historical events becoming the manifestations of the necessary movement of Geist through natural history. The profoundly progressivist vision that attends this conception of historical necessity, as well as the notion that the moments of thought that make up its phenomenological counterpart are necessary in relation to the totality of thought, prove among the most controversial and abiding elements of Hegel's legacy.

The balance of Hegel's works individually and systematically explore the consequences and foundations, in quite different domains, of these early insights. Hegel's aesthetic theory plays a much smaller part in the various declensions of the System than does the aesthetic judgement in Kant, and his discussions of the sublime a role less prominent yet. The conception of literature that Hegel advances openly is fundamentally a cognitive, thematic one: the literary work can serve to reveal the nature of the world, can help make clear the relationship that obtains between 'world' and 'man' – but in the sensuous form of an intuition, which must always remain preliminary and external to the genuine revelation of that relationship in thought as a concept (Begriff) or in religion as a figurative representation (Vorstellung). Thus his crucial treatment of Sophocles' Antigone in the Phenomenology of Spirit and in the Lectures on Aesthetics – decisive in the development of theories of tragedy, from the work of A. C. Bradley to that of Walter Kaufmann or Northrop Frye, and the more recent work of John Winkler – considers the characters in the work as concretizations or reflections of the experience of conflicting claims, Antigone herself becoming a concrete allegorical representation of the notion of inherent contradiction (she is enjoined to obey the law of the gods requiring appropriate funeral rites, and to obey the public, human law that the gods sanction and that Hegel emblematized in the figure of Creon, a law that in this case forbids the burial of her brother). On this understanding, the play concludes by asserting the necessary emergence of civil society from the concretization of its constitutive contradictions, Antigone's sacrifice presenting physically for the play's audience (hence merely as an intuition) what would become, considered under the aspect of its concrete universality, an object of conceptual reflection (*Begriff*). Both Marx and Engels, and with less nuance early twentieth-century marxist critics like Franc Schiller, Mikhail Lifschitz and especially the Lukács of the period from *History and Class Consciousness* (1923) to his *The Young Hegel* of 1948, take from Hegel the sense that the aesthetic, and literature in particular, constitutes in this way a preliminary (if in some instances also a necessary) moment in the formation of thought or ideology – corresponding to the 'intuitive' certainty afforded by sensuous representation, which yields under the pressure of its excessive abstractness to the mediate experience afforded by conceptual reflection – rather than a concrete or instrumental intervention in a specific historical circumstance.

This, then, is the defining *philosophical* context that frames the 'return to Hegel' in the years immediately preceding and following the Second World War. That 'return' is characterized – especially in France, as Michael Kelly has shown (1983, 1986) – by a tension between two dominant interpretative traditions. The first, centred upon Hegel's earlier works, turns on an *eschatological* interpretation of the Hegelian system that partly captures those works' reliance on Böhme, and partly reflects the religious determinism that runs through Hegel's career. On this account, the form assumed by Absolute Knowledge at the conclusion of the *Phenomenology of Spirit* reflects a philosophically achieved position, 'after' which nothing new can strictly speaking be thought. That Hegel embodied this form in the concrete historical figure of Napoleon (whose battered fortunes might raise some questions about his absoluteness) does not affect the heuristic claim, or the Kantian individualism that can return with it: the position of totality achieved in and by means of the *Phenomenology of Spirit* assumes the shape of an Idea regulating the movement *and content* of 'my' thought. The motor of the dialectic's machinery, under this description, is not so much *contradiction* as it is the triad of *desire, negativity* and *recognition*, the central terms in Kojève's *Introduction to the Reading of Hegel* (1947); the work that this dialectical machine performs is *Bildung*, or education. The second interpretative tradition, centred upon Hegel's later works and of a generally socialist inclination, understands the dialectical method as a means to achieving social change, representations (both broadly cultural and literary in particular) as the reflection or externalization of social contradictions, and philosophy, literary criticism and theory as ways of provoking a reflective understanding or internalization of the social and material conditions of the work's production and reception. The stress remains on the primary contradictions in social relations, and the locus of this 'internalization' of contradictions becomes not man – as in the 'anthropological' or humanistic Hegelianism that flows from Kojève's work – but the broader notion of ideology. The characteristic triad of reflection as externalization, dialectical method and reflective internalization can nonetheless be arranged in ways almost as explicitly deterministic as obtains in eschatological readings of the Hegelian system, as in Lifschitz's work or in the Lukács of *Studies in European Realism*, where it occurs again under the aspect of the *necessary*, 'peculiar' synthesis in what Lukács calls 'the central category and criterion of realist literature', the *type*.

Much of the polemic concerning the 'return to Hegel' in postwar Europe flowed as much from continuities as from the tension between these two approaches. Allegiances were never very stable within the two camps, and in the immediate postwar period certain eccentric figures or texts not easily classified in either proved to be at least as influential in forming Hegel's reception. Such is the case in Germany with Heidegger, whose comments on Hegel in *Being and Time* (on Hegel's 'conception of time', ¶82), in the 1942–43 course Heidegger devoted to the *Phenomenology of Spirit* and in the published essay deriving from that course, the crucial 'Hegel's Concept of Experience', had a significant impact in both Germany and France; with Bertolt Brecht's criticism and plays, whose 'estrangement' effects (*Verfremdungseffekt*) put great pressure on the 'organic' synthesis of realistic representation, and closely correspond to the mode of *irony* and to the logic of *contradiction* in Hegel; so too with thinkers associated with what would come to be called the Frankfurt School, like Walter Benjamin and especially Theodor W. Adorno, already in the middle 1930s sketching out what would become his immensely suggestive account of the 'critical category' of *totality*, in *Negative Dialectics* (1966). For Adorno, the imperative to 'convict' totality or merely mythic thought finds expression methodologically in what could be called a re-literarization or a re-rhetoricization of the dialectic – a procedure that cannot be squarely fitted into either an eschatological or a classically materialist account of Hegel's reception. Adorno's closest followers in Germany and the United States have followed Adorno in seeking to define the nature of the 're-literalized' negative dialectic. Critics and philosophers more evidently in the Frankfurt School tradition – Jürgen Habermas in particular – have in contrast adopted a position on the Hegelian legacy that partly reacts to the mixed terms of Adorno's critique, generally objecting that the role Adorno assigned to aesthetics in his approach to Hegel could more properly be assigned to an explicitly *social, communicative* or *intersubjective* understanding of language use (rather than a literary or a merely rhetorical one).

In France the lines between the 'anthropological' and the materialist receptions of Hegel were no firmer, and Kojève's more immediate influence did little to settle them. Georges Bataille and Jacques Lacan – among the most influential of Kojève's students – would take from Kojève's prewar seminars on Hegel a vocabulary and set of approaches that they developed and changed dramatically and fruitfully in the following decades; Maurice Blanchot, reading Hegel through Kojève as well as Heidegger, would in his novels and criticism provide the most explicitly *literary* extension of this vocabulary. Bataille's early writings dwelt inchoately on themes and terms (the insistence of abjection, sacred terror, genuine thought understood as excremental) that would find formal echoes in Kojève's reading of Hegel a decade later. By the time of *Inner Experience* (1943) and even more pointedly in work from the 1950s, the elaboration of Kojèvian themes and terms had been married to an explicit (if entirely heterodox) marxist engagement, in a combination whose deployment of the term 'transgression' in the place of the Hegelian term 'contradiction' and the Kojèvian term 'desire' fits only obliquely the Kojèvian goals of anthropological 'education' – bringing 'man closer to the idea which he makes for himself'. Maurice Blanchot devoted chapters of *The Work of Fire* (1949) to a critique of Hegel's account of the merely 'external' nature of symbolic art, which is faulty, suggests Hegel, because the exteriority of the image never coincides fully with its spiritual content (a more highly mediated form of art being required to achieve such a coincidence. Likewise, Blanchot's enigmatic concluding essay to *The Work of Fire* turns on an interpretation of the *Phenomenology of Spirit* undertaken explicitly through an encounter with Kojève's *Introduction to the Reading of Hegel*, Blanchot's famous description of the 'two slopes of language' amounting to a rewriting of the dialectic of Hegelian aesthetics, with a node of contradiction no longer described in the earlier language of 'symbol', 'fault' and 'correspondence'.

So too with Lacan was the idiosyncratic revision of Hegel's vocabulary first adopted, brought into contact with Heidegger's work, and then dramatically shifted. Not only does Lacan's elaboration of the structural function of desire as lack (of a real object) flow directly from Kojève's analysis of the desire for recognition in the *Phenomenology of Spirit*'s dialectic of Master and Slave, much of the development of both the technique and the theory of Lacanian criticism occurs *by means of* readings of Hegel's work, and often in confrontation with thinkers who serve as proxies for Kojève and for Hegel. However firmly he condemned Hegel's residual 'humanism', Lacan's engagement with the philosopher's work lasted till the end of his career. Thus, for example, his addresses on 'Subversion of the Subject and Dialectic of Desire in the Freudian Unconscious' and 'Position of the Unconscious' published in *Ecrits* (1966) bear on the ways in which Freud 'reopens' the term 'desire' to 'the play from which revolutions spring, the hinge between truth and knowledge' that Hegel, Lacan writes, associates with the form of 'desire, *Begierde*, where the ... minimum connection the subject has to ancient knowledge, is guarded so that truth will be immanent in the realization of knowledge'.

By the time that *Hegel et la pensée moderne* appeared in Paris (1971; collecting essays and presentations from Jean Hyppolite's 1968 Collège de France seminar on Hegel's *Logic*), and in great measure on account of the conceptual and terminological revisions of Kojèvian Hegelianism in the work of Bataille, Adorno, Lacan and Blanchot, the heuristic distinction between programmatically marxist renderings of Hegel and an 'anthropological' or humanist Hegelianism was no longer tenable. What Fredric Jameson announced in 1990 as the 'impending Hegel revival' may be said to have begun in Europe and the United States with the exhaustion of that opposition, with the importation into the field of dialectics of the psychoanalytic concepts of over- and under-determination, and with the rediscovery of the notion of 'hegemony' in the work of Antonio Gramsci.

This incipient 'revival' of Hegel in France, Italy and the US has largely been defined in answer to the dramatic revisions of Hegelianism in the work of Louis Althusser and Jacques Derrida from the middle 1970s forward. The description that Louis Althusser provided in 1967 of the means by which 'individuals' become 'subjects' in given societies – famously phrased as the 'interpellation' by ideology of individuals into an existing subject-position where 'I recognize myself' – bears traces of a determinist approach to the work of Marx and Hegel, the interpellating function of ideology having material means (state apparatuses of different sorts) but in fact a structural status clearly imagined with certain psychoanalytic and Hegelian formulations in mind. Althusser's Hegelianism, however, is qualified. From 1962 onwards he argued both for distinguishing between Hegel's vision of society as a 'totality' and Marx's vision of it as a 'complex whole, structured in dominance', and for understanding that Marx's claim to having 'inverted' the Hegelian dialectic was only a 'metaphor for a real materialist transformation of the figures of the dialectic' (as he puts it in the 1975 *Is it Simple to be a Marxist in Philosophy?* (1990)), a 'real transformation' which Marx never provided explicitly. Coordinating the 'materialist' alternative to the idealist dialectic with the description of a structured society required the development of three concepts intended to clarify the deterministic relation between structure and event still palpable in Althusser's early reading of Hegel. The first two formed an integral part of Althusser's published work in the decade from 1965 to 1975. The concept of 'aleatory materialism', the third and last that Althusser developed in an exploration of the materialist dialectic that would lead him toward what he eventually called a 'philosophy of the encounter', remained inchoate, formulated in interviews and unpublished works. Its debt to Heidegger, and to Althusser's own earliest understanding of Hegel, is palpable: 'A philosophy of the *es gibt*', he writes in 'Le courant souterrain ...' (1994) 'of the "it's given thus" ... "opens" onto a vista that restores a kind of transcendental contingency to the world'. The 'transcendental contingency' of Althusser's conception of matter constitutes his last, perhaps his most controversial contribution to the dismantling of the residual categories of 'necessity' and of 'determination' in the Hegelian legacy.

Like Althusser's, Jacques Derrida's engagement with Hegel is constant, fruitful and resolutely unassimilable to any single tradition of reception. As is also true for much of the *Tel Quel* group, his earliest work on Hegel is firmly Bataillean: the fundamental essay on 'Hegelianism', 'From a Restricted to a General Economy' in *Writing and Difference* (1967), works from Bataille's Kojèvian essays to provide a striking account of a productively 'empty' and analogic use of Hegelian *Aufhebung* to 'designate the transgressive relation linking the world of sense to the world of non-sense'. For Derrida this relation is bi-directional, embedding the 'naive conscience' of philosophy (Absolute Knowledge, the philosophy of reflection, the Book) within the world of non-sense, and the world of non-sense (madness, death, writing construed as *écriture*) within that of sense. The consequences of this 'transgressive' (and no longer simply dialectical) re-description of the relation between sense and non-sense are taken in political terms: the movement between Book and writing can be read 'as a reactionary or as a revolutionary movement, or both at once'. The Bataillean strain, and this early insistence on the necessary 'emptiness' of Hegelian *Aufhebung*, are never far from Derrida's treatments of Hegel.

Beginning in the 1980s, and with increased coherence in the decades since, an 'unfamiliar' Hegel has indeed begun to emerge from the interaction of the Althusserian, Derridean and Lacanian critiques of the Hegelian orthodoxies. In the US, the development of 'American' deconstruction in the late 1970s and early 1980s occurred very much under the aspect of a sympathetic critique of Hegelianism remarkably close to that found in Adorno and in Derrida, though inflected with a different and characteristic interest in the question of the philosophical work's *literariness*. In the work of critics like Paul de Man, Andrzej Warminski, Rodolphe Gasché, Timothy Bahti and others a highly rhetoricized Hegel emerges. More overtly psychoanalytic 'returns' to Hegel have included the work of Henry Sussman and especially of Judith Butler, whose 1987 *Subjects of Desire: Hegelian Reflections in Twentieth-Century France* set out the articulation between the stress on embodiment found in the languages of Husserlian phenomenology, and the legacy of Kojèvian 'desire' in Derrida, Foucault and others. In subsequent work Butler has developed influential descriptions of gender performativity, of materiality and of the Hegelian and Freudian postulation that one comes to 'be' through a dependency on the Other. Most explicitly in chapters on Althusser and on the 'Unhappy Consciousness' section of the *Phenomenology of Spirit* in her *The Psychic Life of Power* (1997), Butler provides an account of the 'vulnerability of strategies of subjection' to the 'capacity of desire to be withdrawn and to reattach' 'blindly', a 'blindness' of desire drawn conceptually from both Lacan's description of the metonymic form of desire, and Althusser's account of the 'aleatory' nature of the event – and in both cases marshalled against a deterministic reading of 'desire' in line with Hegelian eschatology.

Butler and Gasché's recent work on Hegel has often been undertaken in open dialogue with such European philosophers as Rosi Braidotti, Ernesto Laclau and Chantal Mouffe (whose *Hegemony and Socialist Strategy* (1985) brought to the fore the political and philosophical weight of the notion of contingency, and provided a far-reaching critique of the Hegelian notion of social totality in terms drawn from Gramsci rather than from Adorno), and especially with the Slovenian Hegelian-psychoanalyst philosophers Mladen Dolar and Slavoj Žižek. Žižek in particular, arguing against Derrida, Gasché and Warminski in a number of publications, suggests that 'tarrying' with the negative moment in the Hegelian philosophy of reflection makes it possible to avoid understanding the distinction between necessity and contingency by means of the 'category of pure formal conversion', and instead to stress the 'undecidable' logic that governs their relation. It is a sign of the productive 'unfamiliarity' of this returning Hegel that in the most recent literary-theoretical and philosophical work about and inspired by him the parallel notions of 'undecideability' and 'contingency', the Althusserian 'encounter' and what Warminski (following Derrida) calls Hegel's 'writing' emerge as a means of envisioning, in Laclau and Mouffe's terms, a 'radical democratic' politics.

Jacques Lezra

Further reading and works cited

Adorno, T. W. *Negative Dialectics*. New York, 1990.
Althusser, L. *Lenin and Philosophy, and Other Essays*. New York, 1972.
—. *Positions, 1964–1975*. Paris, 1976.
—. *Philosophy and the Spontaneous Philosophy of the Scientists & Other Essays*, ed. and intro. G. Elliot. London, 1990.
—. *Ecrits philosophiques et politiques*, Vol. I. Paris, 1994.
—. *For Marx*. London, 1996.
—. *Reading Capital*. London, 1997a.
—. *The Spectre of Hegel*. London, 1997a.
— and Navarro, F. *Filosofia y marxismo*. Mexico, 1988.
Barnett, S. (ed.) *Hegel After Derrida*. London, 1998.
Bataille, G. *Inner Experience*. Albany, NY, 1988.
Benhabib, S. *Critique, Norm, and Utopia*. New York, 1986.
Blanchot, M. *The Work of Fire*. Stanford, CA, 1995.
Bourdieu, P. *Distinction: A Social Critique of the Judgement of Taste*. Cambridge, MA, 1984.
—. *The Logic of Practice*. Stanford, CA, 1990.
Brod, H. *Hegel's Philosophy of Politics*. Boulder, CO, 1992
Butler, J. *Excitable Speech*. New York, 1997.
—. *The Psychic Life of Power*. Stanford, CA, 1997.
—. *Subjects of Desire*. New York, 1999.
— et al. *Contingency, Hegemony, Universality*. London, 2000.
Cassirer, E. *Kant's Life and Thought*. New Haven, CT, 1981.
Croce, B. *What is Living and What is Dead of the Philosophy of Hegel*. New York, 1969.
Deleuze, G. *Nietzsche and Philosophy*. New York, 1983.
—. *Kant's Critical Philosophy*. Minneapolis, MN, 1984.
— and Guattari, F. *Anti-Oedipus*, preface M. Foucault. Minneapolis, MN, 1983.
—. *A Thousand Plateaus*. Minneapolis, MN, 1987.
de Man, P. *Aesthetic Ideology*. Minneapolis, MN, 1996.
Derrida, J. *Writing and Difference*. Chicago, 1978.
—. *Margins of Philosophy*. Chicago, 1982.

—. *Glas*. Lincoln, NE, 1986.

—. *The Truth in Painting*. Chicago, 1987

Descombes, V. *Modern French Philosophy*. Cambridge, 1980.

Dworkin, R. M. *Taking Rights Seriously*. Cambridge, 1977.

Foucault, M. 'The Subject and Power', in *Michel Foucault: Beyond Structuralism and Hermeneutics*, eds B. Dreyfus and P. Rabinow. Chicago, 1983.

—. 'What is Enlightenment? Was ist Aufklärung?', in *The Foucault Reader*, ed. P. Rabinow. New York, 1984.

—. 'Kant on Enlightenment and Revolution', *Economy and Society*, 15, 1, February 1986.

—. *Mental Illness and Psychology*. Berkeley, CA, 1987.

Guyer, P. (ed.) *The Cambridge Companion to Kant*. Cambridge, 1992.

Hamacher, W. *Pleroma: Reading in Hegel*. Stanford, CA, 1998.

Hegel, G. W. F. *Hegel's Philosophy of Right*. Oxford, 1965.

—. *Hegel's Science of Logic*. London, 1969.

—. *Hegel on Tragedy*, eds and intro. A. and H. Paolucci. New York, 1975.

—. *Aesthetics: Lectures on Fine Art*. Oxford, 1975.

—. *Phenomenology of Spirit*. Oxford, 1977.

—. *Elements of the Philosophy of Right*, ed. A. W. Wood. Cambridge, 1991.

Heidegger, M. *Holzwege*. Frankfurt, 1950.

—. *Being and Time*. New York, 1962.

—. *Kant and the Problem of Metaphysics*. Bloomington, IN, 1962.

—. *What is a Thing?* Chicago, 1968.

—. *Hegel's Concept of Experience*. New York, 1983.

Höffe, O. *Immanuel Kant*. Albany, NY, 1994.

Horkheimer, M. and Adorno, T. W. *Dialectic of Enlightenment*. New York, 1972.

Hyppolite, J. *Studies on Marx and Hegel*. New York, 1969.

—. *Figures de la pensée philosophique*. Paris, 1971.

—. *Genesis and Structure of Hegel's 'Phenomenology of Spirit'*. Evanston, IL, 1974.

—. *Logic and Existence*. Albany, NY, 1997.

Jameson, F. *Late Marxism*. London, 1992.

Kant, I. *Observations on the Feeling of the Beautiful and Sublime*. Berkeley, CA, 1981.

—. *Critique of Judgement*. Indianapolis, IN, 1987.

—. *The Metaphysics of Morals*, trans. and ed. M. Gregor. Cambridge, 1996.

—. *Critique of Practical Reason*. Cambridge, 1997.

—. *Critique of Pure Reason*. Cambridge, 1998a.

—. *Groundwork of the Metaphysics of Morals*. Cambridge, 1998b.

Kelly, M. 'The Post-War Hegel Revival in France: A Bibliographical Essay', *Journal of European Studies*, xiii, 1983.

—. 'Hegel in France Today: A Bibliographical Essay', *Journal of European Studies*, xvi, 1986.

Kojève, A. *Introduction to the Reading of Hegel*. Ithaca, NY, 1980.

Lacan, Jacques. *Ecrits*. Paris, 1966.

—. *Ecrits: A Selection*. New York, 1977.

—. *The Ethics of Psychoanalysis, 1959–1960*. New York, 1992.

Laclau, E. and Mouffe, C. *Hegemony and Socialist Strategy*. London, 1985.

Lefebvre, H. *Dialectical Materialism*. London, 1974.

Levinas, E. *Totality and Infinity*. Pittsburgh, PA, 1969.

Lukács, G. *History and Class Consciousness*. Cambridge, MA, 1971.

—. *Studies in European Realism*. London, 1972.

—. *The Young Hegel*. Cambridge, MA, 1976.

MacIntyre, A. C. *After Virtue*. Notre Dame, IN, 1981.

Pinkard, T. *Hegel: A Biography*. Cambridge, 2000.

Propp, V. *Morphology of the Folk Tale*. Austin, TX, 1968.

Rawls, J. *A Theory of Justice*. Cambridge, MA, 1999.

Ricoeur, P. 'Symbole et temporalité', *Archivio di Filosofia*, 1–2, 1963.

Sartre, J.-P. *What is Literature?* Cambridge, MA, 1988.

Sloterdijk, P. *Critique of Cynical Reason*. Minneapolis, MN, 1987.

Smith, B. Herrnstein. *Contingencies of Value*. Cambridge, MA, 1988.

Stern, R. (ed.) *G. W. F. Hegel: Critical Assessments*. London, 1993.

Sussman, H. *The Hegelian Aftermath*. Baltimore, MD, 1982.

Taylor, C. *Hegel*. Cambridge, 1975.

Theweleit, K. *Male Fantasies*. Minneapolis, MN, 1987.

Warminski, A. *Readings in Interpretation*. Minneapolis, MN, 1987.

Weiskel, T. *The Romantic Sublime*. Baltimore, MD, 1976.

Wimsatt, W. K. and Beardsley, M. C. *The Verbal Icon*. Lexington, KY, 1954.

Žižek, S. *The Sublime Object of Ideology*. London, 1989.

—. *Tarrying With the Negative*. Durham, NC, 1993.

—. *The Indivisible Remainder*. London, 1996.

—. *The Ticklish Subject*. London, 1999.

3. Johann Christian Friedrich Hölderlin (1770–1843)

During his lifetime, more than half of which (1806–43) was spent in mental illness, Friedrich Hölderlin's work and thought was largely unappreciated. Although his Swabian compatriots sought to reclaim him as a poet of the 'homeland', the critical reaction to his lyric work was overwhelmingly negative, so that a collected edition (incomplete as it was) had to wait until 1846. Furthermore, biographical interest in Hölderlin's personal destiny (fostered by the interpretations of Wilhelm Waiblinger, who began visiting him in 1822) overshadowed engagement with his work for most of the nineteenth century.

However, Hölderlin's novel *Hyperion*, published in two volumes in 1797 and 1799, was widely appreciated, and a second edition appeared in 1822. The Romantic authors Bettina and Ludwig Achim von Arnim (1785–1859 and 1781–1831) and Clemens Brentano (1778–1842) held not only *Hyperion*, but some of Hölderlin's lyric work in highest esteem. Through the editorial efforts of Gustav Schwab (1792–1850) and Ludwig Uhland (1787–1862), an incomplete volume of Hölderlin's collected poetry was published in 1826. Finally, the Young Germans' reception of Hölderlin culminated in Alexander Jung's 1848 monograph *Friedrich Hölderlin und sein Werk*. This book influenced the philosopher Friedrich Nietzsche (1844–1900) whose sustained engagement with Hölderlin can be traced back to 1861. It focused, in particular, on the form of what Bothe calls 'the poetic-philosophical discourse (Bothe 1994, 51) and on Empedocles, a tragic character.

During the second half of the nineteenth century, however, Hölderlin scholarship was largely inspired by a scientific-positivist mentality. The most perceptive interpretation in this spirit is probably Emil Petzold's (Petzold 1986), which gives due weight to Hölderlin's utopian-democratic, if not anarchist, political orientation, and to the originality of his thought, as well as to his interlinking of Hellenism with Christianity. By contrast, the most problematic is the psychopathologically inspired work of Wilhelm Lange-Eichbaum (Lange 1909), whose dubious claim to fame relies on its passing psychiatric criteria of 'normality' off as aesthetic-intellectual valorizations.

It was not Nietzsche's own reception of Hölderlin, but elements of his philosophy of art, of history and of 'life' that entered into the transformation of Hölderlin studies at the beginning of the twentieth century, inaugurated by the work of Wilhelm Dilthey (1833–1911) and Norbert von Hellingrath, who fell at Verdun in 1916. Dilthey's influential study *Das Erlebnis und die Dichtung (Lived Experience and Poetry)*, first published in 1906, exalts Hölderlin's poetic stature in an unprecedented manner, while also idealizing him as a visionary (in keeping with the philosopher's understanding of art as non-rational cognition) and depriving his work of both its speculative and socio-political dimensions.

Hellingrath, who had discovered the manuscripts of Hölderlin's late hymns and of his Pindar translations, brought out a collected edition with commentary, in four volumes, the final one of which was published posthumously in 1917. His key concerns are re-mythologization, a conception of language as functioning autonomously rather than communicatively, together with a focus on its musical-incantatory rather than semantic character, the exaltation of German poetic diction in its supposedly unique relation to the ancient Greek, and a view of Hölderlin's entire work as constituting fundamentally a single poem. The most disturbing aspect of Hellingrath's Hölderlin interpretation, however, is its tacit assimilation of Hölderlin's notion of the 'fatherland' to the nationalist rhetoric of his day, coupling it with the idea of the cultural mission and elect status of Germany – the 'secret Germany' envisaged by the poet Stefan George and his circle, of which latter Hellingrath was a member. These construals prefigured the National Socialist distorted interpretation (which did not shy away from textual alteration) and ideological appropriation of Hölderlin in the 1930s and early 1940s. Moreover, all these strands of thought entered in highly complex ways into the powerful readings of Hölderlin that are central to the thought of Martin Heidegger. So did the poetic engagement with Hölderlin on the part of the Austrian poet Georg Trakl, and of Rainer Maria Rilke, although Heidegger remained unresponsive to the inscription of Hölderlin in the work of Paul Celan.

Heidegger, who devoted three lecture courses to Hölderlin's hymns as well a volume of essays of 1936–68, *Erlauterungen zu Hölderlins Dichtung* (Heidegger 1971), understands his own thought in important ways as an 'interlocution' with Hölderlin who articulates the essential being (*Wesen*) of poetry as bringing language to reveal the being of beings, in a modality of revelation that does not violate being's self-withdrawal. Furthermore, Hölderlin, for him, limns the essential-historical self-understanding of his people and of the West.

Heidegger's thought and the Hölderlin translations by Heidegger scholars such as Jean Beaufret and François Fédier have stimulated and influenced an ongoing tradition of French Heidegger interpretation, ranging from the Catholic theological perspective of Jean-Luc Marion to poststructuralist readings by Maurice Blanchot, Jean-Luc Nancy and Philippe Lacoue-Labarthe. A different approach characterizes the biographically and politically oriented labours of Pierre Bertaux. Given the complexity and vitality of both the French and the German scholarship, Hölderlin reveals himself to be a figure of contemporary theoretical importance rather than a precursor in the usual sense.

Life, work and thought

Hölderlin's birth in Lauffen in the Duchy of Würtemberg placed him squarely in a pietist milieu of introspective religiosity (as well as of bourgeois prosperity) that was suspicious of the arts and remote from the cosmopolitanism of the major academic centres. His twice-widowed mother sought to channel her son's high intellectual, literary and musical gifts into the secure career of a small-town or rural pastor, which he always found uncongenial. He received a theological and classical education, first at the monastic boarding school of Maulbronn, then at the Tübingen theological academy. His master's thesis concerned *The History of the Fine Arts Among the Greeks and Parallels between the Sayings of Solomon and Hesiod's Works and Days*. At the Tübingen academy, he formed a close and lasting friendship with the future philosopher G. W. F. Hegel, which was joined, in 1790, by the younger F. W. J. Schelling. Hölderlin's role in the development of German idealism was formative rather than merely receptive. His friendship with the lawyer and revolutionary activist Isaak von Sinclair, which lasted until the latter's death in 1815, also began in Tübingen.

The odes and hymns of his early poetic creativity show both the strong influence of F. G. Klopstock and Hölderlin's characteristic exalted diction. They are concerned with themes such as freedom, harmony, truth, beauty, humanity and nature – topics too abstract to allow them to be poetically fully successful. They also reveal his deep and lasting sympathy for the ideals of the French Revolution, and a nostalgic self-identification with the culture of ancient Greece.

Philosophically, he had studied Plato, Spinoza, Leibniz and Rousseau, and, beginning in 1790, he immersed himself passionately in a thorough study of Kant, and later of Fichte, whose lectures he attended in Jena in 1795 and whose thought he discussed with Hegel. He understood Kant's philosophy to be fundamentally oriented toward the liberation of reason from any form of heteronomy. It resonated, for him, with his own cultural critique that saw an original order of freedom perverted into an order of legality, and with his understanding of the French Revolution as seeking to bring about 'a reign of love', where the ideal and the real are no longer disjoint. At the same time, he criticized a hegemony of reason that subordinated the senses, feeling and creative imagination. Kant's notion of the 'thing in itself' attested, for him, to the fundamental unknowability of the enigma of reality by reason alone. By contrast, love is understood as the power to institute interrelations, enabling one ultimately to think the whole, which Kant's philosophy appeared to him to be incapable of.

He criticized Fichte's thought for leading to the dead-end of an isolated ego. His argument is that pure being cannot be understood as identity; for identity presupposes separation. The difficulty is how to think being as both divisible and without separation.

These philosophical explorations, as well as investigations of the relationship of antiquity to modernity, of the possibility of a 'mythology of reason', of the relation between poetry and philosophy, and other theoretical topics are articulated in a series of essays that he often wrote for the purpose of clarifying and developing his own thoughts, rather than with the intent of publication.

After the conclusion of his studies, he accepted a post as private tutor to Charlotte von Kalb's son Fritz, which took him first to Waltershausen near Jena, then to Jena and Weimar. The position was mediated by Schiller, whom Hölderlin venerated, and who published a number of Hölderlin's early works in periodicals that he edited. The position did not ultimately prove successful. Soon after its termination (after a stay in Jena and a precipitous retreat to his mother's house in Nürtingen), Hölderlin accepted another position as private tutor with the Gontard family in Frankfurt (1796). Here his educational programme and relationship to his pupil Henri proved successful, but his passionate and reciprocated love for the lady of the house, Susette Gontard, whom he called Diotima, brought his employment to an abrupt and emotionally painful end in 1798. He retreated to Homburg, the home of Sinclair.

His work on *Hyperion*, which had continued over some seven years, came to fruition with the publication of the two volumes in 1797 and 1799. The Frankfurt period also brought an intense philosophical interchange with Hegel, whose own position there as private tutor Hölderlin had mediated. His poetic work during this period is marked by formal innovation. In particular, he adopted and perfected the asclepiad and alcaic strophe forms, developing their expressive potential and writing epigrammatic odes. A number of important lyric works, such as *Stimme des Volks, An die Deutschen, Die Heimath* and *Diotima* took form during this period. However, the culmination of Hölderlin's lyric creativity was still to come.

Given that *Hyperion* is the one work by which Hölderlin was generally known in the nineteenth century, a brief discussion of it is called for. The novel is composed of letters written by the title character, an eighteenth-century Greek (the subtitle calls him 'a hermit in Greece') to his German friend Bellarmin. The letters are retrospective and reflective, revealing Hyperion's life struggles and their resolution. Although the novel is generally considered to be a *Bildungsroman* or novel of personal formation, this has been disputed on the grounds that it is not fundamentally concerned with a personal itinerary, but with a self-consignment to nature (for Hölderlin nature has Spinozan resonance and is a notion akin to that of Being) which gives one poetic entitlement. Hyperion has lost the spontaneous union with nature characteristic of naive consciousness or of childhood through the separative force of a rational quest; his 'eccentric path' (the centre being union) cannot seek to regain it, but must realize a new and higher form of union out of estrangement. His loving mentor is Adamas, whose pronouncement 'God in us' leads him to envisage a social order of free, autonomous individuals. In his friendship with the freedom fighter Alabanda, he seeks to realize this vision in battle, but he soon encounters the power of violence to become an end in itself, rather than remaining subordinate to a higher purpose. In estrangement from Alabanda, he meets the ideal figure of Diotima who tells him that it is enough to be or to live, and that, in the 'divine world', there can be neither masters nor slaves (1976 XI, 768). Their separation is made necessary by his 'eccentric path', and her subsequent death leads him to become, as she had foreseen, an educator of his people through the written word, and a 'priest' of nature in keeping with Hölderlin's understanding of the sacrality of the poet's vocation.

A key work of Hölderlin's first Homburg period – a time during which he sought in vain to establish himself as an independent writer – is his tragedy *Empedocles*, which he had already begun to work on in Frankfurt. It is extant only in three fragmentary versions, together with the theoretical essay 'Ground for Empedocles'. This body of work leads directly on to the theory of tragedy that Hölderlin developed during his second Homburg period (1804–6). The challenge addressed in the three successive versions is that the title character (whose thought is not that of the pre-Socratic philosopher but Hölderlin's own) cannot just choose to embrace death for reasons of his own. Rather, his death must be called for by 'the destiny of his time', or the historical destiny of his homeland.

Hölderlin follows here his understanding of Greek tragedy as the most severe of poetic forms, constrained to purge the tragic events of any merely accidental factors (it is also for this reason that he chooses temporally and culturally remote protagonists). The action is to show forth no mere human dilemma, but a divine process.

Hölderlin achieves this ideal in the third version, but only at the cost of consigning all action to the past. Empedocles here unifies in his individual person the 'aorgic' element of nature (linked to what Hölderlin calls *Todeslust*, a desire for death) and the 'organic' element of human measure, and he does so at a time of the most acute historical opposition of these principles. Since, however, the unification is purely individual and cannot enter into the life of the people, it must by tragic necessity be destroyed. Tragedy is revealed here as intimately bound up with far-reaching historical changes (*Zeitenwende*).

The first Homburg period yielded some major odes, hymns and elegies. The Pindaric hymn *Wie wenn am Feiertage* (*As on a Holiday*), which opens directly upon Hölderlin's late hymnic work, dates from 1800. However, much of the particular importance of this period lies in its rich harvest of philosophical and poetological essays. These address the relationship between philosophy and poetry (philosophical insight forms the basis of poetic practice but cannot grasp the 'higher interconnection'), between art and nature, ancient and modern poetic practice, and questions of poetic form. A key essay for the theory of tragedy is 'Das Werden im Vergehen' ('Becoming in Perishing'), which concerns the relationship of poetry to history, and the tragic law governing both history and nature.

In June of 1800, Hölderlin left Homburg for a brief stay in Nürtingen, followed by a sojourn of several months with his friend C. Landauer in Stuttgart. This happy period gave rise to serene poetry, such as *Der Gang aufs Land*. Hölderlin was able to support himself in Stuttgart by giving private philosophy lessons, but he nevertheless decided, in January 1801, to accept a new position as tutor in Hauptwil, Switzerland. His employment was terminated after only three months, but his experience of the majestic Swiss alpine landscape was for him (always deeply involved in the study of landscape) of great poetic importance. It is mirrored, for instance, in the late hymn *Der Rhein*. The elegy *Heimkunft. An die Verwandten* reflects his homeward journey across the *Bodensee*.

At the end of 1801, he left Germany once more to take on a position as private tutor with the consul D. C. Meyer in Bordeaux, France. This position was likewise of short duration, but important for him in that it allowed him to experience, in the southern landscape and southern culture, the essential presence of antiquity. In late June 1802, Susette Gontard died of an infectious illness. In the same month, Hölderlin arrived in Germany (first Nürtingen and Stuttgart) in a condition of nervous exhaustion and agitation aggravated by grief. By the autumn, he was nevertheless able to begin intensive work on the hymn *Patmos* (dedicated to Count Hessen-Homburg), initiating a period of intense lyric creativity. Through Sinclair's efforts, Hölderlin's translations of Sophocles's *Oedipus Tyrannos* and *Antigone*, together with two difficult but important theoretical essays, were published in 1804, but their reception was distressingly negative, since their idiosyncrasies were ascribed to the poet's rumoured 'madness'. They were staged only in 1951.

Sinclair also procured (and financed) a nominal position as court librarian for Hölderlin in Homburg, which he held until the autumn of 1806, when his mental condition deteriorated to the point that he was forcibly institutionalized, only to be released the next year as incurable. At this time, the master carpenter Heinrich Zimmer (who admired *Hyperion*) offered to take over the patient's care. Hölderlin remained until his death at

Zimmer's home in Tübingen, where his room in the 'tower' commanded a beautiful view, and where, besides his flute, a gift piano was at his disposal.

Several significant changes are evident in Hölderlin's late poetry, which constitutes his supreme lyric achievement. Firstly, the hymnic form predominates over those of the ode and elegy (the latter predominated in 1800), together with a turn to free verse (still written in strophes). Secondly, philosophical reflection and questioning is now incorporated into the poems themselves, which indicates a privileging of the hermeneutic over the visionary mode. The poet's vocation to mediate the holy and to interpret the sacred (divine and heroic) names of history is not the role of a seer, but of a seeker. Finally, this late period is the time of Hölderlin's 'patriotic turning'; but one must guard against reading the adjective in any nationalistic sense. Hölderlin (who had included a famous invective against the Germans in *Hyperion*) now turns toward his native country envisaged in terms of its 'Hesperian' relationship to 'Oriental' Greece, in keeping with the quasi-dialectical philosophy of history elaborated in his Remarks on Sophoclean tragedy. If Germany is to be the place of a new cultural and spiritual flowering, the reason lies, for Hölderlin, in the thoughtfulness and quietude he found among its people. Significantly, he portrays Germania (in *Germanien*) as a priestess and as unarmed.

Some of the late hymns (notably *Griechenland*) are hermetic, but in others such as *Andenken* or *Mnemosyne*, the hermeticism is tempered by a compelling beauty. Heidegger's Hölderlin essays and lecture courses address chiefly the late hymns, including the great stream hymns.

Apart from developing, as already noted, a philosophy of history and carrying forward the theoretical elucidation of tragedy begun during the first Homburg period, the difficult 'Remarks' on Sophoclean tragedy introduce the notion of a 'categorical turning' through which God and man must part from each other, leading to the tragic perdition of the protagonist. The formal analysis highlights the *caesura* as the inscription of this turning.

Hölderlin continued to write poems during his illness. These are generally short rhymed poems of transparent simplicity, but also of a certain rigidity, showing none of the audacity of thought and diction of the poet's lucid work. Perhaps, however, they realize in their own way Hölderlin's belief that what is most exalted stands revealed in the most inconspicuous.

Theoretical importance

The theoretical issues raised by Hölderlin's work are far-reaching, given not only his original researches in poetics and the theory of tragedy, but also and above all the fact that, far from merely drawing on philosophy, he was a well-trained creative philosopher in his own right. His philosophical thought, moreover, is integral to his poetic achievement.

The key Hegelian motifs of spirit seeking to grasp itself through a self-exteriorization in nature and history, together with a dialectical understanding of historical process, are largely Hölderlinian in their incipience. Hölderlin's insightful articulation of the dialectical bond between the cultures of ancient Greece (and more remotely India or the Orient) and Occidental Hesperia (see his 'Remarks on Antigone') are crucial to Heidegger's own efforts to think the 'historical destiny' of the West and the crisis of his time.

The dialectical structure of Hölderlin's historical analyses also informs his poetics. For instance, his theory of the alternation of tones, formulated around 1800, presupposes the dialectical principle that one's 'ownmost' is what is most difficult to realize. Far from coming naturally, it requires the challenges of opposition and estrangement to achieve fruition. Thus the 'ideal' (intellectual-contemplative) tone fundamental to the tragic mode not only calls for a countervailing tone that constitutes the work's 'art-character' (here the heroic), but the tension between these must be mediated by the previously excluded tone (the naive) if the basic tone is to come into its own convincingly. Moreover, the poetic work can only return, as it must, to its original basic tone at the completion of its progressive development by passing through the 'counter-rhythmic interruption' of the *caesura*.

Spirit and dialectics aside, however, Hölderlin thinks otherwise than Hegel, for reason is not, for him, sovereign and capable of grasping absolute reality, but rather the latter poses an always 'hyperbolic' challenge to human thought. In this fundamental conviction, Hölderlin's thought is, as Heidegger puts it, transgressive of metaphysics. Although he remains committed to intrinsic truth (and willing to formulate the grand narratives that Lyotard regards as defining modernity), he anticipates postmodern insights both by his recognition that metaphysical-systematic knowledge of reality as a whole is inachievable, and by his refusal to grant reason sole or sovereign access to truth. Indeed, the hyperbolic challenge to think reality remains, for him, compelling because, where reason comes up against its limits, the senses and feeling remain receptive to intimations of truth.

Truth is not, for him, fundamentally univocal but pluridimensional, and the challenge to think it is a challenge to cultivate openness to new thought-forms and dimensions of experience. Here, one may note, Hölderlin's trans-metaphysical thought is entirely in harmony with his anarchist political persuasions. It is also this challenge of voicing a non-univocal truth (or, more conventionally expressed, of 'saying the holy') which makes for the intensely self-reflective character of Hölderlin's poetic practice – a self-reflective mode of writing that is, of course, carried forward by poets such as Rilke and Celan. Finally, responding to the hyperbolic challenge of truth is, for Hölderlin, always a matter of exposure and risk. The lightning bolt as which the god reveals himself may leave only ashes, or the visionary poet may find himself 'struck by Apollo'. In contrast to the German idealist paradigm of converting negativity into spiritual gain (a paradigm that fails before the horrors of the twentieth century), Hölderlin's thought can countenance disaster and irrecuperable loss, yet it resolutely repudiates nihilism.

Véronique M. Fóti

Further reading and works cited

Allemann, B. *Hölderlin und Heidegger*. Zürich, 1954.
Beck, A. and Raabe, P. *Hölderlin. Eine Chronik in Text und Bild*. Frankfurt, 1970.
Beyer, U. (ed.) *Neue Wege zu Hölderlin*. Würzburg, 1994.
Binder, E., and Weimar, K. *Friedrich Hölderlin. Studien von Wolfgang Binder*. Frankfurt, 1987.
Böschenstein, B. and Rider, J. le (eds) *Holderlin vu de France*. Tübingen, 1987.
Bothe, H. *'Ein Zeichen sind wir, deutungslos'. Die Rezeption Hölderlins von ihren Anfängen bis zu Stefan George*. Stuttgart, 1992.
—. *Hölderlin: Zurhrung*. Hamburg, 1994.
Courtine, J-F. (ed.) *L'Herne: Hölderlin*. Paris, 1989.
Gaier, U. *Hölderlin*. Tübingen and Basel, 1993.
Heidegger, M. *Erläuterungen zu Hölderlins Dichtung*. Frankfurt, 1971.
—. *Hölderlins Hymne 'Der Ister'*, Sommersemester 1942, GA, vol. 53; *Hölderlins Hymne 'Andenken'*, Wintersemester 1941/2, GA, vol. 52; *Hölderlins Hymnen 'Germanien' und 'Der Rhein'*, Wintersemester 1934/35: all in *Heidegger Gesamtausgabe*. Frankfurt am Main, 1976–.

Henrich, D. *Hegel im Kontext*, 4th rev. edn. Frankfurt, 1988.

Hölderlin, F. *Sämtliche Werke*, Grosse Stuttgarter Ausgabe, eds F. Beissner and A. Beck, 15 vols.
    Stuttgart, 1943–85.

—. *Sämtliche Werke*, Frankfurter historisch-kritische Ausgabe, eds D. E. Sattleer and W. Greddeck, 20
    vols. Frankfurt, 1976.

—. *Friedrich Hölderlin: Poems and Fragments*. Cambridge, 1980.

—. *Hölderlin: Hymns and Fragments*. Princeton, NJ, 1984.

—. *Hölderlin. Essays and Letters on Theory*, ed. T. Pfau. Albany, NY, 1988.

Jamme, C., and Pöggeler, O. (eds) *Hölderlins letzte Homburger Jahre (1904–1906)*. Bonn, 1988.

Lacoue-Labarthe, P. *L'Antigone de Sophocle, suivi de La Césure du spéculatif*. Paris, 1978.

Lange, W. *Hölderlin – Eine Pathographie*. Stuttgart, 1909.

Lernout, G. *The Poet as Thinker: Hölderlin in France*. New York, 1994.

Petzold, E. *Hölderlin's Brod und Wein. Ein exegetischer Versuch*. Sambor, 1896.

Szondi, P. *Hölderlin Studien. Mit einem Traktat über philologische Erkenntnis*. Frankfurt, 1967.

Warminski, A. *Readings in Interpretation*. Minneapolis, MN, 1987.

4. Karl Marx (1818–1883)

Although Karl Marx did not compose any sustained piece of writing on aesthetics or literature, he exerted an enormous influence on literary theory and criticism of the twentieth century. Trained as a philosopher in the left Hegelian tradition, Marx is most noted for his contributions to political economy and for his revolutionary political activities. Because his theories about capitalism and about the history of human development encompass society in its entirety, his thought has relevance for art and literature. Marx was educated in the classical tradition and had a tremendous knowledge of European literature. His observations on authors, literary texts and related matters, when combined with the comments of Friedrich Engels, his lifelong associate and collaborator, comprise two large volumes. But these remarks rarely consist of extended discussions: most often they amount to allusions or casual references, more decorative than substantive in nature. The most frequently cited passages of direct literary concern are the criticism of Eugène Sue's serialized novel *The Mysteries of Paris* in *The Holy Family*, the debate with Ferdinand Lassalle over his drama on Franz von Sickingen, and occasional prescriptive comments in the late letters of Friedrich Engels. But the impact of marxism is only partially related to these discussions. Much more important for subsequent writers was the emphasis on the embeddedness of all culture in social and economic relations. Although critics such as Georg Lukács, Antonio Gramsci, Louis Althusser, Raymond Williams, Theodor Adorno and Fredric Jameson have differed significantly on what Marx meant and how one should apply his insights to literary texts, they all agree on the fertile connection between a socioeconomic realm and the arena of culture. Marx's greatest achievement for literary studies was his insistence that literature is never entirely autonomous, and that it represents a mediated ideological statement about genuine social struggle.

Born in Trier in 1818 into an assimilated Jewish family that soon converted to Protestantism, Marx attended the local Gymnasium (college preparatory high school) and in 1835 the University of Bonn, where he was supposed to follow in the footsteps of his father Heinrich and study law. The following year he secretly became engaged to Jenny von Westphalen, whom he married in 1943; of their four children, only two survived their childhood years. In 1836 Marx transferred to Berlin, where he soon became interested in Hegelian philosophy. After his dissertation on Democritus and Epicurus was accepted at the University of Jena in 1841, he turned to journalism, editing for a time the *Rheinische Zeitung* in Cologne until it was banned in 1843. Radicalized by his tenure as editor, Marx was forced to leave Germany and take up residence in Paris in 1843. Here he met Friedrich Engels, the son of a wealthy north German businessman, who had just returned from an extended stay in England. Marx moved to Brussels in 1845, but returned to Germany briefly during the revolutionary years of 1848–9, when he edited the *Neue Rheinische Zeitung*. Expelled in the aftermath of the unsuccessful revolution in 1849, Marx and his family settled in London, where he spent the rest of his life in poverty researching and writing on various topics, mostly on current events or issues pertaining to political economy, and contributing to the organizational efforts of the communist movement. Adversely affected by the death of his wife Jenny and his oldest daughter in the early 1880s, and already in ill health due to years of hardship, Marx died in 1883.

Marx's earliest writings revolve around a critique of religion, which he initially conceived as the preliminary task of any radical philosophy. In the first and only issue of the *Deutsch-französische Jahrbücher* in 1844, he tackled the thorny issue of Jewish emancipation in the notorious essay 'On the Jewish Question'. Although the essay has been frequently controversial because of Marx's derogatory remarks about Jewish business practices, his central argument is that emancipation is incomplete if it entails only religious or political and not a total human emancipation: for Marx genuine emancipation is not achieved with the extension of rights to certain religious groups, but only with a radical refashioning of the total social order. He argues along the same lines in his famous 'Critique of a Hegelian Philosophy of Right', the second essay he included in the *Deutsch-französische Jahrbücher*. In the celebrated comparison between religion and opium, he claims that our concern with the afterlife diverts our attention from the pursuit of happiness in this world. Religion represents the self-alienation of human beings, and just as the critique of religion reveals the true character of belief, so too philosophy should set itself the task of clarifying the obfuscatory aspects of the real world. The trajectory in this important essay starts from a critique of religion and proceeds through philosophy to politics and revolution. Already at this stage in his development Marx had determined that negation in the realm of thought was insufficient: if historical progress is going to occur, there has to be a real struggle involving a historical agent that will propel history forward. The proletariat, as the only class that could represent society as a whole, is appointed the task of redeeming society. Philosophy and the working class hold the hope for the future: the essential task is not just the interpretation of the world, but its wholesale transformation.

In his writings prior to the *Communist Manifesto* Marx often resorted to concepts adopted from his predecessors in order to analyse the economic predicament of the proletariat. A case in point is the notion of 'alienation', which figures prominently in the *Economic and Philosophic Manuscripts*, composed in Parisian exile in 1844. The term is appropriated from G. W. F. Hegel and Ludwig Feuerbach. Hegel admitted nature into his system as the self-alienation of Spirit; thus he maintains that man as a natural being is the self-alienation of the Absolute or of God. Feuerbach holds precisely the opposite position, with which Marx largely concurred: God is self-alienated man, the essence of man abstracted and made alien or strange. In the 1844 *Manuscripts*, however, Marx conceives alienation as the key to a critique of political economy. The basis for his analysis is the observation that under capitalist forms of production the product of labour does not belong to the labourer. Not only is the product thus alienated from the worker, appearing to him as an object belonging to another, it is also the source of wealth for another (the capitalist) and therefore contributes to the bondage of the worker in the production process. The more the worker produces, the more enslaved he is by the alienated products of his labour. This most general and primary form of alienation is in turn the origin of supplemental types that extend into the anthropological realm: the worker is also alienated from the production process, from the essence of the human species (since its essence lies in production), from nature, from other human beings and from himself. The capitalist mode of production, which deprives the worker of the product of his labour, is thus the root cause of all generalized manifestations of social alienation.

Obviously dissatisfied with the anthropological assumptions contained in his discussion of alienation in the 1844 *Manuscripts*, Marx avoided the term in his subsequent writings, referring at one point derisively to 'alienation' as a term he employs so that philosophers will understand him. The notion of alienated labour, however, survives and becomes a cornerstone of Marx's theory in *Capital*, where it is discussed under a somewhat altered label: the fetishism of commodities. Proceeding from an analysis of the commodity form, Marx argues that the fetishism of commodities arises from a specific social arrangement, when commodities are taken to the marketplace and acquire exchange value. If we can decipher the mysterious notion of value, a social hieroglyph, then we can understand what is occurring under conditions of capitalist production. In exposing the production process, however, Marx does not seek to return us to a pristine state prior to alienation, but rather to provide a general methodological principle for modern social phenomena. His central point is that our reflections on social life are necessarily distorted by the confusion wrought by commodity fetishism. The notion of commodities as natural products of human society and development has led us to confound nature and history. The result is a series of false and misleading starting points for political economists, who repeatedly consider derivative phenomena (money, prices) as essential, while regarding the essential as natural. Fetishism of commodities is thus associated with false consciousness, as well as with epistemological inadequacies in bourgeois ideology, and this field of association contributed to its centrality in Georg Lukács' *History and Class Consciousness*, where it reappears as reification or in the notion of an 'administered society' in the writings of the Frankfurt School.

A second central notion in the early writings of Marx is 'ideology'. At issue in the 1840s was a clarification of Marx's views in contrast to the convictions of other left Hegelians and socialists of the times, and Marx, along with Engels, who began collaborating with Marx during the mid 1840s, devoted two longer treatises to this task: *The Holy Family* and *The German Ideology*. Although these works do not explicitly define ideology, it is apparent that Marx associated this notion in the first instance with the abstraction and idealism that is ultimately derived from Hegelian thought. Marx himself had developed from Hegelian philosophy, so in a sense these writings were both a self-critique and an endeavour to carve out a position different from those of his former associates. Hegelians, he argues, remain in the realm of a religious critique, not because they concentrate solely on religious matters, but because they reduce the various critiques they make – of politics, law, morals – to a religious essence. They want to combat deficiencies in the real world by opposing the phrases associated with these deficiencies, and therein they remain entrapped in a particularly German ideology. They propose changing consciousness, but only in so far as this change entails interpreting reality differently – not, as Marx will suggest, by changing reality. By contrast, Marx advocates in *The German Ideology* a materialist basis for analysis. Eschewing ideological explanations for political and social problems, he explains even consciousness and language as dependent on a material basis. Ideology is thus opposed here and elsewhere to 'science' or to views that originate in a materialist analysis of the social order. Ultimately ideology, ideals and ideas are based in the interests of a class seeking to maintain or to gain hegemony, and to the extent that literature contains ideological material, it too participates in class struggle.

The culmination of Marx's early theoretical development and his practical activities in organization appears in the *Manifesto of the Communist Party*. Commissioned by the Communist League as a set of foundational principles, the *Manifesto* contains much spirited writing, but is an uneven document. The third section incorporates Marx and Engels's criticism of other socialist and communist movements, while the second section, betraying the original catechism form in which Engels sketched the initial draft, answers hypothetical questions and corrects widespread misconceptions about communism. Most interesting is the discussion of the role of the bourgeoisie in the first part of the work. Marx considers the bourgeoisie to be a unique and essentially revolutionary class: all previous ruling classes have taken a conservative stance toward production, attempting to limit it and thereby preserve their hegemonic social position. By contrast, the bourgeoisie needs to revolutionize production constantly, introducing more efficient means to increase productivity. Thus the bourgeoisie, which was once a revolutionary class in the historical sense that it opposed and overthrew the feudal order, retains an aspect of its revolutionary promise even after it has gained power. In imposing a rational order on production, however, the bourgeoisie has also revolutionized the ideological sphere. Gone are the feudal superstitions and traditional notions that fettered individuals to a medieval hierarchy. The bourgeois era has not eliminated exploitation and misery; it has merely lifted the veil of religious and political guises that formerly legitimated oppression of the lower classes, and substituted brute force and the cash nexus. Thus despite its despotic role in contemporary society the bourgeoisie has propelled history forward, simplifying class conflict, introducing a new ideological structure, and paving the way for its own downfall by introducing its own grave-diggers: the proletariat.

By the time of the *Manifesto* the place of culture and literature was defined by its role in class struggle. Marx conceived of cultural phenomena as secondary and dependent on a more basic economic order, and the classical and most concise statement of this relationship is contained in the 'Preface' to *A Contribution to the Critique of Political Economy*, published in 1859. Marx begins by defining what he means by the economic base, introducing two important notions: relations of production and productive forces. In other texts Marx explains that the productive forces consist of raw materials and the instruments of production, which together are called the means of production, as well as labour power. Means of production and labour power exist in any epoch, in any human society; changes in productivity, however, are implemented by modifications of one or more factors: technological advances, for example, may increase productive potential, but production can also be augmented by an increase in the work week. What defines an economic mode of production, however, is not the amount produced, but the relationship human beings have to the productive forces, determined largely by ownership of, or effective control over, the productive forces. In slave-holding societies, for example, the ruling classes own both the means of production and the labour power of individuals, while the slaves own nothing. Under capitalism, the proletariat owns only its labour power, which it is compelled to sell on the marketplace in order to survive. Although there is no precise relationship, certain types of relations of production correspond to the development of productive forces. In general slave-based societies are agricultural, while industrial economies are capitalist.

The real foundation of a society is its economic base. But arising from this base is a superstructure, which Marx defines in terms of legal and political matters: despite the insistence of most commentators, Marx does not connect the superstructure with cultural phenomena; instead it appears to contain institutional elements of governmental and judicial significance. However, corresponding to the economic base are also forms of 'social consciousness': the ideas, ideals and ideologies of a social order, which presumably include its philosophy, religion, literature and art. Marx makes it clear that the mode of production determines the social and intellectual sphere: the real social being is located in the economic structure, while consciousness is an epiphenomenon, dependent on the more fundamental realm of production and the relations of production. The struggles and conflicts that occur in this superstructural realm are ultimately derived from a primary arena of contradictions in the base. We must therefore distinguish carefully between the self-consciousness of a given epoch, what it thinks of itself and how it portrays itself, and what this consciousness really represents in objective terms. With this theoretical perspective Marx advocates what Paul Ricoeur would later call a 'hermeneutics of suspicion': in order to accomplish a Marxist interpretation the critic must recognize that the foregrounded ideology is a subterfuge, and that the real meaning of ideas and forms in literature and art is derived from their role in a more fundamental sphere. While the contradictions in the economic realm can be determined with scientific precision, Marx suggests that the legal, political, religious, philosophical and aesthetic struggles, which are no more than the way in which individuals become conscious of contradictions and fight them out, are often more elusive and ambivalent.

Indeed, Marx recognizes in other writings that the relationship between artistic production and economic production is neither simple nor direct. Progress in the economic sphere, which is easily measured in terms of increased productivity, does not necessarily mean a concomitant advance in art. The times of great art do not necessarily correspond at all to what is occurring at the material foundation of society. What we can say, however, is that certain types of artistic products correspond to definite modes of production. The Greek epics, for example, are obvious products of an undeveloped society. Since they are based on Greek mythology and employ a different relationship to natural phenomena, we cannot imagine the production of similar epics in industrial societies, where we encounter steam engines, trains, and telegraphs. Achilles' heroism cannot be reproduced in the same fashion in an age of gunpowder, and the oral nature of the epic seems in doubt with the advent of the printing press. In short, the conditions under which the heroic epic prospered no longer obtain. Explaining the way in which art belongs to its own times, however, is much easier than trying to understand why we enjoy art from the past. Marx asks why we can still appreciate Greek art, now that we are living under enormously changed circumstances. His tentative answer, that we recognize in the Greeks the childhood of humanity, indicates that Marx was not able to integrate all aspects of aesthetics into his historical schema.

The theoretical considerations that Marx sketched for the history and interpretation of literary texts was supplemented in his work only occasionally by concrete case studies. Although Marx exhibits a thorough knowledge of the classics, of Shakespeare and of modern literature in general, only twice does he comment at any length on a particular novel or play, and in both cases the works are known more for Marx's criticisms than for their own literary merit. The first occasion occurred in the 1840s, when Marx discussed Eugène Sue's popular novel *Mysteries of Paris* in *The Holy Family*. Like most of this polemical text, the sections on Sue's novel deal harshly with a work that seems at first glance very close to the socialist and philosophical concerns of Marx and Engels. The novel champions the working class, and Sue evidences obvious sympathy for the proletarian cause. Marx, however, felt that the work was trite and contrived, and that Sue himself was a sentimental, petty-bourgeois, social fantast. In the extended discussion Marx actually writes less about Sue and his work than he does about a particular piece of criticism of the novel, written under the pseudonym Szeliga (Franz Zychlin von Zychlinski), which praises its artistic and ideological merits. In the context of *The Holy Family* Szeliga is portrayed as the typical speculative idealist of the Hegelian school, who was unable to penetrate to the economic realities of the capitalist world, remaining instead on the level of conceptual abstraction that precluded effective critique.

The second longer commentary occurred in 1859, when Ferdinand Lassalle, a leader of the socialist movement in Germany, composed a historical drama entitled *Franz von Sickingen*. The play was written to capture in literary form the experiences of the failed revolution of 1848, but Lassalle chose to project backward and selected for his hero a knight whose revolutionary aspirations during the peasant revolts had similarly ended in defeat. In a letter to Lassalle Marx notes aesthetic deficiencies in the text: the characters are too abstract and not sketched in as full and interesting a fashion as they could be. But his main criticism involves the inaccuracy in depicting the class struggle. For Marx, Sickingen, a free knight struggling to retain the privileges and rights of his class, represents a declining social order; his failure, although tied to the historical predicament of his age, cannot be separated from his position in the social hierarchy, and his campaign against the emperor and the princes, however much this campaign coincides with the interests of the peasants, is undertaken to restore a reactionary system, not to advance history. The real tragedy of the revolution, therefore, is not represented by Sickingen's demise, but by the defeat of progressive elements in the cities and the peasants, who never play an active role in Lassalle's drama. As a consequence of his misconstrual of the class situation, Marx accuses Lassalle of idealistic representation: Sickingen is a mere mouthpiece for progressive views, which he may have held in reality, but which do not legitimately belong to him historically as a member of a declining class. In Marx's critique we encounter the foundation for class-based criticism: implicit in his remarks is the demand that fictional or fictionalized figures represent the views of their class.

The dominant style of fiction in the nineteenth century was realism, and Marx's theory, as well as his comments on specific works, validates a class-conscious variant of realist portrayal. Among the most important remarks on realism, however, were those made by Engels a few years after Marx's death in letters to the novelists Minna Kautsky and Margaret Harkness. Although Engels praises the work of both writers, he suggests their novels may not be realistic enough. He explains that when he speaks of realism he means typical characters in typical situations, not simply the accurate mirroring of historical detail. In Harkness's novel, for example, Engels criticizes the passivity of the proletariat: all help for the working class comes from above; the workers appear unable to organize themselves, which may have been the case earlier in the century, but now is simply incorrect. With regard to Kautsky's work Engels claims that she has not always succeeded in producing types, which he defines as a figure that retains individuality while representing more general dimensions of social relevance. His main concern, however, is that these engaged novelists do not degenerate into tendentiousness. The question of the appropriateness of 'tendency' in art was a frequently discussed topic among committed writers of the mid and late nineteenth century, and both Marx and Engels seem to advocate that authors refrain from injecting their personal sentiments or ideologies into their fiction. They favoured epic narratives in which the writer and her/his views recede into the background. In his letter to Kautsky Engels states that tendency is not in itself inappropriate, but that it must originate in the situation and plot, and not be something added from the outside. And writing to Harkness, Engels maintains that the true realist, which is synonymous with the genuine artist, may represent a progressive view of reality even if the author him/herself has no sympathy with radical causes. Balzac, a favourite author of both Marx and Engels, is the best illustration of someone whose politics were regressive, but whose adherence to realism compelled him to portray the aristocracy, whose views he shared, with bitter satire, and the republicans, whom he disliked, with admiration. The lesson is that tendentiousness is artistically undesirable and unnecessary if a perspicacious writer comprehends and captures social reality dispassionately.

The legacy of Marx's views on literature parallels to a degree his general reception. Among the social democrats Franz Mehring applied basic tenets from Marx and Engels in his numerous contributions to early socialist literary criticism. In the twentieth century Marx's works were fruitfully developed by various critics. Writers such as Walter Benjamin and Theodor Adorno, associated with the Frankfurt school, emphasized the dialectical and creative quality of literary criticism; they were equally adept at close reading and ideological criticism, but they recognized that Marx had to be brought into play with twentieth-century concerns if he was to be relevant. Structuralist marxists, such as Lucien Goldman, Louis Althusser and Pierre Macherey, focused their attention on ideology and consciousness, advancing our understanding of how form and content unite in an uneasy totality. Georg Lukács, perhaps the most prolific marxist critic of the twentieth century, was influential for philosophically based criticism of the Frankfurt School, but he also contributed many works that advanced a more dogmatic stance toward Marx, especially in Eastern Europe. In the Soviet Union and other Eastern bloc countries, one often encountered a version of marxist criticism that elevated Marx's occasional and historically conditioned remarks to inviolable doctrine. Socialist realism, at its best a continuation of nineteenth-century realism, at its worst an artificial and mechanical application of realist features to socialist content, was promulgated in the 1934 Party Congress of the Soviet Union by Andrey Zhdanov, and thereafter Zhdanovism became synonymous with Stalinist cultural politics. Although the ideological strictures on criticism loosened gradually during the 1970s and 1980s, in many communist circles socialist realism and its attendant restrictions remained official policy until just a few years before the decline of Soviet influence in Eastern Europe.

Robert C. Holub

Further reading and works cited

Althusser, L. *For Marx*. New York, 1969.

Anderson, P. *Considerations on Western Marxism*. London, 1976.

Arvon, H. *Marxist Esthetics*. Ithaca, NY, 1973.

Bakhtin, M. *Rabelais and His World*. Cambridge, 1968.

Baxandall, L. and Morowski, S. (eds) *Karl Marx and Friedrich Engels on Literature and Art*. New York, 1974.

Eagleton, T. *Criticism and Ideology*. London, 1976a.

—. *Marxism and Literary Criticism*. Berkeley, CA, 1976b.

Frow, J. *Marxism and Literary Criticism*. Cambridge, 1986.

Goldman, L. *The Hidden God*. New York, 1964.

Goldstein, P. *The Politics of Literary Theory*. Tallahassee, FL, 1990.

Jameson, F. *Marxism and Form*. Princeton, NJ, 1971.

Lukács, G. *The Historical Novel*. New York, 1962.

—. *History and Class Consciousness*. Cambridge, 1971.

Macherey, P. *A Theory of Literary Production*. London, 1978.

McLellan, D. *Karl Marx: His Life and Thought*. London, 1973.

—. *The Thought of Karl Marx*, 2nd edn. London, 1980.

Marx, K. and Engels, F. *Über Kunst und Literatur*, 2 vols. Berlin, 1967.

—. *Collected Works*, 50 vols. London, 1975–.

Nelson, C. and Grossberg, L. (eds) *Marxism and the Interpretation of Culture*. Urbana, IL, 1988.

Prawer, S. S. *Karl Marx and World Literature*. Oxford, 1976.

Solomon, M. (ed.) *Marxism and Art*. New York, 1973.

Trotsky, L. *Literature and Revolution*. New York, 1925.

Tucker, R. C. *The Marx-Engels Reader*. New York, 1972.

Williams, R. *Marxism and Literature*. Oxford, 1977.

5. Charles Baudelaire (1821–1867) and Stéphane Mallarmé (1842–1898)

In ways unprecedented in mid- and late-nineteenth-century Europe, both Charles Baudelaire and Stéphane Mallarmé created critical aesthetics of alterity where literature and criticism no longer acted as each other's Other. No longer were literature and criticism, for either writer, to be understood as necessarily opposing or complementary, yet distinct, counterparts to each other. Instead, the two writers practised their respective critical poetics of modernity – all the distinctions notwithstanding – as mixed genres: literature as criticism, and criticism as literature. Their work responded to a sense of cultural, political and epistemological crisis framed by the changes late-nineteenth-century France experienced in moving into modernity. In so doing, Baudelaire and Mallarmé instrumentalized strategies that shifted, and shattered, the modalities hitherto associated with literature and criticism as separate entities. Oxymorons and contradictions functioned as allegorizing dynamics to divide identities from within, *pars pro toto* fragmented and dematerialized wholes, and self-reflexivity foregrounded language's metaphoricity as common to both: these strategies significantly reconfigured the identities of both literature and criticism. Walter Benjamin wrote that Baudelaire's aesthetics 'indicated the price for which the sensation of the modern age may be had: the disintegration of aura in the experience of shock' (1968, 194). It might be said, in turn, that decadence, symbolism, modernism and the avant-garde movements all reverberated with the aesthetic after-shocks of the disintegration of aura. However, they also rebuilt their respective aesthetics with those same tools and experiences: disintegration, shock, fragmentation and a focus on the shared medium of literature and criticism – the language of the other which, paradoxically, was now closer and closer to becoming the same language. Today, Baudelaire's and Mallarmé's work in this area continues to raise crucial questions concerning the identity of literature and criticism. What, or who, defines the literary? Who uses the term, to what purpose and for what audience? Where, when and how can we separate the literary from the non-literary? Equally importantly, their questions challenged the respective relationships both literature and criticism have had, and have today, with institutional identities – academic, aesthetic, pedagogic and political. Finally, and yet perhaps most urgently for us at the start of the twenty-first century, their work prompts a thorough questioning of constitutive and/ or critical roles of literature-as-criticism in the ways we understand identity in linguistic, cultural, national or international terms.

Their radical rethinking of criticism as/in/through literature, and vice versa, presents key common elements that we will review before addressing in greater detail their different ways of working with these shared elements. Each poet-critic felt addressed by, and addressed himself to, the particularities of his historical time: both were poet-critics embedded in the space and time of their present. No longer did these poet-critics set themselves apart and above. They had departed from earlier nineteenth-century Romantic aspirations of the poet as privileged seer or visionary. For both Baudelaire and Mallarmé, their contemporary contexts – not past history or mythology – provided the primary materials for their literary-critical projects. In this way, their distinctive aesthetics of modernity were attuned to and responsive to questions posed by their changing times.

In Baudelaire's case, his work was shaped by the political transitions preceding, and during, the 1848 Revolution, and then most profoundly by the culture and politics of the Second Empire and by the loss of Paris as it existed before Haussmannization. These changes constructed a new urban space and new modes of sociality. Forms and norms of relationality (self/other, subject/object, individual/group) were redefined and recreated; conventional aesthetic equations between beauty, morality and the natural world no longer absorbed the shocks, nor echoed the reactions, that a rapidly modernizing capitalist society sent through the subjective experiences of the axes of time and space. Baudelaire addressed the inadequacy of conventional aesthetic, political and ethical answers by sketching out new roles for the artist (the dandy, the *flâneur*, the poet as ragpicker (*le chiffonnier*) who recycles rubbish through literary creation), new aesthetic values (the immediacy of subjective effect, an unsentimental poetics of urban abjection, beauty located in artifice), and new arenas for artistic inspiration (the street, the crowd). Mallarmé, in contrast, is one of the first poet-critics to emerge from what was, in Third Republic France, a new social group of writers: the state-employed teacher-writer, author of *Les mots anglais* (1876). References to Third Republic pedagogic, institutional and cultural contexts for the poet-critic thread their way through his prose writings, particularly *La Musique et les lettres* (1894).

Although the work of both poet-critics played, and plays, a decisive role in the developments within French literature and culture, both were also actively involved in literary-critical endeavours outside of their own national and linguistic literary tradition. In Baudelaire's case, his translations of the works of Edgar Allan Poe, and in Mallarmé's case, his work as teacher/scholar of the English language, gave them both strong contacts with the English language, with English and American literature, and with English and American writers and critics. Most influential, however, on the subsequent nature of their critical work is that the contact went beyond the exchange of ideas: both had first-hand experience of writing in a foreign language. At a time when other French writers and critics were advancing various forms of literary and cultural nationalism – from the benign, to the virulent as was the case with Maurice Barrès – the work of Baudelaire and Mallarmé challenged the ideological assumptions formative of national genealogies, literary heritages and protectionist equations between language and culture. One could say that they were un-French in this conventionally most 'French' of areas: the identification of language and culture. Their experiences working in another language afforded them valuable insights, so to speak, into the ways their own language and culture were, in fact, also foreign or other to themselves. This perspective is one Ruth Robbins and Julian Wolfreys find in Baudelaire's economy of the eye, where 'identity becomes something dependent on the other reflecting the self back to the self' (1999, 27). In the visual realm too, then, our identity, Baudelaire shows us, is constituted through interchanges, necessarily outside of the self, and not primarily through interiority.

Closely related to the last commonality of approach is their eschewal of what Flaubert would call literary-critical *lieux-communs*, or *idées reçues*. Just as their experience of the otherness of their own language provided them with critical perspectives on the ideological risks implicit in overvaluing the Frenchness of literature and culture, they both demonstrated a powerful critical energy of insider-outsiders to shake, if not blast away, the clichés of past literary-critical conventions, and to disabuse their readers of spurious forms of aesthetic consensus. For example, what passed for criticism, or what others idolatrously worshipped as 'art' was never spared in their writings. Rosemary Lloyd puts it well, when commenting on Mallarmé's enthusiasm in *Symphonie Littéraire* (1866) for the innovative poetic strategies of Théodore de Banville, where she refers to Mallarmé's horror of the 'rhetoric of literature' (Lloyd 1999, 82). At a time in French literary criticism where the biography-based approaches of Sainte-Beuve held sway, Mallarmé's elimination of the subjective from poetry forced, and still forces, a rethinking of literary criticism and a critical awareness of excess (biographical) baggage. Likewise, as indicated by the immediate censorship in 1857 of six poems in Baudelaire's *Les Fleurs du Mal*, Baudelaire does not simply voice his hostility to stultifying consensus through his art criticism, as in the *Aux Bourgeois* section of his 1846 Salon (*Curiosités Esthétiques*, 97); his own resolutely modern aesthetics shattered consensus about what counts as art.

Baudelaire's work as poet-critic, and specifically as art-critic, began in the 1840s when two distinct aesthetic legacies of romanticism existed in French culture. First, the influence of Victor Cousin's first complete translation of Plato into French (1822–40), and of his subsequent publication of his Sorbonne lectures – delivered from 1822 onwards under the title *Du Vrai, du Beau, et du Bien* (1853) – flourished in romantic Platonism. The work of Vigny and Lamartine, among others, exemplified this approach: the poet created texts intended to awaken in readers a sense of the Ideal essence, to find analogies between the visible (natural) world, and the invisible (Ideal) one. The natural world was central to this strain of romanticism because poets saw in it a symbolic or hieroglyphic form for the deciphering of the Ideal, and saw poetic language as the tool for such deciphering. While Baudelaire rejected in this the focus on Beauty (in its capitalized, idealized exclusivity), his aesthetic project infused temporality and corporeality into romanticism's poetic analogies and correspondences. From a vertical aesthetics of desired transcendence of the material world, Baudelaire de-sublimates and re-embodies an aesthetics through creating horizontal, sensory, correspondences: synaesthesia, or the verbal translations between the senses. Baudelaire's rejection of an exclusive Ideal of Beauty – Platonic, classical or invariable as any system defines it – found articulation in prose poems such as *Chacun sa chimère* and *Le Fou et la Vénus*, and also in poems from *Les fleurs du mal* such as *La mort des artistes* and *Les Plaintes d'un Icare*. Here, Baudelaire presents the artist self-destructively consuming himself in the impossible creative struggle with immutable Beauty.

The recorporealizing of poetic correspondences that Baudelaire derives, and reroutes, from a Platonic strain of romanticism exists alongside a different approach to beauty found in the work of Stendhal. Unlike Victor Cousin's Platonic yoking together of the triad of Beauty, goodness and the real (of Platonic essences), Stendhal's work in *De l'amour* (1822) and *Racine et Shakespeare* (1823) presents beauty as relative; here, beauty is dependent upon feelings, passions, circumstances, locations (to name but a few variables). Baudelaire's impatience with an exclusive fixation on Platonic approaches to Beauty re-emerges clearly in his article on the *Exposition Universelle* of 1855. Here, he mocks an imaginary contemporary doctrinaire of Beauty whose ways of seeing leave him figuratively blind to all beauty that falls outside of his own aesthetic system: such a critic 'would blaspheme life itself and the natural world' (CE, 213). Baudelaire takes the relativity of beauty several steps further than his Romantic predecessors when he asserts that, 'What is beautiful is always bizarre', (CE, 215). Emphasizing the significance of 'life itself' to beauty, and the importance of the individual particularities that 'see' beauty in the bizarre, Baudelaire's aesthetics promoted the subjective perspective of the artist's imagination to central place. Decidedly non-mimetic and non-descriptive, Baudelaire's aesthetics were defined in his *Salon de 1846* as a way of feeling, a beauty that bears the mark of individual passions. However, despite intimations of Rousseau here, Baudelaire's larger project, elaborated in the series of essays comprising *Le Peintre de la vie moderne* (1863), and specifically *L'Éloge du Maquillage*, exposed Rousseau's equations between idealized pasts, nature and virtue as so much primitivist romanticizing of a fictionalized past. The passing jab at Rousseau, however, serves merely as the conceptual prelude to Baudelaire's central aesthetic argument for the ubiquity of artifice, and, more importantly, not simply for the superiority of artifice over nature – as he is often understood to be arguing. Baudelaire goes further than merely disrupting literary-critical conventions here, since he presents the naturalness of the desire for artifice in all cultures – human and animal – at all times, be they so-called 'primitive', 'civilized', 'natural' or 'decadent' cultures.

What we see here is that just as Baudelaire's title for his collection of poems, *Les Fleurs du Mal* (1857) offers us a dynamic oxymoron framing his aesthetic practices, so too does Baudelaire's argument about artifice take the form of an oxymoron: natural artifice. Indeed, in *De L'Héroïsme de la Vie Moderne* (1846), when he gives a definition of the multiple forms of beauty, he uses the same rhetorical structure: 'All beauties contain . . . something eternal and something transitory – something of the absolute and something of the particular' (CE, 195). Baudelaire reinforces and multiplies the dynamic duality to make it the distinctive, and defining, feature of the beauty of modernity in *Le Peintre de la vie moderne*. Baudelaire builds an entire aesthetics resting on such dynamic oxymorons. For example, his practice of writing 'prose poems' deploys the same structure, but transfers it to the re-articulation of conventional categories of genre. This final example makes it clear that the oxymoron is not simply a rhetorical ornament, but performs a structuring function for Baudelaire – it gives form to Baudelaire's critical concepts – and in so doing, unites the literary to the critical, both in methods and goals.

One of the most creative critical approaches to this feature of Baudelaire's work has come in the work of Christine Buci-Glucksmann (1989), who studies this dynamic in Baudelaire's writing – the non-dialectical maintenance of contradictions – which she argues is central to Baudelaire's aesthetic of modernity, but is equally important to the writings of Walter Benjamin in the *Arcades Project* (1935). Through an oxymoron of her own, 'Baroque reason', she emphasizes the un-Reasonable, grotesque and paradoxical logic at work through this literary-critical aesthetic specific to modernity. Pointing to the proliferation of such non-dialectical contraries (i.e. which resist recuperation or hierarchical resolution) in Baudelaire and Benjamin's writing, she contends that they constitute an allegorical figuration of an Other (modernity) not as a directly oppositional nature to the modernity of narratives of progress, but rather as an alterity that sustains the very production of further non-dialectical oppositions. For Buci-Glucksmann, this Baudelairean and Benjaminian aesthetic of modernity combines the critical with the destructive, and hollows out from within the founding, and governing, representations of modernity that are buttressed by linear time, narratives of progress, faith in science and rationality. Doubling and destroying the 'substantial' model of modernity, baroque reason opens, through allegory, onto an alterity whose medium is a theatricalized space of figuration within the frame of representation. Allegory here in Buci-Glucksmann's usage works to destroy and demystify the appearance of completeness adhering to representations of reality, producing it instead as ruins and fragmentation. For Buci-Glucksmann, it is a strategy both writers use to make visible the ambivalences – of history, time or subjectivity – through freezing or neutralizing non-dialectical contradictions.

Buci-Glucksmann's study of the allegorized figuration of a baroque reason offers one of the most helpful paths into theorizing Baudelaire's representations of women, and their relationship to his aesthetics of modernity. This she undertakes by according centrality to Benjamin's work on the prostitute. Benjamin sees nineteenth-century mass prostitution resulting in a hyper-visibility of the prostitute's body, a change that had aesthetic repercussions, Buci-Glucksmann argues, by invalidating the figure of woman as mediator of a divine and immortal love, and representation of ideal feminine beauty. Departing from this analysis, Buci-Glucksmann suggests that the nineteenth-century reconfigurations of the visibility and invisibility of the woman's body inevitably rebounds on masculinity. In any binary organization of socio-sexual space, one term cannot shift without having an impact on the other. The disembodied, masculine observers of feminine bodies, deprived of their idealized, feminized mediators of love, project onto the ubiquity of the prostitute's body the precariousness, if not mortality, of masculinity itself. Baudelaire's poems abound in representations of decaying, ageing or dead feminine bodies, just as they eroticize the dead female body as in *Une Charogne*. Buci-Glucksman's analysis offers a nuanced response to such representations in Baudelaire's work. She considers them both as reactive, misogynist, masculinist counter-projections triggered by an awareness of the mortality of a specific historical formation of masculinity; yet, she argues, they can also seen as potentially 'progressive' literary-critical ways of making visible the effects of the capitalist commodification of bodies.

Buci-Glucksmann is one of many critics who offer readings of the critical work performed by the self-reflexive dynamic doubling so characteristic of Baudelaire's writing. Jean Starobinski's study, *Mélancholie au miroir* (1989), links Baudelairean melancholy to a dynamic doubling of the self. No longer is this the romantic melancholy of solitary contemplation in a stark natural landscape of ruins. Instead, Starobinski shows how Baudelaire's melancholic reflexivity develops out of, and yet transforms, the reflexivity of early nineteenth-century German romantic irony to produce the artist's necessary self-critical duality: the self takes itself as its other, its ironic, self-deriding, double, as we see in the lines of 'Héautontimorouménos' where the poetic subject is both victim and executioner, persecutor and persecuted. When we turn to Mallarmé, such staging, or performing, of intrapsychic dramas – one form of the theatricalizing of a poetics of alterity – moves far away from Baudelaire's subjective impressions on embodied, material subjects. Instead, language takes the stage, and its effect on the reader's imagination takes over.

Mallarmé's theatrical poetics of alterity engaged several interrelated dimensions of spacing (*l'espacement*) – e.g. the white page, blanks, silence and punctuation – all of which destabilized any unquestioned certainties about literature's identity. His work did this through making explicit the process of reading, the work (and role) of the reader, and by switching the focus onto the effect – rather than the meaning – of the poem. To say that Mallarmé's poetry produces its own space is to invoke, first, Mallarmé's notion that the reader produces or stages, the poem. By designating the reading process as a *mise en scène* in the reader's mind, Mallarmé emphasizes that we do not receive the poem as a finished product whose meaning pre-exists either in the poet or in the poem. Mallarmé's dramatizing of poetry demands that readers focus on enunciation, on how, rather than what, the poem means, i.e. on its effect. It demands that the reader's own staging of the poem finds its cues by attending to the poem's placement and spacing on the page (the typography, the typeface, the spacing, the metrics). To struggle with the words as discrete entities, extracted from the configuration of the poem itself, is to remain attached to signification, i.e. to what the poem means. Mallarmé's poetry leads us away from signification, and instead to configuration, to text and paratexts, to what is present as well as to the interdependence of presence and constitutive absences. Implicitly theorized here is that verse exists only because blank spaces separate and join the verses.

Since Mallarmé's poetry and prose is simultaneously creative and critical, as we see above, its material practices simultaneously theorize their practice. As he writes in an 1867 letter to Eugène Lefébure, the modern poet is first and foremost a critic. He uses the tools of his literary art – signs – the twenty-four letters of the alphabet, as he puts it in *La Musique et les lettres* (*Oeuvres Complètes* 1945, 646) the way that other literary critics theorize through reasoning, doctrines, manifestos, argumentation or philosophical concepts. His writings combine verse through spacing with the staging of language as performative. Implicitly theorized here is an understanding of spacing that goes beyond blankness and whiteness on the page. Spacing also designates a wide range of differences and similarities in language – phonological, grammatical, rhythmic, and semantic – that are all equally constitutive of verse. In *La Musique et les lettres*, Mallarmé likens the concept of spacing to the spaces separating the different notes in a musical scale. A piece of music doesn't mean anything as such, and yet its contingency is also absolutely necessary within the terms of its form, be it a performance of a sonata in A minor or of a minuet in C major. Analogously, Mallarmé suggests, a poem doesn't mean any one thing, yet its concrete realizations are both contingent and necessary. Language once estranged (though never entirely severed) from any referential, representational or realist expectations – once put under the theatre lights in its otherness – offers the materials from which the reader stages, or produces, the poem's previously unformulated, and unprogrammable, network of relationships as an 'effect' *in* and *on* the reader's mind (OC, 635–57). Words become dislodged from any 'proper' meanings and perform, as in a musical score, in relation to each other, reflecting each other's multiple facets (OC, 366). In Saussurean terms, Mallarmé's spacing intensifies and multiplies all the potential permutations of effect between signifier and signified within the sign and among signs.

Mallarmé's creative and critical poetic practices, by unpeeling language from the reassuring plasterwork of referential illusions, coax readers to explore language's perfor- mativity and have fostered a wide range of creative and critical responses in the twentieth century. A survey of critics' respective emphases affords a useful comparative analysis of the different critical constructions of Mallarmé that readers encounter today. Maurice Blan- chot, one of the his most rigorous readers, analyses the poet's deliberate erosion of the reader's default position – to rely on language's referentiality – and asks what it can mean, given this effacing of straightforward referentiality, to say that literature 'exists'. For example, if language makes things present by abstracting properties from them – as in metonymy, to take but one of many examples – thereby negating them, and absenting them, what kind of existence does literature have (Blanchot 1955)? For Blanchot, Mallarmé's writings gain their singularity by signalling to us that the only way to establish any relationship with death is through language because its strange mode of 'being' lies in its very un-being, an insight he finds compellingly demonstrated in Mallarmé's *Igitur*. While Jacques Derrida, in *La Double Séance* (1972), continues and develops Blanchot's path, in the intervening years appears the monumental 650-page study by Geneva School phenomenologist, Jean-Pierre Richard, *L'Univers imaginaire de Mallarmé* (1961), a pub- lication which sets the stage for an emblematic intergenerational critical struggle which takes Mallarmé as its text and pretext.

Rather than through approaching Mallarmé's spacing as a bridge concept that recasts epistemology in terms of processes of signification (as does Blanchot), Richard approaches space thematically through an exhaustive analysis of Mallarmé's representational figures of space (i.e. the themes of blankness, death, whiteness, sterility, absence). Undertaking the work as a thematic critic, Richard's phenomenological training leads him, first, to project a 'totalizing' analysis (Richard 1961, 14) of the dominant motifs of Mallarmé's writings (space being only one among them) and then to aspire to a comprehensive understanding of the modes, methods and strategies of the creative consciousness at work. In a phrase, Richard aims to discover the 'sensibility in his [Mallarmé's] logic, and a logic to his sensibility' (Richard 1961, 38) through two critical methods: deciphering (the herme- neutic goal) and assembling the parts (the combinative goal). What is immediately clear from this brief description is that Richard shifts the production of the poetic effect away from the reader and back onto the author. Furthermore, although he tracks Mallarmé's poetic syntax (which implies that relationality is central to his analysis), his selection of motifs and themes contains, and transfers, the dynamic potentiality of performative readings to the static structures of a pre-existing, governing, thematic syntax of a creative consciousness. Richard's inventory of themes constituting the architecture of Mallarmé's poetry is outstandingly meticulous and thorough. For that reason, *L'Univers* stands as an 'incontournable' [Fr. essential reading; a text to be reckoned with or not to be ignored], and controversial, scholarly text for any aspiring scholar of creative critical writing in the wake of Mallarmé. However, just as significant to the trajectory of critical thought, is the response it provoked from the perspective of another rigorous reader of Mallarmé – Jacques Derrida – who considers Richard's analysis a distortion of crucial premises underlying Mallarmé's work.

Derrida's response to Richard (Derrida 1972) marks a critical watershed, and yet not only for an understanding of Mallarmé. The Derrida/Richard differences also present an important and lucid exposition of key explanatory elements underlying poststructuralist readers' 'issues' with, if not disdain for, thematic criticism; this approach bore (and still does) the stigma of critical opprobrium in the US Academy during the late 1980s and early 1990s, before cultural studies reinvigorated and relegitimated thematic approaches through different methodological tools, e.g. new historicism's emphasis on culture as the unit of analysis as opposed to phenomenology's emphasis on the individual's creative consciousness. As a debate triggered by Mallarmé's work, and which bears the mark of a specific intellectual moment in the paths of academic theorizing, it merits close examination.

Taking Gérard Genette's lead (Genette 1962), Derrida faults Richard for psychologism in the latter's mapping of Mallarmé's thematic syntax. That is, he disputes Richard's use of an expressive aesthetic framework to interpret Mallarmé's text, and points out that such a premise runs counter to Mallarmé's stated aesthetic of impersonality in *Crise de vers* (OC, 366), i.e. the goal of yielding 'initiative' to the words themselves, or rather to a given reader's staging of the web-like interrelationships among the multiple registers of multifaceted signs. Further distortions are embedded in Richard's approach, Derrida argues, because psychologizing readings remain necessarily oblivious to the play of the signifier (the very materiality of language). To psychologize implies a (Hegelian) dialectical reading which sublates the materiality of the words on the page in the name of a higher meaning (the signified, or what Richard posits that Mallarmé intended). Derrida returns us to Mallarmé's spacing as concept, rather than theme, and by connecting the ways signification spaces and grounds epistemology, Derrida aligns spacing with the differential character of language. Supporting his argument with a reading of Mallarmé's short prose text *Mimique*, Derrida demonstrates the ways Mallarmé's text undoes Platonic assumptions that mimesis is derivative of Ideal, or True, essential forms. *Mimique*, Derrida argues, posits that the supposed Ideal forms are always already within representation as imitations which do indeed accrue an essential aspect – i.e. they become naturalized – but are nevertheless imitations of originary imitations, not of Ideas: his reading of Mallarmé, concludes Derrida, shows us that we find copies, not originals, at the supposed source of origination.

Where Derrida finds an undoing of Platonic assumptions in Mallarmé's practices of spacing, Jean-François Lyotard interprets spacing from the standpoint of two related and enduring intellectual passions in his own work: his exploration of the processes and practices of aesthetic avant-gardes ranging from Mark Rothko to Sam Francis, and his tenaciously sensitive probing of discourse for the corporeal gestures or pulses of affect. In *Discours, figure* (1971), Lyotard views Mallarmé's disruptive reconfigurations of spatiality as, in his terms, 'figural' ruptures where the sensible (form, shape) bursts through discursive meaning. Just as Sam Francis considers that colour in his paintings holds a feeling until it finds articulation in discourse, Lyotard privileges Mallarmé's spatiality as a form holder for the as-yet unarticulated. However, together with Lyotard's work, it is undeniably in Julia Kristeva's doctoral thesis, *La Révolution du langage poétique* (1974), that we find a sustained argument linking Mallarmé's spacing to non-discursive outlets of affect.

Kristeva offers a firmly psychoanalytically framed, and loosely politically oriented, interpretation of Mallarmé's practice of throwing into relief the functions of spacing. Theorizing the pre-Oedipal chora (the semiotic (*le sémiotique*)) as the space excluded by, yet formative of, the symbolic and social order of language, she interprets Mallarmé's spacing as so many ruptures, interruptions and eruptions which mark the rhythms and corporeal drives of unarticulated affect as it breaks through discursive meaning. By taking the symbolic, social and bourgeois orders as synonyms of each other, Kristeva's case for the 'revolutionary' political force of Mallarmé's semiotic disruptions of language stretches its analytic reach awkwardly and unconvincingly between text and the context of Third Republic France, ultimately getting lost somewhere in between. There is copious critical response to Mallarmé's revolutionary poetics, so the concept of revolution is completely justified here. However, Kristeva's programmatic approach to the overall meaning of spacing keeps the lid on the potentially revolutionary ruptures and reconfigurations of relationships between reader and text, between literature and its others.

In conclusion, it is perhaps important to ask where Baudelaire and Mallarmé seem to be leading criticism in the wake of our recent *fin de siècle*? Taking my lead from Ellen Burt (1999), I would suggest, as I have throughout, that both writers' consciousness of their foreignness to themselves – linguistically, culturally – is an address we cannot afford to ignore if we are to think our way through the dilemmas posed by identity. As Burt comments, '. . . one of those futures [of the text] is of a political life not bounded by the limits of nationalism and the national language . . .' (1999, 125).

Elizabeth Constable

Further reading and works cited

Baudelaire, C. *Curiosités Esthétiques, L'Art romantique et autres oeuvres critiques de Baudelaire* [CE]. Paris, 1990.
Benjamin, W. *Illuminations*. New York, 1968.
Blanchot, M. *L'Espace littéraire*. Paris, 1955.
Buci-Glucksmann, S. *La raison baroque de Benjamin à Baudelaire*. Paris, 1984.
Burt, E. *Poetry's Appeal: Nineteenth-Century French Lyric and the Political Space*. Stanford, CA, 1999.
Derrida, J. *La Dissémination*. Paris, 1972.
—. 'Mallarmé', in *Tableau de la littérature française*. Vol. III. Paris, 1974; 'Mallarmé', in *Jacques Derrida: Acts of Literature*, ed. Derek Attridge. New York, 1992.
Genette, G. 'Bonheur de Mallarmé?', *Tel Quel*, 10, 1962.
Gould, E. *Virtual Theater: Virtual Theater from Diderot to Mallarmé*. Baltimore, MD, 1989.
Johnson, B. *Défigurations du Langage Poétique: La Seconde Révolution Baudelairienne*. Paris, 1979.
—. *The Critical Difference*. Baltimore, MD, 1981.
Kristeva, J. *Révolution du langage poétique*. Paris, 1974.
Lloyd, R. *Mallarmé: The Poet and his Circle*. Ithaca, NY, 1999.
Lyotard, J.-F. *Discours, figure*. Paris, 1971.
Mallarmé, S. *Oeuvres Complètes*, ed. H. Mondor [OC]. Paris, 1945.
Richard, J.-P. *L'Univers imaginaire de Mallarmé*. Paris, 1961.
Robbins, R. and Wolfreys, J. 'In the Wake of . . . Baudelaire, Valéry, Derrida', *The French Connections of Jacques Derrida*. New York, 1999.
Starobinski, J. *La mélancholie au miroir*. Paris, 1989.

6. Friedrich Nietzsche (1844–1900)

Friedrich Nietzsche was perhaps the most original and provocative German writer of the nineteenth century. A classical philologist by training, he held a professorship at the University of Basel from 1869 to 1879 before retiring and becoming a freelance author. His writings, which were composed from the early 1870s until the outbreak of his insanity at the start of 1889, covered a wide range of topics in the fields of aesthetics, art, ethics, religion, psychology, politics and sociology. As a philosopher he broke away from the conventions of traditional philosophical prose, employing various innovative forms and rhetorical strategies to construct arguments. Much of his mature work consists of aphorisms; one of his most important books, *Thus Spoke Zarathustra*, is structured as a parody of the Bible and contains parables and maxims of high symbolic value. During his own lifetime Nietzsche's writings were known to only a small circle of admirers. In the preface to one of his last works, *The Antichrist*, Nietzsche wrote: 'Only the day after tomorrow belongs to me. Some are born posthumously', thus predicting exactly the course of his popularity after his death. During the first decades of the twentieth century Nietzsche rapidly became one of the most influential thinkers. Few European authors or critics of the early twentieth century were unaffected by some aspect of Nietzsche's thought; in philosophical circles he was championed by such celebrated thinkers as Martin Heidegger, Karl Jaspers, Jean-Paul Sartre, Jacques Derrida and Michel Foucault; and although Sigmund Freud would downplay his impact, his insights into the workings of the psyche were obviously seminal for the development of the psychoanalytic movement. Because of his elusive style and the often obscure nature of his philosophical message, Nietzsche's writings have been able to bear a wide variety of interpretations, and although not all of his followers would have been welcome to Nietzsche himself, they attest to the immense vitality of his thought.

Nietzsche's earliest published writings dealt with issues in classical philology and are of interest only for specialists. His first book written for the general public, *The Birth of Tragedy from the Spirit of Music*, can be considered an attempt on Nietzsche's part to combine his academic training with his enthusiasm for the composer Richard Wagner. Nietzsche had met Wagner in 1868, and the two men had quickly become friends, although Nietzsche, who was Wagner's junior by thirty years, was clearly subservient to the already celebrated composer. Nietzsche had much in common with Wagner: as an amateur musician himself – Nietzsche composed and played the piano – he appreciated Wagner's innovations and grandiose musical projects. The two men also shared an admiration for the pessimistic philosophy of Arthur Schopenhauer and a longing for the renaissance of cultural greatness in Europe. Nietzsche imagined that Wagner would be the leader of a vast cultural movement, and their friendship was based to a degree on the common dedication to a sacred artistic cause. At one point Nietzsche even imagined giving up his professorship at Basel in order to devote himself full-time to publicity for Wagner and his opera house, which was constructed at Bayreuth and completed in 1876.

The Birth of Tragedy is thus a work of celebration, enlisting classical studies in order to promote the Wagnerian cause. In his initial arguments Nietzsche explains the origins of Greek tragedy as the confluence of two tendencies or spirits in the ancient world: the Apollonian and the Dionysian. The first of these terms, the Apollonian, is associated first and foremost with dream, but it is also related to illusion, since illusion involves something that appears to us in the mind's eye, something that takes definite and limited form. The Apollonian also entails the principium individuationis (principle of individuation), for this principle operates precisely as a limiting of chaos, as a cutting out from the flux of phenomena some limited and individual portion. The Apollonian is thus a representational principle, referring to the artistic and epistemological tendency that allows something else to appear or take form. By contrast the Dionysian is first introduced to us as intoxication in contrast to the Apollonian dream. Like the Apollonian, it encompasses a field of association rather than a precise definition. At times Nietzsche likens it to a frenzied, instinctive, unconscious unity; at other points it is associated with oblivion and self-forgetting; and on occasion it becomes more ominous, reminding us of the cruelty and absurdity of existence, of the suffering of the human being and the torments of life on earth. In the Attic tragedies of Aeschylus and Sophocles the Apollonian and Dionysian are united: the anarchic, inchoate Dionysian force finds expression through the Apollonian form or appearance.

The final sections of the original Birth of Tragedy – ten sections addressing the rebirth of the tragic spirit in Wagnerian opera were added after completion of the original text – trace the fall of Greek tragedy. Responsible for the demise are two figures: Euripides and Socrates. Nietzsche accuses Euripides of removing the genuine tragic element by eliminating the tragic chorus, which contains the primeval Dionysian impulse, and by introducing characters from everyday life. Euripides, however, is portrayed as the agent of an even more destructive and powerful force, represented by the figure of Socrates. Indeed, Euripides' dramas are based on an aesthetic Socratism. As the representative of the new rationality, Socrates necessarily opposes the Dionysian mysteries, and henceforth the real opposition in western culture becomes one between Dionysus and Socrates. In art the Socratic principle advocates realism, the copying of appearances, rather than essences, the depiction of the world as it exists for us. But Socratic thinking also extends into the realm of epistemology and ethics, where Socrates promotes the intelligibility of the world and virtuous conduct according to universal tenets. The good, the true, and the beautiful thus come into harmony in the Socratic worldview, destroying the fragile synthesis of Apollonian and Dionysian, the pinnacle of cultural achievement in the western world. Ultimately Nietzsche hopes to regain this synthesis in the nineteenth century, and his advocacy of the Wagnerian project stems from his belief that greatness in art can again be attained in the modern world.

The remaining works from Nietzsche's earliest period, the Untimely Meditations, likewise revolve around his relationship to Wagner and his championing of cultural renewal in the recently united Second German Empire. The first of these Meditations was directed against the smug philistinism of bourgeois life; the third Meditation lauded Schopenhauer, the intellectual bond between Wagner and Nietzsche, as an exemplary 'educator'; and the fourth Meditation is devoted entirely to Wagner himself and the celebration of his Bayreuth opera house. But Nietzsche also concerned himself with the pedagogical aspect of cultural renewal, and an unpublished lecture series, as well as the second *Untimely Meditation*, 'On the Advantage and Disadvantage of History for Life', focused on the deficiencies in educational practices in Germany. Nietzsche argues that German youth are receiving too much historical education, and that as a result they are inhibited from action and from great accomplishments. Distinguishing among a monumental, an antiquarian and a critical notion of history, he claims that each has distinct advantages, but that any sort of historical education, if promulgated to an extreme, will be ultimately pernicious. Nietzsche's goal is not universal education or an educated populace, but a pedagogical practice and corresponding institutions that will foster the production of greatness. Eschewing the apparent progress detected by his contemporaries, he writes that the goal for humanity does not lie in an end, but in its highest specimens. *On the Advantage and Disadvantage of History*, like most of his earliest work, is a plea for a fundamental change in culture so that genius and greatness will once again hold sway.

Nietzsche's middle period, which stretches from 1876 until 1882, is marked by three momentous changes. In his personal life he broke off his friendship with Wagner and distanced himself from the intellectual world of the tightly knit Bayreuth circle. He also moved further away from classical studies, and although he continued teaching until 1879, in his last years as a professor he was either on leave or repeating courses previously offered. The second change concerns the predominant themes in his writings. Nietzsche continued to devote some attention to culture, but he was no longer solely or primarily concerned with the renaissance he felt imminent in the earlier part of the 1870s. He began to cover a wider range of themes, influenced by earlier writers, in particular the French moralists of the seventeenth and eighteenth centuries. The change that was most easily detectable was his increased willingness to explore topics from philosophy proper, and the beginning of reflection on moral issues in a more serious fashion. But we also find consideration of other matters: science (especially physiology and biology), society (the question of women's rights and socialism), politics, national character and art. His measured stance in these reflections, his willingness to examine matters from various angles, his rejection of dogmatism and desire to search for deeper truths, are all characteristic of this phase of his writing. The youthful vibrancy of his earliest essays gives way to a more sovereign, thoughtful and pensive tone. A third change involves a new style of writing. The four books he published over this five-year period – *Human, All Too Human* (1878 and 1879), *The Wanderer and His Shadow* (1880), *Dawn* (1881) and *The Gay Science* (1882) – were all written in aphorisms. Nietzsche found his own style in this middle period. He was never comfortable with the essay: it demanded too much sustained writing and logic, too much systematic thought and rigorous method. The aphorism allowed him to develop his strengths, which involved sudden insight rather than sustained reflection, the quick sketch of a problem and its solution rather than the patient elaboration of a thought.

The scepticism characteristic of these middle years, combined with a fascination for natural science, led Nietzsche to a consequentially anti-metaphysical position in which he rejected all absolute values, ideals and dualistic models. Increasingly he came to believe that thoughts, ideas, consciousness, language and values are the means men use to deflect attention from our instinctual, biological life. Within this general criticism of metaphysics Nietzsche articulates one of his most noted hypotheses: the death of God. Formulated first as a parable in *Human, All Too Human*, Nietzsche presents God as a deceased and omniscient prison warder, whose demise has no visible effect on the prisoners he had formerly overseen. In aphorism 125 in *The Gay Science*, the death of God is announced by a madman who claims that God has been murdered. The crowd of unbelievers to whom he delivers his message remains unfazed, and the madman concludes that he has come too early, that the news of such an enormous event travels slowly. Significant for Nietzsche's thought is that he does not advocate a simple atheism. Nietzsche distinguishes between ordinary non-believers, who may be associated with the Philistine population of Germany and Europe in his times, and a select group of non-believers, like himself, who have a premonition of the enormous significance of the death of God. God is not simply a divinity; he stands for the entity that provides ethical substance for one's action, and meaning and purpose for life. At one point in human development God occupied a central position in our existence. But the recognition of his demise in the course of human history must entail more than disbelief in a divinity: if our emancipation is to be complete, the death of God must also liberate us from the epistemological and ethical constraints placed on us by any metaphysical system.

If God is no longer the centre of our universe, then humankind is thrown back upon itself and forced to create its own meaning. In his mature work Nietzsche begins to map out a complex conceptual framework for the philosophy of the future. Its initial and most elusive form occurs in *Thus Spoke Zarathustra*, the four-part work many critics consider his magnum opus. In *Zarathustra* Nietzsche highlighted notions that would become the most controversial in his thought. Among the best known terms he introduced is the 'overman' or 'superman'. The 'overman' is characterized by overcoming; Nietzsche conceives of man as a bridge or tightrope between an animal existence and a being that has yet to appear but that is logically possible. The 'overman' is meant as a conception of what we might become if we can breed a new and superior type of human being, if we can create ourselves anew and rid ourselves of the pernicious traditions that have enslaved us. The notion has obvious evolutionary overtones: Nietzsche describes our path from worm to ape to man, and claims that our current state of affairs is one that will also be surpassed. The human species is not the final development in evolutionary history, but an intermediate stage that will itself cede to a higher order of being. The 'overman', however, does not express Nietzsche's agreement with Darwin's theory of evolution, but rather his answer to it. The creation of a new type will not depend on natural selection, the Darwinian mechanism that Nietzsche felt produced only the mediocrity of 'modern man', but on wilful determination.

Along with the overman the highlight of *Zarathustra* for most philosophical interpretations of Nietzsche's writings is the teaching of eternal recurrence. Although this notion had been introduced already in *The Gay Science*, it is presented as the climax of Zarathustra's wisdom. Sometimes advanced as a daring hypothesis, at other times as a doctrine, eternal recurrence states that all things will happen again and have already happened exactly as they are happening now. From Nietzsche's notebooks it is clear that he believed eternal recurrence to be a scientific truth. Drawing on the first law of thermodynamics, which maintains that energy is conserved and finite, and the infinite nature of time, Nietzsche concluded that all configurations of matter that are now achieved must have occurred before and must occur again. So certain was Nietzsche that eternal recurrence was true that he even argues with the second law of thermodynamics, which postulates the tendency toward a state of equilibrium: if equilibrium were possible, Nietzsche reasoned, then it would have already been attained, and since it has not yet been attained, it is not possible. The importance of Nietzsche's notion of eternal recurrence, albeit based on a superficial understanding of science, lies in the ontological and ethical realm. It describes an unusual state of existence that is finite yet recurring, and demands that we act in such a way that we would welcome a recurrence of our actions. For Nietzsche eternal recurrence thus implies an affirmation of being, an *amor fati* or love of fate, since only by embracing life and its possibilities do we live a fulfilled existence.

The third and perhaps most controversial concept that is seminal for *Zarathustra* is the 'will to power'. The notion came into disrepute in part because after his death Nietzsche's sister Elisabeth published a collection of aphorisms from Nietzsche's literary remains under this provocative title. It lent Nietzsche's philosophy an aggressive profile and brought it into the proximity of politics and nationalist aspirations, both of which Nietzsche himself deplored. At the very least it suggests a ruthlessness that contrasts sharply with the genteel manners of nineteenth-century Europe, and no doubt Nietzsche championed the will to power as a provocation to his contemporaries. It is an ill-defined term, but in most cases it appears as the essence of life itself and the sole principle for all occurrences. It is clearly separate from the will of any individual; it is akin to a life force, a monistic tenet that is the ultimate source of all organic and inorganic activity. Because it is highly speculative and totalizing some commentators have seen the will to power as a metaphysical premise, as a substitute for the God Nietzsche declared deceased. But Nietzsche's radical anti-metaphysical stance suggests he had something else in mind, and various critics have found ways to save him from regressing into a metaphysical trap. Will to power may itself be Nietzsche's anti-metaphysical position; in this view it would be tantamount to an inversion of the metaphysical values that Nietzsche elsewhere opposes. It can also be conceived as a statement derived ultimately from science: given Nietzsche's frequent recourse to physics and physiology, will to power could express something about elemental states of energy that are responsible for all substance and thus for all motion and activity. Finally, some observers have suggested that will to power is simply Nietzsche's perspective on things, his view, no better and no more correct or truthful than any other view, but one that can overlay all phenomena and serve as an explanation. Will to power would be something on the level of psychology, a part of our or Nietzsche's interpretation, but not an objective principle of the world. This notion of will to power fits well with Nietzsche's much heralded 'perspectivism', but it contradicts statements that appear to posit will to power as a cosmological precept.

Zarathustra announced a philosopher of the future, and the conceptual universe Nietzsche creates in this book is meant as a basis for future thought and action. But Nietzsche's writing after *Zarathustra* takes up a task that is just as necessary: the revaluation of values. In order to refashion our current value system, Nietzsche investigates how it came into being. His first major area of concern was morality, in particular the morality associated with the Judeo-Christian tradition. In *Beyond Good and Evil* and *On the Genealogy of Morals*, where he undertakes his most thorough examination of western ethics, Nietzsche posits two different value systems, one based on notions of 'good' and 'bad', another on the binary pair 'good' and 'evil'. At some point in the past the former system of values, which Nietzsche regards as noble or aristocratic, was prevalent. The label 'good' was the result of an affirmation of self, and the designation 'bad' arises out of strength and the recognition of something low or common. In time, however, a priestly caste develops from this noble system of values, and from physical weakness it begins to affirm a quite different system of values. As a means of asserting itself against the nobles the priestly caste invents the notion of evil for those who are more powerful. Thus the original deed of the 'herd or slave morality' is a negation, a symptom of *ressentiment* or rancour, and 'good' is refashioned as the term applied to the powerless, the weak, the sick. Nietzsche's mythologized history of values is meant less as an empirical description of humankind's development than as an explanation of how we have forfeited our original instincts and natural drives for the abstract and debilitating ideals of the civilized, Christian world.

Nietzsche is not an ethical philosopher in that he does not propound a system of ethics or basic moral principles. Rather, he is a historian or 'genealogist' of morals, interested in investigating how we have become what we are. The elements of his genealogical method are historical studies, especially legal history, philology, in particular the examination of etymologies, and psychological intuition. With these tools he seeks to answer questions such as 'how did human beings become creatures entitled to make promises?' His answer is that as a species we have undergone a long history of punishment that eventually made us regular and reliable. Indeed, underlying the veneer of civilization and the moral precepts that facilitate social cohabitation is a legacy of cruelty and torture. Nietzsche argues that part of our moral conscience emanates from the debtor – creditor relationship, where the debtor paid by putting his body at the disposal of the creditor, allowing him to inflict upon him an equivalence in suffering. We should not be deceived into thinking that we have become more civilized today; in our current state of sham and denial we are simply unable to face our true nature. After the fact we have accounted for punishment in different ways, giving it an acceptable rationale, but we thereby ignore its origins and function in creating a moral human being. Guilt and bad conscience, by contrast, do not originate in punishment according to Nietzsche. Instead, they are the result of an internalization of aggressive drives. With the war against the instincts that is part of Christian morality we have gradually developed from happy, adventurous, nomadic semi-animals to the domesticated, self-incarcerated, repressed, calculating creatures of the modern world.

Although Christianity was not at the root of our miserable condition – the fall begins, Nietzsche suggests, with Socrates and especially with Plato in the ancient world – it has been the foremost ideology of *ressentiment* in our long history of decline. In the works of his middle period Nietzsche had analysed religion in general as an attempt to reinterpret our experience, and he singled out Christianity in particular for its incompatibility with science and for its fantastic mythology: it is a piece of antiquity that does not fit well in the modern era. In his later works, however, Nietzsche assaults Christianity for placing humanity in an impossible situation. Hypothesizing that religion originates in a debt we owe to our forefathers, which eventually leads to a deification of ancestors, Nietzsche remarks that Christianity presents us with the unique situation in which God himself sacrifices himself for humankind. Christ dispenses our obligation to God himself, but in so doing, he places us only further in his debt. The Christian divinity heightens and exacerbates our bad conscience. We preserve and increase our guilt because we can never live up to the conduct prescribed for us, and exacerbate our guilt further by projecting a perfect creditor, one who even sacrifices himself for us his debtors, and in whose debt we will therefore remain into eternity.

Much of Nietzsche's later work is thus preoccupied with a genealogy of Christianity. What is significant about the Judeo-Christian heritage is that it represents the most drastic and consequential overturning of natural values, of instincts and of aristocratic ethics. In *The Antichrist*, where Nietzsche articulates his most sustained assessment of the Christian tradition, he notes that Judaism initially promulgated the 'correct' and 'natural' relationship to things. From its origins as a 'natural religion' Judaism took a decisive turn when it developed a 'denatured' God and the notions of 'sin' and 'blessing'. The turn to a supreme being who makes ethical demands on a people, who is conceived in terms of conscience and abstract morality, initiates a downward path for European civilization. Accompanying this change is the advent of a priestly caste that assumes authority over the people. The hegemony of the priest means that all natural behaviour, everything that formerly emanated from the instincts and contained value in itself, is ritualized and conferred with a new value, an anti-value resulting from a desecration of natural existence. Christianity represents an extension and continuation of the regime of the Jewish priesthood. The difference between Christianity and Judaism is that the former negates the remnants of the older Jewish religion and thus turns religion into an unremitting advocate of self-abnegation. Nietzsche views Christ's rebellion against the Jewish priesthood as the destruction of the vestiges of natural hierarchy remaining in Judaism. Christ is the original anarchist; his death on the cross is not for our moral guilt, but for his own political guilt in attempting to overturn an established order. In Nietzsche's worldview the Christian religion originates in a revaluation of values that is anti-instinctual, democratic and antithetical to natural hierarchies.

Nietzsche's 'immoral', anti-Christian, anti-democratic and vitalistic message was not received well during his own conscious life. Shortly after his mental breakdown in January of 1889, however, his fame, promoted successfully by the enormous efforts of his sister, began to spread throughout Germany and Europe. By the time of his death in 1900, he was already well known, mostly as a cultural critic, among prominent circles of European intellectuals, and he became a significant figure for the literary and cultural elite for much of the twentieth century. His advocacy of cultural renewal, his hatred of middle-class smugness and his own brilliance as a prose writer were his most attractive features during these years. During the two world wars, however, Nietzsche's reputation became embroiled in political controversy: many Germans championed him as an ultra-nationalist, while many non-Germans believed him to be the spirit of aggression and racism. His bellicose language, especially the easily misunderstood parables in *Zarathustra*, and his remarks on the history of religion became especially important. After the Second World War, Nietzsche was rehabilitated in Germany and the West as a philosopher, a process that was initiated in the 1930s and 1940s with the seminal works of Martin Heidegger and Karl Jaspers. Reinterpreted by each successive generation, Nietzsche has been claimed at times by phenomenology, hermeneutics, existentialism, analytical philosophy, poststructuralism and deconstruction.

Robert C. Holub

Further reading and works cited

Aschheim, S. E. *The Nietzsche Legacy in Germany 1890–1990*. Berkeley, CA, 1992.
Bergmann, P. *Nietzsche: The Last Antipolitical German*. Bloomington, IN, 1987.
Clark, M. *Nietzsche on Truth and Philosophy*. Cambridge, 1990.
Danto, A. C. *Nietzsche as Philosopher*. New York, 1980.
Derrida, J. *Spurs: Nietzsche's Styles*. Chicago, 1978.
Foucault, M. *Language, Counter-Memory, Practice: Selected Essays and Interviews*. Ithaca, NY, 1977.
Gilman, S. L. (ed.) *Conversations with Nietzsche*. New York, 1989.
Hayman, R. *Nietzsche: A Critical Life*. New York, 1980.
Heidegger, M. *Nietzsche*, 4 vols. New York, 1979–84.
Holub, R. C. *Friedrich Nietzsche*. New York, 1995.
Janz, C. P. *Friedrich Nietzsche: Biographie*, 3 vols. Munich, 1978.

Jaspers, K. *Nietzsche: An Introduction to the Understanding of His Philosophical Activity*. Tucson, AZ, 1965.

Kaufmann, W. *Nietzsche: Philosopher, Psychologist, Antichrist*. Princeton, NJ, 1974.

Magnus, B. and Higgins, K. M. (eds) *The Cambridge Companion to Nietzsche*. Cambridge, 1996.

Mittasch, A. *Friedrich Nietzsche als Naturphilosoph*. Stuttgart, 1952.

Nehemas, A. *Nietzsche: Life as Literature*. Cambridge, MA, 1985.

Nietzsche, F. *The Genealogy of Morals*. Garden City, NY, 1956.

—. *The Gay Science*. New York, 1974; trans. as *Joyful Wisdom*. New York, 1960.

—. *Thus Spoke Zarathustra. The Portable Nietzsche*, ed. W. Kaufmann. Harmondsworth, 1961.

—. *The Birth of Tragedy, The Case of Wagner*. New York, 1966.

—. *Kritische Gesamtausgabe: Werke*. eds G. Colli and M. Montinari, 30 vols. Berlin, 1967–.

—. *Twilight of the Idols The Portable Nietzsche*. Harmondsworth, 1968.

—. *Human, All Too Human*. Cambridge, 1986.

—. *Untimely Meditations*. Cambridge, 1983; as *Modern Observations*, ed. W. Arrowsmith. New Haven, CT, 1990.

—. *The Complete Works of Friedrich Nietzsche*. Stanford, CA, 1995–.

—. *The Genealogy of Morals*. Oxford, 1996.

—. *Beyond Good and Evil*. Oxford, 1998.

Nietzsche-Studien. Internationales Jahrboch for die Nietzsche-Forschung. Berlin, 1972–.

Solomon, R. C. (ed.) *Nietzsche: A Collection of Critical Essays*. Notre Dame, IN, 1980.

Strong, T. *Friedrich Nietzsche and the Politics of Transfiguration*. Berkeley, CA, 1988.

7. Sigmund Freud (1856–1939)

Through his invention of psychoanalysis Sigmund Freud deeply altered how western culture thought about itself. Few as skilled in the art of writing have had so profound an impact on medical, political and other practical discourses as Freud had, and fewer still are the men of science who, like him, have produced so important an effect on philosophical thought and artistic works. Freud's *oeuvre* is large – there are twenty-three volumes in the *Standard Edition* – yet, such is the classical clarity of his prose that in the whole of his *corpus* there seems never to have been a single wasted word.

The subject matter of Freud's essays is, however, anything but classical. An experiential core (and failing that, a textual one) lies at the heart of every bit of Freud's writing – experience that, viewed with Freud's courageously honest eye, refuses to lend itself easily to stock narrative treatments or standard literary contrivances. To honour his own unasserted gaze, Freud had to invent fresh narrative strategies: under his pen *the case history* became a new art. Freud perfects a process of writing 'the case' and in doing so discovers, develops and enriches the two key psychic structures of *neurosis* (hysteria, obsessionalism) and *psychosis* (the paraphrenias: schizophrenia, paranoia). Written between the years 1905 and 1918, these histories are exemplary of Freud's psychoanalytic process and of his virtuoso literary style.

In the 'Dora' case (1905, *SE VII*), Freud demonstrated vividly how the *hysteria* he had studied with Josef Breuer earlier (1893–5, *SE II*) 'speaks' through a young girl's gestures and acts, rather than through her words, and belies her verbal discourse. Along the way Freud also painted an unforgettable portrait of Dora, caught in parental love triangles and sexual intrigues that have left her little way out except the hysteric option. With her, Freud also finds that his analytic procedures stumble: he begins to discover how mysterious woman is.

In the 'Ratman' case (1909, *SE X*), Freud recounts, in rather horrifying detail, the psychic impulses behind a young man's obsessive fantasies of torture by rats. The young military officer's socially approved behaviours have become unbearable compulsions for him. In the analysis, Freud discovers that guilt toward his dead father (who makes ghostly appearances in which he 'commands' the Ratman to kill himself) is the key.

In the only case where Freud discusses psychosis, 'Psycho-Analytic Notes on an Autobiographical Account of a Case of Paranoia' (1911–12, *SE XII*), Freud analysed Dr Daniel Paul Schreber, but he did so by reading Schreber's memoirs, not by treating him. Schreber was a prominent jurist in Germany who fell ill with paranoid delusions when he was in his fifties. In the history of his mental illness, Schreber described in vivid and complete detail his psychotic system, in which he was 'called upon' to repair the flawed universe by allowing himself to be ravished by God, becoming God's 'wife' and bearing God's children.

In the 'Wolfman' case ([1914–18] *SE XVII*) Freud showed – in stunning variety and over many decades – how a repression disrupts the amorous life and physical well-being of a Russian émigré patient. The repression had proceeded, Freud discovered, from an unrecallable 'primal scene' in the patient's infancy, where, Freud hypothesized, he had witnessed his parents making love. That scene is retroactively inferred by the analyst from the patient's dreams (one of which regards a tree where wolves sit) which lead to his unconscious fantasies. The primal scene is thus the single factor that insistently warps and blunts the Wolfman's capacity for enjoyment throughout his life.

The significance of Freud's use of exquisitely shaped prose to portray as well as to analyse the aberrations of the mind (and the body it affects) lies in what it is trying to present: the singular structure of unconscious mental phenomena. Thus it is that Freud's case histories do not merely offer the finished results of an analysis, but also its working through, its process: Freud's narrative style reflects the gradual unfolding of an unconscious *knowledge* that remains only partially revealed, in fits and starts, to both the analyst and the patient. And their respective understandings are rarely in harmony, rendering the task of writing a challenge.

Freud also found his style constrained by the nature of his material. By this is meant less the content than the bizarre form that the mental phenomena he discovered assume. He had found, for example, that 'the mind' interacts and intersects with language and speech. But this language is shaped by formal elements for which literary and philosophical history provide no useful models:

1. by the psyche's aberrant *temporality* (*Nachträglichkeit*, unconscious memories, screen memories, repetition);
2. by the psyche's peculiar relation to *speech* (the *parapraxis* or Freudian slip, the disguised sexual *symbol*, the *symptom*);
3. by the variety and peculiarity of the psyche's tools of *representation* (*Darstellung, Vorstellung, Vorstellungsrepräsentanz, condensation, displacement, the dreamwork*); and
4. by the psyche's deployment of several different kinds of *negation* (Freud distinguishes three kinds: regation [*Verneinung*], denial [*Vernichtung*] and foreclosure [*Verwerfung*]).

Freud had first fully described the origin and operations of these mechanisms in a masterwork, *The Interpretation of Dreams* (1900, *SE IV*). His deciphering of the psyche's strategies of representation through the hieroglyphic character of dreams remains one of Freud's capital achievements, comparable, for some, to the discovery of the Rosetta Stone. Indeed, if we had only three of Freud's works we would have a rich, important and seemingly finished *oeuvre*: *The Interpretation of Dreams* (1900, *SE IV and V*), which demonstrates the astonishing variety of the verbal and pictorial distortions deployed by an unconscious wish that seeks to break through repression and declare itself; *The Psychopathology of Everyday Life* (1901, *SE VII*), which examines the formal mechanisms by which the unconscious disrupts discourse; and the volume on *Jokes and Their Relation to the Unconscious* (1905, *SE VIII*), which completes the main work Freud undertook to demonstrate that language is disturbed by the presence of the unconscious even in the most ordinary, everyday behaviours and events.

Of course, Freud did more. He gave the world of art and letters a shock that went well beyond his disclosing the subterranean machinations of disguised desire. The fact is that Freud outraged many people – and not simply for the 'historicist' reason that he was treating matters that were censored under Victorian 'politeness', since his work continues to stir controversy today. (For example, one might refer to the Jeffrey Masson-Janet Malcolm disputes over his seduction theories, or the public outcry over the Smithsonian Institution's exhibition in honour of the 100th anniversary of the *Interpretation of Dreams*.)

At first glance, Freud seemed mainly bent on shaking up a placid society with the news that it is constantly beseiged by an unwelcome guest, the Unconscious. Freud dramatized its presence and made it all the more shocking by insisting on its *sexual* character: the hidden wishes that formed its substance were not only for forbidden sex, their very sexualization was tied to events that occurred in infancy. In his *Three Essays on the Theory of Sexuality* (1905, *SE VII*) and 'My Views on The Part Played by Sexuality in the Aetiology of the Neuroses' (1905–6, *SE VII*), Freud closely observed infants (who lack the means of verbalization; *in-fans* = without speech) and young children. He discovered there the makings of all subsequent forms of adult sexual behaviours, from fantasies to inhibitions, from homosexuality to perversion. He also studied the effect that tabooing sexual knowledge had on children: he examined the accounts young children, kept in the dark about 'the facts of life', devise to explain away the sexual energy they feel in their bodies (and sense in their parents), not to mention the inexplicable advent of a new baby – see 'On the Sexual Theories of Children' (1907, *SE IX*) and the interesting case of 'Little Hans', which consists of a father's reports to Freud regarding his son's fears and of Freud's return commentaries ('Analysis of a Phobia in a Five-Year-Old Boy', 1909, *SE X*). The father was an early devotee of Freud's, the mother had been Freud's patient, and on the birth of a younger sister Hans developed multiple phobias.

More than Freud's insistence on sexuality, what continues to surprise thinkers everywhere today is that he introduced an unheralded complexity into concepts and words that had previously been more simply understood. He had to: he was describing an indescribable entity – the *Unconscious* – whose presence, force and operations could only be inferred from the phenomena he was the first to single out for analytic attention. The Unconscious, which 'knows no negation', is not merely a temporarily backgrounded thought or perception; it is a mind-within-the-mind. Yet it is not entirely 'in' us, either. The Unconscious is in fact structured and determined by our intimate links to others – to parents, siblings, social and sexual rivals, *et al.* – and to language. Its presence is only 'given away' through slips of the tongue, unsuitable gestures or compulsive acts. These alone are how the Unconscious indirectly manifests itself.

What is the Unconscious? Its contents are comprised of only one thing: a repressed wish (*Wunsch*) that cannot be resolved through a verbal articulation: a desire that cannot speak its name. Since verbalization is one of the only 'satisfactions' society permits us, a repressed wish (i.e. one lacking the means of verbalization) will adopt a variety of circuitous forms to sustain its energy and psychic force. To counter it, the mind energizes itself to bar the injection of this unspeakable desire into social relations. Such a wish may be for forbidden incest, but also for other unavowable, things like murder; it is mainly, but not exclusively, sexual in character. Forced back, the unavowable wish does not disappear, but crystallizes into a fully staged *fantasy*. Elaborated and re-elaborated in the unconscious this fantasy constitutes what Freud calls the 'other scene' [*andere Schauplatz*].

When Freud developed psychoanalysis, he seemed at first to be answering philosophy's traditional demand for the fully examined life (e.g. Socrates' or Kant's questions, 'What can I know?', 'What must I do?', etc.). But Freud's theory also traced its descent to 'hard' science. He was trained as a neurobiologist and as a physician and he greatly admired the work of his near contemporary, Charles Darwin, to whose books *The Descent of Man* and *The Expression of the Emotions in Man and Animals* Freud referred on numerous occasions.

Freud in fact represented a philosophical conundrum. More than anyone had thought possible, he fulfilled the Delphic oracle's challenge to 'Know thyself', the *Nosce te ipsum*. But his 'answer' managed to question, to an unprecedented degree, the very status of *knowledge* itself. He shook the most fundamental assumptions about the very *language* in which human knowledge is conveyed, and he further shook the presumption that human beings actually *desire* to know themselves. For Freud had found that in the very structure of thought itself lay a necessarily unthought, unknowable portion.

The foundations of his 'scientific' side were also disturbed by Freud. Freud's discovery meant that human *biology* was as much or more subject to the *laws of language* and *culture* as it was to the *laws of nature*. The analysis of the psyche had demonstrated irrefutably that the *organic logic* of the *human* body (its natural, teleological functionality) is supplanted wholesale by another logic: the *logos* of speech or language. It is a logic that ruins natural logic, and therefore makes it possible for the mind (made out of logos – reason, speech) to affect the body and make it ill. As Lacan once put it: 'people feel the weight of words'.

Freud's philosophical and scientific revolution thus had the same root: a mind with an unnatural relation to nature; a body that affected, and was even more fundamentally affected by, the mind. How did this come about?

Freud theorized that human mental life originated in a unique way, and he worked these theses out carefully in two early papers, the unpublished (by him) *Project for a Scientific Psychology* (1895, SE I) and the 1911 essay, 'The Two Principles of Mental Functioning' (*SE XII*). He never really deviated from this initial vision.

For Freud, the specifically *human* mind was indebted neither to the 'innate ideas' Cartesian rationalism hypothesized, nor to pure experience, as British empiricism and the neurobiological sciences Freud studied, presumed. Freud believed, instead, that human mental life was initially *driven* into existence by being deprived of its 'nature' in a singular fashion. An animal always finds a way to fulfil its natural needs; if not, it dies. But the *human* mind does not accept this simple split of life from death, of satisfied from unsatisfied needs. Refusing to credit 'necessity', faced with a situation where satisfaction is impossible, the human mind concocts a third solution quite different from the animal's forced choice to eat or to die. Instead it devises an alternate *satisfaction*: Freud calls hallucination or *fantasy* our first acts of mentation. Using the emptied maternal breast as his paradigm, Freud shows that even the smallest infant will construct mental substitutes for the satisfaction – the milk – that has been withdrawn. The breast, which no longer supplies nourishment, is recalled as a 'lost' enjoyment made 'present' again to a mind which enjoys it in fantasy. Thus provisionally satisfied, the infant will stay in that mental space until 'reality' finally intervenes and requires active effort to gain nourishment. According to Freud, once humans substitute mentally fabricated satisfactions of their needs that cannot be actually fulfilled, *mental life* as we know it begins. Necessity, *Ananké*, and thus Death remain the cardinal denial of human mental life, and Freud later says that no ego can really believe it is anything but immortal.

The core of human 'consciousness' is therefore formed by a fundamental discounting of 'reality' in favour of what we might call 'metaphor': the substituting of some *image* for some *thing*, which is also the basis of language itself. Freud came to believe that *mental life* as such was specifically designed to shut out the *knowledge* of brute reality (the real absence or real presence of the satisfying thing). At the same time, however, *another knowledge* – precisely of that brute reality – also persisted underneath its metaphorical replacements. As 'conscious' cultural and mental forms (spurred by the drives, and rooted by metaphor and fantasy) became more complex, unconscious knowledge also flowered secretly in equal measure. This hidden twin of conscious thought took thus the paradoxical form of an 'unknown knowledge': the knowledge we had elected *not* to know for the simple reason that we had also elected to *think*.

When Freud founded the new art and science of psychoanalysis he based it entirely on the desire (his own, primarily) to know and to bring this *unconscious knowledge* to the light of rational discourse. But it could not be *his* desire alone. His desire to know had to be doubled: the *analyst's desire to know* about the patient's unconscious must be matched by the *patient's* desire. This underground knowledge had gone, buried by what Freud calls *repression* (*Unterdrängung*), which finds Freud likening the analytic process to an archaeology.

Psychoanalysis quickly became institutionalized as a healing art, in and out of fashion ever since. But after Freud, the *arts* have rarely dispensed with him. It was, tellingly, Leonard Woolf's Hogarth Press that published Freud's works in English translation as they were being written; his wife, Virginia Woolf, and their Bloomsbury Circle mingled socially and intellectually with the Freudians. Later, the French New Wave (Sarraute, Robbe-Grillet) would have been unthinkable without Freud, likewise film. In Alfred Hitchcock's *Spellbound*, *Marnie* and *The Birds* psychoanalysis is thematized; Fritz Lang's *Secret Beyond the Door* makes direct use of psychoanalytic technique and references psychic temporality, and Marguerite Duras' *Hiroshima, mon amour* has been likened to a case history. In her film *Détruire, dit-elle*, Duras says of a forest a female character is afraid to enter: 'The Forest is Freud'.

Freud's work has intrinsic literary interest: the myriad disguises obscuring the reality of sexuality in human affairs; the mis-steps in the spoken word that betrayed cloaked desires; the intimations of an 'other stage' where repressed scenarios of rivalry and romance are granted fantasy stagings – this is also the stuff of plays, novels and poetry. Freud himself used literature: a Shakespeare play (*The Merchant of Venice* in 'The Theme of the Three Caskets', 1913, *SE XII*; *Hamlet* in Mourning and Melancholia', 1915, *SE XIV*), a Goethe poem (Goethe appears in nearly every volume; one example is 'A Disturbance of Memory on the Acropolis', 1936, *SE XXII*), novels by the Russian Dostoevsky ('Dostoevsky and Parricide', 1928, *SE XXI*) and by the Danish Wilhelm Jensen (*Delusions and Dreams in Jensen's Gradiva*, 1906–7, *SE IX*), a story by John Galsworthy (in *Civilization and its Discontents*, 1929, *SE XXI*), not to mention the plays of Sophocles' *Oedipus* cycle whence Freud formulated the 'Oedipus Complex' as the nucleus of the neuroses ('Further Remarks on the Neuro-psychoses of Defence', 1892, *SE III*). He wrote about 'Psychopathic Characters on Stage' (1905, *SE VII*), and in his 'Creative Writers and Daydreaming' (1907, *SE IX*) he located the *fantasy* art deploys as partially Unconscious and partially social. Unlike *unconscious fantasy*, artistic fictions admit of others' participation in a forbidden enjoyment: for example, fictionalized sex and murder.

To some, literature seems diminished by psychoanalysing it. Freud, however, granted art and literature theoretical importance. Freud updated Aristotle's *catharsis*, wondering just why in art social taboos can be violated with impunity and even socially rewarded. In 'Instincts and Their Vicissitudes' (1915, *SE XIV*) Freud began modelling key psycho-analytic concepts on *aesthetic production*, especially *sublimation*, one of the psychic transformations of *drives* into acceptable mental productions.

With the advent of the First World War in which the venerable Austro-Hungarian Empire lost its cultural dominance to the younger British one, the stable society that Freud had taken for granted disappeared and his work now took a different turn: away from the micro-behavioural toward larger cultural assessments. He was particularly concerned with the impact culture has on the psyche. Culture [*Kultur*] – the English 'civilization' – not only smoothes over brutal reality (which remains 'known' only to the Unconscious and its attendant fantasies) but is itself an ongoing source of fresh dilemmas for human existence.

Around the First World War Freud produces some of his most complex concepts. They blend socially recognizable personality traits and behaviours with analysis of their unconscious roots: narcissism, melancholia, repression. At this time he also elaborates the theory of the *drives* (usually, but incorrectly, translated as 'instincts'). *The Papers on Metapsychology* (*SE XIV*) contain these conceptually rich notions as well as Freud's pensive, haunting 'Thoughts for the Time on War and Death' (1915), an essay whose expression and conception alike continue to interest students of literature (MacCannell 2000).

Freud's original 'cultural critique' had a frankly 'mythic' character: *Totem and Taboo* (1913, *SE XIII*). Later he evolved a more anchored and structured discourse concerning socio-cultural life: in 'Beyond the Pleasure Principle' (1920, *SE XVIII*), *Group Psychology and the Analysis of the Ego* (1921, *SE XVIII*), *The Future of an Illusion* (1927, *SE XXI*), *Civilization and its Discontents* (1928, *SE XXI*) and his final major work in this area, *Moses and Monotheism* (1939, *SE XIII*). Freud systematically pursued the psychology of human groups, from the primal horde (run dictatorially by a ferocious Ur-Father who hates and persecutes his sons) through to modern 'artificial' groups, whose Leaders 'love' and nurture those under their command. Freud, rather chillingly, saw the outlines of the first still present in the second, with guilt for a dead father the key to a group's integrity.

Freud painted vividly our discontents (*Unbehangen*) with group life. While his critique of culture was first taken in the eighteenth-century way, i.e. as a conflict between simple, 'natural' man's 'instincts' and arbitrary social laws that forbid them, Freud was telling a far more complex truth. That the *drives* simply contest the constraints of civilization is an illusion: for, Freud found, the drives are in fact only produced by civilization itself. Conversely, without the spur of the drives, civilization and culture have no incentive for further elaboration, the mind is impelled to no new labours: *Drive* (translated as 'instinct' by Strachey), Freud writes, is 'a measure of the demand made on the mind for work' ('Three Essays on Sexuality', *SE VII*, 168).

In Freud's quite vivid pictures of our anguished relation to other people, he also made it clear that only the *civilization* (*Kultur*) we hold in common grants us *human* status. The sacrifices 'the common work of civilization' demands of us make us *sick*, but it is less because our 'animal' parts rebel against cultural constraints, than because culture produces in us *drives* which by their very nature *must* remain unsatisfied. Culture itself generates the unconscious *excess* that spurs it to further elaborations, just as mentation produces a blank absence of knowledge that it then must work to fill.

For Freud the fundamental and insoluble dilemma of human existence is that our *Drives* demand recognition by civilization, but our civilization commands their misrecognition – because it is itself their source. *Drive*, as *excess* energy, is unique and specific to human being, the by-product of our increasing mental activity and an accelerating metaphoric translation of our raw experience. The more we try to contain drives, the less able we are to recognize that inhibitions only generate more drives. We have to try dissipating or discharging the excess energy of drive without resorting to repressive codes and regulations which only enflame, rather than quell, *drive*. The great self-regulatory principles human life has traditionally devised ('the pleasure principle' and 'the reality principle') go only so far and cannot ultimately attenuate the capital drive in us: *death drive*. *Death drive* is the logical extension of a mental life formed by the denial of biological necessity and reality: human beings will defer the satisfaction of their drives at the expense of life itself.

Thus, when Freud took psychoanalysis past the pleasure and reality principles with the radical concept of the *Death Drive* (which he drew from Sabrina Spielrein, a patient, and systematically formulated in 'Beyond the Pleasure Principle'), he posed a major challenge to Aristotelian and neo-Aristotelian assumptions that 'balance' is inherent to and indispensable for social organization, aesthetic works and individual ethics. The simple fact is that we must live with a certain inherent imbalance, an imbalance that is key to human mental health and illness alike.

Freud's complex picture of our relation to civilization was often given simplified treatment in its applications, sometimes with significant effects. Leslie Fiedler, a professor at the State University of New York, Buffalo (a campus that still has a Center for Psychoanalysis and Culture), was among the first American critics to push literary studies beyond textual analysis toward the broad cultural horizon Freud's work implies. Fiedler's *Love and Death in the American Novel* (1960) was frankly Freudian, and deeply disturbed the then genteel world of literary criticism that leaned heavily on aesthetic philosophy and maintained a near-Victorian decorum. So was American critic Norman O. Brown's *Life Against Death; The Psychoanalytical Meaning of History* (1959) and his *Love's Body* (1966). Europeans, of course, had long taken a similar tack, often blending Freud with Marx: Theodor W. Adorno (1967, 1987), and Herbert Marcuse (1955, 1964) were among those who first used Freud's critiques of 'civilization' to attack capitalist culture.

Marcuse, Max Horkheimer and Adorno promoted the Frankfurt School's unique synthesis of Freud and Marx. Walter Benjamin, their Frankfurt School colleague and Adorno's close friend, became known to the English-speaking world in the 1960s with the translation of some of his essays. While working in the field of culture criticism, Benjamin inflected Freud differently from his friends, and ended by deploying Freud in a highly original and insightful manner. Benjamin's way of reading rivalled Freud's in complexity, but Benjamin rarely took up a Freudian concept without making it his own. His essay 'On Some Motifs in Baudelaire' (1973) makes free, but not inaccurate, use of Freud's 'Beyond the Pleasure Principle' to imply that the material culture surrounding this 'lyric poet in the age of high capitalism' had become much like the primordial brew in which Freud had immersed his pre-mental sentient beings. Benjamin focused on the 'shocks' and 'stimuli' that in Freud's 'BPP' overwhelms primitive creatures. These shocks force them to form consciousness as a shield against, rather than a prolongation of, experience. Benjamin analogized Freud's mythic neurological 'shocks' to the inassimilable horrors of modern capitalism and its advancing technologies.

The use of Freud made by 'ethnic' critics, begun by Leslie Fiedler (1955), turned Freud into a crucial ally against the erasure of social and cultural difference that the New Criticism had made one of its tenets. Fiedler's and Brown's books startled literary studies into awareness of the social as well as sexual dimensions in literature. When they appeared the 'age of conformity' in the United States was drawing to a close (as new cultural movements like the Beats gained momentum) and the politicizing of academic and public discourse was about to begin. Freudianism came to the fore as a natural ally of both movements.

Yet official twentieth-century literary criticism in Anglo-America had, in fact, already incorporated several strains of 'Freudianism' though without ever making Freud's methods and theories a focus of outright debate. There were not yet declared Freudians like Frederick Crews (who later turned against Freud), but certain individualist critics like Kenneth Burke, Lionel Trilling and Leon Edel knew Freud well, and diverted him to their own purposes. Burke, for example, did not necessarily agree with Freud, but he did not reject him entirely; instead, Burke placed grammatical mechanisms and rhetorical under-pinnings beneath 'Freudian' insights.

Stanley Edgar Hyman's influential collections of literary critics (*The Armed Vision*, 1948, and *The Critical Performance*, 1960) were intentionally eclectic. They aimed to introduce the students present at the dawning of *literary theory* to a variety of approaches, ranging from the marxist one of Christopher Caudwell's to the New Critics. Hyman's strongest sympathies lay with Kenneth Burke, who connected rhetorical concerns to contemporary social issues and sought to make literature 'equipment for living', often by adapting Freudian topics and methods to this end. (See Burke's use of Freud's 'On the Antithetical Meaning of Primal Words'.) Hyman also befriended Burke's brilliant student Erving Goffman, who published a respectfully yet playfully deviant remodelling of Freud for social analysis, *The Presentation of Self in Everyday Life* (1959). Goffman's highly modified Freud influenced cultural critics like Dean MacCannell (*The Tourist*, 1976) and Michel de Certeau (*The Practice of Everyday Life*, 1984). In the same era, Canadian theorist Marshall McLuhan's 1951 cultural critique in *The Mechanical Bride* had a distinctly 'Freudian' tinge.

Freud's intensive scrutiny of language, speech and rhetorical devices intrigued literary specialists who might otherwise have seemed incompatible in sensibility with Freud's overt sexual focus and broad cultural scope. Thus it was that Charles Kay Ogden, an aesthetic philosopher, and the eighteenth-century specialist I. A. Richards wrote *The Meaning of*

Meaning; a Study of the Influence of Language Upon Thought and of the Science of Symbolism (1927) and indirectly encouraged Anglo-American criticism to draw inspiration from Freud.

Ogden and Richards tapped into two different, though kindred, psychological approaches (Freud's and Will James') to tackle the question of *meaning*. To Ogden and Richards 'meaning' seemed to have a necessarily subjective as well as an objective side. Richards had disagreed with his teacher G. E. Moore's thesis that words *can* say what we mean. (Richards, in despair over his arguments with Moore, at one time intended to become a psychoanalyst.) Together with Ogden, Richards hoped to make their work on the 'subjective' side of meaning as rigorously logical and 'scientific' as Moore's on the 'objective' side, an enterprise in the spirit of Freud's inquiry. The pair drew on the *sign* defined by Charles Sanders Peirce (the American whose philosophy of *Pragmaticism* (*sic*) inspired William James, his best friend) to designate the literary sign's way of 'meaning'. (Incidentally, both Derrida and Lacan elected Peirce's sign over Saussure's, Lacan because of his friend Roman Jakobson, a Peircean semiolinguist.) At the same time, Ogden and Richards included essays on the *social meaning* of signs and *symbols* by the Freudian anthropologist Bronislaw Malinowksi in their influential book.

New Criticism held a firm line against 'Freudian' interpretations of literature and its authors, as the famous essay on the 'Intentional Fallacy' by William K. Wimsatt and Monroe C. Beardsley in Wimsatt's *The Verbal Icon* (1954) attests: its New Critical stand against psychobiographical criticism is quite plain. Yet in some way, even an anti-Freudian New Criticism prepared the ground for accepting Freudian thought. The New Criticism, after all, had an immense appetite for the intrinsic ambiguity of verbal expression, for emotional and moral ambivalence in literary tone, and for hidden ironies in poetic personae. In some students' minds this translated into a potential tie to Freud's 'unconscious' – although there was in fact no true theoretical basis for making such a connection.

Finally, in France, the linguistic analysis of Freud is deepened in the work of Nicholas Abraham and Maria Torok, who reanalysed Freud's Wolf Man purely on the basis of the signifer in *The Wolfman's Magic Word*. American critics Avital Ronell and Laurence Rickels have used their work.

By the mid-twentieth century Freudian criticism was drawn out of its more or less comfortable closet by two circumstances that proved fateful for Freud's place in the subsequent literary critical canon. One was the historic entrance of *women*, as writers, literature professors and critics, into the growing field of modern language studies. The other was the development, in France, of Jacques Lacan's Freudian School, which marked deeply the direction of literary criticism there, and of Derridean deconstruction, which critiqued but also used Freud's close attention to the operations of language. The appearance of a 'French Freud' exerted significant pressure on literary theory and criticism in the United States and the United Kingdom; Freud, for the first time, became the explicit topic of open and impassioned debate.

The movement of women into the literary profession provided a forum for contesting from within certain of Freud's views of 'civilization and its discontents'. After all, within that civilization, Freud granted women an exceedingly minor role: 'Women represent the interests of the family and of sexual life. The work of civilization has become increasingly the business of men; it confronts them with ever more difficult tasks and compels them to carry out instinctual sublimations of which women are little capable' (*Civilization and its*

Discontents, 1929, *SE XXI*, 103–4). This made women themselves into one of the 'discontents' 'civilized' man had to put up with.

Indeed, Freud made so little theoretical room for the woman who might labour productively as a creative writer or as a critic that it seems unlikely for women to follow him – at least not without strong dissent. It is a therefore a perpetual surprise that Freud found as many 'daughters' as he did to continue his line of thought, despite his patently patriarchal attitude. Freud's express misogyny ('an individual woman may be a human being in other [than sexual] respects', 'On Femininity', 1933, *SE XXII*, 119), his focus on fathering, his constitutional resistance to recognizing the female portion in cultural transmission, etc., did not prevent a great many women from finding him fascinating.

For Freud was also exceptional in his sympathy *to* women – he had listened, after all, to the hysterics and had spoken for them when they could not speak for themselves. Significant numbers of his earliest followers were women: H. D., Marie Bonaparte, Joan Riviere, Melanie Klein, Lou Andreas-Salomé and, of course, his daughter Anna (Appignanesi and Forester 1992; and Wright 1992). One of the most intriguing pieces of early 'Freudian' literary criticism is Princess Marie Bonaparte's study of sadism, mourning and necrophilia in the work of Edgar Allan Poe (1933) for which Freud wrote the glowing introduction. Bonaparte, a patient of Freud's and his staunchest French supporter, also authored the first psychoanalytic study of *Female Sexuality* (1953).

By the 1970s, New Zealander Juliet Mitchell had seized upon Freud and his French variant, Jacques Lacan, for the critical study of women *in* literature and of literature *by* women. Her books (1974, 1984), in tandem with her 1982 collaborative translation of (and commentary on) Lacan's and the *école freudienne*'s Feminine Sexuality (with Jacqueline Rose) appreciated Lacan's updating of Freud for women. With Mitchell's lead, many British and American women critics entered the field, including Elizabeth Abel, Elizabeth Wright, Naomi Segal, Parveen Adams, Madelon Sprengnether, Teresa Brennan, Alice Jardine and Jane Gallop (along with many men, of course), though they were as often inspired the French Freud of Lacan and the French feminists Hélène Cixous, Luce Irigaray and Julia Kristeva as by Freud himself.

Clearly, it was Freud's translation through Lacan that encouraged a path for Freudian literary criticism *by* women, particularly women drawn to 'cultural critique'. Partly contesting and partly advancing it, they focused on Freud's apparent exclusion of women from culture, ethics, social justice. In 'Femininity' Freud had, for example, claimed that the psychic space reserved for social justice was crowded out in woman by her envy of male power – and of the penis [*penisneid*]. Freud's pithy pronouncements made it seem impossible for women to produce cultural insights: woman was, after all, 'a dark continent' where the reason's light was extinguished; woman had a weak Superego; her psychic make-up evolved not from civilizing *guilt* (the guilt for murdering the father incurred by the brothers in *Totem and Taboo*) but simply from *shame*, by which Freud meant fear of exposing her lack of a penis. If woman's genitalia are exposed, they resemble, Freud said, the Medusa's head (1940, *SE XVIII*) that turns men to stone, (i.e. sexually arouses them, but also petrifies them with forebodings of their own death – the ultimate castration).

Why did women persist in looking to Freud? Freud's preponderant desire was to know *about* women, and this singular, perpetually refreshed desire was part of his irresistibility to them. He famously asked, 'What does a woman want?' in a letter to Marie Bonaparte; he wondered openly why femininity was 'a riddle wrapped up in a mystery inside an enigma'. His sheer interest in women seemed sufficient cause for one female critic after another to pause at the edge of his stream of misogyny for a deeper drink. It was, after all, the hysteric's sadly blunted efforts to break through male imposed limits that inspired Freud to create his theory in the first place. Its keystone, the thesis that language had its 'dark' side, also found women had been culturally forced to occupy that obscure space. Freud's theory proved that that was an accident of history and a problem to be solved. Unlike the 'anatomy' that Freud once called our 'destiny' (by which he meant that our organs of excretion and of procreation were inalterably entwined, not that a biological and mental sex were inevitably matched up), our *language* gives sex a culturally embedded *place*. There is no naturally assigned *fate* for each sex. Once Jacques Lacan's exposition of masculine and feminine positions in language made this crystal clear, everything Freud had said about women could be reassessed. (In his *Encore Seminar XX* (1975) Lacan identified two distinctive logics of *feminine* and *masculine* that relieved both sexes of their biological designations and hence of their anatomical 'destiny' – see Copjec (1994).)

The most recent turns of Freudian criticism by women now combine the practice of Freud's strong 'formalism' and textual precision with the surer footing women have gained in his field of cultural critique, a footing enabled largely by Lacan: Joan Copjec (1994), Juliet Flower MacCannell (1991 and 2000), Renata Salecl (1999), Hélène Cixous and Catherine Clément. Even rhetorical critics like Shoshana Felman (1987) have oriented recent work to cultural criticism via psychoanalysis (1991). Other women have taken up the practice of psychoanalysis, like Michele Montrelay, Monique David-Ménard, Julia Kristeva (1980 and 1989) and Luce Irigaray.

At present, there remains both great hope for and great suspicion of Freud for literary and cultural criticism – in equal doses of committed enthusiasm and staunch anti-Freudianism.

Juliet Flower MacCannell

Further reading and works cited

Abraham, N. and Torok, M. *The Wolf Man's Magic Word*, preface J. Derrida. Minneapolis, MN, 1986.

Adorno, T. W. *Prisms*. London, 1967.

—. *Aesthetic Theory*, eds G. Adorno and R. Tiedemann. London, 1984.

Appignanesi, L. and Forrester, J. *Freud's Women*. New York, 1992.

Benjamin, W. *Charles Baudelaire: A Lyric Poet In The Era Of High Capitalism*. London, 1973.

Bonaparte, M. *Edgar Poe, Étude psychanalytique*. Paris, 1933.

—. *Female Sexuality*. New York, 1953.

Brown, N. *Life Against Death*. Middletown, CT, 1959.

—. *Love's Body*. New York, 1966.

Cixous, H. and Clément, C. *The Newly Born Woman*, intro. S. M. Gilbert. Minneapolis, MN, 1986.

Copjec, J. *Read My Desire*. Cambridge, MA, 1994.

De Certeau, M. *The Practice of Everyday Life*. Berkeley, CA, 1984.

Felman, S. *Jacques Lacan and the Adventure of Insight*. Cambridge, MA, 1987.

Fiedler, L. A. *An End to Innocence*. Boston, 1955.

—. *Love and Death in the American Novel*. New York, 1960.

Freud, S. *The Standard Edition of the Complete Psychological Works of Sigmund Freud*, eds J. Strachey and A. Freud, 24 vols London.

Goffman, E. *The Presentation of Self in Everyday Life*. Garden City, NY, 1959.

Hyman, S. *The Armed Vision*. New York, 1955.
—. *Critical Performance*. New York, 1956.
Kristeva, J. *Desire in Language*. New York, 1980.
—. *Black Sun*. New York, 1989.
Lacan, J. *Le Séminaire. Livre XX. Encore*, ed. J.-A. Miller. Paris, 1975.
— and the école freudienne. *Feminine Sexuality*, eds J. Mitchell and J. Rose. New York, 1982.
MacCannell, D. *The Tourist: A New Theory of the Leisure Class*. New York, 1976.
MacCannell, J. F. 'The Regime of the Brother', in *Opening Out*, ed. T. Brennan. London, 1991.
—. *The Hysteric's Guide to the Future Female Subject*. Minneapolis, MN, 2000.
McLuhan, M. *The Mechanical Bride*. Boston, 1967.
Marcuse, H. *Eros and Civilization*. Boston, 1955.
—. *One Dimensional Man*. Boston, 1964
Mitchell, J. *Psychoanalysis and Feminism*. New York, 1974.
—. *Women: The Longest Revolution*. London, 1984.
Ogden, C. K. and Richards, I. A. *The Meaning of Meaning*. London, 1936.
Salecl, R. *Spoils of Freedom*. London, 1994.
Wimsatt, W. K. Jr. *The Verbal Icon*. Lexington, KY, 1954.
Wright, E. *Psychoanalytic Criticism*. New York, 1992.

8. Ferdinand de Saussure (1857–1913) and Structural Linguistics

Much of the contemporary theoretical project finds its linguistic origins in the intellectual history of structural linguistics and semiotics. The analysis of the social construction of signs, moreover, has influenced the emergence and direction of various political genres of literary criticism, including feminist criticism and cultural studies, among others. As the study of signs, semiotics refers to the analysis of cultural and social referents, especially regarding their impact upon various modes of human behaviour.

Swiss linguist Ferdinand de Saussure advanced the study of signs further as a form of 'semiology' because of its attention to socially and culturally inscribed codes of human interaction. Often considered to be the founder of modern linguistics, Saussure constructed a theory of language whose intellectual legacy continues to resonate within scholarly circles, as evinced by A. J. Greimas's (1917–92) contemporary achievements in terms of semiotics and discourse theory. In addition to his postulation of a social-semiological metatheory, Saussure's influence includes his identification of the places of *langue* and *parole* in language and literary study.

Saussure's theories of signs recognizes the systemic codes and socialized conventions that characterize languages and the manner in which they become internalized by members of a given culture. Understanding that signs both implicitly and explicitly convey information between members of that culture, Saussurean semiotics addresses the nature of the speech acts and non-verbal gestures that mark human discourse communities. Although it quite obviously intersects with Charles Sanders Peirce's earlier linguistic philosophy of signs and their arbitrariness, Saussure's postulation of the sign attempts to elucidate the signifying system itself, rather than merely interpreting the instance of signification. For Saussure, the sign consists of two inseparable aspects, the signifier and the signified. The signifier refers to a set of speech sounds in language, while the signified functions as the meaning that undergirds the sign itself. Eschewing Peirce's theories regarding the objectivity and subjectivity of language, Saussure's semiology contends that the senses of identity or uniqueness of all aspects of language emerge via the differences inherent in that language's network of linguistic relationships, rather than through a given language's objective features. This concept demonstrates Saussure's paradoxical argument that in a given language system 'there are only differences, with no positive terms' (Culler 1981, 21). The importance of Saussure's discoveries finds its origins in the linguist's anticipation of language, in the words of Bertil Malmberg, as an 'abstract, superindividual system' (1967, 9). As with Peirce's theory of signs, however, Saussure's conceptualization of language recognizes the arbitrariness of speech acts and their invariable historical and cultural contingency.

Saussure's postulation of *langue* and *parole* – and their substantial impact upon language study – also demonstrate his significant contributions to twentieth-century linguistics and literary criticism. Saussure's philosophy of language argues that the fundamental aim of semiotics is to understand the concept of *langue* (language) as a possible result of *parole* ('word'). For Saussure, *langue* refers to the basic system of differentiation and combinational rules that allows for a particular usage of signs; *parole* connotes a single verbal utterance, as well as the employment of a sign or set of signs. 'In separating *langue* from *parole*,' Saussure writes, 'we are separating what is social from what is individual and what is essential from what is ancillary or accidental' (Culler 1981, 24). Saussurean linguistics contends, moreover, that signs lack signification in themselves and only accrue meaning via their relationships with other signs. The inherent differences among a set of given signs share, then, in the creation of their meaning. In Saussure's philosophy, David Holdcroft writes, '*langue* is social because it is the product of face-to-face communicative interchanges between members of a linguistic community, each of whom, as a result of these interchanges, has a similar representation of it' (1991, 27). Saussure's comprehension of language's inherently social particularity reveals its autonomous nature and the ways in which it conforms to the norms and linguistic requirements of a given historical or cultural era.

This latter distinction regarding the central philosophy of Saussurean semiotics necessitates the discussion of two additional aspects of the linguist's system of language study, the notion of the phoneme and Saussure's social-semiological metatheory. As the smallest basic speech sound or unit of pronunciation, Saussure's ground-breaking conceptualization of the phoneme represents a signal moment in the history of linguistics. It allows us to distinguish between two different utterances in terms of their measurable physical differences. According to Jonathan Culler, Saussure's postulation of the phoneme provides us with a means for comprehending the 'social significance of objects and actions' and for registering the 'judgements and perception' that a given speaker evinces, often unconsciously, when using a given language in a given historical instance (1991, 81). Having established his concept of the phoneme, Saussure demonstrated that the linguistic system in its entirety can be understood in terms of a theory of syntagmatic and paradigmatic relationships. The former involves the study of language in relational sequences, while the latter refers to the oppositional relationships that exist between linguistic elements that can

replace one another. Saussure employed a similar system for understanding the relationships between phonemes, which he explained in terms of their synchronic and diachronic
structures. A phoneme exists in a diachronic, or horizontal, relationship with other
phonemes that precede and follow it. Synchronic relationships refer to a phoneme's
vertical associations with the entire system of language from which individual utterances –
or, in regard to the auspices of literary criticism, narratives – derive their meaning.

Saussure's elucidation of the synchronic and diachronic relationships that exist in
language and literary study anticipated a number of later theoretical advances in literary
criticism, particularly in terms of the advent of new historicism. They also formed the basis
for what many of Saussure's expositors refer to as his social-semiological metatheory. Paul J.
Thibault describes this system as a 'unitary or self-consistent, rather than a totalizing,
social-semiological metatheory'. In addition to attempting to fashion a theory that
addresses languages of all types, Saussure's metatheoretical approach to semiology offers,
in Thibault's words, 'a structured system comprising the resources which social agents use to
make meanings in systematic and socially recognizable ways in a given culture' (1997, 19).
The resources to which Thibault refers include the typical lexicogrammatical patterns and
relations of the language system. Perhaps more importantly, these resources also include
linguistic systems for making meaning in other semiotic modes such as the visual image, the
human body, and music and other non-verbal modes for the social construction of
meaning. *Voluntarism*, one of the central concepts in the linguist's social-semiological
metatheory, involves the voluntary reduction of language to a kind of social institution
that depends, in Saussure's words, 'more of less on our own will' (Thibault 1997, 23). In
short, we use language as a transparent and often non-semiotic naming mechanism that
affords us with a means for reflecting the extralinguistic realities in which we live. The
concept of *voluntarism* underscores the ways in which we both consciously and unconsciously exploit language as a system for constructing our own social realities.

By demonstrating the social dynamics inherent in language via such mechanisms as the
social-semiological metatheory, Saussure has influenced generations of linguists and
literary critics regarding this significant and ground-breaking facet of language and literary
study. The subsequent linguistic achievements of Greimas, for instance, reveal the
powerful impact of Saussure's intellectual legacy upon the future course of structuralism
and structural linguistics. Using many of Saussure's discoveries as his scholarly points of
departure, Greimas derived his theories of language as a mechanism involving what he
described as the interdependent, 'reciprocal presupposition' of its elements. For Greimas,
structural linguistics finds its origins in Saussure's social-semiological metatheory, a system
of thought that Greimas later reconceived in terms of the roles of knowledge and power in
the social construction of language. Saussurean linguistics provided Greimas with a
mechanism for clarifying semiology as a language system, Schleifer writes, 'marked by
double articulation, hierarchy, and neutralization' (1987, 181). Because semiotics offers a
valuable paradigm for examining the nature of cultural codes and social conventions, a
number of literary critics, structural anthropologists and psychoanalytic theorists have
explored semiology's interdisciplinary applications – from Barthes and Lévi-Strauss to
Lacan and Kristeva, among a wide range of others. Michel Foucault, for example,
developed a form of semiological study for addressing changing medical interpretations
of disease systems, treatment methodologies for insanity and our frequently shifting
perceptions of human sexuality. Frederic Jameson lauds Saussure's semiological achievements as 'a liberation of intellectual energies'. Saussure's imaginative approach to language

study, Jameson adds, 'is that of a series of complete systems succeeding each other in time' and the product of 'a perpetual present, with all the possibilities of meaning implicit in its every moment' (1972, 5–6). As with Peirce before him, Saussure articulated a new vision of semiotics that continues to impact the study of language and literature.

Kenneth Womack

Further reading and works cited

Barthes, R. *Elements of Semiology*. New York, 1967.
Culler, J. *Ferdinand de Saussure*. New York, 1976.
—. *The Pursuit of Signs*. Ithaca, NY, 1981.
Eco, U. *A Theory of Semiotics*. Bloomington, IN, 1976.
Harris, R. *Reading Saussure*. London, 1987.
Hawkes, T. *Structuralism and Semiotics*. London, 1977.
Holdcroft, D. *Saussure: Signs, System, and Arbitrariness*. Cambridge, 1991.
Holland, N. *The Critical I*. New York, 1992.
Jameson, F. *The Prison-House of Language*. Princeton, NJ, 1972.
Koerner, E. F. K. *Ferdinand de Saussure*. Braunschweig, 1973.
Lévi-Strauss, C. *Structural Anthropology*. New York, 1972.
Malmberg, B. *Structural Linguistics and Human Communication*. Berlin, 1967.
Saussure, F. de. *Course in General Linguistics*. New York, 1959.
Schleifer, R. A. *J. Greimas and the Nature of Meaning*. Lincoln, NE, 1987.
Thibault, P. J. *Re-Reading Saussure*. London, 1997.

9. Edmund Husserl (1859–1938)

Edmund Husserl founded the philosophical movement of phenomenology, a movement that was subsequently extended into two broad traditions of literary criticism: phenomenological criticism and poststructuralism. Husserl began his philosophical career by questioning the origin and possibility of meaning. Husserl's earliest work, including his *Philosophy of Arithmetic* (1891), explained meaning through a theory of psychologism: here, meaning is explained as the mental activity of an actual subject or psyche (Husserl 1970a). (So, the meaning of an arithmetical equation would be nothing more than the process of addition occurring in the mind of an individual.) Husserl's early psychologism was subsequently attacked by Gottlob Frege and as a consequence Husserl went on to formulate his theory of transcendental phenomenology, a theory which rejected both psychologism and historicism (1974). As Husserl argued in his late work, *The Crisis of the European Sciences* ([1936] 1970b), both psychologism and historicism explain meaning by describing the formation of concepts from *within* the world: for psychologism meaning is the act of an individual psyche; for historicism meaning emerges from historical contexts. (On a psychologist account the origin of geometry would be explained by referring to the mental acts of its founder, Euclid. On a historicist account geometry could be explained by referring to the Ancient Greek context from which it emerged.) Against these *explanations* of meaning, Husserl argued that the meaningful activity of consciousness was *absolute*: in order to experience a world we need to constitute that world meaningfully. Meaning is not an activity within the world – within history or mind – for it is only through meaning that any world is possible. Furthermore, for Husserl psychological and historicist explanations of the emergence of meaning could not account for the truth or ideality of meaning. The meaning of ideal entities, such as geometrical formulae or numbers, transcends the mental acts of individuals and the collective contexts of historical epochs. The truth of a mathematical equation is true, regardless of its specific context or its particular mental occurrence. Such ideal entities may initially require a factual or material origin (such as the inscription of formulae by the first geometer). But these factual, empirical or material inscriptions express a *sense* which is infinite (infinite, because $2 + 2 = 4$, for example, is true regardless of historical context, specific language or any finite mental act). Husserl's main task, therefore, was twofold. On the one hand he wanted to acknowledge the ideality of meaning: concepts and numbers have a sense that transcends both their material inscription and specific mental acts. On the other hand, and in contrast with Frege, Husserl wanted to avoid simply positing a separate reality for ideal entities (as in realism where the meaning of numbers and logical formulae exists independently of any subject). Husserl negotiated this problem of meaning through his theory of transcendental phenomenology and transcendental subjectivity, articulated in *Ideas* ([1913] 1982). Ultimately, this required Husserl to question the very concepts of being and existence that underpinned the problems of meaning he was investigating.

Husserl was insistent that we ought not to assume some foundation for meaning – such as the mind, history or logic – for any such foundation would itself have to be founded. Husserl therefore set himself the task of providing a foundation for all domains of meaning. In order to secure the truth of ideal meanings and not rely on already assumed foundations (such as the subject of psychologism or the logic of an already constituted science) Husserl argued that we needed to 'bracket' or 'suspend' all our current explanations and theories about the foundation of existence. This bracketing (or *epoche* as Husserl termed it) has two consequences. First, we need to attend to just what is experienced without assuming some ground or foundation; that is, we should consider only what appears – phenomena – and not posit some origin outside experience. This leaves us with a domain of pure immanence; here, we just attend to what is given and we avoid interpreting that givenness. Immanence is 'pure' in this sense because we do not see experience as the experience *of* an external world or as the experience *of* some psychophysical subject. We just attend to what is given, immanently, without taking this immanence to be the sign of anything other than itself. The second consequence of this bracketing or *epoche*, according to Husserl, demands going back to 'things themselves'. Hussserl described his phenomenology as a positivism. We take our experience as it is given. When we experience a thing, Husserl argued, we don't experience perception or sense data; we experience the thing itself. This means that attention to the pure immanence of experience also includes the experience of things. The task is, therefore, not to explain how we get from mind to world – for this assumes that there is an opposition. We need to explain how experience, taken immanently, is always already experience of a world. When we look to the pure immanence of experience we don't see sensations, data, perceptions or pictures of the world; we experience the world itself. Everyday experience is always experience of a world that we take to be present; it is an error of sceptical philosophy to ask how mind reaches the world.

Husserl begins his approach into the possibility of truth by taking everyday experience (or what he terms the 'natural attitude') as his object of inquiry. Husserl argues that we ought to take experience just as it appears and suspend or bracket any assumptions we might have regarding its ultimate existence, truth or foundation. Husserl begins his critique of the 'natural attitude' by arguing that it already contains certain metaphysical assumptions. In everyday experience we assume that we are subjects who then experience some independent world. We assume that the world exists independently of our experience and that we then discover this world through experience. Furthermore, we also assume that we, as subjects, are also beings within this world. And so, Husserl argues, the natural attitude already has some understanding of existence or being. In the language of phenomenology, there is a transcendence in the very immanence of experience. Experience is already experience *of* what is other than itself, or what transcends (transcendence).

In the natural attitude we assume that there is some real world or being, and that this world includes subjects who then come to know objects. We assume that subjects are a part of the world. Rather than assume that there are two types of beings – subjects and objects – Husserl begins his process of doubt by suspending this natural attitude and just attending to experience or what is given. Phenomenology will just examine experience or phenomena, and we will *then* ask how it is that we experience the world *as objective*. In this process of bracketing (or the *epoche*) Husserl likens his approach to Cartesian doubt. But he argues that Descartes's doubt was not sufficiently radical. For Descartes still assumed some object – the subject or *res cogitans* – which would explain all other objects. When Descartes concludes that 'I think therefore I am' he is right in arguing that the one thing we can't doubt is the stream of experience. But he is wrong to say that this experience is located in a thinking substance or mind. Descartes, according to Husserl, was caught in the natural attitude: the assumption that the world is an object for some experiencing subject.

Against this natural attitude Husserl formulates a theory of transcendental subjectivity. Here, the subject is not an assumed thing or substance *within which* experience of the world is located; nor is the subject a thing within the world. The transcendental subject is not a thing, but a process of constitution or 'synthesis' that then makes the experience of any thing possible. Husserl formulates this theory of the transcendental subject by examining the presuppositions of the natural attitude and the very experience of objective being. How is it possible that we experience something *as existing*? How is something taken to be present or real? When we experience a thing as existing or as present we do so because we have a certain connectedness of appearances. A thing is never given all at once; rather, the very character of the object is that it is experienced through time from a series of perspectives. Immanuel Kant had already argued that the very nature of objectivity relies on the synthesizing activity of an experiencing subject. Where Husserl differs from Kant is over the status of the transcendental subject. For Kant, the subject synthesizes experience into a coherent unity, and the subject is able to do so because there are universal or a priori categories through which the received world is ordered. For Husserl, by contrast, the categories through which the world is synthesized are not located in some prior synthesizing subject. Categories are not imposed by an experiencing subject; categories are constituted within the synthesis of experience. The difference between Husserl and Kant is difficult to grasp, but we could say that for Kant there is a subject who synthesizes the world. For Husserl, by contrast, there is synthesis; and it is from this synthesis that subjectivity and objectivity are then constituted.

It is this refusal to locate synthesis *within the subject* that differentiates phenomenology from Cartesianism and Kantianism. There is not a subject who then comes to know an external world. Rather, there is synthesis, or the temporal connectedness of experience, and it is from this passive synthesis or temporal flow that we then are able to think of experiencing subjects and an experienced world (Husserl [1893–1917] 1991). For Husserl, previous theories of metaphysics had remained within the natural attitude; they had assumed that there were subjects who then cognized an outside world. Against this assumption of a boundary between an interior subject and an outside world, Husserl asks how this distinction between subject and object, or interior and exterior, is constituted. He concludes by arguing that objectivity and exteriority are constituted from within experience. When we take something as an existing thing we constitute it in a coherent series of perceptions (temporally) and locate it outside ourselves (spatially). Husserl referred to this character of experience as *intentional*. Consciousness, he argued, is always consciousness *of* some thing – even if this intended object is ideal (such as number), psychological (such as a feeling) or material (such as a thing). Through his theory of intentionality Husserl radically redefined the nature of subjectivity. It's not that we have a subject who then grasps or comes to know the world; consciousness is not a thing or substance that then relates to an outside or material substance. On the contrary, consciousness is always a relation, or transcendence, to what is beyond itself. If we examine experience without the metaphysical presupposition of a separate subject, then we see that experience is always intentional, always directed toward some object. The very phenomena of experience are not experienced as isolated mental data, but as experiences *of objects*. When I perceive a chair, I perceive the thing itself and not some mental picture or representation.

Objectivity is not something that precedes experience but is given through experience. The condition for the possibility of objectivity is just a certain mode of experiencing; an object remains the same through time, and a material object is located in external space. This means that time and space aren't things we experience but transcendental conditions for experience: the very notion of experience demands that we receive something other than ourselves. And so all experience is intentional, related to some object. Husserl referred to this intended object as a *noema*; in so doing he expanded the notion of possible objects of consciousness beyond material things to ideal objects (such as numbers, logical propositions or geometrical formulae). The natural attitude, by contrast, begins from a highly limited interpretation of being – the spatio-temporal thing – and then asks how consciousness can know such things. Husserl, however, insisted on various modes of givenness which would open up domains of objective being that were not reducible to spatio-temporal being or the psychical being of mental entities. The most important instance of this insistence on the objectivity or transcendence of the *noema* was Husserl's argument for *ideal being*. Numbers, logical forms, geometric formulae and so on are not objects in the material world, nor are they fictions or mental entities imposed by a subject. They are essences that can be intuited by any subject whatsoever. Husserl was insistent on the possibility of the intuition of essences. When the geometer describes a formula for triangularity she is formalizing what she intuits as an essential law for any possible triangle. The same applies to number; these entities are not just psychological, for they are given to experience as essential forms for any possible experience. When I think of the number four, for example, I am directed towards an objectivity that is not reducible to my isolated experience; this ideal object cannot be reduced to a psychological phenomenon. The system of number must have had its original constitution from within experience, and then have been given some material symbol or signifier. But the signifier or written number formalizes a meaning that can always be returned to or intuited by any experiencing subject. The *meaning* of an ideal object has an essence that cannot be reduced to an isolated subjective experience or an arbitrarily imposed system. This is where Husserl differs from psychologism, historicism, structuralism and realism (Tragesser 1984). The ideal object has a worldly genesis; it must have been intuited and constituted at some point in empirical history. But once constituted the ideal object is infinitely repeatable and transcends any worldly context. The truths of Euclidean geometry, for example, have an empirical origin in an inscribing subject and a historical moment. But the truths of geometry are true, and remain true, regardless of this factual origin. And it is always possible for us to retrieve the original sense or meaning of these essences.

What Husserl grapples with, in this constitution of the ideal object, is what Jacques Derrida refers to as the 'opening to infinity' (1973). The ideal object has a finite and contextual genesis, but once constituted it exceeds all finitude. The concept of truth, for example, must be articulated in a specific language and a specific time; but, once inscribed, the very concept of truth enables us to think of that which exceeds any finite context. There is, on the one hand, the original subject event or act and, on the other hand, that towards which the act is directed. Any truth must originate in some act of experience (the *noesis*), but *as true* what is experienced goes beyond the particular act. Husserl therefore distinguished between the *noesis* (the active subjective constitution of this object) and the *noema* (the object intended or aimed at). The *noesis* is the 'really inherent' component of meaning; it is the particular mental act undertaken by the subject. The *noesis* is that aspect of experience that can be attributed to the synthesizing activity of the subject. For any object I can recognize its original constitution by some perceiving subject. When I think of 'four' I have some specific *noesis* (either the signifier 'four' or '4', or four perceived objects), but this specific *noesis* is directed towards an object, the *noema*. This *noema* is more than just the concept of four; it is what is meant or intended in the experience. This means that there can be *noematic* unities prior to concepts. We can perceive or intend some sense, Husserl argues, without yet having a formalized concept of that object. There is still, though, a *noesis* and a *noema*: an act – of perception, imagination, memory – and an intended object – a thing, feeling or essence. Every perceptual act aims at some transcendence or intended object, some *noematic* pole, even if there is not an explicit concept for that *noema*. We may have the general concept of red, but I can also have a *noesis* or perception that aims at this quite specific shade. The *noema* is not just 'redness'. Indeed I can intuit the singular essence of this specific shade of red, such that though I have perceived it once I discern a quality that I could perceive again independent of this experience now. An essence is not a generalization from experiences, nor is it the effect of imposing concepts on experience. Essences are intuitable precisely because experience is always more than a mental act; it aims at something beyond itself, given in presence. Let us imagine that I have an experience of a cat; the *noesis* is just that particular perception, from a certain angle, of this furry animal. (I could also remember or imagine the same cat, but these would be different noetic acts. And so memory or imagination aren't weaker forms of perception; they are quite different kinds of experience.) The *noema* is the objective pole; I take this experience to be the experience *of* a cat. This experience can be confirmed and the *noema* can be fulfilled; I go on having coherent experiences that confirm my first perceptions. Or, the experience can be frustrated; what I took to be a cat was actually a doorstop or a soft toy. What Husserl emphasizes in his theory of perception and its poles of *noesis* and *noema* is that consciousness always intends some object and it does so in a particular way: both from a certain perspective but also with a certain type of regard. I don't just encounter the ideal object four or the material being of the cat; each *noema* is given in this or that particular way, as this specific *noesis* or *noetic* act. I relate to the object as desired, remembered, perceived, imagined, feared or represented.

This distinction between the *noesis* and *noema* challenges the natural attitude's interpretation of the world as some form of objectivity that we then experience. The 'world' includes a number of different modes of givenness, and we need to attend to the way differing *noetic* acts relate to essentially different *noema*. We ought not to privilege one form of *noesis* – such as sense perception – and then see all other forms of experience as derived from that. Nor should we regard sense perception as a weaker or unreliable form of knowledge as opposed to logic or mathematics. Each region within the world, Husserl argues, has its own specific way of being known. It's the nature of perception, for example, to relate to its objects as 'actually existing'; it's the nature of fiction to relate to its objects 'as imagined'; and it's the nature of logic to operate as the synthesis of any possible subject. The *noesis*, the act of experience, already relates to different types of objectivity. And this means that we shouldn't restrict ourselves to one form of entity – the objects of perception – to explain all other forms, such as values, logical truths, concepts or numbers. If we examine the phenomena themselves then we are given all sorts of modes of being, including ideal objects, fictional objects and material things. The material thing, far from being the basis of knowledge and subjectivity, is only one particular mode of experienced objectivity. The very essence of the material thing, if we examine the domain of phenomena, is constituted from a concatenation of coherent appearances. It's not that there is a spatio-temporal world that 'we' only grasp in some partial way through experience. It is the very essence of spatio-temporal being that it is given in a series of perceptions and perspectives. The very meaning of 'object' is something that is located in space and remains through time; it is essential to the *noema* of objectivity that it be grasped in a temporal series of perceptions and from a specific point in space. Even a divine intuition, Husserl insists, could not know an *object* absolutely, for it is the very essence of objectivity to be known and experienced in time and space. The objects of memory, logic, desire and imagination have their specific modes of givenness. A memory is not a weaker version of a perception, and a logical proof is not a stronger form of certainty than a perception. It's not as though we have an experience and then work out whether it's a memory, fiction, perception or logical necessity. Different domains of objects are given in essentially different ways. It would be incoherent or absurd, Husserl argues, to dogmatically assert the existence of two types of thing (subjects and objects) and then ask how one of these things (materiality) appears to the other (subjectivity). Rather, the only coherent manoeuvre is to assume the originary or primordial status of appearing. There is appearance – or phenomena – and from this appearing we then conclude that there is a subject who experiences and a world that then appears. The natural attitude – the assumption of the subject as a being who encounters other beings – occurs *after* the original event of appearance. The natural attitude has already made a decision about being; it has assumed that being is something external that then appears to a subject. But Husserl puts appearance or phenomenality before all such interpretations.

Husserl therefore begins his 'transcendental reduction' as a methodological or epistemological manoeuvre: we must bracket all presuppositions about existence and just examine what appears. But this epistemology then leads to a new ontology: it's not that there is a being or presence that then appears; being or presence is constituted from an *absolute* domain of appearance. Husserl therefore refers all being and existence back to the lifeworld or *Lebenswelt* (Husserl 1970). Through time and history certain meanings, forms and languages are constituted. When we experience the world we do so through these sedimented and formed meaningful unities. But because meaning emerges from the flow of experience it is always possible that we can return to the very genesis of meaning. As an example, Husserl demonstrated how the truths of logic should not just be accepted as a static system, for it must always be possible to see the essential truth of these forms. Philosophy ought to be just this responsibility of reason: not the acceptance of truths as things given to experience but the grounding of truth back in the very possibility of experience.

The consequences of Husserl's phenomenology lie in two broad areas: the theory of the subject and the theory of meaning. If we bracket all previous assumptions and begin philosophy from just that which appears, then we are forced to recognize the primacy of conscious life. Any object or being is the outcome of a series of appearances. In the beginning are the phenomena, or pure immanence, and all objectivity is determined from this original domain. This is why Husserl describes his phenomenology as a transcendental idealism; any reality or being can only be understood as having been constituted in the intentional life of consciousness. A complexity arises when we examine just what this consciousness is. Husserl was critical of both Descartes and Kant for assuming that the subject was a type of thing that then imposed the forms of time and space upon the world. For Husserl time is not ideal – the way in which a pre-temporal subject then constitutes a world – time is transcendental. Time is neither subjective nor objective; it is from the flow of time that subject and object are constituted. If we ask who or what constitutes this flow of time then we are at risk of falling back into the natural attitude. For Husserl, the constituted flow of time is not undertaken *by* a subject; the subject is constituted in this temporal synthesis. Perhaps Husserl's most difficult idea, and one that turned the whole subjectivism of phenomenology on its head, was the idea of passive synthesis. Rather than assuming that there are ideal subjects who then form the world through the medium of time, Husserl argued for the primordiality of time. There just is the transcendental flow of time, a flow within which the subject and object can then be formed or constituted (1991). It's true that if we take any being or thing we see it as the outcome of a synthesis of perceptions, but any thought of a being *who synthesizes* would itself be the result of a synthesis. We might say, then, that consciousness is not a thing that synthesizes; it is the event of synthesis from which all things are then rendered possible. Far from being a self-present and identical ground or basis for the world, Husserl's transcendental subject is just this dynamic, synthesizing and pre-objective power or event of synthesis. This leads the way, of course, for a critique of the very use of the word 'subject' or 'consciousness' to describe this event of synthesis. Both Martin Heidegger and Jacques Derrida radicalized Husserl's theory of synthesis in order to criticize subjectivism. If the subject is nothing other than the event of temporal synthesis then it may be more appropriate to locate time as the original event (Heidegger [1927] 1996) or do away with the possibility of an origin altogether (Derrida 1973).

Husserl's phenomenology not only disrupted the very possibility of an originating or self-present subject, it also redefined the very problem of meaning. Husserl argued that all experience was, in some way, meaningful. I always experience the world *as* this or that specific, or intended, being. Meaning is not something we add on to the world. In order to have a world at all experience must originally intend or aim at some unity. But meaning for

Husserl also opens up a domain of ideality beyond any specific experience, and does so from experience itself. Let's say that I perceive four objects. The number four is more than just this specific mental event. Indeed I can intuit *both* these four specific things *and* the essence of four. Husserl argued that we could intuit essences and that we did so from singular or specific experiences. When the concept of four functions in mathematics it is no longer tied to a specific perception but can now extend beyond any finite perception or sense and be repeated infinitely. For Husserl, this theory of the intuition of essences and the constitution of ideality solved the problem of realism versus psychologism. Ideal objects are intuited in finite and empirical circumstances – such as this particular experience of four things – but we can then constitute a logical system (such as the system of number) which can repeat this essence infinitely and independent of all content and specificity. Husserl therefore recognized that the being of ideal objects exceeded specific mental events; they were more than psychological phenomena. But Husserl also resisted realism. Numbers don't exist in some 'third realm' of forms awaiting their apprehension by experience. They are constituted within experience, but then refer to an object or form of any possible experience. This means that the forms of pure logic are forms of possible experience. They must have a finite and empirical origin; but this empirical origin is just the recognition of a form of experience *in general* – not this or that finite experience but what must be true for any possible experience. The formality and ideality of logic or mathematics is constituted by an intuition of the essence of a specific experience. In non-formal domains of meaning, such as natural and literary language, there is more specific content. Thus Husserl's theory of meaning opens the way to consider concepts in terms of their greater or lesser degrees of idealization and formalization. Certain meanings – such as those of logic – refer to possibilities of experience in general, and they do so by abstracting from particular content. Other meanings, such as the concepts of a particular language, cannot be translated and repeated across languages. They are less capable of formalization. Literary language, particularly poetry, would be the least susceptible to formalization. But a literary work still has an ideal content or *noematic* core. The meaning of *Hamlet*, for example, lies above and beyond any particular edition or performance. Each reading and each performance is a specific reactivation of the work's infinitely repeatable ideal content. Certain elements of both the work and performance are at the ideal end of the spectrum of meaning; the work relies on certain essential and necessary logic forms – such as time, space, identity and extension. But there are also other ideal objects in the work – the personality of Hamlet, for example – that cannot be entirely freed from the specific textual determination. And there are also specific and local literary effects that are irreducible to meaning and idealization. The use of rhyme, meter and alliteration would not be capable of translation and formalization. At an even more specific level there would be quite singular effects in any work that are not repeatable or formalizable – the specific material form of this edition or this performance. We might say, then, that Husserl's theory of meaning opens up a spectrum of different levels of formalization and conceptuality. Ideal concepts are true for any possible experience and can be repeated infinitely regardless of context (and here we would include the forms of mathematics and logic). Other meanings are less repeatable. I might experience this particular shade of red in this particular instance. I still perceive an essence, but it is singular. The consequences of Husserl's argument that meaning occurs through a process of formalization that constitutes essences from the finitude of experience have been extended in post-Husserlian phenomenological criticism. Hans-Georg Gadamer argued that literary works have an essential core that is then varied with each activation or performance (1989). Further, this essential core and the original concepts are also reconfigured and added to with each subsequent performance. There is not a strict boundary between the formal concepts of philosophy and the specific meanings of a literary text. In each case meaning is only possible through reactivation of the text. In each reactivation the work is intended or made meaningful according to its specific context or lifeworld. Rather than accept concepts or meanings as static forms that we then apply to experience, Gadamer argued that we needed to see concepts as ongoing syntheses of experience. And experience is not an isolated subjective event. On the contrary, because experience is nothing other than a meaningful relation to the world it already relies on the concepts and forms of language and others. The phenomenological tradition of criticism extended Husserl's location of all meaning and being within experience. Texts do not have meanings that we then uncover; the meaning of a text is nothing other than its continual and possible interpretation. But this does not mean that we have lost all objectivity or ideality of a text; for as Husserl argued, ideal objects are constituted through time and history. The meaning of *Hamlet*, for example, occurs through a series of interpretations but also exceeds any single interpretation. There is now the ideal object of the meaning of Shakespeare's play. This ideal object emerges from the finite fact of the original textual inscription, but the play's meaning exceeds any particular edition, copy or performance and can be reactivated infinitely.

Claire Colebrook

Further reading and works cited

Derrida, J. *Speech and Phenomena, and Other Essays on Husserl's Theory of Signs*. Evanston, IL, 1973.
Fuchs, W. W. *Phenomenology and the Metaphysics of Presence*. The Hague, 1976.
Gadamer, H.-G. *Truth and Method*. New York, 1989.
Heidegger, M. *Being and Time*. Albany, NY, 1996.
Husserl, E. *Cartesian Meditations*. The Hague, 1960.
—. *The Idea of Phenomenology*. Dordrecht, 1964
—. *Phenomenology and the Crisis of Philosophy*. New York, 1965.
—. *The Paris Lectures*. The Hague, 1967.
—. *Philosophie der Arithmetik. Mit ergänzenden Texten*, ed. L. Eley. The Hague, 1970a.
—. *The Crisis of European Sciences and Transcendental Phenomenology*. Evanston, IL 1970b.
—. *Logical Investigations*. London, 1970c.
—. 'Letter to Frege: July 18, 1898', 'The Frege-Husserl Correspondence', *Southwestern Journal of Philosophy*, 5, 1974.
—. *Ideas Pertaining to a Pure Phenomenology and to a Phenomenological Philosophy, First Book: General Introduction to a Pure Phenomenology*. The Hague, 1982.
—. *On the Phenomenology of the Consciousness of Internal Time*. Dordrecht, 1991.
Ingarden, R. *The Cognition of the Literary Work of Art*. Evanston, IL, 1973.
Macann, C. *Four Phenomenological Philosophers*. London, 1993.
Mohanty, J. N. *Husserl and Frege*. Bloomington, IN, 1982.
—. *Phenomenology: Between Essentialism and Transcendental Philosophy*. Evanston, IL, 1997.
Ricoeur, P. *Husserl: An Analysis of his Phenomenology*. Evanston, IL, 1967.
—. *From Text to Action*. Evanston, IL, 1991.
Tragesser, R. S. *Husserl and Realism in Logic and Mathematics*. Cambridge, 1984.

10. Phenomenology

'Phenomenology' names the most decisive development in philosophical thought since the beginning of the nineteenth century. Its significance is first and foremost philosophical, but in so far as all movements in literary theory and criticism have a basis in philosophical thought, the importance of phenomenology for the understanding of literature cannot be underestimated. This can be seen in the attention that phenomenology pays to aesthetics, but even more so in that phenomenology accomplishes a *linguistic turn*, with all its implications as to a theory of literature. While there are specific strands of literary theory that understand themselves explicitly as belonging to phenomenology – in particular the hermeneutic movement of Hans-Georg Gadamer and Paul Ricoeur – nearly all twentieth-century ideas of literary criticism have been engendered by the phenomenological movement, especially structuralism, poststructuralism and deconstruction.

Indeed, as French phenomenologist Maurice Merleau-Ponty said, phenomenology is either everything or nothing (1964). Consequently, phenomenology seems to be of such breadth and complexity that in the following it is only possible to sketch the basic outlines necessary to understand its importance for modern criticism generally. In the course of this outline phenomenology may appear more homogeneous than it really is.

The first book of phenomenology was written by G. W. F. Hegel under the title *Phenomenology of Spirit*. This book concerns an account of the appearance of human spirit, where 'spirit' designates human reality as a historically and culturally integrated reason sedimenting in human consciousness, in art and in political institutions. But why does this book speak of the 'phenomenon' rather than the 'appearance' of spirit? For the two millennia before Hegel, philosophers have generally tried to make the world intelligible by distinguishing appearances from that which appears in them. For example, when Immanuel Kant separated the transcendental form of subjectivity from the actual existence of any one human being then we see the latter as an appearance of the former. Without such a separation we would have to presuppose that the actually existing human being determines the idea of the human being as such; this is what philosophers call 'psychologism' and regard as one of the worst forms of relativism. In other words, philosophers have always distinguished appearance from the absolute that appears in it and which consequently makes appearances intelligible and the world inhabitable. The 'absolute', then, stands for a reality absolutely independent from any mediation.

From this perspective it might be said that phenomenology is the philosophy that realizes the moment at which, as Friedrich Nietzsche says, the true world, as opposed to the world of appearances, has become a myth. An appearance, on the one hand, is something through which something else appears. A phenomenon, on the other hand, and according to its original Greek meaning, is something that shines through and by itself. Hegel expresses this in his book in the form of a relatively inconspicuous sentence, when he writes that 'the supersensible is appearance *qua* appearance' (1977, 89). What Hegel means is that there is nothing which would give meaning to the world without itself being a part of it. Rather, the world is understood as the temporal constitution of its own meaning – it gives rise to the absolute from within itself. In this respect phenomenology is the movement of the overcoming of metaphysics and the realization that, again in Nietzsche's words, 'with the real world we have also done away with the apparent one' (1998, 20).

What are the consequences of such a thinking? *First*, that all truth becomes historical in so far as essences constitute themselves throughout history. This is to say that both the development of philosophical thought and human sensibility itself are in an essential sense historical. *Second*, phenomenology turns against 'theory' understood as the idea of a thinking independent from what it thinks about; and it consequently turns against representation, that is to say against the idea of truth as a thought corresponding to a piece of reality. *Third*, phenomenology becomes the main opponent of any objectivism and hence an essential critique of the rationalism of the Enlightenment. *Fourth*, phenomenology relinquishes the instrumental idea of thinking: in so far as thinking does not represent a lever that can be applied to the world from the outside, the different modes of thinking are themselves understood as an integral part of that reality. From here phenomenology is led to the concept of *description*. *Fifthly*, if thought and its activity are real elements of the world rather than simple means to represent the world, then language gains a special importance in terms not only of understanding the world, but much more essentially in terms of any actual mode of inhabiting the world. If words can no longer be understood as the mere appearance of an ideal meaning, then our whole conception of the world as grasped through language is affected. As Michel Foucault put this, metaphysics is when one claims that there is first of all a thought and then its expression in language. Yet language, to remain with our terminology, is not the appearance of a thought but its phenomenon; in other words, anti-metaphysics or phenomenology is when one claims that there is first of all language and then, by way of its mediation, the constitution of meaning. Hegel expresses this insight by arguing that language is more truthful than our opinions and conscious intentions. In it we directly contradict what we mean to say. Martin Heidegger formulates this strange insight in its clearest form when he says that 'we do not say what we see, but rather the reverse, we see what *one says* about the matter' (1985, 56). From here one can see that phenomenology, in as much as it makes even the sensibility of the human being subject to the historical codification of language, radicalizes the question of history by making it the sole content of philosophy.

The implications of this for an understanding of literature are not to be underestimated, in so far as philosophical texts themselves are no longer seen as instantiating an ideal meaning, but rather are grasped from out of their historical development, so that we find here the origin of the 'death of the author' as that instance that determines the meaning of the literary work. The literary or philosophical text becomes always, in every age, anew. Its origin has to be sought in history rather than in a 'real' historical writer.

Yet, while these points appear straightforward, they harbour a wealth of contradictions: the stress placed on history seems to contradict that placed on description; the opposition to any objectivist philosophy seems to disagree with its apparent positivism; the claim that the world is just what it is conflicts with the determination of being through becoming, that is with the phenomenological theme of constitution; the turn towards 'the things themselves' stands opposed to the claim that the world is first of all given by language.

And even if we solved these problems, we would still have to confront all the arguments that have led philosophy for the best part of 2,400 years to claim that there has to be something independent from this world of experience in order to explain 'the fact of knowledge', that is to say, the meaningfulness of the world.

But phenomenology does not submit easily to criticisms regarding the incoherence of its concepts. It has to a certain extent left the realm of the principle of non-contradiction behind, not only in as much as Hegel understands contradiction as the primal mover of history, but also in that logical contradiction cannot 'overrule' the perceived world. As Merleau-Ponty points out, contradiction would only be permissible as an argument against phenomenology 'if we could put a system of eternal truths in the place of the perceived world, freed from its contradictions' (Merleau-Ponty 1964).

Phenomenology hence moves between metaphysics and positivism, between idealism and realism, between the modern natural sciences and the humanities, between logic and psychologism, between linguistics and relativism, threatened by each of them and yet without coinciding with any. It is thereby especially concerned with its relation to the modern natural sciences, in so far as these have attempted during the nineteenth and twentieth centuries to dominate the discourse of science generally.

One way to get this problem into focus is by contrasting the 'first beginning' of phenomenology in Hegel and Nietzsche, with its 'real' beginning as a discipline and distinctive strand of philosophy in the work of Edmund Husserl. Husserl is often called the 'father' of phenomenology; yet we never understand a child as a mere expression of its father. As with every child, many of its features were decided long before its father was even born, while it, once born, sets out on its own way.

Having described the development of phenomenology from Hegel onwards, it might come as a surprise that Husserl is led to it from the perspective of the question of pure mathematics and hence from a stance that determines phenomenological investigation in complete abstraction not only from the history of philosophical thought, but from all historical reflection. Husserl understands phenomenology first and foremost as a defence against psychologism and relativism as they arose at the end of the nineteenth century. Yet the problem pursued in his early work is the same as that already described, namely the problem of conceiving an *a priori* that determines all empirical understanding of the actual world, without locating such an idea in a transcendent realm. On the ground of this question he tries to found the possibility of an absolute science or a *mathesis universalis*, which is to say a universally valid teaching, under the title of *Transcendental Phenomenology*.

What is phenomenology? As we said, it is an understanding of the world that does not separate the subjective experience of the world from the experienced objects themselves. How can one experience the world directly, without taking this experience as a mere appearance of the 'real things' behind our experience? Husserl's answer is quite straightforward and similar to Descartes's, in that he refers us to the immediate nature of conscious experience. When we see a door, for example, we neither experience a difference between the actual door and its image that our eyes have let through into our consciousness, nor do we regard this image in our head while suffering from an uncertainty concerning the 'real' door through which we wish to pass. Our experience does not at all suffer from a duality of subject and object, but is rather characterized by a unity of seeing and the seen. This is not to say that I confuse myself with the door, but that the impression of immediacy in my experience arises from a correlation between my seeing and the thing seen at any one moment. In so far as what we mean when we speak of 'seeing' and 'the seen' are first of all processes 'in' consciousness, Husserl calls this correlation by its Greek name, that of *noesis* (the act of thinking) and *noema* (the thing thought). The idea of immediacy breaks up when we think about this correlation: maybe we would have confused ourselves with the door, if it was not the case that we 'see' or intuit a difference between the immediate presence of a thing, on the one hand, and its essence, on the other.

This thought allows Husserl to depart from the naive restriction of thinking to the representation of present ideas, to include the greater part of the life of the human soul: objects that are not given to sight, like music or pain, for example; emotions, like fearing or loving; other conscious activities, like remembering, striving, hoping, etc. Husserl's terminology permits us to consider the world of our experiences in its immanent unity, thereby avoiding the question of how the subject could ever reach out from its inner experience towards a world understood in opposition to it. Phenomenology thus undercuts the 'mind–body problem' which had stifled modern philosophy since Descartes.

Husserl originally stands, alone among the 'great' phenomenologists, on the side of a rationalistic intuition identifying the question of conscious knowing with the constitution of the world. Philosophical thought, as he says, is fully determined through its epistemological position, that is to say, philosophy *is* the theory of knowledge (1973). Husserl pursues, in the best Kantian tradition, the attempt to constitute the world according to a theory of judgement as he had opened it up in his first major work, the *Logical Investigations* (1900). We tend to identify the concept of science with the methodology of the modern natural sciences, but to speak of a rigorous science of phenomenology does not mean that the phenomenologist would begin to experiment with objects and record results, nor that her aim consisted in the manipulation of objects. The idea of science derives from Greek antiquity and has always been an integral part of philosophy. Its idea concerns a systematic questioning and ascertaining of knowledge generally. The modern natural sciences are then only one idea of how such a securing of knowledge is possible. Phenomenology has to remain quite independent from these regional ontologies – that is, from sciences that have a specific subject area and that constitute their methods accordingly, so that these methods depend on a prior unreflected presupposition regarding the nature of the objects to be investigated – in so far as it regards experience by bracketing off any preconceptions about it. That is to say, it undercuts the naive convictions of the natural sciences, sedimented in what Husserl calls the natural attitude or common sense. Phenomenology cannot become a function of the natural sciences as they have determined our worldview through their unrivalled success, rather it ultimately pushes for a radically new foundation of these sciences.

Husserl's investigations are, then, more and more drawn to history and language and, fulfilling their claim to a return to the things themselves, he finally arrives at the conception of the lifeworld as opposed to the objectified world of the natural attitude. A short look at *The Vienna Lecture* (1935) will show that Husserl developed the idea of phenomenology in a direction that, finally, fits comfortably into the lineage turning from Hegel and Nietzsche to the later phenomenological strands of the twentieth century.

The starting point of *The Vienna Lecture* is the acknowledgement that Europe, and that is to say the history of philosophy, is in crisis. What might surprise us today is that, in 1935, during a time pushing towards the Second World War, and a time that forced Husserl, who was Jewish, to flee his home, his analysis of this crisis nonetheless centres on the insight that Europe suffers from a misguided rationalism which first appeared with the Enlightenment. In this lecture he describes phenomenology as always having been concerned with the fight against objectivism and he identifies German idealism, including Hegel, as the philosophical force that had first taken up this struggle. The phenomenological reduction, known as the *epoche*, thus becomes not only an epistemological tool for ascertaining the foundations of objective knowledge, but a method by which Husserl proposes to turn against scientism. Phenomenology cannot be a dependent discipline grounding the validity of the natural sciences: 'it is a mistake for the humanistic disciplines to struggle with the natural sciences for equal rights. As soon as they concede to the latter their objectivity as self-sufficiency, they themselves fall prey to objectivism' (1970, 297). In contrast, transcendental phenomenology sets out to ground the natural sciences, but so that in that process they will change beyond recognition. 'There are only two escapes from the crisis of European existence: the downfall of Europe in its estrangement from its own rational sense of life, its fall into hostility toward the spirit and into barbarity; or the rebirth of Europe from the spirit of philosophy through a heroism of reason that overcomes naturalism once and for all' (299).

Today this sense of a crisis seems to have disappeared and in so far as it was described as a crisis coming from the depths of European history, such a swift dissipation might convey the idea that it never was real. And in fact, what Husserl called a misguided rationalism is often represented by us as a short period of irrationalism, following the destruction of which Europe has re-established the link to its Enlightenment tradition. Taking another look at the twentieth century, this history might appear in a different light. Despite certain developments in the sciences, which have born out the claims of phenomenology, in terms of the 'hostility towards spirit' we have advanced relentlessly. By far the clearest characterization of our age stems from a letter that Martin Heidegger wrote in 1967 to a friend:

> In the 'sciences' today reigns a progressively positive stance towards cybernetics and its possibilities. In 'philosophy' there is 'logical positivism', which by means of its theory of language pushes itself more and more to the fore. All these tendencies have to be countered with a principled re-consideration – although we cannot hope for any short term success. Everywhere there will be 'cells' of resistance, formed against the impetuous power of technology. These cells will inconspicuously keep thinking awake, and they will thus prepare the reversal, for which 'man' will cry, in a day yet to come, when the general devastation will have become insupportable. (Heidegger 1987, 352)

Martin Heidegger's first major work *Being and Time* undertakes to show that the epistemological understanding of the world as constituted by positive, affirmative judgements, that is the identification of truth and knowledge, derives from a practical understanding of our relation to things. He argues that our general idea of action as preceded and motivated by rational deliberation is quite mistaken. Rather we think about something in a theoretical mode only once it has lost its integration within the world of action. Thus we use, for example, a hammer without any reflection up to that moment when its handle breaks and our intentions are 'broken' with it. In this way all theoretical engagement in the world is considered a second order phenomenon. This point might appear rather obvious, so that one might wonder what Heidegger is up to. The admirable analytic of the existential modes of our 'Being-in-the-World' can be misunderstood as a positive philosophical doctrine to a degree that even empiricists have begun to like that work, if it were not for its strange elaboration on 'the question of Being'. This 'question of Being' is, first of all, another attempt at understanding the differentiation between the actual thing in front of me and that which Husserl called an essence. It is indeed only through a consideration of this question that the reader comes to realize that the whole book is, as Heidegger says himself, metaphysical, attempting to show that metaphysics has always understood the idea of Being from out of the everyday concerns with beings. We might even say that metaphysics has kept too close to objects – so that they eventually became blurred. Thus arose the idea that it was too abstract, so that to correct it one consequently attempted to tighten one's grip on reality. In this sense metaphysics concerns the abolition of *action at a distance* in favour of a mechanistic understanding of the world. The point this book demonstrates is that the history of metaphysics ends quite logically with its realization in the objectivism of technology, while phenomenology attempts to understand the difference between Being as such and the being of beings, hence suspending the identification of truth and knowledge. The task of phenomenology, according to Heidegger, is then the *Verwindung* – an overcoming in the sense of mourning – of metaphysics. While many commentators have insisted that Heidegger never tried to criticize objectivism in this early work, but rather tries to ground the traditional notion of truth as the adequation of thought and reality, one only needs to think of the aim of phenomenology to return to 'the things themselves'. In other words, phenomenology cannot restrict itself to founding a new philosophy or to ascertaining the methodological structure of the natural sciences, nor can it afford to indulge in the general quibble about positions and worldviews, which are often taken for the task of philosophers. It does not even take a stance for or against technology or the natural sciences, but rather attempts to respond to the needs of a historical situation.

Phenomenology is then not only a historical science, but also places itself as a historical movement, in so far as it is determined by the attempt to find an answer to the alienation effected by a 'misguided rationalism'. This is again clear already in its 'battle-cry' *back to the things themselves*, in so far as it is only possible to go 'back' to these 'things' in as much as one departs from a prior alienation. Phenomenology is, accordingly, thinking in the 'age of complete meaninglessness', as Heidegger calls our time in the opening pages of his seminal lectures on *Nietzsche* (1961).

It sounds more and more as if phenomenology was a rather pessimistic philosophy. It criticizes our age in the most extreme ways while itself being limited to description. But does phenomenology really only describe what has happened after the fact? Already for Hegel the human being can sustain its spiritual existence only in so far as it grasps its history by way of this philosophical mode of description. As Merleau-Ponty says, left to itself perception is ignorant of its own accomplishments; we are hence not only describing what has happened, i.e. the world understood as fact, rather philosophy concerns itself with that which precedes facts and which thus somehow is involved in their constitution.

One of the major questions after Husserl thus becomes the question of the ontic-ontological difference, i.e. of the relation between the *a priori* and the empirical. Both Husserl and the early Heidegger, in unison with most traditional philosophy and thus the natural sciences as well, refuse to allow any possibility that experience could recoil on the transcendental or ontological level. 'From matters of fact nothing ever follows but matters of fact' as Husserl says in *Ideas I* (1982, 17). As we have seen, Husserl concludes from this point the necessity of a methodological revision of the sciences. Later on, in Heidegger and in Merleau-Ponty, this question turns into the much more radical formulation of a correlation between our experience and its transcendental ground. When Heidegger speaks about the 'co-origin of word and thing' as the basis of a turn within the ontic-ontological difference – away from the formulation of the two distinct levels and the consequent problem of their interaction towards the thought of the difference itself – and when Merleau-Ponty formulates the 'primacy of perception' as a nascent logos, phenomenology turns finally to the abolition of the appearing world, in the sense outlined by Nietzsche. In other words, phenomenology sets out to come to terms with metaphysics by 'dropping' transcendental philosophy. This task Heidegger prepares in the thought of a 'history of Being', in so far as it breaks with the metaphysical understanding of Being as universal and hence eternal. The very idea of eternal truths, as he writes in *Being and Time*, is the last remnant of Christian theology in philosophy (1962, 272). This possibility of experience recoiling onto the *a priori*, we have already seen – if unexpectedly – in the case of metaphysics itself as a determination of Being according to our everyday concern with beings.

It is for this reason that phenomenology is not a new empiricism. To talk about such a recoiling of experience onto the *a priori* seems to imply that reason is determined by sense-perception, while in actual fact we are looking initially at an interaction which finally gives rise to an understanding of an expressed immanence. Merleau-Ponty finds a first approach to such an understanding in the form of Gestalt psychology, which realizes a unity of objective and introspective psychology, in that it avoids the artificial separation of a spiritual inside from a mechanistic outside of the mind. The task of the phenomenologist is then to draw the philosophical conclusions from such an approach. Following Heidegger's existential analytic of *Dasein* – his interpretation of the human being as neither determined by its *ratio* nor by its animal being, but rather in its *being-there* – Ludwig Binswanger similarly develops *Daseinsanalyse* as a novel approach in psychoanalysis that attempts to escape the latter's naturalist assumptions.

In all the concreteness of such a return to the 'perceived world', the radicality with which phenomenology assails our common understanding makes the whole enterprise appear highly paradoxical. And while philosophy has from its inception been understood as paradoxical, we often succumb to common-sense arguments. It is no wonder, then, that in a discussion following Merleau-Ponty's paper on *The Primacy of Perception*, a monsieur Bréhier summarizes his impression of phenomenology by saying that 'I see your ideas as being better expressed in literature and in painting than in philosophy. Your philosophy results in a novel' (Merleau-Ponty 1964, 30).

This criticism, half absurd and half true, leads us to one of the most beautiful texts of the phenomenological tradition – Merleau-Ponty's *Eye and Mind*. In this text Merleau-Ponty attempts to show the way in which our experience of seeing, which is exemplified in the painter's relation to the visible world, structures our general understanding of the world. Departing from an analysis of the impact of the discovery of perspective in Renaissance painting on the development of Descartes's philosophy, he argues that a closer study of painting would lead to another philosophy. Already in *The Phenomenology of Perception* (1945), Merleau-Ponty had linked the question of the body to the question of language itself and we have seen that language and sense-experience are essentially linked. Here Merleau-Ponty carries these insights further to develop the thought of the incarnation of vision in speech, which tries to understand the language of phenomena, arising from the cross-over of the intending body and the flesh of the world. It is in this respect that Merleau-Ponty contrasts the experience of painting with the ideology of cybernetics.

The phenomenologist does not describe language as does a linguist, who investigates language in so far as it is an object of theoretical inquiry. Rather, the phenomenologist realizes that language lies at the root of any questioning. Consequently, Heidegger demands an end to all 'philosophy of language', in so far as such a philosophy, by raising linguistics to the level of philosophy, unwittingly introduces an essentially flawed idea of language.

The discussion of language as predetermining sense-experience had, initially, led Heidegger to the formulation of the hermeneutic circle, that is, to the realization of the circular structure of understanding. This is conceived as follows: the natural attitude proposes that there is first the positive presence of a state of affairs, which the human being then attempts to understand in order to master the world. Once understood, this state of affairs is represented by positive affirmative judgements. The phenomenologist, on the other hand, recognizes that there is always the need for an *a priori* in order to make an actual understanding possible. Yet, this *a priori* is not simply conceived as a universal form determining the way in which the intellect deals with experience. Rather it has to have a 'content' as well, which is to say that I already need to know what I want to find out. Thus the acquisition of knowledge appears impossible. Unless, that is, what one knows about the thing beforehand is quite wrong, in other words is a prejudice. In that sense hermeneutics – that is, the science of interpretation – claims that one has to have an (erroneous) understanding of a thing in order to be able to get to know it. But this is also to say that this path, starting out from error, cannot be teleologically oriented towards any absolute truth. For that very reason the history of Being is characterized by Heidegger as the 'errancy' of the human being.

These ideas show that it is not far from the early Heidegger to the later one, who refers, in *On the Way to Language*, to the poet Stefan George: 'where word breaks off no thing may be' (1982, 141). In the same way as the painter, for Merleau-Ponty, attains the unity of seeing and seen, so the poet, for Heidegger, finally gets in touch with the common origin of word and thing. From here it follows that language does not consist of an ideal unity of empty words endowed with ideal significations. Rather language accrues as a significance of an originary being-in-the-world. To clarify this point, it should by now have become evident that it is impossible to understand the development of Heidegger's reflection on language by making a distinction between 'later Heidegger's questionable view that language *makes possible* significance' and a 'more plausible view defended in *Being and Time*', namely 'that all significance is sayable' (Dreyfus 1991, 354), in so far as Heidegger is, from the early 1920s on, on the way to the former claim, while what is here called the 'more plausible view' describes an intellectualism that Heidegger never defended, certainly not in *Being and Time*.

Hermeneutic theory, especially in the work of Gadamer and Ricoeur, develops from the idea of the ontological essence of language. The idea of hermeneutics derives originally from the interpretation of the scriptures; hermeneutic theory applies this idea of inter-pretation to literature and life. Like most of twentieth-century philosophy it draws its inspiration from Hegel, Husserl and Heidegger. According to this theory, language is at home in literature and especially poetry. These do not describe particular functions of language, rather they are the natural ground in which language sustains its life. This living language can then be made to signify in the everyday situations of determinate judgement. In relation to the metaphysical idea of language this is quite contradictory. On the basis of metaphysics one would have expected that, first and foremost, language exists in the form of determinate judgements like 'this is a yellow stone' or 'now it rains' before one could use these same sentences in literary works. But already the fact that art stands at the beginning of all civilization grants a hint as to its primordial nature. Likewise Kant had written in his

Critique of Judgement (1790), that aesthetic judgements precede determinate judgements, but here, in the claim of hermeneutics, it is furthermore argued that we can only speak and communicate due to the poetic life of language in poetry and literature.

It is clear, then, that we cannot regard language as originally a means of communication. That is to say, that we cannot understand literature as a means by which an author attempts to 'communicate' with us. In literature, more so than in the everyday use of language, language speaks. In literature, then, language exists as the house of Being, in so far as it is only through language that there can be things and hence a world for us. When Heidegger said, in *Being and Time*, that there is Being only as long as there are human beings, then that is not so much because these humans can summon Being by way of their language; instead the human being is summoned by language to a world. Phenomenology thus counters the modern misinterpretation of Aristotle's determination of the human being as the animal that 'has' language. In so far as this is an essential definition, it cannot signify an animal that first exists and then, as well, 'has' the ability to speak. Instead it is a being that *is* only in so far as in speaking it sustains its bond with language. It then seems that it would be more correct to say that language has or speaks us. From this insight the whole question of subjectivity becomes questionable, as in the order of language the other always precedes me in my being. It is from this perspective that Heidegger turns against the anthropological account of language, which makes of it the symbol of the human being.

On account of this thinking of language we might now understand Sartre's answer to the question *What is Literature?* Sartre speaks, in a text with this title, of *engaged literature* which has often been understood as a version of literature subordinated to ideological ends. But Sartre says 'engaged literature'. In other words, it is literature itself that is engaged, rather than an author, whose idea it might be to sway our moods with beautiful words. This is not to say that writing is not an action and that the writer is not 'engaged' in her writing, but not only does Sartre often use accentuation marks when speaking of an 'engaged' writer, more importantly, the writer can only be engaged when being carried by the essence of literature itself. This engagement of literature cannot even be broken by the author. Sartre claims, accordingly, that it is impossible to write an anti-Semitic novel (1967, 46). The literary work is written by an author but its creation is not accomplished before it is read by its readers. The work thus appeals to the reader, that is it issues an appeal, and it can only appeal to the reader as a human being partaking in the revelation of the world. Yet in so far as author and reader are not 'working together' at it – that is, in so far as this creation does not leap over their separation by way of a prior and conscious intention – the work is created due to the engagement of literary language with the freedom of the human being. That is to say, it becomes impossible to make a novel demand that one should negate the freedom of other human beings, in so far as language is the original bond to these others. Certainly, people can sit down and write novels with the firm intent to stir racial hostility, and somebody who takes up such a book might solely be interested in finding a like-minded writer to reconfirm his prejudice and hatred. But in that case such a reader is reading a pamphlet written in pseudo-literary form. As soon as this reader actually reads such a book and partakes in the revealing of language, the intent breaks itself and the novel effects the opposite of what it was conceived for, namely an insight into the inhumanity of racism and the ethical prevalence of the other. To the act of writing one can then apply Sartre's definition of freedom, according to which real freedom does not consist in being able to do whatever one wishes, but in being able to wish what one can do.

Phenomenologists have, in their attempt to return to the things themselves, rediscovered the world. That is to say they have enabled philosophy to deal with the whole of our life, without having to ostracize our emotional and spiritual life (Husserl); they have introduced a thinking of our Being-in-the-world on account of a thinking of Being (Heidegger); they have uncovered the reality of the other human being (Sartre) and the primordial nature of ethics (Lévinas); they have reintroduced that recalcitrant being, the body, into philosophical thought (Merleau-Ponty); and they have liberated literature from its enslavement to representation (Ingarden, Blanchot).

Ullrich Michael Haase

Further reading and works cited

Bernasconi, R. *The Question of Language in Heidegger's History of Being*. Atlantic Highlands, NJ, 1985.
Bernet, R. et al. *An Introduction to Husserlian Phänomenologie*. Evanston, IL, 1993.
Dreyfus, H. *Being-in-the-World – A Commentary on Heidegger's Being and Time*. Cambridge, MA, 1991.
Embree, L. et al. *Encyclopedia of Phenomenology*. Dordrecht, 1997.
Gadamer, H.-G. *Truth and Method*. London, 1975.
Hegel, G. W. F. *Phenomenology of Spirit*. Oxford, 1977.
Heidegger, M. *Being and Time*. Oxford, 1962.
—. *Poetry, Language, Thought*. New York, 1971.
—. *Nietzsche*. San Francisco, 1979.
—. *On the Way to Language*. New York, 1982.
—. *History of the Concept of Time*. Bloomington, IN, 1985.
—. *Zollikoner Seminare*. Frankfurt, 1987.
Husserl, E. *Cartesian Meditations*. The Hague, 1960.
—. *The Idea of Phenomenology*. The Hague, 1973.
—. *Ideas Pertaining to a Pure Phenomenology and to a Phenomenological Philosophie*, vol. I. The Hague, 1982.
—. *The Crisis of European Sciences and Transcendental Phenomenology: An Introduction to Phenomenological Philosophy*. Evanston, IL, 1987.
Ingarden, R. *The Cognition of the Literary Work of Art*. Evanston, IL, 1973.
Jauss, H. R. *Aesthetic Experience and Literary Hermeneutics*. Minneapolis, MN, 1982.
Lyotard, J.-F. *Phenomenology*. New York, 1991.
Merleau-Ponty, M. *Phénoménologie de la perception*. Paris, 1945.
—. *The Primacy of Perception and other Essays*. Evanston, IL, 1964.
Nietzsche, F. *Twilight of the Idols*. Oxford, 1998.
Ricoeur, P. *The Conflict of Interpretations*. Evanston, IL, 1974.
—. *The Rule of Metaphor*. Toronto, 1977.
Sallis, J. *Delimitations*. Bloomington, IN, 1986.
Sartre, J.-P. *What is Literature?* London, 1967.
—. *Being and Nothingness*. London, 1969.

11. Gaston Bachelard (1884–1962) and Georges Canguilhem (1904–1995): Epistemology in France

In the English-speaking world the name Gaston Bachelard is associated with an excavation of the phenomenology of the poetic imagination. In texts such as *The Poetics of Space, Water and Dreams, The Psychoanalysis of Fire* and *The Poetics of Reverie*, Bachelard has established a reputation for a dissection of the poetic imagination that he defines in terms of its distance from the non-phenomenological techniques of modern science (Bachelard 1994, 156). However, in France Bachelard's reputation lies primarily in the field of the history and philosophy of science, and the particular epistemological revolution he inaugurates and which counts among its heirs, such figures as Georges Canguilhem and Michel Foucault. Author of over a dozen substantial works in this latter field, the status of Bachelard's writing and its significance for debates over epistemology in twentieth-century France cannot be overstated.

The coexistence of these different styles of works in the collected oeuvre of Bachelard is remarkable because the material dealt with in the works on the poetic imagination is described in Bachelard's epistemological works as part of the complement of epistemological obstacles that hamper the development of science. It is one of the tasks of the epistemologist to conduct a 'psychoanalysis' of the scientific mind with the aim of identifying and clearing the sedimentations of pre-scientific conceptualizations. The status of phenomenology in each genre of his work is instructive here: for the imagination the relation to the 'given', as for instance the psychic state elicited by an image that conveys intimacy, is of an entirely different order to that of the status of the 'given' in modern science, which is defined as the procedures and techniques under which the 'immediate' must give way to the 'constructed' (Bachelard 1968, 122–3). Rather than a phenomenology, science is a 'phenomeno-technics'. For natural observation and the objects which supply it contemporary science substitutes phenomena that are in a radical sense constructs of the equipment and procedures of scientific practice. Scientific concepts, in turn, only win their scientific status if they are able to be realized in their technicality (Bachelard 1938, 61).

This technical character of contemporary science supports Bachelard's insistence on a double differentiation of science from common sense, which gauges truth in terms of the immediacy of sensations (Canguilhem 1979, 179), and from the history and epistemology of science as it has conventionally been practised. Against both forms of understanding which transport to science a false concept of historical continuity, Bachelard argues for the discontinuous nature of contemporary scientific development (Bachelard 1953, 211). The implications for the philosophy of science of the break contemporary science represents with other forms of understanding, as well as the accelerated time of contemporary science in which internal epistemological breaks are the norm, are significant. It is, Bachelard argues, only at the level of particular examples that the philosophy of science can give general lessons (Bachelard 1953, 223). And Bachelard's polemic against philosophy is as a consequence directed to the attachment of philosophy to metaphysical precepts. This attachment obscures the pertinent characteristics of modern science and determines traditional philosophy as part of the armoury of obstacles with which science contends. In this essay we will examine the nature of the relationship between Bachelard's formulation of a historically situated but normative epistemology and the self-consciously revolutionary character of the contemporary hard sciences before turning to examine Canguilhem's modifications of Bachelard's epistemology for his own work in the life sciences.

Twentieth-century physics awards priority to arithmetic over geometry and demotes thereby the spatial measurement assumed by pre-scientific experience. This transformed procedure for scientific method also entails a transformation of the methods of philosophical thought. The latter needs to follow the actual procedures through which the sciences attain knowledge. As a first measure, the dependence of philosophy on scientific development requires discarding the perspectives of idealism and realism: the former for its basis in the faculties of an epistemological subject and the latter for its presumption of a unified texture of reality. These perspectives are irrelevant in the face of the mathematicization of the natural sciences. Indeed it is the primacy of mathematicization which underpins Bachelard's account of the constructions by which contemporary science departs from pre-scientific intuitions and the precepts of traditional metaphysics (Privitera 1995, 8).

Against the traditional philosophical approaches to science that had prevailed in the French university system, Bachelard develops a new doctrine of applied analysis for the historical development of the truth-producing practices of the sciences. Dispensing with the ascription to science of a static universalism, Bachelard's approach stresses the necessary mobility of the sciences, which he views as determinate practices in need of regional epistemologies. Canguilhem, along with Foucault and Bourdieu, follow Bachelard in ascribing a privileged status to science: for each figure, the truths of science are located in the contemporary practices of science and thus considered in terms of their historical provisionality. The key for this new style of epistemology, a style scripted by Bachelard as a philosophy of the 'new scientific mind', is that the qualification of scientific truths as historical is not tantamount to a tolerance for relativism.

Bachelard's method for the new history of the sciences is an applied rationalism whose key features are the constructed nature of the scientific object, the development of science by epistemological breaks and the role of the epistemologist as the dialectician of scientific concepts. The regional areas in which Bachelard develops this applied rationalism are those of the hard sciences.

For Bachelard, reason is transformed by the different processes of regional epistemologies. A given knowledge at a given point in its history covers the processes within which experiments are constructed, previous scientific notions corrected and the formulation of standards of proof undertaken. Even within the disciplines of physics and chemistry different forms of reasoning apply. These differences make any single philosophy inappropriate for any given determinate science and discount the fallacious generic category of the sciences, disclosing the need for a dispersed philosophy of regional sciences. As philosophy is apprised of the need to follow the contemporary development of science, so too reason is not, as it is in Kant, a regulative faculty whose ideas give an external horizon towards which science develops. Rather, reason is formed within the specific practices of determinate scientific knowledges and the normative values that regulate these knowledges are those of their current scientific practice.

Bachelard's epistemology defends itself against the charge of historical relativism through a conception of the development of science by the dialecticization of existing scientific concepts. This process develops over two stages: first, epistemological errors are identified by the emergent scientificity so that a rectified science with an enlarged basis can proceed (Bachelard 1968, 24). The conception of history that underpins this exercise cautions against relativism not just in the obsolete status of the prescientific past but in the sanctioned status of this past as the material for dialecticized concepts through which a particular science is expanded. Despite Bachelard's emphasis on the historical discontinuity under which a determinate present may re-evaluate the past, the reconstructive developmental logic under which science develops attests to the strong normative dimension of his philosophy of science.

In *Le nouvel esprit scientifique* Bachelard argues that the rational experimental methods of contemporary science produce the phenomena they study. Hence it is impossible to separate the methods of science from their theoretical fabric: the establishment of determinate scientific facts is the work of the application of a coherent technique (Bachelard 1934, 176). Scientific method is 'rational' as its very object exists in light of its theoretical justification. A phenomenon such as a transuranian element is not an empirical given but a realization of a theoretically based technique that organizes and structures materials according to a preconceived plan (Tiles 1984, 139–40). It is this aspect of contemporary science that Bachelard's epistemology reflects in his view that it is in the practice of science that its objects and its own norms are produced. Further it is because scientific activity carries its own changing criterion for its existence that epistemology as the study of science deals with a historical process (Lecourt 1975, 26).

In modern science, reality becomes a function of the theoretical technique under which it is realized. And the scientific validity of a theory consequently comes to depend on its realization within its sphere of application. This means both that the norms of scientific practice derive from their terrain of application and that any abstraction of scientific theory from this context of practice extracts science from addressing the problems that make it at all meaningful. Correlatively, the constitution of new axiomatic systems are produced not on an unsubstantiated beginning but via the questions of pre-existing theories with which they effect a structural break or rupture. The primacy of experimental practice and the absence of any efficacious metatheory makes discontinuity a feature of the progress of science as each constitution of a new scientific region always implies an epistemological break (Privitera 1995, 14).

The dialectic that is one of the agents of this break does not entail a reduction of the pre-existing scientific theory to falsehood. Instead of a simple rejection of its predecessor the new scientificity places it in a perspective that allows for the enlargement of the basis of scientific inquiry (Bachelard 1968, 115). For instance, wave theory is a historical rupture in the evolution of modern science. Its synthesis of Newtonian and Frenellian thought determines its status as a historical synthesis, i.e. a synthesis built on past science whose own form depends on an epistemological act (Canguilhem 1979, 182). The norm of rectification that organizes the concept of the epistemological rupture in Bachelard conceives of negation as what supports a new mode of calculation rather than a link between contemporary science and the primordial concepts that it 'deforms' (Canguilhem 1979, 186). As contemporary science is a technical and theoretical construct the dialectical progress of science consists in the transformation of the very principles of existing knowledges (Bachelard 1953, 224). This perpetual process of transformation is also an aspect of the culture of contemporary scientific psychology in which anxiety and doubt are necessary companions of discovery. The philosophy of scientific knowledge, correlatively, is an 'open' one which works on the unknown and seeks in reality 'that which contradicts anterior knowledge' (Bachelard 1968, 9).

The dialectic of science includes the moment of rupture from what is now classed as a pre-existing ideology (obsolete history) and the reorganization of the emergent scientificity along with the determinate past form of science (sanctioned history) that is part of the reorganization. This dialectical history is recurrent because the history of the sciences is continually evaluated from the normative laws of contemporary scientific practices (Canguilhem 1979, 182). It is here that the specific tasks of the new philosophy of science emerge. Epistemology is a historical exercise because its object is the specific history of the discipline it examines. But it is also critical as it aims to separate scientific practice from the ideologies that are obstacles to its progress. As the 'defeat of irrationalism' and 'the most irreversible of all histories', the recurrent history of science is a history that is *able* to be recurrently judged and valued (Bachelard 1951, 27). It is this history, applied by Bachelard to the hard sciences of chemistry and mathematical physics, that Canguilhem will take up in the sciences of life.

It is risky to want to present in the form of general principles either Canguilhem's epistemology or his practice of writing the history of science. Such an enterprise would come across many formidable obstacles. His awareness of the specificity of the object of various sciences, whose operational concepts follow their own specific historical rhythms, turns him away from wanting to frame a general epistemology (Canguilhem 1979, 19). This epistemological prudence is further reinforced by the fact that his chosen area is the philosophy and history of the life sciences whose rigor cannot be modelled in mathematics, which also means that the process of formation and rational purification of their concepts cannot be reduced to logical developments of theories. Canguilhem warns against 'the use of hindsight to bring out the latent implications of a theory [that] risks making history seem straightforward and linear when in reality it was far more complex' (Canguilhem 1988, 105). Still less does he think that the heuristic principles of history of the sciences can be applied indiscriminately. This is true even of the principle of epistemological recursion or that of discontinuity. The former was originally developed for the study of mathematical physics and nuclear chemistry, and while it may be 'broadened' (but not 'generalized') to other 'areas of the history of science', it cannot be so 'without a good deal of reflection about the specific nature of the area to be studied' (Canguilhem 1988, 14). As for the epistemology of discontinuity, it 'is appropriate to a period of accelerated change in science' whereas the 'epistemology of continuity has a natural affinity with periods in which knowledge is just awakening' (Canguilhem 1988, 16). The complex process of scientific progress is underlined by the fact that success in one science does not necessarily cause or even entail progress in another; at times it may actually hinder it: 'the success of medical microbiology delayed the inception of a biochemistry of microbes' (Canguilhem 1988,

115). History can belie the scientific claims of a theory, just as, inversely, it may bestow the dignity of science on a theory that was regarded as ideology by many in its inception time. This is what happened, according to Canguilhem, to Darwin's theory of natural selection which had to wait for population genetics to receive experimental proof and hence properly scientific credentials (Canguilhem 1988, 104–6).

Having made these rather brief cautionary remarks, we must nonetheless take due note of the two fundamental thematics which give orientation to his understanding of the history of science and of the significance of (scientific) knowledge. With regard to the former, we may put forth the idea that for Canguilhem, as for Bachelard, the history of science is an inquiry that 'mimics' the practice of the scientist, notwithstanding the fact that it 'is not a science and its object is not a scientific object' (Canguilhem 1979, 22). As to the latter, Canguilhem consistently maintains throughout his philosophical career that scientific activity in general must finally be grounded in the normative activity that life as such is. This is not to deny the autonomy of the sciences, i.e. to question the truths of science in an external fashion, but to make clear that these truths are preceded by a normative decision in favour of the true, which can only be understood in reference to the normative character of the living's relation with its environment. If it is true that 'there is no other truth but that of science' it is also true for him that the idea of science is not scientific, that is it cannot be scientifically justified (Canguilhem, in Balibar 1993, 58–62).

The study of the progress of the sciences requires that the historian adopt a standpoint within scientific discourse. A history of science that intends to go beyond a mere recounting of pronouncements claiming to state the truth (because sanctioned by their contemporary scientific norms) and reveal 'the order of conceptual progress' in a specific science has to bring to bear on its history a theory of what counts as scientific knowledge. This measure, whose precise formulation is epistemology, is provided by the 'present notion of scientific truth' grounded in 'the present scientific culture' that contains a whole series of norms from those of instruments of experimentation to those of methods of observation and proof, to heuristic principles for formulating problems. The epistemologist proceeds from the present model of science toward the beginnings of a science which is the object of study, so that only a part of what was thought to be science is affirmed to be scientific. On the other hand, the reference of the epistemological notion of scientific truth to the present norms of scientificity makes it clear that for Canguilhem this measure is never more than a 'provisional point of culmination' of a history. Only by being historical is epistemology scientific in the sense that it mimics the scientific discourse in which the claim to truth is precisely governed by the possibility of critical correction, and is thus inherently historical: 'If this discourse has a history whose course the historian believes he can reconstruct, it is because it is a history whose meaning the epistemologist must reactivate' (Canguilhem 1988, 4–18). By the same token, the epistemologist's history of a science can never be a definitive history since each new constellation of scientific norms carries with it the possibility of a modification in the trajectory of the conceptual progress that the history of that science must trace. Such modifications range from shifts in emphasis to constructions of new trajectories. The recursive nature of history of the sciences in Canguilhem, which he takes over from Bachelard, sets him apart from the positivist tradition, which views history as a continuous and cumulative progress of the mind determined by 'logical laws', whose stages are thus fixed once and for all (Andreski 1974, 19–64). The history of science is truly a history, that is a series of ruptures and innovations (Canguilhem 1988, 116).

The historical modesty of Canguilhem's idea of epistemology also distinguishes his practice from the 'epistemological inquisition' that he detects in the approach of analytic philosophy to the history of science. The analytic philosopher takes the present standards of scientific theory as a complete doctrine and reduces the task of the historian to a meticulous application of these standards to a past science, thus becoming blind to the fact that the past of a present-day science is not the same as that science in the past. A homogeneous history of science, resting its case on a supposed continuity of intention or the identity of terms, suppresses the radical discontinuity within a science of successive object-constructs which are in fact precipitations of a whole gamut of factors irreducible to theoretical implications. The doctrinal epistemology that guides this history proceeds from an attitude that makes it fall prey in the present to a scientistic realism against which its epistemological scruples were meant to protect it vis-à-vis the realistic claims of a past science. The attitude in question sees scientific truths as statements of fact or definitive expressions of various characteristics of reality rather than provisional results of the constructions of the scientific work.

Scientific truths are not descriptions of a given reality, more sophisticated (because more precise or more penetrating) versions of the common-sensical or sensual knowledge. In a very important sense, a science becomes scientific for Canguilhem no less than for Bachelard because it breaks with its 'prehistory' in which it sought its objects in the sensible world already given. It becomes scientific, in other words, from the moment that it manages to create its own object with its own theories and instruments. 'In sum', writes Canguilhem, 'scientific proof is a work since it reorganises the given, since it produces effects without natural equivalent, since it constructs its organs' (Canguilhem 1979, 192). The historian of science must, here too, follow the lead of scientific practice, must mimic this latter – and on two levels. Firstly, history of science must take its bearings from the epistemological task of reconstructing 'the ways and means by which knowledge is produced' (Canguilhem 1988, 7). Not producing scientific knowledge does not mean that philosophical epistemology has nothing to say in relation to the conditions of production of knowledge. No factor that has had a role in the production of a specific scientific concept – be it the state of contemporary technology, the model of scientificity formulated in an adjunct scientific domain, practical and pragmatic requirements imposed by the economy or political system, or the ideologies and myths and metaphors of the social imaginary – should be left out of the history of that science on the pretext that it is not considered scientifically relevant by the present norms of scientificity. For Canguilhem 'there is no history of science which would be *only* history of science', as Balibar puts it (Balibar 1993, 66), since science is precisely a 'progressive process of purification governed by *norms of verification*' (Canguilhem 1988, 39). Hence, the importance for the history of science, in Canguilhem, of 'scientific ideology' and the care with which he describes its relation with science. On a second level, the historian must make her own the awareness of the scientist that her object is not given but constructed and that the question of knowledge is not that of getting close and seizing hold of the object but rather that of producing consistent results. The historian who views the history of science as a record pure and simple of scientific truth, having failed to recognize the role of 'scientific ideology' in the history of the formation of a scientific concept, ends up producing a 'false consciousness of its object. The closer the historian thinks he comes to his object, the farther he is from the target'. Just like the scientist, 'the historian cannot accurately see any object that he does not actively construct. Ideology is mistaken belief in being close to truth. Critical knowledge knows that it stands at a distance from an operationally constructed object' (Canguilhem 1988, 39–40).

For Canguilhem the history of science is 'one of the functions of philosophical epistemology' (Canguilhem 1979, 23). It is thus never simply a history recounted but first and foremost a history judged. Bachelard sought in mathematics the principle of orientation for this judgement; accordingly, in his thought, the 'axis of epistemological evaluation is in effect provided by the vector of mathematization, which defines the direction in which the rationalist activity of the physical sciences is accomplished' (Fichant 1993, 39). Canguilhem's philosophical epistemology, by contrast, takes its bearings from the question of the 'vital meaning' of knowledge, which one may say constitutes the point of convergence of his reflections on biology and medical sciences and practice. For him, knowledge is fundamentally the activity of forming and deploying concepts; and this latter is itself, as Foucault puts it, 'one way of living', that is one way of exchanging information with the environment (Foucault 1991, 21). The two concepts that in effect allow Canguilhem to question knowledge from the perspective of life, namely normativity and error, are in fact the two that define the manner of the existence of the living.

In *The Normal and the Pathological* Canguilhem defines life as 'polarized activity', or more precisely 'a form of reactivity polarized to the variations of the environment in which it develops' (Canguilhem 1991, 130) or as 'polarity and thereby even an unconscious position of value' (Canguilhem 1991, 126). There is an original form of judgement of value which coincides with life as such. The living beings do not confront their environment as an ensemble of facts but as a structure of vitally meaningful possibilities and demands 'centered on them' (Canguilhem 1991, 284). 'Even for an amoeba, living means preference and exclusion' (Canguilhem 1991, 136). The norm is what determines the normal starting from a normative intention. Being normal means to be normative, that is, being able to transcend the already existing norms toward establishing new ones (Canguilhem 1991, 196–7). This ability marks out a 'margin of tolerance' vis-à-vis the environment's inconstancies and hence a certain degree of independence from it. A normal environment is the one that allows the living to be normative, and accordingly, a 'norm of life is superior to another norm when it includes what the latter permits and what it forbids' (Canguilhem 1991, 182). Physiology's very definition of the normal, in the sense of functional constants of regulation, is derivative of the concrete exchanges which the organism conducts with its environment. If the normal state designates the habitual state of the organs and functions, this habitual state is itself the effect of a dynamic equilibrium between the demands of the environment and those of the organism; it is the precipitation, more or less temporary, of the normalization of the organism's relations with the environment, so that the functional and morphological constants are in the final analysis expressions of a concrete vital order (Canguilhem 1991, 162). In the same vein, disease does not consist in the absence of norms. 'Disease is still a norm of life but it is an inferior norm in the sense that it tolerates no deviation from the conditions in which it is valid . . . The sick living being is normalized in well-defined conditions of existence and has lost his normative capacity, the capacity to establish norms in other conditions' (Canguilhem 1991, 183). The definition of life as normative activity constitutes Canguilhem's conceptual point of departure for the redefinition of not only physiological terms but also biological ones such as 'species' (Canguilhem 1991, 143). More importantly, perhaps, he places human technology and through this human knowledge too in the perspective of 'vital normativity' that characterizes life in general. 'All human technique, including that of life, is set within life, within an activity of information and assimilation of material' (Canguilhem 1991, 130). Man's 'desire to dominate the environment' which he pursues by means of technology is in fact the flourishing of the 'organic vitality' (Canguilhem 1991, 200–1). And knowledge is 'an anxious quest for the greatest possible quantity and variety of information' (Canguilhem 1979, 364).

The 'discussion with an environment' for the purpose of stabilization of a vital order, that life is for the living being, is primordially a normative activity (Canguilhem 1991, 198). Living is already a judgement of value, not just a division into positive and negative but also, as normative, a devaluation of what exists in the form of power to transcend it and establish new norms and hence a new normality. The normal is thus 'the norm exhibited in the fact' (Canguilhem 1991, 243) and norms 'refer the real to values, express discriminations of qualities in conformity with the polar opposition of a positive and a negative' (Canguilhem 1991, 240). This is why, as we said, the environment is always already confronted as vitally significant, as meaningful. The 'a prioris' of meaningful experience are given by life and not, as in Kant, by the subject. 'To define life as a meaning inscribed in matter is to acknowledge the existence of an a priori objective that is inherently material and not merely formal' (Canguilhem 1979, 362). But this primordial materiality of meaning also makes human meaning radically contingent – not only because the mutation that is the origin of all species, of the multiplication of life, is in fact nothing other than 'an error of heredity' or a 'misinterpretation of genetic information', but also because, in the case of human being, 'life would by error have produced a living thing capable of making errors'. There is a specifically human error which is, Canguilhem says, 'probably one with human errancy. Man makes mistakes because he does not know where to settle'. Man's way of negotiation with the environment is movement; he gathers information 'by moving around, and by moving objects around, with the aid of various kinds of technology'. Canguilhem places error, human errancy, at the origins of human technology and science. 'Man is the living being separated from life by science and struggling to rejoin life by science' (Canguilhem 1975, 105–6). Does this mean that human being somehow has to be perpetually dissatisfied with the meaning already given, and first of all with the judgement that life is? 'If the a priori is in things, if the concept is in life, then to be a subject of knowledge is simply to be dissatisfied with the meaning one finds ready at hand. Subjectivity is therefore nothing other than dissatisfaction' (Canguilhem 1979, 364). But this also means that human being is the living being that cannot but be normative with regard to meaning itself: she is compelled by life itself, by 'the limitation of life's finality', by the surplus of the possible over the real, to question life; she is driven to a search for reasons to live (Canguilhem 1991, 281). 'But to pursue such a goal is also to discover reasons not to live' (Canguilhem, in Delaporte 1994, 384). Human being is the living being that is capable of living a meaning, a normative judgement, that may turn out to be an absolute devaluation of the fact of living (Canguilhem 1979, 183–6). In this case, one may perhaps say that being human is, for better or worse, a compulsion to meaning.

Alison Ross and *Amir Ahmadi*

Further reading and works cited

Andreski, S. (ed.) *The Essential Comte.* New York, 1974.
Bachelard, G. *Le nouvel esprit scientifique.* Paris, 1934.
—. *La formation de l'esprit scientifique.* Paris, 1938.
—. *L'Activité Rationaliste de la physique contemporaine.* Paris, 1951.

—. *Le matérialisme rationnel.* Paris, 1953.
—. *The Philosophy of No.* New York, 1968.
—. *The Poetics of Space.* Boston, 1994.
Balibar, E. 'Science et vérité dans la philosophie de Georges Canguilhem', *Georges Canguilhem: Philosophe, historien des sciences*, ed. François Delaporte. Paris, 1993.
Canguilhem, G. *La Connaissance de la vie.* Paris, 1975.
—. *Études d'histoire et de philosophie des sciences.* Paris, 1979.
—. *Ideology and Rationality in the History of the Life Sciences.* Cambridge, MA, 1988.
—. *The Normal and the Pathological.* New York, 1991.
—. 'Le cerveau et la pensée', in *Georges Canguilhem: Philosophe, historien des sciences*, ed. François Delaporte. Paris, 1993.
Delaporte, F. (ed.) *A Vital Rationalist.* New York, 1994.
Fichant, M. 'Georges Canguilhem et l'Idée de la philosophie', *Georges Canguilhem: Philosophe, historien des sciences*, ed. François Delaporte. Paris, 1993.
Foucault, M. *The Archeology of Knowledge.* London, 1972.
—. 'Introduction'. *The Normal and the Pathological.* New York, 1991.
Hyppolite, J. 'Gaston Bachelard ou le romantisme de l'intelligence', in *Hommage à Gaston Bachelard.* Paris, 1957.
Latour, B. and Bowker, G. 'A booming discipline short of discipline', *Social Studies of Science*, 17, 1987.
Lecourt, D. *Marxism and Epistemology.* London, 1975.
Markus, G. 'Changing Images of Science', *Thesis Eleven*, 33, 1992.
Privitera, W. *Problems of Style.* Albany, NY, 1995.
Rabinow, P. *Essays on The Anthropology of Reason.* Princeton, NJ, 1996.
Tiles, M. *Bachelard, Science and Objectivity.* Cambridge, 1984.

12. Jean Paulhan (1884–1969) and/versus Francis Ponge (1899–1988)

Jean Paulhan and Francis Ponge not only share strong biographical and ideological origins in common (both were originally from the South of France (Nîmes), and born into protestant and free-thinking families), they also had an intense personal relationship (too complex to be called simply 'friendship') which lasted their whole lives. A chief editor of the NRF (*Nouvelle Revue Française*), the leading literary journal between the two World Wars, Paulhan took the decision to publish Ponge's first book (*Douze petits écrits*, 1926). After this, he functioned for Ponge as a kind of literary and intellectual mentor, and their correspondence spans a period of almost fifty years (1923–68).

Nevertheless, aside from the biographical elements, one might be tempted to insist more heavily on all that separates Paulhan and Ponge. The first is seen as a critic (some readers hardly even know that he also wrote *fiction*). The latter is considered exclusively a poet, and even the poet of one single masterwork, *Le Parti pris des choses* (1942), whereas most of his writings are definitely *anti-poetical* in tone and scope. Furthermore, the first represents much of the very diverse and, perhaps, antagonistic tendencies brought together (and not necessarily reconciled) in the NRF, with its typical blending of a rather left-wing political involvement and an almost neoclassical sense of taste and well-written French prose, sharp, clear and witty at the same time. The latter, on the contrary, now appears as one of the greatest French poets of the century, who, together with the Belgian author Henri Michaux, has revolutionized our very conception of poetry (and probably of literature and even language in general). Paulhan is also almost ignored by contemporary readers. His (still very incomplete) Oeuvres complètes is long sold out, and many of his books are really hard to find. Ponge, however, has been widely adopted and even cherished by the literary and educational institution. His complete works have entered the ne plus ultra of French editorial chic, the 'Pléiade' series, and is taught at all levels, from elementary schools to PhD programmes (in France, these programmes are all fixed by the Ministry of Education, not freely chosen by the schools or faculties). And finally, whereas Paulhan has been at the (invisible) centre of French literary life, making and unmaking books, authors and careers as an almighty but hidden God, Ponge has occupied a small but well lit margin of it, and his work has been claimed by every imaginable literary and philosophical school of the twentieth century.

But do biographical (and ideological) convergences, on the one hand, and literary (and institutional) divergences, on the other, keep both in balance? In fact, one should add here one or two elements which tie together Paulhan's and Ponge's writing and thinking, and which do so in such an inextricable manner that one can really consider these two authors, if not as each other's intellectual alter ego, than at least as two perfect examples of what French modernism stands for between, say, 1920 and 1970: the first element is the metapoetical turn of their literary and critical practice; the second is the way their poetics has always been defined by the authors themselves in political terms.

The literary career of Jean Paulhan merges almost completely with the life of the NRF, co-founded by André Gide and some of his friends (Paulhan becomes the journal's first editorial assistant in 1920, running the journal from 1925 on). This merging does not of course imply that Paulhan's biography is monolithic or simple. First, Paulhan's editorial functions (not only at the NRF, but very soon at Gallimard, France's most important publisher, and, after the Second World War, in the global literary field) constituted him as a very double personality. A typical go-between, having to defend the interests of writers as well as publishers, he developed an extraordinary sense of diplomacy (or hypocrisy, as his enemies liked to put it). In order to preserve the mutual goodwill of both camps, he became a master of literary, social and political tactics. During the German occupation, he managed for example to keep running the NRF under German censorship (he only resigned when the Nazis decided to give the NRF to a collaborationist writer, Drieu la Rochelle), while at the same time being very active in clandestine publishing and in political Résistance. His incredibly rich correspondence, most of which still remains an unknown continent for copyright reasons, reflects the vastness of his socio-literary networks, and the exceptional human qualities which made him the real 'pope' of French literature during more than forty years (although after the Second World War the prewar NRF monopoly was rudely challenged by successful newcomers such as Les Temps modernes and Tel Quel). For his editorial work, he regularly used pseudonyms, and for many years people believed he was really the author of the pornographic cult-novel Histoire d'O (in fact written by his mistress and collaborator, Dominique Aury).

If Paulhan published only small books (and often very small ones, as far as size or length is concerned), he never ceased to write fiction and essays. His fiction entails mostly short stories (Paulhan never wrote a full-length novel) and is more or less autobiographical. *Le Guerrier appliqué* (1917), for instance, a very unconventional book on his war experiences, remains key reading on the First World War. His *Guide d'un petit voyage en Suisse* (1947) is a mini-travelogue which is also a wonderful example of 'applied philosophy'. Paulhan's essays display a wide range of topics and themes, yet they have only one major subject: language (occasionally language and art, but often either language or art; however, in any case, the questions raised are comparable). From his very first publication on Madagascar proverbs (*Les Hain-Tenys*, 1913), to the paramount essay-books which are *Les Fleurs de Tarbes* (published in 1941, but prepared and rewritten for more than two decades) and the posthumous *Les Incertitudes du langage* (1970), Paulhan never stops turning around the mystery of language, its use, its meaning, but most of all its beauty. For the study of language, however ambiguous and deceptive its results may be, ends always with a kind of epiphany, Beauty and Truth being the final steps of Paulhan's reflection on these matters (his peculiar sensibility to the mystery of language and life explains also why so many readers discover a touch of Oriental mysticism in his work).

But what is language? Paulhan distinguishes three major elements, which appear to have major consequences for other than strictly linguistic speculations.

First, language is a system, where no element ever has meaning by itself, and where meaning both depends on use and context and is permanently shifting. This was indeed the great lesson of Paulhan's study of the so-called 'hain-tenys', small pieces of oral poetry containing more or less stereotyped proverbs which were used in Madagascar in verbal contests (Paulhan spent some years in that colony, and became very hostile towards French colonialism). Speakers of two camps exchange poems and proverbs until one of them finds a proverb-rich poem so well-formed and well-formulated that it blocks the answer of the other, reducing the opponent to silence. Of course, whether a 'hain-teny' is well-formed and well-formulated or not depends not on the utterance itself, but on the context. An oral contest is not the repetition of a stereotyped set of questions and answers, but an open *performance* always full of surprises.

Second, as the 'hain-tenys' example already makes clear, every language is a strange combination of 'stereotyped' and 'original' utterances. However, this does not imply that the very distinction of the two categories can be established once and for all, since speakers and listeners can have different opinions on the degree of 'frozen-ness' of an expression, or since the very use and re-use of stereotypes can alter the perception of its characteristics, and so on.

Third, language is for Paulhan also much more than just a symbolic human activity among others. It always reveals a certain way of thinking, and should therefore be understood as a synthesis of the human mind – an idea that structuralism will of course exploit on a very large scale in later decades. (Paulhan, however, who always links human life and the universe, resembled more a mystical anthropologist of language than a die-hard structuralist.)

The literary and human consequences of these observations are, at least for Paulhan, easy to understand, and he uses his knowledge of hain-tenys *pragmatics* to end a violent discussion on *literary terrorism* (the subtitle of his *Fleurs de Tarbes* runs: 'La Terreur dans les Lettres'). For the terrorists (whom he calls unhappy rhetoricians) linguistic invention and, perhaps, all language, inevitably become a set of stereotypes preventing the speaker from 'expressing' his or her feelings and experiences in a natural, spontaneous way. Hence, in order to 'free' the subject's speech, the terrorist proposes to 'exclude' all stereotypes, and in fact all rhetorics and all literary devices, from the field of writing, making a plea for 'natural', i.e. non literary speech. Thanks to his experience of the 'hain-tenys', which he considers paradigmatic of all human language, Paulhan manages to explain to what extent the conflict between the terrorists and their antagonists, the rhetoricians, is a false one, since it does not take into account the role of context and the specific use of an utterance.

These linguistic and literary stances are then 'transferred' by Paulhan to other areas, such as ethics and politics. Yet since language and life are not opposed, but mutually comprehensive, such a 'transfer' is not just a language-inspired interpretation of life, but a logical consequence of linguistic analysis itself. After the Second World War, the spirit of tolerance which had always impregnated his literary and artistic writings takes an overtly political dimension. Paulhan's battle against literary terrorism becomes a battle against terrorism and political intolerance *in se*. A very influential leader of the 'patriotic' writers' committee born during the *Résistance*, Paulhan publicly fights the prosecution of collaborationist writers, while at the same time strongly affirming the autonomy of literary speech as an illustration of free speech and anti-terrorist play.

Although the third element of Paulhan's definition of language sounds rather outdated nowadays, the influence of Paulhan's writings and work are widely acknowledged. In an era of political correctness, his efforts to avoid major tensions between those who believe that words are 'just words' and those who are convinced that words are 'anything but words' continue to be, in France at least, regularly mentioned with great approval. And Paulhan's own writing, that never-ending rewriting exceeding the limits of any fixed text, book or genre, has become exemplary of new conceptions of authorship and textuality. In that respect, just as with regard to the relationships between writing and politics, the link with Ponge is not difficult to establish, notwithstanding the many other differences between the personalities and literary achievements of the two authors.

At first sight, and contrary to Paulhan's case, life and writing are separated in the example of Francis Ponge by an almost unbridgeable gap, at least at the anecdotal level. After a surrealist beginning (or is it already an intermezzo?), Ponge was obliged to take a job in order to make a living for his family. His marriage put an end to his economic freedom, and all his life he would have to fight poverty. In later texts, he described himself as 'proletarized' by labour: first due to low wages in the 1930s, then due to periods of unemployment, before and after the Second World War, exemplified by his break with the Communist Party (his membership was maintained from 1936 to 1947, and during the first years after the war he worked for a communist newspaper). At the same time, the very difficult material conditions in which he had to write cannot be separated from what is at stake in his writings (during the period he wrote Le parti pris des choses, he was allowed only twenty minutes a day to write, having to work at least twelve hours a day and being too tired to write more). The poetry Ponge wrote is indeed not a form of petit-bourgeois escapism. On the contrary, the way Ponge thinks of poetry and practises it stubbornly signifies an absolute and complete denial of any escapism whatsoever. Poetry is an act of resistance, poetry is politics, and is therefore useful and necessary. However, this act of resistance can only be meaningful if at the same time it is directed towards poetry itself, towards the destruction of ways of writing poetry which maintain the gap between text and life, or literature and politics.

As with so many other angry young men of his generation, Ponge had been seduced by the radicalism of the surrealist movement. Very soon, however, he discarded Breton's vision of language and art, and his vision of their relationship with reality, as false and naive, as inauthentic and unrevolutionary. Indeed, whereas the surrealist revolution tends to despise any given reality and the objects of the given world, favouring instead the world of illogical *trouvailles* and dreams, of the unconscious, of the free association of literary metaphors, Ponge realized that literature must commit itself with the world and its objects, rather than with the subjective feelings of the poet. In order to become truly revolutionary, literature must be real, it must stick to the things themselves, and do everything to serve the world occluded by subjective illusions. Refusing the petit-bourgeois and belle-lettrist vision of writing in a surrealist mode, he then began pursuing an ideal of radically impersonal writing which seems anti-poetic, but which was, for him, the only possible embodiment of revolutionary poetry. This was also the project to which he would remain faithful throughout his life. Despite many variations in tone and political orientation, Ponge wanted his writing to be a revolutionary disclosure of the world itself, the very act of writing being of course also one of its aspects.

While one might distinguish four major steps in his poetic career, it is not possible to establish a real gap between these, each new step being in fact a more explicit version of what was already contained in earlier forms. His second book, *Le parti pris des choses* (1942), a small collection of short pieces of poetic prose, illustrates the more traditional side of his objective poetics. Claiming 'one rhetorics for each object', Ponge reinvents in this book a typically French genre, i.e. the 'poésie en prose'. He cuts it of from its lyrical basis, and replaces it by a 'cold', descriptive mode aiming to do justice to both the materiality of the world and that of the word. When describing, for instance, the 'crate', Ponge not only evokes the referential side (for instance by explaining where you can find such things in Paris), but also mentions some aspects of its own, verbal materiality (for instance by detailing the words which surround it in the dictionary, which is the other place where you can find 'crates' certainly). And, as the example already shows, the very choice of many of the objects described in the book also bear this anti-poetical, materialist attitude (later he will give as a major example the oyster, with a famous comment on the 'accent circonflexe' one finds in the French writing of the word 'huître'). What Ponge wants is to 'say the world (and thus also the words)' in its most humble appearances, not to conceal it by poetical and subjective nonsense.

A new step in his writing is seen in *Proêmes* (1948), an experiment in the blurring of boundaries between the text and its critique, between writing a poem and writing a comment on the poem itself. Of course, many texts of *Le parti pris des choses* already contained such a 'metapoetical' level, but with *Proêmes* Ponges makes a decisive opening towards the fusion of several text-types, and more particularly leaps into the mixing-up of the so-called 'finished' and 'draft' versions of a text. His exceptional familiarity with painting and with the artist's workshop was undoubtedly of great help for the understanding of his own poetical practice.

Le parti pris des choses and *Proêmes* had made Ponge famous, at least in the inner circles of the literary in-crowd. Greater public recognition and honour arrived only in the 1960s. But by the time that people really started reading the books from the 1940s, Ponge was already experimenting with new works, whose importance, although widely and officially acknowledged, was barely understood by many readers. In a book such as *Pour un Malherbe* (1965), the combination of texts, drafts, comments, critiques, quotations, etc., is transformed into a tri-dimensional book-object, which is also a sumptuous masterpiece of typography. (Under the influence of the favourite subjects of his art criticism, such as Braque, Picasso or Fautrier, Ponge's writing had become more and more a scrambling of words inspired by the scrambling of colours on the canvas.) Simultaneously, *Pour un Malherbe* is an autobiography, and also a poetic and political manifesto. Ponge invokes the authority of Malherbe, the Renaissance poet who decisively transformed first French poetry, and afterwards French language itself. As far as poetry is concerned, Ponge thus strongly identifies himself with the man who put an end to the domination of the Ronsardian (in fact Petrarchan, subjective and lyrical) tradition in France and substituted it with a more rational, cold, objective mode of writing. (Ponge was here thinking also of Latin, as a language and as a literature, where texts were carved in stone, and he put an increasing emphasis on the historical and structural continuity between Latin and French.) As far as language is concerned, Ponge elaborates a renewed theory of poetry as civil and political action, of poetry firmly rooted in the institutional organization of both the language and the country itself. Ponge's insistence on the necessary encounter of poet and king, and on their common action in the life of the nation, will later be explained by some as a right-wing 'dérive' [right-wing drift; drift to the right] of his politicization of poetry (these are the years of General de Gaulle and Pompidou), and provoke long-lasting controversy.

In the final phase, then, Ponge released not just the typographic version of a text's adventures, but displayed the whole 'workshop' (once again, the pictorial connotations of this programme are evidently present), and included in books such as *La fabrique du pré* (1971) and *Comment une figue de paroles et pourquoi* (1977). This politics of writing and publishing really accomplishes what Ponge had always asked from poetry: that is, the articulation of an act, a text in action, this act becoming life itself. Writing, performing, living, thinking become a whole.

The reading and interpretation of Ponge follows closely the history of literary and critical theory in the twentieth century. Ponge has been read, as has been claimed, within almost every important critical and political current since the Second World War: communism and marxism, phenomenology, existentialism, structuralism, *Tel Quel* and *TXT* materialism, nationalism, deconstruction and – nowadays – the reborn, strongly psychoanalytically oriented philology called genetic criticism. One should stress, however, that there has always existed a strong tension between the author's intention and his readers' interpretations. From the very beginning of his creative labour, Ponge opposed misreadings of his work. The fear of political recuperation of his writings (for instance by the French Communist Party in the first years after the Second World War) may have been one of the most significant arguments in Ponge's decision to incorporate ever more explicitly in his texts their own 'reader's companion', so that the radical novelty of his anti-poetry would be revealed and misreading blocked as much as possible. That he firmly encouraged during the 1960s the materialist-textualist interpretation of his work by the *Tel Quel* group (the studies conducted by Derrida in later years relied heavily upon the essential insights and preferences of this period) may suggest, and for some even suffices to prove, that this was the ideal reader-response for which the author was looking. In fact, nothing is less sure, since at the same moment he made with Philippe Sollers the interview-book which still today determines the larger public understanding of his work, Ponge had started writing very different texts and inventing new, overtly nationalistic and patriotic auto-interpretations for which there was certainly no room in the 'orthodox' textualist-deconstructionist viewpoint.

Francis Ponge always opposed totalitarianism, fascist as well as communist, while simultaneously always trying to escape from too rigid (or too flattering) criticism. For Ponge, the core business of interpretation is always to be accomplished by the individual reader in a personal encounter with the text, and this encounter has to be renewed in every new reading. Ponge's texts are not objects, but acts, and as such they can never be repeated twice. With him, poetry became performance once again.

Jan Baetens

Further reading and works cited

Badré, F. *Paulhan le juste*. Paris, 1996.
Baetens, J. '– Je m'appelle Jacques Maast', *Poétique*, 78, 1989.
Bersani, J. (ed.) *Colloque de Cerisy, Jean Paulhan le souterrain*. Paris, 1976.
Derrida, J. *Signéponge*. Paris, 1988.
Farasse, G. *L'Ane musicien*. Paris, 1996.
Gleize, J.-M. *Francis Ponge*. Paris, 1988.
Paulhan, J. *Le Guerrier appliqué*. Paris, 1930.
—. *Les Hain-Tenys*. Paris, 1939.
—. *Les Fleurs de Tarbes*. Paris, 1941.
—. *Guide d'un petit voyage en Suisse*. Paris, 1947.
—. *Oeuvres complètes*. 5 vols. Paris, 1966–70.
—. *Les Incertitudes du langage*. Paris, 1970.
—. *Correspondance avec Francis Ponge* (1923–68). Paris, 1986.
Pérez, C.-P. *Entretiens de Francis Ponge avec Philippe Sollers*. Paris, 1997.
— (ed.) *Le clair et l'obscur*. Paris, 1999.
Ponge, F. *Douze petits écrits*. Paris, 1926.
—. *Le Parti pris des choses*. Paris, 1942.
—. *Proêmes*. Paris, 1948.
—. *Pour un Malherbe*. Paris, 1965.
—. *La Fabrique du pré*. Geneva, 1971.
—. *Comment une figue de paroles et pourquoi*. Paris, 1977.
—. *Oeuvres complètes*. Paris, 1999–.
Syrotinski, M. *Defying Gravity*. Albany, NY, 1998.
Veck, B. *Francis Ponge ou le refus de l'absolu littéraire*. Liège, 1993.
Vouilloux, B. *Un art de la figure*. Lille, 1998.

13. György Lukács (1885–1971)

Philosopher, political theorist and literary critic, György Lukács was an influential marxist intellectual who made pioneering contributions to the study of literature and culture, in spite of the controversy that often surrounded his work. In literary theory, he took the first decisive steps toward a systematic marxist aesthetics based not only on formal criticism, but also on economic sociological and historical analysis. Particularly influential in this regard have been *The Theory of the Novel* (1916), which Lukács wrote before he joined the Communist Party, and *The Historical Novel* (1937). Inspired largely by the dialectics of Hegel, these two works offer historical typologies of literary forms that have influenced such diverse marxist projects as Lucien Goldmann's *The Hidden God* (1955) and Fredric Jameson's *The Political Unconscious* (1981). An advocate of realism, Lukács also initiated a formative debate for marxist literary theory on the politics of expressionism and modernism in general, eliciting notable if sometimes scathing critical responses from such prominent marxists as Ernst Bloch, Theodor Adorno and Bertolt Brecht (see Bloch et al. 1980). Most importantly, Lukács developed the groundbreaking concept of reification in his celebrated work, *History and Class Consciousness* (1923). An original extension of Karl Marx's theory of commodity fetishism, this seminal concept proved to be a major influence on the critical theorists of the Frankfurt School, including their associate Walter Benjamin. It also shaped the thinking of existential marxists like Maurice Merleau-Ponty as well as the New Left movement of the 1960s, especially in the case of Guy Debord's *The Society of the Spectacle* (1967). In exerting such influence, Lukács has come to be widely regarded as a founding figure of western marxism.

Born into a wealthy Jewish family in Budapest, Lukács began his road to marxism as a young aesthete deeply opposed to the ills of modern society. Overwhelmed by a sense of futility, the young Lukács was primarily preoccupied with the tragic division between art and life, falling under the influence of Søren Kierkegaard, Friedrich Nietzsche, Fyodor Dostoyevsky and Henrik Ibsen. At the universities in Berlin and Heidelberg, where he acquired his lifelong interest in German philosophy, Lukács' already acute sense of the socio-economic problems of modernity was further intensified under the tutelage of three eminent sociologists, Georg Simmel, Emil Lask and Max Weber. With the outbreak of the First World War, Lukács became utterly despondent. His tragic sense of the modern condition confirmed, he wrote his *Theory of the Novel* 'in a mood of permanent despair over the state of the world' (12). In 1918, after the success of the Russian Revolution and the subsequent collapse of the Austro-Hungarian Empire, Lukács joined the Hungarian Communist Party (HCP) formed by Béla Kún. His conversion to Marxism marked the beginning of his hopeful sense of political commitment. Along with this newly acquired optimism came a period of intense political activity spanning most of the 1920s, during which time Lukács set aside his literary and aesthetic concerns. In the short-lived Hungarian Soviet Republic, he served as the Deputy Commissar of Public Education and as the Political Commissar of the Red Army's fifth division. As a political exile in Vienna and Berlin, he also played a significant role in the émigré HCP from 1919 to 1929, becoming deputy leader of the Landler faction. A major political activist, Lukács even attended the 1921 Third World Congress of the Communist International in Moscow, where he met Lenin personally.

Lukács political writings of the time, however, were generally not well-received by Soviet authorities. The most significant expression of his political views appeared in *History and Class Consciousness*, the central essay of which, 'Reification and the Consciousness of the Proletariat', theorizes the revolutionary emergence of the proletarian subject out of the dehumanizing forces of capitalism. The work as a whole was strikingly non-dogmatic, making the claim that what was orthodox about Marxism was not its doctrine, but its method: dialectical materialism. For this reason, among others, *History and Class Consciousness* was immediately condemned as heretical by the Comintern Congress in Moscow (its non-doctrinaire views were ultimately more influential among Western European intellectuals). A similar fate befell Lukács' controversial political document, 'The Blum Theses' (1925), mainly because it urged communists to collaborate with bourgeois politicians in Hungary (see Lukács 1972). Faced with increasing dogmatism in the Party following the death of Lenin in 1924, Lukács eventually was forced to retract many of his political views and finally, in 1929, to retire from active politics, although he returned briefly for the ill-fated 1956 Hungarian uprising led by Imre Nagy, who made Lukács his Minister of Culture.

In the 1930s, Lukács resumed his literary and philosophical pursuits, which were now bound up with countering the unreason of fascism and developing a proper marxist aesthetic. In Berlin (1931–3) and then in Moscow (1933–45), he turned his attention to a systematic critique of expressionism and modernism, portraying them as forms of decadence that paved the way for the rise of fascism by universalizing alienation, relativism and fragmentation, rather than seeing them as effects of capitalism. In his numerous essays written for *Internationale Literature, Das Wort* and *Die Linkskurve*, which later appeared in his *Essays on Realism* (1948), *Studies in European Realism* (1950) and *Writer and Critic* (1970), Lukács opposed such forms with a marxian theory of realism that underscored the importance of objective representation, narrative and humanism, as well as the progressive politics of the anti-fascist Popular Front. He was primarily interested in the novel, hoping that his critical efforts would halt the ongoing dissolution of its classic nineteenth-century form, which Lukács traced out fully in *The Historical Novel*.

To many western intellectuals and artists at the time, most notably Bertolt Brecht, it appeared as if Lukács were defending the narrow party doctrine of socialist realism which was developed by Joseph Stalin and Maxim Gorky and promulgated by A. A. Zhdanov, but Lukács' views were much more tolerant, if not always directly stated. Not only did he argue against the reduction of literature to propaganda, he also defended certain bourgeois writers whom he called 'critical realists', the most well-known contemporaneous example being the German novelist Thomas Mann. Basically, in contrast to the theorists of socialist realism, Lukács was concerned not only with content, but also with form. In his opinion, the two were dialectically related, as they were for Marx. Later, after the death of Stalin, when a more open discussion of literary matters was possible, Lukács more clearly distinguished his dialectical understanding of realism from orthodox socialist realism, first in *The Meaning of Contemporary Realism* (1958), a critique of modernism that also illuminates Lukács' distinction between critical and socialist realism, and then in *The Specificity of the Aesthetic* (1963), a systematic but less well-known codification of his theory of realism.

As a complement to his critique of modern experimental art forms, Lukács also attempted a critique of modern philosophy, which culminated with the publication of his *The Destruction of Reason* (1952), a lengthy critical overview of 'irrationalism' in the history of German philosophy beginning with Friedrich Schelling. For Lukács, post-Enlightenment philosophers such as Arthur Schopenhauer, Nietzsche and Martin Heidegger were as responsible for the rise of Nazism as the expressionists because, in disparaging understanding and objectivity and promoting the idea of an unchanging human condition, they undermined the basis of collective opposition to fascism, serving the interests of capitalism by contributing to the creation of passive subjects. Like the expressionists, they endorsed a mythological vision of the isolated individual, ignoring the socio-historical processes responsible for that distinctive modern development. In Lukács' opinion, the true philosopher, like the realist writer, must attempt to grasp and reflect the objective world, to serve the democratic interests of humanism. Lukács' posthumously published *The Ontology of Social Being* (1976), which he laboured unsuccessfully to complete in his final years, was to have systematized his views on the matter.

Informing the different phases and projects of Lukács' career is a developing interest in holistic methodologies that is motivated by a profound concern with overcoming the alienation of the modern world. At first, in his largely metaphysical and pessimistic pre-marxist work, Lukács tends to deploy a holistic approach that is based on establishing a normative ideal totality by which to judge his subject at hand. Occasioned by the author's own tragic sense of estrangement and nostalgia, the ideal totality typically takes the form of a lost organic community or an absolute literary form, both of which are juxtaposed with the modern dissolution of art and the increasing anarchy and chaos of modernity. The result is often an unusual combination of sociology and metaphysics. The most well-known instance of this peculiar approach appears in *The Theory of the Novel*, a philosophical and historical study of the novel's origin and development. In this intensely lyrical work, Lukács idealizes the Greek epic, from which, he claims, the novel descends. Following the lead of Hegel, he argues that the epic form is the representative genre of an organic and stable world, of an intrinsically meaningful social totality in which individuals feel at home. Without exhibiting a conscious sense of time, change or alienation, it arises out of and gives expression to a closed, homogeneous world of innocence, community and immanent meaning, giving form to a metaphysical totality of being in which there is no conflict between self and world, essence and life, subject and object.

With the onset of the individualism and relativism of modernity, however, the favourable social conditions necessary for the production of the epic are undermined. As a result, the epic is transformed into the novel, the representative form of a world emptied of intrinsic meaning and value, a world of insecurity, contingency and eternal homelessness in which individuals live tragically estranged from one another, painfully aware of the gap between what is and what ought to be. In an elegiac tone, Lukács proceeds to develop a stark contrast between the classical epic and the modern novel, pointing out that the form of the latter is marked by a growing concern with irony, self-reflection, time and individual psychology, especially the sense of disillusionment and unfulfilled desire. Although he dimly sees some hope for a renewed epic in Dostoevsky's works, Lukács finally renders a negative judgement on the novel, 'the epic of an age in which the extensive totality of life is no longer directly given, in which the immanence of meaning in life has become a problem, yet which still thinks in terms of totality' (1971b, 56). Having evaluated the novel's historical development in terms of its increasing inability to grasp and represent the totality of its world, Lukács famously concludes that 'the novel is the epic of a world that has been abandoned by God' (88).

In his first marxist work of political theory, *History and Class Consciousness*, Lukács exchanges such metaphysically tinged views of totality for a more materialist understanding of holism, revealing a new sense of optimism. Inspired by a Hegelianized version of marxism, he argues here that the developing class consciousness of the proletariat is favourably positioned to overcome the alienation of the modern world, which is now more explicitly described as a result of the rise of capitalism. The intellectual means by which it can do so is the dialectical method, a materialist approach to the study of society whose main objectives are to grasp the concrete totality of capitalism, to understand its historical development, and to project the likely course of its future progress. Based on Marx's assumption that the social relations of every society form a whole, it strives for a systematic mediation between all the seemingly autonomous social and material entities of the modern world, working against the superficial empirical sense of fragmentation endemic to capitalist societies, combining theory and practice. In political terms, the dialectical method also discloses the underlying but often obscured fact of capitalism, namely that it is not a natural or necessary state, but a historical condition that is sustained by social relationships. It thus provides the proletariat with the opportunity to realize its full human potential, to become conscious of itself as an active agent in the creation of history.

For Lukács, such a holistic dialectical awareness is the necessary precondition for the revolutionary transformation of society, and the great irony is that the very material conditions of capitalism itself allows for the possibility of this revolutionary develop-ment. The key assumption behind this view is that the commodity form is 'the central, structural problem of capitalist society in all its aspects' (1971a, 83). Accompanied by such social phenomena as the division of labour, the rationalization of the work process and extensive bureaucratic control, the commodity form is initially responsible for the alienation of the proletariat because it separates workers from the finished products that they produce. Objectifying the proletariat, it reduces them to the status of commodities, since they are forced to sell their labour to survive. The commodity form also destroys the organic social bonds that characterize pre-capitalist societies because it conceals the labour that goes into its production, transforming human beings into passive consumers. The result is that social relationships become mystified; they take on the appearance of things, assuming a kind of unreal or phantom objectivity (reification). The proletariat, in turn, becomes more and more contemplative, as they are filled with the sense of isolation and detachment. Estranged from themselves, they become subject to the debilitating illusion that capitalism is the natural order of things, their sense of space prevailing over their sense of time. Most importantly, they lose their ability to grasp society as a whole.

For Lukács, however, this condition is only temporary. It is characteristic of societies that are only partially dominated by the problem of commodities. In the modern world, where the commodity form has finally permeated capitalist society in its entirety, the proletariat has a new centralized position because the social structure of capitalism is now completely based on the exploitation of labour. According to Lukács, if the proletariat could only become conscious of itself as a commodity, they would of necessity become conscious of the structure of society as a whole. In doing so, they would overcome reification and regain the conscious sense of freedom and creativity proper to humanity. They would realize, in other words, that capitalism is a set of social relations between people and thus subject to change. If acted upon, such a revolutionary consciousness would make the proletariat both the subject and object of history because, in striving to transform the objective material conditions of capitalism, the workers would be putting theory into practice, overcoming their subjective sense of alienation as they create the classless society.

Although Lukács subsequently critiqued some of the assumptions behind this optimistic portrait of the proletarian revolution, he later indicated that *History and Class Conscious-ness* at least rightly 'reinstated the category of totality in the central position it had occupied throughout Marx's works' (1971a, xx). Lukács might have also indicated that it re-established the importance of the category of totality for his own work, not, however, as some kind of idealized norm, but as a guiding objective for a flexible materialist methodology concerned with conceptualizing the concrete moment of capitalism. As with Marx's works, this dialectical materialist understanding of totality, which is always linked to furthering the ends of the socialist revolution, occupies a central position in the writings that follow *History and Class Consciousness*. It is the substance of Lukács' more orthodox political work on the thought of Lenin, who 'always saw the problems of the age as a whole' (1997, 10), and it is the implacable standard against which he critiques modern philosophical trends such as existentialism (see Lukács 1948).

More significantly, Lukács' dialectical materialist understanding of totality is also the basis of his approach to aesthetics. As he explains in 'Art and Objective Truth' (1954), a true work of art is a carefully wrought 'reflection of life in its total motion, as process and totality' (1970, 39). In other words, it is an objective representation of society that discloses the underlying laws governing its structure and development. Far from being a mere photographic reproduction of the real world, it is the product of an intellectual and artistic process of selection and arrangement in which content is shaped into a unified form. Consequently, the defining feature of Lukács' realist aesthetic is a distinctive synthesis of the particular and the general, the accidental and the necessary, appearance and reality. As a 'concrete totality', it attempts to present, in compressed form, a microcosm of society as a whole. Its social function, as in the case of the dialectical method, is to combat the alienation and fragmentation of capitalist society by providing 'a truer, more complete, more vivid and more dynamic reflection of reality than the receptant otherwise possesses' (36).

As Lukács more fully explained in two memorable essays, 'Narrate or Describe?' (1936) and 'The Intellectual Physiognomy in Characterization' (1936), a totalizing reflection of reality is dependent on the use of narrative and 'typical' characters. Narration allows for the depiction of the dynamic and contradictory character of reality. At its best, it reveals society to be an ongoing historical process. 'Typicality', on the other hand, allows for the mediation between the general and the particular. When used properly, it combines a regard for the individual traits of characters with a simultaneous recognition of their various class and social positions. Through such a technique, Lukács explains, realist writers manage the difficult task of revealing the stratified totality of society that the reflection of objective reality requires. Taken together, typicality and narration allow for the overall possibility of a complete dialectical presentation of reality in art, which for Lukács is best exemplified in the classic 'historical' novels of Sir Walter Scott and Honoré de Balzac, as well as in the later novels of Leo Tolstoy and Thomas Mann.

To this dialectical theory of realism, Lukács adds a holistic view of literary forms in which the category of totality is equally prominent. Instead of narrowly focusing on literature in-and-of itself, Lukács develops a more comprehensive critical practice in which literary forms are correlated with the historical developments out of which they emerge. The most celebrated example of this materialist approach is *The Historical Novel*, whose ambitious goal, as Lukács states in the Foreword, is 'to show how the historical novel in its origin, development, rise and decline follows inevitably upon the great social transformation of modern times; to demonstrate that its different problems of form are but artistic reflections of these social-historical transformations' (17). In accomplishing his objective, Lukács demonstrates that the origins of the historical novel in Scott and Balzac lie in the revolutionary crises of the early nineteenth century, when people all over Europe suddenly became conscious of the fact that their own existence was historically conditioned (19–30). Lukács' contention is that the novel realistically reflects this general 'historical consciousness' through its concern with narrative development, social conflict and representative characters.

After the failure of the proletarian revolution in 1848, Lukács argues, realism lapses first into naturalism and then into formalism, both of which lose their sense of totality as capitalism regains and extends its control. Like realism, naturalism focuses on objective description, but it does so without a narrative sense, presenting random empirical details, succumbing to what Lukács calls 'description' or 'reportage'. It is further distinguished from realism in that it depicts human beings as victims of cataclysmic forces beyond their control. Formalism, on the other hand, in Lukács' account, is marked by a growing solipsism, as indicated in such movements as symbolism, expressionism and surrealism. Like naturalism and its relative impressionism, it focuses on accidental details, but it adds a greater concern with interiority, with the random flow of consciousness. Its typical technique is montage or some kind of spatial form. In each case, Lukács explains, an alienated vision of humanity is developed. The realistic novel's dialectical understanding of society as continuously shaped by human labour is exchanged for an illusory world of lifeless autonomous things no longer under human control. In place of the objective world of realism stands a subjective world of fragmentation. History becomes a backdrop, time appears to stand still and narrative falls by the wayside. An existential rather than a historical sense of humanity begins to emerge.

To account for these various traits historically, Lukács argues that they are symptoms of reification, once again linking the concerns of *History and Class Consciousness* with his aesthetic theories. In his opinion, both naturalism and formalism are shaped by the logic of commodity fetishism. Just as the mystified appearance of the commodity form conceals its basis in the exploitation of labour, so do naturalistic and formalistic works obscure the underlying reality of their time. For this reason, Lukács condemns both movements, claiming that they capitulate to capitalism through their various efforts to undermine objective representation. For this reason also, in *The Meaning of Contemporary Realism*, Lukács criticizes modernism, noting that its rejection of history and its elevation of style and allegory mark a further breakdown of narrative, as well as a further intensification of subjectivity (see 1963, 17–46). Lukács, in this regard, is no crude determinist. While he links literary forms to historical conditions, he finally accords a great deal of emphasis to the theoretical ability to overcome those conditions, the key to which, in the case of fiction, is the totalizing perspective of narrative, the literary equivalent of the dialectical method. Ultimately, this emphasis on striving for totality, which is linked to a humanist concern with overcoming alienation, is the main theme of Lukács' marxist work.

As persuasive and influential as Lukács' defence of totality may be, many subsequent theorists, directly or indirectly, have attempted to call it into question. In the 1960s, for instance, Louis Althusser's structural approach to marxism opposed the kind of humanism that Lukács advocated, stressing the so-called 'epistemological break' separating the young humanist Marx from the older scientific Marx. In the 1970s, the poststructuralist Jean-François Lyotard critiqued totalizing 'master narratives', even as a more general critical climate questioned whether linguistic reference was possible at all. More recently, with the advent of post-marxism in the 1980s and 1990s, theorists like Chantal Mouffe and Ernesto Laclau have questioned the traditional view of class consciousness on the grounds that it does not do justice to the complexities of culture, gender, race and ethnicity. A further problem discrediting this view in the minds of many is its link to the notion of a Leninist 'vanguard' leading the way of the masses.

Whatever the limitations of his thinking may be, Lukács now occupies an important position in the history of literary theory. Because of his ground-breaking studies on literature and culture, he is a canonized figure in most accounts of the early development of marxist theory. But Lukács is not just a historical relic. He is also important for contemporary theory, especially for the ongoing study of modernism and postmodernism.

Most notable in this regard is Lukács' influence on the wide-ranging work of the leading American marxist critic Fredric Jameson, whose defence of periodization, dialectics, totality, narrative, cognitive mapping and realism is indebted to his study of Lukács (see Bloch 1980, 196–7; Jameson 1971, 160–205; 1981, 13, 50–6; Lukács 1983, 1–8). Through Jameson, Lukács' insights on the relationship between reification and the rise of modern literary forms have had a decisive influence on theoretical attempts to historicize modernist and postmodernist culture. For this reason, Lukács' work is still relevant. In many respects, he has pointed out the way to a materialist assessment of twentieth-century culture.

Mitchell R. Lewis

Further reading and works cited

Bernstein, J. M. *The Philosophy of the Novel*. Minneapolis, MN, 1984.

Bloch, E. et al. *Aesthetics and Politics*. London, 1980.

Corredor, E. L. *György Lukács and the Literary Pretext*. New York, 1987.

— (ed.) *Lukács After Communism*. Durham, NC, 1997.

Goldmann, L. *The Hidden God: A Study of the Tragic Vision in the Pensées of Pascal and the Tragedies of Racine*. New York, 1964.

Jameson, F. *Marxism and Form: Twentieth-Century Dialectical Theories of Literature*. Princeton, NJ, 1971.

—. *The Political Unconscious*. Ithaca, NY, 1981.

Kadarkey, A. *Georg Lukács: Life, Thought, and Politics*. Oxford, 1991.

Királyfalvi, B. *The Aesthetics of György Lukács*. Princeton, NJ, 1975.

Lukács, G. *A modern dráma fejlödésének története*. Budapest, 1911.

—. *Existentialisme ou marxisme?* Paris, 1948.

—. *Studies in European Realism: A Sociological Survey of the Writings of Balzac, Stendhal, Zola, Tolstoy, Gorki and Others*. London, 1950.

—. *The Meaning of Contemporary Realism*. London, 1963.

—. *Writer & Critic and Other Essays*. New York, 1970.

—. *History and Class Consciousness*. Cambridge, MA, 1971a.

—. *The Theory of the Novel*. Cambridge, MA, 1971b.

—. *Tactics and Ethics: Political Essays, 1919–1929*, ed. R. Livingstone. New York, 1972.

—. *Soul and Form*. London, 1974a.

—. *Heidelberger Ästhetik, 1916–18*, eds G. Markus and F. Benseler. Darmstadt, 1974b.

—. *Heidelberger Philosophie der Kunst, 1912–14*, eds G. Markus and F. Benseler. Darmstadt, 1974c.

—. *The Young Hegel*. Cambridge, MA, 1976.

—. *The Ontology of Social Being*. 2 vols. London, 1978.

—. *The Destruction of Reason*. Atlantic Highlands, NJ, 1981a.

—. *Essays on Realism*, ed. R. Livingstone. Cambridge, MA, 1981b.

—. *The Historical Novel*. Lincoln, NE, 1983.

—. *Die Eigenart des Ästhetischen*, 2 vols. Berlin, 1987.

—. *German Realists in the Nineteenth Century*. Cambridge, MA, 1994.

—. *Lenin: A Study in the Unity of His Thought*. London, 1997.

Sim, S. *Georg Lukács*. New York, 1994.

14. Russian Formalism, the Moscow Linguistics Circle, and Prague Structuralism: Boris Eichenbaum (1886–1959), Jan Mukarovsky (1891–1975), Victor Shklovsky (1893–1984), Yuri Tynyanov (1894–1943), Roman Jakobson (1896–1982)

The historical confluence of Russian formalism, the Moscow Linguistics Circle, and the Prague structuralists in the first three decades of the twentieth century acted as one of the most significant and formative influences upon the direction of literary theory and criticism during the latter half of the century. Their various insights into narratology, linguistics and literary interpretation provided later scholars with the intellectual foundations for the structuralist project. Led by such figures as Victor Shklovsky, Boris Eichenbaum, Jan Mukarovsky, Yuri Tynyanov and Roman Jakobson, among others, Russian formalism resulted from the work of two groups of Russian literary critics and linguists, including the Moscow Linguistics Circle (founded in 1915) and the Society for the Study of Poetic Language (founded in St Petersburg in 1916). Russian formalists eschewed the notion that literature could best be understood in terms of such extra-literary matters as philosophy, history, sociology, biography and autobiography. Initially, they employed formalism as a derogatory term for the analysis of literature's formal structures and technical patterns. As Russian formalism's ideology became more refined, however, the concept began to assume more neutral connotations. Russian formalists – as with the Prague structuralists who would champion Russian formalism's critique after their suppression by the Soviet government in the 1930s – argue that literature functions upon a series of unique features of language that allows it to afford the reader with a mode of experience unavailable via the auspices of ordinary language.

Russian formalists refer to these special features of literature as *literaturnost*, or a particular work's 'literariness'. In a 1921 essay, Jakobson writes that 'the object of literary science is not literature but literariness, i.e. what makes a given work a literary work' (Steiner 1984, 23). A Russian-born linguist, Jakobson was professor at the Higher Dramatic School, Moscow (1920–33) and Masarykova University, Brno, Czechoslovakia (1933–9), before emigrating in 1941 to the United States, where he later assumed posts at Columbia University (1943–9), Harvard University (1950–67), and the Massachusetts Institute of

Technology (1957–67). In addition to founding the Prague school of structural linguistics and phonology, his name would later become nearly synonymous with our universal concepts of structuralism as an intellectual movement of considerable influence upon the nature and direction of the twentieth-century theoretical project. For Jakobson, the concept of *literaturnost* underscores the distinctive features inherent in the various discourses and linguistic forms of literature. More specifically, the notion of literariness refers to the internal relations, within a given literary work, among the linguistic signs and signifiers that comprise such formal features of literary study. In *Russian Formalism* (1984), Peter Steiner writes: 'If all literary works were literary, but some at a given moment were more literary than others, it is not an unchangeable essence but a changeable *relationship* among works that constitute literariness' (114). In short, the concept of literariness resides within the relational spaces established by a text's capacity for utilizing literary or poetic language.

Expositors of Russian formalism often ascribe the relational aspects of the formalist critique to Kantian notions of unity, meaning and the organic structure of art. The Russian symbolist Andrey Bely (1880–1934) based his conception of symbolism on Kant's theories regarding the relationship between art and other modes of human experience. In 'The Symbolization of Meaning', Bely profoundly influenced the course of the formalist methodology through his analyses of 'the unity of form and content' and 'the unity of cognition in the forms of experience' (Thompson 1971, 60). While anti-symbolists such as Shklovsky challenged the arguments of Bely and the other progenitors of Russian symbolism, Shklovsky recognized the interpretative value of understanding a given literary work's form in terms of its relationship with the notions of content and experience. Although terminological battles characterized much of early Russian formalism, Shklovsky's 1916 essay, 'Art as Device', provided formalists with a significant touchstone in their quest to establish their own form of intellectual and theoretical unity. Shklovsky's essay advanced a theory of narrative prose in which the author introduced the concept of *priem*, or 'device'. In addition to distinguishing between the aims of literary scholarship and the empirical sciences, the idea of the device afforded Shklovsky with the means for postulating the textual mechanism responsible for the literary structures and effects that distinguish literary modes of experience from the properties of ordinary language. As Jurij Striedter observes in *Literary Structure, Evolution, and Value* (1989), Shklovsky's groundbreaking study of *priem* resulted in 'the thesis that art is nothing but the consistent application and effect of such devices' (23).

Shklovsky advanced Russian formalism's differentiation between ordinary language and artistic discourse by highlighting art's ability to provide avenues of fresh perception that allow us to recognize new dimensions of reality and aesthetic value. Shklovsky contends that art accomplishes this end through its 'defamiliarization' of the world. In addition to revealing the artistic devices that account for artistic effect, Shklovsky hypothesized that this defamiliarizing concept of *ostranenie*, or the 'making strange' of things, finds its origins in literary, as opposed to ordinary, language. While Jakobson, among others, argued that *ostranenie* neglected to account for the artistic essence of poetic language, Shklovsky's analysis of estrangement acted as a defining moment for incipient Russian formalism because of the manner in which it imbued the movement with a significant and much needed sense of intellectual and artistic relevance. Simply put, *ostranenie* provided literary critics with a means for comprehending Russian formalism's goals for understanding the origins of art's creative and transformative vitality. Shklovsky's concept of defamiliarization involves two distinct concepts, including the idea that estrangement challenges conventional notions of linguistic and social perception, thus forcing the perceiver to reconceive his or her relationship with the world. Secondly, *ostranenie* focuses the perceiver's attention upon the literary work, as well as its contingent possibilities for defamiliarization and for undermining the ordinariness inherent in the extra-textual world. As Striedter notes, the innovative and polemical nature of *ostranenie* is underscored by its ramifications in terms of the literary tradition and the concept of canonicity: 'If literature gains and maintains effectiveness only through defamiliarization, once the newly created forms become canonized and thereby automatic, they, too, must be made strange once again. The theory of defamiliarization', Striedter adds, 'flows into a theory of literary evolution as a "tradition of breaking with tradition"' (24).

As with *ostranenie*, Shklovsky's explorations of *syuzhet* (plot) produced a variety of meaningful revelations regarding the role (or lack thereof) of plot in literary works. In a 1921 essay, 'Literature beyond Plot', Shklovsky devotes particular emphasis to works of 'plotless' literature. Shklovsky demonstrates that the dissolution of traditional plot conventions allows for a kind of literary evolution because of the manner in which it forces writers to experiment with new themes and devices. Shklovsky's article yields two significant conclusions in terms of Russian formalism's methodological aims. First, Shklovsky underscores the various ways in which plot experimentation ultimately serves as a catalyst for a given genre's structural evolution – an important aspect of Russian formalism, particularly in terms of the movement's interest in organicism. Second, Shklovsky challenges the boundaries inherent in our understanding of the concept of genre. Rather than functioning as a fixed canon that operates in terms of a set of firm rules and procedures, genre also exists in Shklovsky's schema as a constantly shifting and evolving mechanism. In his own discussions of plot and their structural role in literary works, Tynyanov takes issue with the latter conclusion, especially regarding Shklovsky's comprehension of literary parody, which he perceives as an automatic and comedic device. In his 1921 article, 'Dostoevsky and Gogol: Toward a Theory of Parody', Tynyanov identifies parody as an organic force that – as with *syuzhet* – operates as an instrument for literary evolution because of the way in which parody simultaneously deconstructs its precursory texts as it constructs new forms of narrative.

As one of the most influential formalists of his era, Vladimir Propp (1895–1970) also formulated a system for understanding the operation of literary works based upon a series of functional elements. A professor of philology at Leningrad University, Propp devoted particular attention to the role of surface detail, literary characters and narratological elements in Russian fairy tales. Recognizing that previous efforts at analysing fairy tales in terms of theme and plot had been intellectually fruitless, Propp opted instead to evaluate the tales via the series of character sequences and narrative tropes that characterize their construction. In *Morphology of the Folktale* (1928), Propp emphasizes the abstract structural elements and their textual function in terms of a given work's artistic and aesthetic whole. Propp's important work on behalf of Russian formalism's critical aims cannot be emphasized enough. As Steiner writes, 'On the most abstract level, he conceived of the fairy tale as a narrative about actions performed by certain characters. And it is the actions, and not the interchangeable characters, that count' (1984, 84). By demonstrating the organic qualities of narrative, Propp succeeded in revealing the nature of the generic, structural components of story. Propp's attention, moreover, to the relational aspects of literature finally afford Russian formalism the capacity to establish general laws regarding the conditions and nature of the structural elements associated with narrative. Propp's achievements in terms of Russian fairy tales also provide formalists with the critical means for articulating their programmatic goals and concerns to other schools and their proponents.

As with *ostranenie*, *syuzhet* and Propp's elucidation of various structural elements, Eichenbaum's conception of *skaz* remains among Russian formalism's most significant contributions to literary criticism. A richly textured narrative technique inherent in nineteenth- and twentieth-century Russian prose, *skaz* refers to literary works in which metaphor, theme and point of view function according to the stylistic requirements of oral narration and folk tales. In a 1918 essay, 'The Illusion of the *Skaz*', Eichenbaum offers a detailed discussion of *skaz* as a literary phenomenon, as well as a vehicle for understanding the fundamental nature of plot as a structural element. In addition to defining plot as the 'interweaving of motifs by the aid of their motivations' (in Striedter 1989, 44), Eichenbaum examines the role of the narrator in establishing the tone of a given plot. In an essay on Nikolai Gogol's 'The Overcoat', for example, Eichenbaum explores the ways in which the narrative serves to create distance between the reader and the plot, as well as between the narrator himself and the story's protagonist. The aesthetics of irony in the story demonstrate the manner in which *skaz*'s structural elements exist in a kind of interrelationship that impinges upon the nature of the reader's textual experience. Eichenbaum's postulation of *skaz* exists as a singular moment within the brief history of Russian formalism precisely because of its illumination of the simultaneous roles of such structural elements as linguistics, stylistics, point of view and plot in our consumption and understanding of narrative.

In one of Russian formalism's most significant instances of narratological innovation, Mukarovsky proposed the concept of 'foregrounding', or the act of placing an idea or element in sharp contrast with the other components of a given work of art. Clearly, estrangement or defamiliarization operates as a kind of foregrounding technique that allows readers to perceive the structural nature of literary language. Jakobson, Tynyanov and other formalists accomplish a similar end in their analysis of such structural matters as metre, alliteration and rhyme. As with such fundamental prose concepts as plot and genre, the notions of metre, alliteration and rhyme function as the organic material via which poetry evolves as a literary tradition. In poetry, metre establishes a kind of progressive force that propels the verse, while alliteration and rhyme, on the other hand, serve as regressive elements because of their reliance upon sound repetition. In other words, formalists such as Tynyanov comprehend poetry in terms of these inherently contradictory forces – the former of which contributes to the organic, evolving nature of poetry as a literary tradition, while the latter operates as a constraining mechanism. Foregrounding various structural elements inherent in verse enables critics such as Tynyanov to isolate these narratological components and identify their role in poetry's textual construction. This process also reveals the unifying mechanisms that undergird works of literary art. For the Russian formalists, unity clearly exists as one of the central principles of literary organization.

As with the Russian formalists, contemporary literary critics and linguists clearly owe a historical and intellectual debt to the efforts of the Prague Linguistic Circle, the group of scholars in the former Czechoslovakia who continued the work of the Russian formalists after their suppression by the Soviet government during the 1930s. Led by such figures as Jakobson, Vilém Mathesius (1882–1945), Lucien Tesnière (1893–1954), and René Wellek (1903–95), the Prague structuralists explored the intersections between linguistics and literary theory. As a group, their examinations of language and other sign systems became more specialized and illuminating after they began to absorb the theories of Ferdinand de Saussure regarding the synchronic analysis of language and its semantic functions. In terms of linguistics, the Prague structuralists' most important achievements include the liberation of phonology from phonetics, as well as Jakobson's work on semantics, Mathesius's revolutionary discoveries regarding syntax and Wellek's theories about literary theory and aesthetics. The advent of the Second World War curtailed their activities, which came to a sudden and precipitous halt after the Nazis closed Czech universities in October 1939. Jakobson continued their work in the interim in the United States; the Prague structuralists resumed their activities in Czechoslovakia in the 1950s, only to be interrupted by the pressures of marxist dogmatism. They reformed during the latter half of the 1950s under the auspices of the Soviet-inspired Czechoslovak Academy of Sciences, an organization that witnessed many linguistic accomplishments in the tradition of the Prague Linguistic Circle, especially the discoveries of such figures as Bohumil Trnka (1895–1984) and Josef Vachek (1909–96), among others. The Prague structuralists enjoyed a revival of sorts during the 1990s after the restoration of democracy in Czechoslovakia.

In an essay commemorating the Prague structuralists' pioneering work in 'Phonology and Graphemics', Vachek attributes one of the group's most enduring achievements to the Praguian conception of the phoneme, which has since become a standard phonological term. Jakobson defines the phoneme as 'a set of those concurrent sound properties which are used in the given language to distinguish words of unlike meaning' (14). By high-lighting the nature and function of the basic unit of phonology, the Prague structuralists were poised to emancipate the study of phonology from the more exclusive terrain of phonetics. Phonology involves the study of speech sounds of a given language and their operation within the sound system of that language. In the contemporary parlance of linguistics, the term refers not only to the field of phonemics but also to the study of sound changes in the history of a given language, i.e. diachronic phonology. The Prague structuralists' innovative research on behalf of phonology resulted in new discoveries regarding the problems of written language and orthography, while also serving as a means for highlighting the interdisciplinary connections between linguistics and narratology. The group's work in the 1930s included similar accomplishments in terms of our larger understanding of semantics and syntax. Through his examination of the Russian case system, Jakobson identified the presence of binary oppositions, a concept that would have an impact on our understanding of morphological units, as well as on the course of structuralism. Mathesius is often credited with having postulated the Prague structuralists' sentence-pattern model of syntax, a morphological mechanism that allows for the analysis of the linguistic signs inherent in every communicative speech act.

While many literary historians acknowledge the Prague structuralists' efforts on behalf of linguistic innovation, the group's significant contributions to our understanding of literature and aesthetics merit attention. Felix Vodichka's (1909–) commentaries on the nature of the literary process and Wellek's attempts at formulating general principles of literary study exemplify this aspect of the Prague structuralists' work. In 'The Con-cretization of the Literary Work: Problems of the Reception of Neruda's Works', Vodichka discusses the role of readerly perception in the literary process, a system that he defines in terms of the authorial subject who generates that artistic text and yet another subjectified other, the reader. Recognizing that the socially produced artistic norms of a given era ultimately share in the construction of literary works, Vodichka demonstrates the ways in which readers perceive narratives based upon their own socially and historically contingent moments of being. A signal moment in the early history of reader response and phenomenological criticism, Vodichka's study of perception theories reveals the manner in which the reading process is encoded by the conditions and structural components inherent in the literary experience. 'The higher structure of the artistic literary tradition is always present as a factor organizing the aesthetic effect of the work if it is to become an aesthetic object', Vodichka writes. 'Therefore the work is understood as a sign whose meaning and aesthetic value are comprehensible only on the basis of the literary conventions of a specific period' (110).

Vodichka's study of readerly perception also established several important inroads into our conception of authorship and its place in the construction of literary works. 'Besides the literary work', Vodichka observes, 'the "author" often becomes related to the developing literary structure. Here, we are concerned with the author not as psychophysical being but, in a metonymical sense, as the unity comprised of the works of a particular author in their entirety' (122). As with the Prague structuralists' Russian formalist precursors, Vodichka's conclusions about the interrelationships between authorship and narrative ultimately demonstrate the significant role of unity in the artistic experience. In his various analyses of the general principles that govern literary study, Wellek acknowledges similar interconnections between a given work's structural elements and its capacity for creating unity. 'The work of art is', Wellek writes in *Theory of Literature* (with Austin Warren, 1942), 'considered as a whole system of signs, or structure of signs, serving a specific aesthetic purpose' (141). By accenting the structural devices that characterize the literary experience, the Russian formalists' and Prague structuralists' critique of literature and language inevitably strives to highlight the roles of linguistic signs, artistic unity and literariness that produce our conceptions of narrative. Their discoveries about the nature of linguistics and literary criticism altered the course of twentieth-century textual scholarship and ushered in a new era marked by an interest in narratology and structuralism. The lingering effects of the Russian formalists and Prague structuralists are evidenced, moreover, by the influential scholarly work of such later figures as Roland Barthes, Mikhail Bakhtin and Fredric Jameson, among a host of others.

Kenneth Womack

Further reading and works cited

Bann, S. and Bowlt, J. E. (eds) *Russian Formalism*. New York, 1973.
Chomsky, N. *Current Issues in Linguistic Theory*. The Hague, 1964.
Erlich, V. *Russian Formalism*. The Hague, 1955.
Fried, V. (ed.) *The Prague School of Linguistics and Language Teaching*. Oxford, 1972.
Jakobson, R. and Halle, M. *Fundamentals of Language*. The Hague, 1956.
Jameson, F. *The Prison-House of Language*. Princeton, NJ, 1972.
Luelsdorff, P. A. (ed.) *The Prague School of Structural and Functional Linguistics*. Amsterdam, 1994.
Pomorska, K. *Russian Formalist Theory and Its Poetic Ambience*. The Hague, 1968.
Propp, V. *Morphology of the Folktale*. Austin, TX, 1968.
Shklovsky, Victor. 'Art as Device', in *Russian Formalist Criticism: Four Essays*, eds L. T. Lemon and M. J. Reis. Lincoln, NE, 1965.
—. *A Sentimental Journey: Memoirs, 1917–1922*. Ithaca, NY, 1970.
—. *Theory of Prose*. Elmwood Park, NJ, 1990.

Steiner, P. (ed.) *The Prague School: Selected Writings, 1929–1946*. Austin, TX, 1982.
—. *Russian Formalism: A Metapoetics*. Ithaca, NY, 1984.
Striedter, J. *Literary Structure, Evolution, and Value*. Cambridge, 1989.
Thompson, E. M. *Russian Formalism and Anglo-American New Criticism*. The Hague, 1971.
Tobin, Y. (ed.) *The Prague School and Its Legacy in Linguistics, Literature, Semiotics, Folklore, and the Arts*. Amsterdam, 1988.
Tynyanov, Y. 'Dostoevsky and Gogol: Toward a Theory of Parody', *Texte*, 1, 1921.
Vachek, J. (ed.) *A Prague School Reader in Linguistics*. Bloomington, IN, 1964.
—. 'Phonology and Graphemics', in *The Prague School of Structural and Functional Linguistics*, ed. P. A. Luelsdorff. Amsterdam, 1994.
Vodichka, F. 'The Concretization of the Literary Work: Problems of the Reception of Neruda's Works', in *The Prague School: Selected Writings, 1929–1946*, ed. P. Steiner. Austin, TX, 1982.
Wellek, R. *The Literary Theory and Aesthetics of the Prague School*. Ann Arbor, MI, 1969.
— and Warren, A. *Theory of Literature*. New York, 1942.

15. Ludwig Wittgenstein (1889–1951)

Ludwig Wittgenstein is one of the most important philosophers of the twentieth century, and the most radical and daring exponent of two of its central modes of thought. As a young student of Bertrand Russell, with a Viennese education that included Kant and Schopenhauer, Wittgenstein developed a severe and rigorous exposition of the Frege-Russell view of language and its representational function. This project, published as the *Tractatus Logico-philosophicus* in 1921, undertakes an account of ontology and the necessary limits of ontology as grounded on the triple relation of logic to proposition to fact to the world, and how this relation determines how we ought to think about the capacities and limits of language. The rest of Wittgenstein's life might be described as an incessant struggle against the bewitching power of this earlier vision, a struggle in which the sheer variety of the particular is brought to bear upon the categorical and austere uniformity of the vision embodied in the *Tractatus*.

For literary theorists, the *Tractatus* is important in several ways. Of most general use will be the fact that the *Tractatus* is sufficiently idealistic in its account of language to make the differences and critiques which Wittgenstein will later spell out applicable to other idealistic theories of language as well, from Saussure to Heidegger to Derrida. The relevance of some of these critiques is considered below.

More particularly, the *Tractatus* also attempts to treat the bedevilling problem of self-reference in formal logic – a problem that will again be at the heart of deconstructive (and even New Critical) approaches to philosophical, literary and psychoanalytic thinking. Russell had shown that paradoxes arise whenever a logical system has sufficient generality to talk about itself: it could then represent well-formed propositions that had the structure of the liar's paradox, which if true would logically have to be false, and if false would logically have to be true. Logic could never guarantee its own reliability, and indeed always seemed to hit a point where it seemed decidedly unreliable. Russell had a sort of jury-rigged system to deal with these problems (the 'theory of types', which disallowed such troubling entities as the set of all sets that do not contain themselves: does that set contain itself or not?). But Wittgenstein saw that such problems might bring us to the heart of subjectivity, since they might be paralleled with Kant's account of the inherent elusiveness of the *I*, the seat of first-person subjective experience (which he called 'the transcendental unity of apperception'). To try to intuit your own subjectivity is to objectify it, and therefore to miss it. The subjective self cannot refer to itself – to its own subjectivity. (Hegel would use the constantly frustrated, constantly renewed attempt at self-reference as the engine for the dynamic production of subjectivity itself, and thus inaugurate the continental philosophical tradition.) In the *Tractatus* Wittgenstein parallels the thinking subject face to face with the world it finds to the eye and the visual field. The eye sees everything within the visual field, but it cannot see itself – it is outside of the field it commands. The subject is outside of the world it can refer to, and language is outside of the things it can sensibly talk about – anything it says about itself, Wittgenstein says, is strictly speaking nonsense (as is, he says, the entire *Tractatus*).

Why should language be paralleled with subjectivity? Are the linguistic paradoxes of self-referentiality internally related to the phenomenological paradoxes of subjectivity? For Wittgenstein they are, since 'The *limits of my language* mean the limits of my world' (5.6) The first of the seven major claims of the Tractatus is: 'The world is all that is the case', and what *being the case* means is being a *fact*, not a thing. The cat is not the case; the *fact* that the cat is on the mat may be. Thus Wittgenstein glosses this by saying that the world is the sum of *facts*, not the sum of things, with the further stipulation that 'the world is determined by the facts, *and* by their being *all* the facts' (1.11: first emphasis mine; cf. 4.52). A fact is something that a proposition pictures, and therefore the interface between language and world is a precise one: on the extreme correspondence theory of truth – the so-called picture-theory of language – that Wittgenstein sets forth in the *Tractatus*, the meaning of the sentence corresponds with the fact of the matter (this is Quine's sceptical formulation), and this attention to facts means not that ontology determines language, but that they both share a more basic substrate, which Wittgenstein calls 'logical space': 'The facts in logical space are the world. The world divides into facts' (1.13–1.2).

Wittgenstein admits, indeed he insists, that a paradox of self-referentiality arises immediately if we add to '*all* the facts' that determine the world the *further* fact that these are all the facts. He is thus led to an extreme account of an isolated and proto-existentialist subjectivity which is an unseizable limit condition to language, the eye or self outside of the world that language pictures and which cannot be pictured because everything that can be pictured can be pictured by language. He thus will end by saying that 'There is no such thing as the subject that thinks or entertains ideas … in an important sense there is no subject' (5.631). But this means finally that subjectivity is the deepest of mysteries ('das Ich, das Ich ist das tief Geheimnisvolle,' he says in a 1916 *Notebook* entry, in the midst of a summer in the trenches in battle) since it is not amenable to any discursive analysis: 'what the solipsist *means* is quite correct, only it cannot be *said* but makes itself manifest' (5.62). Because it cannot be said, Wittgenstein will end the *Tractatus* affirming in his most quoted statement, 'Whereof we cannot speak, thereof we must be silent' (7; I quote the well-known 1922 translation of this aphorism).

The *Tractatus* has been much more influential in the history of literature than in literary theory, and one should mention the important role it plays in both Joyce and Beckett's thinking about language. Beckett's *Watt* with its desperately logical main character depicts a Wittgensteinian hero come face to face with his own subjectivity through his attempts to master logical space. Beckett read the *Tractatus* aloud to Joyce when the latter was writing *Finnegans Wake* and a line in *Watt* is almost a direct quotation from the *Tractatus*: 'Do not come down off the ladder, Ifor, I haf taken it away', Erskine jokes, which alludes to Wittgenstein's conclusion: 'My propositions serve as elucidations in the following way: anyone who understands me eventually recognizes them as nonsensical, when he has used them – as steps – to climb up beyond them. (He must, so to speak, throw away the ladder after he has climbed up it.)' (6.54).

The closest analogue in literary theory to the claims of the *Tractatus* may be found in Blanchot: his sense of the alien alterity of the subject, in literary if not in logical space, is similar to the early Wittgenstein's and his account of 'passivity' and infancy (the subject *infantus*, before or beyond language) in the 1960s and after has much in common with Wittgenstein's sense of the subject as a limit of the world. People have naturally attempted to compare the early Wittgenstein with Heidegger's sense of the relation of being and language, but what Russell called Wittgenstein's mysticism – especially in the ethical passages of the *Tractatus* – is considerably closer to the critiques of Heidegger in Blanchot and Levinas than it is to the mysticism in Heidegger himself.

But Blanchot and also Levinas display far more attention to the subjectivity of the other (of *autrui*) than the emphasis on solipsism in the *Tractatus* might seems to give Wittgenstein title to. His later work justifies the comparison, however, since even as it mounts the most powerful critique ever made of the *Tractatus* and the logicist ambitions it arose from, it continues an exploration into the nature of subjectivity and its relation to language that highlights and clarifies the ethical claims of the *Tractatus*.

The most important work by the later Wittgenstein is *Philosophical Investigations*, an unfinished book published posthumously but which comes closest to Wittgenstein's own vision of how he wished to publish his later thought. The fundamental break that *Philosophical Investigations* represents with the *Tractatus* is in its denial that it is the business of language to picture the world. *Philosophical Investigations* sets forth a powerfully non-representational view of language. Language is used for countless things: there are –

> *countless* kinds [of sentence – *Satz*, translated as 'proposition' in the *Tractatus*]: countless different kinds of use of what we call 'symbols', 'words', 'sentences'. And this multiplicity is not something fixed, given once for all; but new types of language, new language-games, as we may say, come into existence, and others become obsolete and get forgotten. (We can get a *rough picture* of this from the changes in mathematics.)
>
> Here the term 'language-*game*' is meant to bring into prominence the fact that the *speaking* of language is part of an activity, or of a form of life.
>
> Review the multiplicity of language-games in the following examples, and in others:
>
> Giving orders, and obeying them –
> Describing the appearance of an object, or giving its measurements –
> Constructing an object from a description (a drawing) –
> Reporting an event –
> Speculating about an event –
> Forming and testing a hypothesis –
> Presenting the results of an experiment in tables and diagrams –
> Making up a story; and reading it –
> Play-acting –
> Singing catches –

Guessing riddles –

Making a joke; telling it –

Solving a problem in practical arithmetic –

Translating from one language into another –

Asking, thanking, cursing, praying.

– It is interesting to compare the multiplicity of the tools in language and of the ways they are used, the multiplicity of the kinds of words and sentence, with what logicians have said about the structure of language. (Including the author of the *Tractatus Logico-philosophicus*.)

The whole of this passage deserves extended comment. Countless kinds of sentences means that there is no *general* form of sentence, nor single structure of niches for the heterogeneous set of forms. (J. L. Austin objected to this claim, but Wittgenstein, more radically determined against systematicity than Austin, believed in the endless possibility of human and therefore linguistic novelty; many of the items on Wittgenstein's list Austin regarded as 'etiolated' or 'parasitic' uses of language, and Jacques Derrida rightly takes the latter to task on this issue.) Wittgenstein insists on a radical multiplicity of language-games. He says that the multiplicity is not fixed or given once and for all and yet at the same time the world that humans inhabit (at a human level) is the world of their linguistic activities and interactions – of their language games. Thus as in the *Tractatus* there is still something essentially synonymous about living in the world and playing language games – there is still a sense in which my language means my world. But Wittgenstein would no longer say that 'the *limits* of language (of that language which alone I understand) mean the limits of my world' (5.62, my italicization). As he says in recantation in the 1928 lecture on ethics: 'The limits of my language? language is not a cage.' And language is no longer something that alone I understand, nor indeed is it the case that *understanding* is the privileged and natural term for our relation to language-games. (This is a good place to contrast Wittgenstein with Davidson and Quine, who begin with a sense of the radical isolation of the human mind from the world around it – an isolation more in keeping with Wittgenstein's views in the *Tractatus* than in the *Investigations*. Wittgenstein's ideas in the *Tractatus* were highly influential on Carnap who was in turn a major intellectual interlocutor of Davidson's teacher, Quine. By the time Wittgenstein was giving the lectures drafted in the *Blue* and *Brown Books*, he was making striking arguments against the existence of what he called 'private languages', a notion of privacy that still survives in Davidson.)

Thus language and the world it inhabits are radically multiple, mutable and free of determination by any epistemological or ontological centre. (Here, Wittgenstein might be compared to the radical empiricism of William James on the one hand – James was perhaps the later Wittgenstein's most important stimulus to thinking, of which more below – and Deleuze on the other, from *Empiricism and Subjectivity* to *A Thousand Plateaus*.)

In the *Tractatus* Wittgenstein had defined the general form of a proposition (*Satz*): 'this is how things stand' (4.5). Like J. L. Austin's constative or locutionary utterance, the proposition wrongly seems the paradigmatic instance of language: a representation of reality. Austin doubts that pure constatives are anything but rare and extreme cases of language use, and suggests that in normal circumstances they are to be met with perhaps only recently and in scientific or technical books. More radical still, Wittgenstein's parenthetical remark on 'the changes in mathematics' means not that maths gives you at least a rough paradigm for the rest of language (this is the logicist or Tractarian viewpoint he now eschews), but that *even* mathematics belongs to a human practice and is itself liable to the sorts of observations and considerations that apply to the countless different language games. This point deserves emphasis, for one of the most important results in mathematical philosophy during the twentieth century was Gödel's Second Incompleteness Theorem, which was a kind of demonstration of the applicability of Russell's paradoxes of self-referentiality to the whole of mathematics of any generalizing power. Wittgenstein, nearly alone among important philosophers of mathematics, had denied the major significance of Gödel's proof, because he alone among major philosophers of mathematics was a thorough-going anti-Platonist: a thorough-going disbeliever in an immutable realm of mathematical truth or falsehood independent of human activity – despite, or perhaps because of, his results, Gödel remained a Platonist to the end. (Even the mathematical intuitionism that he found congenial, while styling itself anti-Platonic, continues to appeal to a Platonic foundation in truth, denying, however, that there may be a truth beyond the possibilities of human construction.) Anti-Platonism characterizes all Wittgenstein's later work, and what we are to notice here is the refusal of a Platonic view of either language or representation. There is no Platonic form of language: there is no canonical mode of representation. Even the propositions of mathematics have a history, and belong therefore to contingency; that history is one of its involvement with human activity and human use.

Wittgenstein's adjurations against the philosophical interest of self-referentiality – adjurations that set him against even in the apparently rigorous mathematical results of people like Gödel – ought to prevent the common misapprehension of Wittgenstein as a kind of genial champion of common-sense – the Wittgenstein put forward most strenuously and most misleadingly by Richard Rorty. Anti-philosophical he may be, but he is not a-philosophical, and his arguments cut sharply at the deepest and most cherished philosophical beliefs. What in particular they cut at – in mathematics as in language as in psychology – is the notion of a governing paradigm, formula, technique, grammar or structure (variously invoked by science, mathematics, logic, linguistics and anthropology) which might provide the rules whereby particular phenomena would arise.

The later Wittgenstein's importance for literary theory is twofold. On a *negative* side, he will unsettle attentive readers coming from a deconstructive or poststructuralist background just as much as he unsettles the Anglo-American partisans of Frege and Russell. The theory of language which various brands of poststructuralism accept is one that continues to see language as largely representational, whether in its ambitions, illusions or aspirations. To show, following Nietzsche, that language constructs the truths and the templates for the truths that it seems to satisfy is still to accept that the major human investment in language is in its representational function. Wittgenstein's tireless denial of the centrality or privileged position of this function cuts deeper than the claims of deconstruction and related poststructuralist theories of discourse, as it avoids their own critiques. This is to say that Wittgenstein denies the most important (although often tacit) claim of poststructuralist theory: that human subjectivity is constituted through the anxious repression of the primal inadequacy of language to represent the very subjectivity that its failure of representation gives rise to. Such a claim arises out of a Hegelian tradition (made central in France by Alexandre Kojève, whose lectures Derrida, Lacan and many others attended) which Wittgenstein came to reject. The multiplicity and variousness of language-games is at the bottom of his rejection of the hypostasis of 'language' at the heart of poststructuralist thought. For Wittgenstein there is no such thing as language, useful as the term is in many contexts. (Similarly, he vexed Russell by denying that there was any such thing as an 'object', though he never denied that there were, say, ink-spots.)

But Wittgenstein's rejection of the hypostasization of language (and a fortiori of language-as-other, of the symbolic order, for example) arises out of a yet more radical view of mental life, a view adumbrated in the *Tractatus*. The later Wittgenstein strenuously denies the usefulness of the appealing notion of a mental state: a state (a feeling, emotion, disposition, etc.) that a mind might be in, and that would belong to a private world separate from the various inaccessible worlds inhabited individually by other minds. (This denial makes him anathema to cognitive psychologists, from Turing on. Turing was Wittgenstein's student at Cambridge, and transcripts of their mathematical disagreements about Gödel, among other things, survive.) Human life, or human subjectivity isn't at bottom for Wittgenstein a way of being but a way of acting. His arguments against the perspicuity of the invocation of mental states and mental contents (what is the content of a state of expectation? of love? of irritation? of intention? of certainty? of knowledge? of self-consciousness? of following a rule? of hope? of anxiety?) rank among the most bracing and powerful passages of his later work. These passages to some extent read like radicalizations of William James: James gives the most fluid and convincing doctrine of the notion of mental contents and states ever propounded, and Wittgenstein goes farther by rejecting the husks represented by the way James formulates his psychological observations and puzzles. James had characterized the privacy of thought as one of its most notable characteristics, but Wittgenstein is concerned to deny this privacy. In a notorious and central passage in *Philosophical Investigations* he writes:

> I can know what someone else is thinking, not what I am thinking.
>   It is correct to say 'I know what you are thinking', and wrong to say 'I know what I am thinking.'
>   (A whole cloud of philosophy condensed into a drop of grammar.) . . .
>   If I see someone writhing in pain with evident cause I do not think: all the same, his feelings are hidden from me. (222–3)

This passage ought to compared to Austin's account of our knowledge of other minds. Language-games are played with others. To have language is to have others: not to *believe in* or to *assume* or to *presuppose* or to *stipulate* others, but to have them in whatever way we have language. Others are: those we use language to interact with. I am no more certain of the meaning of the word *hand* than I am that others exist whom I can touch with my hand.

The result of Wittgenstein's arguments – which by their nature cannot be well-summarized because there is no general doctrine governing them – is to see something like how robust the human psyche is, and yet how fragile that robustness is. Wittgenstein teaches us that we have certainty, but he also teaches us what certainty is, and whatever it is it's not the metaphysical buttress that philosophers have thought it was. Too many people – both admirers and detractors – stop at Wittgenstein's arguments for the psyche's robustness and do not see the fragility that is its obverse. Belonging to the world in countless ways, there are countless ways that the self may be dispossessed from the world, and not just the handful of ways that anxiety about the capacities of representation would designate. There are countless ways of being dispossessed, and therefore the experience of dispossession may itself become endless.

The influential continental thinkers that the later Wittgenstein is in many ways closest to are Blanchot and Merleau-Ponty (heavily influential as they are on Derrida and Lacan respectively). Like them he has a Proustian sense of the unutterable complexity of human experience and of the correspondingly vast region of potential estrangement from experience within experience. That potential for estrangement is already suggested in the *Tractatus*, when he says that there is no such thing as a thinking subject, that the philosophical self does not belong to the world but is its limit. Even in the *Tractatus* the self has nothing to do with mental states, and the array of experience is everything we possess, and therefore everything from which we are dispossessed. Later this will mean that the world that we live in is the only world we have; the things that we do are all that there is to do, and outside of this is not some Platonic or Kantian world to which the subject belongs, but a place where subjectivity is experienced without being able ever to consolidate itself as an independent entity. This is where Wittgenstein is like Proust, in the heartbreaking sense that he gives of the endless variety of the world which nevertheless is not various enough to cure the final isolation and impoverishment of a self all the more estranged from the world as it belongs all the more wholly to it.

William Flesch

Further reading and works cited

Baker, G. P. and Hacker, P. M. S. *An Analytical Commentary on Wittgenstein's 'Philosophical Investigations'*. Oxford, 1983.

Bouveresse, J. *Wittgenstein Reads Freud*. Princeton, NJ, 1995.

Cavell, S. *Must We Mean What We Say?* Cambridge, MA, 1976.

—. *The Claim of Reason*. Cambridge, MA, 1979.

—. *A Pitch of Philosophy*. Cambridge, MA, 1994.

Crary, A. and Read, R. *The New Wittgenstein*. London, 2000.

Dreben, B. 'Quine and Wittgenstein: the Odd Couple', in *Wittgenstein and Quine*. eds R. Arrington and H. J. Glock. London, 1996.

Floyd, J. 'Wittgenstein on 2, 2, 2 …', *Synthese*, 87, 1991.

Friedlander, E. 'Heidegger, Carnap and Wittgenstein: Much ado about nothing', in *The Story of Analytic Philosophy*, eds A. Biletzki and A. Matar. London, 1998.

Goldfarb, W. 'Metaphysics and nonsense', *Journal of Philosophical Research*, 22, 1997.

Hallett, G. *A Companion to Wittgenstein's 'Philosophical Investigations'*. Ithaca, NY, 1977.

Kripke, S. *Wittgenstein on Rules and Private Language*. Cambridge, MA, 1982.

McGuinness, B. *Wittgenstein, A Life*. Berkeley, CA, 1988.

Monk, R. *Wittgenstein: The Duty of Genius*. New York, 1991.

Quinney, L. *Literary Power and the Criteria of Truth*. Gainesville, FL, 1995.

Shanker, S. *Wittgenstein and the Turning Point in the Philosophy of Mathematics*. Albany, NY, 1987.

Staten, H. *Wittgenstein and Derrida*. Lincoln, NE, 1984.

Wittgenstein, L. *Tractatus Logico-philosophicus*. London, 1961.

—. *On Certainty*, eds G. E. M. Anscombe and G. H. von Wright. Oxford, 1969.

—. *Philosophical Investigations*. Oxford, 1972.

—. *The Blue and Brown Books*. Oxford, 1975.

—. *Wittgenstein's Lectures on the Foundations of Mathematics: Cambridge, 1939*, ed. C. Diamond. Ithaca, NY, 1976.

—. *Remarks on the Foundations of Mathematics*, eds G. H. von Wright, R. Rhees and G. E. M. Anscombe. Oxford, 1978.

—. *Notebooks, 1914–1916*, eds G. E. M. Anscombe and G. H. von Wright. Oxford, 1979.

—. *Zettel*, eds G. E. M. Anscombe and G. H. von Wright. Oxford, 1981.

16. Martin Heidegger (1889–1976)

Martin Heidegger succeeded Edmund Husserl as the major philosopher of the phenomenological movement. Both Heidegger and Husserl regarded phenomenology as the very beginning of true philosophical inquiry: attention to phenomena is directed to what appears, to what is given or shows itself. Phenomenology, therefore, tries to approach the question of being without assuming any prior interpretation of what being is. It does not, for example, ask whether there *are* such beings as numbers, essences or meanings, for such questions presuppose that we know what it means to exist. Both Husserl and Heidegger were far more concerned with understanding what it means to say that something exists.

Whereas Husserl regarded his own philosophy as a radical beginning that broke free from all previous philosophies, Heidegger insisted on the necessarily historical location of any metaphysics. Heidegger's work is usually divided into two broad periods, although there is much debate about the significance of the divide. The first period, prior to the *Kehre* or 'turn', is dominated by Heidegger's *Being and Time* (1927). The main focus of *Being and Time* is '*Dasein*' (or 'there-being'), a term which resists translation precisely because Heidegger was trying to avoid the language of subjectivity, consciousness or man. Such terms, Heidegger argued, presupposed a starting point. What we need to do is begin our questioning in a more radical manner, and not assume that we know what 'mind', 'subject' or even 'thinking' mean. Heidegger begins *Being and Time*, just as Husserl began his phenomenology, with the very problem of beginning: how is it possible to begin metaphysics without presupposing some founding being? According to Heidegger we ought not begin by asserting the existence of some original *being*. Rather, we should assume nothing more than the *question* of being. This is why Heidegger refers to '*Dasein*' rather than man, consciousness or subjectivity. *Dasein*, or 'there-being' is just that point from which being is questioned. *Dasein* is just that being who is capable of asking the question of being. The problem with the history of metaphysics is that it has traditionally begun by assuming the existence of some founding being – such as matter, or man, or subjectivity. Instead of assuming some foundation, *Being and Time* provides an analysis of the being who questions and lays foundations. The first part of *Being and Time* is therefore taken up with what Heidegger refers to as 'existential analysis'. This existential analysis does not begin with a theory or definition of what *Dasein* is but examines all the ways in which we experience ourselves, and then asks how our existence is possible.

Heidegger is, quite justifiably, included in the tradition of existentialism. Although his work needs to be differentiated from other existential thinkers, notably Jean-Paul Sartre, he does insist on the general existentialist claim that we ought not to assume some founding essence that has certain immutable qualities that are then played out in our actual existence. Sartre insisted that our existence precedes our essence: our being is the outcome of the decisions and events of our life. Heidegger argues that it is our essence to 'ek-sist', or to 'dwell' with being (1998, 248). He rejected the traditional opposition between essence (the pure form) and existence (the actualization of that form). Instead, 'ek-sistence' is the essence of a being who is nothing other than its relation to being. By existence Heidegger refers to all the ways in which we live in the world: our past, the complexity of our present, and our directedness towards a future. This is why he uses the term 'Dasein' rather than 'human'. Humans are usually defined as rational animals – beings within the world who then have reason, beings who have an essence. Dasein, by contrast, is not a being who bears certain qualities (such as reason or humanity); Dasein exists by disclosing a world or being.

Heidegger begins his analysis of Dasein by inquiring into how it is possible to form the question of being. What would be the appropriate point from which to ask the question of being? Heidegger insists that we can't just seize upon any specific thing and then ask what being is in general. Being is not a generalization that we gather from examining a collection of beings, for we need to have some understanding of being beforehand in order to say that any single thing 'is'. So being must have a meaning that cannot be reduced to just collecting all the different uses of the word. We cannot, Heidegger insists, begin the question of being from the beings that we have as present before us. Instead we should begin the question of being by looking at the being who is asking the question. For only if we understand how it is that we form the question of being will we be able to understand just what it is we are questioning. The being who is capable of questioning being is Dasein and examining Dasein is an existential analysis. An analysis of Dasein is existential because unlike other beings or entities Dasein 'is' only in so far as it relates to a world. Dasein is not a self-present substance that then comes to know a world. Dasein is always already being-in-the-world.

It might seem that Heidegger's inquiry is circular: we begin to answer the question of being by asking about the being who is asking the question. But Heidegger insists that this circularity is felicitous. The idea of an argument that would not be circular presupposes that there could be some pure point outside our own existence from which we could begin our inquiry. Against this Heidegger insists on the 'hermeneutic circle' of all questioning: we must assume some starting point for the question, but the course of questioning will also illuminate and redefine the point from which we began. And so against the assertion of Dasein as yet one more founding being Heidegger insists that Dasein is a way of interrogating the formation of philosophical foundations. The history of metaphysics has been dominated by the assertion of some grounding presence – such as mind, God, matter, spirit or man – but what has been forgotten is the question of just how such a grounding presence is possible. Heidegger will, in contrast with this tradition of ground laying, ask about Dasein and how Dasein is capable of questioning presence or being. (How is it possible to interrogate grounds or foundations; how is it that we can move beyond any simple assertion of presence and question being?) The fact that we can ask the question of being tells us something about being and how being is made present. It is only possible to ask the question of being if we are already presented with beings. Initially, then, the question of being always begins from a relation to specific beings. We can only ask about being in general because we already exist in relation to the beings of a world.

Heidegger also insists that the question of being is not some empty category imposed by philosophers upon the world. Our questioning power is crucial to the very possibility of having a world. In order to have a world at all, in an everyday sense, we must already have some understanding of being. We have an implicit, but not theoretical, concept of being.

In our day-to-day lives, however, we live this 'pre-ontological' relation to being in the mode or beings that are *Zuhandenheit* or ready-at-hand. Our relation to the world is not objectified or cognized as a subject–object relation. On the contrary, our world is present in the form of projects, purposes, activities and a totality or horizon of meaningful activity. Before we think of the world as simply 'being', and before we understand ourselves as subjects who *know* a world, our world is a world of projects and purposes. Our original relation to the world is one of care or concern (*Sorge*) and not knowledge. The world is not an object to be known but a totality of involvements and possibilities. Indeed, as Heidegger insists, the very being of the world, the fact that we have a world that we take as existing, is grounded upon a prior purposeful 'projection': an understanding of our world as there for our possible becoming and activity. It's not that we have a world that we then come to care about and add values to. Rather, it is *from care* (or some concerned relation) that our world is given. This is why an existential analysis must be primary. Before we can ask about the being of the world we need to understand the ways in which this world is already given in everyday existence. And the condition for any world being given is the concerned existence of *Dasein*.

Heidegger therefore describes a number of what he refers to as existential categories. These categories describe not this or that particular world or *Dasein*, but the very possibility of any world. These categories are not culturally relative; they are possibilities of existence for any world at all. It would not be possible to exist without the categories of care, mood, being-with-others or 'thrownness'. For example, any *Dasein* at all is always 'thrown'. We are not born as individuated subjects who then take on a history, language and culture. On the contrary, we exist only through our specific historical and cultural locale; we are 'thrown'. We are already given a specific set of possibilities for existence. But these are *possibilities* (and not determined attributes). And so alongside the category of thrownness, Heidegger also insists on the category of 'care'. We can only have a 'world' at all with the overall category of care. Care is the way in which we are always directed towards a world and our future projects. A world is never a meaningless object or matter but is always this world at this time with these possibilities. (Even the seemingly blank world of scientific description is possible only because of scientific projects and aims.) Our world is not some blank data to which we add values; there is no world other than the one disclosed through our purposes and projects. Care – a concerned relation to what is other than ourselves – is an existential category, something that would structure the existence of any possible *Dasein*. The world of 'reality' or 'theory', Heidegger insists, is only possible once we have abstracted from the world of everyday concerns, and this world that responds to the look of theory is itself the outcome of specific concerns (the projects of epistemology, science or observation). Initially and for the most part, Heidegger insists, we relate to the world, not as objective matter that is there to be known, but as a meaningful totality given through this or that mood. (And so mood or 'attunement' is another existential category.)

The question then arises, of course, as to how we move from this involved and concerned relation to the world, to the objectifying theoretical attitude – such as science or philosophy – where the world is perceived as inert presence (or *Vorhandenheit*) for a disengaged viewing subject. Heidegger has two ways of answering this question. The first way is his description of the emergence of the objectification of the world in its inauthentic manner. For the most part we dwell in the world in a mode of involvement and concern. We are, therefore, not aware of the *being* of the world, for we are always caught up with specific beings. However, it is precisely this everyday involvement with beings that usually comprises an inauthentic understanding. We imagine that the world is simply 'there' quite independent of our relation to it or our existence. Because we are so involved in an object world, we don't see the world as specifically *ours*. More importantly, Heidegger argues, we don't see it as a *world*. We think we just encounter objects, despite the fact that in order to perceive any single object an entire world must be presupposed. Any single thing is understood, Heidegger insists, only from within a totality of meaningful projects. If, for example, I perceive a hammer, then I already have all the meanings of what a tool is, what building is and what activity is. In everyday understanding, then, Heidegger insists that the world – or what is nearest to us – is precisely what we do not see. I see identifiable things only because I live as being-in-the-world, but it's this totality of meanings that makes up my world that I do not see. Philosophy, or the theoretical attitude, has also according to Heidegger 'passed over' the understanding of the world. So if Heidegger insists that everyday existence already bears within it the tendency to objectify its world and forget its constitutive involvement, he also makes this claim regarding philosophy and science. Because these disciplines are concerned with knowing and interrogating the world, they forget that there is a world of meaningful projects and concerns before we come to ask the question of being or 'reality'. When the scientist or philosopher asks about being she isolates a being as a separate object devoid of meaning and purpose. But, this way of looking, Heidegger argues, presupposes a world. For in the theoretical attitude I regard the thing in a particular way, abstracted from its everyday use and meaning. I regard it in the manner of 'mere thing in general'.

This is why, Heidegger insists, philosophy has historically asked the question of being *ontically*. It has always taken a particular being or thing (the ontic) as the beginning of its inquiry, but it has not asked *how* it is that we come to know or experience things. This would be an *ontological* question: not the question of this or that being, but the question of how any being at all can be. When we question the world we have tended to do so from the standpoint of those beings around us. We imagine that consciousness or the subject is just one type of being that must then come to know other types of beings, such as objects. We 'pass over' the *ontological* dimension of the world. Heidegger therefore wants to insist on the difference between the ontic and the ontological: the ontic dimension is that of specific beings; the ontological is what allows any being to appear. If I ask you what being means and you point to an object and say, 'This is a being', you are giving me an ontic definition. You are just offering me another being. But if you try to explain what being is *as such* you give me an ontological definition. You might say that being is spirit, or God, or matter. Now Heidegger insists that these sorts of answers, despite their efforts, are still *ontic*; they still define being by pointing to some particular being. An ontological definition would not just point to a present being, but would account for the very possibility of being or how things become present. How is it that we say that something *is* at all? According to Heidegger it is only when we really question the very possibility of being that we are capable of thinking at an ontological level. In *Being and Time* Heidegger tries to think both *Dasein* and world at an ontological level. *Dasein*, for example, is not a thing but is an *existence* that is directed to what is other than itself. The *world* properly considered is *ontological* – rather than ontic – because it is not some *present* thing but that horizon through which things appear.

The world is what enables any thing to come to presence. In order to experience a thing I must grasp it through some understanding – 'as' this or that specific thing – and from some mood or comportment. This is so even if I relate to the thing in a theoretical manner, for here I take the thing as 'mere object' and my mood is one of 'mere looking'. All being is therefore given from some world, and the question of being is possible only because we exist in a world in the manner of involved concern (being-in-the-world). If we think of the world ontically (as a collection of things) we don't really understand what our world is. For the world is not a set of objects we encounter; the world is a meaningful totality of other persons, history, projects, languages and practices. The world is a totality of understanding that is not itself a thing; it is what makes any thing possible. The world is not just what is immediately seen; it is what is presupposed in any act of looking.

However, it's precisely because our everyday involvement is so concerned with beings that we fail to really ask the question of being or the world properly. We merely take one form of being – the being of objects – and then use this understanding to question being in general. Metaphysics has largely been caught up in this failure of the question of being, for it has always answered the question of being by deciding upon some specific being as always present and grounding – the being of the subject, of God, of matter or the idea. (And the thought of this grounding being has always taken the form of an object: we imagine consciousness to be a type of thing, or God to be the highest being.) But Heidegger also describes an *authentic* emergence of the question of being. In his later work Heidegger had isolated certain moments in the history of philosophy and certain forms of art and poetry that opened the possibility for an authentic question of being, even if these possibilities were not taken up. Kant, for example, asked how metaphysics was possible. In so doing he *almost* disclosed that we are beings capable of questioning our world, and so we are not self-present 'subjects' (Heidegger 1990). Certain poets, such as Hölderlin, also described the emergence of the world through language and concern (Heidegger 1971). And ancient Greek philosophers had not yet reduced being to mere objectivity (Heidegger 1984). But Heidegger nevertheless argued that the authentic question of being had generally been forgotten. In his later work Heidegger spent most of his time rereading the history of metaphysics to see how being had been forgotten. In *Being and Time*, though, Heidegger describes the ways in which the authentic question of being might emerge from everyday existence or being-in-the-world.

Heidegger describes the emergence of the sense of ownness and authenticity through a specific mood or attunement. While all our activity is undertaken in a certain mood, such that we never view the world in an empty and objective gaze – for this would still be a specific mood – there are certain moods that disclose our relation to the world. They enable us to see our world *as a world*. Heidegger looks at anxiety or *Angst* as that mood *within* the world that enables us to becomes aware of the world in general. In anxiety, as opposed to fear, I am in a state of dread but there is no specific object of my anxiety. I may *fear* an earthquake or a plane crash, but in this case my worldly mood is directed to, and caught up in, an object. I am still within the general horizon of life's meaning. In anxiety, however, my concern has no object. Because of the absence of any specific object to which my concern might be directed, I am brought up against my relation to the world in general. I am no longer immediately involved with my world, relating to this or that specific being. I have the sense of a relatedness towards the world – that there is some 'thing' that I dread – but there is also *nothing* as such that I fear; my anxiety has no specific being as its object. In fact, anxiety often occurs when the world breaks down. In everyday existence I accept the meaning of my world, without that world being specifically *mine*: I catch the bus, do my job, go home and pay my taxes. Anxiety might enter my world, however, when such meaning is lost: if on my way home I see a destitute woman whose very existence discloses the 'comfort' of my world, or if there is some natural disaster that disrupts the rhythm of everyday life. In such cases I may no longer 'have' a world unselfconsciously. The world seems no longer mine or homely, but not because I have some other world or object in view. I am no longer caught up in the meaning of my world. I am brought back from being absorbed in the world of everyday things, and so the very specificity or limit of my world is made apparent.

In *Being and Time* Heidegger has three ways of describing the ways in which *Dasein* becomes aware of its existence or becomes authentic. In the mood of anxiety, I feel my difference from the world without relating to any specific object. I don't know *what* I fear. But Heidegger also describes the call of conscience; here I become aware of existence not through the world, as in anxiety, but through my own being. In conscience my 'morality' is silenced and I am called to decide. This occurs when I realise that my world has been decided not by myself but by the 'they'. If, for example, the government I have elected engages in a war I don't approve of, or if I see a film that foregrounds the contingency of my moral codes, then I realize that the world is, or has been, constituted by a meaning that *I* did not decide. The voice of conscience, then, does not repeat internalized values. On the contrary, it silences received values so that we are thrown back on our own decision. The very 'silence' of conscience can disclose my everyday moral axioms as derived, given or empty. Authentic conscience for Heidegger lies in *not* hearing the voice of everyday morality. It is because there is no given and immutable morality that I can hear the silent voice of conscience; in *not* telling me what to do, or in saying nothing, conscience 'calls' me to decide. Finally, *Dasein* can also emerge from inauthenticity – where it merely under-stands itself as a thing – through being-towards-death. If I truly know that I am going to die then I am forced to confront the specificity and finitude of my lifespan. Inauthentically, I imagine that I will get around to doing things 'some day'; I will give up smoking, donate to charities and quit being unreliable. But if I accept that my death is imminent and truly possible, and that no one can die for me, then I am compelled to decide on my existence. If I am going to act I must do so within this life which is wholly mine. And because my lifespan is finite there are only so many possibilities for me; I must decide and act resolutely.

What Heidegger describes through the three 'existentials' of anxiety, conscience and being-towards-death, is the opening of a world-transcending attitude from within the world. (Heidegger does not just assume that there is a properly transcendental attitude that philosophers ought to adopt. Rather, he shows how any attitude, including the attitude of metaphysics, emerges from a concerned relation to, and understanding of, the world.) For the most part we are concerned with objects, and don't pay attention to the horizon of meanings and purposes that constitute the world in which those objects appear. For an object is only perceivable *as* this or that specific thing because there is a system of meaning and understanding within which it is located (a world). In anxiety, however, this horizon of meaning and the totality of purposes breaks down. Anxiety is that existential mood that discloses the very possibility of existence in general. In anxiety I am no longer caught up in my immediate and purposive existence, and I am brought up against existence in general: that there is a world and that it is not exhausted by the horizon and meaning of my specific existence. In being-towards-death, I am brought back to the specificity of my existence. If I am conscious of myself as one who will die at a certain time, then I am brought up against the particularity and finitude of my existence. Only certain possibilities and projects are open to me. I can act, inauthentically, as if there were no specific limit to my life – as if, all things were open and possible indefinitely. Or, I can act authentically, aware that death inscribes a limit to my life. I live for this amount of time at this point in history, and I must face that limit and undertake my projects accordingly.

Heidegger extended this notion of historical resoluteness and the authenticity of the decision in the work and lectures that followed *Being and Time*. In particular, he suggested that the practice of philosophy and the German university needed to be recalled to its own possibilities (Heidegger 1959). It is this aspect of his work that has attracted criticism from philosophers and political theorists who believe that Heidegger's philosophy bears more than a contingent relation to Nazism. It is an uncontested fact that Heidegger did join the National Socialist movement. The more contentious issue is whether Heidegger's manifestly non-political works, in particular *Being and Time*, are tainted with either Nazi ideology or philosophical tendencies that would support such an ideology. Ostensibly, *Being and Time* and Heidegger's work on this history of philosophy strives to think at a level that is pre-political, not concerned with specific cultural or historical values, but with the essential factors that would make such values possible. The issues surrounding Heidegger's politics and its relation to his philosophy are extremely complex, not least because Heidegger saw his entire philosophical project as disengaged from any anthropologism or any theory of values. He was not, he insisted, offering a moral definition of man, humanity or values. Rather, he was trying to understand how such grounding concepts emerge in the first place. How is it that we have come to think of ourselves as subjects who relate to the world? How is it that we think of ourselves as having a specific and self-present essence? How did the human or subjectivity come to function as a grounding moral and metaphysical concept? For an existential analysis will show that the human cannot be the beginning of a metaphysical inquiry, precisely because the very concept of the human is an effect of the entire history of western metaphysics and a series of embedded decisions. This is why Heidegger insisted that his distinction between authenticity and inauthenticity was not a moral distinction. Moral concepts and values, such as those of humanism, are only possible because we are beings who exist, or who can decide on the meaning of our world. The opposition between authenticity and inauthenticity is not a distinction between values but describes the ways in which we think of the origin of values. And so Heidegger was critical of many of the philosophies of his time that argued that the world is constituted through systems of values. What this left out of account, Heidegger insisted, were the deeper questions of how there is a world in general and how ideal forms, such as values, are presented. And so on the one hand, Heidegger's work is placed *before* any politics, for Heidegger is not concerned with this or that political system of values but how it is that we came to think of the world in terms of valuation, quantification and calculation. On the other hand, this critique of value philosophy and his broader critique of the fall of metaphysics into merely technical questioning do seem to resonate with the conservative philosophies of his time. What characterizes Heidegger's work as a whole is just this difficult relation between the supposedly 'primordial' questions of philosophy and the 'merely' anthropological or political questions that Heidegger sets himself against.

Death and anxiety, with the ownness or authenticity they allow, are explicitly 'existential' themes in Heidegger's *Being and Time* which might seem to have little to do with the vast amount of his later work criticizing the history of metaphysics and the forgetting of the question of being. But a clear distinction between Heidegger's early work on *Dasein*'s existence and his later work on the history of being is not possible. A connection can already be seen in the complex relation between authenticity and inauthenticity. Much of Heidegger's language in *Being and Time* would seem to suggest that there is something lamentable or morally culpable about the 'fall' of *Dasein* into inauthenticity. But a closer look shows that Heidegger sees the inauthentic as an essential possibility of being. His use of moral language therefore raises complex ethical questions. If there is no pure origin and if being is initially given in a 'fallen' and ontic understanding, then the attainment of authenticity will not be a simple retrieval of what is proper. Authenticity requires that we recognize that we are essentially distanced from being, or already fallen. For Heidegger, *Dasein* is initially and originally fallen: that is, we undertake our day to day existence without a consideration of being and without an attention to the horizon of our world that makes any being possible. But this is because of the very character of being. We never perceive or apprehend being in general; we only encounter this or that being with this or that meaning. It is because being never presents itself as such that we tend to answer the question of being with this or that already presented being. In anxiety, however, we are brought up against the very possibility of specific and presented beings. We only have present beings because we have a world – a general horizon of meanings and purposes through which any being is given. If that horizon of meaning is disrupted then we can become aware that any present being is always grounded upon that which is not present: the general comportment or relation to existence that constitutes our world. We only have beings because we anticipate some world within which each specific being can then be located. The condition for a being, then, is some 'fore-having' or anticipation of being in general. Each being is therefore effected through *transcendence*, or a *relation* of existence towards a world. When our 'world' no longer coheres (as in anxiety) then we become distanced or estranged from beings. But this authentic moment of anxiety must emerge from an initial and inauthentic involvement in the world. The 'fall' into the everyday attitude that is oblivious of being is no accident or mishap. We can only ask the question of being because we have already been presented with beings.

The problem with the history of western metaphysics has been that it has not recognized the essential fallenness of *Dasein* or the essential concealedness of Being. Philosophers have defined being as though it were simply present for viewing, like any other object. What we need to recognize, Heidegger argues, is that for any being to be present, it must have been presented. This means (a) that it emerges from non-presence, (b) that this emergence occurs through time and (c) that this presented being will therefore never be fully present. When we ask about being, then, we should not seize upon this or that presented being, but should try to think or disclose the very possibility of presentation in general. In *Being and Time* Heidegger takes this essential possibility to be time. Time is not some subjective form through which we view being (for this would locate time 'in' the subject). Nor is time some objective container, as though beings were located 'in' time. For the very notion of a being – as that which remains present – is already a temporal notion. Time is neither subjective nor objective; it is only through time that the relation between subject and object is possible. Heidegger, therefore, goes one step further than Kant. Kant had argued that in order to think of any being at all we must presuppose time, and that time was therefore an *a priori* condition for the knowledge of being. But Heidegger points out that these terms – *a priori* (what is prior) or condition (what is already given) – are already temporal. It's not that we need to *presuppose* time to think of being; being *is time*. *Dasein* is, therefore, not a subject or consciousness who then temporally constitutes the world, as though *Dasein* 'had' temporality as one of its forms. *Dasein* just is temporality: an existence or projectedness towards a future from some past.

When *Dasein* takes itself as an already presented being, placed within time, it understands itself inauthentically. And this parallels any metaphysics that asks the question of being as though being were a presence to be reached or encountered by a questioning subject. When *Dasein* recognizes that it is nothing other than the temporal movement of its own existence, then *Dasein* has the possibility of acting authentically. Similarly, metaphysics ought to question being with an awareness that being is not something present lying passively in wait for the question. Being will always be determined according to the form of the question. Only in recognizing the constitutive force of the question, as a way of existing towards the world, will metaphysics be authentic or responsible. Being *as such* is not given; being is that which 'gives' beings. To answer the question of being is always to offer some particular understanding of being. And this understanding is also anticipated by the question. If, however, we are brought to the awareness of *Dasein* as just that being who can question being, then we are also brought to the event of ontic-ontological difference. We always begin our inquiry through some specific being (the ontic), but there is one type of being that is capable of relating not just to this or that being, but to being in general (the ontological). For the most part, metaphysics has answered the ontological question (of Being) through an ontic understanding (a specific being). But there is one being (*Dasein*) that offers an opening into the ontological, and this is *Dasein* in so far as *Dasein* can *question* being. If we *can* ask the question of being, then this shows that we have the capacity to think beyond this or that given (ontic) being and think the possibility of being, or how it is that we are given any being at all. In *Being and Time* Heidegger had privileged the questioning power of a *Dasein* aware of its historical locatedness and authentic possibilities.

In his later work, Heidegger focused less on the questioning power of *Dasein* and more on the general movement or history of being. But just as his early existential analyses had stressed that the fall into inauthenticity was no accident, so his critique of western metaphysics acknowledges that there is no pure origin to which thought might return. Metaphysics is at once the question of being, but the very emergence of the question must also have already determined being in a certain way and from a certain world. We can never, then, arrive at some ontological ground that is fully disengaged from its ontic origins. And this means that philosophy is *most fallen* or most blind when it has failed to attend to the essential fall or blindness that renders it possible. Heidegger, therefore, insists that philosophy is never a pure and objective theoretical view from nowhere. When it does understand itself as pure *theoria* this is because it has substituted its own specific relation to the world, for a determination of the world in general. Heidegger therefore sets himself two tasks in his critique of metaphysics. The first is *Destruktion*, which examines the history of metaphysical questions and illuminates their points of blindness, the ways in which they have already decided on the nature of being. The second is his positive task of reformulating the very grammar and logic of metaphysics to allow the question of being. In the phase of *Destruktion* Heidegger will show how the terms of a question or text undermine the explicit aims of that text. The clearest example of this is his attention to the visual metaphors that ground philosophy. Words like *theoria* and *eidos* are tied etymologically to looking. The word 'idea' has come to mean – particularly in idealism – the complete and self-present grasp of identical being. But if we think about looking or appearing more deeply, we realize that we can only look at something that is other than ourselves. Looking is a relational term, and describes a directedness to what is not immediate and already given. Metaphysics, however, has been decided on the determination of a 'look' that is at one with itself, a look that is not relational but is a complete and self-present self-appearing. Heidegger wants to take these terms of presence back to their original world-relatedness. Before the metaphysical look of the self-present idea, there must have been a look directed towards a world. We can only think the pure self-regarding look of theory *after* the look that relates to what is other than itself. Heidegger goes through western philosophy looking at a number of terms – such as logic, the subject, idea or *techne* – and shows how these concepts emerge from an original world-relatedness that becomes objectified and forgets its specificity and locatedness. (*Logos* originally meant a saying-gathering *of the world* but has now become reified into a 'logic' that operates independent of any being; *subjectum* originally referred to the content or foundation of a judgement but has now come to mean the 'subject' that can know and ground himself; *eidos* was originally a look at what was given, now the 'idea' has come to mean that which determines all experience and givenness; and *techne* was originally a practice or art for ordering the world but in modernity has become a technology to which all practices and purposes are subordinate.)

There is a conservative and nostalgic aspect to Heidegger's thought, and this is disclosed in his positive prescriptions for the future of philosophy and thinking. Much of Heidegger's later work was taken up with retrieving the question of being from its history of translation away from its Greek origin. Heidegger imagined that through poetry we could confront the very emergence of our world. While everyday language repeated words as so much adequate and ready-made material, poetry reopened the *relation* between word and world, allowing us to retrieve the very possibility of thinking. But Heidegger also anticipated some of the more radical themes of poststructuralism. If it is the case that we only encounter beings and can never think being in general, then this means that thought is essentially ungrounded. Any attempt to think the origin of being will already be caught up in a world of specific beings. The origin can be thought only after the event. Metaphysics cannot have some proper ground or origin, for any offered ground would be the outcome of philosophical grounding. Metaphysics can only be responsible, then, when it recognizes the 'abyss' of thinking. There is not a ground or presence that is then presented to a knowing subject. Rather, there 'is' presencing, from which being is given and which then enables the possibility of the metaphysical question.

Claire Colebrook

Further reading and works cited

Dreyfus, H. *Being-in-the-World: A Commentary on Heidegger's Being and Time, Division 1.* Cambridge, MA, 1991.
Heidegger, M. *An Introduction to Metaphysics.* New Haven, CT, 1959.
—. *What is a Thing?* Lanham, MD, 1967.
—. *What is Called Thinking?* New York, 1968.
—. *Identity and Difference.* New York, 1969.
—. *Poetry, Language, Thought.* New York, 1971.
—. *The Question Concerning Technology and Other Essays.* New York, 1977.
—. *On the Way to Language.* San Francisco, 1982.
—. *Early Greek Thinking.* New York, 1984.
—. *Kant and the Problem of Metaphysics.* Bloomington, IN, 1990.
—. *Basic Writings*, ed. David Farrell Krell. San Francisco, 1993.
—. *Basic Questions of Philosophy.* Bloomington, IN, 1994.
—. *Being and Time.* Albany, NY, 1996.

—. *Pathmarks*, ed. W. McNeill, Cambridge, 1998.

Macann, C. (ed.) *Critical Heidegger*. London, 1996.

Macomber, W. B. *The Anatomy of Disillusion: Martin Heidegger's Notion of Truth*. Evanston, IL, 1967.

Polt, R. *Heidegger: An Introduction*. Ithaca, NY, 1999.

Sallis, J. (ed.) *Reading Heidegger: Commemorations*. Bloomington, IN, 1993.

Taminiaux, J. *Heidegger and the Project of Fundamental Ontology*. Albany, NY, 1991.

Wolin, R. (ed.) *The Heidegger Controversy: A Critical Reader*. Cambridge, MA, 1993.

17. Antonio Gramsci (1891–1937)

Antonio Gramsci's significance in critical theory largely rests on *The Prison Notebooks*, which details the politics of culture from within a marxist framework, but one that escapes economic determinism and respects the complex, mobile and contradictory dynamics of social interaction. His writing is a fundamental touchstone for postwar left reconsiderations of culture, particularly those that reject high-low culture distinctions, but Gramsci's widespread influence has often come at the cost of abstracting his terminology from the larger context of his work and historical crises that impelled its shape. Gramsci is frequently called on to authorize new critical trajectories, but rarely comprehensively read in ways that think through the impetus for his work – proletarian revolution. Because *The Prison Notebooks* were written while Gramsci was isolated within a fascist jail, published posthumously and had to wait until 1971 for the first major English translation, this selective reading partly comes as a result of interpretations formed by the post-1960s retreat from class as an integral category and western revolution as a foreseeable outcome. But the degree to which critics quote or interpret Gramsci outside of, or in contravention to, his historical context and concern about the relation of the Communist Party to the disempowered is the extent to which these citations become either ornamental or self-aggrandising.

Born in rural Sardinia to an Albanian-Italian clerk and local mother, Gramsci grew up in poverty after his father was imprisoned for embezzlement. Moving to industrialized Turin on a university scholarship, Gramsci ended his study after ill health, financial distress and increasing involvement in socialist politics and journalism. As part of *L'Ordine Nuovo's* (*The New Order*) editorial collective, he focused on the labour militancy of the 1919–20 Turin Factory Councils, which organized workers by their workplace rather than trade, and seemed to be an Italian equivalent to the Soviets that helped catalyse the Russian Revolution. When management occupied the factories and the government intervened, the movement was defeated and the Italian Socialist Party split. On one side, Gramsci and others formed the Italian Communist Party (PCI), while, on the other, Mussolini organized the far right Fascist Party, which later occupied the government. During the early 1920s, Gramsci was sent to Moscow and Vienna to represent the PCI in the Communist International (Comintern), where he became actively involved in debates about international left strategy. Returning to Italy in 1924 as head of the PCI, he was elected senator during Mussolini's rise to dictatorship. Arrested shortly thereafter, Gramsci was given a political show trial and sentenced by a fascist judge to twenty years' imprisonment. In jail, he began keeping notebooks on cultural and political issues, the work that his reputation largely depends on. This history is crucial to approaching Gramsci's *Prison Notebooks*, since it contextualizes their motive and form.

Although university trained, Gramsci is perhaps unique among this encyclopaedia's subjects for not writing within or for the academy. Typical of the left autodidactic tradition, Gramsci's writing, in its journalistic and carceral phase, does not look to university debates, readers or protocols of presentation. *The Prison Notebooks* exist to reflect on severe political defeat, the crushed worker's movement that set the stage for the rise of Italian fascism amid an international containment of revolutionary movements. There is little in his writing about economics, since he takes the analysis of capitalism's physics as definitively stated by Marx. Instead, he investigates the relation of culture to politics in order to ask: why did not the revolution spread beyond Russia; what prevents the transition to global socialism; and how does Fascism maintain power? Gramsci's self-critical investigation into his own situated experience and commitment to a 'marxism without guarantees', which abandons the sureties of historical teleology, makes his work especially resonant for progressive critical theories that attempt to address the left's increasing marginalization amid the dominance of insurgent conservatism after the 1960s. Similarly, Gramsci influenced pre-1989 internal critiques of the Eastern Bloc's 'actually existing socialism', like DDR dissident Bahro's *The Alternative* (1981).

The conditions of *The Prison Notebooks*' production pose the challenge of triple encoding for contemporary readers. The foremost difficulty is that Gramsci often resorted to elliptic phrases to confound the prison censors who secured the journals. Sometimes it is easy to reconstitute Gramsci's intention, like the substitution of 'philosopher of action' for 'Marx', but, at other times, it is hard to discern when Gramsci is creating terms to stand in momentarily for traditional marxist concepts or when he is forging new terminology to flesh out concepts that were incompletely or poorly developed in previous marxist writings. A further hurdle is that Gramsci's signposting assumes a reader conversant with nineteenth-century left writings (not only marxist ones) and Comintern debates of the 1920s and 1930s, many of which were either narrowly circulated or never appeared in print form. Without some familiarity with these debates, it becomes harder to capture Gramsci's intentions and interventions. Finally, *The Prison Notebooks* are just that, draft notebooks. Because Gramsci functionally died in prison (he was released to a guarded hospital shortly before collapsing from a brain haemorrhage), he never came close to assembling an authoritative version for publication. While Gramsci was a precise writer who did redraft some sections, a number of his prescient breakthroughs, like the 'Americanism and Fordism' section that analyses modernization and sexuality, is little more than a sketch. Contemporary readers must almost train themselves to read Gramsci intuitively, a task that has frequently led students to rely on the mediation (and agendas) of secondary criticism. As if these hurdles were not enough, the Anglophone readership has only had a portion of the notebooks translated. Though the most frequently used edition, Hoare and Nowell-Smith's *Selections from the Prison Notebooks* (1971), is masterful, it cannot act as a proper substitute for a complete edition, a project now thankfully underway. Despite these challenges to reading him, Gramsci's vocabulary and concepts ground projects like cultural materialism, 'history from the bottom up', Althusser, Balibar and Poulantzas's work on ideology and classes, Birmingham School Cultural Studies, postmarxism, economic debates about postindustrialism/postfordism, and postcolonialism, such as the writing of Said, Spivak and the Subaltern Studies group.

If one theme animates *The Prison Notebooks*, it is the redefinition of the term 'intellectual'. Gramsci rejects the notion that an intellectual is someone endowed with a greater capacity for thought and freedom from material relations. No one is 'unintellectual' in Gramsci's view because everyone has a 'particular conception of the world' and 'line of moral conduct' (Gramsci 1971, 9) even if this sensibility, what Gramsci calls 'common sense', is vague, incoherent or rife with contradictory attitudes. It is not mental brilliance that makes intellectuals, but how subjects achieve the social function of being an intellectual. 'Because it can happen that everyone at some time fries a couple of eggs or sews up a tear in a jacket, we do not necessarily say that everyone is a cook or tailor' (9). Indeed, Gramsci mainly uses *dirigente*, which is poorly translated as 'intellectual' and is better understood as conductor, organizer or, more simply, activist. A fashion magazine writer about cosmetics is no more or less an intellectual (*dirigente*), in Gramsci's sense, than a philosophy professor, since each promotes confidence in the prestige of their object (commodity beauty or abstract meditation). What distinguishes *dirigente* is their varying organic relation to social formations resulting from class, or class-faction, interests. Gramsci differentiates between what he calls 'traditional' and 'organic' *dirigente*, although his terminology is confusing, since both kinds are organic to their respective formations and the difference cannot simply be captured in terms of left–right categories. The traditional intellectual works out of an already existing institutional matrix and mode of social organization, while the organic intellectual emerges from new, oppositional ones. Marxist professors are not automatically organic intellectuals for Gramsci, despite their commitment to anti-bourgeois strategies, because, whatever the left academic's 'local' message, her or his prestige and authority to speak comes from their credentialization within a traditional structure, the university, that continues to aggravate social divisions through the mental/manual hierarchy created by the awarding of diplomas and academic promotion. If the same professor spoke within a 'people's university', which addressed non-dominant groups in ways that did not mimic the traditional university's values of 'excellence', then the scholar would be more 'organic'. One model might be Gramsci's own involvement with the *The New Order*, which provided the Turin Factory Councils with a forum. A 'traditional' journalist-intellectual writing on the strikes would invoke 'objectivity and neutral reportage', while not questioning the links between the newspaper and the factory's owners, but an organic journalist-intellectual would analyse current events in to help create labour confidence in their new modes of interaction. Gramsci's perception that the agents of knowledge emerge from material sites of truth-production is congruent here with Foucault's writings on discursive formations and the creation of disciplines. A second aspect of the organic-traditional distinction is that the more a set of intellectuals becomes embedded within traditional structures, the more they paradoxically believe themselves to be self-defining, even though their self-declared liberation from class (fraction) simply registers what might be called the secret of the 'intellectual-fetish'. Just as Marx began his analysis of capitalism's system of exploitation with the secret of the 'commodity-fetish', Gramsci uses the traditional intellectual's false autonomy to unpack the larger political economy of cultural power.

While Marx only offers a glimpse of what non-commodity relations might look like, Gramsci uses Machiavelli's *The Prince* to illustrate how an organic intellectual might act. Machiavelli's treatise on power is distinctive because 'it is not a systemic treatment, but a "live" work in which political ideology and political science are fused in the dramatic form of a "myth"' (125). Machiavelli broke from traditional formats by writing neither an idealistic utopia nor dry scholastic review. Instead, he composed an advice notebook, but one for a feudal prince he knew was neither ignorant of power-dynamics nor capable of mastering them. Machiavelli's purpose was to publicize these manoeuvres for 'those not in the know' (135), the proto-bourgeoisie who were not yet capable of enacting these tactics but were beginning to confront a moribund feudal society. Machiavelli's representation of the prince was thus a 'concrete fantasy which acts on a dispersed and shattered people to arouse and organize its collective will', where the populace's spontaneous (unorganized) passions were guided to action. This dialectical exchange provides the example for the 'modern prince', which is no longer be an individual (the favoured subject of bourgeois liberalism) but a 'complex element of society' – the (communist) political party (129). Gramsci's trajectory is always from the individual to collective subjects, and the organic *dirigente* is really about groups, not an individual's choice. The party's role is twofold. First, its collective internal operations offer the first glimpses of potential social alternatives, it is a 'concrete fantasy'. Secondly, it engages with popular 'passions' so that the party does not 'traditionalize' itself through bureaucratic, rather than democratic, centralism, rather than the mass, where it could disastrously mistake itself as the historical agent of change and delegate itself as the gatekeeper for deciding the timing of political action. Gramsci believes the party's self-assured isolation was a major cause in the post-1918 revolutionary failures, and, in prison, he recalls Marx's thesis that the educator himself needs education (the *dirigente* must be directed from below).

The question of intellectuals opens the way to reconsider the relation between state and civil society. Gramsci's axiom is that politics is defined by the 'dual perspective' where power arises out of the varying, yet always present, ratio of coercion and consent, violence and persuasion. Gramsci never believes that liberal democracy excludes raw, physical violence (the police, army, punitive legislation) from its arsenal, it has merely become more economical in its use. Close to Weber's claim that the state has a monopoly of legitimate violence, Gramsci believes that rule by oppression is resource-draining and cannot sustain broad-based power over time. For power to be durable it must also be persuasive, educative and work to promote a consensus typified by the acceptance of a common sense, the implicit, unspoken assumption of the everyday and 'naturalness' of civil society and its hierarchies. Gramsci calls this consensus *hegemony*, which he sees as manifested through a three-phased process of group collectivization and strategic alliances. The first is the 'economic-corporate' moment when 'a tradesman feels *obliged* to stand by another trades-man, a manufacturer by another manufacturer, etc. but the tradesman does not yet feel solidarity with the manufacturer' (181). A second 'economic' step is when there is a 'solidarity of interests among all the members of a social class'. Until this point, rule still mainly relies on coercion, but consensual hegemony is achieved when groups 'transcend the corporate limits' of pure economic self-interest and move to an 'ethical-political' phase so that they 'become the interest of other subordinate groups'. When a class (or class fraction) incorporates other social elements so that subaltern common sense, or 'sponta-neous philosophy', becomes protective of the leading class(es), hegemony is achieved. One kind of hegemony is nationalism, whereby the working class support the local bourgeoisie against the interests of far-away workers.

Hegemony does not 'destroy' antagonistic interests, but, in Raymond Williams's phrase, incorporates them, and the 'ethical-political' moment of hegemony is manifested by the rise of a 'historic bloc'. The historic bloc is more than a codeword for class; a bloc is the coalition of social groups, the networks of alliances that can cross class lines. The model

Gramsci draws from is the *Eighteenth Brumaire of Louis Bonaparte*, where Marx described how the future Napoleon III constructed a historic bloc that enlisted the peasantry against their economic-corporate interests, within a regime that included their historic enemies, the Parisian underclass, and was dominated by financial interests. While one fraction usually dominates a bloc, it is also subject to intrinsic pressures arising from trying to keep the constellation of interests pacified. Blocs have these crises of *cultural capital* because their membership is always restless and internally competes for place of preference and right to command the resources that a bloc garners, but a bloc can protectively adapt to economic and political crises because, like parliamentary cabinet reshuffles, it can swiftly reorganize by rehierarchizing its constituent members, perhaps expelling some or including new ones, to respond to changed conditions.

There are immediate advantages of Gramsci's model of hegemony and historic blocs for cultural theory. First, it frees us from a negative model of ideology as false consciousness where dominated groups are simply overwhelmed by dominant ideology, a vertical suppression akin to what Foucault calls the repressive hypothesis. Because hegemony is the complex product of consensus and coercion, it allows us to understand culture as the product of multiple desires and sources of institutional pressures that are not always easily aligned. Since hegemony is as much about getting subjects not to say 'no' as it is for them to clearly say 'yes' to a historic bloc's rule, hegemony can draw in, or articulate, subjects based on aspects of their allegiances in non pre-determined and often highly ambiguous ways. A further advantage to Gramsci's open conception of culture is that hegemony can also describe the relation between intellectuals and the state, a problem that Althusser specifically followed.

Perry Anderson (1976–7) argues that Gramsci's use of *hegemony* is inconsistent throughout *The Prison Notebooks*, which sometimes seems to oppose civil society hegemony to state violence and then sometimes bundles hegemony as an ideological apparatus of the state's armament, to use Althusser's formula. The confusion arises only if one insists, against Gramsci's method, on a scheme of ahistorical, static binarization. Gramsci dissents from the classical view of the state as simply the instrument of the ruling class. Instead, he views the modern state as the 'unstable equilibria' (182) or field of contestation among classes, which is not simply monopolized by the bourgeoisie. Since the state 'integrates' competing interests, it prevents the expense of dominating through violence. Historically, the state was one of Hobbesian violence as the medieval nobility retained power on the basis of its economic-corporate interests. When a nascent group, like the bourgeoisie, achieved the advanced point of the 'ethical-political', it transformed the state into a hegemonic device by having it 'integrate' competing interests and regulate the historic bloc's internal tensions with the creation of a *dirigente* of *dirigente*, the civil servants who help determine what ought to be a bloc's composition.

The state can act as the bloc's glue because it offers various *dirigente* status by investing them with honorifics or licensing, an act that draws the *dirigente* toward the State as the latter increases the former's status within their original group by making it seem as if the *dirigente* are responsible for preserving a group's inclusion within the bloc, a mystification whereby 'political questions are disguised as cultural ones and as such become insoluble' (149). Because the historic bloc state has various kinds of preferment, it is able to lure a social group's *dirigente* away from their original allegiance by offering greater benefits of security and establishment. Gramsci calls this process *transformism* (or passive revolution), when a bloc reorients itself by fusing oppositional elements in order to contain the open expression of class conflict. A recent example of transformism is the post-Thatcher/Reagan phenomenon of liberal opposition parties assuming governmental office only to further the political agenda of their conservative predecessors, a case where 'what is at stake is a rotation in governmental office ... not the foundation and organization of a new political society' (160).

With the concepts of hegemony and historic blocs, Gramsci turns to discuss the kinds of counter-hegemonic tactics, such as the *war of movement* and the *war of position*. The *war of movement* is likened to a 'classic revolution', which uses a swift, decisive strike to topple the state. This kind of attack succeeded in Tsarist Russia because the obsolete state, lacking any compensatory civil society, quickly fell when faced with popular resistance. The situation is more complicated in the West, where states have more and more complex kinds of blocs to call on when faced with crisis. This situation calls on a *war of position*, or an attempt to create a counter-hegemony, like an alliance between the city (proletariat) and countryside (peasants) that would give it more organizational option. For these reason, Gramsci argues that cultural hegemony must exist alongside, but not necessarily before, political rule if a counter-hegemony is to last. Otherwise, any labouring-class rule will be short-lived because it can be easily outflanked like the Paris Commune. Worse yet, a precipitous defeat throws the defeated into the arms of charismatic forces who promise stability and protection. This is Gramsci's theory of the rise of fascism, a situation he generically calls *Caesarism*, where a momentary stalemate between exhausted antagonists creates the opportunity for the rise of a group which has the stamina to lead and dictate the terms to all the opponents. Caesarist solutions can either be reactionary, like the fascists, or progressive, like Cromwell's Commonwealth, but all will need to develop a new bloc or otherwise quickly fall.

Yet, Gramsci also fears that too great an emphasis on the war of position can weaken subaltern resolve and make a group's *dirigente* lose patience and switch sides. Like the dual perspective of force and persuasion, movement and position must work in dialectical tension. As new blocs become stronger they can hazard gambits of movement to further desegregate the solidarity of the traditional bloc. A counter-hegemony can delegitimize the traditional state by creating a crisis of confidence by attracting the old bloc's members so that the old bloc implodes because it can no longer maintain the architecture that covers its competing interests. If the new bloc's *dirigente* refuse to continue acting as the regulators in the same way that the old ones did, then we have a picture of how the state may 'wither away' in a socialist regime. *The Prison Notebooks* did not fully investigate this process of deconstruction. The horizon of *The Prison Notebooks* is the illustration of what a socialist society might be like after it has conquered the bourgeois one. But *The Prison Notebooks* remain Gramsci's *Grandsire*, incomplete because he was not allowed a life long enough to revise it. The task of critical theory today is to build on Gramsci's foundations and imagine what a 'post' *Modern Prince* would contain.

Stephen Shapiro

Further reading and works cited

Althusser, L. *Lenin and Philosophy and Other Essays*. London, 1971.
Anderson, P. 'The Antinomies of Antonio Gramsci', *New Left Review*, 100, November 1976–January 1977.
Bahro, R. *The Alternative in Eastern Europe*. London, 1981.

Buci-Glucksmann, C. *Gramsci and the State*. London, 1980.

Cammett, J. *Antonio Gramsci and the Origins of Italian Communism*. Stanford, CA, 1967.

David, J. A. (ed.) *Gramsci and Italy's Passive Revolution*. New York, 1979.

Fiori, G. *Antonio Gramsci*. London, 1970.

Gramsci, A. *Selections from the Prison Notebooks*, eds Q. Hoare and G. Nowell Smith. London, 1971.

—. *Selections from Political Writings, 1910–1920*, ed. Q. Hoare. London, 1977.

—. *Selections from Political Writings, 1921–1926*, ed. Q. Hoare. London, 1978.

—. *Selections from the Cultural Writings*, eds. D. Forgacs and G. Nowell Smith. London, 1985.

—. *Prison Notebooks*. Vols 1 and 2, ed. J. Buttigieg. New York, 1992.

Guha, R. and Chakravorty Spivak, G. (eds) *Selected Subaltern Studies*. Oxford, 1988.

Hall, S. *The Hard Road to Renewal*. London, 1988.

— et al. *Policing the Crisis*. London, 1978.

Hunt, A. *Marxism and Democracy*. London, 1980.

International Gramsci Society. http://www.italnet.nd.edu/gramsci/index.html.

Joll, J. *Gramsci*. London, 1977.

Laclau, E. *Politics and Ideology in Marxist Theory*. London, 1977.

Luxemburg, R. *Rosa Luxemburg Speaks*. New York, 1970.

Marx, K. and Engels, F. *Selected Works in One Volume*. New York, 1968.

Mouffe, C. (ed.) *Gramsci and Marxist Theory*. London, 1979.

Poulantzas, N. *Political Power and Social Classes*. London, 1973.

Sassoon, A. Showstack (ed.) *Approaches to Gramsci*. London, 1982.

Simon, R. *Gramsci's Political Thought: An Introduction*. London, 1991.

Sorel, G. *Reflections On Violence*. Cambridge, 1999.

Williams, R. *Problems in Materialism and Culture*. London, 1980.

18. Walter Benjamin (1892–1940)

The work of German literary and cultural critic Walter Benjamin is one of the most influential sources for postwar literary, historical and cultural studies. Benjamin studied German literature and philosophy but he also travelled widely in Europe and wrote about European cities, and translated Baudelaire and Proust in the 1920s. Introduced to Zionism in 1912 when he was twenty, this interest was supplemented by a friendship with Gershom Sholem (1897–1982) which he formed three years later and carried on in letter form after Sholem left for Palestine in 1923. Sholem's comments on Benjamin are important (see Smith 1985, 51–89). His marxism was formed by association with the Riga-born communist and theatre director Asja Lacis in 1924 (see Benjamin 1979, 45), who introduced him to Brecht in 1929, for a friendship and influence that lasted the rest of his life. The central event of Benjamin's life was the rejection of his monograph on German tragic drama by the University of Frankfurt when it was submitted as a *Habilitationsschrift* in 1925, which subsequently became his only book published in his lifetime (see Benjamin 1977a). This failure to qualify for university teaching committed him instead to a lifetime of freelance writing and broadcasting, and to being patronized by other members of the Frankfurt Institute of Social Research, such as Adorno and Horkheimer, who nonetheless published his work in the Institute's journal, the *Zeitschrift für Sozialforschung*. It produced work towards a project which Benjamin referred to as the *Passagen-Werk*, which he began working on in 1927, and of which the work on Baudelaire (Benjamin 1973), and the essays 'The Work of Art in the Age of Mechanical Reproduction' (Benjamin 1970), 'Central Park' (Benjamin 1985) and the 'Theses on the Philosophy of History' (Benjamin 1970) are some offcuts.

Benjamin's studies of Goethe, Baudelaire, Kafka, Proust, allegory and surrealism have influenced literary criticism, while his cultural critique has been felt in subsequent work on architectural theory, urban space, photography, technology, film and fashion theory and work on the politics of everyday life and in the concept of 'visual culture'. His work has engaged studies of memory; it has been important for theories of Fascism as a cultural phenomenon; it engaged with the power of war in modern societies in the texts on Jünger (Benjamin 1999, 312–21); his essay on violence (Benjamin 1979, 132–55) has influenced legal theory via Derrida (Derrida 1992). While obviously original, Benjamin's writings can be seen to exist in an active dialogue with Brecht, and with Adorno, who as Benjamin's most important interlocutor had his own positions with regard to committed and autonomous art, and the 'culture industry' most challenged by Benjamin. While attempts have been made to link Benjamin to Heidegger and to deconstruction, the depoliticizing strains of this must not take away from his work's engagement with marxism and the task of thinking culture and politics together. The choice of writers Benjamin commented on as a 'literary historian' aligns him with modernism: his work on the loss of experience and of memory, and on art in the new conditions of 'distraction' identifies him with postmodernist arguments. No contemporary critic working on social or cultural theory has been able to neglect Benjamin, and numerous commentaries and articles – often whole issues of journals such as *diacritics*, *Critical Inquiry* and *New German Critique* – have explicated one aspect or another of a very complex and disparate set of issues.

In what follows, an attempt is made to chart some aspects of his writings – which are still not wholly available in English translation – by looking at the movement in Benjamin between the work on German tragic drama (*Trauerspiel* – 'mourning play', or even 'funeral pageant' – i.e. the Baroque dramas of the German seventeenth century) and the uncompleted work on the nineteenth-century Paris Arcades: in other words, Benjamin's work of the 1920s and of the 1930s. In *The Origin of German Tragic Drama*, Benjamin aligns the concepts of history, allegory and *Trauerspiel* together and reads them in contrast to the dominant literary forms of myth, symbol and tragedy. He takes these as idealizations of destruction, ways of finding imaginary compensations from suffering, and supporting the idea that art has the entitlement to make some total and privileged statement about history and society (Benjamin 1977a, 166, 176). Benjamin's critique of the notion that art can reveal the 'totality' of relationships within society sets him against Lukács. The reading of history in relation to fragmentation that Benjamin works with persists to virtually the last thing he wrote, the 'Theses on the Philosophy of History' (1940), the year of his suicide on the Spanish border to avoid falling into the hands of the Nazis. The 'Theses' are Nietzschean in their aphoristic style and in their subject-matter, which quotes from Nietzsche's 'On the Uses and Disadvantages of History for Life' from the volume *Untimely Meditations*, which is a title with resonances in Benjamin's writing (see Benjamin 1977a, 166). The 'Theses' illuminate the earlier work on the *Trauerspiel*; they also give a rich context for understanding Benjamin.

In these 'Theses', the historian as a 'historical materialist' – working not with any idealist frame of reference, but from a materialist standpoint, but not with the rigidities of

Hegelian-Marxist dialectical materialism – opposes himself to a positivist and idealizing 'historicism'. Historicism effectively devalues the present in favour of a past with which it identifies and feels empathy with, which means it is informed by nostalgia. Its empathy is dangerous because it means siding with the victors – who have, after all, written the history books. (This is Benjamin at his most Brechtian.) Historicism also regards history as a development towards the present in a 'chain of events' so that history is seen as a 'continuum' (Benjamin 1970, 258, 259, 263). Yet the present is also seen, by this token, as transitional, which is again a form of devaluing it (Benjamin 1970, 264). Benjamin resists that narrative of development which degrades both the past, because its function is only to lead towards the present, and the present, because that is inferior to the past and only transitional, by stressing *Jetztzeit* – 'the presence of the now' – which he describes as a moment 'shot through with chips of Messianic time' (Benjamin 1970, 265). The present moment, though one of danger and of crisis, is also marked by what in Derrida's terms might be called *différance* – those elements which do not fit or contribute to the totality, and which also promise a complete reversal of everything, a redemption akin to revolution, breaking with the idea of history as linearity, cause and effect. Benjamin never sees his interest in history as describing historical conditions which have ended. For him 'the great writers . . . [work] . . . in a world that comes after them, just as the Paris streets of Baudelaire's poems, as well as Dostoevsky's characters, only existed after 1900' (Benjamin 1979, 48). Or, to put it in the terms of 1931, in an essay entitled 'Literary History and the Study of Literature':

> 'What is at stake is not to portray literary works in the context of their age, but to represent the age that perceives them – our age – in the age during which they arose. It is this that makes literature into an organon of history; and to achieve this, and not to reduce literature to the material of history, is the task of the literary historian. (1999, 464)

To put these antagonistic things together – the present and the past – is not to conflate but to achieve a new 'constellation', remembering – in a typical Benjamin aphorism, 'ideas are to objects as constellations are to stars' (1977a, 34).

Benjamin replaces historicism's belief in progress and the continuum of history with his vision of the fleeting 'angel of history', who sees not a chain of events but 'one single catastrophe which keeps piling wreckage upon wreckage and hurls it in front of his feet' (1970, 259). Elsewhere Benjamin makes the point 'that things "just go on" *is* the catastrophe' (1985, 50). History under this gaze becomes the record of the usual failures, ruins and fragments, and of the fate of things 'untimely', and allegory, the mode of the *Trauerspiel*, may be most appropriate for it, since allegory, in contrast to the symbol, is the mode which advertizes failed equivalencies and correspondences. Benjamin speaks of the 'majesty of the allegorical intention: destruction of the organic and living – the extinguishing of appearance' (1985, 41). Allegory and melancholy go together; Benjamin discusses Dürer's engraving of Melancholy, where the figure of melancholy sits with unused and unusable fragments at her feet, and where no object possesses a 'natural creative relationship' to the human subject (1977a, 140). Allegory refuses natural relationships; melancholy knows its experience is alienated and that the fragment or ruin is all that survives, and to see history as fragmented, an allegorical and melancholic vision, disallows it from being seen as the march of progress, calls attention to what writing 'history' omits, and allows for the putting together of fragments in a different configuration – a different constellation. 'Melancholy betrays the world for the sake of knowledge', Benjamin writes, meaning that melancholia (like Hamlet's) rejects sensuous immediate knowledge, 'but in its tenacious self-absorption it embraces dead objects in order to redeem them' (1977, 157). Hamlet's interest in skulls will come to mind: this is Benjamin the collector. When Benjamin writes that 'allegories are in the realm of thoughts what ruins are in the realm of things' (1977a, 178) he pairs allegory and ruins and makes thinking allegorical, indirect and committed to hollowing out systems of thought into their opposite, into the non-systematic. The allegorist, then, has a destructive character (see Benjamin 1979, 157–9).

This may be illustrated as when, in correspondence, Sholem told Benjamin that his work, with its Jewish Messianism, would be regarded by marxists as counter-revolutionary and bourgeois, and as simply purveying ambiguities (i.e. as giving no fixed direction). Benjamin replied that his writings, while they might be counter-revolutionary from the Party's point of view, would not, for that reason, be at the disposal of the counter-revolution, but would be 'denatured', 'definitely and reliably unusable for the counter-revolution at the risk that no one will be able to use them' (Sholem 1981, 228–33). Ambiguity and allegory become essential in Benjamin in the effort to 'wrest tradition away from a conformism that is about to overpower it' (1970, 257).

'Untimely' writing will not fit the times, so 'no poem is intended for the reader, no picture for the beholder, no symphony for the listener' (Benjamin 1970, 69). If it did, that would deny the alienated status of the reader and of the author as producer. It would also suggest, considering modern urban space, that it is impossible to find adequate images of the city, when the city itself is nothing but images, and is like nothing but itself. The city becomes Benjamin's topic in a way that shows his indebtedness to the sociologist Georg Simmel, who had written about the new forms of mental life produced by the metropolis, and whose lectures in Berlin Benjamin had attended in 1912 (see also Benjamin 1973, 38). In 'Paris – the Capital of the Nineteenth Century' (1935), often seen as a clue to the unfinished *Passagen-werk*, Benjamin reads Baudelaire, whose poetry shows 'profound duplicity' (1973, 26) as a melancholic and allegorist (1973, 170), as though he inherited from the writers of the *Trauerspiel*, and he emphasizes how (like them) Baudelaire's images possess a calculated disharmony between image and object (1973, 98). Images are no longer expressive; Baudelaire could even say that his goal in poetry was 'the creation of a cliché' (1973, 152). Benjamin sees ambiguity as central to nineteenth century 'high capitalism' and he defines it as 'the figurative appeal of the dialectic, the dialectic at a standstill'. A snapshot arrests time in a standstill: hence Benjamin's interest in photography is symptomatic. 'This standstill is Utopia, and the dialectical image therefore a dream image. The commodity clearly provides such an image: as fetish. The [Paris] arcades, which are both house and stars, provide such an image' (1973, 171). The dialectic appears in an ambiguous figuration, but in the image – which is not the image of one thing – it has been arrested, so that the image can be deciphered (Benjamin recalls how the French revolutionaries of 1830 fired at the church clocks to arrest time in the present (1970, 264)).

The 'dialectical image', which is therefore double, is one of Benjamin's most complex thoughts (Jennings 1987). Adorno who also used the term, thought of the image's doubleness being between its essence and its appearance, which would imply the possibility of making a distinction between the true and the false. Benjamin's method, because it is not caught in Adorno's marxism, is the antithesis of this: it does not imply ideology-critique. It does not work on the basis of presupposing the existence of an empirical truth where criticism frees the mind from illusions. Rather, Benjamin argues that 'sundering truth from falsehood is the goal of the materialist method, not its point of departure ... Its point of departure is the object riddled with error' (Benjamin 1973, 103). The work of art cannot be thought of as something simply to be appreciated for its truth, for, as Benjamin will put it in the 'Theses', 'there is no document of civilization which is not at the same time a document of barbarism' (1970, 258). The image which must be deciphered dialectically is not the image of one thing, but is like a folded fan which can be opened up to reveal something multiple (1979, 75), or, like the photograph, it can, by interrupting a flow of events, show an 'optical unconscious' (1979, 243). As when Benjamin writes that in visiting Moscow one gets to know Berlin (1979, 177), and as with montage the image is overdetermined, revealing both past and present, so this doubleness, being both the marker of present alienated reality as fetish, and its opposite, (something Utopian), can only be seen in the light of redemption. The Paris arcades, nineteenth-century shopping malls, which were made vivid to Benjamin through the 'profane illumination' (1979, 227) provided by the surrealist Louis Aragon's novel *Paysan de Paris*, give an example of a dialectical image: houses and stars together because of the way they are lit (with glass roofs), inside and outside at the same moment. When in the 1920s Aragon saw the Passage de l'Opéra, built in the 1820s, it was as a nearly depopulated human aquarium, the ruins of what Benjamin identified as both a nineteenth-century Utopia and of nineteenth-century capitalism (Benjamin 1973, 157–9; Geist 1983, 117–9). The passages, whose name implies no staying, no lingering, represent unconscious dreams realized in architecture. Commodities viewed in the strange light of the passages possess the reality of being the nineteenth-century's dream-images. The ambiguous status of the commodity appears in its character as fetish: Marx said, discussing fetishism, that in capitalism, relations between people assumed 'the phantasmagoric form of a relation between things' (in Smith, 277). The ambiguous world of the images and of the commodity is for Benjamin the phantasmagoria, possessing 'the sex-appeal of the inorganic' (1973, 166). Benjamin notes how, in Baudelaire, the fetish itself speaks, which, as writing, shows Baudelaire's 'empathy with inorganic things' (1973, 55). There is no getting free of the phantasmagoria, but when the image is at a standstill, within that fetishistic structure may be seen the ruin, like the fragments of the *Trauerspiel* study, to be taken out of the continuum of history, and to be seen in the light of redemption. Indeed, we can recognize 'the monuments of the bourgeoisie as ruins even before they have crumbled' like the Passage de l'Opéra (Benjamin 1973, 176), ruins because they are always phantasmagoric.

Modern experience is the experience of ruins, just as the angel of history sees things as ruins; melancholia works with the ruins of experience, which is a way of implying that experience is now impossible, the thesis developed by Giorgio Agamben, the Italian translator of Benjamin, in his *Infancy and History*. 'Some Motifs in Baudelaire' (Benjamin 1973, 110–21) confronts the loss of experience (*Erfahrung*) in modernity, which includes the loss of a communicable past, the loss of storytelling, and the erasure of memory, all things which threaten or diminish the possibility of a reversal in the present. In urban modernity, under the experience of shock, which Benjamin takes to be definitional for modernity, consciousness is screened so that such experiences do not enter memory, a point Benjamin derived from Freud, so that the experience that dominates is the lived experience of the moment (*Erlebnis*). The overwhelming power of information in newspapers, to comment on which Benjamin turns to Karl Kraus, impoverishes awareness in that it blocks off what happens in the present from possessing a relation to experience.

Storytelling, as opposed to the giving of information, produces a way of thinking that can work allegorically or outside the categories of the continuum of history – a story 'resembles the seeds of grain which have lain for centuries in the chambers of the pyramids shut up air-tight and have retained their germinative powers to this day' (Benjamin 1970, 90). Proust's work recalls the importance of involuntary memory, and the difficulty of its existing in the conditions of modernity, since only 'what has not been experienced explicitly and consciously, what has not happened to the subject as an experience' can become part of involuntary memory (Benjamin 1977a, 114). Benjamin associates the loss of involuntary memory with modernity, and its effect is to produce only silence through the loss of communicable experience (1970, 84). The angel (the messenger) of history is also speechless. A crisis in articulation may be compared with what Benjamin argues about Kafka, whose work reveals the 'sickness of tradition', the power of an inert tradition with, nonetheless, the received authority of truth. The weight of tradition leads to speechlessness, for Kafka belonged, Benjamin says, to a tradition whose truth had lost its transmissibility. 'Kafka's real genius was that he tried something entirely new: he sacrificed truth for the sake of clinging to its transmissibility, its haggadic element. Kafka's writings are by their nature parables. But it is their misery and beauty that they had to become *more* than parables. They do not modestly lie at the feet of the doctrine as the haggadah lies at the feet of the Halakah' (1970, 147). The argument draws on a distinction between the Jewish Halakah as the law, the letter, and the haggadah meaning story, troping, free elaboration. Benjamin's Kafka, who is also autobiographical for Benjamin, is committed to free storytelling at the level of parable – writing 'fairy tales for dialecticians' (1970, 117) – narratives which operate as dialectical images, containing in them the power of the false, the non-true, not narratives illustrating some known doctrine.

In Benjamin the text stands outside its positioning within the historical continuum and memory is not a mechanical recall of something determinate, since through involuntary memory the past comes back in different contexts and can be laid hold of, to be rearticulated with the present. This accounts for so much personal memory in Benjamin, for example his writing of his childhood in Berlin, with the intention to let nothing be lost. Benjamin speaks about drawing a diagram of his life, and thinks in terms of a labyrinth; in another moment he thinks about losing one's way in a city, as though the city (Paris) was a labyrinth (Benjamin 1979, 314, 298). A narrative of personal existence becomes like Borges's 'garden of forking paths', not a linear pattern; memory and the city – both of which confuse temporality – come together as indescribable structures, incapable of conceptualization. While memory becomes more important, it is not clear that it can be memory of anything. This point becomes more and more insistent in Benjamin, as in the 'Theses' he says he 'wishes to retain that image of the past which unexpectedly appears [the power of involuntary memory] to man singled out by history at a moment of danger'. The image is 'the spark of hope in the past' (Benjamin 1977a, 257). Similarly, in what is nearly the last 'Thesis', a fact only becomes historical 'posthumously' (1970, 265), not because it is has a causal relationship to something else. It is born later on, in the present. This power of an afterlife is for Benjamin Messianic.

The need to overcome the power of reactive forces which link tradition – which includes in it involuntary memory – to conformism – thereby making it like Kafka's tradition – motivates Benjamin's most famous essay, 'The Work of Art in the Age of Mechanical Reproduction' ([1936] 1970, 219–53). New technological reproducibility takes art forms out of their placing within a historical continuum. Unless the work of art undergoes reproduction, it can be experienced only as repetition, which is empty; reproduction means change and hence implies singularity, difference.

What withers at this point is the work's 'aura', which gives what Benjamin calls 'the unique phenomenon of a distance'. Bourgeois culture gives to the work of art the appearance of distance – distance in time, distance from the experiences and the situation of people, existing in a world of its own. Although the aura is already disintegrating in urban modernity in the experience of shock (1973, 154), it is kept alive in the concept of the work of art, and it makes visible a mysterious wholeness of objects; it is like a halo, giving to art a cultic authority, or a fetishistic status. Fading of the aura is like the loss of the idealizing symbol within the *Trauerspiel* as the melancholy allegorist reduces everything of the systematic, apparently unified world to rubble. Reproducing the work in different forms and also in different media, in making the aura decay, changes people's reactions towards art, brings them close to it, and compels upon people a new type of attention. Whereas 'art' is supposed to require concentration, to appreciate its aura, now the dominant state in which it can be absorbed is distraction. The art form that best illustrates distraction is architecture, 'the reception of which is consummated by a collectivity [not the single privileged consumer] in a state of distraction'. The modern person now performs certain tasks in a state of distraction, and film is the medium above all which produces the public 'as an examiner, but an absent-minded one'.

The three substantial points here – art coming out of its continuum, the decay of aura and the democratization this implies, and the state of distraction – are reminders of a then contemporary crisis that Benjamin, in 1936, knew he was part of. The work of art which is reproduced endlessly gives the opportunity for a new creation of the spectacle within fascism. It also allows for a new separation of forms of art – into those requiring attention, which can, on account of this, be refetishized, and into those which induce in the spectator or listener only distraction. The 'conservative modernism' that is constitutive of fascism can pretend to be upholding standards and so keep art at a distance, but at the same time fascism makes its appeal by its powers of technological reproducibility (consider the use the Nazis made of the cinema). For Benjamin, the potential of technological reproducibility is to politicize art, not to re-auraticize it, as fascism is likely to do. In the last statement of 'The Work of Art', he accuses fascism of aestheticizing politics and concludes that 'Communism responds by politicizing art' (1970, 244). This gives not only a theory of fascism which connects with Guy Debord's 'society of the spectacle' and makes it clear that fascism is not a cultural as much as a political movement (requiring, for instance, a psychoanalytic inquiry into its appeal), it also at the time led to an engagement with Adorno on the subject of using art (which, for Adorno, meant treating art as though it was something instrumental), and on the differences between committed and autonomous art. Most crucially, Benjamin raises the question of how both art and politics would be moved on if the challenge of the last sentence was taken. Certainly, it implies a redefinition of both contemporary art and politics.

If the aestheticization of the political produces, ultimately, fascism, it is part of a wider aestheticism which is content with surfaces, with phantasmagoria, and finds its apt symbol in the 'flâneur', the nineteenth-century idler in the city, who thinks of himself as separate from the commodity-world, but who is not, for the intellectual is also on sale, and so is also part of commodification (Benjamin 1973, 34). That the flâneur is male has become the subject of studies drawing on Benjamin of women's relationships to the city (Wilson 1991). Benjamin's work probes below surfaces; this goes right back to his essay on Goethe's *Elective Affinities* where he distinguishes 'critique', which he practises, from 'commentary'. The former is concerned with the elusive truth-content, which is not, however, anything determinate, the latter with the subject-matter (Benjamin 1996, 297–8). The flâneur 'who goes botanizing on the asphalt' (1973, 36) in thinking that he can give a taxonomy of city types and of city life, by doing so makes the artificial appear natural – which is the definition not only of what symbolism as opposed to allegory does, but of what ideology does.

Yet the flâneur is also an image for Benjamin himself (1979, 299), for the flâneur also undertakes a trip into the city's past, which is also the city's unconscious, and links, as an idea, to the city's 'passages' as labyrinthine. The flâneur is a figure of melancholy because he can also see the city passages as dead, like a corpse (and he is inside the dead thing), as 'dialectics at a standstill' in the sense that there is no movement there, rather the abolition of movement. 'The devaluation of the world of objects in allegory [the theme of the *Trauerspiel* book] is outdone within the world of objects itself by the commodity' (1985, 34). It is because the commodity allegorizes and as a dead thing invades everything – Benjamin even calls the souvenir a 'relic' – something dead, hollowed out, a fragment (1985, 48) – that the person who looks can be nothing else than melancholic. The allegorist dealt with fragments which had the status of ruins; Baudelaire is the type, for Benjamin, of the flâneur who sees that the commodity now has that status, and has also performed the work of the allegorist. Since the intellectual is also part of the commodity, the sense of death is everywhere. Yet if the commodity brings about this awareness, then it is also doing what the work of the *Trauerspiel* does – it reveals things as needing redemption, not as under the phantasmagoria. To return to the argument of 'The Work of Art in the Age of Mechanical Reproduction', the fantasy of the work of art still possessing its aura keeps the notion of everything being the same; it keeps appearances going. Technological reproduction has the possibility of working like the power of allegory; it breaks down the sense that art, like everything else, still works in a continuing tradition.

Jeremy Tambling

Further reading and works cited

Benjamin, W. *Illuminations*, ed. and intro. H. Arendt. London, 1970.
—. *Charles Baudelaire: A Lyric Poet in the Era of High Capitalism*. London, 1973.
—. *The Origin of German Tragic Drama*. London, 1977a.
—. *Understanding Brecht*, intro. S. Mitchell. London, 1977b.
—. *One Way Street and Other Writings*. London, 1979.
—. 'Central Park'. *New German Critique*, 34, 1985.
—. *Selected Writings Vol. 1: 1913–1926*, eds M. Bullock and M.W. Jennings. Cambridge, MA, 1996.
—. *Selected Writings Vol. 2: 1927–1934*, eds M. W. Jennings et al. Cambridge, MA, 1999.
Brodersen, M. *Walter Benjamin: A Biography*, ed. M. Dervis. London, 1996.
Buci-Glucksmann, C. *Baroque Reason: The Aesthetics of Modernity*. London, 1994.
Buck-Morss, S. *The Dialectics of Seeing*. Cambridge, MA, 1989.
Derrida, J. 'Force of Law: The Mystical Foundation of Authority', in *Deconstruction and the Possibility of Justice*, eds D. Cornell et al. London, 1992.
Eagleton, T. *Walter Benjamin Or, Towards a Revolutionary Criticism*. London, 1981.
Frisby, D. *Fragments of Modernity*. Cambridge, 1985.
Geist, J. F. *Arcades: The History of a Building Type*. Cambridge, MA, 1983.
Huyssen, A. *After the Great Divide: Modernism, Mass Culture, Postmodernism*. Bloomington, IN, 1986.
Jennings, M. W. *Dialectical Images*. Ithaca, NY, 1987.

Lunn, E. *Marxism and Modernism*. Berkeley, CA, 1982.
McCole, J. *Walter Benjamin and the Antinomies of Tradition*. Ithaca, NY, 1993.
Roberts, J. *Walter Benjamin*. London, 1982.
Sholem, G. *Walter Benjamin: The Story of a Friendship*. Philadelphia, 1981.
Smith, G. (ed.) *On Walter Benjamin: Critical Essays and Recollections* Cambridge MA, 1988.
Steinberg, M. (ed.) *Walter Benjamin and the Demands of History*. Ithaca, NY, 1996.
Wilson, E. *The Sphinx in the City*. Berkeley, CA, 1991.
Wolin, R. *Walter Benjamin: An Aesthetics of Redemption*. New York, 1982.

19. Reception Theory: Roman Ingarden (1893–1970), Hans-Georg Gadamer (1900–2002) and the Geneva School

Reception theory may be defined as reflection on the role of the reader in the constitution of the meaning of texts. The philosophers and literary critics discussed in this essay did not, like later critics, consciously describe their work as 'reception theory', nor did they participate in a comparably collective enterprise. Nevertheless, they can be considered as the first generation of contributors to reception theory, in so far as each gives an account of the act of reading a text in which this act plays an essential role in determining its meaning.

The most influential of these accounts has been that of Hans-Georg Gadamer. In *Truth and Method*, he sets out to describe the kind of knowledge produced in the human sciences, which he argues has been misrepresented since the Enlightenment. The fundamental error, in his view, has been to think of the human sciences as analogous to the natural sciences. Since Descartes, scientific research has been based upon the principle that the discipline of reason by method protects against error. The inductive method of the natural sciences, in which laws are induced from the verified results of controlled experiments and predictions made on the basis of these laws, has therefore been the model with which scholars in the human sciences have, more or less explicitly, conceived of their own procedure. For Gadamer, this is a mistake, as the inconsistency of the best attempts to justify the claim to truth of the human sciences in this way suggests. The truth which emerges in disciplines such as literary criticism, history and philosophy is not attained by the kind of method which characterizes the natural sciences.

In Gadamer's view, the first philosopher clearly to understand this was Heidegger. In *Being and Time*, the latter revolutionized the concept of understanding by describing it not as a kind of method which can be applied to the texts which the human sciences take as their objects but as an essential characteristic of human existence as such. Gadamer sets out to develop the significance of this account of understanding for the process of reading and interpretation. The first consequence is that the ideal which characterized historicist accounts of interpretation, such as those of Schleiermacher and Dilthey, namely a purely objective attitude that avoids interpreting the text in terms of the interpreter's concerns, must be abandoned as a fiction. As Heidegger showed, all understanding has a 'fore-structure', or set of already formed experiences, perceptions and concepts, in whose terms the object to be understood appears as such (Heidegger 1962, 192). This is also true of textual interpretation.

Gadamer traces historicist hermeneutics back to the Enlightenment critique of religious tradition, and in particular to its challenge of the dogmatic interpretation of the Bible. In general, the Enlightenment aims to decide the truth or falsity of historical texts by rational principles alone, and without the prejudice which derives from the acceptance of external authority. Gadamer, however, denies that this is possible. He calls it a 'prejudice against prejudice' (1989, 270), by which he means that the opposition of reason to tradition in such hermeneutics is not a self-evident principle but the result of a specific act of judgement, which determines subsequent interpretations. It is, in short, a pre-judgement, or 'prejudice' (*Vorurteil*). Until the Enlightenment, this term did not only have the negative connotation of an unfounded judgement, Gadamer points out, but also indicated a preliminary judgement which may later prove either true or false. A hermeneutics that seeks to give a proper account of the act of interpretation must reinstate the positive connotation of the concept of prejudice and recognize that no interpretation takes place without it. There are, in short, 'legitimate prejudices' and the fundamental question for hermeneutics is how these are to be distinguished from those which critical reason should oppose (277). This question leads Gadamer to the concept of authority. He accepts the Enlightenment distinction between faith in authority and the individual use of reason, but denies that authority is therefore never a source of truth. The Enlightenment distorted the concept of authority, Gadamer argues. It is not a kind of blind obedience, opposed to the free use of reason, but rather is 'based ... on an act of acknowledgement', namely that the other, in a given case, is better informed or has greater insight than oneself. It is of the essence of authority so conceived, therefore, that what he, she or it says 'can, in principle, be discovered to be true' (280). This is the kind of authority that a layman grants a doctor, for example, or an engineer, or that a student grants a teacher. While the former takes the latter's word as that of one better informed than himself in a particular field, he could, in principle, acquire the information necessary to verify its truth.

The most important source of authority to be discredited in the Enlightenment was that of tradition. This also, in Gadamer's view, is mistakenly opposed to reason, since to preserve a doctrine in a tradition is as much a rational choice as to reject it. Tradition is not an inert body of doctrine that must be passively accepted, but rather 'needs to be affirmed, embraced, cultivated' (281). The important aspect of the concept for Gadamer is that, for the finite and temporal beings that we are, tradition, or discourse that comes to us from the past, never simply constitutes an object of knowledge, over against which we stand as knowing subjects, but rather is the very ground in which we stand. 'We are always situated in traditions', he writes, and therefore study traditional materials not as objects independent of us but as elements of the very same process by which our knowledge of them is determined (282). This is why the human sciences cannot be conceived by analogy with the natural sciences, since the latter's object-in-itself simply does not exist in them. Gadamer describes textual interpretation 'less as a subjective act than as participating in an event of tradition' (290), in which the past and the present mutually determine one another. The prejudices or preconceptions which we bring to our interpretation of a text, that is, are determined by our situation at the conjunction of a series of given traditions, and these traditions themselves are developed and altered by our interpretation.

Gadamer's term for the effect of history in understanding historical material is *Wirkungsgeschichte*, or 'history of effect'. His ideal of a good interpretation, that is of one which attains to the truth possible for our finite and temporal understanding, is one determined by *wirkungsgeschichtliches Bewusstsein*, or 'historically effected consciousness'. He describes this as consciousness of the 'situation' in which one interprets, namely a historically determined present with its specific limits. Gadamer calls these limits, which include the interpreter's prejudices, the 'horizon' of his situation. Historicist hermeneutics aimed to reconstitute the author's past horizon and to determine the meaning of the text within that horizon, and without reference to that of the present interpreter. Not only does this suspend the claim to truth of the text – Gadamer compares it to a conversation in which one listens to one's partner only in order to understanding the meaning of his words – but it also wrongly assumes that the present horizon of the interpreter is closed. In fact, Gadamer argues, 'the horizon of the present is continually in the process of being formed', above all by encounters with those of the past (306). In interpreting historical texts in terms of the prejudices determined by our historical situation, we do not merely confirm these prejudices, but test them. In many cases, we discover that the preconceptions we brought to the text are not justified as we read it. This experience of 'being pulled up short' by the text brings to our attention the challenged prejudices and leads us to question their validity (268). Not only do we interpret a text in a way determined by our present horizon, that is, but the past horizon we reconstruct from it also determines that of the present. Gadamer calls this process the 'fusion of horizons', and argues that properly acknowledging and describing it is the task of hermeneutics (307).

Gadamer's views that prejudice is necessarily a part of interpretation, and that such prejudice derives from the interpreter's situation in tradition, have been criticized by neo-marxist scholars such as Jürgen Habermas. The latter argues that prejudices can become the object of rational reflection and thereby no longer function as prejudices. A student who accepts the views of his teacher on authority can, on reaching maturity, reflect upon those views and, if he sees fit, reject them. Habermas writes, 'Gadamer's prejudice for the rights of prejudices certified by tradition denies the power of reflection' (1990, 237). Not only can tradition be rejected in this way, but it often should be, since it imposes itself upon us by force. This criticism, which would be justified with respect to a conservative view of tradition, cannot be applied to Gadamer's theory of interpretation, however, since the latter takes account of it. Tradition, for Gadamer, is a process of conflict between the past and the present, and the kind of ideology-critique that Habermas has in mind is an example of precisely such conflict. Gadamer writes that 'tradition itself is no proof of validity' and must be accepted or rejected on reflection (1986, 286). His point is simply that such reflection does not occur outside tradition, but is necessarily determined by it and constitutive of it. In fact, Gadamer has constructed a comprehensive descriptive theory of interpretation which applies to every act of literary theory and criticism from Leavis to Derrida. While this theory does lead to a certain relativism, in which no single correct meaning of a text can be isolated, it can equally be argued that there is no supra-historical norm with respect to which historically situated interpretations can be described as relative.

Whereas Gadamer's hermeneutics derives from Heidegger's existential account of understanding, Roman Ingarden came to literary theory in working out his relationship to the phenomenology of Edmund Husserl. It seemed to Ingarden that the literary text was a kind of object that could not be given an adequate phenomenological description in terms of Husserl's transcendental idealism. The literary text is neither an entirely ideal object, like numbers or geometrical figures, since it comes into being at a determinate point in time and is subject to certain changes. Nor is it an entirely real object, existing in space and time, since it is comprised of sentences, which are composites of ideal units of meaning. He describes it as an 'intersubjective intentional object', which means that it derives both from acts of the author's consciousness and from the concepts upon which he draws in these acts (Ingarden 1973a, 14). Since these concepts are ideal, the work is available in identical form to an infinite number of readers, and so transcends the consciousness of its author and readers at the same time as it depends upon them.

Ingarden sets out to expound the specific nature of the literary object so conceived. He argues that it is a 'formation constructed of several heterogeneous strata', each of which determine one another and the work as a whole (1973b, 29). These strata he defines as follows: (1) the word-sounds and the higher-order phonetic formations composed of them; (2) the meaning-units and the higher-order sentences and groups of sentences composed of them; (3) the 'schematized aspects' or the ways in which the objects and actions portrayed by the meaning-units are represented to the reader; (4) the 'represented objectivities' portrayed in this way. The literary text is constituted firstly by the word-sounds, which are apprehended as 'typical phonic forms' rather than as concrete sounds, and which 'carry' the fundamental meaning-content of the work (1973b, 37). Ingarden describes the act of meaning something as an 'intentional' act, which means that it is necessarily an act of meaning something in particular, and describes this meant thing as an 'intentional object' or the 'intentional correlate' of the act. The intentional correlates of sentences, in which nouns typically combine with verbs, he calls 'states of affairs'. When such sentences are combined into higher-order semantic systems, such as a novel or a lyric poem, the states of affairs are combined into the represented 'world' of the text. Ingarden ascribes to such texts a 'borrowed' intentionality, since, once complete, their intentional objects are no longer the direct correlate of the author's acts of meaning them, but are, as it were, the trace of these acts. He writes, 'Of the originally intended purely intentional object, there remains, so to speak, only a skeleton, a schema' (1973b, 127).

This schematic quality characterizes the stratum of the objects and actions represented by the meaning-units of the text. These objects Ingarden calls 'purely' intentional objects, since they have no real existence outside the author's initial act of intending them. The essential difference between real and represented objects is that, whereas the former are fully determined, existing in every respect in this particular way as opposed to that, the represented objects of a literary text are characterized by numerous 'spots of indeterminacy', in which their properties are undescribed in some respect (1973b, 249). In the portrayal of a given character in a novel, for example, we may not be told how tall he is, what his voice sounds like, what he does in between the episodes in which his actions are narrated, and so on. The world represented by the literary text is 'only a schematic formation', whose spots of indeterminacy can be filled out by the reader in an infinite number of ways (251). These indeterminacies are partly removed by the 'aspects' of the represented objects presented to the reader. The aspects of an intentional object are 'that which a perceiving subject experiences' of it, as opposed to the object itself, which is inaccessible in its entirety (1973a, 56). In a literary text, a character may appear acoustically, such as Wilfred Owen's sergeant – ' "I takes 'is name sir?" ' – or visually, like Eliot's Princess Volupine, with her 'meagre, blue-nailed, phthisic hand'. Similarly, a scene may be described in meticulous detail, so that we have the impression that there are no almost gaps in the represented space or time, as in certain realist novels, or we might simply glimpse disconnected moments and events, as in certain modernist poems.

Because of the schematic structure Ingarden ascribes to the literary work, he makes a sharp distinction between the work and its 'concretizations', that is the new intentional objects constituted each time a reader performs the act of reading the work. He writes: 'Every literary work is in principle incomplete' and in need of supplementation by a reader (1973b, 251). This supplementation occurs as the reader actively intends the sentences of the text as the objects of his act of reading, so that their 'borrowed' intentionality becomes real again. As a result of this process, many of the spots of indeterminacy at the level of the represented objectivities are 'filled in' by the reader in acts of imagination. In this 'complementing determination' of the object-stratum of the text, Ingarden writes, the 'co-creative activity of the reader comes into play' (1973b, 53). He regards this activity as an 'art' (1973a, 309). A good reader, that is, will fill in the indeterminate parts of the work in a way that corresponds adequately to those which it has determined. This is true also at the level of the aspect-stratum of the text. 'The reader must perform a vivid representation in reading', Ingarden writes, in order internally to experience, or 'intuit', the text's objects in the multiple ways in which their aspects represent them (1973a, 57). The good reader will not merely understand sentences which represent the text's objects acoustically, that is, but will imaginatively intend the objects of such sentences as heard sounds. Furthermore, he will actualize not just any aspects of the represented objects in this way, but only those suggested by the text. The 'life' of the literary work, for Ingarden, consists in the history of these concretizations, transposed into critical discourse, which can influence and be influenced by both one another and the cultural norms of a given age.

Ingarden's theory of the text has been more favourably received than his theory of reception. His account of the interrelated strata of a literary work, although rarely used in practice, in fact provides a structure for very thorough formal analyses of the ways in which texts construct meanings and achieve effects, both in themselves and in comparison to other texts. His distinction between the text and the reader's concretization has proved to be of lasting value, but needs considerable supplementation. In particular, his concept of the correct concretization demanded by a text is difficult to sustain, since, as Gadamer has shown, reading is a more interactive practice than merely filling in a text's blanks. As Wolfgang Iser writes, Ingarden takes account only of a 'one-way incline from text to reader' rather than a 'two-way relationship', in which the reader both brings his own historically and otherwise determined conceptions to the text and allows these conceptions to be challenged (Iser 1978, 173). He does not, in short, account for the historical situation of the reader. Furthermore, while Ingarden's aesthetic approach deals plausibly with the question of aesthetic value, it limits literary criticism to an account of the constitution of such value, and so also neglects the historical situation of the text.

In contrast to Ingarden's emphasis on the intentional structure of the literary text, the literary critics of the Geneva School aim principally to describe the consciousness itself that the reader encounters there. The school takes its name from the association of many of a group of intellectually and personally associated scholars with the University of Geneva. Most prominent among them are Marcel Raymond (1897–1981), Albert Béguin (1901–57), Georges Poulet (1902–91), Jean Rousset (b. 1910), Jean Starobinski (b.

1920) and Jean-Pierre Richard (b. 1922). Despite significant developments of individual interest, all six of these critics practise what Poulet calls the 'criticism of consciousness' (Richard 1954, 9).

In 'Phenomenology of Reading', Poulet argues that the object which emerges from the book in the act of reading is a consciousness, 'the consciousness of another', which allows the reader to enter into its processes of thought and feeling (Poulet 1969, 54). Like Ingarden, he argues that the objects represented by the signs of a literary text take on a more concrete existence when they are actualized by a reader. Poulet argues that, in reading, these objects lose their materiality and assume a new existence, independent of their basis in signs, in the 'innermost self' of the reader. They become purely 'mental entities' dependent for their existence as such on the mind of the reader in which they exist. This dependence means that the unreal world of a read book has the advantage over the real world of not being opposed to the consciousness of the subject who perceives it. Poulet describes the objects that emerge in reading as 'subjectified objects', whose nature seems to the reader to be consubstantial with that of his own consciousness (55). For Poulet, this is a source of value – it is the 'greatest advantage' of literature that it frees us from our usual sense of the incompatibility between our consciousness and its objects.

It is a further characteristic of the objects of a read book that they do not have the autonomy of real objects but are the thoughts of another subject. In reading, Poulet writes, 'I am thinking the thought of another' (55). I become the subject of another's thoughts and feelings, and his mental world becomes mine. But who is this other? It is not exactly the author himself, Poulet argues, although criticism will benefit from as much historical and biographical detail about him as possible, since his life is 'translated' into the work (58). This translation is 'incomplete', however, and what the reader encounters is an 'analogy' of the author's lived experience. The work has a life of its own – indeed, it is a 'sort of human being' – which it lives in the reader while he gives it existence (59). Criticism is the reader's record of the relationship between the consciousness which emerges in reading the work and his own consciousness. The critic's task, for Poulet, is to describe the characteristic qualities of the consciousness he experiences in a given author's works, and to retrace in them the initial moment of self-consciousness upon which it is based (1972, 48). This is the method of Poulet's own critical studies, such as the *Studies in Human Time*, in which he traces the different experiences of temporal existence expressed in the works of a series of literary and philosophical authors.

In 'The Critical Relation', Jean Starobinski responds to the challenge of structuralism, and, like Poulet, argues that the primary fact of reading is the effect of the 'living world' of the text upon the reader (Starobinski 1989, 11). Structural analysis is necessary in order to demonstrate the derivation of this world from the material signs in which it has its basis. But it must not be forgotten that these signs constitute a 'world within a larger world', in which the structure of the work implies a structuring subject (118). Although the author is inaccessible to the critic except through his own textual works and those of others, nevertheless the critic can and must 'interrogate him *in* his work by asking the question, "Who is speaking?"' (121). Formal analyses of the text, that is, are not ends in themselves, as in structuralism, but can be used to establish an 'intentional trajectory', or the specific nature of the subjectivity coming to expression in the text. Criticism, for Starobinski, must avoid not only the pitfall of too great a subservience to the text but also that of too close an adherence to a method which does not allow the individuality of the text to appear. The ideal mode of criticism, he argues, combines both the 'methodological rigour' of verifiable analytic techniques, and 'reflective openness' in which the subject of the work is thereby allowed to speak in his individuality (126).

Starobinski exemplifies this dual approach in studies such as *Jean-Jacques Rousseau: Transparency and Obstruction* (1988). Here, through numerous close textual analyses, he traces certain fundamental 'symbols and ideas that structured Rousseau's thought' (xi). He argues that Rousseau's experience is such that he both desires a transparent, or purely present, relationship to himself, others and the world, while also desiring to overcome the obstructions that he constantly finds to interrupt such a relationship. Starobinski traces these motifs in Rousseau's fiction, letters, autobiography, philosophy of history, pedagogy and musical theory, and argues that they constitute a 'constant element in Rousseau's life and imagination' (126).

Without the phenomenological framework in which Ingarden describes the intentionality of literary texts, the Geneva critics' fundamental claim to encounter a consciousness in the text lacks convincing support. As J. Hillis Miller points out, their criticism has its roots in the romantic tradition, and it contains a number of romantic presuppositions whose validity can be questioned (Miller 1966, 305). The concept of a fundamental state of pure consciousness, which precedes interaction with its objects, has been challenged by phenomenology, and the concept of pure self-consciousness has been convincingly criticized by Jacques Derrida. As the latter shows, signs mediate presence to oneself, and it is difficult therefore to imagine either that a literary text expresses a previously formed self-consciousness or that it constitutes the formation of such a state, as the Geneva critics believe. Even those who pay greatest attention to the formal aspects of a text, such as Starobinski and Rousset, relate those forms back to modes of consciousness without addressing the question of their transparency. Since the subjectivity encountered in a text is available in no other way than through the text, there is no way of checking the claims of the Geneva School accurately to have reconstructed it, and in practice their results differ considerably. Nevertheless, the Geneva critics' characterizations of the subjective structures expressed in the works of their authors remain impressive. If one accepts that the objects of their analyses are rhetorical constructions rather than expressions of subjectivity, and that literary criticism is not limited to the analysis of these constructions alone, their work remains illuminating.

Luke Ferretter

Further reading and works cited

Béguin, A. *L'Âme romantique et le rêve*. Paris, 1946.
Falk, E. H. *The Poetics of Roman Ingarden*. Chapel Hill, NC, 1981.
Gadamer, H.-G. 'Rhetoric, Hermeneutics and the Critique of Ideology', in *The Hermeneutics Reader*, ed. K. Mueller-Vollmer. Oxford, 1986a.
—. *The Relevance of the Beautiful and Other Essays*, ed. Robert Bernasconi. Cambridge, 1986b.
—. *Truth and Method*. London, 1989.
—. *Gadamer on Celan*, eds R. Heinemann and B. Krajewski. New York, 1997.
Habermas, J. 'A Review of Gadamer's *Truth and Method*', in *The Hermeneutic Tradition*, eds G. L. Ormiston and A. D. Schrift. Albany, NY, 1990.
Heidegger, M. *Being and Time*. Oxford, 1962.
Holub, R. C. *Reception Theory*. London, 1984.
Ingarden, R. *The Cognition of the Literary Work of Art*. Evanston, IL, 1973a.

—. *The Literary Work of Art*. Evanston, IL, 1973b.
—. *The Ontology of the Work of Art*. Athens, OH, 1989.
Iser, W. *The Act of Reading*. London, 1978.
Lawall, S. N. *Critics of Consciousness*. Cambridge, MA, 1968.
Miller, J. Hillis. 'The Geneva School', *Critical Quarterly*, 8, 1966.
Poulet, G. *Studies in Human Time*. Baltimore, MD, 1956.
—. *The Interior Distance*. Baltimore, MD, 1959.
—. 'Phenomenology of Reading', *New Literary History*, 1, 1969.
—. 'Poulet on Poulet: The Self and the Other in Critical Consciousness', *diacritics*, 2, 1972.
—. *Proustian Space*. Baltimore, MD, 1977.
Raymond, M. *From Baudelaire to Surrealism*. London, 1961.
Richard, J.-P. *Littérature et Sensation*. Paris, 1954.
—. *L'Univers imaginaire de Mallarmé*. Paris, 1961.
Rousset, J. *Forme et signification*. Paris, 1962.
Starobinski, J. *Montaigne in Motion*. Chicago, 1985.
—. *Jean-Jacques Rousseau: Transparency and Obstruction*. Chicago, 1988.
—. *The Living Eye*. Cambridge, MA, 1989.
Weinsheimer, J. *Philosophical Hermeneutics and Literary Theory*. New Haven, CT, 1991.
Wellek, R. *Four Critics*. Seattle, WA, 1981.

20. The Frankfurt School, the Marxist Tradition, Culture and Critical Thinking: Max Horkheimer (1895–1973), Herbert Marcuse (1898–1979), Theodor Adorno (1903–1969), Jürgen Habermas (1929–)

Beginnings

The *Institut für Sozialforschung* (Institute for Social Research) of Frankfurt University was opened on Sunday, 22 June 1924, thanks to an endowment from the son of a millionaire, the marxist Felix Weil, who wanted to create a German equivalent of the Marx-Engels Institute in Moscow in the hope that a foundation of this kind would be of use to a future German Soviet Republic (Wiggershaus 1994, 24). The Institute was thus unusual among German academic institutions in openly espousing marxism as its paradigm for studying the historical socialist and labour movements, economic history and the history of political economy. Kurt Gerlach was nominated as the first Director of the Institute, but he died before he could assume his duties. His successor, Carl Grünberg, despite his sympathy for 'scientific' marxism as a methodology, did, however, uphold the Institute's official independence of the socialist and communist parties (the original proposed name for the Institute – Institut für Marxismus – had been discarded for this reason), even though most of his colleagues, i.e. the Institute's assistants and doctoral students, happened to belong to Germany's various communist groupings.

Grünberg retired after suffering a stroke in 1927 and was succeeded as Director of the Institute in October 1930 by the thirty-five-year-old Max Horkheimer, who was also given a chair in social philosophy at the university. The choice of Horkheimer, who had studied philosophy under the anti-Kantian Hans Cornelius, was something of a surprise since his involvement with the Institute up to that point had been minimal, and his socialist or communist affiliations not very evident – the suspicion was that he owed his appointment in large part to the fact that he was more acceptable to colleagues at the university than his openly marxist predecessor had been. Horkheimer, who quickly showed himself to be an adroit intellectual entrepreneur, ambitious both for himself and the Institute, prompted a switch of emphasis in the Institute's research programmes from social and economic history to social theory. He also placed more weight on collective and interdisciplinary work and brought psychoanalysis within the purview of the Institute's research interests (primarily by appointing Erich Fromm to the Institute). A further change occurred in 1932 when Horkheimer replaced Grünberg's empirically oriented journal *Archiv für die Geschichte des Sozialismus und der Arbeiterwegung* with the more theoretical and interdisciplinary *Zeitschrift für Sozialforschung*. The Institute's older members remained broadly wedded to Grünberg's version of materialism, i.e. a 'positivistic' materialism inspired by Engels and Kautsky with its stress on the inexorable 'laws' of capitalist development, while younger members followed Horkheimer in moving towards a non-monistic Hegelian marxism that owed its provenance to Lukács's *History and Class Consciousness* (1923). It could in fact be argued, as Martin Jay has, that the intellectual agenda of the Frankfurt School involved a repristination of the concerns of the so-called Left Hegelians of the 1840s, especially in so far as both groups were concerned to formulate a philosophy of social praxis that involved giving the Hegelian dialectic a more materialist cast (Jay 1973, 42). The Frankfurt School was not simply post-Left Hegelian and marxist, because its intellectual agendas under Horkheimer were also inflected by the legacy of Nietzsche (with its emphasis on perspectivalism and the need to acknowledge the irreducible element of invention in thought) and Max Weber (who compelled social thinkers to deal not just with the history of institutions and the history of production and technology, but also the history of rationality and rationalization). These interdisciplinary concerns were notably less evident in the work of the members who had been appointed by Grünberg.

Prominent 'older' members of the Institute included the economic historian Karl August Wittfogel, best-known for his work on 'hydraulic societies' and the so-called Asiatic mode of production; Franz Borkenau, another economic historian, who did most of his work on the ideological transformations associated with capitalist development; and Henryk Grossman, also an economic historian, who worked on a wide range of topics, including the theory of capitalist accumulation and crisis developed in his best-known work *The Laws of Accumulation and Collapse*. All three had Communist Party affiliations (Grossman with the Polish rather than the German party) and were supporters of the Bolshevik Revolution and its aftermath in the USSR (though Borkenau became disenchanted with the USSR and subsequently severed his links with the German Communist Party).

Of the 'younger' members, the most prominent at the inception of the Institute was Horkheimer's close friend and trusted colleague, Friedrich Pollock, who served briefly as interim Director before Horkheimer was permanently appointed to the position. Pollock, an economist like Grossman but with a training that also included studies in philosophy under Hans Cornelius, was, unlike Borkenau, Grossman and Wittfogel, sceptical about the USSR's capacity to realize the ideal of human emancipation it purported to serve. More importantly for the work of the Institute, the ever-loyal Pollock supported Horkheimer in his efforts to press the Institute in new intellectual directions, especially the revision of the theoretical foundations of marxism that began to take shape under the latter's leadership. In time an inner circle devoted to this objective would form itself round Horkheimer, consisting of Pollock, Theodor Adorno, Herbert Marcuse, Leo Lowenthal (who was the *Zeitschrift's* managing editor) and Erich Fromm.

Max Horkheimer

Horkheimer's inaugural lecture on assuming the Directorship of the Institute, 'The Current Condition of Social Philosophy and the Task of an Institute of Social Research' ('Die gegenwärtige Lage der Sozialphilosophie und die Aufgaben eines Institutes für Sozial-forschung'), provided a conspectus of the current state of social philosophy in relation to its historical precursors. Clearly attempting to set out an intellectual framework for the Institute's future research programmes, Horkheimer constructed a narrative of crisis to account for the trajectory of German social philosophy. According to Horkheimer, German idealism had made the individual the basis of social action, while Hegel had in the end subordinated the individual to the state, and Schopenhauer's philosophy, which in this sense was 'ahead' of Hegel's, reflected the decisive breakdown of philosophic confidence in an objective totality (Jay 1973, 25). Later thinkers – including the Marburg neo-Kantians, Scheler, Hartmann and Heidegger – would struggle without real success to restore this lost sense of an objective totality or to compensate for its demise. Turning to the present, Horkheimer saw social philosophy not as a homogeneous endeavour ensuing in an incontrovertible body of truth predicated on the uncompromised availability of the notion of totality (this guiding intuition for future work in philosophy owing a great deal to Nietzsche's intellectual legacy), but as an interdisciplinary materialism, buttressed by empirical analysis, with contemporary social problems as its focus (the inspiration for this being the Hegelianized marxism that was to dominate the Institute's research under Horkheimer's leadership).

   Horkheimer sought to retain the key elements of the Hegelian dialectic – its emphasis on the essential constructedness of knowledge, the dynamic movement of history – while rejecting Hegel's idealism, which pushed the dialectic to a premature conclusion by insisting that the unfolding of absolute Spirit culminates in a final abolition of the split between subject and object, so that contradictions not resolved in the world will be resolved in Spirit's higher unity. Hegel, in countering the dogmatisms of scepticism and relativism, had succumbed to his own brand of dogmatism. As Horkheimer says:

> Insofar as [Hegel's] method ... still belongs to an idealist system, he has not freed his thought from the old contradiction. His philosophy too is ultimately characterized by the indifference to particular perceptions, ideas and goals which belong to relativism, as well as by the transforma-tion of conceptual structures into substances and the inability to take theoretical and practical account of the dogmatism and historical genesis of is own thought. (1978, 415)

On the other hand, says Horkheimer, the proponents of 'diamat', the deterministic marxism of the Second and Third Internationals, turn marxism into an equally unacceptable and similarly 'closed' dialectic despite their professed desire to turn Hegel's idealism 'on its head'. Social contradictions will not be abolished by some pre-given historical guarantee or telos, as the 'diamat' marxists thought, but only by the practices of concrete historical subjects. The materialist dialectic is necessarily 'unconcluded', and this because thought can never exhaust reality: social reality is not a totality that is available qua totality to consciousness, and it follows that there 'is no general formula for handling the interaction of the forces which must be taken into account in particular theories; the formula must be searched out in each case' (Horkheimer 1986a, 29). Relations between forces, subjects and objects must be grasped historically, and the particularity of the historical and social must be refracted into thought if thought is to do justice to the singularity of the processes and events that constitute the historico-social domain. The social totality can be posited and knowledge of it can be sought, but its constituents are not fixed and they are not therefore epistemically transparent. This is the necessary starting-point for any theory of the relation of truth to historical and social reality.

Most of Horkheimer's thinking on the question of the relation of truth to social reality occurred in the most intellectually active phase of his life, i.e. the period between 1930 and 1945. Central to his thinking on this subject were the propositions that a properly materialist theory of truth and judgement would be one that had the critique of ideology at its core, that praxis is the basis of the verification of judgement, and that interdisciplinary research, some of it with an empirical emphasis, involving economists, historians, sociologists, philosophers and psychologists is crucial for a marxist critical theory capable of avoiding the Scylla of idealism and the Charybdis of the positivism and determinism of 'diamat' (Held 1980, 183).

Horkheimer's attempt to work out a new dialectical logic along the above-mentioned lines amounted to a version of what we today would probably call standpoint theory. Since reality is complex and dynamic and marked by contradiction among its elements, and its subjects and objects are constantly affected by this dynamism and contradiction, the (marxist) theory of this reality has to relate, at a higher level, the particularities of these elements and the inevitably particularized perceptions and apprehensions of them. In this way an appropriately marxist theoretical knowledge of society is achieved through the creation of ensembles of the knowledges afforded at each particular standpoint (Horkheimer 1978, 432–3).

In two other major essays, 'The Latest Attack on Metaphysics' ('Der neueste Angriff und die Metaphysik') and 'Traditional and Critical Theory' ('Traditionelle und Kritische Theorie'), Horkheimer extended the ideological critique of judgement and truth under capitalism made in his earlier articles to the human sciences (geisteswissenschaften). The former essay (Horkheimer 1937) was largely an attack on the then dominant logical positivism, portrayed by its author as a repristination of the age-old nominalist tendency. The logical positivists, by confining the sphere of reason to what was immediately visible in the natural order, made it impossible for there to be a rational conception of society, since the desire for a better world was taken by them to involve a 'mere evaluation' (and hence ultimately 'meaningless') and therefore beyond the purview of rational inquiry. The restriction of speculative reason to the domain of experience and the split between this reason and value initiated by Kant therefore finds a decisive culmination in logical positivism. The latter essay (Horkheimer 1986b), perhaps Horkheimer's most famous, charges 'traditional theory' with an inability to move beyond liberalism, with its prescription of piecemeal reform and a concomitant refusal to seek a transformation of the social totality, while 'critical theory' by contrast takes such a transformation to be rationally determinable and within the compass of human agency.

Horkheimer's theoretical positions were set by the late 1930s, and his best intellectual work was almost done. He was of course to remain productive: the collaboration with Adorno on *Dialectic of Enlightenment* remained ahead, and the shepherding of the Institute through the travails of exile was a major undertaking calling for resourcefulness and administrative acumen. After the Second World War Horkheimer's thinking veered in a more conservative direction (even if he continued to believe that the human demand for happiness is irreducible), and though lionized by the student radicals of the late 1960s like the other members of the Frankfurt School, he disapproved of their aims and aspirations, and his work took on a politically quietistic and increasingly theological turn. So much so that in 1958 he wanted the young Jürgen Habermas removed from the Institute (which had moved back to Germany in 1950) for an article – 'On the Philosophical Debate over Marx and Marxism' – that argued against an abstract philosophy of history in favour of a practically-oriented philosophy of history aimed at the transformation of society (Wiggershaus 1994, 554).

Herbert Marcuse

Born in Berlin, Herbert Marcuse, like Horkheimer and Adorno, came from a family of affluent middle-class assimilated Jews. He studied with Husserl and Heidegger, preparing his *Habilitationsschrift* (subsequently published as *Hegel's Ontology and the Foundation of a Theory of Historicity*) under the supervision of the latter. Relations between Marcuse and Heidegger became strained during the deteriorating political situation in Nazi Germany, and Marcuse broke with Heidegger before he could be employed as his mentor's assistant at Freiburg. Now without the prospect of a job at Freiburg, Marcuse relied on Husserl's good offices to take up his case with the Rector of Frankfurt University, and after a favourable review by Adorno of *Hegel's Ontology* in the *Zeitschrift für Sozialforschung*, Marcuse was added by Horkheimer to the staff of the Institute in 1933. Like many of the Institute's staff, he went into exile, ending up in the United States, where he became a major intellectual catalyst for the 1960s new left. Unlike Adorno, Horkheimer and Pollock, Marcuse did not return to Germany after the war, though he died there while on a visit in 1979.

Marcuse was more explicitly committed to marxism as a theoretico-practical paradigm than were Horkheimer and Adorno, and in addition to his studies of Hegel, his work encompassed analyses of German fascism and the stages of capitalist development, a study of Soviet marxism, a synthesis of Freud and Marx, and many publications in which he outlined a detailed vision of non-repressed life in a post-capitalist society. He also had a more positive conception of the revolutionary transformation of society than his life-long friends Adorno and Horkheimer, and there was sharp disagreement between them when Marcuse enthusiastically supported the 1960s radical student movement.

Marcuse's best-known work, *One-Dimensional Man*, began by sharing Horkheimer's and Adorno's concerns regarding the viability in capitalist societies of a creative social criticism. Reification nullifies the possibility of such a criticism, says Marcuse, because:

> Technical progress, extended to the whole system of domination and co-ordination, creates forms of life (and of power) which appear to reconcile the forces opposing the system and to defeat or refute all protest in the name of the historical prospects of freedom from toil and domination. Contemporary society seems to be capable of containing social change –

qualitative change which would establish essentially different institutions, a new direction in the productive process, new modes of human existence. (11)

Technology has generated affluence (the Heideggerian resonance is evident), and affluence, by freeing people from wants, has effectively undermined any real impulse to oppose the system: the working classes now identify with the system, which has become a benign totalitarianism in the process, precisely in order to safeguard their opportunities for consumption. If Horkheimer and Adorno were unable to identify a form of revolutionary agency capable of overturning today's totally administered societies, Marcuse thought there was just such a radical force in these societies, namely 'the substratum of the outcasts and outsiders, the exploited and persecuted of other races and other colours, the unemployed and unemployable' (200). These excluded individuals have broken with the culture of the market (or rather the market has broken with them), and while Marcuse depicts them as a potential counter-force to capitalism, he notes with caution that what they proffer 'is nothing but a chance':

> The critical theory of society possesses no concepts which could bridge the gap between present and future; holding no promise and showing no success, it remains negative. Thus it wants to remain loyal to those who, without hope, have given and give their life to the Great Refusal. (201)

Critical theory therefore provides a theoretical underpinning (in the form of a philosophy of consciousness with its concomitant philosophy of society and social forces) for the Great Refusal. Marcuse, like its other first-generation exponents, took a wide-angled look at the social reality of the regnant phase of capitalist development, produced a scintillating and prescient analysis of it, but could in the end only endorse one affiliated political principle: unrelenting negativity.

Theodor W. Adorno

Theodor Wiesengrund Adorno's father came from a prosperous assimilated Jewish mercantile family. His mother, born Maria Calvelli-Adorno della Piana of a Corsican noble family, was a successful professional singer before her marriage (Wiesengrund, his father's name, would be dropped after Adorno left Germany in 1934 to go into exile). A precocious talent in both musical aesthetics and philosophy, Adorno had known Horkheimer since 1922, when they were both members of Hans Cornelius's seminar on Husserl. Having obtained his doctorate on Husserl's philosophy under Cornelius, Adorno went to Vienna in 1925 to study musical composition with Alban Berg. His talent for composition not matching his gift for philosophy, Adorno returned to philosophy and took his *Habilitation* under Paul Tillich (Horkheimer was one of the other examiners) in 1931 with a thesis titled 'The Construction of the Aesthetic in Kierkegaard' that was published two years later.

In his 1931 inaugural lecture 'The Actuality of Philosophy' ('Die Aktualität der Philosophie'), Adorno presented an overview of philosophy whose lineaments were to feature consistently in his thinking for the rest of his life. Equating idealist philosophy with Hegelianism (with Husserl's thought constituting a final reduction of the Hegelian system), Adorno rejected this philosophy's 'pretension of totality' in ways that strikingly parallel the similar rejection of the idealist versions of totality that was to be found in Horkheimer's social philosophy:

> Whoever chooses philosophy as a profession today must first reject the illusion that earlier philosophical enterprises began with: that the power of thought is sufficient to grasp the totality of the real ... Philosophy which presents reality as such today only veils reality and eternalises the present condition. (1977, 120)

Finding idealism to be in disarray by the 1930s, Adorno further characterized it as a highly abstract reductive system beset by internal contradictions and antinomies. Though he took issue with Hegel, Adorno and Hegel shared the conviction that philosophy's thought-forms were those of culture and society as well. For both the history of philosophy is coextensive with the history of consciousness. The breakdown of classical idealism made it necessary to recast philosophy, and the prolegomenon to this was an immanent and systematic critique of idealism's propensity for 'identity thinking' (i.e. its positing of a constitutive homology between subject and object and thought and reality). Only a truly dialectical philosophy could overcome the old problems, and a path be paved for philosophy that was neither trivial nor contradictory (1977, 130). Adorno proposed that the immanent critique of philosophy take the form of a critical hermeneutics: while the task of science (*Wissenschaft*) is research, 'that of philosophy is interpretation', so that (and here the influence on Adorno of Walter Benjamin's work on German tragic drama and Goethe's *Elective Affinities* is very evident):

> philosophy persistently and with the claim of truth, must proceed interpretatively without ever possessing a sure key to interpretation; nothing more is given to it than fleeting, disappearing traces within the riddle figures of that which exists and their astonishing entwinings. The history of philosophy is nothing other than the history of such entwinings. (126)

Adorno also maintained that sociology is the basis of this critical hermeneutics, since cultural and intellectual objects express, in mediated form, the existing modes of production in society. Philosophy's basis is thus irreducibly materialist and historical – ideas arise from history, and classical idealism disintegrated because it overlooked this truth (128–9). The task of a materialist philosophy is to show how idealism is destroyed by the social contradictions it expresses and effaces in a simultaneous movement, and to 'demystify' the bourgeois thinker's pretensions to totality and completeness. Influenced as much by Freud (who had already been used by Adorno in his doctoral thesis) as by Marx in this view of philosophy as a form of demystification, Adorno's 'logic of disintegration' sought to pave the way for an emancipatory philosophy that eschewed the 'identity thinking' of the classical philosophical systems. The critical theorist cannot change reality – only the labour of human subjects to change material and social conditions can do this. But by destroying, internally, the hold of conceptual systems on reality, critical theory makes possible the discovery of potentially liberating possibilities that are inherent in humans and things. By freeing objects from our deadening hold, and sustaining a sense of possibility, 'immanent criticism' preserves a place for utopian impulses. In the following years Adorno used this method of an 'immanent criticism' to undertake rigorous technical examinations of Kant, Hegel, Husserl and Heidegger (this was in addition to the study of Kierkegaard that constituted his *Habilitationsschrift*).

As was the case with Horkheimer, changing historical circumstances affected Adorno's own estimation of the possibility of a utopian transformation of society. Stalinism made him sceptical of the utopian possibilities afforded by an 'official' marxism, and Auschwitz and Hiroshima condemned the past that had led up to them and placed the future under the shadow of total catastrophe. Hence, says Adorno, 'life has changed into a timeless succession of shocks, interspersed with, empty, paralysed intervals' (1974, 54). Those who survived Auschwitz are burdened by the guilt of having survived:

> The only responsible course of action is to deny oneself the ideological misuse of one's existence, and for the rest to conduct oneself in private as modestly, unobtrusively and unpretentiously as is required, no longer by good upbringing, but by the shame of still having air to breathe, in hell. (1974, 28; see also 1973, 362–3)

In such a hell, 'our perspective of life has passed into an ideology which conceals the fact that there is life no longer' (1974, 15). Contemporary culture has become completely reified, because it is now so dominated by the exchange mechanism that the social and political forces which underlie our society are no longer fully comprehensible: 'no society which contradicts its very notion – that of mankind – can have full consciousness of itself' (1967, 26). Life is inescapably ideological – 'Things have come to pass where lying sounds like truth, truth like lying' (1974, 108). However, while truth may be difficult, even impossible, to determine, we should not allow ourselves to be terrorized by this fact (1974, 69). Human consciousness no longer has a purchase on the absolute, but truth is still possible, even in a totally reified society. These are seemingly contradictory assertions, and Adorno freely admits to being guilty of this contradiction:

> After everything, the only responsible philosophy is one that no longer imagines it had the Absolute at its command; indeed philosophy must forbid the thought of it in order not to betray that thought, and yet it must not bargain away anything of the emphatic concept of truth. This contradiction is philosophy's element. (1998, 7)

Only when alienation is overcome will it be possible for men and women to think the absolute. But 'the emphatic concepts of truth' cannot be relinquished since they are the only things which contradict the heteronomous reality of the present. Distorted social arrangements can be revealed for what they are – the untruth – only when these distortions are confronted by an ideal which makes apparent the gap between the ideal (or 'concept', to use Adorno's terminology) and reality (or the 'object'). Truth is therefore to be sought in the act of negating existing social reality, and so for Adorno the desire for truth is equivalent to desiring utopia: 'To want substance in cognition is to want a utopia' (1973, 56). Truth is also to be identified with that which enables us to live with oppressing others:

> A new categorical imperative has been imposed by Hitler upon unfree mankind: to arrange their thoughts and actions so that Auschwitz will not repeat itself, so that nothing similar will happen. (1973, 365)

Critical thinking is quintessentially negative and dialectical; it aspires to call continually by their names, instance by instance, all the expressions of alienation which imperceptibly dominate human thought and existing institutions. His unremitting brilliance notwithstanding, Adorno was sometimes too slapdash in his use of such key notions as *alienation*, *truth*, *reconciliation*, etc., and though he did refer in several of his essays to the class struggle, it is not clear what exactly he took this struggle to entail or what he considered its possible outcomes to be. This reluctance or reticence brought him into conflict with the student radicals of the 1960s, and by the time of his death (1969) he had been repudiated by the student movement.

Adorno's intellectual range was astonishing, and little or nothing in the human sciences escaped its compass: philosophy, musicology and musical aesthetics, social psychology,

political theory, sociology, literature, art, film theory and educational theory are significantly represented in his oeuvre. Unlike Horkheimer and Herbert Marcuse, who are hardly
read today, his writings (along with those of Walter Benjamin) seems somehow to be ahead
of us, to have a future beyond their current reception, and even as one acknowledges their
problems, Adorno's texts constitute at the same time a salutary and dazzling provocation for
those wanting to reflect on the characters of our times.

Jürgen Habermas

Jürgen Habermas was Adorno's assistant, and is widely regarded as the most distinguished of
the 'second generation' of the Frankfurt School. Other members of this generation include
Oskar Negt, Klaus Offe and Albrecht Wellmer, though none has been as prominent as
Habermas, the author of over twenty books and several dozen major articles and reviews.

Habermas's first major philosophical work, *Knowledge and Human Interests* (*Erkenntnis
und Intresse*), took from Kant the notion that reason has universal presuppositions, and
from Hegel the notion that reason undergoes historical development, to provide a theory of
the conditions of possibility for our emancipation from the structures of power and
ideology. Three significant departures from the First Frankfurt School soon showed
themselves in Habermas's writings: (a) an interest in the theory of rationality, and in
particular its *reconstruction* (some have argued that Kant is more important for Habermas
than Hegel and Marx); (b) an interest in language, especially the speech-act theory of
Austin and Searle, as opposed to consciousness; and (c) a willingness to engage with
Anglo-American philosophy, in particular Pierce and G. H. Mead (in addition to Austin
and Searle). Commonalities do exist of course, in two areas especially: (a) the shared
interest in emancipation; and (b) the conviction that the human lifeworld is to be
safeguarded from the depredations of technology and its accompanying instrumental
rationality.

Habermas's magnum opus *Theory of Communicative Action* (*Theorie des kommunikativen
Handelns*) views society as a multi-tiered amalgam of symbolic structures open to 'communicative understanding', that is as a totality bound by a system of rules of discourse and
action that are shared by its participants. These rules constitute a 'discourse ethics', the
basis of which is a practical procedure for achieving a non-coercive rational discourse
involving free and equal protagonists. In this procedure, each member of society is required
to take the perspective of all the others, generating a complex of perspectives that ensues in
an overarching 'we-perspective' from which all can test their norms to see if these norms
can constitute the basis of a genuinely shared practice. In this way a pragmatic ideal is
established, an ideal that has to be embodied in actual speech-situations if democratic
arrangements are to be implemented and sustained. Habermas has achieved a blend of the
utopian and rational that some have nonetheless found unconvincing (is a very slightly less
than ideal procedure still capable of generating norms that can be accepted as valid?).
Horkheimer's idea of an interdisciplinary theory of social emancipation is given a kind of
realization in Habermas's delineation of this 'universal pragmatics', but Habermas's staunch
commitment to a universal rationality would not be shared by the first generation of the
Frankfurt School. In fact, a case can be made for suggesting that the intellectual legacy of
Horkheimer and Adorno has crossed the Atlantic and found its current stopping point in
the work of Fredric Jameson, who in addition to producing exemplary commentary on
Adorno, has, among other things, extended the latter's extraordinary insights into late

capitalism as a totality inhering in our cultural forms (an insight not much to be found in the Habermasian organon) in ways that Adorno himself could scarcely have anticipated. (Jameson's use of the Althusserian notion of a structural totality gives his account of late capitalism a scope and pertinacity not available to Adorno, who invoked the notion of totality, but only negatively, as a heuristic device in his immanent critique of capitalism. Totality for Adorno is the source of utopian counter-images bespeaking the reconciled life that can be pitted against the distorted life we are compelled to live under capitalist dispensations. It is precisely that – utopian – whereas for Jameson, even as he remains faithful to Adorno, totality is indispensably involved in any attempt to map (and mapping is always a practico-theoretical operation) the cultural and political operations that are constitutive of capitalism.)

The Frankfurt School has given the present-day theorist of culture a powerful meta-language for grasping and comprehending the innumerable forms, and ensembles of forms, through which historicity, temporality and the present coalesce with the capitalist mode of production to produce social and cultural reality. Elements of this metalanguage appear dated or are no longer serviceable for some of us today. But its productive scope has been substantial, its influence immense and salutary.

Kenneth Surin

Further reading and works cited

Adorno, T. W. 'Cultural Criticism and Society', in *Prisms*. London, 1967.
—. *Negative Dialectics*. London, 1973.
—. *Minima Moralia*. London, 1974.
—. 'The Actuality of Philosophy', delivered in 1931. *Telos*, 31, 1977.
—. 'Why Still Philosophy', in *Critical Models*. New York, 1998.
Arato, A. and Gebhardt, E. (eds) *The Essential Frankfurt School Reader*. Oxford, 1978.
Connerton, P. (ed.) *Critical Sociology*. Harmondsworth, 1976.
Habermas, J. *Knowledge and Human Interests*. Boston, 1971.
—. *Theory of Communicative Action. Volume One. Reason and the Rationalization of Society*. Boston, 1984.
Held, D. *Introduction to Critical Theory*. London, 1980.
Horkheimer, M. 'Der neueste Angriff und die Metaphysik', *Zeitschrift für Sozialforschung*, 6, 1, 1937.
—. 'On the Problem of Truth', in *The Essential Frankfurt School Reader*, eds A. Arato and E. Gebhardt. Oxford, 1978.
—. 'Materialism and Metaphysics', in *Critical Theory: Selected Essays*. New York, 1986a.
—. 'Traditional and Critical Theory', in *Critical Theory: Selected Essays*. New York, 1986b.
— and Adorno, T. W. *Dialectic of Enlightenment*. London, 1979.
Jay, M. *The Dialectical Imagination*. London, 1973.
Marcuse, H. *One Dimensional Man*. London, 1968.
Wiggershaus, R. *The Frankfurt School*. Cambridge, MA, 1994.

21. Mikhail Bakhtin (1895–1975)

Mikhail Bakhtin has been hailed by Tzvetan Todorov as 'the most important Soviet thinker in the human sciences and the greatest theoretician of literature in the twentieth century' (1984, ix), and has had a serious impact on the thinking of literary critics as diverse and distinguished as Roman Jakobson, Wayne Booth, David Lodge and Julia Kristeva. By any standards he is a stunningly original thinker, whose work has implications for philology, semiotics, philosophy (especially ethics and aesthetics), psychology and cultural anthropology as well as for literary history and criticism. Yet virtually his entire life passed in obscurity, not only from the viewpoint of the West but within the Soviet Union as well. The son of a bank manager, Bakhtin was born in Orel, south of Moscow, and like his older brother Nikolai studied classics at Petersburg University (1913–17). He and his family moved to Nevel to avoid some of the hardships of the Civil War in Petersburg, where Bakhtin dominated a group of intellectuals, the first 'Bakhtin circle', including the linguist and musicologist Valentin Voloshinov, the Jewish philosopher M. I. Kagan and the philosopher and literary scholar Lev Pumpiansky. Soon much of the group moved to Vitebsk, where they were joined by Pavel M. Medvedev, a critic who had some official standing with the government.

In 1920 Bakhtin married Elena Okolovich, who would be his lifetime caretaker. During this period he suffered from osteomyelitis of the left leg as well as a typhoid infection of the right; eventually that leg would be amputated and his health always remained precarious. Still, throughout the mid-1920s Bakhtin was quite productive, working on a number of essays and monographs in aesthetics and moral philosophy (some of which has been translated under the title *Art and Answerability*) as well as an early version of his book on Dostoevsky; the surviving notebooks show him moving away from the neo-Kantianism of Ernst Cassirer and Hermann Cohen which had been an important influence. In 1924 he returned to Leningrad, where he was granted a small medical pension but lived in relative obscurity; his friends' involvement in religious questions tended to isolate them, and indeed in 1929 Bakhtin was arrested, apparently for his questionable religious affiliations, and sentenced to ten years in the Solovetsky Islands camp. Meanwhile, *Problems of Dostoevsky's Creative Works* had been published to some acclaim, and some of his influential friends, including Gorky, managed to have his sentence commuted to six years' 'internal exile' in Kazakhstan, probably saving his life. During the early 1930s he held a variety of menial jobs, occasionally lecturing and drafting essays, until in 1936 Medvedev found him a position teaching at the Mordovia Pedagogical Institute in Saransk, about four hundred miles west of Moscow.

In the late 1930s, fearing a purge of the faculty, Bakhtin moved to Savelovo. He published some reviews and finished a book on the novel of education, the publication of which was stopped by the war. Only fragments of it survive. Meanwhile several of his circle, including Medvedev, were executed or died in camps. By 1940 he had prepared a doctoral dissertation for the Gorky Institute on 'Rabelais in the History of Realism' but the war postponed his defence. After teaching in secondary schools awhile, in 1945 he returned to the Pedagogical Institute, eventually becoming Chairman of the Department of General Literature. In 1946 his defence was rescheduled but increasing ideological repression during the Zhdanov period postponed his degree until 1952. And then – probably because of the politically dubious nature of his writing – he was awarded only a candidate's degree.

During the late 1950s his old formalist antagonist Shklovsky mentioned the Dostoevsky work respectfully, as did Jakobson, and by 1960 several young Russian scholars, believing him dead, were making efforts to republish that book. Bakhtin was persuaded to revise the book and the final years of his life were marked by increasing recognition and many more material comforts. Both the surviving formalists and the Tartu semioticians (on the left) celebrated him, as did a young group of Russian Orthodox scholars (on the right). Bakhtin's ability to appeal simultaneously to thinkers of widely divergent positions has continued to characterize his work during its reception in Europe and the Americas. Meanwhile, during his last years he worked on the Rabelais manuscript (which was published in 1965), his notebooks and a host of earlier manuscripts he wished to revise. In 1973 the semiotician Vyacheslav Ivanov claimed that Medvedev's book *The Formal Method in Literary Scholarship*, a critique of formalism published in 1928, was actually written by Bakhtin, as were *Freudianism: A Critical Sketch* (1927) and *Marxism and the Philosophy of Language* (1929), both signed by Voloshinov, and several essays published under Voloshinov's name. Bakhtin did not conclusively either affirm or deny these assertions, and by 1975 he was dead. His final words were 'I go to thee' – perhaps addressed to his beloved wife, who had died in 1971, or perhaps not.

Bakhtin has been claimed by formalists and their successors the structuralists as one of their own, and he shares with both of them the conviction that language must be the fundamental key to analysing and evaluating art and experience. Poststructuralists, beginning with Julia Kristeva (1980), often claim him as a precursor because his attack on the notion of a unified speaking subject as the guarantor of *logos* and his vision of language as inevitably a patchwork of citations anticipates poststructuralist positions. Marxists have claimed him because of his conviction that language is always already ideological and his championing of the dispossessed and admiration for 'the people'. Anti-marxists often see him as a religious thinker, pointing out the parallels between his work and that of Martin Buber, with its highlighting of the 'I–Thou' relation. He is a hero to a neo-Aristotelian like Wayne Booth because he proposes analytic categories for thinking about narration, like a formalist, but also clearly sees literary issues as ethical.

The question of the disputed texts exacerbates some of these issues, since the Voloshinov and Medvedev works are much closer to conventionally marxist thought than are the works published under Bakhtin's name. At this point, though, it is probably the consensus of scholars that while the disputed texts may indeed incorporate many of Bakhtin's ideas, they are not directly his work. But although Bakhtin is not a conventional marxist, neither are most of the western marxists such as Althusser, Adorno or Benjamin. His approach and values are certainly more 'sociological' and anti-idealist than was the work of most Anglo-American literary critics up until the last twenty years. But he is unlike both marxists and many contemporary theorists in his opposition to 'theoretism', the explanation of human phenomena by invoking a set of abstract rules, norms or analytic categories. He is not himself a wholly systematic thinker, and the state of being 'unfinished' or 'unfinalizable' is in fact one of his highest values and is basic to his definition of humanity.

Bakhtin's idea of the self is radically dependent upon others; the self, for him, is an act of grace, the gift of the other. Human consciousness is formed only in a process of perpetual negotiation with other selves by way of their 'languages'. Selfhood is supremely social, and a person who grew up without ever having been exposed to speech would not be fully human for Bakhtin. For Bakhtin, in a way, intersubjectivity precedes subjectivity. Paradoxically, while consciousness is where Bakhtin locates selfhood, consciousness for him is fundamentally linguistic, and thus in his terms an extraterritorial part of the organism. As he remarks, language 'lies on the border between oneself and the other' (Bakhtin 1981, 293). In his early writings on self and other Bakhtin points out that every person benefits from the 'surplus of vision' that others enjoy in looking at him or her and incorporate that vision into their vision of themselves even while opposing or partially assenting to it. So by definition one's finalizing vision of another is never adequate; people, like successful characters in novels, 'do not coincide with themselves'. Bakhtin has little interest in the unconscious, and ascribes to consciousness most of the conflicts, contradictions and complexities that Freudians see in the interaction of conscious and unconscious minds.

Language, the semiotic system that most interests Bakhtin, is not an abstraction for him. He is always concerned with *parole* – the individual instance of speech – rather than *langue* – the system that orders speech. From Bakhtin's perspective, formal study of language systems is useless – and the early Formalists were essentially wrong-headed – because it ignores the way in which speech is always rooted in a particular material situation that contributes a significant part of its meaning. The 'sentence' is objective and can be reiterated, but the 'utterance' is unique and unrepeatable. Further, language is always, in Bakhtin's terms, ideological: that is, each utterance carries with it the aura of a particular idea-system (which may be more or less explicitly political) out of which it was spoken. The most significant aspect of an utterance for Bakhtin is what he terms its addressivity, its quality of being in some respect spoken *toward* someone. Bakhtin calls for a 'metalinguistics' or a 'translinguistics' which would investigate not merely the forms of language but the kinds of material situations in which speech occurs, because each speech act involves not only a theme but at least two interlocutors plus an invisible 'third', a 'superaddressee' providing an imagined absolutely just response – God, human conscience, 'the people', science, etc. (Bakhtin 1986, 126). Bakhtin uses the term 'heteroglossia' to refer to the fact that speech, in so far as it is always embodied in a particular situation, is always multiple, always a mixture of languages which themselves can be further reduced. Everyone participates in numerous 'languages of heteroglossia', each of them claiming privilege. Obviously one of the problems of such a system is to establish any sort of final typology, but Bakhtin was happy to generalize about language types in a strictly provisory way. Toward the end of his life he was wrestling with the problem of what he termed 'speech genres', 'whole utterances belonging to particular generic types' (Bakhtin 1986, 89).

The key to understanding language for Bakhtin is that 'our speech, that is, all our utterances (including creative works) is filled with others' words, varying degrees of otherness or varying degrees of "our own-ness", varying degrees of awareness and detachment. These words of others carry with them their own expression, their own evaluative tone, which we assimilate, re-work, and re-accentuate' (Bakhtin 1986, 89). Thus language is always 'double-voiced', embodying both the language of the speaker (itself an amalgam of that speaker's important interlocutors such as parents, lovers, intellectual influences and so forth) and any immediate or anticipated addressee, towards whom the speaker may linguistically assume a great variety of postures. To a remarkable degree, Bakhtin's theories of self – other relations, of language and consciousness, of ethics and of literature interpenetrate and support one another, so that Gary Saul Morson and Caryl Emerson have offered the term 'prosaics' to suggest both the way Bakhtin's thought is always rooted in the ordinary, the everyday and the immediate and the way his literary system elevates the prose genres over the poetic ones (Morson and Emerson 1990). To a great extent, the 'actor' or 'performer' of Bakhtin's philosophical and ethical writings is the same as the 'author' of his later specifically literary ones, and both groups of writings celebrate the confrontation with alterity.

For literary criticism, Bakhtin's most important essays are probably 'Epic and Novel', 'From the Prehistory of Novelistic Discourse' and 'Discourse in the Novel', all collected in *The Dialogic Imagination* (1981). In an unsystematic but highly suggestive way he lays out a theory of literature that inverts most of the classical assumptions about the hierarchies of writing and what constitutes formal excellence. First, he opposes the novel and its earliest hellenic forms, such as the dialogue, the symposium or Menippean satire, to epic and lyric poetry (and, less convincingly, drama too), arguing that the prose forms are superior in that they are dialogic – founded upon and constituted by dialogue – whereas poetry always tends toward the monologic, the state of a single, authoritative voice. In his book on Dostoevsky, Bakhtin argues that that novelist most fully realized the potential of the form and that his aesthetic process is best described as polyphonic, referring to the interplay between the author's own language and the fully realized languages of his protagonists. While in one sense no real speech or writing can be truly monologic, Bakhtin uses the term to refer to patriarchal, authoritarian, consciously ideological speech that reifies and totalizes; the authorial speech of Tolstoy seems this way to Bakhtin, as opposed to the polyphonic speech of Dostoevsky, in which we can easily find dialogized heteroglossia, a living dialogue of worldviews. In the genuine novel, Bakhtin claims, 'the "depicting" authorial language now lies on the same plane as the "depicted" language of the hero, and may enter into dialogic relations and hybrid combinations with it' (1981, 27–8). Indeed, it can be said that in the fully realized novel the 'author participates in the novel (he is omnipresent in it) *with almost no direct language of his own*. The language of the novel is a system of languages that mutually and ideologically interanimate each other' (1981, 47).

Bakhtin is at his most formalist in categorizing dialogical relations in the novel, although he does so very differently in different works. He talks of the enormous number of ways in which language is stratified – by genres and sub-genres of literature (lyric, oratorical, penny-dreadful), by social professions (lawyers, businessmen, politicians), by social differentiations among groups, by artistic circles, journals and even particular artistic works, all 'capable of stratifying language, in proportion to their social significance' (1981, 290). But his main interest is reserved for different ways in which the language of the author may interact with other languages in the novel. For example, he explores what he terms 'character zones' in novels, areas of the text in which the authorial language changes to reflect the consciousness of a character even when that character is merely mentioned by the author and no direct attempt is being made to represent his or her thoughts. Much later and independently, the critic Hugh Kenner described this as the 'Uncle Charles effect', in reference to a passage in James Joyce's *Portrait of the Artist as a Young Man* where Stephen Dedalus's Uncle Charles 'repairs' to the outhouse, where he finds the air 'salubrious' – a passage that Wyndham Lewis, missing the point, attacked as inflated late-Victorian prose. A character zone is a clear example of heteroglossia; another is the way the novel form uses incorporated genres – short stories, songs, poems, newspaper stories, scholarly or religious genres, for example, as well as the familiar confession, letter, diary and so forth. This is another strength of the novel for Bakhtin, and shows how it is not simply another genre of literature but a 'super-genre', capable of assimilating all the others.

In *Problems of Dostoevsky's Poetics* Bakhtin gives his most elaborate schema for classifying novelistic discourse (1984, 199). His first category is direct, unmediated discourse directed exclusively toward its referential object – essentially, the monologism of the author (and thus something not found in a true novel). The second category is objectified discourse – in other words, a character's speech. Bakhtin notes that this can be more or less 'typed', and in so far as it is *not* typed, the relationship between author's and character's speech approaches dialogue. Double-voiced discourse, or discourse with an orientation toward someone else's discourse, is the third category, and the one that Bakhtin finds crucial. There are several sub-types of double-voiced discourse, the first of which he terms 'unidirectional' and 'convergent'. Examples of this type include stylization, the narration of an independent narrator, the unobjectified discourse of a character who is in part an authorial spokes-person, and first-person narration. One might note that the author is fundamentally sympathetic to all these voice-types. The reverse is the case with 'vari-directional double-voiced discourse' (where the voices are 'divergent'), including parody, the discourse of a character being parodied and 'any transmission of someone else's words with a shift in accent'. The last sort of double-voiced discourse is the reflected discourse of another in which the other discourse exerts influence from without, including the 'hidden internal polemic' (where another's language is being contested without ever being explicitly identified), the discourse 'with a sideward glance' toward someone else's discourse (which is never directly addressed but is indirectly highly influential in producing the speaker's language), or a rejoinder of a dialogue (either explicit or hidden). Elsewhere, Bakhtin deploys very different paradigms, but his main areas of interest remain.

A second characteristic of the novel which is not derivable from his concept of dialogism is the form's participation in a sense of life Bakhtin labels carnival, from the medieval ritual celebration. It is a simplification but perhaps helpful to say that if dialogism is the novel's proper form, carnival underlies its optimal content; the true novel is *carnivalized*. Carnival is probably Bakhtin's most influential formulation, and unsurprisingly it is also the most easily susceptible to abuse. As he develops the notion, principally in *Rabelais and His World* (1968) and *Problems of Dostoevsky's Poetics*, carnival embodies a kind of folk wisdom that celebrates the body and opposes all forms of authority. It is 'a pageant without footlights and without a division into performers and spectators' (Bakhtin 1984, 122). Bakhtin derives his utopian notion of carnival from various medieval celebrations in which a sort of 'licensed misrule' was practised, usually through mockery directed toward the Church and the town's established hierarchy. Often the mighty were ridiculed and a fool was crowned and uncrowned and there was general indulgence in 'base' pleasures of the body. Bakhtin emphasizes the free and familiar contact among people in carnival without regard to hierarchies, in 'carnival mésalliances', as well as the free indulgence in blasphemy and profanation. For Bakhtin carnival expresses the 'joyful relativity' of all structure and order, and through its celebration of the 'bodily lower stratum' affirms a perpetual organic process of birth and death, nourishment and decay, that is wholly transindividual. Although Bakhtin interprets carnival as almost entirely oppositional, it should be noted that many historians view this officially tolerated ritual as a mere 'safety valve' whose effect is to reaffirm the dominant power.

Most kinds of symbolic expression associated with carnival Bakhtin finds in 'carnivalized' literature, including the all-important carnival laughter, the ritual exchange of insults, parody, creative blasphemy, crowning and decrowning, the highlighting of base bodily functions, including sex, ingestion, defecation and urination, drunkenness, flatulence and a host of material appetites. Carnival levels all pretence, and in literary formulation tends toward a 'grotesque realism' that Bakhtin celebrates as the natural form of 'unofficial culture'. Rabelais's works are for Bakhtin the best examples of the tendency of the novel toward carnivalization, though he finds many traces of carnival in Dostoevsky as well. Indeed, Bakhtin traces two separate stylistic lines of development for the novel. One of them originates in the relatively monological language of the 'Sophistic novels' and runs through the medieval novels of gallantry, the Baroque novel and the fictions of Voltaire; the other is rooted in the dialogues and in Menippean satire, the works of Apuleis and Petronius and runs through the uncategorizable works of writers like Rabelais, Sterne and Dostoevsky. The Second Line, as Bakhtin calls it (1981, 371–88), shows the novel's fundamentally dialogized relationship to heteroglossia, while the First Line tends toward objectification and monologism. And as it happens, where the First Line usually strikes a serious tone and involves itself in idealizations, the Second Line is more or less carnivalized from the beginning. Bakhtin's implication is that the traditional genealogy of the novel culminating in the social realism of Stendhal, Austen, Trollope, Balzac, Thackeray and James is actually a diversion from the more anarchic and fertile line running through Rabelais, Cervantes, the picaresque novelists, Goethe, Hugo, Dickens, Sterne – and perhaps, in the twentieth century, writers like Joyce, John Barth and Thomas Pynchon.

A final term of Bakhtin's that has found some currency in contemporary literary criticism is the chronotope, a coinage that literally means 'time-space' and that Bakhtin uses to refer to the characteristic qualities of these parameters within any given fictional genre. Unusually, Bakhtin gives primacy to neither, and is particularly interested in their interaction. His discussion of the chronotope of the Greek 'adventure novel of the ordeal' (200–600 AD) and of the 'adventure novel of everyday life' – Apuleius's *Golden Ass* and Petronius's *Satyricon* – somewhat resembles European phenomenological criticism of the 1960s in its attempt to give the 'inner sense' of a literary universe, in which both time, space, causality, selfhood and other fundamental categories of experience can be deployed in a variety of ways (1981, 86–129). Bakhtin may well have been forced to develop the idea of the chronotope because he is determined to trace the origins of the amorphous form of the novel through its ancient precursors, including locations (such as Menippean satire) where few critics had looked for pre-novelistic traces. But because Bakhtin's idea of the destiny of the novel is something very different from social realism, he re-maps the literary past in radical ways, highlighting texts ignored by most literary historians of the novel.

R. Brandon Kershner

Further reading and works cited

Bakhtin, M. M. *Rabelais and His World*. Cambridge, MA, 1968.
—. *The Dialogic Imagination: Four Essays*. ed. M. Holquist. Austin, TX, 1981.
—. *Problems of Dostoevsky's Poetics*, ed. and trans. C. Emerson. Minneapolis, MN, 1984.
—. *Speech Genres and Other Late Essays*, eds C. Emerson and M. Holquist. Austin, TX, 1986.

—. Art and Answerability: Early Philosophical Essays by M. M. Bakhtin, eds M. Holquist and V. Liapunov. Austin, TX, 1990.
Bakhtin, M. M. Medvedev, P. N. The Formal Method in Literary Scholarship, Cambridge, MA, 1985.
Clark, K. and Holquist, M. Mikhail Bakhtin. Cambridge, MA, 1984.
Kristeva, J. Desire in Language: A Semiotic Approach to Literature and Art. New York, 1980.
Lodge, D. After Bakhtin. New York, 1990.
Morson, G. S. (ed.) Bakhtin: Essays and Dialogues on His Work. Chicago, 1986.
— and Emerson, C. (eds) Rethinking Bakhtin. Evanston, IL, 1989.
—. Mikhail Bakhtin: Creation of a Prosaics. Stanford, CA, 1990.
Todorov, T. Mikhail Bakhtin: The Dialogical Principle. Minneapolis, MN, 1984.
Voloshinov, V. N. Marxism and the Philosophy of Language. Cambridge, MA, 1986.
—. Freudianism: A Critical Sketch, eds I. R. Titunik and N. R. Bruss. Bloomington, IN, 1987.

22. Georges Bataille (1897–1962) and Maurice Blanchot (1907–)

Georges Bataille's collected works comprise twelve volumes and Maurice Blanchot's available record of publication indicates a similar output. This output and the overall quality of this production are extraordinary, although, remarkably, more of a rule than an exception in the intellectual landscape to which both belong (one can mention, among others, Levinas, Lacan, Foucault, Barthes, Deleuze and Derrida). One ought to pause further to contemplate an even more extraordinary fact – namely, what kind of writing these thousands upon thousands of pages of Bataille's and Blanchot's writing (and those of other figures just mentioned) contain. Consider, for example, the passage closing Blanchot's short essay on serial music via Thomas Mann's *Doctor Faustus*, 'Ars Nova', included in *L'Entretien infini* (*The Infinite Conversation*). In the space of six pages, the essay itself traverses an immense array of themes, ideas, works and authors – Mann, Schönberg, Lukács, Adorno, Benjamin and Paul Klee, among them (1993, 345–50). It would be difficult to give a full list, since many themes and authors, while implicitly addressed, are not explicitly named, for example Kant, Hegel, Nietzsche and Derrida. Having accomplished this already remarkable feat, Blanchot, in closing, brings into consideration Georges Poulet's *The Metamorphoses of the Circle*, to open yet another set of trajectories. These trajectories traverse just about the richest conceptual space imaginable, even though and because this richness is made possible by that which is irreducibly inaccessible to any knowledge, however encompassing or deep. As will be seen, an analogous epistemology emerges in and defines Bataille's vision as well. Ultimately, this space is defined as, in Blanchot's famous title phrase, 'the space of literature'. Blanchot writes:

> I ask myself why, along with this book the whole history of criticism and culture closed and why, with a melancholy serenity, it seemed at the same time to send us off and to authorize us to enter a new space. What space? Not to answer such a question, certainly, but to show the difficulty of approaching it, I would like to invoke a metaphor. It is nearly understood that the Universe is curved, and it has often been supposed that this curvature has to be positive: hence the image of

a finite and limited sphere. But nothing permits one to exclude the hypothesis of an unfigurable Universe (a term henceforth deceptive); a Universe escaping every optical exigency and also escaping consideration of the whole – essentially non-finite, disunified, discontinuous. What about such a Universe? Let us leave this question here and instead ask another: what about man the day he accepts confronting the idea that the curvature of the world, and even of this world, is to be assigned a negative sign? But will he ever be ready to receive such a thought, a thought that, freeing him from fascination with unity, for the first time risks summoning him to take the measure of an exteriority that is not divine, of a space entirely in question, and even excluding the possibility of an answer, since every response would necessarily fall anew under the jurisdiction of the figure of figures? This amounts perhaps to asking ourselves: is man capable of a radical interrogation? That is, finally, is he capable of literature, if literature turns aside and towards the absence of the book? A question the *Ars Nova*, in its neutral violence, has already addressed to him. And in this it was indeed a diabolical art: Thomas Mann was finally right. (1993, 350)

It is not possible to offer a reading of this passage here. Indeed, the question is how one can possibly approach a text, such as Bataille's and Blanchot's, that such passages paradigmatically represent. Extending the trajectories indicated above, the passage conjoins modernist art with modern mathematics and science: the key references include non-Euclidean geometry (here of negative curvature); Einstein's general relativity, in part based on this geometry; and modern cosmology, based on both. This network is further extended to modern philosophy and, in particular, the radical epistemology that defined twentieth-century thought. Thus, even leaving aside the pre-Socratics, especially Heraclitus (whom Blanchot considers in this context in *The Infinite Conversation*), the notion of the unfigurable has its genealogy in the ideas of, among others, Kant, Hegel, Nietzsche, Heidegger, Bataille, Lacan, Levinas and Derrida. Blanchot also draws upon legal philosophy and theology. The combination is remarkable both in range and in bringing these subjects into a complex, irreducibly non-simple, yet cohesive, arrangement. In question is not even so much the intertextuality of Blanchot's text but a richly interlinked conceptual work, which is primarily responsible for this extraordinary density. Arguably, the most remarkable quality of Blanchot's, or Bataille's, thought is that of discerning proximities, one might say radical proximities, between what appears to be so heterogeneous and distant. Far from being exceptional, passages of that kind are found in the immediate vicinity of virtually every point of Bataille's and Blanchot's writing. How, then, is one to approach such works, even if one could leave aside the incessant reciprocity of the relationships between Bataille's and Blanchot's work, further enriching and complicating both texts?

In confronting this task here, I have decided (the possibilities are as abyssal as the impossibilities) to offer a discussion of the architecture of some among their major concepts and/in their networked interrelationships within and between their texts. I understand the term concept itself in the sense that Gilles Deleuze and Félix Guattari give it in their *What is Philosophy?*, rather than, as is more customary, as an entity established by a generalization from particulars, or indeed 'any general or abstract idea', as they argue, via Hegel, a key figure for both Blanchot and, especially, Bataille, and one of the inspirations for the present approach as well (Deleuze and Guattari 1994, 11–12, 24). A philosophical concept in this sense is an irreducibly complex, multi-layered structure – a multi-component conglomerate of concepts (in their conventional sense), figures, metaphors, particular (ungeneralized) elements and so forth. This view allows one to absorb Bataille's and Blanchot's conceptual entities, or those, such as 'différance', introduced by Derrida under the heading of 'neither terms nor concepts'. (Bataille's and Blanchot's concepts are often entities of this type as well.) Philosophy itself is defined by Deleuze and Guattari as the creation of new concepts in this sense, and even 'concepts that are always new' (1994, 5). Nietzsche would speak of philosophy and philosophers of the future, which view defines as much Bataille's and Blanchot's thought as Nietzsche's own. Both Bataille's and, especially, Blanchot's fiction or, in their own terms, literature can be, and here will be, correlated with this conceptual-philosophical view, in part because their conceptual architecture is defined by both in terms of and through work(s) of literature.

Bataille

If one could *sum up* Bataille's experience, thought and writing in a single phrase (it is crucial that in fact one cannot), it would be his own phrase, 'encounter with the impossible', 'the impossible' itself eventually (in one of his last published works) used by Bataille as his title (1991 – see 'Preface to the Second Edition', 9). This statement must be understood not so much in the sense that these are shaped by an encounter with the impossible, but instead in the sense that they *constitute* this encounter or are reciprocal with it. Nor can one say that Bataille's experience or thought precede and are then (re)presented in his writing; these relationships, too, are defined by a more complex and interactive reciprocity. Accordingly (in parallel with Derrida's 'neither a term nor a concept' of writing) I shall here speak of Bataille's writing as designating this multi-reciprocal field. This multi-reciprocity is one of the effects of the efficacity to which Bataille's 'encounter with the impossible' aims to relate in an irreducibly oblique fashion, or, in Blanchot's terms, in the form of non-relation, for it cannot be done otherwise. This encounter would also constitute a form of, as Bataille calls it, 'sovereign' practice, even though and because the impossible itself in question cannot be *mastered* by any knowledge (in particular, in Hegel's dialectical sense of mastery (*Herrschaft*)). It is irreducibly 'unknowable', the term correlatively employed by Bataille. Bataille terms the relevant aspect of the sovereign practice itself as 'unknowledge (*nonsavoir*)'. Thus Bataille's writing *is* his experience – the experience of existing at 'the (extreme) limit of the possible' and on the threshold of the impossible (the phrase recurs throughout *L'Expérience intérieure*). This, however, can only be said if one uses the term 'experience' in Bataille's sense of 'interior experience' (*expérience intérieure* – sometimes translated as 'inner experience'), in juxtaposition to the classical concept of experience, understood as the experience of presence and particularly of consciousness. As Derrida points out:

> 'that which *indicates itself* as interior experience [in Bataille] is not an experience, because it is related to [no consciousness], no presence, no plenitude, but only to the 'impossible' that it 'undergoes' in torment. This experience above all is not interior; and if it seems to be such because it is related to nothing else, to no exterior (except in the mode of nonrelation, secrecy, and rupture), it is also completely *exposed* to torment – naked; open to an exterior; with no interior reserve or feeling; profoundly superficial. (1980, 272; translation modified)

The phrase 'encounter with the impossible' occurs in *Inner Experience* (*L'Expérience Intérieure*), where the concept is developed via Blanchot's *Thomas the Obscure*. The book is an instalment, along with *Guilty* (*Le coupable*) (1988a), and *On Nietzsche* (*Sur Nietzsche*) (1990), of what was originally conceived of as *La somme athéologique* – both a quasi-autobiographical 'summing-up' of this encounter and a conceptualization, or philosophy, of interior experience. At the same time, the atheological or, more generally, a-ontotheological nature of this encounter and of this summing-up makes them rigorously unsummable. (Following Heidegger and Derrida, ontotheology here designates any form of determination, idealist or materialist, equivalent to the theological determination in positing a single fundamental agency, overt or hidden, which would uniquely or unconditionally govern or control nature, history, interpretation and so forth.) Thus Bataille's writings 'de-cohere', as it were, away from any *attempt* to link them to classical, for example, dialectical, or indeed any conceivable wholeness (understood as an unambiguously determinable arrangement of parts). I stress 'attempt' because one cannot here think in terms of some (logically or ontologically) pre-existing coherence from which one then 'de-coheres'. Bataille's practice is defined by un-totalizable but mutually engaging – heterogeneously interacting and interactively heterogeneous – relationships among various problematics, terms, concepts, fragments and other elements of Bataille's text or genres (essays, theoretical treatises, fictions and so forth). One encounters a very different form of organization, which is a consequence of Bataille's radical epistemology, here at work in and deployed by his own writing. (The same argument would apply to the work of Blanchot and a number of other figures mentioned above.)

It may be useful to give a summary of the key features of this epistemology in this context. The particular elements involved interact and are organized: that is, we may meaningfully consider collective configurations of them as having structure. This organization, however, does not fully govern the functioning of each of these elements in their particularity, thus allowing them to assume independent significance – ultimately to the point of defying any attempt to define them by any denomination. Bataille's writings continuously enact configurations of that type, which is essential to what he calls 'sovereign' discursive and conceptual practice, sovereign writing, and necessary for the writing (in the above sense) of sovereignty itself. They do so even as, and by virtue of the fact that, they equally submit and pursue (sovereignty being impossible otherwise) that which escapes even these far-reaching dynamics, or indeed anything; Bataille's writings, in their contigorations, figure that which is irreducibly inaccessible, ultimately inaccessible even as inaccessible, or as 'that'. For, the efficacity itself of the interplay of the (organized) collective and (singular) particular elements, or of either type of 'effects', to begin with, appears to be irreducibly inaccessible, and hence cannot be 'mastered' by any means. It cannot be assigned any available or conceivable terms, such as 'underlying', which makes Bataille appeal to the (irreducibly) 'unknowable' and, in conceiving of this (ultimately in turn inconceivable) process itself, to 'unknowledge'. Nor, however, can (the alterity of) this efficacity be postulated as existing in itself and by itself, as anything to which inaccessible properties can be assigned. Accordingly, the unknowable is not something excluded from the domain or the configuration governed by the logic in question, as an *absolute* other of it, which would return the situation to a classical regime, by enabling one to master the unknowable by exclusion (sovereignty is never mastery). Instead it is irreducibly linked to this configuration and made the efficacity of the effects that define it. It may be added that it is even more the necessary (non)relation to this alterity-efficacity than the fragmentary multiplicity of writing (which is merely one of its effects) that Blanchot refers to (via 'the neutral' and 'the fragmentary') by 'the absence of the book', or Derrida by 'the end of the book and the beginning of writing' (1974).

The situation may appear paradoxical, even impossible, which in part makes Bataille speak of 'the encounter with the impossible', while, however, making the encounter itself with this impossible possible. Indeed it does lead to an epistemology that is complex and difficult, and for some impossible to accept. What is experientially or otherwise intolerable to some, but would be affirmed by and is a necessary condition of interior experience and sovereignty, is that this irreducible loss of meaning is in fact the *efficacity* of meaning, ultimately of all possible meaning. Emerging at the limit of the possible and at the threshold of the impossible, sovereignty accepts and welcomes this type of knowledge or (or accompanied by) unknowledge, defined by Bataille as the process of relating to this unknowable. In other words, in question is not merely a renunciation of a further analysis but the recognition that, at a certain point, any further analysis is in principle excluded. This impossibility, however, does not preclude, but instead enables, a rigorous analysis of the effects of this unknowable efficacity. Hence, according to Bataille, 'it would be impossible to speak of unknowledge [for example, as 'unknowledge'] as such, while we can speak of its effects' (this sentence is omitted from the text published in '*Conférences* 1951–1953'). Conversely, 'it would not be possible to seriously speak of unknowledge independently of its effects' (1962, 5; *Oeuvres Complètes*, VIII, 219).

The conception just outlined is remarkable, even if not altogether unprecedented (it is found in Blanchot and several other figures mentioned here). It is equally remarkable that this 'calculus', formulated in a rather scientific, almost mathematical mode by Bataille himself, is used and indeed developed by Bataille in considering such ordinary human effects as laughter and tears, which are specifically in question in the elaborations just cited. That is, except that these are neither ordinary nor even 'human' in any classical sense we can give to this word. Indeed they are joined with, and coupled to, such (more conventionally) extraordinary effects as sexual excitation, poetic emotion, the sense of the sacred, ecstasy, sacrifice and the death of God (OC, VIII, 567–8, 592). The conjunction itself of a rigorously formal theoretical framework and something that is, at every level, outside any formalization (in any conceivable sense) is characteristic of Bataille. Now, however, this conjunction itself is given a rigorous epistemological justification by virtue of the fact that these effects, the absolute uniqueness of each occurrence of such phenomena, are formalized as irreducibly unformalizable, while *accessible*. By contrast the efficacity of all effects involved, manifest in 'the sum of all these effects' (OC, VIII, 592), is irreducibly inaccessible, unknowable. How such effects conspire to form, as they sometimes do, rich and complex orders is itself mysterious. By the same token, it cannot be seen as mystical, in the sense that one of the rigorous consequences of the sum of these effects is that no single, omnipotent agency behind them can be postulated. One can speak here of the death of God, in the broad sense of theological-like thinking wherever it is found.

Bataille's own writing becomes a particular case of this epistemology and logic, which would define the epistemology and logic of reading accordingly. This epistemology would never allow (Bataille himself or his readers) a rigorous 'summing-up' of Bataille's (interior) experience and writing under a single non-provisional rubric such as 'encounter with the impossible' or 'encounter' and 'the impossible', however effective it may be conceptually, rhetorically or strategically. The impossible and unknowable in question entails and is the efficacity of these impossibilities as well. It is, however, also the efficacity of the immense possibilities offered to and enacted by Bataille's writing, or offered to his readers, even if 'insurmountable possibilities'. Bataille himself speaks of 'the abyss of possibilities' (*Inner Experience*, 1988b, 103). A seemingly paradoxical but in fact logical consequence of

Bataille's epistemology is that impoverishment and abundance, loss and excess, the impossible and the possible, the unknowable and the richness of knowledge, or a suspension of logic and its most rigorous use all reinforce and enable each other.

It follows that, in approaching Bataille's 'encounter with the impossible', one cannot bypass other major concepts introduced by Bataille and/in their irreducible interactions anymore than Bataille himself could avoid multiplying his concepts, strategies, textual styles and so forth. It would not be possible to properly explain here all of these concepts or the connections among them, even leaving aside that the considerations just given would make it an interminable process. I shall, accordingly, only delineate some of them, which are arguably the most crucial from the concept-oriented perspective here adopted. Beyond those already indicated, in particular interior experience, they include unknowledge, sovereignty, restricted and general economy, chance, and literature and poetry. As follows from the preceding discussion, one can (always provisionally) centre, and some readers have, one's treatment otherwise – on sacrifice, gift, eroticism, ecstasy, expenditure, heterology or literature. I shall comment on some of these as I proceed.

The concept of unknowledge defines the nature and structure of our knowledge in relation to the epistemological situation here outlined. The ultimate nature of unknowledge is itself inaccessible: we cannot know how we ultimately know anymore than what is ultimately responsible for the things (objects of knowledge) that we can know. As I have stressed, however, even though unknowledge places an irreducible limit upon all knowledge, it brings into play the limits of the known and the unknown, the knowable and the unknowable, the possible and the impossible, and of the relationships between them and their limits. Other terms, such as the representable and the unrepresentable, the thinkable and the unthinkable, and so forth would be considered within the same conceptual field.

By analogy with the science of political economy, 'general economy' is defined as the science (theory) of sovereignty. Bataille juxtaposes general economy to classical or 'restricted' economies, such as that of Hegel's philosophy or Marx's political economy. Restricted economies would claim or aim to contain or compensate for irreducible indeterminacy, loss and non-selective – excessive – accumulation within the systems they describe, at least in principle, if not in practice, thus making all expenditure in principle productive. Both fundamentally base their analysis of human practices on the idea of consumption or productive (or at least accountable) expenditure, rather than on (also) taking into account sovereign practices. The latter are assumed to be irreducible by general economy and the engagement with them defines sovereignty, the primary concern of general economy, defined as the science of sovereignty, in whatever domain the latter emerges. As Bataille writes:

> The science of relating the object of thought to sovereign moments in fact is only a *general economy* which envisages the meaning of these objects in relation to each other and finally in relation to the loss of meaning. The question of this *general economy* is situated on the level of *political economy*, but the science designated by this name is only a restricted economy – restricted to commercial values. In question is the essential problem for the science dealing with the use of wealth. The *general economy*, in the first place, makes apparent that *excesses of energy are produced, which by definition cannot be utilized. The excessive energy can only be lost without the slightest aim, consequently without any meaning.* This useless, senseless loss *is* sovereignty. (OC, V, 215–16, emphases added)

Sovereignty, thus, relates to the radical irreducible loss of meaning, which is by the same token also always excessive, in particular with respect to its containment within the experience of presence, consciousness and meaning. It is primarily as such that sovereignty is juxtaposed to the Hegelian mastery or lordship, always linked to meaning, in particular in giving meaning to the loss of meaning, even though Hegel's analysis of death and sacrifice also brings them into a close, almost infinitesimal proximity as well (although the subject is crucial throughout Bataille's work – see especially 'Hegel, la mort, et le sacrifice' (OC, XII, 326–45)). The practice of a general-economic theory may be 'sovereign' or a form of interior experience. Conversely, a given case of interior experience, such as Bataille's, may acquire aspects of scientific investigation, even though his works presenting it, such as *Inner Experience*, are quite different from the more conventionally theoretical genre of, say, *The Accursed Share*, *Theory of Religion* and related works.

It is crucial that general economy always entails a rigorous deployment of restricted economy. These relationships are irreducible in so far as general economy is the science of the relationships between that which can be accessible by restricted-economic means (which may be the only means of accessibility we possess) and that which is inaccessible by any means, whether those of restricted or those of general economy. Sovereignty, too, must be understood as an ultimately inaccessible part of interior experience. It is experienced or felt (in unknowledge) as unmanifest and unmanifestable in and through the force of its manifest effects, of which we can speak. Short of engaging with these efficacious dynamics and the resulting interactions, one always ends up with a restricted economy, even if in the name of excess, indeterminacy, loss of meaning and so forth. According to Bataille: 'It is regrettable that the notions of "productive expenditure" and "nonproductive expenditure" have a basic value in all the developments of my book. But real life, composed of all sorts of expenditures, knows nothing of *purely* productive expenditure; in actuality it knows nothing of purely unproductive expenditure either' (1989b, 12). This point is often missed by Bataille's critics and admirers alike, which leads to significant misunderstandings of Bataille's works, specifically by assuming him to (uncritically) privilege or idealize expenditure, loss and so forth.

One of the inevitable consequences or correlatives of these considerations is a radical concept of chance, which Bataille argues to be inaccessible to 'the calculus of probability' (1988a, 76). In accordance with the preceding discussion, it would be inaccessible to any conceivable form of calculus, human or divine, which rigorously suspends all theological determination. In other words, this chance is irreducible not only in practice (which may be the case classically as well) but also in principle. There is no knowledge, in practice or in principle, that is or will ever be, or could in principle be, available to us and that would allow us to eliminate chance and replace it with the picture of necessity behind it. Nor, however, can one postulate such a (causal/lawful) economy as unknowable (to any being, individual or collective, human or even divine), but existing, in and by itself, outside our engagement with it. This qualification is crucial. For, some forms of the classical under-standing of chance allow for and are indeed defined by this type of assumption. In part proceeding via Blanchot's *Aminadab*, *Guilty* develops this concept of chance especially powerfully (1988a, 69–86), although Bataille's remarkable notes to 'Conférences 1951–1953' (OC, VIII, 562–3, 564–7) offer a necessary supplement.

Bataille's work may appear to be and has often been associated with and even defined by elements that are traditionally seen as counterparts of (philosophical) rigour – such as poetry, chance, play, eroticism, ecstasy, laughter and other, from the classical or traditional perspective, non-philosophical or counter-philosophical elements. Bataille's writing, however, is rigorous, as well as productive of knowledge. Indeed, for the reasons explained above, it rigorously requires the utmost intellectual, philosophical and logical rigour, even a rigour comparable (although of course not identical) to that of mathematics and the natural or exact sciences. Moreover, they refigure the non-philosophical elements listed above, by relating them, as effects, to (the efficacity of) the unknowable and unknowledge.

Accordingly, Bataille's concept of literature or poetry, including as practiced in his own writing, must be seen as bringing together that which is rigorously scientific or formal, and that which is rigorously (scientifically) outside any scientific treatment or formalization. Thus it conjoins the knowable and the unknowable, classical knowledge and sovereign unknowledge, and so forth. For Bataille, literature or poetry is, in our culture, the highest or the most intense form of the encounter with the impossible and/as of the writing of sovereignty, and, reciprocally, the sovereign writing of inner experience. Naturally, the terms themselves 'literature' and 'poetry' are given a special sense, although this sense manifests itself more readily in some conventional practice of both. (Literature and poetry are not always the same in Bataille, but I shall here suspend the difference between and nuances of these two terms in his work.) As Bataille writes, 'poetry, laughter, ecstasy are not the means for other things', especially not the means for knowledge, as, say, philosophy would require. 'In the [Hegelian] "system", poetry, laughter, ecstasy are nothing. Hegel gets rid of them in a hurry: he knows of no other end than knowledge' (1988b, 111). However, this hidden, subterranean, subversive, Dionysian invasion of poetry, laughter and ecstasy into philosophy is not only inevitable but opens new possibilities for philosophy itself, even if philosophy, as it has constituted – or instituted – itself so far may not want or cannot pursue these possibilities.

Both in relation to his own practice and in general, the association of experience and writing at the extreme limit with poetry or literature is found throughout Bataille's works. He often has in mind more conventionally literary works (as in the essays assembled in *Literature and Evil*), but far from exclusively so, especially in his own case. For poetic experience and writing define Bataille's non-fictional and overtly theoretical works – indeed, one might argue, more so than his fiction. I refer again especially to *Inner Experience*, *Guilty* and *On Nietzsche*. These works must also serve here as paradigmatic examples of Bataille's style. I cannot here consider, beyond the discussion given earlier, specific aspects of writing that result – their ruptured, fragmented structure, their multiple genres, their autobiographical or auto-eroto-biographical aspects, or their engagements with chance – defined by the sovereign epistemology. The possibility of such works, however, is a crucial point that allows one to rethink the possibilities of both literary and philosophical writing.

Bataille describes his own (interior) experience and writing as follows: 'in the desire for an inaccessible unknown, which at all cost we must situate beyond reach, I arrive at this feverish contestation of poetry' (*Inner Experience*, 1988a, 137). Bataille's interior experience and writing fundamentally reflect – indeed, as I said, they are – this experience, they are this chance and this necessity. Moving towards and opening, and then unfolding the unknown and, finally, the unknowable, they reflect and are necessitated by vertiginous – abyssal – oscillations between the known and the unknown, the knowable and the unknowable, the possible and the impossible. One is almost tempted to speak, paying well-deserved homage to Hegel's grand conception (and with Hölderlin in mind), of the vertigo – 'the abyss above' – of oscillations between absolute knowledge and absolute unknowledge. The radical – but never absolute – unknowable at stake in Bataille, however, would, in the same vertiginous abyss, suspend all absolutes, positive and negative, the very absoluteness of the absolute. 'Non-knowledge attained, absolute knowledge is no longer anything but one knowledge among others' (1988b, 55). One cannot quite speak of attaining non-knowledge either. For it is defined by anguish. It is anguish, the uneliminable anguish of the unknowable.

Blanchot

Blanchot summed up his life and writing for us himself, when he said in an autobiographical statement, indeed a micro-autobiography: 'born in 1907 and dedicated his life to literature'. (Naturally, this statement requires caution, for example, given the right-wing political journalism of the 1930s, and the fragmentary nature of Blanchot's autobiographical writing (in the present sense) need not only involve epistemological complexities here considered (although these continue to play a key role). By and large, however, the statement is true from about 1938 on.) The unsummable nature of this summing up (of both Blanchot's experience and work and of literature) is analogous to that of Bataille's 'encounter with the impossible', in part because what is at some point called 'the space of literature' and, then, 'speech' ('plural speech') and 'writing' (including his own) are structured analogously to the spaces of Bataille's unknowable and unknowledge. Ultimately the very possibility of literature, as writing and as reading, may be imperiled. Blanchot will speak of 'the death of reading, the death of writing'. This ultimate abandonment even of literature itself rather than only of culture (both high and low cultures, whose complicity in both directions Blanchot understood so penetratingly) may well be a culmination of Blanchot's lifelong dedication to literature and his most radical insight. This insight is helped by the key literary figures he considers, perhaps especially Hölderlin, Mallarmé and Kafka (although many others considered by Blanchot may be mentioned, Beckett, Woolf and Duras among them). *The Space of Literature* (1951) defines the epistemology of this space in its radical terms perhaps for the first time. *L'Entretien Infini* (*The Infinite Conversation*) (1969), where the 'construction' of this space proceeds by joining Levinas and Bataille (although Hegel, Nietzsche and Heidegger remain as crucial here as elsewhere in Blanchot), and then *The Writing of the Disaster* (1980) takes this epistemology to its ultimate limit just indicated, to 'the death of reading, the death of writing', the culmination of Blanchot's lifelong meditation on the relationships between death and literature or/as all writing. These works will here serve as the main signposts (admittedly too few and far between) in navigating through Blanchot's immense oeuvre.

I am speaking of the 'spaces' analogous to rather than identical to those of Bataille, in part because, while the epistemology is fundamentally parallel and while an often parallel network of concepts is at work, often somewhat different aesthetic, cultural and political aspects of literature itself are stressed. First of all, Blanchot's concept of literature is defined primarily against the background of literature in its more conventional sense, often by selecting a particular set of authors and reading them accordingly. In this respect, a writer of fiction and philosopher (again, in Deleuze and Guattari's sense of a creator of concepts) as he is, Blanchot remains a literary critic, arguably the most philosophical critic of this century. (He does have competition in such figures as Walter Benjamin, Mikhail Bakhtin and Paul de Man.) As a result, there emerges a somewhat different (from Bataille's) cluster of concepts and relations to 'the unknowable' (the latter concept is shifted as well). The very concept of the *space* of literature is specifically Blanchot's, too. It must be kept in mind, however, that, following, among other things, Heidegger's concepts of spatiality (specifically, the spatiality of *Dasein*) and consistently with the radical epistemology in question, space in this sense may not be conceivable and especially visualizable. Hence, in a certain sense it is not spatial in any sense available to us. The enactment of this 'space' in his own work, by and large, takes place more in his fictional works, in contrast to Bataille's (non-fictional) autobiographical writing, although some of Bataille's fictions can be read in this way as well. (Nor are these works scientific, or quasi-scientific, treatises of the type of *The Accursed Share*.) Some non-fictional works, critical and philosophical, contain elements of such an enactment and a few, such as *The Writing of the Disaster* and, to some degree, the earlier *Le Pas Au-Delà* (*The Step Not Beyond*) (1973) could be seen in these terms throughout, while others in more fragmentary ways, which, however, is part of the unsummability in question. (Conversely, some of Bataille's fiction functions similarly as well.) From *Thomas the Obscure* and (its quasi-sequel) *Aminadab*, his fictions become massive allegories of, to stay for the moment with Bataille's terms, the unknowable and unknowledge, and are used as such by both Bataille and later on by Derrida. I here use the term allegory also in de Man's sense, in turn entailing an analogous radical epistemology, which also makes these works allegories of allegory itself.

The political and ethical dimensions of these allegories remain crucial. In general, one would be mistaken to identify Blanchot's criticism or philosophy, let alone his fiction, with any form of, to use de Man's term, aesthetic ideology. As has been rightly stressed by a number of recent commentators, just as, and reciprocally with, philosophical-epistemological ones, the political and ethical dimensions are crucial, and indeed irreducible, in Blanchot's work, in particular proceeding via Bataille (the political) and Levinas (the ethical). Derrida's recent works, such as *The Politics of Friendship* and *The Specters of Marx*, or Deleuze's commentary on and usage of Blanchot's concept of friendship, or of course Bataille's work, may serve as significant examples of deploying these aspects of Blanchot's (as well as Levinas's and, more implicitly, Bataille's) work. In short, as is Bataille's, Blanchot's work is defined by complex heterogeneously interactive reciprocities between all these dimensions, as they invade and pass into each other.

I shall, then, here consider Blanchot's key concepts by traversing, with the preceding discussion of Bataille in mind, this space of reciprocities, proximities and difference between Bataille and Blanchot themselves. I shall use Blanchot's passage with which I began here as a guide, for it contains in a condensed form arguably the most crucial and most radical elements of Blanchot's epistemology and of his conception of literature. Accordingly, although Blanchot is compelled to engage with the network of terms whose multiplicity or dissemination cannot in turn be contained, as does Bataille, I shall here focus on the unfigurable and literature. The latter itself is conceived as a 'radical interrogation' of the unfigurable, or more accurately (we cannot interrogate the unfigurable 'itself' but only its effects), is shaped by an engagement with the unfigurable. Literature, thus, involves processes similar to Bataille's unknowledge as relating to the unfigurable/unknowable by means of, returning to Blanchot's terms, non-relation. In *The Infinite Conversation* Blanchot ultimately questions the adequacy of interrogation itself, however radical, he questions the very form of 'questioning', which appears to define all of our intellectual history. These conceptions and this agenda are intimated already in such earlier works as *The Space of Literature* and *La livre à venir* (*The Book to Come*) which already intimate the *death* of the book to come or, as will be seen, perhaps even of literature to come.

I shall, again, bypass the immense thicket of Blanchot's concepts and metaphors, and his brilliant usage of the epistemology of modern science (which is found in Bataille as well), specifically geometries of negative curvatures and modern cosmology based on Einstein's general relativity. Here, cutting though this thicket of concepts, is Blanchot's 'definition' of the unfigurable:

> Nothing permits one to exclude the hypothesis of an unfigurable Universe (a term henceforth deceptive); a Universe escaping every optical exigency and also escaping consideration of the whole – essentially non-finite, disunified, discontinuous. What about such a Universe? ... But will he ever be ready to receive such a thought, a thought that, freeing him from fascination with unity, for the first time risks summoning him to take the measure of an exteriority that is not divine, of a space entirely in question, and even excluding the possibility of an answer, since every response would necessarily fall anew under the jurisdiction of the figure of figures? But will he ever be ready to receive such a thought, a thought that, freeing him from fascination with unity, for the first time risks summoning him to take the measure of an exteriority that is not divine, of a space entirely in question, and even excluding the possibility of an answer, since every response would necessarily fall anew under the jurisdiction of the figure of figures?

The radical exteriority or alterity at stake in these propositions takes on a role analogous to the unknowable in Bataille, as considered earlier. As we recall, Blanchot adds, however: 'This amounts perhaps to asking ourselves: is man capable of a radical interrogation? That is, finally, is he capable of literature, if literature turns aside and towards the absence of the book?'

Blanchot, thus, associates both radical interrogation and the radical unfigurability with literature, even uniquely with literature, even when other fields of human endeavour are at stake, such as serialist music, discussed in 'Ars Nova', or perhaps even modern mathematics and science. That literature would assume for Blanchot the primary role in essentially and radically structuring the space of all art and even culture (or/as counter-culture) is not surprising. That radical interrogation, as conceived by him, signals the ultimate departure from literature – the death of literature, both of writing and of reading – rather than (this could be expected) only from culture, is more remarkable. As I said, *The Writing of the Disaster* will invoke both the death of writing and the death of reading more directly. Accordingly, literature itself (in any way we know it or even can conceive of it) may have to be sacrificed in the process, or rather it may no longer be possible at this limit. That is, such an interrogation may no longer function as literature in any conceivable sense that is meaningful or even definable within our culture, even though the latter appears to permit (including in legal terms) us to apply this term to virtually anything. To begin with, again, analogously to Bataille's unknowledge, at stake here is a process to which no name can apply. Secondly, 'literature' cannot be seen as a 'neutral' name, free of cultural or politico-ideological appurtenances, specifically aesthetic ideology. Blanchot's concept of the 'neutral', a key element of the epistemology and conceptual architecture under discussion here (and, again, of the reciprocity of Bataille's and Blanchot's thought), is designed with these complexities in view.

Once this type of space, the space defined by its relation to the unfigurable (or the unknowable), is introduced, two particular aspects of inhabiting this space, of practice within it, emerge. The first is the exploration (or more generally, knowledge) and productive deployment of whatever is possible under the conditions of the irreducibly unfigurable, and, as we have seen, much and, in a certain sense, everything is possible under these conditions, the best classical knowledge included. Accordingly, new and extraordinarily rich and productive possibilities of knowledge, philosophy, culture, literature or politics do emerge – but, again, *under these conditions*. The second aspect, on the other hand, is the exploration or, to begin with, the experience (interior experience) of existence at the threshold of or in relation to the unfigurable itself, and, as Nietzsche understood, the circumference of knowledge has many such boundary points (Nietzsche 1967, 97–8). Besides, by definition, this exploration is interminable, at least at some of such points, such as those where Blanchot's (*The Space of Literature* and *Le Pas Au-Delà* are perhaps especially graphic examples here, as the latter title indicates) and Bataille's work takes us. Blanchot's (or, again, Bataille's, or other figures' here mentioned) writing is defined and made possible by the complex interplay of both of these aspects. It is, however, especially the second that defines the existence in the space of literature, defines literature, for Blanchot and Bataille, or de Man (but, for a contrast, not necessarily or not in the same way for Derrida or Deleuze).

It may be useful to comment from this vantage point on Blanchot's earlier reading of Beckett in 'Where now, Who now?' Blanchot sees Beckett's *The Unnamable* as 'a decentered book deliberately deprived of every support'. 'It elects to begin precisely where there is no possibility of going on and persists stubbornly in staying there, without resorting to trickery or subterfuge, and stumbles on for three hundred pages'. It follows, first, that 'aesthetic considerations are out of place' in this case. Ultimately, as I said, it may not be possible to speak about literature any longer, certainly in any sense hitherto available. Alluding to Mallarmé's idea of the book, which will contain the whole world (Blanchot has written on the subject extensively), Blanchot suggests that 'what we have before us in *The Unnamable* is not a book because it is more than a book'. I would add, it is not literature because it is more than literature. Or rather, it is both more and less than a book, more and less than literature. 'It is a direct confrontation with the process from which all books derive – with the original point at which the work is inevitably lost, that always destroys the work, but with which an ever more primal relationship has to be established'. Accordingly, 'The unnamable is indeed condemned to drain the cup of infinity' (Blanchot 1982b, 192–4). 'Infinity', however, is here used in (or close to) Levinas's sense in *Totality and Infinity*, as connoting the radically unfigurable, designated by Levinas himself as Autrui – an absolute alterity, exteriority, otherness – which also links, especially for Blanchot, Levinas and Bataille. This infinity (un-finity may be a better name or un-name) unnamably names the radically unnamable, unfigurable, unknowable – in the black space which Beckett invokes and in which everything, all light and all enlightenment, are as inescapably Beckett's 'caged beasts born of caged beasts born of caged beasts born of caged beasts', as we ourselves are (1958, 386). These themes, developed in full measure later in Blanchot, lead to the complex relationships between the ethical and the literary, as indicated earlier. Art, most particularly literature – this is, for Blanchot, the message of Beckett's work, or of other key figures he considers – 'requires that he who practices it should be immolated by art, should become other, not another, not transformed from the human being he was into an artist [like, say, Thomas Mann], with artistic duties, satisfactions and interests, but into nobody, the empty, animated space where art's summons are heard', and ultimately the summons of the death of art. The answer to the question 'why art should require this metamorphosis' is to be 'found in the process by which the work of art, seeking its realization, constantly reverts to the point where it is confronted with failure. ... It is this exploration ... that makes artistic creation such a risky undertaking – both for the artist and for art', especially since one must risk and sacrifice art or literature itself – that is, try to make sure that it ultimately dies as a result (*The Sirens' Song*, 1982a, 196). Naturally, this would worry 'men of culture', 'men of taste', as Blanchot calls them, writers such as Thomas Mann or Georg Lukács among them, in contrast to Kafka, Beckett or Duras, or the composer Adrian Leverkühn, Mann's protagonist in *Doctor Faustus*. According to Blanchot, however, this is also the one thing, ultimately the only thing, that makes art an important activity. 'It is because *The Unnamable* makes us realize this in the bluntest possible way that it is more important than most of the [so-called] "successful" books published'. Blanchot concludes: 'Let us *try* to hear this voice ... And let us try to go down to the world into which sinks, henceforth condemned to speak, he who in order that he may write dwells in a timelessness where he must die in an endless dying' (197–8). This is this voiceless voice, the unwriteable writing of literature as a non-relational relation to the unfigurable, ultimately unfigurable even as unfigurable, in all of its aspects and implications (artistic, philosophical and political) that becomes or, again, has always been the lifelong dedication of Blanchot's work and that culminates in the death of writing, the death of reading of *The Writing of the Disaster*.

And yet, most disturbingly to the men of culture and taste, such as Mann or Lukács, it is the engagement with the radical unfigurability that appears to make possible all conceivable figuration, and the best figurations, old and new, have in fact or in effect always drawn on this radical unfigurability. Whether in this picture the unfigurable is seen as ultimately defeating figuration, in particular as 'literature', or giving it a chance, however small, is a complex question. As I said, there are significant differences on this point between different thinkers – such as Heidegger, Benjamin, Bataille, Adorno, Blanchot, Barthes, Derrida and de Man, with Blanchot, and de Man, arguably, offering us the least hope here. One might argue that Heidegger, Bataille, Derrida, Barthes and Deleuze are still enamoured with literature as a particular and even privileged form of intellectual practice. By contrast, Blanchot and de Man (especially in their late works) would see literature as crucial but ultimately secondary to the radical interrogation of the radically unfigurable. This view may also be seen as a complex and ambivalent reading of Hegel's famous announcement of 'the death of art' in his *Aesthetics* in 1830.

Whether it is possible as literature, or possible at all, radical interrogation compels us to explore as yet unimagined curvatures of thought, literature and culture, or of the physical universe, and to ask very radical questions concerning them. When, however, as in *The Writing of the Disaster*, at stake become the death of writing, the death of reading, the death of literature, the question is no longer only whether we are capable of literature or writing, if writing becomes the absence of the book or transgresses other currently available forms of it (say, hypertext or other computerized forms of it). Instead the question is whether we are capable of writing if writing itself becomes the absence or the death of writing. Radical interrogations in literature or elsewhere, for example in modern science, may extend the limits of both knowledge and the unknowable well beyond those of which we can conceive now, to forever more complex forms of both figuration and the impossibility of figuration. A truly radical interrogation may or may not be ultimately possible. Either as possible or as impossible, it appears to be ever more necessary, even though and because it may lead us to the death of reading, the death of writing, the death of literature, even the death of interrogation – perhaps to the beginning of something else in this unfigurable ununiverse, in the ununiverse of the unfigurable. If we are lucky, if – 'caged beasts born of caged beast born of caged beasts born of caged beast' – we can ever be so lucky. For Blanchot's *The Writing or the Disaster* also reminds us – indeed this is what the *writing* of the disaster would 'be', if one could assign any ontology (or 'itself-ness') to either this writing or disaster itself –

that it is even more difficult to forget than to figure, or unfigure, the darkness that inhabits and surrounds all these figures – Dante, Hölderlin, Nietzsche or Leverkühn (or Marlow's, if perhaps not Goethe's, Faust), the universe, or innumerable others amid still darker disasters of modernity that defeat silence and speech, or writing – disasters unwriteable and unspeakable, but also unsilenceable. This is a darker, more tragic message of Blanchot's work, but it cannot stop this work itself, the work of writing, the work of reading.

Arkady Plotnitsky

Further reading and works cited

Bataille, G. 'Conférences sur le Non-Savoir', *Tel Quel*, 10, 1962.
—. *Oeuvres Complètes* [OC], 12 vols. Paris 1970–88.
—. *Visions of Excess*, ed. A Stoeckl. Minneapolis, MN, 1985.
—. *Guilty*. New York, 1988a.
—. *Inner Experience*. Albany, NY, 1988b.
—. *Theory of Religion*. New York, 1989a.
—. *The Accursed Share*. New York, 1989b.
—. *On Nietzsche*. New York, 1990.
—. *The Impossible*. San Francisco, 1991.
—. 'Hegel, la mort, et le sacrifice', OC, XII.
Beckett, S. *The Unnamable*. New York, 1958.
Bident, C. *Partenaire invisible*. Editions Champ Vallon, 1998.
Blanchot, M. *The Sirens' Song*. Bloomington, IN, 1982a.
—. *The Space of Literature*. Lincoln, NE, 1982b.
—. *The Writing of the Disaster*. Lincoln, NE, 1986.
—. *The Infinite Conversation*. Minneapolis, MN, 1993.
—. *The Blanchot Reader*, ed. G. Quasha. New York, 1999.
Botting, F. and Wilson, S. (eds) *The Bataille Reader*. Oxford, 1997.
— (eds) *Bataille: A Critical Reader*. Oxford, 1998.
Deleuze, G. and Guattari, F. *What is Philosophy?* London, 1994.
Derrida, J. *Of Grammatology*. Baltimore, MD, 1974.
—. 'From Restricted to General Economy: Hegelianism without Reserve', in *Writing and Difference*. Chicago, 1980.
Gill, C. B. (ed.) *Blanchot: the Demand of Literature*. London, 1996.
Hill, L. *Blanchot: Extreme Contemporary*. London, 1997.
Holland, M. *The Blanchot Reader*. Oxford, 1995.
Levinas, E. *Totality and Infinity*. Pittsburgh, PA, 1969.
Nietzsche, F. *The Birth of Tragedy and the Case of Wagner*. New York, 1967.
Poulet, G. *The Metamorphoses of the Circle* [1961]. Baltimore, MD, 1967.
http://lists.village.virginia.edu/~spoons/blanchot/mb_french_chronological.html.
Stoekl, A. (ed.) 'On Bataille', *Yale French Studies*, 78, 1990.

23. Bertolt Brecht (1898–1956)

Bertolt Brecht is not generally known as a theorist – at least not to English-speakers with access only to his poetry, some of his plays and limited, if serviceable, translations of a fraction of the critical and theoretical essays (Brecht 1965, 1977, 1992). The view of Brecht as a theatre artist corrupted by politics, who allegedly dismissed the audience's empathetic response to emotion on stage, in the name of reason and alienation in the theatre and out, still prevails in Britain and North America in publications like *The New York Times* or *The Economist* as well as in writing by some academics. This view not only misses Brecht's contribution to theatre and film from Canada to the Philippines, Finland to South Africa, and the impact of his example on renowned directors such as Peter Brook and Jean-Luc Godard, as well as on activists using performance for politics. It also obscures the intensity of the interaction between Brecht and mid-century theorists of *modernity*, modernism, realism and the relationship between aesthetics and politics, especially Ernst Bloch, György Lukács, T. W. Adorno and Walter Benjamin, as well as his impact on the political and cultural theory of younger intellectuals, from those associated with the Frankfurt School in Germany, especially Alexander Kluge, to marxists and others in France, from Roland Barthes to *Cahiers du Cinéma*, and on materialist critics in Britain identified with cultural studies or the film theory of *Screen*. In the United States, Brecht's theory has had a more modest impact outside the purview of Brecht specialists, although feminists as well as marxists have found his work useful including, very recently, Fredric Jameson.

This essay will focus on key critical terms developed by Brecht out of theatre and film practice in Weimar Berlin (1920s–1932) and in the German Democratic Republic (GDR–1948–56) and reflection in exile in Scandinavia and the United States (1933–47). It will also examine the appropriation of these terms by his contemporaries and successors and explore the theoretical implications of methodological differences. Like his contemporary Benjamin, but unlike the professional academics Lukács and Adorno, Brecht wrote experimentally rather than systematically, and published 'creative' and 'critical' texts together in collections called *Versuche* (essays or experiments). Many of Brecht's theoretical insights appear in dramatic form – such as the *Messingkauf* (lit. buying brass; fig. acquiring material for use; Brecht 1965; 1998, v. 22), a dialogue among philosopher, actor, dramaturge and a worker, probably the stage electrician, about the value of art, play and instruction in the theatre. They also appear in parables, such as *Me-ti, Buch der Wendungen* (Brecht 1998, v. 18), whose playful subtitle, meaning 'book of changes' or 'turns of phrase', appropriates the example of Mo-ti (Chinese philosopher; ca. 480–400 BCE) to represent not a system of thought but a series of encounters among a commentator (Me-ti), a Brechtian poet (Kin-jeh) and figures representing the marxist classics, Marx (Ka-me) and

Lenin (Mien-Leh), and their successors from Trotsky (To-tsi) to Stalin (Nien) to the dissidents, Rosa Luxemburg (Sa) and Karl Korsch (Ka-osch), the exiled philosopher Brecht called his 'Marxist teacher' (Brecht 1998, 22, 45; Knopf 1996, 2, 447–76; Gross, in Mews 1997, 168–77). Even his most systematic theoretical statement, the *Short Organum for the Theatre*, first published in 1949 (Brecht 1998, 23, 65–97, 289–97; 1992, 179–205, 276–81) and named after the Renaissance thinker Francis Bacon's *New Organon for the Sciences*, is a series of aphoristic observations.

As 'organum' or 'tool' implies, Brecht used his own terms and those of others as tools for investigating and refunctioning (*Umfunktionieren*) the world as well as the stage, page or screen. This does not mean that in his hands ideas became merely instruments (although critics like Adorno argue as much) but rather that ideas, as Marx argued, are determined by social being and political struggle; they emerge out of material practice and should be tested against it. Although he admired Lenin's revolutionary example, Brecht borrowed most directly from the teaching of dissident marxist and ex-Party member, Karl Korsch, who, like Antonio Gramsci, favoured a philosophy of practice with critical attention to the specific relations of economic and cultural phenomena rather than a generalized theory of economic determinism (Kellner, in Mews 1997, 284). Brecht's marxism was neither doctrinaire nor opportunist, but rather a practical and playful engagement with Marx's 11th thesis on Feuerbach: 'The philosophers have always sought to understand the world; the point, however, is to change it'. His artistry was likewise pragmatic; although he continually experimented with new forms and techniques of performance – from gestic acting and Verfremdung (critical es*trange*ment) of character and action in epic – or, more precisely, *epicizing (episierend)* – theatre to the pleasurable and instructive representation of social contradiction in dialectical theatre – he always returned to the question of function. He was thus critical of those, such as Lukács, who remained attached to an apparently immutable form of realism represented by the nineteenth-century novel, and willing to discard techniques that become reified and absorbed as commodities by capitalism (as estrangement and montage have been absorbed by advertising) and thus no longer facilitate a realistic critique of same.

The central, often mistranslated term of Brecht's critical practice is *Verfremdung*. Brecht himself began using the term in an essay written in 1935, 'Alienation Effects in Chinese Acting' (1992, 91–9) in response directly to the estrangement effect – as least for European spectators – of the Chinese opera star and female impersonator Mei Lanfang and indirectly to the theory and practice of the Russian formalists, especially the radical left faction represented by playwrights Vladimir Mayakovski and Brecht's friend, Sergei Tretyakov (1992, 99) rather than the literary theorist Victor Shklovski, who developed the concept of *ostranenie* (defamiliarization). Although John Willett's mistranslation 'alienation' has stuck, the first English translation (published in 1936 as 'The Effects of Disillusion in Chinese Acting'; Brecht 1998, 22, 960) better captures the original sense: undoing theatrical illusion so as to encourage the audience to understand and thus critique the world off as well as onstage (1998, 22, 401). A decade before he coined the term, however, Brecht and his contemporaries in the fertile experimental theatre of 1920s Berlin, such as director Erwin Piscator, designer Caspar Neher and composers Kurt Weill, Hanns Eisler and Paul Hindemith developed the theory out of practice work with techniques that they associated with epic rather than dramatic theatre. Although Brecht called epic theatre 'non-Aristotelian', his antagonist was not so much Aristotle as the sentimental operetta or the Wagnerian *Gesamtkunstwerk*, whose elaborate stage machinery, plaster sets and rousing

music enveloped the audience in illusions and fake emotion. In Brecht's most programmatic opposition between epic and dramatic theatre, published in the first volume of
Versuche (1931), 'epic' signifies narrative voice and point of view, shown in discrete scenes
linked by montage rather than the 'dramatic' manipulation of suspense and sudden
reversals of bourgeois theatre; in acting by quotation and representation of the gest of
the actor towards the character rather than unrestrained emotional embodiment and
identification; in separation of the elements such as music and scene design rather the
sentimental harmonizing of music and emotion (1992, 37–46; 1998, 24, 78–85). Although
this programmatic statement opposed 'sensations' and 'emotions' to 'recognition' and
'decisions', Brecht went on to argue, in 'Theatre for Pleasure and Theatre for Instruction'
(written in exile in 1935) that he was not against emotional identification (and in fact
recommended it to actors studying their roles) or against pleasure in art for all involved, but
rather against the manipulation of emotion, in art as in politics; where the 'dramatic
theatre spectator' sees 'nature', 'great art' and 'inescapable' suffering, the 'epic theatre
spectator' should see both the art of the representation and the critical exposure of the
causes of suffering (1992, 71; 1998, 22, 110). Estrangement in Brecht's usage is thus
precisely *not* the 'alienation' of labour, which the early Marx borrows from Hegel's master–
slave dialectic, but, as the marxist philosopher Ernst Bloch suggests, the critique of that
alienation (Bloch 1972, 3–9).

   Although *Verfremdung* has been closely associated with the specific stage techniques
mentioned above, Brecht continually renegotiated this association, refunctioning techniques for critical representation and for thinking *as* intervention (*eingreifendes Denken*).
Verfremdung depended on commitment and on opinions and objectives (*Ansichten und
Absichten*), without which, he writes in the Short Organum, 'we can represent nothing at
all' (1992, 196; 1998, 23, 86). His understanding of commitment was, however, always
concrete. Where Jean-Paul Sartre's *engagement* remains a romantic notion of the author's
appeal to the reader's 'feeling for freedom' (1949, 40), Brecht focuses on the enactment of
critique. The gest, in Willett's archaic translation of Brecht's *Gestus*, carries the original's
associations of gist and gesture, meaning and bearing (Brecht 1992, 42). In carriage, tone
of voice and interaction, as well as in gesture, the gest conveys the actor's attitude to and
social engagement with her action (1998, 22, 329–30; 1992, 104). More broadly, it
applies to the producers (director, designer, composer as well as actor) and the means
(material and apparatus) used to represent the 'socially significant gest' of the production
as a whole, as well as those of its constituent parts (1998, 22, 158; 1992, 86), without,
however, losing sight of the representation of contradiction (1998, 23, 288; 1992, 277).
Faced with audiences that happily ducked contradictions (as did the enthusiastic
bourgeois audience humming 'Mack the Knife' from *The Threepenny Opera*, his most
popular and profitable play), Brecht proposed the *Lehrstück* (learning play), which
dispensed with audiences and even with the theatre apparatus. Scripts like *The Exception
and the Rule* and *He who says yes/He who says no*, accompanied by several options for
performance and discussion, offered non-professional players such as workers or students a
model for learning through performing controversial action without the pressure of
aesthetic standards so as to test the implications of that action hypothetically as well as
realistically (1998, 22, 351; see Schoeps in Mews 1997). It is this model, used by
communists and youth groups in 1920s Germany, which informs political enactments
from workers' agitprop in 1930s America to the role-playing of social conflict of the
forum theatre pioneered by Augusto Boal for non-professional groups with limited

resources since the 1960s and modified for local performance from the American inner city to Southern African rural slums.

Faced with the complexity of the culture industry in advanced capitalism, however, critique has to use more craft. As Brecht argues, telling the truth about society requires art and cunning as well as courage (1998, 22, 74–79). Showing the act of production and the institutions that sustain capitalist productive relations is key because the act of showing makes visible the social relations otherwise reified in the commodity formation that, as Marx reminds us, treats social relations as relations between things. However clear the picture, on stage, screen or photographic image, the picture alone will not ensure a realistic representation of capitalist society or serve the radical functional transformation (*Funktionswechsel*) of art in society (1998, 21, 439; 22, 265). The workings of the apparatus should be made visible. Noting that 'a photograph of the Krupp factory or of AEG says almost nothing about these institutions', Brecht argues that the 'reification [*Verdinglichung* or thingification] of human relations' and the commodification of art renders obsolete mimetic notions of realistic representation in photographic reproduction and makes imperative the analysis of all levels of production, from the actor's gestic repertoire and the photographic apparatus to the construction and funding of theatres and the publishing and film industries (21, 469).

Some of Brecht's most trenchant comments on the commodification of art, the culture industry and the challenge of critique in areas other than theatre (especially film, photography and radio) appear, like the preceding remark, in *The Threepenny Lawsuit*, which he wrote as part of the action against the Nero film company for softening the film treatment of *The Threepenny Opera* in 1930. Although not apparent from the fragment published in English (1992, 47–50), this essay plays a fundamental role not only in Brecht's theoretical development but also in his influence on contemporaries such as Benjamin, successors such as Enzensberger and Kluge, and antagonists such as Adorno (Giles 1997). Tracking the 'deconstruction' (*Demontierung*) of the author's work (especially the critique in the play of the capitalist as criminal) and its reconstruction, like some second-hand car (1998, 488), as a commodity standardized to the demands of a mass-market audience for films about glamorous outlaws, Brecht anticipates Adorno's argument about the commodification of art under the culture industry (see Adorno 1997, 16–18, 225–61). Arguing that no work of art, however transcendentally universal, is untouched by the apparatus (*apparatfrei*) and that even the autonomy of art, its apparent lack of effect or consequence (*Folgenlosigkeit*) (Brecht 1998, 21, 512), is not untouched, Brecht anticipates the work of Herbert Marcuse (Adorno's colleague at the Frankfurt School) and his comments on the social function of this apparent functionlessness of art: the representation of a beautiful illusion of happiness in a world of oppression (Marcuse 1968, 95–101). Brecht's analysis of the penetration of art by the apparatus and thus the transformation of mystery into commodity reappears in Benjamin's 1936 essay on the 'work of art in the age of its technical reproducibility' (Benjamin 1980, 2, 437–507), whose original title emphasizes the standardization of art by technological (*not* mechanical) reproduction. Benjamin's idea of the aura, the authority and authenticity of art, destroyed by capitalist conditions of reproducibility and replaced by the 'rotten – in the sense of decaying – spell' (*fauligen Zauber*) of the commodity (Benjamin 1980, 2, 477, 492) and the assertion that the reality of photographic representation only appears to transcend the apparatus (458, 495) echo Brecht's analysis of the transformation of art's autonomy or 'functionlessness' into a commodity.

The troubled relationship between art and apparatus, autonomy and *engagement* exercises Brecht, Benjamin and Adorno, but in different ways. Although Benjamin repeatedly praises Brecht's formal innovations, such as the gest, the separation of the elements and the relaxed audience (Benjamin 1973, 3, 21, 15), the last of which reappears in his argument (drawing on film critic Siegfried Kracauer as well as Brecht) for the distracted audience (1980, 465, 504), it is this insistence on the institutional determination of art, including the apparent autonomy of art from the institution, that brings Benjamin closer to Brecht than Adorno. To be sure, Adorno recognizes that autonomy is a 'social fact' (1997, 1) and a response to commodification rather than a complete escape from it (2), but he rejects Brecht's 'abolition of aesthetics' (1992, 20; 1998, 21, 202) and Benjamin's destruction of aura, arguing instead that art can critique society only when it is autonomous and exercises critique only by its autonomy, by 'merely existing' as an art work (Adorno 1997, 226) rather than overtly criticizing existence. In his theory, explicit commitment compromises autonomy because it amounts to advertising and therefore complete commodification. This ideal of the uniqueness and the disinterestedness of the autonomous work links Adorno to the idealist aesthetics of Kant and Hegel; his insistence that the work match an autonomous *idea* does not allow a theory of the institution mediating between the antinomy of 'art' and 'society' and therefore leaves no room for the pragmatic negotiation at different levels of mediation that characterizes Brechtian theoretical and theatrical practice. Although the sharp rejection of Brecht's tendentious 'message in art' as a 'clandestine accommodation with the world' (Adorno 1977b, 193) that characterized Adorno's essay on 'Commitment' (initially published in *Der Monat*, funded by the Cold War institution, the Congress on Cultural Freedom (Willett 1998, 227), in 1962, just after the erection by the GDR of the Berlin Wall had inspired renewed anti-communist attacks on Brecht) gives way in his *Aesthetic Theory* (1970) to the possibility that 'commitment is a higher level of reflection than tendency; it is not just out to correct unpleasant situations . . . [but] aims at the transformation of the preconditions of situations' (1997, 246), Adorno remains committed to form rather than function, rather than, as Brecht has it, refunctioning different forms to different occasions of resistance.

Brecht did not live to read Adorno's critique but his case against the formalist and therefore *unrealistic* tendency of Lukács's theory of realism has some relevance for Adorno as well. To be sure, Adorno attacks Lukács for dogmatically dismissing all modern art as 'decadent' and thus for relapsing into a reactionary defence of immutable tradition rather than the critical realism he claims to advocate (Adorno 1977a, 154–5) and argues instead that the truly modern work of art resists society by refusing to represent it: 'art's asociality is the determinate negation of a determinate society' (1997, 226). But, from Brecht's point of view, both would be idealists to the extent that they insist that art conform to an ideal form, whether that ideal is represented by Balzac's 'realist' depictions of nineteenth-century Paris or Joyce's and Beckett's 'modernist' resistance to linear narratives and transparent reflection. Both also invited Brecht's pragmatic protest, in that they claimed that only art conforming to their respective models would offer an effective critique of actually existing capitalist society.

It is against creeping idealism in modernist and realist critical theory that Brecht defines realis*tic* cultural practice. Lukács's assertion, published in 1938 in *Das Wort* (which included Brecht among the editors but was published in Moscow under the shadow of the show trials against dissident communists), that 'so-called avant-garde literature' was 'anti-realist' (Lukács 1977, 29) because it remained at the level of 'immediacy' (37), apparently refusing 'to mirror objective reality . . . to shape the highly complex mediations in all their unity and diversity' (43), reiterates the orthodox opposition between capitalist decadence and socialist realism, defined by its 'representation of the achievements of socialism and the socialist individual in the present and future' (Zhdanov 1981, 21). Brecht's response, which neither *Das Wort* nor the Comintern-funded *International Literature* would publish, hints at this political pressure by arguing that Lukács's notion of realism was not only unrealistic but also *alienated* from reality (*Wirklichkeitsfremd*) (Brecht 1998, 22, 456; 1977, 70; trans. modified). Lukács's insistence on the normative status of the nineteenth-century novel was thus formalist not only in fixing on a single form to the exclusion of others but also in denying the undeniable reality of modern life that would not fit in outdated forms. The totalizing narratives of so-called socialist realist novels were politically as well as aesthetically unrealistic, in that they offered formal rather than real solutions to the social problems they depicted (1998, 458; 1977, 72). In the GDR of the 1950s, Brecht returned to this problem, objecting to the heroic novel of 'socialist arrival' that provided only fictional solutions to real problems (1998, 23, 259; 1992, 267) and arguing instead that socialist artists should show not only 'victories' but also 'the threat of defeat or else [they would give rise to] the error that victories were easy' (1998, 25, 422; Kruger 1994). Realistic representations are therefore risky; their realistic character depends not only on their accuracy, but also on their capacity to test existing models and means of representation against the pressing demands of a changing reality while maintaining a sense of humour and invention (1998, 22; 409; 1992, 109; 1977, 82). 'Fighting realism' is serious business, but it requires a light rather than a heavy hand: 'The world is certainly out of joint and it will take powerful movements to put it together again, but among the instruments that might serve, there is one, delicate, breakable, which requires handling with ease [*leichte Handhabung beansprucht*]' (1998, 22, 817; 1965, 94; trans. modified).

This articulation of a necessary and delicate balance between the serious business of transforming reality and the light hand needed to represent that transformation artfully and critically is Brecht's signal contribution to contemporary and present-day debates on the art of politics and the politics of art, but it has also been the source of conflicting interpretations of his work. While Lukács and his successors among the GDR bureaucrats and Communist Party officials in France and elsewhere attacked Brecht for an allegedly formalist and anti-realist attachment to avant-garde experiments, structuralists found in *Verfremdung* a semiotic imperative, a self-reflexive attention to the arbitrariness of signs, and poststructuralists or deconstructionists a deferral rather than a consolidation of meaning. Louis Althusser, maverick member of the French Communist Party (PCF), finds Brecht's theatre materialist to the extent that it makes visible the latent structures of recognition in and of the audience rather than simply dishing up an ideologically correct story (1969, 142–51). Roland Barthes, influenced by marxism but no PCF member, praised Brecht in 1957, a few years after the Berliner Ensemble astonished French audiences for 'breaking the Zhdanovian impasse' by 'separating ideology and semiology' (1972, 71). He argues that Brecht's formalism is semiotic, ' a protest against the confines of . ... false Nature; ... in a still alienated society, art must be critical ... the sign must be partially arbitrary' (75). Writing for the poststructuralist magazine *Tel Quel* in 1963, he hailed Brecht as a deconstructionist *avant la lettre*, who 'affirmed meaning but did not fulfil it' in a theatre that did not 'transmit a positive meaning (this is not a theatre of the signified) but show[s] that the world is an object to be deciphered (this is a theatre of the signifier)' (1972, 263). A decade later, in his more reflective memoir, Barthes acknowledged that a radical semiotic reading of Brecht dodges his commitment to fighting realism in the name, perhaps, of the play of the signifier. Noting that he would prefer to 'live with little politics', he quotes Brecht's meditation on the choice between being the 'object' or the 'subject' of 'politics' (Brecht 1998, 22, 304) as though it were Brecht's reproach to Barthes himself (Barthes 1977, 70–1) but also notes that Brecht never quite solved the problem of representation that he posed in the case of the Krupp photograph. In Barthes's view, 'time, history ... the political ... resist copying' or at least the imitation that can be rendered visible in the gest of an actor (1977, 154).

This tension that Barthes notes between Brecht's committed and semiotic moments, between the imperative to render history visible and the arbitrariness of the signs to do so, reappears especially in cinematic appropriations of Brecht to craft what might be called a self-reflexive or cunning realism. In Jean-Luc Godard's 1967 film *La Chinoise*, one of several of his films to use techniques borrowed from Brecht, Maoist students debate the power of the names of their forebears; Brecht's name remains on the classroom board and the screen as others are erased. While the kind of play and pleasure evoked by the street slogans of May 1968 owed more to the situationists' inheritance of dada and to the erotic liberation theory of Marcuse, then based in California, the writing of Godard and his fellows in *Cahiers du Cinéma* (especially 1968–72) reflected Brecht's influence. Radicalized by May 1968, *Cahiers* shifted from celebrations of the classical American cinema to politically charged analyses of cinematic sign systems. Collectively written articles such as '*La Vie est à nous* [by Jean Renoir]: A Militant Film' (Browne 1990, 68–88) drew on Brecht's practical example – here his film, *Kuhle Wampe* (1932), made with composer Eisler and director Slatan Dudow – as well as his theoretical imperatives, especially those of refunctioning form and institution and of the necessary light touch of the instrument of analysis (characteristic of the director Renoir). The English appropriation of *Cahiers'* example and with it a 'new' cinematic Brecht appeared in *Screen* magazine from 1974. Where *Cahiers* in this period consistently emphasized Brecht's 'fighting realism', articles in *Screen's* first special issue on Brecht played out a tension between celebrations of a poststructuralist Brecht as advocate for the play of the signifier (by the Barthes scholar, Stephen Heath) and a more militant defence of realism (Colin MacCabe; both in *Screen* 1974), reflecting not only the absence of anything approaching the revolutionary turmoil of May 1968 (and equivalents in Germany and Italy) but also local academic battles about 'Continental theory'. Where Heath and MacCabe used Brecht's example as a way of arguing for forms that could be both realistic and avant-garde, the older marxist critic, Raymond Williams, retained a certain scepticism about the claims for radical form, arguing that 'certain techniques . .. once experimental and actual shocks. .. have become the working conventions of . .. commercial art' (Williams 1989, 62).

In West Germany during the 1960s and 1970s, the growth of the student movement and the extra-parliamentary opposition to what was seen as the erasure and therefore normal-ization of the Nazi past and the ongoing undemocratic character of the West German state provided the occasion for a revival of the leftist cultural and political theory of the Weimar Republic, including Brecht, whose fighting realism challenged the political quietism and cultural elitism of the Frankfurt School, represented above all by Adorno in his role as professor and director of the institute until 1969. After years of Cold War repression, Brecht reappeared not only as the subject of influential scholarly studies of his most radical theatre and political work (Brüggemann, Steinweg) but also as the inspiration for programmes for the critical refunctioning of the media. Critic Hans Magnus Enzensberger drew on Brecht's utopian formulation of two-way radio as well as Adorno's condemnation of the culture industry in his discussion of community-based alternatives to the 'consciousness industry'. Sociologist Oskar Negt and film-maker and Frankfurt scholar Alexander Kluge developed the idea of the *proletarian* public sphere, the sphere of working-class experience and aspirations which excluded or marginalized the legitimate or bourgeois public sphere by drawing on Brecht's critical reflections on the transformation of media institutions to challenge the concept of the bourgeois public sphere developed by another Frankfurt scholar, Jürgen Habermas. If in the 1970s the name as much as the example of Brecht offered the German New Left a touchstone for revival, twenty years later after the centenary of his birth (1998) Brecht is still the subject of debate in the united Germany, even if some dismiss him as a dead classic.

While Brecht and Brechtian terms entered the general intellectual culture of Europe more than a generation ago, his name resonates almost exclusively in academic circles in the United States, and then usually among Germanists and theatre scholars. His theoretical writings lack the prestige (and syllabus space) granted his contemporaries Benjamin and Adorno or his successors from Barthes to Kluge, although they have been recently picked up by feminists (e.g. Diamond) as well as the doyen of marxist criticism in the United States, Fredric Jameson. Yet even this brief review of Brecht demonstrates his original and lasting contribution to the debates of his day, on the aesthetics and politics of realism and modernism, and his anticipation of many current critical preoccupations, especially the interest in performance and performativity as terms of theoretical and not just theatrical analysis. Rereading Brecht as theorist now not only revitalizes the historic connection debates about aesthetics and politics; it also reminds us that the performative character of the enactment of critique was theorized long before the current Anglophone fashion generated belatedly by readings of J. L. Austin and Judith Butler.

Loren Kruger

Further reading and works cited

Adorno, T. W. *Aesthetic Theory*. Minneapolis, 1997.
Althusser, L. *For Marx*. London, 1969.
Barthes, R. *Critical Essays*. Evanston, IL, 1972.
—. *Roland Barthes by Roland Barthes*. New York, 1977.
Benjamin, W. *Understanding Brecht*. London, 1973.
—. *Gesammelte Schriften*, ed. R. Tiedemann, 12 vols. Frankfurt, 1980.
Bloch, E. '*Entfremdung, Verfremdung*: Alienation, Estrangement', in *Brecht*, ed. E. Munk. New York, 1972.
— et al. *Aesthetics and Politics*, ed. R. Taylor, afterword, F. Jameson. London, 1977. Includes: Adorno 1977a: 'Reconciliation under Duress'; Adorno 1977b: 'Commitment'; Bloch 1977: 'Discussing Expressionism'; Brecht 1977: 'Against Georg Lukács'; Lukács 1977: 'Realism in the Balance'.
Brecht, B. *The Messingkauf Dialogues*. London, 1965.
—. *Werke: Grosse Kommentierte Berliner und Frankfurter Ausgabe*, eds W. Hecht et al., 30 vols. Frankfurt, 1988–98 (cited as Brecht 1998).
—. *Brecht on Theatre: The Development of an Aesthetic*, ed. and trans. J. Willett. New York, 1992.
Browne, N. (ed.) *Cahiers du Cinéma, 1969–1972: The Politics of Representation*. Cambridge, MA, 1990. Includes: Narboni, Pierre and Rivette 1990: 'Montage'; Comolli and Narboni 1990: 'Cinema/Ideology/Criticism'; Bonitzer et al. 1990: '*La Vie est à nous*: A Militant Film'.
Brüggemann, H. *Literarische Technik und soziale Revolution*. Hamburg, 1973.
Diamond, E. *Unmaking Mimesis*. London, 1997.

Enzensberger, H. M. *The Consciousness Industry*. New York, 1974.

Giles, S. *Bertolt Brecht and Critical Theory*. Bern, 1997.

Hecht, W. *Brecht-Chronik*. Frankfurt, 1996.

Knopf, J. (ed.) *Brecht Handbuch: Vol. 1: Theater, Vol. 2: Lyrik, Prosa, Schriften*. Stuttgart, 1996.

Kruger, L. 'Stories from the Production Line: Modernism and Modernization in the GDR Production Play', *Theatre Journal*, 46, 1994.

Marcuse, H. *Negations*. Boston, 1968.

Mews, S. (ed.) *A Bertolt Brecht Reference Companion*. Westport, CT, 1997. Including: Mews 1997: 'Introduction'; Grimm 1997: 'Alienation in Context: On the Theory and Practice of Brechtian Theater'; Schoeps 1997: 'Brecht's *Lehrstücke*'; Gross, 'Dialectics and Reader Response: Bertolt Brecht's Prose Cycles'; Kellner 1997: 'Brecht's Marxist Aesthetic'; Mews 1997: 'Annotated Bibliography'.

Negt, O. and Kluge, A. *Public Sphere and Experience: Towards an Analysis of the Bourgeois and Proletarian Public Spheres*. Minneapolis, MN, 1993.

Sartre, J.-P. *What is Literature?* New York, 1949.

Screen, special issue on Brecht, 15, 2, 1974. Includes: MacCabe, 1974: 'Realism in the Cinema: Notes on Some Brechtian Theses'; Barthes, 1974: 'Diderot/Brecht/Eisenstein'; Mitchell, 1974: 'From Shklovsky to Brecht'; Brewster 1974: 'A Reply': Heath 1974: 'Lessons from Brecht'.

Steinweg, R. *Das Lehrstück: Bertolt Brechts Theorie einer politisch-ästhetischen Erziehung*. Stuttgart, 1972.

Suvin, D. *To Brecht and Beyond*. Totowa, NJ, 1984.

Völker, K. *Brecht: A Biography*. New York, 1978.

Willett, J. *Brecht in Context*. London, 1998.

Williams, R. *The Politics of Modernism*. London, 1989.

Zhdanov, A. A. 'Soviet Literature: The Richest in Ideas, the Most Advanced Literature', in *Problems in Soviet Literature. Reports and Speeches of the First Soviet Writers Congress*, ed. H. G. Scott. Westport, CT, 1981.

24. Jacques Lacan (1901–1981)

Psychoanalyst Jacques Lacan was one of the most influential thinkers of his time. The linguistic, philosophical and political scope of his *theory of the subject* stirred intellectuals and artists in his native France and all over the world. He was a faithful interpreter of Freud, but he freely incorporated artistic, mathematical and philosophical insights into his own psychoanalysis without subordinating the Freudian field to any of them. It has been said with reason that Freud took root in France mainly through Lacan. Though he published relatively little in his lifetime, Lacan drew fascinated critical attention whenever his writing made its rare appearance. As his yearly seminars began being transcribed, edited (by his son-in-law, analyst Jacques-Alain Miller) and disseminated in French (1975–98) and English (1978–98), a number of Freudian schools modelled on Lacan's also began training clinicians, in France and out (e.g. Québec, Italy, Spain and Latin America). In 1980 Lacan dissolved the École Freudienne de Paris that he had founded in 1964, and refounded it in its current form, the *École de la Cause Freudienne*. It is not, however, the only Lacanian school extant in Paris.

The Lacanian path into literary criticism is an indirect one. Lacanianism came in fits and starts like the Freudianism to which it strictly (if creatively) adheres. In the United States, a flurry of initial interest was sparked by Lacan's rare American visits to literature and humanities programmes at Johns Hopkins University in 1966 and to MIT and Yale University in 1973. In contrast, by the late 1970s in France Lacan's name had spread beyond the clinic to appear in the broadest spectrum of critical orientations: structuralism, deconstruction, feminism, philosophy, film studies and cultural critique.

A good example of how Lacan's French influence intersected with literary study and criss-crossed the Channel and the Atlantic is Hélène Cixous. Cixous is a James Joyce specialist, poet, playwright and literary theorist who founded *Etudes féminines* in France and promoted the critical concept of *écriture féminine*. In her ground-breaking book on hysteria, *The Newly Born Woman* (co-authored by Clément) Cixous cited Lacan to contest Freud's narrower views of women (1975, 9, 19, 29, 35–6).

If Lacan's work nourished a certain feminist thought, supporting its objections to Freud's patriarchal evaluation of woman, feminist Luce Irigaray resisted what she saw as Lacan's own 'phallogocentricism' (to use Derrida's term). Irigaray viewed Lacan's emphasis on the crucial role language plays in subject formation as lending undue aid and comfort to culture's traditional repression of the feminine. In a series of highly innovative texts Irigaray protested what she felt was Lacan's support for the primacy of a phallic linguistic model that structurally consigned woman to cultural inferiority. If, as Lacan believed, language is the indelible foundation of human being, to Irigaray its very grammatical structure excludes the feminine. Human society, life in common, conceptually depends on the existence of a grammatical 'third person' – always 'It' or 'He' and never 'She'. To Irigaray, an analyst and a trained philosopher, Lacan's *big O Other* was too close to this 'third' person that conceded nothing to woman, and she broke with Lacan. Still, unlike other deconstructive theorists of gender (e.g. Judith Butler) Irigaray appreciated Lacan's attention to sexuality as indispensable for feminist politics. Lacan's logic of *sexuation* (see Copjec 1994, 201–36) remained necessary to support all 'difference' and crucial for any theory of rights. Irigaray writes: 'Equality between men and women cannot be achieved without a *theory of gender as sexed* and a rewriting of the rights and obligations of each sex, *qua different*, in social rights and obligations' (1993, 13).

Leading French theorists viewed Lacan as a systematic thinker whose theses demanded recognition and, often, contestation. Philosopher Gilles Deleuze, with Félix Guattari, is often presumed to include Lacan in his attack on traditional psychiatry. Yet Deleuze and Guattari found Lacan fruitful for their schizoanalysis, particularly his radical reorientation of psychoanalysis toward psychosis, femininity and the passing of the Oedipus complex (i.e. the advent of the superego) and away from Oedipal neurosis. In *Anti-Oedipus*, their 1972 study of capitalism and schizophrenia, Deleuze and Guattari recognized the importance of Lacan's *objet a* (1977, 27n). In 1980 their *1000 Plateaux* echoed Lacan's attention to courtly love, *desire, lack* and *jouissance* (1987, 154–6).

However multiple the points of Lacanian insertion into literary criticism – through feminism, the clinic, film studies and political analysis – it was the French *philosophical* battles *over* Lacan that first captured Anglophone literary attention. In these debates the great bone of contention was always the status of *literature* in Lacan's work. The question of literature-and-psychoanalysis had more than literary significance for philosophy. Since these intra-French philosophical arguments eventually exercised great influence in England and North America (largely through comparative literature and critical theory programmes) and set many terms of theoretical debates still ongoing, they demand more than passing mention.

By 1973, French philosophy began to engage Lacan over specifically literary issues. In that year two young philosophers who had embraced Jacques Derrida's critique of Ferdinand de Saussure mounted an attack on Lacan from a similar angle. Saussure, and the structuralists who followed his semiological method, were said by Derrida (1967) to have overvalued *speech* to the detriment of the material, *written sign* that merely 'recorded' it. Lacan was linked to structural linguistics through his invocation of Saussure's semiotic sign (an image plus a concept, a signifier and signified) and by virtue of his close friendship with Peircean semiolinguist Roman Jakobson. Jakobson had linked the metaphoric/metonymic axes of speech to both mental problematics (aphasia) and literary ones: for Jakobson, the interplay between the two tropes formed the respective axes of poetry and realist prose. His discovery paralleled Gregory Bateson's thesis on the genesis of schizophrenia as a linguistic 'double bind' between metaphoric and literal. When Lacan's translator Anthony Wilden linked Lacan to Bateson in his 1972 *System and Structure*, Lacan's 'structuralist' identity seemed confirmed.

Speech was the crucial focus of Saussurean and Jakobsonian linguistics. In his *De La Grammatology* Derrida called attention to the fact that the material conveyance of the sign (by what he called *écriture* – writing) had been overlooked by semiolinguists, and he argued that it was the actual support of any signifying force in speech. Writing was more than the 'writing down' of speech events (*paroles*); *écriture* was the very condition of possibility of speech, the sine qua non of the arbitrariness and free play of even oral signifiers.

With an eye on Derrida's critique, Philippe Lacoue-Labarthe and Jean-Luc Nancy trained their sights on Lacan, for whom speech *and* the material mark ('letter') were both key analytic concepts. In a short book, *Le Titre de la lettre* (1973) they investigated Lacan's thesis that the subject is a '*parlêtre*', a pun-word meaning both *par lettres* (i.e. through or by means of letters or literature) and *parle être* (speaking being). In their book the pair contended that despite Lacan's attention to 'the letter' his interpretive method remained locked into the letter as inferior handmaiden to 'authentic' voice and 'original' speech. Speech, the analytical medium (the talking cure of 'free association' in the presence of an analyst), exemplified the Saussurean error locating authentic 'truth' only in speech. According to them, Lacan refuses the 'strategy of the signifier' (1992, 135–6) wherein truth is never one and final. Indeed, the oral signifier is structured so that speech itself is always already 'written' in a polysemic, plurivocal 'text' in which meaning is deferred and irreducible to a singular 'truth'. For them Lacan has misplaced confidence in the revelation of truth through authentic or 'full' speech (1992, 83–9).

Lacan was a clinician and not a philosopher or a literary critic but the two philosophers responded so strongly with good reason. By the late twentieth century literature and philosophy had come to be intensely implicated in each other's fate. After Nietzsche (and Heidegger) philosophy was enmeshed in literature and vice versa. Poetry especially was regarded as a unique attention to logos and to the non-prosaic being it produced. To modern thinkers interpreting literary texts it had great philosophical significance. Lacoue-Labarthe and Nancy saw Lacan's interpretative method as a function of a reductive truth that threatened to obscure literature as a source of primary philosophical insight.

In his recent responses to Lacoue-Labarthe philosopher Alain Badiou, critic and sometime playwright, argued that, to the contrary, Lacan was never caught inside the paradigm of literary-philosophy, and that Lacan instead adumbrated a philosophy for *after* the era of anti-philosophy opened by Nietzsche. Philosophy, for Badiou, does not find its 'end' in literature, its fulfilment in poetry as the Heideggerian 'age of poets' asserts. That age is drawing to a close permitting poetry to be relieved of the ethical burdens philosophy has laid on it; for Badiou, Lacan's role in preparing the new stage of philosophy will have been crucial. Lacan advanced philosophy's cause by radicalizing, undercutting and reframing one of its conditions of possibility (1999, 43–4, 81–4, 88–91). To Badiou, Lacan's singular contribution to philosophy's renewal is his refurbishing of the conceptual grounds of *love*, one of Badiou's four fundamental 'conditions' of philosophy (politics, love, the matheme and art).

To adopt either Badiou's or Lacoue-Labarthe and Nancy's evaluation would be, however, to relieve Lacan of any *serious* literary or critical consequence. Thus it is somewhat ironic that it was philosopher Jacques Derrida's critique of Lacan that assured the analyst his place in literary critical history. Derrida opened the question of Lacan's insistent *letter* in the unconscious on specifically *literary* grounds informed by but not ruled by philosophical problematics.

Derrida was institutionally linked to the university space carved out for 'practitioners of the unconscious' at the University of Paris VIII-Vincennes, where he, Foucault, Deleuze, de Certeau, Serge Leclaire, Georges Canguilhem, Jacques-Alain Miller and Hélène Cixous all taught (Roudinesco 1990, 553). Derrida, along with Deleuze, lent political support to Lacan's continued teaching at the *École Normale Supérieure* when Lacan was threatened with expulsion in 1969 (Roudinesco 1990, 539). Yet, when Derrida's reproach to Lacan's 'applied' literary criticism of Poe's *Purloined Letter* in his 1954 seminar (Lacan 1988, 175–205) appeared in *Critique* (and then in *Yale French Studies*) in 1975, it was regarded as an attack that turned many away from using Lacan for literary criticism. Derrida nevertheless rendered an oblique homage to Lacan, transforming Lacan's 'practice of the letter' into his own expanded concept of *écriture*, a homage later made explicit in his essay, 'For the Love of Lacan' (Derrida [1990] 1998, 39–69).

Derrida's complaint in his 1975 article, 'The Purveyor of Truth', is related to Lacoue-Labarthe and Nancy's: that Lacan chiefly relies on extra-textual truth – the 'clinical' truth of the (phallically organized) unconscious – to bolster the act of interpretation. Derrida notes that the 'truth' of the Lacanian unconscious is manifested in the *letter*, a letter that, as Lacan quipped, always 'arrives at its destination'. Derrida takes this to mean that the analyst 'reads' a subject's unconscious truth rather than the play of textuality that constitutes it. For Derrida, Lacan thereby invokes the presence of some 'thing', some transcendental signified, without adequate attention to the textual dimensionality into which the letter is woven. Literary texts have only truth-effects; to overlook how these effects are produced is a monumental error. To Derrida, Lacan's literary approach is modelled too much on an analyst–patient model, which prizes 'full' speech, and even that model, for Derrida, ignores the 'dead' letter always already conditioning speech acts. Despite Lacan's focus on the *letter*, to Derrida Lacan's critical method remains trapped in a true-speech model.

Yet a closer look at the 'literariness' of the letter Derrida delineates in 'The Purveyor [literally, the postman] of Truth' situates why Lacan's letter-object is inspiring new uses for Lacan in literary criticism. Derrida takes Lacan's 'letter' on three levels: literal (the letters the text is composed of), metaphorical (the missive addressed to an other) and metonymic (it stands for 'letters' or literature, the body of which it is a fragment). For Derrida, Lacan's letter is insufficiently literary. Derrida takes Lacan's dictum concerning the letter's 'destination' to mean its *proper* destination, i.e. that Lacan believes the letter will always find its 'true' or proper 'meaning'; that its message is always received by the proper addressee (the analyst); and that a letter always finds its appropriate location, its proper place, in the body of a text and in the body of texts (literature). Such destining of the letter constitutes a closed circuit that is simply untenable for literary works, since writing can neither predict nor limit its addressees nor claim to possess a singular, transmissible meaning. Meaning, Derrida reminds us, is created solely by relaying a *promise* of meaning from signifier to signifier: it is found neither as offstage obscenity nor as truth buried in the unconscious. A missing or out-of-place letter (like the '*a*' Derrida inserted into *différance*) is 'symptomatic' only of a purely *textual* unconscious, readable on the surface.

Derrida's second complaint is that the transcendental signified or singular truth lies in the Lacanian unconscious and that Lacan sees all textual symptoms (letters) referring to it – the *phallus*: 'indivisible and indestructible ... like the letter which takes its place ... indispensable to the circulation of propriety' (Johnson 1980, 124). If the phallus is *the* 'truth', *the* meaning of a literary text, Derrida rightly concludes that reading as such would cease, and that therefore Lacan and psychoanalysis are wrong for literature. Gayatri Spivak succinctly posed the problem another way: 'All precautions taken, literary criticism *must* operate as if the critic is responsible for the interpretation, and, to a lesser extent, as if the writer is responsible for the text' (1977, 224) To put the unconscious (and Lacan's 'letter' is frankly 'in' the unconscious) at the centre of literary interpretation reduces *meaning* to the *phallus* and blocks the consciousness and 'responsibility' Spivak says are criticism's crucial and necessary fiction.

Was Lacan's *letter* really about elevating phallic truth over 'secondary' representation, however? Did Lacan genially ignore the way texts generate both truth and meaning as *textual effects*? Did the inevitable 'arrival' of Lacan's letter at its 'destination' mean that the *letter* bore a 'full' meaning, and successfully closed an open communication circuit? It would be difficult to comprehend Lacan's critical resurgence if this were the case. A different perspective on the letter for Lacan finds his '*letter*' precisely *not* the representative of the *phallus*, but its *opponent*.

In Lacan's system, the *phallus* is purely symbolic. It is indeed the centre of a centred unconscious (the Symbolic Order), the point where all four coordinates of the subject (the self, the self-image, the subject and the big O Other) are balanced (see Lacan's 'L Schema'). Phallic centrality accrues its merely virtual but dominating psychic power by repressing the Real. The letter, on the other hand, emerges *in* the very Real that the Symbolic represses. Derrida's sympathies with the letter were thus correctly Lacanian, though to him Lacan appeared a phallocrat. Clinically, symbolic balance is the goal, but culturally and literarily the 'feminine' letter gains a crucial ascendancy.

Interestingly, when Lacan responded to critiques of his 'letter' he did so not to Derrida but to Philippe Lacoue-Labarthe and Jean-Luc Nancy, sending the two a 'Love Letter' in his 1972–3 seminar on feminine sexuality, *Encore*. Once this 'love letter' appeared in English (in Mitchell and Rose 1982) it touched off a wave of critical interest in Lacan that concurred with Derrida's resistance to the phallus. Feminist criticism in particular intuited something rebellious at work in the *letter* that precluded its standing-in for the phallus. Instead (and despite his mischievous pronouncements regarding feminine sexuality in it) Lacan's *Encore* (*Seminar XX*) showed the *letter against* the phallus. For Lacan the agency of the letter in the unconscious was *not* 'phallogocentric', but feminine and literary.

Kant had put non-purposive enjoyment at the heart of aesthetic feeling. Lacan, too, analysed *enjoyment* (*jouissance*) by closely attending to the letter. He discovered varieties of enjoyment – feminine, perverse, abusive, phallic – but negatively. He saw these varieties of *jouissance* as all forms of an excess that is specifically excised from all the discourses. Discourses are precisely woven to exclude, shield or disavow this excess *jouissance*.

To Lacan, all traditional ethics and aesthetics deal with excess by weaving 'discourses' as fictions of harmony (which always fails). In contemporary life, the accent has now fallen on transgression, disruption and imbalance. Modern life, that is, highlights the presence of excess and as such it throws the aesthetic principles of Aristotle and the ideals of Kant into question. *Sublimation* and *perversion* are for Lacan characterized by excess (they both *overestimate* their object), and they thus have come to the fore in modernity. Sublimation elevates the excess to dignified heights (e.g. the Lady in Courtly Love); perversion's passion is for the object's overwhelming *jouissance* (e.g. the fetish).

Contrary to Derrida's assumption, then, Lacan's *subject* is not the sociological or political subject of structuralism, or the subject of positive law. For Lacan, the *subject* is nothing except a pure function of its *object*. In other words, the Lacanian *subject* is not a conscious rational, philosophical subject. Nor is the object that defines it empirical in character, for it is pure excess.

Significantly, Lacan's 'overvalued' object at the core of the subject is nothing more nor less than a *letter*, the 'object *little letter* a' (*objet petit a*). By means of this psychic 'object-letter', the *subject* becomes the subject of *unconscious* fantasy as well as of the Symbolic-phallic unconscious. The subject is subject of the unconscious *because* its object is the 'object *little letter* a', the hinge point of the *unconscious fantasy*. This fantasy is what conflicts with and contests the phallically centred, symbolically organized unconscious.

The *letter* traces a Lacanian path for psychoanalytic theory and practice. Lacan calls '*letter*' the mark or imprint left on the *body* by *jouissance*, a *jouissance* that is repressed by language. Against its repression the letter rebels by *stamping* itself on the subject's body. Moreover, the 'body' it inscribes itself on is no ordinary, organic body. It is a 'body' already shaped by language – and that language has banished *jouissance* from its domain. Lacan put it thus: the symbol is the murder of the Thing.

For Lacan, *a subject's symbolic body* is not a *biological* body; it is a body that no longer follows organic logic but instead the logic of the signifier. Language rips the body from its animal niche and deports it into a force field and system of logic entirely distinct from those ruling animate organic life. This violent imposition of language (or symbolic law) denatures the subject and opens it to its specifically human dimensions: reason, thought, social relations. Lacan writes: '[Man] thinks as a consequence of the fact that a structure, that of language – the word implies it – carves up his body, a structure that has nothing to do with anatomy' (1990, 6). The effect of language, whose avatar is the (phallic) *signifier*, is thus to reconstitute the body through words that substitute for what they displace: *metaphors* (see *Seminar I*, 1953–4, and *Seminar III* on psychosis, 1955–6).

Language thus divides a *subject* from its 'being', replacing the body ruled by natural law with one that complies only with the laws of language. Lacan formulated this as *alienation* – or the 'castration of the subject by the signifier'. The phallus, a merely symbolic form of an animal organ (the penis), in this context becomes the very signifier of the entire process of signification: a master *signifier* S_1, the absent centre around which the Symbolic Order is arrayed, the cardinal element 'responsible' for the *orderly* reconfiguration of the body as a logical body. It civilizes the subject, and undertakes the stewardship of society under the rule of chiefly male elders that it silently authorizes and 'guarantees'. The Father, and his Name, 'represent' this S_1.

A deceptively simple set-up like this is, however, not long to be believed. The *phallus* is by no means the sole factor in the formation of the subject nor of the social order for Lacan. While language (etymologically, tongue and blade), makes the subject's body into a *body-without-organs*, what it 'carves' off is something that only its action produces (and that is never fully lost): *jouissance*. That is, the 'phallic signifier' banishes enjoyment (*jouissance*) from the body that is under its sway – and that *body* protests the expulsion much the same way those oppressed by civilization may silently and, at length, openly rebel against the constraints and discontents they endure. (Deleuze had a horror of domestic animals because they are subject to symbolic laws with no means of contesting them.)

In Lacan, what comes directly up against the phallus is the *letter*. How? Non-empirical, *jouissance* is the after-effect of the 'carving' action of the signifier, whose cut produces a material loss of raw energy. This 'lost' energy returns as *drive* (*pulsion*), i.e. not as physical energy, but as energy *psychically represented*. Jouissance is thus a complex concept. What is expelled by language is not real 'enjoyment' in the ordinary sense, but a *psychic* discharge modelled on a *neurotic* one. In the *organic* body, discharge is release, fulfilment, brute enjoyment. It is relief from the pressure of the excess energy of external and internal stimuli. In the *logical* body, jouissance is only *fantasied* discharge, only a fantasm of *satisfaction* and *need*.

Psychic energy, as drive, latches onto the body wherever the body is not fully under the (phallic) signifier's sway, e.g. primarily in the genital zones, where it appears as 'sex drive'. But it can pop up anywhere in the logicized/language-made body, for like that body, drive is only the after-effect of the *word*. The 'excess' psychic energy (*jouissance*) cumulates, Lacan observes, and when it does it tends to stamp itself on bodily *orifices* and their *rims* (lips, eyelids, anal rings and vaginal labia, etc.) – wherever the continuity of the logical-body encounters an interruption or gap (*Seminar XI*, 1978, 200).

It is crucial to note how Lacan's thesis regarding the constitutive effect of language differs markedly from that of *structuralism*. Structuralism sees language as a *positive force*, like Foucault's discursive practices that coercively shape the subject and imprint its arbitrary social character. Lacan took the *opposite* position. For him, the subject is *hollowed out* by language; the crucial impact of the symbol lies not in what it actively *marks on* the subject, but in what it *takes from it*. Language subtracts *being* from the subject: the *signifier* replaces the *jouissance* of being with a promise of meaning. And its spectral companion, the *letter*, hollows out a void into which psychic *jouissance* floods.

In his 1964 seminar Lacan made a diagram of *alienation* that illustrates the 'subject' as ontological *lack* (*manque-à-être*), produced by a double linguistic-ontological lapse. The diagram consists of two overlapping circles (Lacan [1964] 1994, 211). Lacan labels one circle 'meaning' and the other circle 'being'. The *subject* emerges in the concrete gap between two signifiers ('being' and 'meaning') where the circles intersect and overlap, i.e. from 'the superimposition of two lacks'. So does *desire* (1978, 214). As its 'being' disappears into 'meaning', the subject is born *as* desire (*libido*). A lozenge-shaped area of 'non-meaning' lies where the two circles intersect and overlap: Lacan calls this the *lamella*, the *libido* or indestructible life-force that surges forth where *meaning* and *being* lapse equally for the subject.

The fact that language requires a leap to produce its twinned fictions of *being* and of *meaning* inaugurates a specific bridging called '*metaphor*'. Interpreters have been quick to assume that the Lacanian subject of *desire* is thus of purely metaphoric confection. True, metaphoric desire is 'the essence of man' for Lacan, as for Spinoza (1978, 275). But this desire (psychic longing, not empirical need) is 'impure', Lacan tells us: it is not *only* symbolic or metaphoric in character. The desiring subject is rather, Lacan says, a *metonymy*.

Why *metonymy*? Metonymy is the trope that evokes *contiguity with* what it stands for ('need', 'hunger') rather than metaphoric *distance from* its referent (e.g. 'hunger-like'). The distinction is extremely significant for Lacan. It means that *desire* remains surreptitiously linked to those real Things that the symbol seemed to have displaced definitively – to have 'murdered'. But, for Lacan, some *real* object of longing, some material residue, some scrap or remnant of the displaced Thing remains at the heart of all desire – as if, for example, a fragment of the satisfying maternal breast (from which everyone must separate) had remained in the unconscious and continued exerting a force of attraction not fully under the control of reason and social rules.

Of course this internal object is not *really* Real. But it is not *only* symbolic. It has psychic density – *jouissance*. Lacan's pronouncement that the Symbolic makes a 'hole in the Real' is thus counterbalanced by the obverse: in every Symbol there remains a (psychic) kernel of the Real; in every Desire lies a fragment of Drive; and in every social Symbolic Order lies a nucleus that contains some Thing, some event, some deed, some group, that can never be symbolically recognized or assimilated.

Through its constitutive signifiers (symbols, metaphors, the phallus) language thus 'organizes' the subject, but it also *disorganizes* the subject: its after-effects produce a strange, inexplicable energy – *libido* – that issues from what is now a *body-without-organs*, not from hormones or natural urges. *Libido* is a powerful (if negative) force whose field is that of *Drive*. The 'object' of satisfaction of *drive* is not empirical: i.e. it is not the *apple* that sates a psychic hunger but the *enjoyment in it*, an enjoyment retrospectively imagined or prospectively projected as inhering in that apple rather than in the mind. Yet in human desire, it is *jouissance* of the apple that counts, not the nutritive and aesthetic elements of the physical apple. The 'emptiness' of the desiring subject (produced by the signifier's repression of the Real) is in fact filled with half-real, half-hallucinated objects of longing, lodged there where the *letter* has opened a space for them, the space of the Drive that undergirds *desire*.

The *objet a* is thus the kernel of Desire, an 'extra-*jouissance*' that is equally desired but avoided. *Drive* overshoots its target; it 'aims' at the *jouissance* in the *object a* but fails to arrive at its destination: complete satisfaction is lethal *for the subject* (1978, 174–86). All drives therefore represent death drive, but never more than *partially*. Their 'circuit' (joining life to death) is unclosed, or an open loop, or an internal 8, or an invagination, such as diagrammed by Lacan throughout *Seminar XI* (1978, 178).

For Lacan, the *subject* forms around the hollow left by the *object a's* stamp, around the lesion where *jouissance* cumulates. Lacan goes further, calling *letters* (*objects a*) the very *subjects* of the unconscious (1978, 242). In 'Kant avec Sade' (1989) Lacan formulated a-phallic subject-formation as $ \lozenge a$, which translates roughly as 'the language-divided subject stamped by the *object a*'. (This is his '*formula of fantasy*'.) Recognizing the Fantasy support of Desire (1978, 185) is what inclined Lacan (from the 1960s on) toward scrutiny of the 'envers' (or obscene underside) of the phallic-Symbolic order, and paved the way for new avenues for clinical and literary application. In his clinic, as in his aesthetics, Lacan's *object a*, *jouissance* and *fantasy* began to take conceptual precedence over his *Symbolic Order*, *phallic primacy* and the *signifier*.

This move accelerated a critical encounter between literature and the clinic that Lacan did not so much produce as reproduce. In France, after all, the first important entrée for Freud had come through literature: the Freudian clinic surged following the fanfare with which Surrealism touted the Freudian unconscious. Lacan, through his studies with Gaëtan de Clerambault (who discovered 'mental automatism' in the criminally insane), found parallels between surrealist procedures, which dramatized the unconscious as automatic writing and bizarre metaphors, and psychoanalysis as a clinical procedure. Poet André Breton, painters Salvador Dali and André Masson (Lacan's brother-in-law), writers Sollers, Camus, Sartre, Leiris and Bataille, among others, facilitated Lacan's freedom to move away from the organic logic that had, up till then, dominated the clinic.

Lacan's personal acquaintance with poets, novelists and theorists of aesthetics accustomed him, from the beginning, to engage aesthetics in his clinical work; the seminars he gave to clinicians include meditations on Claudel, Gide, courtly love and Baroque poetry, James Joyce and E. A. Poe. Social scientists and philosophers assisted Lacan part of the way on his route: Lévi-Strauss, Jakobson, Merleau-Ponty. But artists were crucial to his thinking. Once, in his 'Homage to Marguerite Duras', (1987), Lacan invoked Freud's belief that artists were out ahead of analysts and cut the path for them.

The Lacanian 'clinic' tracks the *letter a* that has been traced on the logical body. The analyst, attentive to the patient's signifiers, finds them knotted around a *jouissance* in (and of) the *symptom*. Patiently locating the signifying chain that encrypts or walls off this *jouissance* like a cyst that interrupts the flowing of the signifier, the analyst's process is one of unknotting. Its goal is to free the patient to function effectively in the Symbolic; to lift off the subject's unconscious domination by the commands of an abusive internal Other ('the Other's *Jouissance*'), and by fantasies of seduction or castration by that 'big O' Other. Analysis cannot fully erase the letter-*object a* the subject has crystallized around; it only brings it to knowledge (*savoir*).

In an artistic and literary context, the structure of the subject remains the same: it is a precipitate of *object a, jouissance* and *fantasy*. But here Lacan's emphasis shifts from *symptom* to *sinthome*. Lacan's most elaborate literary analysis was *Le Sinthome, Seminar XXIII* in which he intersected a clinical diagnosis of James Joyce with an analysis of Joyce's aesthetic production: *writing*. For Joyce, whose 'psychical structure' was psychotic (according to Lacan), writing was prophylactic against the threat of psychopathology. How? The answer lies in the structure of the *sinthome*.

In the *symptom* signifiers knot themselves around a hollow left by the letter's stamp, a hollow filled with a threatening *jouissance*. The symptom is a damming-up of jouissance that also provisionally halts the freeplay of signification. The *sinthome*, too, is a place of accumulated psychic excess (surplus *jouissance*). But here excess *jouissance* is bound *to* a signifying formation, one that permits signification – but also dammed-up *jouissance* – to flow again. The *sinthome*-signifier is penetrated with a *jouissance* that the *signifier* a priori excludes, only here pathological *jouissance* is transformed into *jouis-sens* ('enjoy-meant'). For Lacan, the *sinthome* is the signifying face of fantasy, not of the Symbol.

Derrida and Lacan come together and apart once more here. Writing, for Derrida, circulates infinitely, combining the virtues of the signifier (commonality with other subjects, avoidance of lethal *jouissance*) with the aesthetic pleasure of literary art. For Lacan, literature's 'letters' are also those *object a*-letters that retain their connection to the Real, to experience and to a *jouissance* otherwise unattainable. Literature, for Lacan, is thus partly signifier (but a signifier frozen up by the *jouissance* it normally excludes) and partly object (but an object made entirely of the 'letters' of its subject's logical body, which nonetheless leave the body to circulate as freely as signifiers).

Lacan's *sinthome* updates and puts a keener edge on Freud's essay on the creative writer's relation to phantasy, wherein art is prized for furnishing a purely fictional, non-threatening satisfaction of censored (because lethal) drives. For Lacan, art is an even more uniquely crucial entity in the story of the subject-as-written-by-language. Lacan's own inimitable writing style has an 'irreducibly literary dimension', says Shoshana Felman comparing him to Stéphane Mallarmé (Clément 1974, 1). For Lacan, art refills the void left by language – but it 'fills' it only with a second void. Lacan's fable of art is the vase: a potter makes a hole in what is already a hole in the Real (1986, 119–21).

Juliet Flower MacCannell

Further reading and works cited

Apollon, W. and Feldstein, R. (eds) *Lacan, Politics, Aesthetics*. Albany, NY, 1996.
Badiou, A. *Manifesto for Philosophy*. Albany, NY, 1999.
Cantin, L. 'The Letter Against the Phallus', *American Journal of Semiotics*, VII, 3, 1990.
Copjec, J. *Read My Desire*. Cambridge, MA, 1994.
Deleuze, G. and Guattari, F. *Anti-Oedipus*. Minneapolis, MN, 1977.
—. *A Thousand Plateaus*. Minneapolis, MN, 1987.
Derrida, J. *De La Grammatologie*. Paris, 1967.
—. 'The Purveyor of Truth', *Yale French Studies*, 52, 1975.
—. *Resistances of Psychoanalysis*. Stanford, CA, 1998.
Irigaray, L. *Speculum de l'autre femme*. Paris, 1974.
—. *Ce sexe qui n'en est pas un*. Paris, 1977.
Johnson, B. *The Critical Difference*. Baltimore, MD, 1980.
Lacan, J. *Le Séminaire. Livre XX*, ed. J.-A. Miller. Paris, 1975.
—. *Le Séminaire. Livre VII. L'Ethique de la Psychanalyse*, ed. J.-A. Miller. Paris, 1986.
—. 'Homage to Marguerite Duras', in *Duras by Duras*. San Francisco, 1987, pp. 122–9.
—. *The Seminar of Jacques Lacan Book II*, ed. J.-A. Miller. New York, 1988.
—. *Television*, ed. J. Copjec. New York, 1990.
—. *The Four Fundamental Concepts of Psycho-Analysis* (Seminar XI), intro. David Macey. London, 1994.
Lacoue-Labarthe, P. and Nancy, J.-L. *The Title of the Letter*. Albany, NY, 1992.
MacCannell, J. Flower. *Figuring Lacan*. Lincoln, NE, 1986.
Miller, J.-A. 'Extimité', in *Lacanian Theory of Discourse*, eds M. Bracher et al. London, 1994.
Millot, C. *Nobodaddy*. Paris, 1988.
Mitchell, J. *Women: The longest Revolution*. London, 1984.
— and Rose, J. (eds) *Feminine Sexuality*. New York, 1982.
Ragland-Sullivan, E. and Bracher, M. (eds) *Lacan and the Subject of Language*. New York, 1991.
Roudinesco, E. *Jacques Lacan & Co*. Chicago, 1990.
Spivak, G. Chakravorty. 'The Letter as Cutting Edge', *Yale French Studies*, 55/56, 1977.
Walden, A. *System and Structure*. London, 1972.
Wright, E. et al. (eds) *Feminism and Psychoanalysis: A Critical Dictionary*. Oxford, 1991.
Žižek, S. *The Sublime Object of Ideology*. London, 1989.
—. *For They Know Not What They Do*. London 1991.
—. *Looking Awry*. Cambridge, MA, 1992.

25. The Reception of Hegel and Heidegger in France: Alexandre Kojève (1902–1968), Jean Hyppolite (1907–1968), Maurice Merleau-Ponty (1908–1961)

The reception of Hegel and of Heidegger in France has followed a somewhat similar curve at a century's distance, oscillating between enthusiastic acceptance based on severe misunderstandings, serious scholarship accompanied by new translations of certain works selected from the abundant productions of both philosophers, and a stubborn rejection, quite often proffered in the name of the traditional virtues of French thought, defined since Descartes by clarity of expression and linguistic transparency. Even if there never was a 'Hegel scandal' in the late nineteenth century as there was a 'Heidegger affair' in the 1980s, constant suspicion dogged the thought of Hegel who was accused and still is – although without real foundation – of having provided Bismarck with a model of imperialist and totalitarian doctrine. Since the reception of Heidegger in France is still a burning issue, entailing not only endless political and ethical discussions but also the whole question of translation, and since most canonical texts by Heidegger are almost unreadable in their current French 'versions' – which has had the advantage of forcing readers to go back to the German text – I will start by following the thread provided by Hegel as a surer guide.

Victor Cousin was the first French philosopher who actually met Hegel: he immediately acknowledged the genius of his interlocutor, admired the force and breadth of his vast syntheses, while remaining a little mystified by a 'scholastic language that was entirely his own'. Their meeting in 1816 in Heidelberg (Cousin explains how a first conversation with Hegel made him miss his coach, and decide to come back to be enlightened) is based on the old mixture of seduction, incomprehension and reciprocal projections that has character-ized the Franco-German intellectual dialogue. In a typically French about-face, the glimpse of Hegel's system led Cousin to name his own philosophy 'eclectism'! It was left to the French philosophers of history such as Michelet and Quinet to salute their noble German precursor from a safe distance, without wishing to engage with the dense riddles of the text.

The first serious Hegelian philosopher writing in French was, curiously, Italian, more precisely, the Neapolitan Giambattista Vico. Augusto Vera, who had been Hegel's student in Berlin during the last years of the latter's life (Hegel died in 1831), started translating his works into French between 1855 and 1878. His translations are precise and rigorous, and are accompanied by long personal footnotes often quoting Hegel's extemporized remarks during his lectures or his correspondence. What is the most striking feature of these translations for us now is that one does not find the *Phenomenology of Spirit* among them: what interests Vera is to reconstruct the Hegelian system, moving gradually from the *Logic* (trans. 1859), the *Philosophy of Nature* (1863–6), the *Philosophy of Spirit* (1867–70) and finally the *Philosophy of Religion* (1876–8). These translations have been completely forgotten and it is a pity, since they allow one to reconstruct the deep impact of Hegel less on the French philosophy of the time than on poets like Stéphane Mallarmé, Villiers de l'Isle-Adam, Jules Laforgue and last but not least André Breton. André Breton, who had read Hegel's *Philosophy of Nature* very closely, found there many crucial images (his meditations on the crystal, or his use of the phrase 'the magnetic fields' are entirely in debt to Vera's Hegel). Vera chose to translate Hegel's concept (*Begriff*) by '*la notion*', in a somewhat weakened version, but one can still see it echo from Mallarmé to the early Breton. But here was perhaps the original sin of the French reception of Hegel: the omission of the phenomenological 'beginning' of the system, an omission that was repaired with a vengeance by Kojève in the 1930s, when Hegel's system can be read entirely from a few key-terms contained in the *Phenomenology*. By that time, the influence of Heidegger's revised Husserlian phenomenology will have contributed a new tone to philosophy.

Surrealism was a key factor in the rediscovery of Hegel, which led to wholesale embracing of the three Hs (Hegel, Husserl and Heidegger) as the new sources of philosophical thinking in France in the 1930s. If Heidegger's philosophy was not perceived in itself at first – at least as a spectacular break with Husserl's rational phenomenology – the rediscovery of Hegel in the 1930s corresponded with both a discovery of history (that is, of elaborating a discourse about contemporary history, which explains the long flirtation of French Hegelianism with Marxism) and a rediscovery of the concrete, of the world out there, at hand's reach as it were. In this general drift, there was a general agreement between the Hs and their various conceptions of what phenomenology can bring to philosophy.

This is why, after a relatively long eclipse, since, despite Vera's efforts, French philosophy at the end of the nineteenth century and in the first decades of the twentieth century took very different paths (Comte's positivistic religion of science led gradually to the institutional domination of a form of epistemological neo-Kantism, both generating the romantic reaction of Bergson's philosophy of intuition and duration), and the late 1920s and early 1930s were marked by a reawakening of an interest in Hegel. Jean Wahl, who had devoted a brilliant thesis to *The Pluralist Philosophers of Britain and the United States* (1920) and several books on Plato and Descartes, did not look like a typical 'Hegelian' when he published *The Unhappiness of Consciousness in Hegel's Philosophy* in 1929. This book was ground-breaking in that it not only returned to the *Phenomenology of Spirit* but also made extensive use of Hegel's early theological writings such as 'The Positivity of the Christian Religion' and 'The Spirit of Christianity', and the fragments on 'Love' and the 'Idea of a System', texts that had only been published in 1905 by Dilthey. Jean Wahl's originality was to take into account Kierkegaard's critique of Hegelian scholasticism, which led him to stress the role of alienation and desire in Hegel's early works, and presents Hegel as a budding existentialist. For Wahl, there is no historical progress without a dialectics of separation between the consciousness and the object it desires: the tragedy of separation and endless longing is experienced by every subject who will have to pass willy-nilly through stages of alienation and despair before regaining hope. Hope is granted above all by the belief that history will continue in its open-ended progress. This version of Hegel calls up more Bloch's 'principle of hope' than Vera's notion of a strict scientific systematicity, while history introduces a process that is unbounded. Later, Wahl was to stress that this historical path led 'toward the concrete' (as in *Toward the Concrete*, 1932), a concrete that would be processed by consciousness as it progressed along, in terms suggestive of a Husserlian influence.

Like Wahl, the second important commentator of that decade, the Russian born Alexandre Koyré, would stress the importance of the earliest texts, but without opposing them to the repressive nature of the System. What matters for Koyré, in a gesture that anticipates Hyppolite's, is to reconcile the subjective dialectics of separation, unhappiness and striving for reunification with the logical aspect of the doctrine. Koyré stresses the originality of Hegel's conception of time, a time that is dominated by the future. This time nevertheless contains a knowledge that will develop itself by establishing links between the future and the past – even if the present is experienced as contradictory and in conflict. Koyré also stresses the anti-theological and rationalistic aspect of Hegel's philosophy: his system aims not at creating another ontology but an anthropology. All these elements would be soon emphasized and even systematically exaggerated by Koyré's friend and disciple, Alexandre Kojève.

Coming like Koyré from Russia, Alexandre Kojevnikoff suddenly made Hegel not only accessible but indispensable to a whole generation. His famous seminars at the École Pratique des Hautes Études delivered yearly between 1933 and 1940 gathered people as diverse and famous as Raymond Queneau, Georges Bataille, Jacques Lacan, Raymond Aron, Maurice Merleau-Ponty, Jean Desanti and Jean Hyppolite. Kojève's wonderful appeal, his intellectual 'sexiness' one might say, lay in his uncanny ability to transform Hegel's abstract prose into a lively philosophical novel, to give blood and vigour to the notion of a 'gallery of images' traversed by the Spirit in the famous simile provided by Hegel on the penultimate page of his *Phenomenology*. Like Koyré, Kojève dismisses the religious element and stresses the anthropological element: 'According to Hegel – to use the Marxist terminology – Religion is only an ideological superstructure ...' (1969, 32). His own starting point is the famous dialectic of the Master and Slave, a key passage in the original text indeed, which nevertheless takes up less than ten pages out of the 600 pages or so of the whole work. But it is a crucial turning point in the analysis of the discovery of reciprocity by consciousness, and the subsequent need to be acknowledged by a consciousness that will also be free that Kojève can bring both Marx and Heidegger to bear on the Hegelian dialectic. Starting from the central insight that the meeting of Hegel and Napoléon in Jena embodies 'absolute knowledge' at the time of the writing of the *Phenomenology*, Kojève reopens the philosophical interpretation of the old historical scandal, well noted by Hegel, that Greek democracies never abolished slavery. This scandal is then linked with the dynamic function of Desire. If Man is ready to sacrifice his biological self in order to satisfy his desire for recognition in the struggle for death that marked the early times of civilization, one would always find certain individuals who accepted servitude rather than lose their life. Thus, after Speech, Desire and Reciprocity, Slavery is the fourth dominant concept in Hegel's anthropology: '... the possibility of a difference between the *future* Master and the *future* Slave is the fourth and last premise of the *Phenomenology*' (Kojève 1969, 42). History thus begins with this difference between Masters and Slaves, and conversely it will end only when this difference is abolished.

The analysis is well known: since the master has risked death in what might appear as a more authentic relationship to his *Dasein* (with echoes of Heidegger's *Being and Time*, the slave is determined by his 'fear of death'), after his victory, the master can bask in his superiority and leave everything vulgar and material to his slave: he will be content with enjoying the benefits of another's labours. The slave, who owns nothing, not even his desires, since he toils to satisfy the master's least whims, nevertheless discovers another kind of authenticity through a work which slowly transforms nature, whereas the master has to satisfy himself with the more and more empty recognition of his peers. The 'truth' of the master is then the slave, since he is the only one who can reconcile work and knowledge, leaving desire for later, when he can reach the end of the cycle leading to Absolute Knowledge. 'The Master appears only for the sake of engendering the Slave who "overcomes" [aufhebt] him as Master, while thereby "overcoming" himself as Slave. And this Slave who has been "overcome" is the one who is satisfied by what he *is* and will understand that he is satisfied in and by Hegel's philosophy, in and by the *Phenomenology*' (Kojève 1969, 47).

The second original element brought by Kojève's reading has been recently revived by Francis Fukuyama, and it is perhaps the most shocking for common sense: it is the thesis of the 'end of history'. For someone who had stressed from the start an anthropological reading while never losing sight of the problem concretely posed by the realization of Absolute Knowledge posed as the last stage of the progression of Spirit through Time, it seemed almost inevitable to assert that the attainment of Absolute Knowledge would result in the elimination of anthropology qua anthropology – that is, in the 'end of man'. A long footnote to the 1938–9 seminar begins by stating almost off-handedly that this is not an apocalyptic vision, but quite the contrary:

> The disappearance of Man at the end of History, therefore, is not a cosmic catastrophe: the natural World remains what it had been from all eternity. And therefore, it is not a biological catastrophe either: Man remains alive as animal in *harmony* with Nature or given Being. What disappears is Man properly so-called – that is, Action negating the given, and Error, or in general, the Subject *opposed* to the object. (Kojève 1969, 158–9)

In this Edenic reverie, wars and revolutions will have disappeared, along with Philosophy as the discourse that accompanied them, while all the arts, passions and the elements of superfluity much needed to fill in an empty time will remain in high demand, since we will be in an endless 'Sunday of Life' (to quote Queneau's witty title). No doubt that snobbism and the 'Japanese' model will play an exemplary role in such a scheme.

It would be idle to try to prove that Hegel never intended this: the 'end of history' belongs to the Hegelian legends skilfully examined by Jon Steward and his collaborators. But as Kojève says in a 1948 letter to the marxist critic Tran-Duc-Thao, his aim was not to find out what Hegel himself meant in his book, but to think with him and from him; he acknowledges that he has unduly stressed the role of the Master and Slave dialectic because he wanted to 'strike people's minds' and offer a new 'propaganda'. As Lacan and many others who have approached Kojève testify, he had only contempt for those who were satisfied with the role of pure intellectuals; he refused all academic honours, and spent most of his life as a high civil servant working on international relations between European states and their former colonies, devising and implementing an original system of aid and compensation. He indeed saw the looming conflict between North and South or between the first and the third world as more fundamental than the issues raised by marxism in terms of industrialization and infrastructure versus superstructure. For him, indeed, the Chinese revolution was only the 'alignment of the provinces' on the scheme already provided by the development of the System.

There was clearly the need for a more scholarly examination of Hegel, and this was to be provided by Hyppolite, who gave the first complete French translation of the *Phenomenology*, then added a systematic commentary, before attempting a synthesis between the earlier and the later Hegel in *Logic and Existence*. One could observe, for instance, how Jacques Lacan slowly moved from a Kojèvian version of Hegel that stressed desire, mirror images and aggressivity, to an ongoing discussion with Hyppolite who was a regular participant in his Seminar in 1954–6. When Lacan states that 'Man's desire is desire of the Other', he is in fact glossing Hyppolite's use of 'The Other' for the object of desire understood as pure alterity or just 'Life'. Unlike Kojève, however, Hyppolite does not take Desire (*Begierde*) for one of the most fundamental concepts in Hegel. And of course, very early in his commentary, he refuses the idea that history might have an end. This would be a 'naive' belief that the system freezes history, and according to him Hegel never fell into that trap. When Hegel famously asserts in the Preface to his *Philosophy of Right* that it is 'just as absurd to fancy that a philosophy can transcend its contemporary world as it is to fancy that an individual can overleap his own age', Hyppolite adds that what matters is the experience of joy and pain in the present, and the awareness that the consciousness seen progressing through various stages in the *Phenomenology* is both a singular and a universal consciousness.

This is the place in which Hyppolite inserts his most systematic and recurrent questioning: if Hegel's thought forms indeed a system, what is the function of this introduction to knowledge constituted by the *Phenomenology*? Why do we have to follow all the divisions and illusions of a consciousness on its way to absolute knowledge, if absolute knowledge is presupposed from the start? He notes that while the *Phenomenology* is the most literary of Hegel's treatises, it is caught up between strong opposites that he names 'panlogicism' on the one hand and 'pantragicism' on the other. We have seen how Wahl had chosen to stress the tragic – even pathetic – elements, in a way that would no doubt impress Georges Bataille: Hegel is indeed the philosopher of the encounter with death and pure negativity, but he also looks at real history and its 'slaughter-bench' without flinching. Hyppolite makes a lot, for instance, of Hegel's interpretation of 'Terror' in revolutionary France. Unlike the first French Hegelians who looked to the German philosopher as someone who helps them go back to history so as to find a meaning in it, Hyppolite is aware of the danger of any philosophy of history that identifies the Real and the Rational: one risks falling into a history of the legitimization of political power, the tragedy of negativity being quickly subsumed by the patience of an overarching concept.

A new tone is therefore sounded just after the Second World War, when Hyppolite published *Logic and Existence* in 1952, an essay that tackles the same problem of the relationship between the 'genesis' of consciousness in the *Phenomenology* and the 'structure' of the concept contained in the *Logic*, but with a different emphasis. This text marks a break with the anthropological readings of Hegel that dominated before the war, and opts resolutely for a quasi-Heideggerian version: if the Logic presupposes the experience of the phenomenon, and if the phenomenology presupposes the concept, none can be reduced to the other, but both are related to the fact that Man is 'the dwelling of the Universal and of the Logos of Being, and thus becomes capable of Truth' (Hyppolite 1997, 187, modified). Curiously, this is Hyppolite's most Heideggerian text, and it sounds very close to Heidegger's 1930–1 lectures on *Hegel's Phenomenology of Spirit*. For instance, Hyppolite writes: 'The Logic's dialectical discourse will be the very discourse of Being, the *Phenomenology* having shown the possibility of bracketing man as natural Dasein' (1997, 42). The

Logic bequeaths us with a fundamental insight into the function of sense: Being is thought absolutely, but only through our existence. An essential difference will therefore constitute the very core of Being: Being projects constantly its own Other, unfolds and generates an inner self-differing. Alert as he was to the Nietzschean and Heideggerian echoes of this thesis, Hyppolite can be said to pave the way to Derrida's and Deleuze's philosophies of Difference – a good decade in advance. Deleuze had noted this point in a famous review of Hyppolite's work, in which he claims that, for Hyppolite, 'Being it not *essence* but *sense*' which allows him to see how Hegel 'transforms metaphysics into logics, and logics into a logics of sense' (Hyppolite 1997, 193), and which entails that the Absolute is *here*, or in other words, that there is 'no secret'. Deleuze points out some difficulties in this Hegelian programme (how can one avoid falling back into the anthropology that has been denounced?) and he suggests that Nietzsche would have been a better guide. At least, it is fascinating to observe how the meeting between Hegel and Heidegger, half-way as it were, predetermines the evolution of French philosophy in the second half of the twentieth century.

This is clearly a far cry from what was at the time felt to be the dominant mode of French phenomenology, a mixture of Husserlian anthropology and existentialism. In 1943, Sartre could still think he was being a true Heideggerian when he merely translated into his own vocabulary two key terms of Hegelian phenomenology, the *Insich* and the *Fürsich* that were readily transformed into *l'en-soi* and *le pour-soi*. By a wilful distortion (since for Hegel what matters is the discrepancy between the way things can be 'in fact' and how they are perceived for a consciousness at a given stage), Sartre returns in fact to a neo-Cartesian dualism opposing the world as positivity (which is in itself) and consciousness as its inverse negativity (since it is always for itself). Sartre's genius is evident in his concrete analyses (of the gaze, of facticity) as if he had borrowed from Hegel and from Hegel only the right to transform philosophy into a novelistic series of vignettes – which would situate him as Kojève's unexpected heir! However, Sartre clearly criticizes what he calls Hegel's 'onto-logical optimism', a logical optimism which would make him trust the truth of the Totality too easily. According to Sartre, there is constantly a sleight of hand by which Hegel thinks he can overcome the singularity of individual consciousness to reach the Whole because the Whole had already been given at the outset. Sartre adds, in a phrase that sounds tantalizing: 'But if Hegel forgets himself, we cannot forget Hegel' (1943, 300). Alas, it is only to add: 'Which means that we are sent back to the cogito.'

Merleau-Ponty will have no difficulty in disentangling several levels of confusion in Sartre's essay, a book he admires in spite of its many shortcuts. The texts he collected in *Sense and Non-Sense* all date from the postwar years, the heady discussions with Sartre and marxist thinkers, and their joint foundation of *Les Temps Modernes*. In a piece on 'Hegel's Existentialism', Merleau-Ponty closes the entire circle of French existentialist variations on Hegel's *Phenomenology*: he first pays homage to Hyppolite's translation and commentary, then moves on to connections with Sartre's *Being and Nothingness* before engaging more decisively with Heidegger's influence. Merleau-Ponty notes that the conclusion of Hegel's major essay could lead one either to join the Communist Party or the Church, and is clearly not a philosophy of the individual choice. In the same way, Heidegger's philosophy has been misconstrued, according to him, as being a-historical, whereas the last part of *Being and Time* contains a philosophy of history. Clearly, in this short piece, Merleau-Ponty is busy pushing existentialism away from its individualistic limitations, so as to confront it with Hegel and Heidegger.

This is what dominates in later texts by Merleau-Ponty, who although he could reproach Sartre for not being marxist enough in the early 1950s, nevertheless kept criticizing the Stalinist doctrine of the French Party. In his posthumous *Notes de Cours 1959–1961* as well as in his unpublished essay that he meant to call '*An Introduction to the Prose of the World*', one can see that Merleau-Ponty's initial debt to Husserl gradually leaves room to a systematic confrontation with Hegel (the very title of 'prose of the world' is borrowed from Hegel) and Heidegger: for both pose the question that was probably still unsolved in Husserl of the links between language and historicity. His last lecture notes on 'the state of philosophy today' sketch an interesting philosophical genealogy: they begin with Husserl, continue with Heidegger and then branch off into Heidegger's reading of Hegel, finally concluding with a confrontation between Hegel and Marx. It looks as if Husserl and Heidegger had been indispensable mediators who would help Merleau-Ponty find 'Hegel and his negativity having descended into the Flesh of the World' (1996, 348). But by that time, the shift in French marxism due to Althusser had started rejecting any trace of Hegelianism in Marx's 'scientific' thought. Whereas Althusser could remark rather positively (in a 1947 review of Kojève) that Kojève's merit had been to show that 'without Heidegger ... we would never have understood the *Phenomenology of Spirit*' (1997, 171), the later recurrent coupling of both Hs was enough to brand them as idealist and unfit to come into contact with real 'theory'.

Jean-Michel Rabaté

Further reading and works cited

Althusser, L. *Early Writings: The Spectre of Hegel*. London, 1997.
Butler, J. *Subjects of Desire*. New York, 1999.
Descombes, V. *Modern French Philosophy*. Cambridge, 1980.
Fukuyama, F. *The End of History and the Last Man*. New York, 1992.
Heidegger, M. *Hegel's Phenomenology of Spirit*. Bloomington, IN, 1988.
Hyppolite, J. *Logic and Existence*. Albany, NY, 1997.
Jarczyk, G. and Labarrière, P.-J. *De Kojève à Hegel*. Paris, 1996.
Kojève, A. *Introduction to the Reading of Hegel*, ed. A. Bloom. Ithaca, NY, 1969.
Matthews, E. *Twentieth-Century French Philosophy*. Oxford, 1996.
Merleau-Ponty, M. *Sense and Non-Sense*. Evanston, IL, 1964.
—. *Notes de Cours 1959–1961*, ed. C. Lefort. Paris, 1996.
Nancy, J.-L. *Hegel: L'inquiétude du négatif*. Paris, 1997.
Roth, M. S. *Knowing and History*. Ithaca, NY, 1988.
Sartre, J.-P. *L'Etre et le Néant*. Paris, 1943.
Stewart, J. (ed.) *The Hegel Myths and Legends*. Evanston, IL, 1996.
Wahl, J. *The Phirolist Philosophies of Britain and the United States*. London, 1925.
—. *Vers la concret*. Paris, 1932.
—. *Le Malheur de la conscience dans la philosophie de Hegel*. Paris, 1951.
Wolin, R. *Labyrinths*. Amherst, MA, 1995.

26. Jean-Paul Sartre (1905–1980), Albert Camus (1913–1960) and Existentialism

Albert Camus would probably turn, once again, in his grave at the allegation that he was an existentialist. But his disquiet is better understood through the uneasiness of his personal relationship with Jean-Paul Sartre, who is more obviously associated with the term, than any genuine incommensurability between their beliefs. It is probably the word *absurdity* that is responsible for the persistence with which commentators have linked Camus and existentialism, and the subsequent connection, for which we might hold Martin Esslin at least partly responsible, between absurdity and the ideas about *being* and *freedom* to which Sartre devoted so much intellectual energy. But the idea of absurdity, of which Camus was so fond, was not plucked from the air. Whatever new inflections Camus might have added to it, the notion of the absurd was integral to the philosophical tradition that most informed the work of Camus and Sartre, and can be found, if not always by name, in the work of Kierkegaard, Nietzsche, Heidegger, Husserl and Jaspers. Camus may have refused the label existentialist, but it is difficult to see his thought as anything other than a celebration of this tradition of existentialist and phenomenological philosophy.

Camus's elaboration of the absurd had much in common with Nietzsche and Kierke-gaard for its sense of exhilaration about the collapse of metaphysics: a recognition that philosophy and religion were incapable of formulating a universal logic which might render human experience intelligible as a whole. Like Nietzsche, Camus had a sense that the absurdity of the universe entailed the freedom of the human being, and that from the negative realization of Godlessness might emerge a positive philosophy of personal existence. This is the movement of his most philosophical collection of essays *The Myth of Sisyphus*, which takes as its starting point the proposition that suicide is the only serious philosophical question. For Camus, the recognition of a total lack of hope, of life's ultimate meaninglessness and of the finality of death is a kind of liberation into an adventure to be experienced exactly by sustaining the recognition of absurdity. Suicide therefore comes to represent a response to misplaced hope, and it is only by liberating oneself from this kind of hope that life becomes an affirmative adventure. Living absurdity, then, is riding on the back of negativity in the full knowledge of life's absence of meaning. From the twenty-first century this can seem like a rather banal recognition, or a kind of nihilism that affirms no particular course of action. But for Camus, the core of absurdity does not lie in the affirmation of any particular programme of action but in the recognition of choice which results from the advantage of having given up all hope. In *The Myth of Sisyphus*, this condition is expressed through a selection of literary examples, of absurd heroes such as Don Juan and Captain Ahab in Moby Dick, who are taken as emblems of strength in the face of pointlessness. Sisyphus himself, who has been condemned by the gods to the perpetual labour of rolling a stone uphill, is an absurd hero who should be understood not as the subject of irresistible divine malice, but as someone who chooses to strive continuously in the knowledge that he can never succeed. For Camus, Sisyphus represents a happier condition than any misplaced hope of success exactly because he proceeds in the knowledge that his labour is fruitless.

Camus's resort to literary examples throughout *The Myth of Sisyphus* is revealing. There is a clear preference for the emblematic literary example over philosophical reason which could be said to characterize his mode of philosophizing in general terms. Existentialism emerges from a suspicion of philosophical reason that invests literary discourse with a new philosophical importance exactly because literature deals with concrete situations and personal experience without the burden of formulating the general laws to which metaphysics aspired. For H. J. Blackham, the preference for the concrete situation over theoretical reason, or for a philosophy of personal existence over metaphysics, is at the heart of existentialism:

> We are given a world whose pretensions must be broken, a world to be both accepted and refused, a life to be built on the further side of despair; knowledge being irremediably incomplete and uncertain throws the weight of responsibility upon personal decision; reason alone can limit reason, and its present duty is to restore the concrete and thus to eliminate the false theoretical problems which have haunted philosophy and illumine the real problems for which there are no theoretical solutions. As each aspect of the human situation is lit up, the light is reflected upon the personal isolation and responsibility of the existing individual at the centre. (1952, 150)

Blackham doesn't quite say so here, but this tenet that the duty of philosophy is to discard unsolveable theoretical problems and turn instead to the illumination of real problems in concrete situations underlies what might be called the existentialist valorization of literature. It is clear in Camus's writing that the novel is a form that allows the exploration of his thinking on the absurd a concrete, situation-based expression that is more appropriate to existentialist themes than the rigours of the philosophical essay. The impact of Camus's notion of the absurd was undoubtedly enhanced as a result of its elaboration not only in the philosophical essays of *The Myth of Sisyphus* (1942), but in his novel *L'Etranger* (1942) and the earlier drama *Caligula* (1939), both of which seemed to set philosophical ideas about absurdity into concrete situations, in modes of writing which forsake reason for what Martin Esslin would later call a direct experiential validity. This relationship between philosophy and literature is one of the preoccupations that most clearly links Camus to Sartre, and in which the themes of existential philosophy can be most directly linked to concerns of literary theory. *The Myth of Sisyphus* is preoccupied with the critique of reason, with the departure from a pure philosophy of reason into a more paradoxical kind of philosophy capable of apprehending the absurd. This paradoxical philosophy lies somewhere between philosophy and literature, so that the writings of philosophers such as Nietzsche, Heidegger, Jaspers and Husserl are understood to have given up the pursuit of universal truths through pure reason and embraced the absurd through an admission of irrationality: hence, for Camus, absurd reasoning is a kind of composite of art and reason which he describes as a 'confrontation of the irrational and the wild longing for clarity' (1942, 26). Reciprocally, Camus claims that 'the great novelists are philosophical novelists, that is the contrary of thesis-writers' and cites Balzac, Sade, Melville, Stendhal, Dostoevsky, Proust, Mallard and Kafka as examples. This tension between the depiction of concrete situations and the kind of philosophical hope that these situations can be rendered intelligible by reason lies at the heart of existentialism. It is the sense of incompletion of one without the other that seems to lie behind Camus's formulation:

> But if in fact, the preference they have shown for writing in images rather than in reasoned arguments is revelatory of a certain thought that is common to [all the great novelists], convinced of the uselessness of any principle of explanation and sure of the educative message of perceptible appearance. They consider the work of art both as an end and as a beginning. It is the outcome of an often expressed philosophy, its illustration and its consummation. But it is complete only through the implications of that philosophy. It justifies at last the variant of an old theme that a little thought estranges from life whereas much thought reconciles to life. Incapable of refining the real, thought pauses to mimic it. (1942, 93)

This is interesting for several reasons. The sense of tension between thought and image helps to explain the place of fiction and drama for existentialist thinkers like Camus and Sartre as a kind return of thought to mimic the real. By this formulation it is the borderline between philosophy and fiction that contains the most energy for what Camus calls absurd creation. From this point of view, existentialism can be seen as an important pre-history to poststructuralist attitudes to fiction and philosophy in so far as they characteristically challenge any rigid line between the two, and celebrate instead a kind of reason pervaded by creativity and a kind of creativity characterized by critical self-consciousness. Derrida's writing, for example, shows the same oscillation between a kind of playful creativity and the rigours of philosophy, the same doubleness of acceptance and suspicion of the possibility of a philosophical or critical metalanguage.

The productive tension between philosophy and fiction seems to operate for both Camus and Sartre, not only as a guiding principle in their own writings, not only as a choice between writing theoretically and writing fictionally, but as a basis for the critical assessment of other writers. We have already touched on this in Camus, who uses the notion of absurdity, and the absurd hero, as a measure of the greatness of other writers. Similarly in the case of Sartre, his own philosophical frameworks are never distant from his critical writings. Sartre's study of Baudelaire (1946) is a well-known example, where the philosophical perspectives of *Being and Nothingness*, Sartre's most influential philosophical tract, are applied to the life of Baudelaire in a process that he called *existential psycho-analysis*. *Baudelaire* is not so much a work of criticism as an account of the writer's failure to live an authentic existence as a result of the death of his father and the remarriage of his mother to a man that he rejected. Refusing the Freudian account of this scenario in the Oedipus complex, Sartre attempts to establish an interpretation which rejects the idea that humans act according to unconscious motives, and turns instead to his own concept of *bad faith*. In *Being and Nothingness*, Sartre sets out a programme for authentic living which consists in the apprehension of one's freedom and the recognition of choice as the determining factor in the existence of any individual. Baudelaire's bitterness towards his father-in-law is seen by Sartre as a special kind of bad faith that he called Being-for-Others. This is a kind of self-absolution from the responsibility that comes with freedom, in which one blames the condition of one's existence on other people, or in which one chooses to see oneself as if someone else. In addition to being a principle for the assessment of Baudelaire as a writer, there are two important aspects of this analysis. The first is that it distances Sartre's thought from Freud, who sees early childhood as the crucial stage of an individual's formation, which then determines the unconscious desires and motives of the adult. To preserve the idea of freedom, Sartre focuses on an event in Baudelaire's life that took place at the age of eight, at which free individual choices become possible, and any evasion of them through the inauthenticity of Being-for-Others is a failure of responsibility. The second is that it distances Sartre from the marxist tradition, which had always refused the idea of the individual as a sovereign or transcendent realm of free choice, and preferred to subordinate questions of the individual to the social system which determined all aspects of inner life.

There is a strange reciprocity here between Sartre's dealings with a writer and the deployment of his philosophical ideas which I think is characteristic of his work in general. There is a feeling that Sartre's life, his philosophical writings, his views on literature, his evaluation of other writings and his politics are all facets of a unified project. In his dealings with Baudelaire there is a cross-contamination between critic and philosopher (also to be found in his 1952 study of Genet and of Flaubert in 1966) that seems to uphold the values of Sartre's own life and work as he describes it in his autobiography. In *Words*, Sartre makes it clear that the fall into bad faith he describes in Baudelaire contrasts with his own eight-year-old moment of authentic responsibility when he decided irreversibly, and against the will of others, to be a writer. And when he returns to Baudelaire in that text, he adds another account of Baudelaire's fall into bad faith, this time in relation to his uncritical acceptance of the romantic myth of a poet in isolation from society and therefore doomed to unhappiness. Again, the contrast with Sartre's own life is difficult to miss. In *What is Literature*, Sartre's well known polemic in favour of a committed literature, a literature whose worth is measured by its oppositional power and its orientation towards social action, the romantic myth of the poet in social isolation is not sufficiently *engagé*. Indeed, *What is Literature* argues that being a poet at all is something of an obstacle to commitment by the very nature of the poetic language:

> The poet is outside language. He sees words inside out as if he did not share the human condition, and as if he were first meeting the word as a barrier as he comes towards men. Instead of first knowing things by their name, it seems that first he has a silent contact with them, since, turning towards that other species of thing which for him is the word, touching them, testing them, fingering them, he discovers in them a slight luminosity of their own and particular affinities with the earth, the sky, the water, and all created things. (1993, 6)

Commitment is the preserve of prose, in which language is capable of transparency to the world, and particularly when the writer's own world is visible beyond the materiality of language. 'You explain this world to me with an image', says Camus in a similar spirit. 'I realize that you have been reduced to poetry. .. So that science that was to teach me everything ends up in a hypothesis, that lucidity founders in metaphor, that uncertainty is resolved in a work of art' (1942, 25). There is a critical attitude at work here that values philosophical lucidity above the excesses of metaphor, and yet at the same time doubts the ability of that philosophical lucidity to describe existence in its concrete quiddity. It is as if good writing must forsake reason, and yet not err so far into literariness that it becomes poetic. There is a kind of self-endorsement in these views, that philosophy should not venture too far from literature, and that literature should stay within the orbit of philosophy.

Sartre's early philosophy describes the condition of freedom as if it were a simple fact, and the concept of bad faith as a flight from that freedom. Literature is often described as existentialist when it represents the condition of existence against a backdrop of absurdity, or where various forms of bad faith seem to fill the meaningless void in an attempt to push back the anguish of responsibility and freedom. Beckett's drama, also much to his chagrin, is often seen in this way. A backdrop of silence is filled by characters whose habitual actions prevent them from apprehending their freedom. Chief among these habits is the meaningless exchange of apparently unscripted dialogue, the main purpose of which is to give characters the impression of existence through interaction with others. The importance of the mutually dependent pair in early Beckett drama seemed to many to be speaking directly to Sartre's description of the bad faith of Being-for-Others, in which one character's existence is affirmed by the perception of the other. But communication is never a very successful or meaningful business for Beckett's characters, who seem to express only the need to continue trying to express in the knowledge that they will continue to fail. It is easy to understand why critics of the mid-century were eager to read Vladimir and Estragon, Hamm and Clov or Winnie and Willie as allegories of Sartre's descriptions of Being-for-Others, and many of Beckett's own pronouncements seemed to indicate the validity of the approach. Characters who are free to leave fail to do so because they believe their existence to be dependant on another (Vladimir and Estragon), characters who think their existence will end if the other leaves (Hamm and Clov), characters whose primary need is the perception, however negligible, of another (Winnie in relation to Willie) or characters who see themselves as another person (Krapp) seem to be advancing a negative view of the absurdity of interaction with others. The negativity here relates more closely to Sartre's rather gloomy analysis of freedom in *Being and Nothingness* rather than to the optimistic affirmation of the absurd that we get in Camus's *The Myth of Sisyphus*. And Beckett's own hostility to the critical interpretation seems if anything to affirm rather than to deny the link with existential categories, communicating as it does with the suspicion of meta-languages and the valorization of literature as a philosophical mode. As he constantly asserted, his plays were mere existents attesting to the ineffability of knowledge, and yet clearly aimed at the representation of an existential condition which defied and mocked the attempts of reason to render it intelligible.

The importance of existentialism for literature and literary theory might then be summarized in the following categories. (1) Fiction and drama were adopted as suitable discourses for the representation of existential themes by Camus and Sartre. (2) The boundary between philosophy and literature became a source of energy for both, valorizing philosophical fiction and literariness in philosophy. (3) The idea of absurdity developed as a philosophical account of the absence of meaning in the universe, and provided a backdrop for fictional and dramatic explorations of bad faith, freedom and the quest for meaning in Sartre and Camus's own writing. (4) Sartre's philosophical writings provided perspectives on language, especially the role of language as a mode of Being-for-Others, and the demotion of poetic language in relation to political commitment. (5) Sartre's existential psychoanalysis was a form of diagnosis which, against Freud and Marx, sought to reveal a moment of fundamental choice, within or outside fiction, which might, really or hypothetically, be consciously changed. (6) Camus's and Sartre's philosophy provides a critical vocabulary beyond existential psychoanalysis for the description of apparently purposeless and futile fictional and dramatic actions. Perhaps most significantly, if we cast forward to contemporary literary criticism and theory, existentialism can be seen as a set of foundations for the reciprocity between theory and fiction that has characterized postmodernism, and particularly the extent to which literary practice and criticism have aspired to forms of social action and political engagement in the aftermath of the more scientific and formalist concerns of the Anglo-American tradition in the mid-twentieth century.

Mark Currie

Further reading and works cited

Beckett, S. *Waiting for Godot*. London, 1956.
—. *Endgame*. London, 1958.
—. *Krapp's Last Tape*. London, 1959.
—. *Happy Days*. London, 1965.
Blackham, H. J. *Six Existentialist Thinkers*. London, 1952.
Camus, A. *The Myth of Sisyphus*. Harmondsworth, 1942.
—. *The Outsider*. Harmondsworth, 1961.
Danto, A. C. *Sartre*. London, 1975.
Macquarrie, J. *Existentialism*. London, 1972.
Patrik, L. *Existential Literature*. London, 2000.
Poster, M. *Existential Marxism in Postwar France*. Princeton, NJ, 1975.
Sartre, J.-P. *Being and Nothingness*. London, 1957.
—. *Baudelaire*. [1946]. London, 1964.
—. *Words*. London, 1964.
—. *Nausea*. London, 1965.
—. *What is Literature?* London, 1993.

27. Emmanuel Levinas (1906–1995)

Anyone interested in literature who decides to read Emmanuel Levinas for the first time will very likely experience an awkward tension that will accompany him or her for book after book. On the one hand, in his philosophical writings especially, Levinas refers to a wide range of canonical dramatists, novelists and poets, most of them French, German and Russian. He affirms that he came to philosophy by reading Russian fiction, and observes that 'it sometimes seems to me that the whole of philosophy is only a meditation on Shakespeare' (Levinas 1987a, 72). His major work, *Totalité et infini* (1961), begins with a line from one of Arthur Rimbaud's prose poems and ends with a line from one of Charles Baudelaire's. He devotes a little book to his oldest friend, Maurice Blanchot, for whose novels and *récits* he has the greatest respect, and he consecrates short, admiring texts to Paul Celan, Edmond Jabès, Roger Laporte, Michel Leiris and Marcel Proust. Simply reading his books will reveal that Levinas can write in a lyrical manner when it suits his purposes, and one may even come to find that in general his prose has unique attractions. Scarcely inattentive to Levinas's philosophical originality or the subtlety of his arguments, Jacques Derrida nonetheless notes that '*Totality and Infinity* is a work of art and not a treatise' (1978, 312, n. 7).

On the other hand, before one has gone very far into Levinas's works it will become sharply evident that he launches one of the most virulent attacks on art since Plato composed *The Republic*. In 'Reality and its Shadow' (1948) we are told that art is 'the very event of obscuring, a descent of the night, an invasion of shadow', that it consists 'in substituting an image for being', that every image is '*already a caricature*' and that 'There is something wicked and egoist and cowardly in artistic enjoyment' (Levinas 1987b, 3, 5, 9, 12). Criticism is to be valued over art, we are advised in the same essay, while in *Totality and Infinity* prose is opposed to poetry, leaving us in no doubt that this is to the former's advantage because prose breaks the 'rhythm which enraptures and transports the inter- locutors' (Levinas 1979, 203). In that same work, Rimbaud who summarily informed his former teacher Georges Izambard that 'I is another [*Je est un autre*]' is given a slap over the wrist: 'The alterity of the I that takes itself for another may strike the imagination of the poet precisely because it is but the play of the same' (Levinas 1979, 37). Since Levinas's ethics, as we shall see, turn on elevating the other over the self this can only be received as a harsh judgement on the French poet and the schools of poetics that draw on his revolutionary statement about the 'I'. Yet Levinas can be even more blunt. In another place he speaks of the 'violence' to be found in 'poetic delirium and enthusiasm displayed when we merely offer our mouths to the muse who speaks through us' (Levinas 1990a, 7).

Quite reasonably, anyone with a literary bent who has taken the trouble to read Levinas will ask whether this tension can be resolved and, if so, how. Although art is a peripheral matter for Levinas, the questions he raises with regard to it lead us directly to the centre of his thought, and so we shall follow them. To begin with, one might think that the tension between admiring and condemning art can be explained by appealing to empirical events in Levinas's life, such as his son's decision to pursue a career in music. (Michael Levinas became a composer, concert pianist and teacher of musical analysis at the Conservatoire de Paris.) At no time, however, does the philosopher change his mind about what he criticizes in the arts. And yet when he writes about art he does not always focus on what he finds most worrying about it. 'Reality and its Shadow' (1948) complains that art is not socially committed, so it is odd to look back only a year before and find in 'The Other in Proust' (1947) an author who recognizes that 'Proust is the poet of the social' (Levinas 1996, 102). 'We distrust poetry' we are told in a 1950 essay on Paul Claudel only to hear in a 1969 essay on the same poet that what 'makes language possible' is in all likelihood 'the very definition of poetry' (Levinas 1990a, 121, 132). In 'The Servant and Her Master' (1966) the Blanchot of *Awaiting Oblivion* is praised for his language 'of pure transcendence without correlation … a language going from one singularity to another without their having anything in common' (Levinas 1996, 148). And, later, in 'Paul Celan: From Being to the Other' (1972), the philosopher lauds the poet in terms he elsewhere reserves for ethics: 'The poem goes toward the other' (Levinas 1996, 41). If Levinas has not changed his mind about art, we must ask whether Blanchot, Celan, Claudel and Proust produce something other than art, as Levinas understands the word, or whether they incorporate a criticism of art in what they produce.

Before we can turn our attention to this matter, though, we must consider another attempt to explain Levinas's ambiguous relation to art by way of his biography. For it is sometimes proposed that the strictures in 'Reality and its Shadow' and elsewhere can be explained satisfactorily by noting that Levinas is a Jew and that therefore he feels bound, at one level or another, to respect the divine prohibition against the making of 'graven images' (Exodus 20: 4). Before evaluating this explanation, we need to grasp the scope of the prohibition in question. The commandment is debated in the Babylonian Talmud (Tractate Rosh Hashanah, ch. 2, 24 a–b), and the conclusion reached there is that that images may be made for public display but only when there is no chance they can be worshipped as idols, and that images may be used for purposes of instruction. Levinas is well aware of this. In Lithuania, as a child of observant Jews, he learned to read the Hebrew Bible in its original language. Then, after a period in which religious studies played little or no part in his life, he returned to them but in a new way. From 1947 to 1951 he devoted himself to studying the Talmud under the strict guidance of M. Chouchani, and starting in 1957 gave papers at the annual Colloquium of Jewish Intellectuals that meets in Paris. So one would expect him to have an informed and nuanced understanding of Torah, including Exodus 20: 4. In fact, Levinas is less interested in the prohibition against images as a religious rule than in something that the rule perhaps bespeaks. He wonders if beneath the commandment there is not 'a denunciation, in the structures of signifying and the meaningful, of a certain favoring of representation over other possible modes of thought' (Levinas 1999, 122).

In the sentence I have just quoted Levinas modulates from religion to philosophy, and it needs to be pointed out that he distinguishes his philosophical from his confessional texts. The five collections of his Talmudic readings, from *Quatre lectures talmudiques* (1968) to the posthumous *Nouvelles lectures talmudiques* (1996), are published by Les Éditions de Minuit, while his main philosophical works, *Totalité et infini* (1961) and *Autrement qu'être* (1974), first appeared with Martinus Nijhoff. This empirical division of his labours sends a clear signal to readers. Even so, the line between the two sorts of writing is hardly continuous or straight. Although he does not cite the Talmud in order to establish a philosophical position, he does not hesitate to quote Scripture in order to amplify or clarify points in his non-confessional writings. As his reflections on Exodus 20: 4 suggest, his philosophical thinking sometimes converges with his reflections on Torah and Talmud. Yet these reflections are not confessions of religious belief. As Levinas observes, his Talmudic readings are neither dogmatic nor theological but are in search 'of problems and truths', a discipline he believes to be necessary 'for an Israel wishing to preserve its self-consciousness in the modern world' (Levinas 1990b, 9). 'Israel', for this Jew, denotes an intellectual as well as a political and religious reality, and the former must not be obscured by the latter.

Philosophy derives from the ancient Greeks, Levinas maintains, but in saying that he is not merely endorsing Alfred North Whitehead's *bon mot* that all philosophy is a series of footnotes to Plato. Rather, he is suggesting that intelligibility itself is underwritten by fundamental Greek concepts: '*morphe* (form), *ousia* (substance), *nous* (reason), *logos* (thought) or *telos* (goal), etc.' (Cohen 1986, 19). Thus understood, intelligibility yields a notion of truth as presence. What is true is present or presentable, and it follows that the present moment, the now, is able to hold very different elements together in a relation of sameness. These elements are 'englobed in a history which totalizes time into a beginning or an end, or both, which is presence' (Cohen 1986, 19). A quite different notion of truth may be found in the Hebrew Bible, Levinas reminds us, one that answers to infinity rather than totality. Biblical truth is a matter of the proximity of God; it turns on a call for justice, a concern for the other person. In contemplating this Hebraic sense of truth, Levinas affirms that 'The other qua other is the Other' [*L'Autre en tant qu'autre est Autrui*]' and consequently that 'The Other alone eludes thematization' (Levinas 1979, 71, 86). Immediately, though, a difficulty appears, one that Derrida was quick to indicate in his reading of *Totality and Infinity*. Can one coherently affirm the Other as infinitely other? 'The other cannot be what it is, infinitely other, except in finitude and mortality (mine *and* its). It is such as soon as it comes into language, of course, and only then, and only if the word *other* has a meaning – but has not Levinas taught us that there is no thought before language?' (Derrida 1978, 114–15). Levinas saw the point of the objection, which perhaps nudged him toward distinguishing the Saying from the Said in *Otherwise than Being* and its satellite essays.

Derrida had pointed out that Levinas was seeking to question philosophy at its deepest level. His was 'a question which can be stated only by being forgotten in the language of the Greeks; and a question which can be stated, as forgotten, only in the language of the Greeks' (Derrida 1978, 133). Plato had spoken of the 'good beyond being' in *The Republic* 509b, and thereby evoked a goodness that does not answer to presence, and Levinas has devoted himself to a radical reinterpretation of Plato's expression. As he says as early as the preface to the first edition of *De l'existence à l'existant* (1947), 'The Platonic formula that situates the Good beyond Being serves as the general guideline for this research – but does not make up its content. It signifies that the movement which leads an existent toward the Good is not a transcendence by which that existent raises itself up to a higher existence, but a departure from Being ...' (Levinas 1988, 15). The issue, then, is how we are to understand transcendence. Levinas condemns the 'false and cruel transcendence' implicit in Greek religion (Bergo, Bergo and Perpich 1998, 9). Transcendence for Hesiod and Homer is conceived as a spatial ascent, and it amounts to idolatry. For all their elevation, the gods are commensurate with humans. To the extent that western knowledge bases itself on the Greeks, it is a secularization of idolatry and a commitment to the value of the same over the other. And to the extent that Christian mysticism is a longing to be taken into the ineffable unity of the Godhead, it too derives from Greek religion. We escape idolatry only when we embark on a transcendence that is not spatial, one that occurs within immanence and disturbs it.

How can one transcend being without understanding the good to be or to confer a higher kind of being? Or, in the words that Levinas will come to use, how can one pass from 'being otherwise' to 'otherwise than being'? Two of the rationalists provide clues, one positive and one negative. René Descartes argued in the third of his *Meditations* that the infinite is not the negation of the finite; on the contrary, since there is more reality in infinite than finite substance, the idea of infinity must precede the idea of the finite. For Levinas, the infinite is the absolutely other, a transcendence that does not generate mystical theologies but that passes in the other's face. Benedict de Spinoza provides the negative clue in his *Ethics*, Book III, proposition six: '*Each thing, in so far as it is in itself, endeavors to persevere in its being*' (Spinoza 1949, 135). Taking Descartes and Spinoza in tandem, Levinas affirms that transcendence consists precisely in yielding one's *conatus essendi*, or self-maintenance in being, in favour of the other person, and this movement from being to the other *is* the good. The 'good beyond being' is thereby wrested from both Platonic metaphysics and religion and is reinterpreted as ethics.

This is not an ethics that depends on choice, for the other person has always and already made a claim on me. At no time did I contract to answer for the other. My responsibility for him or her comes from an immemorial past which has never been present. Levinas's entire thought, in all its density and difficulty, is contained in this original rethinking of Plato's thought about the good. Once formulated, it is tirelessly explored, so that Levinas's mature work can be regarded as so many variations on a theme, although some of these variations are themselves breathtaking in their daring. There is a considerable distance between *Totality and Infinity* and *Otherwise than Being*, to cite only the most dramatic and important instance, but before we can understand either the drama or the importance we must retrace our steps and go back to the beginning, as Levinas himself does in essay after essay.

A philosopher has many beginnings, and Levinas is no exception. One could cite the Plato who broaches 'the good beyond being', the Descartes who writes of the idea of the infinite, the Spinoza who formulates the *conatus essendi*, the Rosenzweig who criticizes totality, or the Bergson who conceives time as duration. More often than not, though, Levinas begins by returning to Edmund Husserl. There is a biographical as well as a philosophical reason for this. After studying at the University of Strasbourg, where he became close friends with Blanchot, Levinas went to the University of Freiburg for the summer semester of 1928 and the winter semester of 1928–9. Husserl had retired from his chair just before Levinas arrived, although he continued teaching throughout the winter semester of 1928–9 until his successor, Martin Heidegger, arrived from the University of Marburg. As it happened, Levinas gave a paper in the last meeting of Husserl's final seminar, which had been devoted to the constitution of intersubjectivity. Levinas's first publications were a review essay on Husserl's *Ideas I* in *Revue Philosophique de la France et de l'Etranger* in 1929, and his doctoral dissertation *The Theory of Intuition in Husserl's Phenomenology* (1930) which led French philosophers, including Jean-Paul Sartre, to German phenomenology. Several further expositions of Husserl's thought followed, along with introductions to Heidegger's bold rethinking of phenomenology in *Being and Time* (1927).

Although Levinas offered patient and thorough explanations of Husserl's phenomenology, which still serve as excellent guides to the subject, he expressed reservations about the master's prizing of theoretical consciousness. In the fifth of the *Logical Investigations* (1899–1901) Husserl had followed Franz Brentano in arguing that intentional experience is either a representation or based on a representation. With *Ideas I* (1913) this thesis is modified, although not sufficiently to concede that non-objectifying acts, such as affection, desire and will, help to constitute objects as meaningful. To be sure, other Husserlian notions – non-theoretical intentionality, the lifeworld, and the lived body – provide ways in which the pertinence of these acts can be acknowledged. But the Husserl of *Ideas I* and beyond holds fast to the view that all non-objectifying acts must ultimately refer to a representation. In other words, perceiving, judging and knowing are granted priority in experience, despite Husserl's claim that being *is* what is experienced. 'This is why the Husserlian concept of intuition is tainted with intellectualism and is possibly too narrow' (Levinas 1973, 94). Over the years Levinas becomes less cautious than that 'possibly' suggests. In the vocabulary of phenomenology, 'intuition' denotes experience in a wider sense than that allowed by empiricists; it includes categories and essences, and makes no presumption about how something exists. (After all, the same thing may be given in a dream, a memory, a perception, or whatever.) Under the influence of Heidegger, which can be detected as early as *The Theory of Intuition*, Levinas releases intuition from the grip of epistemology, and attends to our ways of being in the world rather than human nature. After the Second World War, however, Levinas distances himself from Heidegger for a mixture of philosophical and political reasons, and develops intriguing phenomenologies of fatigue and insomnia that exceed the frame of *Being and Time*. And in the decades to follow, he focuses on what precedes representation and interrupts it: what calls 'the face' or 'infinity' or 'the Other'.

Although Levinas never abandons phenomenology as a method, he unfolds it in his own way. Husserl heavily underlined the importance of the *epoché* or phenomenological reduction. It must come first, he says, and it must be prepared for with the greatest care. In the reduction the thesis of the natural standpoint – that reality is simply objective – is suspended. We shake off the unexamined metaphysics that we habitually absorb from science, and are left instead with experience as concretely lived. This experience can then be examined in all its originality and richness. For Levinas, Husserl's endless refining of the reduction from *Ideas I* to *The Crisis of European Sciences* (completed in 1937) leads more surely to a sterile methodology than to 'the things themselves' as promised in the *Logical Investigations*. The freedom of the reduction is the freedom of theory. Misled by granting representation pride of place in intentional life, Husserl offers no account of how the reduction is based in life as it is lived, and the reduction ends up looking uncomfortably like the natural attitude it seeks to suspend. According to *The Theory of Intuition*, the reduction is hampered by 'the intellectualist character of intuition' (Levinas 1973, 158). Later, in *Totality and Infinity*, we are told more magisterially that the 'very possibility' of the reduction 'defines representation' (Levinas 1979, 125).

It follows that the reduction will always have the effect of objectifying the other person, making a vulnerable singular individual into a representation. Consequently, the *epoche*, as formulated by Husserl, plays little role in Levinas's philosophy. What is alive in phenomenology, he thinks, is the invitation for 'consciousness to understand its own preoccupations, to reflect upon itself and thus discover all the hidden or neglected horizons of its intentionality' (Cohen 1986, 14). Intentionality, the thesis that consciousness is always consciousness of something, is of the greatest importance for him for two reasons. First, intentionality is not an attribute of consciousness but is subjectivity itself. No one is imprisoned in their minds or their selves. And second, because it is outwardly directed, intentionality contains the thought of otherness. In phenomenology, an object is not only given to consciousness but also modified according to the many horizons of intentionality. In no way is this a fall from the objective to the subjective, for the thought that constitutes the object as meaningful has already been solicited by that object. Phenomenology involves a passage from asking *what* we are thinking about to *how* we are thinking about it, and in making that move we find ourselves inquiring how an object has been positioned in and by consciousness. Here, then, at the very centre of phenomenology, Levinas finds what will destroy the hegemony of representation. For 'representation already finds itself placed within horizons that it somehow had not willed, but with which it cannot dispense' and so 'an ethical *Sinngebung*', a bestowing of meaning that is ethical not epistemological, 'becomes possible' (Levinas 1998a, 121).

It is one thing to become possible, another to be realized. The ethical *Sinngebung* occurs not with objects, which can be grasped by consciousness, but with faces which cannot be mastered. When I encounter the other as other, Levinas argues, my act of perception is interrupted thereby preventing any correlation of other and self. An ethical event occurs in a social space that is curved upward in favour of the other. So it is a non-theoretical intentionality that is operative here, although even that will be disturbed by the face. Without having to say a word, this absolutely singular individual addresses me in the mode of command: the face says, 'Thou shalt not kill' and (so Levinas adds in his last writings) 'Do not leave me to die alone'. At first one might think of the critical philosophy, and indeed Levinas can sound very Kantian when he remarks, 'The kingdom of heaven is ethical' (Levinas 1981, 183). Unlike Kant, however, Levinas focuses on the call from the singular other to the singular self, and does not venerate a universal moral law. The silent address is received by me alone, and I alone can accept responsibility for this other person. I respond by saying, as Samuel did, 'Here I am' and in doing so accept responsibility for the other, testifying not to the truth of a representation but to the glory of the infinite. Mortality is therefore witnessed in terms of the *other*'s finitude and weakness, not mine; and this marks what Levinas came to regard as a vast gulf between himself and Heidegger. As Heidegger brilliantly argues in *Being and Time* § 53, death is always my ownmost possibility, indeed the possibility of the impossibility of my existence. I am individuated by anticipating my end. Confronted by the nothingness that awaits me, I experience anxiety: not as a psychological state but as an ontological attunement.

For Levinas, the ultimate question is not 'To be or not to be' but how things stand with the other person. It is not nothingness that is truly frightening but the sheer impersonality of being, what Levinas dubs the *il y a* or 'there is'. We see Levinas emerge as an independent thinker when he titles his 1947 volume *De l'existence à l'existant*. The crucial movement imagined here is from the priority of anonymous being, which interests Heidegger, to the priority of the other person. On Levinas's analysis, the other confronts me in my enjoyment of being, and in recognizing that I am responsible for this other person I cede my place in being and become being-for-the-other. This is the way we escape the horror of the *il y a*. Levinas calls the move from being to being-for-the-other holiness, which for him is an ethical rather than a religious value. The phased counterpart of holiness is the sacred, which he understands by way of institutional religious practice. One can of course be holy within the world of the sacred, yet the sacred can easily lead one away from authentic holiness. It can even involve us in what Lucien Lévy-Bruhl calls 'participation', a state in which emotional experience gains us access to the supernatural. Levinas views this state with increasing distrust and comes to associate it with poetry as much as religion.

The passage to authentic holiness is more heavily marked in *Otherwise than Being* than in *Totality and Infinity*. 'The soul is the other in me', we are told in the later work (Levinas 1981, 191, n. 3), and indeed the whole treatise is a radical attempt to reformulate subjectivity by way of relations with the other person. If Levinas is a humanist, his is a 'humanism of the other man', as the title of one of his books puts it. Responsibility, here, does not relate to the consequences of one's free choices but indicates a state to which one has been elected by the other. 'The word *I* means *here I am*', Levinas ventures, and adds that 'The self is a *sub-jectum*; it is under the weight of the universe, responsible for everything' (Levinas 1981, 114, 115). The asymmetry between self and other which was everywhere apparent in *Totality and Infinity* is pushed to an extreme in *Otherwise than Being*, so that the self is 'obsessed' with the other, 'persecuted' by him or her and held 'hostage'.

If one is tempted to object to Levinas that his ethics are utopian, he would be the first to agree. First, they are utopian in the literal sense that I am required, in responding to the other, to yield my place in being. I thereby create 'a profound utopia' (Levinas 1998b, 145). Second, it needs to be stressed that Levinas is not describing or prescribing normative moral behaviour but merely seeking to show that the ethical has a meaning that is irreducible to representation. Ethics is not morality: the distinction between the two is sharp though not complete. Were there only I and the other in the world, I would owe everything to the other, but as soon as a third party appears, this asymmetry cannot hold sway. There is a call for justice by the third person, which brings reciprocity into play. And yet the fundamental asymmetry between the Other and the Self is supremely important, Levinas thinks. Without it, society would be in danger of becoming totalitarian. Even a small gesture such as saying 'After you' before a doorway indicates that ethical asymmetry interrupts the symmetry of morality.

In *Otherwise than Being*, communication is held to be complete only when one assumes responsibility for the other person. Levinas redraws communication from the perspective of ethics, rather than from social linguistics. In the same move he thoroughly reinterprets the phenomenological reduction. Distinguishing the Saying from the Said, he observes that the true reduction, 'the going back to the hither side of being', is none other than going back 'to the hither side of the said' (Levinas 1981, 45). It should be noted that Saying (*le dire*), should not be confused with Martin Buber's notion of dialogue, which presumes the self and other to stand on the same level. Still less should it be confused with Heidegger's *Sage*, which is also translated as 'Saying' and which the German philosopher regards as 'the being of language in its totality' (Heidegger 1982, 123). On the contrary, Saying for Levinas is an escape from being and totality; it is an addressing of oneself to another, an interruption of a settled or settling state of affairs. Inescapable as it may seem, the language of action is nonetheless misleading here, for Levinas stresses that one is *already* the hostage of the other person and so, strictly speaking, Saying bespeaks a passivity beyond the well-known dialectical duo of activity and passivity.

What is said in an address to the other is less important than that the self responds to a trace of the infinite there, and takes responsibility for this person. Inevitably, even the most naked and vulnerable Saying eventually becomes deposited in a Said: the transcendence of ethical openness becomes mired in ontological immanence. This very text is an example. The hesitations, doublings and unsayings that characterize Levinas's prose end up being smoothed out in a short encyclopaedia article. And yet the Said can be unsaid: Levinas prizes philosophy in this regard, trusting in its untiring ability to start from scratch and rethink a problem. By way of contrast, theology cannot do this, he suggests, although he seems to regard the Queen of the Sciences very narrowly, as a thematizing of a Said and a destruction of true transcendence. Theologians will object, and with reason; it is hard to recognize Karl Barth, Karl Rahner or Jürgen Moltmann – to name only a handful of the French philosopher's contemporaries – from this perspective. Levinas is more favourably disposed toward poetry than theology, for poetry can unsay itself, although in different ways than those practised by the philosophers.

Thinking of Blanchot, Levinas notes that 'the word poetry, to me, means the rupture of the immanence to which language is condemned, imprisoning itself. I do not think that this rupture is a purely aesthetic event. But the word poetry does not, after all, designate a species, the genus of which would be art' (Levinas 1996, 185, n. 4). That Blanchot writes prose, not verse, does not matter in the slightest. 'Poetry', for Levinas, is taken to interrupt representation, the image or ontology, and to be a response to the fleeting trace of the infinite in the face of the other. Poetry is not merely one of the arts, and verse has no monopoly on poetry. It is a name for that which disturbs representation. Where art freezes the other in an image, or indulges itself in the delights of incantation, poetry is by contrast a saying and an unsaying; it is therefore coordinate with transcendence, as understood ethically rather than religiously. Or to say the same thing in slightly different words, poetry interrupts art. This is not an apology for the avant garde; on the contrary, it is an elevation of ethics over aesthetics. What interests Levinas in avant-garde poetics – Blanchot, Celan, Jabès and Leiris, for instance – is that their work follows a trace and does not present a mimetic image. Presumably, though, this response to the trace could also be seen in other writers, in people as different as Jonathan Swift and Samuel Johnson, William Wordsworth and John Keats, Roberto Juarroz and Eugenio Montale.

Kevin Hart

Further reading and works cited

Bergo, B. and Perpich, D. (eds) 'Levinas's Contribution to Contemporary Philosophy', Graduate Faculty Philosophy Journal, 20, 2–21, 1, 1998.
Bernasconi, R. and Critchley, S. (eds) Re-Reading Levinas. Bloomington, IN, 1991.
Chalier, C. and Abensour, M. (eds) Emmanuel Lévinas. Paris, 1991.
Cohen, R. A. (ed.) Face to Face with Levinas. Albany, NY, 1986.
Davis, C. Levinas. Cambridge, 1996.
De Boer, T. The Rationality of Transcendence. Amsterdam, 1997.
Derrida, J. Writing and Difference. London, 1978.
—. Adieu to Emmanuel Levinas. Stanford, CA, 1999.
Eaglestone, R. Ethical Criticism. Edinburgh, 1997.
Gibbs, R. Correlations in Rosenzweig and Levinas. Princeton, NJ, 1992.
Heidegger, M. On the Way to Language. New York, 1982.
Lescourret, M.-A. Emmanuel Levinas. Paris, 1994.
Levinas, E. The Theory of Intuition in Husserl's Phenomenology. Evanston, IL, 1973.
—. Totality and Infinity. The Hague, 1979.
—. Otherwise than Being or Beyond Essence. The Hague, 1981.
—. Time and the Other. Pittsburgh, 1987a.
—. Collected Philosophical Papers. The Hague, 1987b.
—. Existence and Existents. Boston, 1988.
—. Difficult Freedom. Baltimore, MD, 1990a.
—. Nine Talmudic Readings. Bloomington, IN, 1990b.
—. Proper Names. Stanford, CA, 1996.
—. Discovering Existence with Husserl. Evanston, IL, 1998a.
—. Entre Nous. New York, 1998b.
—. Alterity and Transcendence. London, 1999.
Llewelyn, J. Emmanuel Levinas. London, 1995.
Peperzak, A. To the Other. West Lafayette, IN, 1993.
Poirié, F. Emmanuel Lévinas: Qui êtes-vous? Lyon, 1987.
Robbins, J. Altered Reading: Levinas and Literature. Chicago, 1999.
Spinoza, B. de. Ethics preceded by On the Improvement of the Understanding, ed. J. Gutman. New York, 1949.

28. Simone de Beauvoir (1908–1986) and French Feminism

Simone de Beauvoir set the agenda for late twentieth-century feminism with her essay on the situation of women, The Second Sex (1949). In this work she framed many of the concepts, presuppositions and problems that have engaged feminists in the last three decades of the century. Yet her importance for the reading of feminism on both sides of the Atlantic has not always been fully acknowledged. Like Sartre, with whom she was closely associated throughout her life, she, for a time, tended to be dismissed, in the light of the triumph of Lévi-Strauss' structuralism and its appropriation by Lacanian psychoanalysis, as an adherent of an outdated existentialism which was excessively individualistic and which took too little account of the determinations of language and the forces of the unconscious. Her status as the canonical twentieth-century feminist was further undermined by various feminist critiques of Sartre's philosophy. These critiques have posed something of a difficulty for feminists, since de Beauvoir often claimed to have been philosophically unoriginal and to have applied Sartre's philosophical system in her works. From the time in 1928, when de Beauvoir began her affair with Sartre, until his death in 1980, the lives of this couple were closely linked. Despite the intense affairs which each of them had with others, they chose to make their relationship with each other essential to their jointly forged identity. They commented on, and corrected, each other's work, saw each other nearly daily when both in Paris, and corresponded regularly while apart. Given that de Beauvoir was so closely associated with a philosophy that began from a Cartesian subjective questioning, she has, from the point of view of postmodernist and poststructuralist feminists, appeared outdated. In an early and very influential paper, Michele Le Doeuff both acknowledged the importance of de Beauvoir as a feminist precursor, but criticized her adoption of existentialist categories (Le Doeuff 1980). In a later book-length discussion, Le Doeuff stressed de Beauvoir's differences from Sartre, and argued that despite her claims to the contrary, de Beauvoir transformed existentialism (1991). The project of saving de Beauvoir for feminism by asserting her originality and independence from Sartre has been taken up by a significant number of English and American feminists during the 1990s (Simons 1995). This is partly in reaction to the earlier tendency, associated with postmodernism and the emergence of feminisms of difference in the 1980s, to cast de Beauvoir as a male-identified, egalitarian feminist, who, despite her importance for the feminist movement, was philosophically misguided.

Both the treatment of de Beauvoir as completely male identified and the depiction of her as quite independent of Sartre involve distortion. The first gives de Beauvoir too little credit for having recognized and developed an account of the situation of women which both related it to, and differentiated it from, the situation of other oppressed groups. The second gives Sartre too little credit for the role he played in the postwar emergence in France of a left-wing critique of oppression which was both anti-Stalinist and anti-capitalist. The version of existentialist marxism that was developed by this couple during the 1940s and 1950s, had a widespread influence. It was disseminated through the journal *Les Temps Modernes* and in the plays and novels written by both authors, which constituted their contribution to a committed literature that they consciously used for political ends.

Late twentieth-century feminism would not have had the character it has had had de Beauvoir not provided her account of woman's oppression. Even those feminists who reject her existentialist presuppositions use concepts that she introduced to explain woman's situation. In particular, the idea that woman is man's other and the observation that woman is always defined in relation to man were original to de Beauvoir and have been constantly repeated. De Beauvoir did not produce an independent philosophical system. Her background, philosophical training and interests were sufficiently close to Sartre's that she was happy to influence the development of his philosophical system through discussion, and through the revisions that she made to his major philosophical works. In general she adopted a very similar philosophical outlook to his, although she was early on more sensitive to the constraints on freedom that arise from social circumstance than he was. The influence on their philosophy of the phenomenology of Husserl and Heidegger led them to take a particular interest in *le vécu*, the lived experience of a particular concrete situation, and from the 1940s onwards, they did much to illuminate the way in which this lived experience emerges out of the constraints of a social situation. The richness of the description of woman's situation in *The Second Sex* owes much to this involvement with capturing *le vecu*, and is one of its great strengths. It has meant, however, that the work has been able to exert an enormous influence, without its philosophical underpinnings being much discussed or very fully appreciated.

This is particularly true in the US, where Betty Friedan, Kate Millett, Shulamith Firestone and Anne Oakley were all more or less inspired by *The Second Sex*, but had read it in the philosophically illiterate Parshley translation and tended to ignore its philosophical commitments. French feminists have also sometimes adopted de Beauvoir's conclusions, while rejecting or ignoring her philosophical premises. Luce Irigaray's *Speculum of the Other Woman* (1974), announces in its title a debt to de Beauvoir's proposition that woman has been man's other. However, its presuppositions are very different to de Beauvoir's existentialism. Irigaray is indebted to Lacanian psychoanalysis, and so she seeks to transform the symbolic order. She accepts the existence of the unconscious, and accepts as a descriptive truth Lacan's claim that the language of consciousness is dominated by the law of the father and a single sexual signifier, the *phallus*. In Sartre's existentialism, by contrast, the unconscious had been replaced by the notion of bad faith. De Beauvoir also rejected the determinism and flight from responsibility that are implicit in Freud's, or Lacan's, psychoanalysis. This allowed her to criticize those elements of psychoanalysis which imply that there is no human freedom while exploiting some of its observations in order to explain women's experience. Irigaray also criticizes Lacan's version of Freudian psychoanalysis, but accepts a basically psychoanalytic framework. In some of her writings the de Beauvoirian idea that woman is other becomes transformed into the idea that there is a feminine language that is other to the masculine symbolic and which can only express itself in ambiguity and madness.

Monique Wittig takes up a different aspect of de Beauvoir's thought. Her influential paper, 'One is Not Born a Woman' (1981), reprinted in *The Straight Mind and Other Essays* (1992), echoes the first sentence of the second volume of de Beauvoir's work. Yet her separatist tendency diverges a great deal from de Beauvoir's ideal, which was for the establishment of a genuine reciprocity between the sexes, in which each would recognize the other as both sovereign subject as well as inessential object. Like some American interpreters of de Beauvoir, in particular, Judith Butler, Wittig seizes on the idea that what woman is has been defined by men, and assumes that a free choice can result in the creation of new genders which do not involve being a woman. This way of reading de Beauvoir comes very close to ascribing to her the nominalism that she rejected in the introduction of *The Second Sex*, and it underplays her emphasis on the real difference in the concrete physical situation of men and women through which they live out their existence.

During the 1950s and early 1960s, de Beauvoir saw the struggle for women's emancipation as part of the wider struggle for the overthrow of capitalist and bourgeois domination. In the early 1970s she was invited to participate in the campaigns of the emerging women's liberation movement in France, and she came to recognize the need for an independent feminist struggle. This was partly due to the recognition that socialism had not brought with it genuine equality between women and men. In 1974 *Les Temps Modernes* published a special issue on the women's movement with the title, 'Les femmes s'entete', and in 1977 the journal *Questions féministes* began, with de Beauvoir as editor. During this period of involvement in the feminist movement, de Beauvoir criticized the emerging emphasis on difference and *écriture feminine* as falling back into essentialist myths, and this no doubt contributed to her being characterized as outdated and male oriented.

Simone de Beauvoir, belonged to a singularly fortunate generation of French women who were able to compete for the *agrégation* in philosophy on almost equal terms with men. This was possible for a short period during the 1920s and 1930s, and has only fairly recently become possible again (Moi 1994, 38–52). She attended lectures at the Sorbonne, and although she was not able to enrol at the prestigious *École Normale* with her male contemporaries, Sartre, Maurice Merleau-Ponty, René Maheu, Raymond Aron and Paul Nizan, she attended lectures there and was included in their discussions as they prepared for the competitive exam. In 1929, de Beauvoir came second in this exam to Sartre, who had failed in the previous year. In doing so she was the youngest person ever to have completed the *agrégation*. Her diaries from this period show her already asking the big 'existential' questions, nostalgic for the certainties of a childhood belief in an Absolute that had been provided by her Catholic background, tending towards despair at the futility of life, uncertain of her own identity and tempted by the immersion of her self in the being of some superior other (Simons 1999, 185–243). The collection of stories *When Things of the Spirit Come First*, which was rejected for publication in the 1930s and finally appeared in 1979, presents, in a fictionalized form, her experiences as a philosophy teacher, and the choices then available to educated bourgeois women of her class, as she conceived them. It also gives a fictionalized account of the death of Zaza, subject of an intense childhood friendship, who was to have married the young Merleau-Ponty, but who died tragically while involved in a conflict with her parents over his suitability as a husband (Francis and Gontier 1987, 83–8). This period of de Beauvoir's life is also recounted in the first volume of her memoirs.

The initiation of de Beauvoir's relationship with Sartre was an important turning point in her life. She says in her memoirs that she felt intellectually dominated by him, despite the fact that all the evidence points to her having been his philosophical equal. And although de Beauvoir claims that she never felt her sex to be a disadvantage while she was young, one can see operating in her life some of the forces of our construction by others that she was later to detail in *The Second Sex*. Comparing her account of her childhood with Sartre's *Les Mots* (1964), one sees that from the beginning his family represented him as a genius, whereas hers recognized her intelligence, but found it a pity that she had not been born a boy (de Beauvoir 1974, 177–8). In the second volume of the memoirs she explains that she did not see herself as a philosopher; she did not aspire to join the elite who attempt 'that conscious venture into lunacy known as a "philosophical system" from which they derive that obsessional attitude which endows their tentative patterns with universal insight and applicability.' She comments: 'As I have remarked before, women are not by nature prone to obsessions of this type' (1965, 221). Unfortunately, this translation obscures de Beauvoir's intentions. In the French text there is no reference to woman's nature, but only to 'la condition féminine' (de Beauvoir 1960, 229). What de Beauvoir is indicating is that, in the light of her upbringing as a girl in a sexist society which did not anticipate and promote female genius, she, like other women, was not prone to the level of arrogance required in order to believe that she would be able to solve philosophical conundrums on which so many great minds have foundered. Whatever the explanation, the 1930s – a period during which Sartre went to Berlin to study Husserl and Heidegger, published *Nausea* (1938) and the philosophical essays that laid the groundwork for *Being and Nothingness* (1943) – were years of relative lack of professional success for de Beauvoir.

Her first attempts at fiction were not published, and it was not until the first years of the war, when she wrote *She Came to Stay* (1943), that she found her literary and philosophical voice. This novel is a fictionalized version of a triangular relationship which existed between Sartre, de Beauvoir and her student Olga Kosakievicz, to whom the book is dedicated. The discussion of the conflict between the consciousness of reality of the protagonist of this novel, Françoise, and the other members of the triangular relationship, Xaviere and Pierre, may well have influenced Sartre's discussion of concrete relations with others in *Being and Nothingness*. If this is the case, then there is every reason to conclude that, without denying de Beauvoir's originality or importance as an influence on Sartre, one can adopt the traditional attitude of reading her novels as applications of many of the schemata outlined in Sartre's work.

The late 1940s were a period of extreme philosophical and literary productivity for de Beauvoir. In 1945, with Sartre, Merleau-Ponty, Aron, Camus, Lieris, Queneau and Olivier, she set up *Les Temps Modernes*, in which she regularly published political, literary and philosophical essays, many of which are only now appearing in English translation. She published her two most obviously philosophical works, *Pyrrhus and Cinéas* and *The Ethics of Ambiguity* in 1944 and 1947 respectively. This period culminated in her two most widely read works, *The Second Sex* (1949) and the novel, *The Mandarins* (1954), for which she received the Prix Goncourt. De Beauvoir's status as a thinker who has shaped the philosophical vocabulary and presuppositions of the late twentieth century is partly obscured by the method that she chose to use, and which she outlined in her essay, 'Littérature et Métaphysique' (1946). There she explains that when young she was torn between the abstract universality of philosophy and the concrete realities of the novel. In order to overcome this conflict she proposes a literature which is concrete, but metaphysically informed. Just as psychology can be treated theoretically, or can inform a novel which deals with concrete events, so too at least some metaphysical outlooks lend themselves to both forms of development (Fullbrook and Fullbrook 1998, 37–51). Following this statement of her desire to illuminate the universal through the concrete she chose to concentrate her efforts on her literary output, and later on her memoirs. Although she does not theorize them as such, the vehicle of the memoir is a perfect means for concretizing a philosophical outlook by locating it in a particular social milieu. De Beauvoir constructs her life story carefully as the story of the emergence of an independent consciousness, its early apprehension of death, its tendency to allow itself to be submerged by others, and its final blossoming as a socially committed, political consciousness devoted to the abolition of oppression and the establishment of an egalitarian world that conforms to the humanist marxism that Sartre expounded in *Critique of Dialectical Reason* (1960). She has been accused of having constructed her biography too carefully, and of having glossed over the moral dubiousness, and emotional cost, of her 'open' relationship with Sartre, in which they remained 'essential' to each other while engaging in other 'contingent' relationships (Bair 1990, 17–18). But this overlooks the philosophical aspect of de Beauvoir's autobiographical enterprise. In *The Second Sex*, she observes that there have been 'sincere and engaging feminine autobiographies but [she says] none can compare with Rousseau's *Confessions* and Stendhal's *Souvenirs d'egotisme*.' She attributes this to the fact that while women have explored the phenomena of the world, they have not attempted to discover meanings, and she asserts that they 'lack metaphysical resonances' (de Beauvoir 1983a, 718–21). In terms of the duality discussed in

'Littérature et Métaphysique', one might say that they have described the concrete and particular, but without attempting to draw from it its metaphysical significance. Her own biography, by contrast, is clearly constructed as a metaphysical journey first towards transcendence and engagement and then into the disturbing realms of old age, which closes off the avenues of transcendent activity and in which the body becomes an obstacle to, instead of an instrument of, transcendent activity. Because of her conscious choice of literature and autobiography as the vehicle for exploring the metaphysical dimensions of existence, her status as a philosopher has been under-estimated. But in taking this approach to the development of metaphysical themes she has been followed by many other French feminists, even those who see themselves as belonging to opposed philosophical traditions. Cixous and Kristeva, in particular, have continued along a path which refuses to choose between literature and metaphysics and have written metaphysical novels, as well as theorizing the psychological and meta-physical elements within literature. In the blurring of the boundary between philosophy and literature which has been characteristic of late twentieth-century literary theory, de Beauvoir emerges as a little acknowledged precursor.

De Beauvoir's philosophical contribution has also been overlooked for the reasons outlined above: the inadequacies of the English text of *The Second Sex*, and the fact that the blossoming of feminism in the 1970s coincided with a widespread rejection of existentialism by a new generation of thinkers intent on establishing their difference from what had gone before. Nevertheless, it is impossible to understand the complex-ities and the limitations of the account of women's oppression that is offered in *The Second Sex* unless one takes into account the philosophical context in which it was produced.

Black, indigenous and third-world women have sometimes criticized the western feminist movement for its elitist and bourgeois orientation. It is important to recognize, however, that at least some of de Beauvoir's thinking in relation to the situation of women was influenced by her exposure to Black American literature, her friendship with Richard Wright and her belief that there were parallels, as well as differences, between the situations of various oppressed groups, blacks, the working class, Jews and women (Simons 1999, 167–84). Sartre, in *Being and Nothingness*, had argued that human free will is the source of value, but that people flee the responsibility that is implied by their freedom and fall into various forms of bad faith. One of these is the spirit of seriousness: the widespread tendency to treat values as givens that have to be obeyed, and as rooted in the essences of things, rather than as residing in the choices of the people who recognize them. A particular form of this spirit of seriousness is Manicheanism, which treats some people as essentially bad and others (usually one's own kind) as essentially good. In her travelogue, *America Day by Day* (1948), de Beauvoir muses on the tendency of the Americans to see the world in terms of good and evil (de Beauvoir 1999, 65–6). In his 1946 essay, 'Anti-Semite and Jew', Sartre had also argued that the anti-Semite takes a Manichean attitude to the world and sets up the Jew as the incarnation of evil, assuming that this evil is an objective reality that justifies his passion rather than a freely adopted passionate attitude. This tendency to structure the world into a pair of opposites is, de Beauvoir thinks, the result of a fundamental feature of consciousness, and she takes from Hegel the idea that 'subject can be posed only in being opposed', an idea which she had already developed in her novel, *She Came to Stay*. The philosophical theory which explains this conflict between consciousness is given its fullest development in *Being and Nothingness*, in the sections on 'The Look' and 'Concrete Relations with Others'.

Sartre begins his mammoth tome with an account of two irreducible regions of being, being for-itself, consciousness, and being in-itself, the material things which are objects for consciousness. Consciousness is defined via the Husserlian dictum that consciousness is always consciousness of something, and from this Sartre concludes that consciousness is never an object of consciousness. This implies that the ego, the self as an object of consciousness, is different from consciousness. Consciousness is transcendent, in the sense that it cannot be identified with any idea or thing in the world. The ego is a thing in the world, an empirical self with a value and meaning derived from free consciousness. The transcendence, or nothingness, of consciousness is the foundation of human freedom. It is often overlooked by feminist interpreters of Sartre that in the middle of his major book Sartre introduces a third irreducible ontological moment, being for-others. In his early essay, 'The Transcendence of the Ego' (1937), Sartre claimed that his theory of being in-itself could solve the problem of solipsism. By the time he was writing *Being and Nothingness*, he had decided that this was a mistake. It seems that it was at this point that his reading of a draft of de Beauvoir's novel, *She Came to Stay*, provided him with a solution to this problem (Simons 1995). In the look of the other I have an immediate apprehension of the existence of others, and feel myself reduced to an object for others. Thus my ego, the object that is myself, is an object for others as well as an object for my consciousness. The fact that I experience the look of the other as a threat to the sovereignty of my evaluation of the world sets up a conflict between consciousnesses not unlike Hegel's, although Sartre refuses to believe that any automatic dialectic of history will resolve the conflict. Sartre then describes two fundamental attitudes to the other consciousness which arise out of this conflict. The attitude of indifference, desire, sadism and hate involves denying the transcendent consciousness of the other, taking one's own consciousness as sovereign and objectifying the other. The attitude of love, language and masochism involves attempting to incorporate the transcendence of the other, accepting one's objectification and adopting an attitude of dependence towards the other's transcendence which is assumed to provide an objective ground of value outside the self. Both of these fundamental attitudes are manifestations of bad faith. In a short section on the Us-object, Sartre suggests that an individual can be objectified as a member of a class and that this is the origin of class consciousness. In 'Anti-Semite and Jew', he uses these schemata to explain the concrete situation of the Jews who find themselves hated by the anti-Semite. There he claims that it is the anti-Semite who creates the Jew.

It is illuminating to read de Beauvoir's *The Second Sex* in the light of this schematic representation of concrete relations with others. If we do so we find that her claim that woman is other amounts to the assertion that women find themselves in a concrete situation in which they are objectified by men. Unlike Jews and blacks, however, who are also objectified as a class, women are scattered among the male population, and this makes them particularly prone to adopt versions of the attitudes of love and masochism, to which de Beauvoir adds narcissism and mysticism. These are all forms of what she calls the fall into immanence in which a conscious subject fails to recognize its transcendence and behaves as though it were a mere thing in-itself, dependent for its meaning on some exterior transcendence.

While I have here emphasized the validity of interpreting de Beauvoir's most influential essay as incorporating structures to be found in *Being and Nothingness*, it should also be recognized that there are differences of detail and of emphasis in the way these schema are developed by Sartre and de Beauvoir. The relationship between their philosophies is currently hotly contested, and a consensus is unlikely to emerge until de Beauvoir's early philosophy becomes more widely available, and until feminists overcome their widespread aversion to taking Sartre seriously. Reading de Beauvoir's early essays, it seems fair to say that one feature which characterizes her method, and differentiates it from Sartre's, is her emphasis on ambiguity. Faced with the choice between the moralism of clean hands and the effectiveness of political expediency in 'Idéalism Moral et Réalism Politique' (1945) she asserts the need for an effective morality. Faced with the choice between the concreteness of literature and the universality of metaphysics in 'Littérature et Métaphysique' (1946) she adopts a method of discovering the universal through the concrete situation. Setting up the situation of humanity in *An Ethics of Ambiguity* (1947), she emphasizes the ambiguity of a consciousness that is flesh, neither determined like a mere material object nor absolutely free like a disembodied spirit. Although she does not consciously develop the theme of ambiguity in *The Second Sex*, there is a sense in which it also haunts this text. Describing the fall into immanence, which she claims has been characteristic of woman's reaction to her situation, she says that this represents a moral fault if the subject consents to it, and if it is inflicted on the subject it spells frustration and oppression. Two incompatible themes seem to war throughout the text. On the one hand woman's situation is one of oppression in which freedom is curtailed. On the other hand women freely submit to the temptations of a situation in which they are able to flee the anguish of moral responsibility. They alienate their freedom in narcissism or love or mystical devotion, rather than consciously taking the responsibility for the world on their shoulders. It is perhaps this ambiguity, which de Beauvoir consciously emphasized, which has allowed so many divergent feminist developments of her text. This may seem to be a fault. But her insistence on not oversimplifying for the sake of a metaphysical system was conscious. And in the light of this emphasis on ambiguity we can see that her resistance to calling herself a philosopher was itself a philosophical stance. She relates that she had no confidence that words could really capture the plenitude of things. Here she is quite at odds with more recent feminists who have tended to reject the idea of a reality beyond words which is only partly represented by them. From de Beauvoir's point of view, words already universalize experience, categorizing different concrete totalities in terms of their shared general features. The philosopher who sets out an abstract system arrogantly universalizes a particular point of view. De Beauvoir resisted this, wanting rather to describe a concrete situation so that others could take from it as many generalities as were still relevant. She succeeded mightily in *The Second Sex*, in which many women of her generation and of later generations have recognized their own conflicts and the outlines of a situation that they share, and which allowed women to come to a fuller consciousness of the concrete realities of their situation. But the subtlety of her philosophical position has been overlooked, and her descendants have tended to adopt one or other of the attitudes which she held in ambiguous tension. The materialist feminists and social constructionists are her most conscious descendants, but they discount the little place that there still exists for freedom and agency in her philosophy of ambiguity. Judith Butler takes the opposite stance, making gender, which is identified with the sexed body, into a free act of performativity and under-emphasizing the constraints of situation. Essentialist feminists of difference are furthest from de Beauvoir's explicit pronouncements, but even they show, in their interest in dualities within the history of philosophy, the marks of her analysis. No contemporary French feminist, has been a completely faithful daughter of de Beauvoir, reproducing her mother's text. Most have repudiated what they take to be her errors. And yet, just as with daughters of flesh and blood who assert their difference from their mothers while reproducing so many of their features, none of the debates within feminism would have developed in the way that they have if de Beauvoir had not set the questions that she did, and had not provided us with the conflicting wealth of observations that make up her most influential text.

Karen Green

Further reading and works cited

Bair, D. *Simone de Beauvoir. A Biography*. London, 1990.
Barnes, H. 'Self-Encounter in *She Came to Stay*', in *The Literature of Possibility*. London, 1961.
Bergoffen, D. *The Philosophy of Simone de Beauvoir*. Albany, NY, 1997.
de Beauvoir, S. *Pyrrhus and Cinéas*, Paris, 1944.
—. 'Idéalism Moral et Réalism Politique', *Les Temps Modernes*, 1, 1945.
—. 'Littérature et Métaphysique', *Les Temps Modernes*, 1, 1946.
—. *The Mandarins*. London, 1960.
—. *Ethics of Ambiguity*. New York, 1962.
—. *The Prime of Life*. Harmondsworth, 1965a.
—. *She Came to Stay*. London, 1965b.
—. *Memoirs of a Dutiful Daughter*. New York, 1974.
—. *The Second Sex*. Harmondsworth, 1983a.
—. *When Things of the Spirit Come First: Five Early Tales*. London, 1983b.
—. *America Day by Day*. Berkeley, CA, 1999.
Francis, C. and Gontier, F. *Simone de Beauvoir: A Life A Love Story*. New York, 1987.
Fullbrook, E. and Fullbrook, K. *Simone de Beauvoir and Jean-Paul Sartre*. London, 1993.
—. *Simone de Beauvoir: A Critical Introduction*. Cambridge, 1998.
Irigaray, L. *Speculum of the Other Woman*. Ithaca, NY, 1984.
Le Doeuff, M. 'Simone de Beauvoir and Existentialism', *Feminist Studies*, 6, 1980.
—. *Hipparchia's Choice*. Oxford, 1991.
Lundgren-Gothlin, E. *Sex and Existence*. Hanover, NH, 1996.
Moi, T. *Feminist Theory and Simone de Beauvoir*. Oxford, 1990.
—. *Simone de Beauvoir: The Making of an Intellectual Woman*. Oxford, 1994.
Pilardi, J. *Simone de Beauvoir Writing the Self*. Westport, CT, 1999.
Sartre, J.-P. *Les Mots*. Paris, 1964.
—. *Being and Nothingness*. London, 1995.
Schwarzer, A. *After the Second Sex*. New York, 1984.
Simons, M. (ed.) *Feminist Interpretations of Simone de Beauvoir*. University Park, PA, 1995.
—. *Beauvoir and the Second Sex*. Lanham, MA, 1999.
Vintges, K. *Philosophy as Passion*. Bloomington, IN, 1996.
Wenzel, H. '*Simone de Beauvoir Witness to a Century*', *Yale French Studies*, 72, 1986.
Wittig, M. 'One is Not Born a Woman', in *The Straight Mind and Other Essays*. Boston, 1992.

29. Claude Lévi-Strauss (1908–)

Claude Lévi-Strauss is the inventor of structural anthropology, which derives its name from one of its major sources of inspiration, structural linguistics. His ideas and theories have provided new ways of approaching many fundamental anthropological problems, such as the nature of kinship ties, the significance of totemism, the purpose of classification or the meaning of so-called primitive myths. As a writer and a thinker, however, his influence extends beyond the field of anthropology. His writings have had an impact, in particular, on French philosophy (even if the impact, here, is most evident in the form of a conflict between anthropology and philosophy), psychoanalysis and literary criticism. He was also, albeit unwittingly, at the origin of what became in the Paris of the 1960s, the intellectual fashion of structuralism.

Lévi-Strauss's first major book was *The Elementary Structures of Kinship*. It immediately attracted the attention not only of anthropologists but also the broader intellectual community. Simone de Beauvoir, who at the time was writing *The Second Sex*, and the novelist and philosopher of the erotic Georges Bataille, were among the first to review it.

Lévi-Strauss wrote most of *The Elementary Structures* (1949) in New York during the Second World War. He had travelled there as a Jewish refugee fleeing occupied France. Once in New York, he attended the lectures of the Prague School linguist Roman Jakobson where he discovered for the first time structural linguistics. The event was to be a decisive one for the history of structuralism. It was the assimilation of this body of thought into anthropology that was to enable Lévi-Strauss to assemble the various half-formulated ideas and intuitions that he had had so far – including meditations brought about by the contemplation of wild flowers on the border of Luxembourg in 1940 – into the fundamental tenets of structuralism. One aspect of linguistic theory that was particularly important to Lévi-Strauss was the emphasis that it placed on the unconscious activity of the mind.

Structural linguistics, as developed by Swiss linguist Ferdinand de Saussure, showed that language, as a social institution, is governed by rules that are unconscious. When we speak with one another, when we string together sequences of sounds into meaningful sentences, we are not normally aware of the organizing rules that govern what we are doing. Lévi-Strauss proposed that other kinds of social institutions, such as the institution of marriage, for example, are governed by unconscious rules of a similar kind.

Just as the role of linguistics is to discover and analyse what determines, at an unconscious level, our use of language, the role of anthropology, for Lévi-Strauss, is to uncover, beyond empirically observed reality, the unconscious structures and schemas that are the basis of social institutions. And, for Lévi-Strauss, access to the level of the unconscious is what guarantees the objectivity of the anthropologist's observations, since it enables him or her to bypass the potentially misleading secondary interpretations of those involved in the phenomena being studied.

How does the recourse to the unconscious apply to Lévi-Strauss's kinship theory? Different cultures have very different ideas about what constitutes a family. Lévi-Strauss shows, however, that the many different types of kinship systems observed by anthropologists are reducible to a small number of recurring elementary structures. Influenced by the seminal essay *The Gift* by French sociologist Marcel Mauss, Lévi-Strauss proposed that marital alliances between groups took the classic form of reciprocal gift exchanges, the gifts in this case being women. He hypothesized that the hidden, *unconscious*, function of kinship systems was to regulate the exchange of women between groups and ensure the continuity of these exchanges. Thus, what Lévi-Strauss terms 'elementary structures of kinship' corresponds to the basic patterns of the exchange of women between social groups.

He distinguished two basic forms of exchange, which he labelled 'restricted' and 'generalized' (the latter is also referred to as 'marriage in a circle'). The model of the first type of exchange is that of a straight swap between two groups. In the second type, 'generalized' exchange, the schema involves at least three groups related so that A gives to B, who gives to C, who gives back to A. Exchange in this case is indirect and hence more risky, but also potentially more rewarding since it involves a larger number of groups.

Another aspect of linguistic theory that has had a major impact on Lévi-Strauss's thought is the discovery that the sound system of a language does not consist of an aggregation of isolated sounds (phonemes) but in the relationships between those sounds. Phonemes have no value of their own; they are negative entities that exist in and through their opposition to other sounds: the sound [p] is only [p] because it is not [b]. Lévi-Strauss's kinship theory adapts this basic insight to anthropology. Previously, anthropologists, such as the great British anthropologist Sir Alfred Radcliffe-Brown, had assumed that the unit of structure from which kinship systems are built is the elementary family, consisting of a man and his wife and their child or children. For Lévi-Strauss, on the contrary, what is elementary is not families, which are isolated units, but the relationships between those units, in other words the systems of affinal alliances brought about by the movement of reciprocity.

The social rule that brings about the exchange of women is the incest taboo. Lévi-Strauss relates the incest taboo to rules of exogamy, which are rules that require marriage outside of a particular group or category of individuals. His conception is that the primary function of the incest taboo is to oblige individuals to marry out. The incest taboo forces the kin group to make alliances with strangers and thereby create a community. The emergence of the incest taboo – the first social rule – is therefore associated with the emergence of human society itself.

Here, too, Lévi-Strauss's understanding is inspired by linguistic theory, in particular the theory of the phoneme. As purely differential units, phonemes are the means by which two domains are articulated: sound and meaning. In a similar way, although at another level, the incest taboo may also be seen as the means by which two domains are articulated, in this case the domains of nature and culture. And, in a similar way that linguistic rules ensure the communication and circulation of words, the rules of exogamy ensure the communication and circulation of women. In the Lévi-Straussian paradigm, the exchange of words and the exchange of women are similar kinds of phenomena.

One of the reasons why Lévi-Strauss turned to linguistics for inspiration was that it had reached, in its recent developments, a degree of scientific rigour that did not exist in other social sciences. Lévi-Strauss hoped that, by using the methods of linguistics, anthropology might be able to work towards a similar level of scientificity. It is this project that often defines the way in which structuralism is portrayed. It is true that, according to his own stated aims, Lévi-Strauss turned to linguistic theory to help him lay down the foundations of scientifically rigorous methods of analysis in anthropology. However, to see Lévi-Strauss's works exclusively in these terms is reductionist, and conceals the overdetermined nature of his writings, and the often speculative and hazardous nature of his interpretations.

It would be misleading to see Lévi-Strauss's work simply as an application of the methods of structural linguistics to anthropology. Often, as is the case with the kinship theory that I have outlined above, linguistics is brought to bear on anthropology by way of extended analogies. Metaphorical thinking is fundamental to Lévi-Strauss's works, as one can see in his invention of such notions as 'bricolage' – a term he used to describe the kind of intellectual DIY used by myths to create new narratives out of the fragments and debris of old narratives – or in his choice of a book title such as *La Pensée sauvage* (the title relies on a pun: 'pensées' are 'thoughts', but 'la pensée sauvage' is also a wild flower, the Viola Tricolor, the implication being that his book is concerned with 'wild' as opposed to 'domesticated' thinking).

Lévi-Strauss's work on primitive myths illustrates even more clearly the duality that opposes the scientist to the imaginative thinker. On the one hand, using linguistic theory, Lévi-Strauss develops a complex methodology for the analysis of myths, which enables a quasi mathematical formalization of their hidden structures. He decomposes myths into the 'codes' that they use (a code is something like a concealed extended metaphor), their 'armature' (the structural schema underlying a myth or group of myths) and their 'message' (what the myth means). But these concepts are themselves metaphors of a kind, approximations, which Lévi-Strauss is the first to admit possess a degree of indeterminacy and even vagueness. The term 'armature', for example, is borrowed from musicology. It comes from the French for a key signature, the symbols placed at the beginning of each stave which indicate the tonality or key of a composition. By analogy, an armature, in mythology, is the hidden schema that provides the underlying principle of structural unity of a myth.

That Lévi-Strauss should have borrowed from musicology is not coincidental. One of the fundamental themes of the *Mythologiques* – Lévi-Strauss's tetralogy on Amerindian mythology which was published between 1964 and 1971 – is the close affinity that exists between myth and music. In the 'Overture' (the parts of this book are named after various musical forms) to the first volume, *The Raw and the Cooked*, it is not Saussure or Jakobson whom Lévi-Strauss identifies as the founding father of the structural analysis of myths but Wagner. One reason for this is that the recurrence of certain musical themes in Wagner's operas, such as the theme of the renunciation of love in the *Rhinegold*, link episodes in the story which appear to be unrelated but which Lévi-Strauss sees as constituting structural variations of one another.

What motivated Lévi-Strauss in his interpretations of myths was to uncover an order behind what, at first, may appear arbitrary or even absurd (he saw Freud's interpretations of dreams as a model in this respect). Amerindian myths constitute surreal narratives that, at first, do not seem to make much sense. And, as in dreams, their content is uncensored. The Amazonian Tucuna myth M354, which serves as the starting point and guiding thread of volume 3 of the *Mythologiques*, *The Origin of Table Manners*, tells the story of the hunter Monmanéki's quest for a wife. After several unsuccessful marriages with various animals, including a frog which he impregnates by urinating in the hole in which it was hiding, Monmanéki marries a fellow human being. This is how the myth concludes. In order to fish, Monmanéki's wife, who possessed magical powers, would separate into two at the waist. Leaving the lower half of her body behind, the torso would swim into a river where the smell of flesh would attract many fish which it would then catch. Through various twists in the narrative, the torso eventually becomes affixed to Monmanéki's back. It begins to starve Monmanéki to death by stealing his food, then defecates all over him. Monmanéki finally escapes and his wife transforms into a parrot and flies away. (See below for an interpretation of this myth.)

The basic hypothesis underlying the *Mythologiques* is that myths come into being by a process of transformation of one myth into another. For Lévi-Strauss myths do not have any meaning in themselves but only in relation to each other and therefore have to be studied in the course of their transformation from one into another in order to unlock their meanings. To illustrate Lévi-Strauss's method is always problematic because wherever one starts one is always breaking into a chain, or even several chains, of transformations. Equally, wherever one stops will always fall short of arriving at a final interpretation, since it is in the very nature of myths to always be in the process of becoming other myths, none of which contains the final meaning.

Each myth is submitted to an analysis which reveals its connections to other myths. These are progressively brought into the picture and in turn analysed. Lévi-Strauss follows step by step the paths indicated by the myths themselves and which correspond to the paths of their coming into being, drawing something like a map of the lines of mythical descent.

For example, in *The Raw and the Cooked*, Lévi-Strauss shows that a Bororo myth (the 'reference myth' M1), which tells the story of the origin of rainwater, is in fact an inversion of another myth (M7–12) told by a neighbouring population, the Gé, which tells the story of how humans first obtained fire from a jaguar. M1 is a myth about the origin of fire metamorphosed into a myth about the origin of water.

As the reader follows these transformations she is taken on a journey from the tropical forests of central Brazil to the state of Oregon on the Pacific Coast of North America. In the process, series of affiliated myths are integrated into broader units and gradually the picture of a total system – compared by Lévi-Strauss to a nebula – emerges.

The underlying theme with which the whole of Amerindian mythology is concerned, according to Lévi-Strauss, is that of the creation of human culture as an order separate from nature. The purpose of Amerindian myths is to try to explain this founding division, and the numerous other divisions that come in its wake, such as that between day and night, land and sea, man and woman, all the way down to those affecting daily life, such as the distinction between edible and non-edible plants. Lévi-Strauss shows that different populations express the theme of the passage from nature to culture using different symbolic 'codes'. In the South American corpus, it is symbolized by cooking, the transformation of raw food (nature) into food that is ready for human consumption (culture). This explains the symbolic importance of fire, the means of cooking, which is seen as a mediating term between earth and the sky, nature and culture. In the myths of the North American corpus, the symbols which are used to encode the opposition between nature and culture change. What marks the passage from nature to culture is no longer the mediation of cooking, but the invention of costumes, ornaments and the institution of commercial exchanges. Where South American myths oppose the raw to the cooked,

North American myths oppose the naked to the clothed, each opposition being in a relationship of transformation to the other.

The *Mythologiques* rest on what constitutes, in effect, a theory of intertextuality (although the word did not yet exist at the time that Lévi-Strauss was writing). Each myth is defined and understood in terms of its intertextual relationships to other myths (one can see, here again, the influence of the linguistic idea that phonemes are purely negative entities, defined entirely in terms of their relationship to other phonemes).

And Lévi-Strauss's role, as mythographer, is to decipher the hidden logic that explains the transformation of one element in one myth into another element in another. The character of the female torso in the Tucuna myth that I have already cited is explained in this way (*Mythologiques*, vol. 3, 'The Mystery of the Woman Cut into Pieces'). She is not an original creation but the South American version of a character that occurs in North American mythology, a woman-frog. Lévi-Strauss's explanation is that the character of the woman-frog expresses *metaphorically* the idea of a woman who in French would be described, also metaphorically, as 'collante' (she won't let go). The female torso affixed to her husband's back expresses the same idea, but literally. Seen differently, one might say that whereas the North American myth relies on metaphor (a relationship of resemblance) to convey its message, the South American myth relies on *metonymy* (a relationship of contiguity). Hence, Lévi-Strauss argues that as we pass from one hemisphere to the other, metaphor converts into metonymy. And it is this rhetorical manipulation that brings about the simultaneous transformation of one mythological character into another.

The myths that are linked in a series of transformations are treated as a cognate group. Each myth in the group, however dissimilar it appears to be from other myths in the group, is related to a common armature, a logico-sensible schema that is the matrix of that transformational group. The schema has no concrete existence. It is a system of interrelated categories or concepts underlying each group of myths and whose features are deduced by the mythographer. It is, as Lévi-Strauss puts it, the virtual chess board on which the myths of a given transformational series play out their respective games.

Myths use such schemas as logical tools to resolve various formally similar problems by linking them together and treating them as one. In *The Origin of Table Manners* (1968), for example, Lévi-Strauss analyses the schema of the canoe journey, to which many of the myths, including the above Tucuna myth, are said to be related. Myths that draw on this schema are all fundamentally concerned with the problem of distance: geographical distance, but also the distance between celestial bodies and the distance between human beings.

The occupants of the canoe are the moon and the sun. In astronomical terms, the problem that the schema enables mythical thought to tackle is: at what distance should the moon be from the sun in order to guarantee the regular alternation of night and day? If the moon and sun become too far apart, says Amerindian mythology, there is a danger that a total disjunction between night and day will occur, resulting in either eternal night or eternal day (in mythology, a common state of affairs prior to the institution of human culture). If they are too close, there is an equally dangerous risk of a conjunction of night and day (resulting in such disruptions as eclipses).

The schema of the canoe journey maps these astronomical concerns onto the social problem of marriage, and the need for human beings to invent the right social institutions for them to live at the correct distance from one another – like the moon and the sun, neither too far nor too close. In this way, the schema establishes a formal homology between the opposition, on the one hand, between night and day, disjunction and conjunction, and on the other, between the two kinds of marriages against which society must guard itself in order to continue functioning properly: an excessively 'distant' marriage, such as the ones that Monmanéki contracts with animal species rather than fellow human beings, and excessively 'close' marriages, such as an endogamous or incestuous marriage, the dangers of which are dramatized by the story of the female torso affixed to her husband's back.

Life in the canoe, at the mid-point in its journey, represents a cosmological and social ideal where moon and sun, husband and wife, each at their own end of the boat, are kept at exactly the right distance from one another to guarantee a harmonious life.

Lévi-Strauss's analyses of myths as transformations of other myths provide him with a general theory of aesthetic creation which, elsewhere in his works, he has applied to other kinds of creations. *The Way of the Masks*, a study of the masks made by the North American Salish and Kwakiutl, is a book about how populations comes to acquire their own distinctive aesthetic style. It shows that different types of masks, belonging to neighbouring populations, form part of an overarching system of transformations within which the style of each mask may be interpreted as a negation of the style of another. Each population borrows stylistic features which it then transforms to make its own. In *The View from Afar*, Lévi-Strauss traces the myth-like transformations that, from Chrétien de Troyes's medieval romance to Wagner's opera, have affected the Perceval legend. And in *Regarder Écouter Lire*, he applies the logic of mythical transformations to classical painting. He identifies transformations in three versions of *The Arcadian Shepherds*, two painted by Nicholas Poussin in the 1630s and one earlier version by Guercino. Lévi-Strauss argues that the three paintings correspond to three stages in a sequence of transformations in the course of which Guercino's original composition is gradually assimilated by Poussin to be reborn as Poussin's *Arcadian Shepherds*. Lévi-Strauss traces, in particular, the transformation of the skull which occupies a prominent position in the earliest version of the painting, is reduced in the second, then disappears in the last, to be replaced by a mysterious female figure whom Lévi-Strauss interprets as the embodiment of death.

The *Mythologiques* has concerned the literary critic perhaps more than any other work by Lévi-Strauss. In it, Lévi-Strauss formulates one of the key twentieth-century theories of myth, providing new hypotheses about the nature of mythical discourse, the processes of creation behind it and its place and function in human society. The *Mythologiques* also demonstrate the application, to over a thousand myths, of an original method of analysis, whose value and limits Lévi-Strauss constantly comments upon at the same time as he puts it into practice.

There is, however, another quite different explanation of why the *Mythologiques* are particularly relevant to critical theory. As both Roland Barthes and Jacques Derrida have remarked about this text, one of its distinguishing features lies in the unusual status of Lévi-Srauss's critical discourse. Derrida describes it as 'mythomorphic' because it has 'the shape of that about which it speaks' (1978, 286). Barthes sees it as partaking in the cultural revolution that has seen the transformation of critical discourse into a literary genre (Barthes 1987). It corresponds to Barthes's ideal of the 'writerly' text, which weaves together many discourses and codes and involves the reader in an active role of production rather than a passive role of consumption.

These views reflect Lévi-Strauss's own concept that if all myths are transformations of other myths, his own interpretations of Amerindian mythology are themselves simply another version of it, its latest transformation to date. And, in this respect, the *Mythologiques* may be seen as a form of literary creation in their own right, a postmodern text made up of a collage of fragments.

Lévi-Strauss's conception of his relationship to the myths that he studies involves, at its very heart, the notion of a playful and creative interaction between myth and mythographer. In *Histoire de Lynx*, the second of two additions to the *Mythologiques*, Lévi-Strauss uses a chess metaphor to describe the mythographer's task. Myths are the opponent, and the aim of the analyst is to guess his opponent's strategy – in the present case, the hidden rules of transformation that connect, like so many moves in the mythical game, one myth to another. And, each time that a myth is told or read (retold, reread) a new game is played, each one revealing new networks of structural relations and hence generating new versions of the myth in question.

Boris Wiseman

Further reading and works cited

Barthes, R. *Critcism and Truth*. London, 1987.
Derrida, J. *Writing and Difference*. London, 1978.
Hénaff, M. *Claude Lévi-Strauss and the Making of Structural Anthropology*. Minneapolis, MN, 1998.
Lévi-Strauss, C. *The Savage Mind*. London, 1966.
—. *The Elementary Structures of Kinship*. London, 1968.
—. *Mythologiques*, 4 vols. London, 1970–81.
—. *Tristes tropiques*. Harmondsworth, 1976.
—. *Structural Anthropology*. Harmondsworth, 1977.
—. *The Origin of Table Manners*. New York, 1978a.
—. 'Preface'. R. Jakobson, in *Six Lectures on Sound and Meaning*. Hassocks, 1978b.
—. *Myth and Meaning*. London, 1978c.
—. *The Way of the Masks*. London, 1983.
—. *The View from Afar*. New York, 1985.
—. *Histoire de Lynx*. Paris, 1991a.
—. *De Près et de Loin: Conversations with Claude Lévi-Strauss*. Chicago, 1991b.
—. *Regarder Écouter Lire*. Paris, 1993.
Mauss, M. *The Gift*. London, 1990.
Paz, O. *Claude Lévi-Strauss: An Introduction*. London, 1971.

30. Jean Genet (1910–1986)

Jean Genet is rare among twentieth-century French authors for the speed with which his reputation became established. The author's personal dramas, his 'canonization' by Jean-Paul Sartre and Jean Cocteau, the *succes-de-scandale* which still helps to sell his books, all contributed to an immense celebrity and large numbers of readers, from very early in his career. Genet's works, the most celebrated are his five novels and five dramatic texts, are marked by his simultaneous criticism of, and participation in, radical politics, as well as his obsession with role-playing and identity; as such they anticipate postmodern apprehensions and techniques. The postmodernism in his works is established, as it were, by an avant-garde writing style, a style which often prompts structuralist or deconstructionist modes of reading because of its inherent difficulty and lack of transparency. As Genet himself said of his own works in an essay in *Tel Quel*, his texts resist simple meanings and dramatize the impossibility of pinning down interpretation (Genet 1967).

One of the most important aspects of Genet's writing is the ways in which it requires a rethinking of the boundaries between art and reality, the aesthetic and the political. Thus, far from erasing the irreducible existence of the real (most often blemished by multifaceted evil, the suffering, the isolation and the marginality of the alienated beings whom he obsessively represents in his texts), Genet instead highlights the boundaries that separate fiction from reality. His aestheticism metamorphoses, one might say, the wounds of humanity: the spiritual misery, principally, and its physical abscesses generated by the division of humanity between those who are hand in glove with the reigning order and those who are excluded or who deliberately exclude themselves (Malgron 1988, 34). Genet's writing, beyond the perverse denial of the castration that it constantly betrays, in its taste for misrepresentation, in its games of veils and mirrors, appears, on the one hand, as an attempt at identity recovery or, if one likes, as a defence mechanism (Derrida 1981). His fiction, an epic which tells of internal suffering, corresponds on the other hand to a double postulation: to declare oneself in order to approach the image which hides within us, all the while constantly dissimulating behind a fictional image reflected in a mirror of illusion (Brook and Halpern 1979, 12).

Autobiographical in scope, his novels and plays illuminate the possibilities of survival among men, and sometimes women, bound together by fierce, unrelenting erotic desire that illuminates and transfigures the 'margins' (Foucault 1994, 119–20). As a chronicler of outcasts, lost causes and the underworld, Genet carefully scrutinizes homosexual, black or Palestinian reality. Though his novels are intricate explorations of the questions of identity, primarily of Genet and the men he loves, his plays are, on the other hand, ritualized means for staging and demolishing identity. Throughout his work, he combines crimes and innocence, obscenities and tenderness, blasphemies and mysticism, and seeks to exhaust his creative desire in an excess of scandalous images and of identity quests which incessantly speak to us of imprisoned and suffering beings (Genet 1991, 41).

Genet's narrative works took six years to write, at the frenetic pace of a novel per year. From 1944 to 1949 they succeeded one another very quickly, *Notre-Dame-des-Fleurs* (1944) (*Our Lady of the Flowers*, 1963), *Miracle de la rose* (1946) (*Miracle of the Rose*, 1965), *Pompes funèbres* (1948) (*Funeral Rites*, 1970), *Querelle de Brest* (1944) (*Querelle*, 1974) and *Journal du voleur* (1949) (*The Thief's Journal*, 1965). In these five texts, which all integrate, more or less directly, autobiographical elements, Genet varied the models successively, using three different versions of the novel form: the autobiographical novel, the novel written in the third person and the journal.

The first quasi-autobiographical novel, *Notre-Dame-des-Fleurs*, was written in jail over an extended time as his manuscripts were constantly confiscated by prison officials. The very circumstances of the story highlight in fact Genet's sexual identity. The story is narrated by a masturbating prisoner, Louis Culafroy, alias Divine, who tells us that the characters he/she describes are products of his/her erotic fantasies conceived under the hot wool blanket of his/her bed. At once man and woman, as a transvestite provided with a double designation, this narrator, cast under the sign of a hybrid nature, excessive and beyond limiting definition (Dollimore 1991, 314), has no intention of settling for only one identity, sexual or otherwise. The story is filled with sexually explicit descriptions of male prostitution, through which Divine transforms him/herself into an uncanny being, neither male nor female, whose dynamics lie in the double negation of sexualized identity that has no stable sex/gender. All the characters created in this work are masturbatory fantasies, characters chosen for that evening's delight. Genet thus defined throughout this first novel the psychological nature of fantasy; the characters themselves often 'dream' their sexual encounters with each other (Genet 1979, 33).

Genet's second novel, *Miracle de la rose*, amounts to a hymn to Harcamone, a French criminal of the 1930s whom Genet would have met at Fontevrault Prison. The author describes his fascination for this murderer, while recalling the years he spent in Mettray prison. This complex, often mystical novel is structured around the development of the author's gay passions. In fact, as Edmund White has suggested, the book's scrutiny of prison life is plotted as the development of a mounting gay passion and the exploration of alternative gay identities in which Genet moves from passive relations with prisoners to assuming butch roles (1993, 75). It explores the tendency of lovers to leave men for more 'masculine' prisoners as well as the nuances of sexual relations between older men and young boys. What stands out above all is the miraculous world in which the action takes place, since Harcamone transforms, in his writing, the hard cold prison in which he lives into a world of gentleness and flowers. The work is presented as a long series of love scenes in which mutual affection between men is revealed, in its own time, as a series of transformations and connections.

In contrast to the two preceding novels, where his protagonists are only mental constructs – even if Harcamone was born of a real individual – in his third autobiographical novel entitled *Pompes funèbres*, Genet presents someone whose existence he has shared. Dedicated to Jean Decarnin, a twenty-year-old communist militant killed on the barricades at the time of the Paris liberation, this work is a direct response to real-life events. The author started it less than a month after the death of his lover, at the height of grief. The book proceeds through a series of impersonations; for instance, Genet and Decarnin become a young German (Erik) and his lover, the burly public executioner of Berlin. Hatred becomes love: the dead inhabit the bodies of the living, as when a survivor eats the dead body of his enemy, believing that by his act of cannibalism, he might simultaneously ingest the virtues of the defeated dead man (cannibals are said to steal the virtues of the defeated through eating their noble organs) (Moraly 1988, 54). The novel can be understood as 'incantatory' (or as literary critics say, performative) in two senses: as a ritual to resuscitate Decarnin (Derrida 1981, 92), and as an exorcism through the profanation of Genet's grief and mourning (Malgron 1988, 71–2).

Genet's fourth novel, *Querelle de Brest*, is narrated in the third person as an episode in the life of a sailor, Georges Querelle, a man without faith or morality, who kills in all his ports of call, and manages neither to be pursued nor even suspected. Through the behaviour and choices of this hero, Genet shows us that the prejudice that makes gays 'unnatural' beings responds to the need that most homophobic individuals have to deny their own homosexual urges. Thus, instead of protesting against this absurd prejudice, Genet accentuates the absurdity of it in his novel, while at the same time representing Querelle's sexual delights as the pleasures of an intellectual nature. This aspect of the novel has made many critics regard *Querelle de Brest* as Genet's strongest book. Its dual themes are repressed homosexual desire and violence (Moraly 1988, 86). Sexual attraction to men is rigidly, bitterly denied, while emerging as a form of hero-worship, a substitute for denied heterosexual desire, or as an expiation for guilt. Because this work is Genet's only non-autobiographical novel, he is paradoxically able to be more personal, if less intimate, than he usually is (White 1993, 290).

Finally, *Journal du voleur*, one of Genet's most accessible novels (Simont 1989, 117), deals with the problem of sanctity and the inversion of values. While explicitly referring to Jean Genet's 'career as a thief', this book is filled with portrayals of his lovers and their strengths and foibles. In his depiction of the criminal underworld and the survival tactics it demands of its inhabitants, the author explores the possibilities of 'camp' and outlines the parameters of a criminal subculture that is openly gay. This personal journal has often been perceived by the critics as a loving recreation of criminal style and language, specifically a representation of the charms of the men Genet loves. For some, however, Genet's glorification of homosexuality-as-revolt leads him to equate it with crime in a manner that the bourgeois world he vilifies understands all too readily (Malgron 1988). A difficulty that his book presents to contemporary readers, say others, is one that besets many of his early novels. He is unwilling to consider specific differences between sexuality and crime, instead focusing obsessively on the links between them (Davis 1994). Despite his minute exploration of a milieu excluded from the social order, Genet neglects to define his sexuality in terms other than those provided by the dominant class: as monstrous, criminal and deviant (Bergen 1993).

Through the constant mix of realism, autobiographical elements, fiction and the stylization which permeates all his narrative works, Genet gives the appearance of having written social novels with postmodern tendencies. Notable instances of realism that are entwined with postmodernity include: the diverse shady settings of *Querelle de Brest* (the realistically portrayed lives of the sailors who stop over in Brest, their communal life in the shipyard, La Feria, the brothel where all the men meet, which function as both real and as symbolic settings); the treatment of war crimes in *Pompes funèbres*, representations which fuse horror and pleasure; and *Notre-Dame-des-Fleurs* with its realistic and yet symbolically colourful setting of the 'little queers of the Pigalle' in Paris between the two world wars. As for the descriptions of the prison world in *Miracle de la rose* and *Journal du voleur*, they are so minutely detailed that Michel Foucault asked Genet to co-author a chapter about Mettray prison for his work on punishment and prisons, *Surveiller et punir* (*Discipline and Punish*) (1975).

Having completed his fifth novel, Genet felt that he had had enough of writing. He had already embarked on a new adventure of addressing theatregoers. 'It was essential', he said, 'to change mindsets and to know that I was writing for an audience that is visible and numerous each time, whereas the reader of novels, especially of mine, is invisible and sometimes hidden' (Malgron 1988, 165). The shift to the stage served as a *processus dénegatif* for the author. Genet gives his characters a voice and no longer speaks in his own name, which gives the impression that he is no longer referring to himself. In the shift to drama Genet does not seek the acceptance of polite society but rather recognition from a growing theatrical audience (Aslan 1973, 28).

His first two plays, *Haute Surveillance* (1949) (*Deathwatch*, 1954), and *Les Bonnes* (1954) (*The Maids*, 1954), which were steeped in tragedy and revealed the sombre spectacle of funerary ritual, together constitute a sort of 'chamber play' or *théâtre intime* – in the sense intended by Strindberg – a theatre in which the action, cut off from the outside world, is centred exclusively on the hero as well as on the quest for an image that leads him inevitably to his death. In these two plays, Genet brought to the stage the socially marginalized figures he had also portrayed in his novels: domestic employees, gangsters, prisoners, as well as prison guards and police officers. The theatre thus extends, at the beginning of Genet's dramatic career, the novelistic universe of the author, where the world of the incarcerated continues to exert a strong influence on him. In *Haute Surveillance*, for example, three ordinary prisoners rot in jail. One of them, Yeux-Verts, is condemned to death. The other two (Maurice and Lefranc) vie for his attention, as though the enormity of his crime and the imminence of his death make him a sacred figure. In this gloomy cage, from which none can escape, Lefranc murders Maurice in the hope of impressing Yeux-Verts and to win his attention away from Maurice. However, Lefranc realizes that he is the victim of Yeux-Verts's betrayal – Yeux-Verts turns him in to the guard. This highly symbolic climax emphasizes here Genet's preoccupation with evil, betrayal and martyrdom.

Similarly, but now within a 'rituel à deux', the play *Les Bonnes* highlights another funerary ritual, which can be summarized as follows. In the opening scene, one of the maids, Claire, impersonates the mistress of the house, Madame, and the other maid, Solange, in turn plays her sister, Claire. In the exchanges between the two sisters, the audience discovers that they have anonymously denounced Madame's lover, Monsieur, as a criminal. The maids in their madness waver between wanting to murder Madame, the real person, and wanting to murder Madame-impersonated-by-Claire. A phone call reveals that Monsieur has just been released from jail. When Madame arrives, Claire prepares a poisoned cup of herbal tea for her. However, Madame discovers Monsieur is free and that he awaits her. She neglects her tea and gaily rushes off into the night. The maids, knowing that the anonymous letter of denunciation will be soon traced to them, begin to plan their own deaths. Claire dresses as Madame and drinks the tea, so that her sister Solange will know a kind of infamy and be denounced as a murderer.

In *Les Bonnes* Genet explores the two sisters' quest for an image and questions the social roles they are assigned as a result of their class status. In his next play, *Le Balcon* (1956) (*The Balcony*, 1958), the scene expands and offers a critique of a whole society; his themes finally open out into the world at large in *Les Nègres* (1958) (*The Blacks: A Clown Show*, 1960) and *Les Paravents* (1961) (*The Screens*, 1962), texts in which racial antagonisms are brought to the fore. Through them, the dramatist reflects on, among other things, the way in which the power at the heart of a social group manipulates the image of the group (which the group projects or wishes to project) to achieve its aim, the absolute quest being, according to the playwright (Genet 1991, 102), the most pernicious form of alienation there is. In *Le Balcon*, perhaps the best known of Genet's dramatic works, the action is set in a brothel, or 'house of illusions', in an undisclosed country. Madame Irma's house is a place where plumbers, bank clerks and chiefs of police come to act out their sexual fantasies as judges, bishops, generals and so on. The illusions must be erotic, complete and undisturbed. When the illusion is broken, when one of the prostitutes breaks his or her role as a criminal or a penitent, the illusion is destroyed. However, while the revolution rages in the city, the clients of the 'Grand Balcony' play out their perverse scenarios. Although they are hidden behind closed doors in the brothel, they feel threatened. Their world and their identities – illusory or real – are on the verge of collapsing. Moreover, power will manipulate, in a clandestine manner, their perverse fantasies and exploit their fear in order to turn them into agents of a well-orchestrated repression.

Whereas the quest for an image is here directly linked to the question of exclusion, it is presented in *Les Nègres* and *Les Paravents* in terms of racial identity and takes a definite political turn. Certain socio-political facts – such as the French colonization in Africa, racism and apartheid – are openly called into question. Written as a vehicle for an all-black cast, Les Nègres consists of three complex intrigues all centring on the murder of a white woman, whose coffin remains in the centre of the stage as a symbol of the Blacks' reaction to white domination. The first intrigue recreates, through a ritual, the rape and murder of the woman. The second is far more obscure. In the course of this intrigue, a series of actions which occur off-stage are revealed to the audience by the character St Nazaire. The third intrigue introduces two characters (Village, the murderer, and a prostitute called Virtue) who, in a discussion, allude to the 'New World' dominated by the Blacks. Perched on a balcony are three 'white' members of the court (a queen, a judge and a governor), while beneath them, black actors theatrically recreate the crime to be judged by the dignitaries. The main action of the play – this reconstruction of the crime before the court – takes the form of a *mise en abyme* or a play within a play, thereby accentuating the process of division that occurs between the dominant (white) and the dominated (black). In addition to this, the play, which centres on a mock trial on-stage while a real trial takes place off-stage, is imbued with an intense sexuality as well as an easy-going transvestism (Blacks play Whites, men play women). Not only are men played against women and Blacks against Whites, but the dead are also constantly contrasted to the living.

Finally, *Les Paravents* – Genet's response to the Algerian war (1954–62) – is literally a work of epic proportions containing nearly a hundred characters. This play details both the war and the relationship between an Arab mother and son – one of the most sophisticated characterizations of a woman in all of Genet's works – in this simple story. Saïd Nettle, a poor worker in an unnamed colony, has a wife, Leila. They both live with his mother and three other members of the Nettle family. Saïd does not get along with his fellow workers on Sir Harold's estate; they ridicule him because his wife is ugly, which leads to fistfights which he always loses. One day, the villagers mock Saïd's mother because her son is an outcast. Then slowly things erode in a sort of moral entropy. The Europeans lose their power and take refuge in self-intoxicating rhetoric. Saïd's mother, almost unintentionally, strangles a French soldier. More and more of the characters die. At the end of the play a trial scene takes place. As with the finale of *Les Nègres*, Genet reminds us that the real danger is that the revolutionaries will all too successfully emulate their ex-masters, that instead of inventing or rediscovering their own culture and values they will simply retain the European system but fill in the blanks with new Arab – or Black – names.

Some critics (Laroche 1997; Malgron 1988; Read and Birchall 1997; Webb 1982) have reckoned that through these plays Genet, oriented towards international politics, applauds the collapse of the colonial system. For example, when he was writing *Les Nègres*, France, with the 1954 defeat of Dien Bien Phu still in mind, finally recognized the independence of Laos, Cambodia and Vietnam. Furthermore, while Nasser organized the Arab League and as the Algerian war got under way, Genet wrote *Les Paravents*, a text which he reworked for years. His theatrical works, following the example of his narrative texts, therefore draw on reality without, however, adopting the principle extolling the virtues of realism. Thus the author only grasps the illusion – fictional and theatrical – to celebrate its deconstruction, or destruction in a flamboyant carnival, celebration and sacrifice of the artificial where the values advocated by the dominant system (linked, amongst other things, to 'norms', to justice and to religion) seem to be subjected to the monotonous wish for power by alienated individuals who, in the work of Genet, wander between life and death (Goldmann 1970, 299).

This Genetian universe, composed of the fringe elements of society, crooks and criminals, in addition to disconcerting many, caused much grinding of pens by commen-tators, such as Georges Bataille (1957), who wished to solve the 'case of Genet' by denouncing as inadmissible the literary use of Evil and crime made by the author throughout his work. Bataille develops a curious denunciation, which he pursues by taking up the principal elements of the Sartrean argument in *Saint Genet, comédien et martyr* (1952). Keeping in mind that, according to Sartre, the works of Jean Genet consist essentially in depicting Evil up to the point of its own destruction, to the point of annihilating Good, if necessary, the author thereby transforms the outcasts of 'polite society' into a chosen people (Sartre 1952, 55); this task, according to the philosopher, consists in denying the normative universe and its values and in placing this negation as the object in the Genetian hero's quest (1952, 117). However, for Bataille, Genet's will, as with the content of his texts, refers, on the contrary, to a generalized negation of the 'forbidden', to a search for Evil pursued without limitation, until the moment when, all barriers broken, man – represented by the author in his fiction – goes into total decline. Judging that he is constantly infringing on the taboos during their transgression, and that he takes refuge in betrayal and in the negation of his readers' expectations (l'horizon d'attente) – ruining any chance of effective 'communication' (1957, 240) with them – the author of *La Littérature et le mal* concludes that Genet can be the 'sovereign' only in Evil and that Evil is never more evil than when it is punished (Bataille 1957, 207). This point of view is refuted, in the early 1980s, by Jacques Derrida in a work entitled *Glas*, in which the critic pursues his research project on the difference of meaning, annular movement, auto-annulation, through which meaning continually differs and is ultimately deferred.

In *Glas*, Derrida shows that the difference between sexes is transformed into opposition by a dialectical movement (1981, 157), which is what a number of critics in *gay and lesbian studies* have been attempting to illustrate over the last few years. *Glas* constitutes a reflection on sexual difference – notably in Genet's work – and at the same time shows how Jean Genet's fiction offers its readers a long series of living antitheses that toll the bell for the Hegelian dialectic, as with the most scathing of Bataille's commentaries. Derrida also reassesses many of the statements in *Saint Genet, comédien et martyr*. For example, while Sartre asserts that Genet's work reverses the hierarchy of traditional oppositions which structure western thought, and says that the world the author invents represents the opposite of 'reality' inasmuch as it is Evil – rather than Good – that constitutes the privileged term (1952, 119), Derrida tends to prove that the imaginary world of Genet is 'different' from the real world without simply being its opposite, thereby maintaining a relationship of displacement with it and not of negation (1981, 92).

Other works by Jean Genet include numerous poems (*Treasures of the Night: Collected Poems of Jean Genet*, 1981), another novel (*Un captif amoureux* (1986), *Prisoner of Love*, 1992), a treatise on ballet (*Madame Miroir*, 1949) and three more plays (*Elle*, 1989; *Splendid's*, 1993; *Le Bagne*, 1994), works that have only begun to be explored.

Alain-Michel Rocheleau

Further reading and works cited

Aslan, O. *Jean Genet*. Paris, 1973.
Barthes, R. *Essais critiques*. Paris, 1964.
Bataille, G. *La Littérature et le mal*. Paris, 1957.
Bergen, V. *Jean Genet: entre mythe et réalité*. Brussels, 1993.

Brook, P. and Halpern, J. (eds) *Genet: A Collection of Critical Essays*. Englewood Cliffs, NJ, 1979.

Cixous, H. *Three Steps on the Ladder of Writing*. New York, 1993.

Davis, C. 'Genet's *Journal du voleur* and the Ethics of Reading', *French Studies*, 48, 1994.

de Man, P. *Allegories of Reading*. New Haven, CT, 1979.

Derrida, J. *Glas*. Paris, 1981.

Dollimore, J. *Sexual Dissidence*. Oxford, 1991.

Foucault, M. *Surveiller et punir*. Paris, 1975.

—. *Dits et écrits. 1954–1988*. Paris, 1994.

Genet, J. 'L'Étrange mot d' …' *Tel quel*, 30, 1967.

—. 'Le Secret de Rembrandt', in *Oeuvres complètes*. Paris, 1979.

—. *L'Ennemi déclaré: textes et entretiens*. Paris, 1991.

Goldmann, L. 'Le Théâtre de Genet. Essai d'étude sociologique', in *Structures mentales et création culturelle*. Paris, 1970.

Laroche, H. *Le Dernier Genet*. Paris, 1997.

Mahuzier, B. et al. (eds) 'Same Sex/Different Text. Gay and Lesbian Writing in French', *Yale French Studies*, 90, 1996.

Malgron, A. *Jean Genet*. Lyon, 1988.

Moraly, J.-B. *Jean Genet. La vie écrite. Biographie*. Paris, 1988.

Naish, C. *A Genetic Approach to Structures in the Work of Jean Genet*. Cambridge, 1978.

Oswald, L. *Jean Genet and the Semiotics of Performance*. Indianapolis, IN, 1989.

Read, B. and Birchall, I. *Jean Genet: Ten Years After*. Haomondsworth, 1997.

Sartre, J.-P. *Saint Genet, comédien et martyr*. Paris, 1952.

Simont, J. 'Bel effet d'où jaillissent les roses … (à propos du *Saint Genet* de Sartre et du *Glas* de Derrida)', *Les Temps modernes*, 510, 1989.

Todd, J. M. 'Autobiography and the Case of the Signature: Reading Derrida's *Glas*', *Comparative Literature*, 38, 1986.

Webb, R. C. *Jean Genet and his Critics: An Annotated Bibliography*. London, 1982.

White, E. *Genet. A Biography*. New York, 1993.

31. Paul Ricoeur (1913–2005)

An encyclopaedia of criticism and theory would not be complete without an entry for Paul Ricoeur. However, Ricoeur does not fit easily into the category of 'theory'. His position as a 'poststructuralist' is in doubt and his few forays into literature seem to gesture toward the sort of textual exegesis which theory has largely displaced. Ricoeur is a classically trained phenomenologist, in the tradition of Husserl and Heidegger, who happens to work at the interface of philosophy and literature. Undoubtedly, his work is part of a wider postwar, cultural shift towards an aesthetic, rather than scientific, paradigm for human knowledge, but he would have little time for many of the more rococo claims of literary theory. However, as a professional philosopher working in the French academy he is perhaps closer to Jacques Derrida (they taught a phenomenology seminar together at the Sorbonne) than any other thinker. Their proximity and difference is revealed in a brief exchange between the two. In *The Rule of Metaphor* Ricoeur criticizes Derrida's essay 'White Mythologies' (Derrida 1982). Derrida replies to this in his essay 'The *Retrait* of Metaphor', suggesting that 'it is because I sometimes subscribe to some of Ricoeur's propositions that I am tempted to protest when I see him turn them back against me as if they were not already evident in what I have written' (1978, 12). In other words, Ricoeur's published objection to Derrida is in fact a point of agreement. However, Ricoeur remains an 'un-deconstructed' Heideggerian and as such his philosophy is of interest to critical theory because it is predicated on the double axis of time and language.

Mario J. Valdés describes Ricoeur and Derrida as the 'the two philosophers whose work has given poststructuralism its two faces of hermeneutics and deconstruction' (Valdés 1991, 22). Derrida and Ricoeur share a Heideggerian view of human activity, which rules out the possibility of an errorless reliable origin. The related positions of Ricoeur and Derrida mean that their work shares a number of philosophical and cultural influences. First, they rely on an understanding of the critical 'hermeneutics of suspicion' advanced by Hegelian Marxism, Nietzsche and Freud. Secondly, both Ricoeur and Derrida's thought is informed by the structural linguistics of Saussure, Jakobson and Lévi-Strauss. However, their work is most importantly characterized by its attention to the phenomenological and existentialist theories developed by Husserl, Heidegger, Marcel, Jaspers, Sartre and Merleau-Ponty. Ricoeur and Derrida separate on the question of a shared intentionality in meaning. Valdés calls Ricoeur a poststructuralist – despite this difference to Derrida in their understanding of meaning – because Ricoeur's work 'has developed over the last two decades and not only has taken structuralism and semiotics into full consideration and responded to them but, most significantly, has built on this debate' (Valdés 1991, 39). Valdés's comments are instructive in two ways. First, he makes clear Ricoeur's debt to structuralism in *Time and Narrative* and so positions his work within the field of narrative theory. Second, it identifies *Time and Narrative* as a site of struggle in the inheritance and development of the phenomenological tradition, particularly in relation to Derrida's project of the deconstruction of philosophy. Ricoeur's hermeneutics and Derrida's deconstruction are not in fact radical opposites but rather possible alternative directions within continental phenomenology, which inform and complement one another. Derrida's philosophical inquiry follows Ricoeur's exemplary studies in the larger economy of European phenomenology, both Derrida and Ricoeur are involved in the same reassessment of the phenomenological heritage since Kant and Hegel. Their work is part of a history of ideas which exceeds the narrow limits of the historical periodization of, what the Anglo-Saxon academy calls, poststructuralism. Ricoeur has identified this project as 'the work of mourning' (Ricoeur 1988, 206) for Hegelian thought, while Derrida's own consideration of the phenomenological tradition constitutes a major preoccupation in his writing.

Ricoeur's early work, such as *History and Truth* and *Political and Social Essays*, encourages a rapprochement between Christian theology (of a distinctly Protestant kind) and socialism (of a decidedly Hegelian variety). These texts are an engagement with the ethical, political and social concerns of their historical moment. They are also spirited defences of humanism, which may account for the relative lack of attention paid to early Ricoeur by critical theory. Even within his mature philosophy Ricoeur will always privilege Being over, say, language or narrative. He suggests an ontological sequence starting from our experience of being in the world and in time – preceding and preunderstood outside of language – and proceeding from this condition towards linguistic expression. Ricoeur's work has tended to find favour with those who have sought an alternative to the displacements proposed by postmodernism. His three volumes, *Freud and Philosophy*,

Interpretation Theory and *Hermeneutics and the Human Sciences*, have been key texts for hermeneutics – sometimes thought of as a conservative reflex within critical theory which wishes to adopt the insights of poststructuralist textual analysis while retaining an idea of stability between text and reader. In *Freud and Philosophy* Ricoeur places Freud in a philosophical tradition of interpretation, providing a well-founded if less energetic counterpoint to psychoanalytic criticism. Similarly, in *The Rule of Metaphor* Ricoeur's analysis of figurative language follows a philosophical genealogy and might be said to be more rigorous if less dazzling than Paul de Man's *Allegories of Reading*, written at the same time. Perhaps Ricoeur's most significant contribution to critical theory is the three volumes of *Time and Narrative*, which provide a sustained meditation on the philosophical tradition, history, literature, aporia and temporality. The rest of this entry will discuss the architecture of *Time and Narrative* as a way of outlining some of Ricoeur's key concerns.

Paul Ricoeur outlines the project of *Time and Narrative* in his interview with Richard Kearney:

> My chief concern in this analysis is to discover how the act of *raconter*, of telling a story, can transmute *natural* time into a specifically *human* time, irreducible to mathematical, chron-ological 'clock time'. How is narrativity, as the construction or deconstruction of paradigms of story-telling, a perpetual search for new ways of expressing time, a production or creation of meaning? That is my question. (1984, 17)

For Ricoeur narrativity is the means by which time can be transformed from a universal constant into an activity of human production. In other words, narrativity is the operation that relates temporality to the production of meaning. However, as the title *Time and Narrative* suggests Ricoeur is well aware of the aporetic relationship that exists between these two concepts. This aporetic relation, in which the conditions of possibility of one figure depend upon the impossible conditions of the other, is outlined by Ricoeur at the opening of Volume 1:

> One presupposition commands all the others, namely, that what is ultimately at stake in the case of the structural identity of the narrative function as well as in that of the truth claim of every narrative work, is the temporal character of human experience. The world unfolded by every narrative work is always a temporal world. Or, as will often be repeated in the course of this study: time becomes human time to the extent that it is organised after the manner of a narrative; narrative, in turn, is meaningful to the extent that it portrays the features of temporal experience. (1984, 3)

The interdependence of time and narrative is complete. Time becomes an activity of human production because it is structured in the form of a narrative, while narrative produces meaning because it represents the structures of time. By 'human time' Ricoeur means, as he tells Kearney:

> The formulation of two opposing forms of time: public time and private time. Private time is mortal time, for, as Heidegger says, to exist is to be a being-towards-death [*Sein-zum-Tode*], a being whose future is closed off by death. As soon as we understand our existence as this mortal time, we are already involved in a form of private narrativity or history; as soon as the individual comes up against the finite limits of its own existence, it is obliged to recollect itself and to make time its *own*. On the other hand, there exists public time. Now I do not mean public in the sense of physical or natural (clock time), but the time of language itself, which continues on after the individual's death. To live in human time is to live between the private time of our mortality and the public time of language. (1984, 20)

This is another aporia that Ricoeur relies upon in his mediation between time and narrative. The 'human time' which narrative both constructs and depends upon is the aporetic consequence of the relation between 'private' time (the mortality of the body) and 'public' time (the temporal experience of the social use of language). This 'public' time is a necessity of the mortality of the body and this 'private' time is made meaningful through the communal use of language. The key issue which Ricoeur's work on narrativity and temporality touches upon in this instance is the relation between language and death (see Vol. 2, 27 and Vol. 3, 270).

Ricoeur's assertion that 'one presupposition commands all the others, namely, that what is ultimately at stake in the case of the structural identity of the narrative function as well as in that of the truth claim of every narrative work, is the temporal character of human experience' may suggest that he is working within the classic phenomenological assumption that narrative is an intentionality of subjective consciousness, rather than the view of narrative suggested by (post)structuralism, that it is a discursive structure which predetermines the subjective operations of consciousness. However, as he explains to Kearney, this is not the case:

> It is both at once. The invaluable contribution made by structuralism was to offer an exact scientific description of the codes and paradigms of language. But I do not believe that this excludes the creative expression of consciousness. The creation of meaning in language comes from the specifically human production of new ways of expressing the objective paradigms and codes made available by language. (1984, 19)

Here Ricoeur is suggesting that another aporetic relation exists within the construction of narrative. Narrative simultaneously represents the structures that determine the possibility of communal linguistic action and is itself constituted by this linguistic action. That is to say, narrative is both constituted by, and constitutive of, the intersubjective process. Ricoeur tells Kearney, 'I would say, borrowing Wittgenstein's term, that the "language game" of narration ultimately reveals that the meaning of human existence is itself narrative' (1984, 17). In this way Ricoeur provides a powerful theory of narrative related to both poststructuralist representations of the subject and a reassessment of the phenomenological tradition.

Having identified the processes of narrativity as aporetic in nature, Ricoeur uses the strategy of aporia to guide his study. He identifies another aporetic figure in the relation between 'fiction' and 'history.' In Volume 3 of the study Ricoeur overlays the two chapters of Section 1, 'The Aporetics of Temporality', and the first two chapters of Section 2, 'Poetics of Narrative: History, Fiction, Time', in order to identify this relation:

> The task of the following five chapters will be to reduce the gap between the respective ontological intentions of history and fiction in order to make sense of what, in Volume 1, I was still calling the interweaving reference of history and fiction, an operation that I take to be a major stake, although not the only one, in the refiguration of time by narrative. (1988, 6)

The avowed aim of this investigation (to demonstrate the shared narrative characteristics of history and literary fiction) comes from Ricoeur's proposal that history and fiction are dependent upon each other in much the same way as time and narrative are interrelated. The structure of literary fiction defines the nature of 'human' time which history describes, while the representation of 'human' time in history provides the material from which literary fictions are constructed. Ricoeur writes in conclusion to Volume 2:

Only after a theory of reading has been proposed in one of the concluding chapters of Volume 3 will fictional narrative be able to assert its claims to truth, at the cost of a radical reformulation of the problem of truth. This will involve the capacity of the work of art to indicate and to transform human action. In the same way, only once the theory of reading has been presented will the contribution of the fictional narrative to the refiguration of time enter into opposition to and into composition with the capacity of historical narrative to speak of the actual past. If my thesis about the highly controversial problem of reference in the order of fiction possesses any originality, it is to the extent that it does not separate the claim to truth asserted by fictional narrative from that made by historical narrative but attempts to understand each in relation to the other. (1985, 160)

For Ricoeur, history and fiction form an aporetic figure in which the nature of the two halves of that figure can only be understood by a determination of their interrelation and the influence one half, continually, simultaneously and irreducibly, plays upon the other:

From these intimate exchanges between the historicization of fictional narrative and the fictionalization of the historical narrative is born what we call human time, which is nothing other than narrated time ... these two interweaving movements mutually belong to each other. (1985, 102)

In order to investigate this mutually dependent figuration between history and literary fiction it is necessary for Ricoeur to adopt a strategy of paradox and to follow the impossible logic of both sides of the figure simultaneously. This is his concern in the first five chapters of Volume 3:

To put this question in more familiar terms, how are we to interpret history's claim, when it constructs a narrative, to reconstruct something from the past? What authorises us to think of this construction as a reconstruction? It is by joining this question with that of the 'unreality' of fictive entities that we hope to make progress simultaneously in the two problems of 'reality' and 'unreality' in narration. (1988, 5)

Only by addressing both halves of the mutually dependent figure simultaneously can progress be made in connection with the problem. In other words, the aporia must be thought through as a whole rather than as the sum of discrete parts. The relation between the two halves of the figure is not merely a question of analytic method but is, says Ricoeur, a question of ontology:

By the interweaving of history and fiction I mean the fundamental structure, ontological as well as epistemological, by virtue of which history and fiction each concretise their respective intentionalities only by borrowing from the intentionality of the other.... I am now going to show [in the introduction to Volume 3, Chapter 8, 'The Interweaving of History and Fiction'] that this concretization is obtained only insofar as, on the one hand, history in some way makes use of fiction to refigure time and, on the other hand, fiction makes use of history for the same ends. (1988, 181)

This aporetic relation between history and fiction is important to Ricoeur because it 'refigures' time to produce what he terms 'human time'.

Ricoeur resists effacing the difference between historical and fictional narratives. Simultaneously, Ricoeur insists that, 'the ultimately narrative character of history ... is in no way to be confused with a defence of narrative history' (1988, 154). What is at stake in this study, and in his suggestion that the production of temporality in a narrative form makes any human experience or understanding of history narrative in nature, is the epistemological status of the question of 'truth' and its relation to narrative. This ultimately suggests that all human understanding is narrative in character. In terms of the question of truth, Ricoeur offers a patient argument that depends upon the aporetic necessity of the interrelation of historical and fictional discourse and their irreducibility. Ricoeur does not imagine historical 'truth' to be a matter of accession to events through the undecideability of textual representation (as a certain poststructuralist materialism might). Rather, he sees it as the determination of events that are themselves cast in the form of a narrative, as a consequence of their relation to temporality. Any poststructuralist discussion of the determination of history necessarily involves an investigation of the question of 'truth'. Ricoeur's hermeneutic Heideggereanism is no different. The difficulty involved in Ricoeur's position is not necessarily the acceptance of this description of the effects of narrativity, but rather the problem of squaring this description with Ricoeur's discussion of meaning and language.

For Ricoeur, the question of 'truth' is not merely a matter of the identification of a disjuncture between real events and their culturally and ideologically specific narrative, or linguistic, representation. Rather, having identified 'truth' as an issue within narrative theory (as it relates to a reassessment, which is also a continuation, of the phenomenological tradition) the value of Ricoeur's work is his determination to realign what Gibson calls 'the narratological imaginary' (Gibson 1996, 3). Ricoeur is not concerned with an absolute imposition of an objective truth. Instead he moves the discussion of 'truth' and its relation to narrative away from a simplistic equation between so-called realist narrative, ideological conservatism and an objective truth, as opposed to a modernist or postmodernist narrative, radical subversion and relativism. He identifies the process of narrativity as offering a 'poetic' strategy (and therefore a productive but ultimately ambiguous one) for the discussion of the aporetic conditions of 'truth' claims. The determination of 'truth' is not an opposition between event and representation but an identification of the aporetic relation between event and narrative production of the event, involved in the possibility of human understanding.

For example, Ricoeur considers the aporetic nature of temporal experience (the opening chapter of Volume 1 would be a case in point). Part of Ricoeur's interest in narrative derives from the inability of a 'purely phenomenological' account of temporal experience to avoid becoming bogged down in the aporias it both discovers and generates. The textual practice of narrative offers a means of working through the paralysis of the aporia. Ricoeur comments in Volume 3:

> The hypothesis that has oriented this work from its very beginning, namely, that temporality cannot be spoken of in the direct discourse of phenomenology, but rather requires the mediation of the indirect discourse of narration. The negative half of this demonstration lies in our assertion that the most exemplary attempts to express the lived experience of time in its immediacy result in the multiplication of aporias, as the instrument of analysis becomes ever more precise. It is these aporias that the poetics of narrative deals with as so many knots to be untied. In its schematic form, our working hypothesis thus amounts to taking narrative as a guardian of time, insofar as there can be no thought about time without narrated time. (1988, 241)

It is Ricoeur's assertion that 'there has never been a phenomenology of temporality free of every aporia, and that in principle there can never be one' (1988, 3). In order to produce solutions to the questions posed by temporal experience Ricoeur considers it necessary to discuss these questions in relation to the narrative structure they constitute and by which they themselves are constituted. He writes, 'our study rests on the thesis that narrative composition, taken in its broadest sense, constitutes a riposte to the aporetic character of speculation on time' (Ricoeur 1988, 11). This is a complicated and detailed strategy inhabited by the figure of aporia. The project of *Time and Narrative* faces the 'difficulty that the aporetics of temporality will reveal, namely, the irreducibility of one to the other.' That is to say, the aporias which Ricoeur investigates are pre-existing concepts within phenomenological inquiry and will thus be approached by a narrative mediation in an already irreducibly complex form. However, *Time and Narrative* also depends upon the intervention of phenomenology to explain the narrative discourse it generates.

The introduction to Volume 3 finds Ricoeur's strategy embracing this paradox:

> We must assume the much greater risks of a specifically philosophical discussion, whose stake is whether – and how – the narrative operation, taken in its full scope, offers a 'solution' – not a speculative, but a poetic one – to the aporias that seemed inseparable from the Augustinian analysis of time. (1988, 4)

This is an inevitable consequence of the route Ricoeur chooses to take in relation to the aporias of temporal experience. He comments in conclusion to the penultimate section of his study:

> Let us first say that, if the phenomenology of time can become one privileged interlocutor in the three-way conversation we are about to undertake among phenomenology, historiography, and literary narratology, this is a result not just of its discoveries but also of the aporias it gives rise to, which increase in proportion to its advances. (1988, 96)

While narrative is a means by which to resolve the aporias of phenomenological inquiry, phenomenology is the necessary means by which to explain the narrative solutions. In this way the very action of Ricoeur's project takes on an aporetic form. The interdependence of the narrative modes of history and literature, and the relation of narratology to phenomenology within Ricoeur's work, as Hans Kellner has pointed out (regarding the two components of the study's title): 'lean upon each other like the two parts of the Christian Bible, the latter part of which is proven true because it fulfils the former, the former part of which is proven true because it prefigures the latter' (Kellner 1990, 229). The value of such a strategy is the challenge and support it presents to other theories of narrative which attempt to examine the impossible simultaneity of aporetic conditions.

One of the difficulties in reading Ricoeur is – as a consequence of his Heideggerian training – his ability to accommodate two contradictory positions within an argument. In this way he allows that argument to unfold by the double logic of these contradictions. When Ricoeur seems at his most contradictory he is also at his most rigorously philosophical. Ricoeur's use of the figure of aporia requires expansion. The analytic technology of *Time and Narrative* most frequently involves a dialectical synthesis of two juxtaposed arguments to produce a third concept. This dialectical third is aporetically figured but not necessarily as a result of the creation of a paradox out of the original two arguments. For example, the dialectical synthesis of Aristotle and Augustine gives rise to the concept of 'human time'. However, the aporia of human time's refiguration in narrative is not a result of an aporetic relation between Aristotle's *muthos* and Augustine's *distentio*. The structure of Ricoeur's three volumes is determined by the logic of this argument. Volume 1 of *Time and Narrative* is divided into two sections 'The Circle of Narrative and Temporality' and 'History and Narrative'. The first section acts as a general introduction to the entire argument of the three volumes; each section is divided into three chapters. In Part 1, Chapter 1 presents a reading of the aporetic experience of time, which is in a dialectical relationship with the concepts of emplotment in Chapter 2; Chapter 3 presents this relationship. Thus, Ricoeur places Augustine in dialectic encounter with Aristotle, and this juxtaposition produces the threefold mimesis outlined in Chapter 3.

Similarly, in Part 3, Chapter 4, 'The Eclipse of Narrative', is related to Chapter 5, 'Defences of Narrative', and this dialectic exchange brings about chapter 6, 'Historical Intentionality'. This logical method applies to the entire three-volume project. Thus, Part 1 of *Time and Narrative* is the introduction to the entire argument, whereas Part 2, on historical narrative, is directly countered by Volume 2 on fictional narrative, with Volume 2 serving as the synthesis to the initial problem of human time created through narrativity. Volumes 1 and 2 find their discussions of historiography and literary fiction dialectically synthesized into Volume 3's preoccupation with phenomenological temporality. Phenomenology is described – in contrast to the aporetic pertinence Ricoeur demonstrates elsewhere – as a 'privileged interlocutor in the three-way conversation' (Ricoeur 1988, 96). The work is characterized by an interest in groupings of three: threefold mimesis, three measurements of time, three interlocutors and, of course, its three volumes. This repeated ternary movement within the work can be identified as Ricoeur's formulation of Hegelian culmination in the sign of the analogue as a methodological dynamic which enacts Ricoeur's 'work of mourning' for Hegel.

It is necessary for the project of *Time and Narrative* to subsume a representative selection of all narrative knowledge into the mediation of its argument. Ricoeur's project is to show that all human experience in the lived world is made temporal (and so understandable) when it is refigured into narrative, fictional or historical. In order to demonstrate this *Time and Narrative* requires a strict methodology, which will draw every heterogeneous aspect of this vast object of study under the singular, ordered (or to use Ricoeur's own term concerning the action of narrative, 'concordant') form of the particular model of narrative Ricoeur appropriates. As a result Ricoeur must take those elements of inquiry which do not fit neatly into a narratologically defined category and demonstrate that they are narrative in character. Ricoeur does this by likening them, by analogy, to a trope from narrative theory. In his own words he 'quasifies' them:

> The concepts of quasi-plot, quasi-character, and quasi-event that I had to construct in order to respect the very indirect form of filiation by which the history that is the least narrative in its style of writing nevertheless continues to rely on narrative understanding. (1984, 230)

Hans Kellner comments upon this method:

> All of this quasi-ness reminds us that the Sign of the Analogue, under which the ship sails, certifies the figurative process, which is the life-blood of *Time and Narrative*; its destination, after all, is a refiguration of time by narrative. Each step of the way involves a turn, a tropological allegorization, by which apparently different pieces of reality (the Sign of Same and Other) are resolved provisionally, into analogues, quasis. In this phenomenological strategy, narrative acts as a middle-level tropological process, mediating parts into wholes, without looking over either shoulder at the lower and higher level protocols of language. Narrative is thus the quintessence of Ricoeur's vision of humanity. (1990, 233)

The 'figurative process' that Kellner identifies as 'the life-blood' of Ricoeur's argument is a figuration of language different from that imagined by deconstruction. For Ricoeur and hermeneutics – as Kellner indicates – the figurative process takes place at a structural level within the unit of the textual whole (character, event) rather than at the level of the signifier or trace.

Ricoeur's use of analogue is not so much a description of the mediating power of the tropological process of narrative but rather a narrative approach to the Hegelian dialectic. Ricoeur's description of the narrative characteristics of historiography, and his attempt to breach the impasse of the aporias of phenomenological temporality, can be thought of as a narrativistic approach to the use of Hegelian thought on issues within contemporary hermeneutics. This use of the analogue can be said to be narrativistic or narrativizing because it translates one tropological operation into another. So, Ricoeur's analogue is a radicalization of Hegel. The problem it ultimately poses for Ricoeur's thematization of the aporia is that the apparent resolution of the signs of the Same and the Other must negate the fundamental irreducibility of both halves of the figure of aporia. In other words, Ricoeur's dialectical ontologizing is in tension with the hauntological process of aporia as Derrida understands it (see Derrida 1993). This mediation denies the radical alterity which constitutes the figure it seeks to describe. While Ricoeur may be fascinated by the figure of aporia, his argument is ultimately at odds with the alterity implied by the aporetic. Ricoeur's mediation of the narrative function as an analogue, by means of the process of analogue, is itself a narrative because it is an imaginary resolution of real contradictions. However, this is not necessarily an argument against Ricoeur, it is merely to identify Ricoeur's position as narrativistic. This is an inevitable consequence of Ricoeur's own argument regarding the necessary expression of temporal experience (and so all textuality) in the form of a narrative. Rather this description of Ricoeur's dialectic methodology may just be a further demonstration of Ricoeur's relation to Hegel and the phenomenological tradition.

Martin McQuillan

Further reading and works cited

Clark, S. H. *Paul Ricoeur*. London, 1990.
Dauenhauser, B. P. *Paul Ricoeur*. New York, 1999.
Derrida, J. 'The *Retrait* of Metaphor', *Enclitic*, 2, 1978.
—. *Margins of Philosophy*. Brighton, 1982.
—. *Aporias*. Stanford, CA, 1993.
Gibson, A. *Towards a Postmodern Theory of Narrative*. Edinburgh, 1996.
Hahn, L. E. (ed.) *The Philosophy of Paul Ricoeur*. Chicago, 1995.
Kearney, R. *Dialogues with Contemporary Continental Thinkers*. Manchester, 1984.
—. *Paul Ricoeur*. London, 1996.
Kellner, H. '"As Real as it Gets …"': Ricoeur and Narrativity', *Philosophy Today*, 34, 3, 1990.
—. 'Narrativity in History: Post-structuralism and Since', *History and Theory*, 26, 1987.
Kemp, T. P. and Ransmussa, D. (eds) *The Narrative Path*. New York, 1989.
Lawlor, L. *Imagination and Chance*. Albany, NY, 1992.
Miller, J. Hillis. 'But are things as we think they are?', *Times Literary Supplement*, 9–15 October 1987.
Reagan, C. E. *Paul Ricoeur*. Chicago, 1998.
Ricoeur, P. *History and Truth*. Evanston, IL, 1965.
—. *Husserl*. Chicago, 1967.
—. *Freud and Philosophy*. New Haven, CT, 1970.
—. *Paul Ricoeur: Political and Social Essays*, eds D. Stewart and J. Bien. Athens, OH, 1974.
—. *Interpretation Theory*. Fort Worth, TX, 1976.

—. *The Rule of Metaphor*. London, 1978.
—. *Hermeneutics and the Human Sciences*, ed. J. Thompson. Cambridge, 1981.
—. *Time and Narrative*, Vol. 1. Chicago, 1984.
—. *Time and Narrative*, Vol. 2. Chicago, 1985.
—. *Fallible Man*. New York, 1986.
—. *Time and Narrative*, Vol. 3. Chicago, 1988.
—. *The Conflict of Interpretations*. London, 1989.
—. *From Text to Action*. London, 1991.
—. *Oneself as Another*. Chicago, 1992.
—. *Figuring the Sacred*. New York, 1995.
—. *Critique and Conviction*. Cambridge, 1997.
—. *The Just*. Chicago, 2000.
Valdés, M. J. (ed.) *Reflection and Imagination*. London, 1991.
Wood, D. (ed.) *On Paul Ricoeur*. London, 1992.

32. Roland Barthes (1915–1980)

None of the theoreticians who has contributed to the radical transformation of literary and cultural studies since the 1960s has a higher profile than Roland Barthes. His name is associated with controversies about the status of literature and the nature of authorship that represent the public face of the postmodern revolution in literary theory. Yet, despite some famous and hard-fought debates, and a strong connection to major movements and practices – such as semiotics, structuralism and poststructuralism – Barthes cannot be identified with a strict or canonical set of principles, methods or ideas, in the same way as Lacan, Derrida or even Foucault. Barthes's career is remarkable for the breadth of the material that he has been able to deal with, from popular culture to the 'high' literary, from music to film and photography, from public textual conventions to the intense and solipsistic space of the purely subjective, even bodily or perverse, experience of reading.

Despite this eclecticism, Barthes's output revolves around a consistent set of issues. Rather than isolating or preferring a single methodology, his work is marked by the subtle adaptation of or exemplary enthusiasm for a range of theoretical terminologies, lifted variously from Saussurean linguistics, Russian formalism, marxism, Lacanian psychoanalysis, Derridean deconstruction and even Nietzschean perspectivism. The project, which these different terminologies needed to serve, was not the derivation of truth or theoretical finitude, but the attempt to enact a kind of avant-gardism of reading, a social and historical practice of which Barthes was the most subtle and articulate practitioner. The issue that defines Barthes's engagement with reading is the subjective value of the slippage between meaning and meaninglessness *as an experience*. At the communal level, shared conventions of meaning-making exhibit a simultaneous political brutality and historical fragility, exemplifying pressure-points in public culture where orthodox groups and values attempt to disguise or naturalize unresolved conflicts or unrepresented tensions. At the subjective level, textual codes and practices position us in a network of conditioned meanings that can only be evaded by the very instability and breakdown that haunts, indeed defines, them. All this is not understood in Barthes as a philosophy of language or even a theory of subjectivity, but as a narratable experience, touching on issues of class, the body and affectivity.

Barthes's first book-length work *Writing Degree Zero* (1953), a compilation of previously published essays, proposes that the problem of the relationship between language and meaning is not only the main subject of modern literature, but the form of its proper engagement with history. Literature must be seen as a historical phenomenon, not transcending it to form a trans-historical institution of unshakeable human or cultural values. It is this engagement with the 'problematics of language' (1967b, 3) that allows literature to renew its purpose by challenging the limitations of inherited conventions and forms. Literary form, like language itself, is imbued with the rich and unknowable traces of all the uses to which it has already been put. It is thus always already radically historicized, grounded in the tradition of previous practices in which the writer has no choice but to work. There is thus no simple free choice for writers of the mode of their creativity, nor are there any forms – like realism – which can convincingly claim to transcend linguistic conventions to produce an unadulterated engagement with the real world. Each literary form is implicated in the society which produces it, and writers inevitably exemplify social meanings outside of and beyond their own specific needs and intentions. The problematizing of language undertaken by writers from Flaubert onwards insistently reminds us that literary conventions can thus no longer be seen as pragmatic or functional options manipulated by writers seeking an outlet for their already existing ideas by way of free invention or free choice. Writing is itself a 'compromise between freedom and remembrance' (Barthes 1967b, 16), in which the new appears only as a complication or transformation of already located conventions. In modern poetry, this disruption of the inherited takes the form of a stripping away of the normal functions of language, till words appear in their most neutral form, their degree zero. In this way 'the consumer of poetry, deprived of the guide of selective connections, encounters the word frontally, and receives it as an absolute quantity, accompanied by all its possible associations' (Barthes 1967b, 48). In prose, the exemplary case is Camus' *The Outsider*, where 'the social or mythical characters of language are abolished in favour of a neutral and inert state of form' (77), which separates the writing from the dictates of 'a History not its own'. The aim here is to create a rupture in the texture of inherited language use, which confronts the reader with both the limitations of socially situated conventions and the possibility of a language expanding beyond them. Readers or 'consumers', as Barthes sometimes calls them, are thus announced as the possible site of a radical disjunction between conditioned meaning and its disruption.

In the mid-1960s, Barthes's work on literature provoked an attack from the more traditional practitioners of literary criticism, largely as a result of his *On Racine* (1960). This book is made up of three essays. The first and longest is an attempt at defining the Racinian 'type', the second a critique of contemporary Racinian theatre production and the third a polemical statement about the value of literary studies entitled 'History or Literature'. The opening essay is indebted to Lacan and Lévi-Strauss, and rests on the premise that the purpose of literary study is not to transmit moral meaning nor advance national culture, but rather to disinter an author's own dynamic and unresolved anthropology. Barthes's Racine presents a world, not of moral enlightenment nor psychological insight, but unresolved violence, intra-familial rivalry and sexual obsession. The role of literature is not to resolve nor evaluate this world, but to present it in its raw state to an audience who must experience it as a provocation. It is no wonder that this view, accompanied by the polemical statements in the book's final essay, constituted a challenge to the conventional role of criticism and literary study. Sorbonne-based Racine scholar Raymond Picard challenged Barthes in a pamphlet *Nouvelle critique ou nouvelle imposture* [*New Criticism or New Fraud*] (1965), which accused the new styles of criticism of being destructive, irrational, cynical and perverse. Barthes's reply in *Criticism and Truth* (1966) endures as one of the most lucid statements of the inadequacies of traditional criticism and the need for an alternative. It rigorously attacks the naivety and pseudo-objectivity of conventional criticism and its untheorized attitudes to signification. In the end, the book restates the key theme of *Writing Degree Zero* that 'a writer is someone for whom language constitutes a problem' (1987, 64), and links it with what will become a central idea in Barthes's thinking: that plurality is the defining quality of literary language. This plurality allows for meaning, but denies its univocity, insisting that any meaning discernible in a text is inevitably accompanied by a variety of other possible meanings that always destabilize its authority. The experience of meaning must also be an experience of that meaning's precariousness.

Although the material analysed is from another dimension of culture altogether – the inadvertent daily practices of the mass media – Barthes's semiotics repeats many of the same understandings of the relation between text and history that were also developed in *Writing Degree Zero*. Most famously assembled into the collection *Mythologies* (1957) and theorized in its appendix 'Myth Today' and the later *Elements of Semiology* (1964), Barthes's analyses of popular culture also attempt to restore to apparently naive communicative processes the complex function that belies their ostensibly transparent and simple motivation. The aim of these pithy and stylish pieces is to undermine 'the 'naturalness' with which newspapers, art and common sense constantly dress up a reality which, even though it is the one we live in, is undoubtedly determined by history' (Barthes 1973, 11). An example is the analysis of the use of language in the trial of peasant Gaston Dominici for the murder of a family of English tourists camped on his farm. The language of the court and the press conspire together to present Dominici's language as alien, and therefore outside of the logic of common sense and social consensus. The result is that the accused is subject to the narrative reconstruction and platitudinous psychology that underprops this common sense, a psychology based on the clichés of popular realist literature. The function of language therefore is not simply to represent Dominici and his supposed crime, but to confirm a whole petty bourgeois worldview as natural and unquestionable, and us all as subject to its logic. This is the primary function of the myths that Barthes identifies, to transform 'history into nature' (1973, 129), to take the specific and contingent logic of a certain historical social system and present it as unquestionable and inevitable, in short as natural.

In 'Myth Today', Barthes analyses this process as a double movement of signification. The simplest model of language use detects a stable signified beneath the material signifier. Beneath the prosecutor's language in the Dominici case lies the apparently simple attempt to reconstitute a sequence of events that clarify and explain a murder. Yet in this speech, both signifier and signified combine to become together a new signifier, this time of a signified with much broader social resonance, the confirmation of a view of psychology that reassures and rationalizes a whole social order. In this double movement from simple transparent sign to complex myth, signification is appropriated from its apparent function into a political historical function. In this way, the artificiality of sign systems becomes apparent: meaning only appears to be natural. It is in fact thoroughly staged to serve complex political and social needs. Myth is thus 'speech stolen and restored' (1973, 125), Barthes writes. It appears to perform a simple communicative function, but this simplicity is contrived. Another set of meanings has intervened which complicate signification by subsuming it into the needs of more elaborate social processes. This complex multi-layering in turn creates the opportunity for the analyst to perform a sceptical reading. Naive language use, if there is such a thing, can be described. Its logic can be endorsed or rejected, but purely on its own terms. The complex double structure of mythical semiotic systems, on the other hand, allows the analyst access to whole historical and social processes that expose not the truth or falsity of single statements, but the logic and culture of whole realities: semiotics is not a way of assessing the truth or falsehood of statements. It is a way of reading a society. There is 'no semiology which cannot, in the last analysis, be acknowledged as *semioclasm*' (1973, 9), Barthes writes. Meaning is thus not the purpose of signifying systems, but merely one of their artifices. The aim of the active reader is to draw attention to such artifices in order to defy the ruse of meaning and reveal the politics of signification.

Elements of Semiology (1964) represents an attempt to give semiotic analysis a more rigorous basis. The book is built around an explanation of four fundamental binary oppositions: *langue* and *parole*; signifier and signified; syntagm and system; and, finally, denotation and connotation. According to the opposition between *langue* (language) and *parole* (speech act), each individual language event is allowed, even predetermined, by the existence of a 'systematized set of conventions necessary to communication' (1967a, 13), that we conventionally call a language. Because speech can only occur within the context of language, yet we only know language by way of speech, the two are in a genuinely dialectical relationship. This distinction allows the analyst to detect the general principles and possibilities behind each act of signification, and also to see how these principles and possibilities are actualized. The second distinction in *Elements* is the conventional and familiar Saussurian one between the two things that constitute the sign, its material substance (signifier) and 'mental representation' (42) or signified. Thirdly, Barthes distinguishes between system (paradigm in more conventional structuralism) and syntagm. The paradigm represents the various options that can be substituted for one another in a cultural practice, and the syntagm the logical sequence which combines them in order. Various words may substitute for one another in the same position in a sentence, and are thus in a paradigmatic relationship to one another within the same system. The order in which they appear in that sentence betrays their syntagmatic relationship. In a famous example, Barthes proposes that the menu in a restaurant replicates the same logic: the alternative dishes within a course are a system; the logical sequence in which they appear (entrées before main course, main course before dessert) is their syntagm. The final binary opposition Barthes outlines is between denotation and connotation, announcing that 'the future probably belongs to a linguistics of connotation' (1967a, 90). This claim exhibits the contradiction at the heart of this semiotic enterprise. Connotation is seen as 'general, global and diffuse' (91), yet Barthes calls connotation a system (91). This paradox foreshadows how attempts at the rigorous constitution of binary oppositions as rock-hard theoretical principles would soon come undone in Derridean deconstruction, a process of which Barthes would become perhaps one of the less philosophically rigorous but more rhetorically influential fellow-travellers. The most severe version of Barthes's semiotic analysis appears in his treatment of the language of the fashion industry in *The Fashion*

System (1967). His next works represent (especially *S/Z* and *Empire of Signs*) an inversion, even parody of this approach, even though the scepticism they imply towards a putatively scientific methodology always respects and relies on the semioclastic will to read across signs and texts for their unconfessed meanings.

Elements ends with a call for a synchronic approach to language, to present not the unfolding meaning of history in process, but 'a cross-section of history' (Barthes 1967a, 98). This ahistorical approach may defy the traditional marxist imperative to always historicize that haunts much of Barthes's early collection *Critical Essays* (1964) and its celebration of Brecht, yet it foreshadows another model of textual politics, one that would become increasingly important and one with which Barthes is strongly identified: the idea that the instability and plurality of signification resist the homogenization on which all author-itarian systems (political, social and intellectual) depend, thus allowing for the contra-diction, inconclusiveness and ambiguity that can be experienced as at least an image of freedom. It is this idea that Barthes now develops into a fully-fledged understanding of textuality, and the horizons of pleasure, and in turn, subjectivity itself.

Barthes's most famous single piece of writing is the short essay 'The Death of the Author' (1968). More than any other piece, this essay has become notorious among those opposed to the poststructuralist influence on literary studies. Here Barthes argues that the under-standing of a literary text in terms of the biography, psychology or historical context of its author is reductive and limiting, and is a misconstruction of the nature of literary language. 'To give a text an Author is to impose a limit on that text, to furnish it with a final signified, to close the writing' (Barthes 1977a, 147). This closure, in turn, collaborates with all authoritarian systems of meaning-making. A style of reading that engages with the plurality of textuality as 'a multi-dimensional space in which a variety of writings, none of them original, blend and clash' (146) challenges such authority, becoming 'an anti-theological activity, an activity that is truly revolutionary since to refuse to fix meanings is, in the end, to refuse God and his hypostases – reason, science, law' (147). Here, reading against meaning liberates us from the constraints of traditional reading institutions, the academy in particular, and allows us to animate the incommensurability, contradiction and difference implicit in textuality. Here is the most succinct version of Barthes's understanding of reading as an avant-garde activity. The later essay 'From Work to Text' (1971) develops many of these same ideas into a comparison between the traditional model of, on the one hand, the closed work located in fixed and knowable sequences of literary filiation and meaning, and the open text, on the other, which expects and inspires an active reading, 'play, activity, production, practice' (Barthes 1977a, 162). This article is largely an attempt to assimilate Julia Kristeva's idea of the 'intertextual', that texts produce their meaning not from their own internal structures and intentions, but from their relationship with other texts. Reading is seen not as an act of consumption, but of collaboration (Barthes 1977a, 163).

Barthes's most sustained piece of literary criticism *S/Z* (1970) brings together many of the themes of these essays and others, such as the influential essay on narratology 'Introduction to the Structural Analysis of Narrative' (1966). *S/Z* is simultaneously the highest version, and a parody of, structural analysis. It is a book-length treatment of Balzac's story 'Sarrasine', breaking the narrative into 561 units, most of which are a few words or sentences long. These units are then analysed in terms of five functional codes: the hermeneutic, which reveals how enigmas are proposed and then dealt with; the semiotic, which reads semes in terms of their simple denotative function; the symbolic, where meanings operate in a polyvalent or reversible form; the code of actions, which plots the sequence of episodes; and, finally, the referential code, which alludes to culturally sanctioned bodies of knowledge. The story is shown to be built around the interrelationship of these codes. Barthes writes: 'to depict is to unroll the carpet of the codes, to refer not from a language to a referent but from one code to another' (Barthes 1974, 55). The illusion of animation in the realist narrative is the result of the simultaneous function of different codes 'according to unequal wavelengths' (61). The slight disjunction between the codes gives the sense of accident and movement we read as the real. *S/Z* is probably most famous for the argument that realism as a literary genre does not present an open window on the world, but is highly structured around codes and conventions of narrative, an argument enlarged in the book's conclusion to become the general credo of postmodern metafiction (a rising literary style of the time) that 'narrative concerns only itself' (Barthes 1974, 213). This view of realism as highly conventionalized appears in Barthes's work as early as *Writing Degree Zero* (see Barthes 1967b, 67).

Systematic structuralist analysis is also a victim of Barthes's method, despite the latter's apparently mathematical order. It is clearly shown that the operation of the text can be broken into constitutive elements, but these function not as impersonal laws or as universal narrative ingredients, but rather as latent textual experiences that only achieve value when read. Reading is itself an active and open-ended process, a 'nomination in the course of becoming, a tireless approximation, a metonymic labour' (1974, 11). Reading then does not aim for the isolation of a fixed set of meanings, nor does it rely on the architectonics of a rigid, closed system of codes that plot scientifically the horizons of the text and limit the possible values it can produce. In Barthes's words, 'reading does not consist in stopping the chain of systems, in establishing a truth, a legality of the text . . . it consists in coupling these systems, not according to their finite quantity, but according to their plurality' (1974, 11). Here we find an early statement of a theme that would become important in Barthes's later work: readers engage and involve themselves with the plurality and dynamism of the textual experience because they themselves are textual. 'This "I" which approaches the text is already itself a plurality of other texts' (10).

This relationship between subjectivity and textuality is developed fully in Barthes's next major theoretical work *The Pleasure of the Text* (1973). What is discernible here is the influence of Lacanian psychoanalysis and its understanding of the relationship between subjectivity and language, though as he asserts in *Roland Barthes by Roland Barthes*, Barthes's use of other systems of thought is never systematic or 'scrupulous', but allusive, impressionistic and 'undecided' (1977b, 150). *The Pleasure of the Text* picks up on many of the themes that had dominated Barthes's work since 1968, especially the image of the text as defined by plurality. Here, however, the focus of this plurality is the subjectivity of the reader, an idea that had been foreshadowed without being thoroughly developed in the conclusion of 'The Death of the Author'. The experience of the text is to be seen as erotic even perverse, and divided between two collaborating types of affective experience: pleasure, which confirms the reader's sense of self and his culture on the one hand, and *jouissance*, or bliss, that flirts with the loss of self on the other. (It is worth noting that this distinction echoes Nietzsche's bifurcation of Greek literature into Apollonian and Dionysian modes. Nietzsche's influence also emerges in Barthes's aphoristic style here.) These two experiences of textuality are always in some kind of contradiction with one another, but it is this very incommensurability that releases the text's erotic potential. Barthes writes 'neither culture nor its destruction is erotic; it is the seam between them, the fault, the flaw, which becomes so' (Barthes 1975, 7). What is crucial to grasp here is the slippage between the possible sites of these different affects. They are both to be understood, of course, as emotional experiences released in the reader. Yet, the 'text of pleasure' and the 'text of *jouissance*' are discussed as qualitatively different kinds of texts. The text of pleasure 'comes from culture and does not break with it, is linked to a *comfortable* practice of reading' (14). The text of bliss, on the other hand, 'imposes a state of loss' and 'discomforts' (14). Texts thus are agents of affectivity. The spontaneity and freedom of the reader's experience is, if not constrained, at least defined by a putative typology of textuality, though Barthes refrains from offering a list of ingredients of each type of text beyond the kind of impressions captured here. Indeed, the source of any such typology is no longer to be objectified in the text itself, but in its reading. The texts are qualitatively different, but this difference is not to be known in their structure nor in their production, but in their consumption. The nature of the text is radically *subjectivized*, and the ideal reading subject is imagined, who 'keeps the two texts in his field and in his hands the reins of pleasure and bliss', who 'simultaneously and contradictorily participates in the profound hedonism of all culture ... and in the destruction of that culture: he enjoys the consistency of his selfhood (that is his pleasure) and seeks its loss (that is his bliss)' (Barthes 1975, 14).

From at least *Mythologies* on, Barthes had identified the text, not only as an object to analyse, but also as a site of experience, whether this experience was understood as consumption, mere reading or as the 'doubly perverse' (1975, 14) entwining of bliss and pleasure. The constant challenge of his career had been to work out exactly how the objective nature of the text and the subjective nature of a reader's experience of it could be qualified and quantified together. It would be naïve to announce that this problem's final and absolute destiny was the model we find here of textual object and reading subject as a kind of chiasmus, a mirror-like sharing of a fundamental linguistic nature. Yet this does seem to represent a point of clarification in Barthes's relationship to this issue that earlier alternatives did not. This is especially true of semiology, the objective potential of which Barthes never seemed to fully believe in, perhaps because it never provided a satisfactory account of the motility and active nature of reading.

Two works which followed *The Pleasure of the Text*, *Roland Barthes by Roland Barthes* (1975) and *A Lover's Discourse: Fragments* (1977), commit themselves to the model of the subject as text. The epigraph to *Roland Barthes* says of the fragmented account of the author's life which follows: 'it must all be considered as if spoken by a character in a novel' (Barthes 1977b, 1). A comparable statement opens *A Lover's Discourse*: 'The description of the lover's discourse has been replaced by its simulation, and to that discourse has been restored its fundamental person, the *I*, in order to stage an utterance, not an analysis' (Barthes 1990, 3). In both these texts, the subject is not something to be analysed or even described, but something to be produced out of the heart of the languages and texts that make subjectivity possible. It is not an entity, but an enactment, and it is not to be known but experienced.

Two important statements in *Roland Barthes* reinforce this point, and it is important to recognize how grounded both these sophisticated and generalizable theoretical remarks are in the intensity of, not just anyone's, but Roland Barthes's own idiosyncratic self-identification. First, Barthes defines his relationship to his own time:

> I am only the imaginary contemporary of my own present: contemporary of its languages, its utopias, its systems (i.e. of its fictions), in short, of its mythology or of its philosophy but not of its history, of which I inhabit only the shimmering reflection: the *phantasmagoria*. (1977b, 59)

Here, subjectivity is only conceivable within the horizons of a thoroughly textualized culture. The tone here, however, is not one of loss, or of limitation, but of stimulation, open-endedness and plurality. If we recall the distant yet resonant argument from *Writing Degree Zero*, that modern literature confronted history by problematizing language, we can see how this statement reconfigures subjectivity as an implicit engagement with the social and intersubjective, even if Barthes is no longer confident in describing it as the historical.

The second statement of interest here links the theorist of subjectivity with the contradictory politics of meaning. Speaking of himself in the third person, Barthes writes:

> Evidently he dreams of a world which would be *exempt from meaning* ... yet for him, it is not a question of recovering a pre-meaning, an origin of the world, of life, of facts, anterior to meaning, but rather to imagine a post-meaning: one must traverse, as though the length of an initiatic way, the whole meaning, in order to be able to extenuate it, to exempt it. (1977b, 87)

The value of the plurality of the text that Barthes had done so much to advertise in the second half of his writing career emerges as the slippage between an encumbering meaning and an imagined post-meaning. It is in the surprise and disorientation that the eruption of meaninglessness into meaning provides that one attains a sense of selfhood.

This argument is developed in Barthes's last major work, his study of photography, *Camera Lucida* (1980). The key theoretical achievement here is the distinction between *studium* and *punctum*, a definition of textual experience not very far from the distinction between the text of pleasure and the text of bliss. The *studium* is an experience of interest in an image, even enthusiasm for it. The *punctum*, on the other hand, thrills and destabilizes, surprises and reveals the subject to itself. Again, the *punctum* is only known as part of the viewer's affective experience, yet it is also an attribute of the text itself. Barthes is able to identify the *punctum* in various of the photos he discusses. The most important example is a photo he does not reproduce of his mother as a child (which he calls the Winter Garden Photograph). This photo which he discovers going through her effects after she has died captures something about her that he is able to recognize and that he had forgotten. The experience is a kind of Proustian epiphany, where one is surprised by a feeling of one's own fleeting authenticity as it emerges from a material re-embodiment of the past. It is this disruption of his normal conception of himself and his mother by a seemingly more real experience of her that revives in Barthes a sense of the 'real', a term that has fascinated and lured him throughout his career. In an argument seemingly oblivious to the image-manipulation that photography has always been subject to, and now of course rendered obsolete by digitalization, Barthes argues for the status of the photographic image as the record of what has literally been. Debate over the veracity of this claim aside, it does provide a useful insight into Barthes's thinking. More than a naive assumption about the deterministic power of the real, Barthes is again asserting that the real is simply an effect. Like subjectivity, reality does not impinge upon us, but is enacted as that location where the text seems to come undone, where the seam between meaning and meaninglessness is under most pressure. Here we experience an intensification of both the sense of the self and of the real. This intensification makes clear the textual nature of both subjectivity and reality. This is not because of the inevitability of textual mediation in our culturally enclosed experience of the world. Texts do not constitute a uniform and unbroken field that wraps us around with representations instead of things. The field of textuality is highly fraught, and ruptured by what we experience as a hypothetical outside that we can never know or validate. Almost invariably these sites of imagined rupture occur where our conventional practices of meaning reach their limit, break down and allow for the meaninglessness that inevitably shadows them. It is this experience of imagined rupture that Barthes sometimes saw as the possibility of a kind of politico-cultural disruption, but that at the end of his career produced not self-consciousness in the traditional humanist sense, but an understanding of textuality as a kind of perpetual re-subjectification.

Nick Mansfield

Further reading and works cited

Barthes, R. *Elements of Semiology*. New York, 1967a.
—. *Writing Degree Zero*. New York, 1967b.
—. *Critical Essays*. Evanston, IL, 1972.
—. *Mythologies*. ed. A. Lavers. London, 1973.
—. *S/Z*. New York, 1974.
—. *The Pleasure of the Text*. New York, 1975.
—. *Image-Music-Text*, ed. S. Heath, Glasgow, 1977a.
—. *Roland Barthes by Roland Barthes*. London, 1977b.
—. *On Racine*. New York, 1983a.
—. *The Fashion System*. New York, 1983b.
—. *The Empire of Signs*. London, 1983c.
—. *Camera Lucida*. London, 1984.
—. *Criticism and Truth*, ed. K. Pilcher Keuneman. Minneapolis, MN, 1987.
—. *A Lover's Discourse: Fragments*. Harmondsworth, 1990.
Calvet, L.-J. *Roland Barthes*. Cambridge, 1994.
Culler, J. *Barthes*. London, 1983.
Hill, L. 'Barthes's Body', *Paragraph*, *11*, 1988.
Lavers, A. *Roland Barthes*. London, 1982.
Moriarty, M. *Roland Barthes*. Cambridge, 1991.
Picard, R. *Nouvelle critique ou nouvelle imposture*. Paris, 1965.
Rylance, R. *Roland Barthes*. Hemel Hempstead, 1994.
Ungar, S. *Roland Barthes*. London, 1983.
— and McGraw, B. R. (eds) *Signs in Culture*. Iowa City, IA, 1989.
Wiseman, M. B. *The Ecstasies of Roland Barthes*. London, 1989.

33. French Structuralism: A. J. Greimas (1917–1992), Tzvetan Todorov (1939–) and Gérard Genette (1930–)

This essay will attempt to give a general synthesis of French structuralist thinking from the 1960s onwards. Yet its focus lies not in a sketch of the historical background of structuralism, however useful (if not indispensable) such a frame of reference may be; the impressive two-volume study by François Dosse offers extensive information regarding the complex networks of relations, persons and influences on the Parisian scene. Rather, I would like to concentrate my discussion on the theoretical and the methodological presuppositions of structuralist thinking, by focusing on the work of three major literary scholars working in (and sometimes against) this productive paradigm in literary studies.

This article consists of two closely interrelated parts. First of all, I will describe the general principles that underlie structuralist thinking. To this end, I will concentrate on three seminal texts: *Sémantique structurale* (1966) by Algirdas Julien Greimas, *Grammaire du Décaméron* (1969) by Tzvetan Todorov, and *Discours du récit* (1972) by Gérard Genette. In the second part, the scholarly career of these three protagonists will be sketched in order to grasp the complexity of their attitude towards structuralist thinking in later years. Thus I hope to demonstrate how the 'structuralists' have gradually come to broaden the scope of their research – in an obvious attempt to cope with the acknowledged limitations of the structuralist project – without, however, having taken recourse to a radical 'poststructuralist' reorientation.

I will indeed argue that, although structuralism may be seen as a historical current in literary studies (roughly situated in the 1960s and 1970s, with its main manifestation in France), its premises still continue to exert a profound influence on our contemporary thinking about literature and culture. Some dreams of structuralism may be declared obsolete or dead; however, structuralism as such, as an ambitious project in the humanities, definitely cannot.

The emergence of structuralism, which can be situated around 1955–60, is related to an important shift in the humanities, which may be roughly characterized as a move from a 'pre-scientific' towards an explicitly 'scientific' approach. In the specific case of literary studies, some younger scholars opposed vehemently the impressionistic and strongly subjective way in which canonized literature was considered. In fact, the analysis of a literary text hardly amounted to anything but a mere paraphrase of its content in a quasi-literary style, clearly intended to enhance its canonized status and its aesthetic merits. This scholarly discourse on literature was severely dismissed as impressionistic (versus systematic) and subjective (versus objective), of local and anecdotal importance only (versus generally valid), as highly normative (versus descriptive-analytical), and finally as literary (versus scientific).

This overall critique, combined with a passionate plea for an entirely new discourse on and method of study of literature, gave rise to an innovative, productive intellectual movement during the 1960s in Paris, which was very soon associated with the name of 'structuralism'. Though controversial in some respects, structuralism almost immediately gained popularity and status among younger scholars. In this respect, it is symptomatic that Greimas' essay on semantics was titled *Sémantique structurale* because the editor thought that adding this fashionable adjective would contribute to its success.

Structuralism coincides with a strong interdisciplinary orientation, in which the pilot-function of modern linguistics was generally acknowledged as a decisive impetus for the scientific reorientation of the humanities in general, and of the discipline of literary studies in particular. Linguistics was supposed to provide not only the theoretical premises but also the concrete methodological tools and the specific concepts for the analysis of numerous phenomena. In this respect, the ideas of Ferdinand de Saussure and Louis Hjelmslev, and, in addition, the paradigm of transformational-generative linguistics primarily associated with the name of Noam Chomsky, proved extremely influential frames of reference.

A supplementary catalysing factor for literary studies was provided by the work of Roman

Jakobson and the anthropologist Claude Lévi-Strauss. In his analysis of social behaviour, Lévi-Strauss endeavoured to go beyond the mere detailed description of empirical data when he set out to seize the mechanisms underlying family relations, myths, rituals and other semiotic practices. He postulated a limited number of fundamental categories (mostly oppositions and homologies), which could be put into practice, modified or combined by means of given transformational principles in order to account fully for the anthropological phenomena. The similarities between this project and the generative model advocated by Chomsky in his *Syntactic Structures* (1957) are striking; the linguist also starts from a limited number of elements and rules in order to generate all possible sentences of a language.

When analysing the classic myth of Oedipus, for instance, Lévi-Strauss (in his *Anthropologie structurale*, 1958) does not restrict himself to one particular textual version. Rather, he constructs his version of the myth as an abstract basic structure from which all particular instances may subsequently be derived. Diversity and specificity thus become secondary to unity and coherence. Moreover, this constructed, 'immanent' level of the 'text' is further rewritten as a fundamental homology of two basic oppositions. One of these oppositions thematizes family relations (underrating vs. overrating of blood relations), the other is related to the origin of mankind (chthonic vs. autochthonic origin). This deep structure analysis results in a paradigmatic interpretation, which reveals the fundamental oppositions at stake in the mythic structure, as well as in a syntagmatic reading, which displays the (chrono-)logical chain of events constituting the mythical plot.

From these preliminary remarks, some basic principles of structuralist thinking may be derived. First of all, structuralists strongly believe in a 'pure', scientific point of view, which is most apparent in their construction of a general theoretical and conceptual framework and, complementarily, in their polemical anti-humanistic attitude. To achieve this ideal, the scholar 'constructs' his object of research, which is subsequently analysed by means of a priori scientific procedures (which are stated to possess universal validity). This analysis resorts to a restricted number of basic categories and oppositions, a set of relations and combinatory principles in order to arrive at more complex and more dynamic structures, and separate, if not hierarchically structured, levels of analysis. Finally, an unambiguously defined conceptual apparatus is considered indispensable to guarantee and to maximize the scientific status of the structuralist enterprise.

A structuralist fascination seems hardly surprising in the case of Algirdas Julien Greimas, since he was, as a professional linguist, first and foremost interested in the construction of a semantic theory destined to analyse linguistic significations. Greimas started as a lexicographer – which accounts for his interest in meaning, in contrast to the almost exclusively syntactic orientation of his fellow-linguists – but gradually he became interested in the way in which isolated word meanings might be combined into larger semantic wholes. In his seminal essay *Sémantique structurale* (1966), Greimas introduces to this end the concept of isotopy, which designates the repetition of certain semantic features in order to enhance the coherence and the homogeneity of syntagms, sentences and, ultimately, of texts in their entirety. Semantic incongruity is subsequently analysed in terms of consecutive isotopies, or else in terms of a clash between different isotopies (e.g. in the case of metaphorical expressions).

In the final chapter of his book, Greimas tries to account for a macro-structural semantics. Relying on Lévi-Strauss's concept of homology and Vladimir Propp's formalist analysis of folktales, he proposes his famous actantial scheme. In fact, the apparent multitude of characters and plots may be reduced to a restricted number of functional roles (or 'actants', in contrast to the actors which operate in a particular narrative) and predicates. First of all, there is the central relation between a subject and an object, a relationship characterized as 'desire'. Next, there is the axis of communication, which relates the sender (the actant provoking the subject's desire, e.g. by expressing a wish or formulating a certain task) to the eventual receiver of the object. Finally, there is the actantial pair of the helper versus the opponent, thematized as the axis of struggle.

In his *Sémantique structurale*, Greimas also proposes – rather succinctly – a syntagmatic model for the analysis of narrative events by postulating a series of tests which the subject has to succeed in completing in a fixed logical order. Later on, this idea is further elaborated and specified. Narratives may be defined as a logical sequence of four phases, which may or may not be realized explicitly in the course of a particular story. First of all, in the Manipulation phase, the virtual subject receives his task through the mediation of the sender. Next, the emerging subject has to obtain the necessary qualifications (knowledge and power) during the Competence phase, before he can really confront and defeat his opponent successfully during the Performance phase. Eventually, the realized subject has to deliver the achieved object to the right receiver in order to get acknowledged as the only true subject. This occurs during the Sanction phase, in which good and evil are separated definitively and the incarnation of the good is rewarded.

A similar fascination for modern linguistics is to be found in Tzvetan Todorov's *Grammaire du Décaméron*, published in 1969. In the programmatic introduction to his study, Todorov pleads for a new science, 'narratology', which would study the essential characteristics of narratives, regardless of their origin and their medium. Although Todorov takes Boccaccio's collection of stories, *Decamerone*, as his main topic of research, the 'grammar' he proposes has obviously far more general (if not universal) pretensions. In this respect, it is not a coincidence that Todorov's text grammar is entirely modelled on Chomskyan linguistic theory.

Todorov takes the 'proposition' (defined as a 'non-decomposable action') as the basic unit of narrative. On a syntactic level, propositions consist of agents and predicates; on a semantic level, they can be analysed in terms of proper names, substantives, adjectives and verbs. Moreover, they may be modified by means of negation and comparatives.

After this first-level analysis, Todorov proposes a theoretical model for the integration of individual propositions into larger sequences. Narratological theory thus takes the form of a structured algorithm: starting from a few basic elements, complex narrative structures are gradually generated by means of combinations, transformations and hierarchical levels. Although the linguistic orientation is dominant on the level of both general argumentation and detailed textual analysis, Todorov's book, however, displays a fundamental ambivalence, which may be considered symptomatic for literary structuralism in general. Indeed, there is a discrepancy between, on the one hand, the detailed (if not exhaustive) analysis of a particular literary text and, on the other hand, the intended level of an abstract (even universalistic) text grammar.

The same holds true for Gérard Genette's *Discours du récit* (1972), which was originally part of a collection of essays, *Figures III*. Taking one particular literary text as his starting point – Proust's *A la recherche du temps perdu*, a masterpiece of literary modernism – Genette presents a general theoretical frame for the analysis of narratives. Once again, linguistic categories seem perfectly suited for describing literary texts as well. Genette borrows the terms 'tense', 'mood' and 'voice' to constitute the basic categories of narrative discourse.

Yet, unlike Todorov, Genette does not entirely resort to linguistics in order to construct his theory. Rather, he integrates the theoretical concepts and the methodological tools developed by traditional literary studies. The specific 'structuralist' dimension of his research lies in Genette's search for conceptual categories that may be applicable to a huge variety of texts. In this respect, he explores the various strategies used to represent the various aspects of temporality: order (chronological versus anachronistic), speed (from ellipsis and summary to descriptive pauses) and frequency (singular versus iterative narration). The chapter on 'Mood' introduces the distinction between the narrator (who tells) and the focalizer (who sees). In his analysis of 'Voice', Genette discusses the various instances of narrative enunciation, in relation to their qualitative position and the level on which they function. Hence, Genette is less interested in the logic of events constituting a plot (in contrast to Todorov) than in the specific modalities of the process of narration itself. In this respect, the influence of Proust's novel of consciousness, which is Genette's exemplary narrative, on his narratological model can hardly be underestimated.

In spite of the at times violent criticism that Genette's proposals have met – a criticism with which the author has endeavoured to cope in his *Nouveaux discours du récit* (1983) – his model undoubtedly remains a stimulating landmark in narratology to the present day.

After the heydays of structuralism, the oeuvres of Greimas, Genette and Todorov have manifested interesting evolutions, in which, perhaps predictably, continuity and discontinuity are precariously balanced. However, one cannot state that, in the cases of these scholars, a major shift of 'structuralism' towards 'poststructuralism' can be witnessed. The protagonists of French structuralist poetics have never drastically deconstructed their initial structuralist project, even though the rather naive dreams of a truly objectivist science of meaning have been largely abandoned. Instead of taking recourse to a deconstructionist or rhetorical stand – as the later Barthes and the members of the *Tel Quel* group have successfully done – Greimas, Genette and Todorov have, each in their own way, tried to compensate for the recognized limitations of structuralism in two ways. On the one hand, they have considerably broadened their field of interest; on the other hand, they refrained from certain structuralist premises and pretensions.

In general, Greimas remains the most typical representative of 'orthodox' structuralist thinking. In fact, he never gave up his dream of constructing a major semiotic theory which would encompass all meaningful phenomena in society: various kinds of texts, but also rituals, human behaviour, emotions, etc. To this end, he continually tried to formulate an adequate metalanguage that would guarantee the scientific character of his enterprise. The landmark for this variant of semiotic research remains the invaluable two-volume *Sémiotique. Dictionnaire raisonné de la théorie du langage*, written/edited in close collaboration with J. Courtés (1979). In fact, Greimas's theory is constructed as a set of hierarchically related metalanguages: the level of 'descriptive' metalanguage is needed to analyse 'objects', but it has also to be validated on the superior levels of a 'methodological' and eventually of an 'epistemological' metalanguage. In the case of Greimas and his followers, theoretical conceptualization and meticulous analysis are thus closely related, since they are intended to sustain and to stimulate one another. In the two volumes *Du Sens* (1970) and *Du Sens II* (1983), Greimas broadens the field of application of his semiotics considerably. He convincingly argues the semantic and narrative dimension at work in all kinds of semiotic constructs: social conventions, a story, a description, as well as fragments from a scholarly essay or a cookbook.

On the other hand, the theory has undergone substantial modifications as well.

Gradually, a shift is noticeable from textual analysis towards the analysis of subjectivity and human experience. Modalities have come to fulfil a decisive role in the discursive construction of narrative sequences and of the rhetoric of subjectivity. Complementary to the level of the enunciated (the story as it is), Greimas stresses the importance of the level of enunciation, i.e. the basic contract between sender and receiver which ought to optimize communication.

From this point of view *Sémiotique des passions. Des états de choses aux états d'âme* (1991) is of crucial importance. In this book, written in close collaboration with Jacques Fontanille, traditionally philosophical subject matter, human passions and emotions, are considered from a semiotic point of view. As a consequence, in order to investigate a passion such as jealousy, the authors start from daily intuitions and their codification in dictionaries in order to describe the actantial and narrative construction of the passion. Next, they reconsider its manifestation in diverse discursive contexts, thus demonstrating both the homogeneity and the crucial variations that are at stake.

In contrast to this thoroughly scientific approach, the short essay *De l'imperfection* (1987) tries to deal with the aesthetic experience in a much more fragmentary, literary style. Taking semiotics as an axiology, Greimas pleads in favour of the so-called 'small ontologies': the delights of secrets and seductions, passion and bodily sensations. The strong scientific rhetoric of his other texts is here replaced by a more frivolous diction, in which examples taken from literature play a central role. Yet, it is not a coincidence that this text was published by a rather obscure publishing house, and that Greimas refrained from referring to it in his other, 'more serious' writings. The same denial (or is it mere ignorance?) is to be found in overviews of French structuralism as well.

Gérard Genette handles the problematic aspects of structuralism in a different way. Like Greimas, most of his work remains largely within the boundaries of the structuralist paradigm. However, at the same time, Genette has managed to establish his own authoritative position, despite the ongoing debates regarding structuralism, owing to his undogmatic position.

In retrospect, one is indeed struck by the fact that Genette has, almost from his early start as a literary scholar, never confined his research to the text as an autonomous, closed universe of meaning. Quite on the contrary, he has taken into account a much broader dimension of textuality. His *Introduction à l'architexte* (1979) studies the problematic relation between individual texts and the categorial concepts of genre and mode. *Palimpsestes* (1982) complicates matters even further, focusing on the crucial question of intertextuality. Genette limits himself in this book to the study of explicit forms of intertextual rewriting (in his terminology the subcategory of 'transtextuality'). Relying on a large variety of examples, taken from different historical periods and different national literatures, he explores a number of transformational relations, ranging from mere imitation to parodies, pastiches and more complex forms of textual transposition. *Seuils* (1987) treats the 'paratextual' elements, which tend to surround a text without constituting an integrated part of it: preface, footnotes, titles, mottoes, blurbs ... This paratextual information, which symbolizes the problematic borders of a text, may fulfil several functions, either in a constructive (affirmative) or in a more deconstructive (ironic or polemic) way.

These publications indicate how Genette tries to account for a large variety of textual phenomena in a deliberate attempt to overcome the limitations of classic structuralism. On the other hand, they still display a major 'structuralist' concern. Instead of drastically deconstructing the concept of text altogether, Genette prefers to explore the marginal zones of inter- and paratextuality in a systematic, coherent and encompassing way. Even the boundaries of texts are thus scrutinized, systematically classified and accordingly analysed. So, in the end, the ideal of a taxonomic structure remains fundamentally unaltered, even though the author frequently underlines the hazardous dimension of his own enterprise. Similarly, his analysis of literary examples pays hardly any attention to their textual and contextual specificity.

Genette's latest publications – the two volumes of L'oeuvre de l'Art, Immanence et transcendance (1994) and La relation esthétique (1997a) – offer a very broad philosophical view on general aesthetics. The first volume considers art as a fascinating combination of immanence (art as a specific object in its own right) and transcendence. The latter term refers to the various ways in which a work of art transcends its own material status: works of art may be copied, transformed and reconsidered throughout history. In this respect, Genette's ideas may be seen as a non-deconstructionist answer to Derrida's concept of iterability and his critique on the logic of origin. The second volume considers the different relation between the work of art and the consumer of art. As such, it complements the rather 'intrinsic' approach of the first book by taking into account the psychological aspects of the aesthetic attention, the aesthetic judgement and, ultimately, the artistic function.

Finally, there is the influential work by Tzvetan Todorov. Although his earliest books were largely consistent with the expectations of structuralism as a scientific framework, Todorov's work was already at that time characterized by an enormous diversity. Instead of opting for a lifelong realization of one and the same theoretical and methodological project (like Greimas did), Todorov prefers to demonstrate the applicability of structuralist thinking to a large variety of literary and cultural phenomena. This very broad field of interest results in a large number of fascinating essays, which formulate a certain problem in a perspicuous yet sometimes rather suggestive manner, rather than analysing it extensively.

Perhaps Todorov's most central text – and obviously one which has become a 'classic' in its own right – is his Introduction à la littérature fantastique (1970). In this brilliant essay, Todorov tackles a major problem in modern Western literature, i.e. the genre of 'fantastic literature'. To this end, several dimensions of literary research are combined in a highly original manner, resulting in the first systematic approach to the genre. First of all, Todorov tries to reconstruct, in accordance with the principles of structuralist narratology at that time, the underlying patterns that yield this 'fantastic effect'. On the level of syntax, the specific concatenation of events contributes strongly to the effect of suspense. On the level of the semantic and thematic organization, Todorov discriminates between themes of the I (e.g. metamorphosis or the multiple personality) and themes of the other (e.g. sexuality, cruelty and death). This apparently intrinsic approach of the genre is, however, supplemented by an analysis of the reading experience. Indeed, fantastic literature leads to a fundamental 'hesitation' in the reader, since he/she cannot decide whether the story is to be believed or not. Hence, the fantastic is situated on the borderline between the marvellous and the uncanny. Finally, Todorov's essay also considers the historical evolution of the genre, an interest that is marginal in most structuralist texts. In fact, Todorov claims that, in our times, the main function of the fantastic, i.e. talking about 'forbidden' taboos, has largely been taken over by psychoanalysis.

In his recent research, Todorov has explored fully these various trajectories. In his work, he has succeeded in demonstrating brilliantly the advantages of a structuralist perspective, while at the same time he transcends the limitations of classic structuralist thinking by taking into account historical components and the experience of the reader as well.

From the 1980s onwards, the growing resonance of Bakhtin's ideas on polyphony and dialogicity has definitely become a major impetus in Todorov's work. Instead of adopting a strictly 'objectivist' point of view, Todorov starts to explore the intricate tension between alterity and identity in various contexts. Several books deal with the images strategically constructed and legitimized by subjects (groups, cultures ...) in dealing with the both seductive and threatening presence of a radical otherness. However, in reverse, this conception of the other fundamentally influences the conception of one's own identity as well. *La conquête de l'Amérique. La question de l'autre* (1982) investigates the coming into being of the 'new' world in the discourse of the Spanish conquistadores, whereas in *Face à l'extrême* (1991) the western trauma of Auschwitz and the excesses of totalitarian societies is discussed.

Nous et les autres (1989) reconstructs the self-image (and the image of otherness) in the history of French civilization. Here as well, the scholarly analysis gradually moves into a more committed strategy of writing, in which the subjectivity of the author and the constructive character of his own narrative are deliberately exploited. In fact, Todorov's recent publications are clearly marked by an important 'ethical turn'. The former anti-individualistic structuralist has become a genuine 'man of letters' who explicitly argues for a new, non-naive form of existential and ethical humanism, in close dialogue with the ideas of French philosophers such as Montaigne and Rousseau. According to Todorov, we have to learn how to cultivate our 'imperfect garden' (*Le jardin imparfait*, 1998): the expression stems from Montaigne. The fact that he recently published an intellectual biography of Benjamin Constant – a narrative of an individual, in his specific socio-historical constellation – is, in view of this humanistic reorientation, hardly a coincidence, nor a surprise.

Dirk de Geest

Further reading and works cited

Culler, J. *Structuralist Poetics*. London, 1975.
Dosse, F. *History of Structuralism*, 2 vols. Minneapolis, MN, 1997.
Genette, G. *Introduction à l'architexte*. Paris, 1979.
—. *Narrative Discourse*. Ithaca, NY, 1980.
—. *Palimpsestes*. Paris, 1982.
—. *Nouveau discours du récit*. Paris, 1983.
—. *L'Oeuvre de l'Art I: Immanence et transcendance*. Paris, 1994.
—. *L'Oeuvre de l'Art II. La relation esthétique*. Paris, 1997a.
—. *Seuils. Paratexts*. Cambridge, 1997b.
Greimas, A. J. *Sémantique structurale*. Paris, 1966.
—. *Du Sens. Essais sémiotiques*. Paris, 1970.
—. *Du Sens II. Essais sémiotiques*. Paris, 1983.
—. *De l'Imperfection*. Périgueux, 1987.
— and Courtés, J. *Sémiotique. Dictionnaire raisonné de la théorie du langage*. Paris, 1986.
— and Fontanille. J. *The Semiotics of Passions*. Minneapolis, 1992.
Scholes, R. E. *Structuralism in Literature*. New Haven, CT, 1974.
Todorov, T. *Qu'est-ce que le structuralisme. 2: Poétique*. Paris, 1968.
—. *Grammaire du* Décaméron. The Hague, 1969.
—. *Introduction à la littérature fantastique*. Paris, 1970.

—. *Mikhail Bakhtine. Le principe dialogique*. Paris, 1981.
—. *La Conquête de l'Amérique*. Paris, 1982.
—. *Nous et les autres*. Paris, 1989.
—. *Face à l'extrême*. Paris, 1991.
—. *Benjamin Constant: la passion démocratique*. Paris, 1997.
—. *Le Jardin imparfait. La pensée humaniste en France*. Paris, 1998.

34. Louis Althusser (1918–1990) and his Circle

Louis Althusser and the more notable members of the circle of students and colleagues that worked closely with him during most of the 1960s (especially Etienne Balibar and Pierre Macherey) are commonly regarded as structural marxists, that is as marxists who adopted the language and general aims of structuralism. The problem with such a categorization is not merely that it remains too general, but rather that it was categorically false. A careful reader of the texts published during Althusser's lifetime could see the ways in which his concerns were not only different from but opposed to those of the structuralist movement of the time. Now, with the posthumous publication of thousands of pages of essays and books, Althusser's very critical and even hostile view of structuralism from the early 1960s has been made very clear. This is not simply a matter of taxonomy: it is impossible to understand Althusser's approach to literature and philosophy without seeing the way in which his major texts were designed as critiques of the fundamental tenets of the structuralist activity.

Perhaps the best way to measure Althusser's distance from and opposition to the structuralist method of textual interpretation is simply to turn to the theory of reading that he proposes in the introduction to what remains his best-known work, *Reading Capital*. The intervention that Althusser intended the work to be, of course, can only be understood in relation to the precise historical and philosophical moment or conjuncture that Althusser hoped to modify. In 1965 structuralism neared the height of its influence. The following year would see the publication of two special issues of important journals devoted to the topic of structuralism. Roland Barthes's manifesto 'For a Structural Analysis of Narratives' was the introductory essay for an issue of *Communications* on structuralism that included such figures as Gérard Genette, Claude Bremond, Tzvetan Todorov and Umberto Eco. A number of Jean-Paul Sartre's *Les Temps Modernes* included essays on the notion of structure by Pierre Bourdieu and Maurice Godelier, as well as an essay extremely critical of structuralism by a member of Althusser's circle Pierre Macherey.

What explained the interest structuralism inspired at this time? It seemed to herald a new scientific understanding of literature whose scientificity was guaranteed by its close relation to linguistics, the sole social science that was thought to deserve the name. According to this method, literature was no longer a realm of original creations by uniquely endowed men and women that concealed hidden meanings and exhibited a beauty that required long experience to perceive, let alone fully to appreciate. Instead, literature was nothing more than a formal system of possibilities, a rule-governed combination of elements into complex entities. An author had no more control over the emergence of these complex entities than a speaker in everyday life has over grammar. Indeed, to speak a sentence or to write a novel is to submit to a set of rules and to enter into a system of which the 'agent' is almost always unaware. Further, if linguistics has discovered the rules governing the combination of phonemes into morphemes and morphemes into words and words into sentences, we have yet to identify the rules governing the combination of sentences into a still higher unity called discourse. To read a text would be to account for the function of every one of its elements in the structure of the whole, as well as to discover the rules governing the combinations of elements into a coherent whole.

Althusser, of course, was a philosopher, not a literary critic. But structuralism had entered the field of philosophy as well, through such figures as Martial Guéroult) who sought to reconstruct the architectonic unity of the statements that comprised a given philosophical text. To a certain extent, Althusser and his circle regarded such an approach as an open rejection of the impressionistic and careless readings that were all too typical of much pre-Second World War French philosophy. In another sense, however, it seemed merely to be an intensification of a traditional reading of philosophical texts as more or less coherently organized wholes. Literary and philosophical structuralism were for Althusser intimately related and both had their origins in Aristotle's notion of literature as the most philosophical of the modes in which reality might be represented. Both sought to demonstrate the existence of internal orders whose sequences followed a chain of cause and effect or argument and conclusion that moved from a logical starting point to an end. It is not surprising, then, that by the mid-1960s at the latest, Althusser viewed structuralism as a variant of a traditional idealism or metaphysics.

It was not that Althusser rejected the idea that previously non-scientific areas of inquiry, especially in the so-called human sciences, could attain scientific knowledge; on the contrary, he felt very strongly especially at this time that marxism represented an epistemological break or revolution that, if permitted, could be set on the road to scientific knowledge of historical phenomenon. His notion of science, however, drawn from such figures as Bachelard and Canguilhem, precluded the notion that a scientific approach to literature or culture would resemble physics or biology or would necessarily entail the use of mathematical models or even quantitative techniques. Such notions could only result from the imposition of *a priori* principles on a field that might well demand different principles, the rationalism proper to it or the region of which it was a part which remained to be formulated in the process of and not before knowing it. Such a regional rationality, to use Bachelard's expression, could by elaborated on the condition that one would identify and reject the concepts whose application appeared 'obvious' or inescapable.

A scientific understanding of the history of human societies, Althusser announced at the beginning of *Reading Capital*, would necessarily begin with 'the most dramatic and difficult trial of all, the discovery of and training in the meaning of the "simplest" acts of existence: seeing, listening, speaking, reading – the acts which relate men to their works, and to those works thrown in their faces, their "absences of works"' (1975, 16). Althusser himself will begin with the question, 'what is it to read' (1975, 15). Rather than attempt to answer this question immediately, as if one could reason and think in a social, historical and philosophical vacuum, or at least could create such a vacuum through a simple will to objectivity, Althusser first examines the notions that govern reading as it is actually practised. Such an examination is far from easy in that its object is among the apparently 'simplest', most obvious acts, the nature of which appears to be an unquestionable given. Althusser, in an assertion that is at least as relevant to the study of literature as to the study of philosophy, argues that our notion of reading is dominated by 'a religious myth' (17). The model of all texts is the Bible; the practice of reading follows the tradition of scriptural interpretation. The Bible is the word of God and as such is the expression of the Divine Logos. If it appears internally inconsistent or contradictory, if certain of its narratives appear incomplete, fragmented or even incomprehensible, the fault is necessarily that of the interpreter. The inspired reader of scripture knows that the text as a whole is an 'expressive totality in which every part is a pars totalis, immediately expressing the whole that it inhabits in person' (1975, 17). In this way reading is an act of reduction of the surface of the text, which presents the appearance of disorder, to the unity beneath the surface.

The relevance of the 'religious myth of reading' (1975, 17) to the study of literature from Aristotle to structuralism is striking. The intelligibility of a text is a function of its internal coherence; a reading consists of showing the way in which every phrase, word and image expresses a central meaning or theme, or alternately, of showing the way in which the smallest identifiable element (even to the letters of which words are composed) possesses a necessary function in the structure of the whole. In fact, this model so dominates our thinking that to merely to question it seems destined to lead to its inverse, the idea that texts are indeterminate and can (be made to) mean anything. To guide him between the extremes of a religious dogmatism (which can masquerade as a science of the text inspired by linguistics) and an empty scepticism that rejoins religion to the extent that it declares texts, like sacred objects, unknowable and ineffable, Althusser turned to 'the first man ever to have posed the problem of reading and, in consequence of writing: Spinoza' (Althusser 1975, 16). Althusser read the *Tractatus Theologico-Politicus* with great care, noting Spinoza's argument that all previous interpreters of scripture had negated and denied the text in its actual state. They approached what was composite, fragmentary and contradictory in the Bible not to explain these, its real characteristics, but to explain them away. Two opposing approaches to texts thus emerged: do we carefully describe and then explain the text as it is in what will inevitably be its real disorder? Or do we reduce this disorder to a more primary order, dividing the text into the essential and necessary and the inessential and the accidental?

Althusser carefully studied the way Marx read the texts of classical political economy and found that he read by drawing a line of demarcation through these texts (although not always and not consciously). The function of this line was to make visible the specific contradiction that these texts exhibited without resolution or even acknowledgement. In the course of their arguments, these works produced conclusions or even in some cases merely evidence that did not support but actually undermined their conclusion but without these discrepancies ever being noted. To describe these phenomena Althusser uses the language of vision: every text is divided between what is visible and what is invisible within it and to it. How can what a text manifests or shows be called invisible? Althusser at this point takes his leave of Spinoza and turns to psychoanalysis, a discipline whose importance in his thought can hardly be overestimated. In saying that what is invisible in a text is not hidden, Althusser refers to the language of psychic defences: the text not only represses, but denies, isolates and splits off those incompatible elements it produces. Althusser calls a reading that seeks precisely to understand a text as much by what it represses as by what it intends to show or say a 'symptomatic reading' (1975, 28).

The use of this language, however, is bound to raise questions. Freud used the language of the defences to describe the forms of conflict proper to human individuals. Does Althusser then hope to trace the defences proper to a given text back to the psyche of its author? We inevitably want to ask, 'whose conflicts are they, anyway?' To the immense chagrin of his numerous and loquacious Anglo-American critics, Althusser dismissed such questions (who makes history, whose actions create social structures) as variants of the model of such questions: who created the universe? To answer such a question is to accept the theological notion of a Creator; Althusser preferred instead to answer the question with another question: what leads us to ask who? The false question (whose conflicts does a text manifest?) can be replaced with a more productive one: what is the cause, or causes of the conflicts proper to texts? Althusser's answer will fortuitously explain not only the causes of textual contradiction, but even of the impulse to ask 'who', that is to know historical phenomena by reducing them to an origin or creator, not God, of course, but Man. To explain the antagonisms that divide every text (including Marx's and his own) he will refer to the existence of something else: ideology.

In the works of the mid-1960s Althusser defined ideology very much in the spirit of Marx's famous discussion of base and superstructure in the *Preface to the Critique of Political Economy*. On the base of a given society (the technological means of production and the relations of production) arises a corresponding system of ideas, culture, religion and law (which often in different and even opposing ways justifies or gives an air of inevitability to the existing order). Ideology is 'the lived relation between men and their world' (Althusser 1970, 213), but one which is primarily unconscious, determining individuals' actions without their being aware of this determination. Following Spinoza, Althusser called this an 'imaginary' relation that is simultaneously illusion and allusion. Individuals' beliefs are not strictly speaking false; it is rather that they invert the relations between cause and effect. (Marx used the figure of the camera obscura which turns the scene viewed through its apparatus upside down to illustrate this notion.) Most commonly individuals believe that they are free, free to work or not to work, free to succeed or fail, to become a garment worker or the chief executive officer of a multinational corporation, depending on whether they have the strength of character or the determination. As Marx put it in *Capital*, they view themselves as 'determined only by their own free will' (1977, 280) and hence remain unaware of the causes external to them that determine them to will and to act as they do. And in the same way that Galileo's discovery of an infinite and thus decentred universe threatened the Roman Church and the doctrines that justified its domination, so a scientific knowledge of history, which would explain events by their causes, could only upset the dominant ideology, that is the ideology that justified the domination of the ruling class. Therefore what Althusser regarded as Marx's scientific discovery of the forms of determination proper to human societies could only be threatening to a host of ideologies which would work tirelessly to discredit and defeat marxism, attempting to obscure by any means necessary a knowledge of social phenomena through their causes.

Few areas were as invested with ideological 'meanings' as art in general and literature specifically. Pierre Macherey's *A Theory of Literary Production*, a work written in the context of the seminars Althusser organized among his students between 1961 and 1968, critically examines the notions that have dominated the study of literature. Macherey treats these notions as 'epistemological obstacles', to use Bachelard's phrase, that block the development of an adequate knowledge of the phenomenon we provisionally refer to as literature. Again, as was the case with Althusser, there can be no question of simply returning to an absolute starting point free of all preconceptions from which we might construct a coherent theory. In *Spontaneous Philosophy* Althusser wrote, 'every space is always already occupied and one can only take a position against the adversary who already occupies that position' (1990, 144). Accordingly, the first half of A *Theory of Literary Production* is devoted to the identification and deconstruction of the theories that occupy the field of literary criticism and interpretation. Macherey finds that although these theories may differ significantly in their conceptualization of the nature and causes of literature, they are, despite their vastly different origins and orientations, united around a single ideological objective. The history of literary criticism is nothing less than the history of attempts to deny the material and historical nature of what we now call literature. To begin with, for a good part of its history, literary criticism, as the name implies, was less concerned about the knowledge than the judgement of works of art. For Macherey, it was not simply that critics used 'timeless' criteria to dismiss and reject popular and even avant-garde forms of literature and thereby preserve the canon that appeared to justify bourgeois civilization. It was even more that the operation of judgement, whether its verdict in a given case was positive or negative, told us nothing about the work in question, only whether or not, or to what extent, it conformed to an ideal norm by definition situated outside literature in its actual existence. For Macherey, the notion that the object of criticism is to discriminate between good and bad literary texts, and then to 'appreciate' the former while dismissing the latter is as absurd as the botanist insisting that only beautiful flowers are worthy objects of study.

It is true, of course, that with the critique of the very idea of a canon, such an approach to literature has fallen into disrepute and now appears only at the margins of academic literary studies. Other means of rejecting the objective existence of literary texts and thus of rendering them unknowable, however, continue to flourish. They claim to seek to make possible a knowledge of literary texts, but they do so only by negating the work in its actual existence, reducing to something other than itself. One of the most common and enduring forms of interpretation that explains a text by reducing it to a truth outside of it is that which views literature as the creation of an author. The very idea of creation betrays the theological origins of the notion of author. Like God, the author creates something out of nothing, an original before which there was nothing. The author begins with an idea and proceeds to realize (if, that is, the individual in question has the proper strength of will) that idea in a work of art or literature. The work of art takes shape in and is the work of a single individual who is its origin and agent. As such, in our societies at least, the author is also owner of the intellectual property that he or she creates. This legal fact alone compels us to recognize that if the world outside the author has any role in the creative process, it is a purely secondary or incidental role; it is present, if at all, as the influences that form the background to creation. If we truly seek the meaning of the work, from this perspective, we had better seek it in the mind of its creator: the intention behind it, of course, but also the secret sorrows and dimly remembered childhood traumas that the author might have transmuted through the alchemy of creation into a genuine work of art.

These ideas, so dominant even now that students can be persuaded to question them only with difficulty, are among the most tenacious obstacles to the study of literature. The notion of creation offers a mystical explanation for the existence of literary works: we seek the causes of a work in an author, as if it already existed and needed only to be translated into speech, colour or sound. But when we seek the causes of this cause, the origin of the origin, we are forced to take refuge in (to paraphrase Spinoza) the sanctuary of ignorance:

genius, talent, spontaneity. For Macherey, these notions are not simply myths that replace a real problem with an insoluble mystery, but are logical consequences of the legal ideology that assigns to every act an actor to be credited or held responsible, that addresses or, as Althusser would later say, 'interpellates' individuals as subjects, that is as actors and owners of themselves who are 'determined by their own free will alone' (1977, 280). Instead Macherey argues that the author is not a creator at all but a producer who neither makes the 'raw material' with which he works nor controls the 'means of production' which allow him to write anything at all. Writing becomes a collective, not individual, process in which authors are constrained to produce according to historical determinations. Literary works thus do not express the intentions or even the mind of their author which, even if they are inscribed in the work, do not control it: they are not made in their creator's image.

There are numerous theories of literature, however, that deny a central role to the author and in doing so might appear to recognize the material existence of the literary work. Marxism is often associated with the position, for example, that literature 'reflects' or 'represents' the reality of its historical moment, apart from which it cannot be understood. In the light of the marxism of Althusser and Macherey, however, this position appears inadequate. While they agree that no work can be understood outside of its relation to the historical determinations that make it what it is, neither the concept of 'reflection' nor that of 'representation' allow us to understand this determination. In fact, such notions rob the work of its material existence by arguing that it 'reflects' a reality external to it as if it were merely a shadow or a dim, fleeting image of what is real. The work, according to such theories, yields its meaning only when it is exchanged for or disappears into the history outside of itself which is its truth. There is something paradoxical about a Marxism that makes literature intelligible only by regarding it as insubstantial (immaterial?), reducible to something more primary beyond itself.

Of course, in opposition, twentieth-century versions of formalism and structuralism (in many cases, explicitly invoking Aristotle) have argued that the meaning of a work derives from the necessity of its form rather than from the author's intentions or psychology (the New Critics in the US even identified an 'intentional fallacy') or from its historical context. The model of a great work was one in which every incident, character and image conspired together to produce the harmony of the whole. Often, especially in the English-speaking world, this view rendered the literary work independent of historical and political determinations, a self-enclosed, self-sufficient whole that stood outside (and usually above) social struggles. But there were other, more complex versions of formalism. György Lukács, steeped in Hegel, argued that in understanding a given historical epoch 'the truth is the whole' (Hegel 1977, 11) (which bourgeois thought artificially divides into separate factors each of which must be studied in isolation). Invoking Aristotle, Lukács sought to show that the architectonic unity of the work of art was nothing less than a recreation of the repressed totality. He cited the particular case of Balzac, a reactionary author who, because he surrendered to the demands of formal unity, produced a body of work that, by revealing the hidden totality of his historical moment, was objectively revolutionary.

From Macherey's perspective, such approaches also refused the materiality or irreducibility of the text. Formalism was by no means incompatible with a normative theory that judges works (in this case according to their degree of internal coherence): Lukács, for example, found Thomas Mann's novels 'superior' to those of Kafka or Joyce. Even more importantly, however, formalism in all its variants itself rejects the objective existence of the text precisely by declaring it to be a totality, each of whose parts contributes to the structure of the whole. Such an approach must distort the text into coherence, rejecting as inessential all that does not contribute to the harmony of the whole, fictively resolving and reconciling the conflicts that disturb every work. For even the most sophisticated formalists, those identified with the structuralist movement, literary works only seem disordered and contradictory on the surface; hidden within them (and texts are thus endowed with a 'depth') is the unity that must be uncovered. Again, Macherey draws on Spinoza's denunciation of biblical interpretation as it was practised before him: commentators have not explained scripture as it is in its disorder, with its discrepancies and inconsistencies, but have explained it away, substituting for it a text of their own device.

For Macherey and Althusser, the literary work and the process of literary production are real, material and historical. Works are neither expressions of a mind nor reflections of a history external to them; they are not coherent totalities and they are all surface, concealing nothing. The disorder and conflict that texts exhibit are the inescapable consequences of their historical existence; how might they escape the struggles that traverse the history of which they are a part?

In opposition to Brecht, whom Althusser admired and wrote about, the alienation effect is not one possible dramatic narrative among others from which it would be distinguished by raising problems without resolving them and by preventing any suspension of disbelief on the part of the spectator. It is instead the effect proper to literature as such in that every text, including Brecht's, says more than it wants to say, exhibits more than it knows or desires, and thereby makes visible the contradictions of the ideology it dramatizes. This does not make art or literature subversive; it merely means that a symptomatic reading of literary texts, among many other realities, may yield a raw material that can be shaped into historical knowledge

Through the 1960s, Althusser's discussion of literature and art, as well as Macherey's work, focused on the problem of reading literature, particularly the 'internal relations' of texts as specific transformation of ideology. With his essay, 'Ideology and Ideological State Apparatuses', his concerns shifted somewhat. Althusser went to great lengths to show that ideology was not a matter of ideas or even representations but of material practices that existed in the form of apparatuses and institutions. Thus literature and art could no longer be understood at the level of the text; one instead had to inquire into the institutions, legal, educational and cultural, in which literary texts were produced and 'read' (interpreted and taught at various levels). Further, Althusser's essay compels us to ask not how individuals come to write or read a text, but how the institution of literature 'interpellates' (that is, constitutes or positions) individuals as authors or readers. Althusser's essay on ideology had an enormous influence (although he himself had little more to say in this vein); its effects may be seen in Foucault's *Discipline and Punish* (which is simultaneously a continuation and a critique of Althusser's notion of ideology), as well as in the field of cultural studies, for which Althusser's text is a kind of founding document.

Warren Montag

Further reading and works cited

Althusser, L. *For Marx*. New York, 1970.
—. *Lenin and Philosophy*. New York, 1971.
—. *Reading Capital*. London, 1975.
—. *Philosophy and the Spontaneous Philosophy of the Scientists*. New York, 1990.

Elliott, G. *Althusser*. London, 1987.
Foucault, M. *Discipline and Punish*. New York, 1995.
Hegel, G. W. F. *Phenomenology of Spirit*. London, 1977.
Macherey, P. *A Theory of Literary Production*. Boston, 1978.
—. *The Object of Literature*. Cambridge, 1995.
—. *In a Materialist Way*, ed. W. Montag. London, 1998.
Marx, K. *Capital, Volume 1*. New York, 1977.
Sartre, J.-P. *Les Temps Modernes*, no. 246. Paris, 1945–.
Spinoza, B. *Tractatus Theologico-Politicus*. New York, 1991.

35. Reception Theory and Reader-Response: Hans-Robert Jauss (1922–1997), Wolfgang Iser (1926–) and the School of Konstanz

The Konstanz School is named after the university founded in the early 1960s in southern Germany on the shore of the Bodensee, or Lake of Konstanz, and it denotes the group of scholars and critics who established in the late 1960s and developed through to the late 1980s the critical orientation known variously as the aesthetics of reception (*Rezeptionsästhetik*), the aesthetics of literary response and effect (*Wirkungsästhetik*), or more broadly as reader-response theory. As a fairly loosely affiliated and liberal academic community, it drew together researchers from various German universities and also formed international links, especially with France and the USA. Its ongoing work was published in a series of volumes, largely untranslated, from 1964 until the early 1980s, under the general title *Poetik und Hermeneutik* (*Poetics and Hermeneutics*). As Paul de Man has observed, the linkage of these two terms indicates the ambition of the project: to unite the formalistic and rhetorical approaches to literature with the interpretative – to understand at once how the literary work is made, how it works and takes effect, how it signifies and what it means. All these approaches are to be incorporated under the aegis of a theory of reception or response. The two most celebrated members of the Konstanz School are Hans-Robert Jauss and Wolfgang Iser, and their work will be the focus of this essay.

A range of philosophical and theoretical influences bear upon the critical positions of Jauss and Iser, which are importantly different from each other, though both centrally affirm the crucial function of reception in the constitution of the work of art, specifically the literary text. Both critics are situated, notwithstanding their claims to radical positions, in firm relation to the major German philosophical tradition that emanates from Kant, and – that major late current deriving from, even as it seeks to reorient, Kantian thought – provides the philosophical grounding for their theorizing. The filiation is from the phenomenology of Edmund Husserl through its development in the reception theory of Hans-Georg Gadamer, Roman Ingarden and the Geneva School, but other approaches – psychoanalytic, sociological and historical – are employed where they are felt to be productive. Reader-response theory seeks to be both eclectic and syncretic.

The Konstanz School is a major tributary, then, to that current of literary criticism which has been generally characterized as the 'turn to' or 'return of the reader' (Freund 1987) and which emphasizes the primacy, or at least the co-primacy, of reception – in particular, reading – in the constitution of the literary text. The reader and the act of reading assume centre stage for this criticism, which seeks to theorize the activity of reading literature, to explore its dynamics, to define its elements and to exemplify and analyse its workings with regard to specific texts. The reader – more abstractly, the process of reading – produces the text as a living entity, an aesthetic object – unread, the text is inert, without effect or value. The literary text is, moreover, a highly complex and special form of language and its reception is equally complex – it is not simply a message issued from an author to be received and deciphered by a reader. Rather, it stimulates both response and interpretation, and these together constitute the activity of reading which, rather than the author alone, creates the literary *work* – something much more than the mere or literal *text*.

In its emphasis on the role of the reader, reception theory clearly, and at times explicitly, counters the assumption of the primacy of the text propounded in New Criticism, which was the dominant critical persuasion when the Konstanz School began to form itself. The New Critical privileging of the textual object, assumed to be largely autonomous – the individual lyric being the most usual, because most convenient, example – is challenged by an approach that seeks to give equal or greater importance and attention to the reader as subject, whose response is understood to be in part directed or stimulated by the text but also to be an exercise of the reader's own imagination, based on knowledge and experience. What has been described as the 'traditional, rigidly hierarchical, view of the text-reader relationship' (Freund 1987, 4) in New Criticism, with the text dominant, and both reader and context firmly subordinated to it, gives way to a theory of the mutuality of text, reader and context in the constitution of the literary work or aesthetic object. Accordingly, reader-response theory (particularly in the work of Jauss and Iser) engages with other critical currents, marxist theory, structuralism, psychoanalytic theory, communications theory and others, since they emphasize variously these different constitutive forces: text, reader, context. It finds in them valuable insights but also, by and large, a restrictive and distorting emphasis on one or other of the constituents. It might be objected that reader-response theory itself gives, by definition, undue precedence to the reader, but its own claim is that it redresses the balance of previous critical theories which have tended toward merely formalist or ideologically motivated models, as in the case of New Criticism and marxism respectively.

Within this general position there are, as I have said, important differences between the two major representatives of the Konstanz School, Jauss and Iser. In part, these derive from their differing academic and intellectual orientations – Jauss a scholar of French literature, with interests covering a wide and diverse historical range, from medieval genre study to the work of Baudelaire and Valéry, but mainly engaged with poetry; Iser a professor of English, whose area of concern is principally located in the more restricted and homogeneous, but also more popular and accessible area of the English novel from its eighteenth-century beginnings to the present day. Iser has clearly been more user-friendly, so to speak, so far as the Anglophone world of literary studies is concerned. More of Iser's work has been translated into English (largely by the author) and Iser has more frequently and consistently been the point of reference in the dissemination of *Rezeptionsästhetik* in Anglophone (and principally American) criticism. In the view of some, though, Jauss has remained the more important and substantial theorist of the two.

A crucial feature of Jauss's development of reader response theory is his emphasis upon the diachronic – the dynamics of literary history. His aim has been to elaborate a historical approach to literature which will replace the assumption of tradition (particularly a national tradition) and the canonical frame established in the nineteenth century with an interrogation of them, drawing on evidence of the historical reception of literature and, more generally, on theorizing the critical and dialectical function of reading in relating and mediating earlier and current understandings of the literary work. This project is polemically adumbrated in Jauss's celebrated essay 'Literary History as a Challenge to Literary Theory', which was his inaugural lecture at Konstanz in 1967, and formed the first chapter of his book *Toward an Aesthetic of Reception*, published in America together with his other major work in English translation, *Aesthetic Experience and Literary Hermeneutics*, both in 1982 (Jauss 1982a, 1982b). In this essay, Jauss challenges views of literary history as given, as a canonically established body of texts, in favour of a conception of that history as dynamic, a continual process of formation, in which the ceaseless interaction between the already received and established and the new and unprecedented in literature ensures an open, ultimately indeterminable though not indefinable dynamic of change and by the same token refuses any teleological idealism. The conception can be interestingly compared to T. S. Eliot's famous pronouncement in 'Tradition and the Individual Talent' that each 'really new' work of art alters the whole structure of the cultural tradition (Eliot 1951, 15). While Eliot's concern is with artistic *creation*, though, Jauss is engaged in theorizing the process of artistic and cultural *reception* – the ways in which the new artwork enters the domain of the already received. As he puts it, 'literature and art only obtain a history that has the character of a process when the succession of works is mediated not only through the producing subject but also through the consuming subject – through the interaction of author and public' (Jauss, 1982a, 15).

Accordingly, historical, social and cultural contexts are all highly important but not, as in the model of literary marxism relayed by Jauss, reducible to crudely determining or determined functions. Nor is the artistic function to be confined to history (Lukács is Jauss's target here), for the formal and rhetorical elements of the work are crucially active determinants and stimuli affecting, indeed producing, its reception and, more largely, inflecting the history of which it is part. (The concept of defamiliarization propounded in Russian formalism is important here.) However, formalist criticism's tendency to dehistoricize the artwork, or to internalize its history as specifically artistic evolution, must in turn be questioned by opening up much further the issue of how the formal qualities of the work stimulate its reception and consequently its impact on a wider social, cultural and historical situation. Jauss sees his project therefore as the 'attempt to bridge the gap between literature and history, between historical and aesthetic functions' (Jauss 1982a, 18), overcoming the limitations of both materialist and formalist approaches, the former viewed as giving undue attention to context, the historical determinations of literary production, the latter seen as overvaluing the text, the formal and aesthetic composition of the literary work, insufficiently related to conditions of historical change. Neither approach pays adequate attention to the reception of the text, the reader or audience or public, whose role for Jauss is crucial. That reception, moreover, is far from being a merely passive process – on the contrary, it is an active determinant in the continual process of historical and cultural formation, a dialectical process of mediation in which new encounters old and both undergo change. Moreover, this dialectic operates no less within the process of reception itself – habits of reading encounter the challenge of new and unprecedented literary works, responses are altered accordingly, and those changed responses work back in turn upon already received work, reformulating the whole literary-historical model. This implies the rejection of an established, positivistically based and purportedly objective canon of literature in favour of a more labile process of canon formation which acknowledges that the individual literary text and relations among texts, past and present, are not fixed but subject to the changes that their renewed reception (or lack of reception) produces. There is a residual conservatism here: Jauss is not seeking to do away with the process of canonization but rather to render it more dynamic, in conformity with what he terms the 'dialogical and at once processlike relationship between work, audience, and new work', forming an 'ongoing totalization' (Jauss 1982a, 19).

The essay concludes with the formulation of seven theses, elaborating further Jauss's new, reception-based model of literary history. Broadly, these seek to ensure that the theory steers a careful middle course between restrictive alternatives – more exactly, that it enables a balance of interests among these alternatives to be sustained. Thus, it must avoid 'the prejudices of historical objectivism' (Jauss 1982a, 20) and enable a conception of canon formation (thesis 1) but also avoid 'the threatening pitfalls of psychology' (Jauss 1982a, 22), that is the dangers of subjectivity, by holding to an 'objectifiable system of expectations', historically verifiable and culturally established (thesis 2). It must recognize the process of historical change but also acknowledge the force of the text's own appearance as new and contemporary (theses 3 and 4); attend to the patterns of evolution within the literary domain and also recognize the individual text's autonomy, giving both diachronic and synchronic analysis their due (theses 5 and 6); and, finally, register the text's relation to history in general but also more specifically to the history of literature in its bearing upon that wider history (thesis 7). These are large ambitions, and reflect perhaps the German tradition of synthetic inclusiveness which finds its apotheosis in Hegel, though Jauss is of course critical of Hegelian idealism. What one might call the 'both-and' tendency is, however, well represented in his theory.

The essay is seminal: most of Jauss's work can be viewed as an extension and elaboration of the theses set out there, applied and developed with reference to a range of areas – art history, genre criticism, medieval and modern French poetry. His other major translated work, *Aesthetic Experience and Literary Hermeneutics*, extends his thinking in broader philosophical terms and, as its title indicates, shifts the concern more toward a generalized and largely abstract elaboration of the relations between aesthetics and hermeneutics – put simply, between literary effect and meaning, respectively. He begins by taking issue with Adorno's aesthetic theory, which he sees as enforcing a view of art as effectual only in its critical and negative functions. Against this, Jauss seeks to endorse the positive pleasure that art provides, a pleasure which involves both an initial surrender of the recipient to the work of art and a process of aesthetic distancing – the Kantian shadow falls across much of Jauss's thinking here. Three 'fundamental categories' of aesthetic pleasure are distinguished and examined in their historical development through the western tradition, from classical antiquity through the medieval period to modernity. They are given Greek names: *poiesis* (the pleasure of making, of artistic creation or recreation), *aisthesis* (the pleasure in the reception of the artwork) and *catharsis* (the pleasure in the emotional communication effected in the artwork).

For Jauss, pleasure – more broadly, aesthetic experience – is important as the primary category of art and its reception, but it is no less important to consider its succession and outcome in understanding, which is where reflection, Jauss's other key term, applies. The two aspects or stages, experience and reflection, are phenomenologically distinct but yet related and both ineluctably embedded in history – here Jauss's debt to Gadamer is explicit. The hermeneutic or interpretative activity of the reader is examined not so much in general and abstract terms, in the way that aesthetic experience was analysed, as through more specific, though still fairly broadly conceived, instances, which occupy the later part of Jauss's study. These include identification with the hero and responses to the comic hero, as well as more closely focused discussions of French lyric, especially Baudelaire. It may be fair to say, however, that Jauss's treatment of aesthetic experience is more substantial and coherent than his discussion of hermeneutics, which tends to take on a more subsidiary and even incidental role in his theory.

The other major representative of the Konstanz School's theory of reception, Wolfgang Iser, may be seen as occupying a contrasting but also complementary position in relation to Jauss – Jauss himself, at least, has viewed Iser's concept of the 'implied reader' as productively partnering his own theorizing of the 'historical reader'. Iser's relatively more narrow focus, very largely limited to the English novel tradition, certainly contrasts with, and perhaps complements, Jauss's much broader ambit. Robert Holub has defined the difference nicely, seeing Jauss as occupied with 'the macrocosm of reception', Iser with 'the microcosm of response' (Holub 1984, 83). Iser's approach, correspondingly more text-based, has been seen as more in accordance therefore with Anglo-American critical traditions, which is why he has proved the more congenial theorist outside the German intellectual arena (Holub 1984, 1992). Iser's concern is with a phenomenology of reading and his most important intellectual debt is to the philosopher and aesthetician Roman Ingarden, while Jauss is engaged with the relation of aesthetics and hermeneutics and owes much in this respect to his teacher Hans-Georg Gadamer.

In his first major work of criticism (Iser 1974), Iser considers an extensive range of English narrative (from Bunyan to Beckett, as his subtitle announces) from the perspective of a phenomenological conception of the reading process. He coins the term 'implied reader' – derived, it is generally agreed, from Wayne Booth's celebrated conception of the 'implied author' (Booth 1961) – to personify a model of this process, in which meaning is established through the interaction of text and reader. Neither text nor reader has autonomy: the text depends on the reader for its meaning to be realized, and the meaning produced by the reader is controlled by the text. Iser's laudable efforts to explicate and theorize this balance of power, so to speak, in the act of reading tend, however, to produce and sustain a fundamental ambiguity and an uncertainty about the status of this 'reader', for which his theory has been criticized. The 'reader' tends at crucial points to become little more than a function of the text and the text in turn more or less simply the articulation of its reading, each pole of the reading relation apt to lose its vaunted polarity.

What is involved, then, in the 'act of reading' as understood phenomenologically in Iser's theory? Firstly, the literary text is viewed, not as an independent or autonomous object, but as an entity constituted in and by its reading, as an 'intentional' or 'hetero-nomous' object, to use Ingarden's terms (1973a, 1973b). Secondly, the text is indeterminate, in the sense that the 'reality' it describes or evokes is incomplete and requires the imaginative and ideational activity of the reader to develop and extend it, to 'realize' it, in effect. Unlike a real object, which is 'all there', so to speak, despite the partiality of any perception of it, the text, though in an elementary sense defined as a real object, a literary structure composed of a certain number of words, is only active and significant as a stimulus to the construction of a virtual world, which is open to any number of realizations ('concretizations', another of Ingarden's terms). On the basis of these fundamental conceptions, derived from phenomenology, Iser formulates a view of literary meaning which resides neither in the text (*qua* object) nor in the reader (*qua* subject) but in the interaction of the two, an interaction which is conditioned by its context. There are then three inseparable though distinguishable elements or aspects to the act of reading: the *text*, which directs its own reading but is also subject to indeterminacy; the *reader*, or more exactly the *reading process*, which realizes the text as the production of meaning through modes of concretization, involving progressive synthesizing of responses and information in order to obtain a coherent and significant result; and the *context* conditioning both text and reading, that is the social and historical norms and assumptions governing both production and reception of any text.

For Iser, though, it is the notion of indeterminacy that is most active and powerful in his scheme of the reading process so far as fiction is concerned, and it carries an evaluative charge. Any text is both available for and worth reading to the extent that it contains 'gaps' or 'blanks' (*Leerstellen*, literally 'empty places') which invite or stimulate the reader to undertake ideational activity in order to fill in these gaps, thus producing a meaning. Such gaps enable and indeed require the reader to contribute to the eventual literary *work*, which is the combination of both textual and reading process, but they do not open the text to the whim of purely subjective interpretation, since they are themselves constructed by the text and in a manner controlled and directed by it. (Here again a certain ambiguity in the apportioning of authority between text and reader is evident.) Ultimately, for Iser this process is valuable in that it promotes a kind of intersubjectivity, or more precisely a displacement of subjectivity, as the subject-reader engages with the object-text and the limits of the self are transcended through relation to the other. The text in its paradoxically limited indeterminacy stimulates the reader's freedom of imagination but resists the arbitrary licence of fantasy; conversely, the reader's ability to activate the text frees it from the illusion of dogmatic completeness and mobilizes its capacity for potentially infinite but, again paradoxically, not undetermined interpretation.

In its sustainedly careful balance and its thoughtful syncretism, Iser's theory merits our respect, but these very qualities are also perhaps what render it ultimately somewhat bland. Its very capaciousness becomes in a way suspect and its even and rather dry tenor give the impression of a slightly stultifying uniformity. Stanley Fish's notorious attack (Fish 1981) in which Iser's theory is denigrated as both uncontroversial and ultimately self-justifying – established not on fundamental epistemological grounds but on agreed protocols of reading which are essentially those of the liberal, cultured and educated European – is perhaps intemperate but also searching, and Iser does not fully engage with it in his response (Iser 1981). Also, while Iser marshals an impressive range of theoretical back-up, so to speak, in support of his theory – he refers to Laingian psychology, communications and speech-act theory, Gestalt psychology, all placed within the basic phenomenological frame – this has the effect of a slightly numbing insistence, a theoretical 'overkill' (Freund 1987, 164), as does the rather repetitious use of exemplification from a limited number of literary texts, the novels of Fielding, Joyce's *Ulysses* and Beckett's trilogy.

Nonetheless, German reception theory, associated with the Konstanz School and with Jauss and Iser in particular, occupies an important and honourable place in the development of literary theory in the second half of the twentieth century. The rather dry academic tone, and the careful, perhaps somewhat ponderous elaboration of argument, together with the syncretic determination of its major exponents make it distinctly less controversial and glamorous than other movements in theory – deconstructionism, poststructuralism – which begin in the mid-1970s to enjoy considerably more attention in the Anglo-American intellectual sphere, so that reception theory on the Konstanz model is quite quickly upstaged. Moreover, the determined elaboration of the theory seems to have ensured a determinate period for its flourishing – roughly, the twenty years or so from its inception in 1967 with the inaugural contributions from both Jauss and Iser. Its subsequent development or transmutation into a 'literary anthropology', as Iser has termed it (Iser 1989), has involved a theoretical diffusing and broadening of concern. As for its provenance, for all its initial situation within the German version of the radicalizing movement of the late 1960s, it does not come out of the blue – like other critical positions which emphasize the role of the reader, it draws upon the phenomenological tradition which stretches back to the early part of the century, and there are significant precursors in the discipline of literary criticism. It is a substantial tributary to a wide and various current of thinking and theory about the importance of reception to the constitution of the literary work – the work of art in general – which has been a major feature of literary theory and criticism in recent years (a selection of works in this area is included in the further reading bibliography to this article).

Jeremy Lane

Further reading and works cited

Amacher, R. E., and Lange, V. (eds) *New Perspectives in German Literary Criticism*. Princeton, NJ, 1979.
Bennett, A. (ed.) *Readers and Reading*. London, 1995.
Booth, W. C. *The Rhetoric of Fiction*. Chicago, 1961.
Eco, U. *The Role of the Reader*. Bloomington, IN, 1979.
Eliot, T. S. *Selected Essays*. London, 1951.
Fish, S. 'Why No One's Afraid of Wolfgang Iser', *diacritics*, 11, 3, 1981.
Freund, E. *The Return of the Reader*. London, 1987.
Garvin, H. R. (ed.) *Theories of Reading, Looking, Listening*. Lewisburg, PA, 1981.
Glowinski, M. 'Reading, Interpretation, Reception', *New Literary History*, 11, Autumn 1978.
Holub, R. C. *Reception Theory*. London, 1984.
—. *Crossing Borders*. Madison, WI, 1992.
Ingarden, R. *The Cognition of the Literary Work of Art*. Evanston, IL, 1973a.
—. *The Literary Work of Art*. Evanston, IL, 1973b.
Iser, W. 'Indeterminacy and the Reader's Response in Prose Fiction', *Aspects of Narrative*, ed. J. Hillis Miller. New York, 1971.
—. *The Implied Reader*. Baltimore, MD, 1974.
—. *The Act of Reading*. Baltimore, MD, 1978.
—. 'Talk Like Whales', *diacritics*, 11, 3, 1981.
—. *Prospecting: from Reader Response to Literary Anthropology*. Baltimore, MD, 1989.
Jauss, H. R. 'Literary History as a Challenge to Literary Theory', *New Literary History*, 2, Autumn 1970.
—. *Toward an Aesthetic of Reception*. Minneapolis, MN, 1982a.
—. *Aesthetic Experience and Literary Hermeneutics*. Minneapolis, MN, 1982b.
Purves, A. C. and Beach, R. *Literature and the Reader*. Urbana, IL, 1972.
Richards, I. A. *Practical Criticism*. New York, 1935.
Rosenblatt, L. *Literature as Exploration*. New York, 1937.

Segers, R. T. 'Readers, Text, and Author: Some Implications of *Rezeptionsästhetik*', *Yearbook of Comparative and General Literature*, 24, 1975.

Slatoff, W. *With Respect to Readers*. Ithaca, NY, 1970.

Suleiman, S. R. and Crosman, I. (eds) *The Reader in the Text*. Princeton, NJ, 1980.

Tompkins, J. P. (ed.) *Reader-Response Criticism*. Baltimore, MD, 1980.

36. Jean-François Lyotard (1925–1998) and Jean Baudrillard (1929–): The Suspicion of Metanarratives

Any thinker who announces the end of an old epoch and the beginning of a new, if they should do so persuasively, will attract special attention above and beyond the relative merits of their argument. In the case of Jean Baudrillard and Jean-François Lyotard both announce, with different rationales for doing so, the end of modernism and the onset of postmodernism. Neither would speak of the 'beginning' of the postmodern, because a central feature of postmodernism is that it reveals all teleology as an organizational myth. Origin is a construction designed to lend legitimacy and a sense of inevitability to a present-day reality. For Lyotard, this 'reality' will be dictated by the general organization of knowledge, as such knowledge is constituted by computer databases, mass media and the Internet. For Baudrillard, too, there is a crisis of legitimacy, and it is also traceable to the rise of mass media. He, however, is more interested in the use of images to construct 'reality', than the gathering and dissemination of knowledge. Both Lyotard and Baudrillard would agree key reference points of an earlier time – morality, proof, history, even reality – no longer function as communal markers for the 'truth'.

As a result, for Baudrillard, 'reality' is what he calls a 'hyper-reality', one where various representations of 'reality' masquerade as 'simulations' of what is real when, in fact, the unauthorized, illegitimate interplay of these simulations *is* our reality, and the myth there is a 'real' reality behind it just another example of the self-legitimating myth of origin no longer viable or believable in postmodernity. Where Baudrillard would point to the interplay of image-generated 'simulations', Lyotard would point to a similar dynamic of word-generated 'play' in various 'language games'. For Lyotard, various language games translate what is in fact undecidable into what is apparently incontrovertible. If images pose as simulations in order to preserve the myth of a reality available to be simulated, language games allow words to constitute themselves into configurative 'proof' of a truth presumed to underwrite them. Whether image or word-based, both theorists demonstrate a profound suspicion about any narrative purporting to explain or represent.

While Lyotard is most explicit in this, declaring that the postmodern can be virtually defined as the 'death' of any 'master narrative' offering to explain everything, Baudrillard makes a similar grand claim when he argues all simulations, in one way or another, exist in order to posit the illusion of a reality that is elsewhere. Disney World, for example, is, according to Baudrillard, an aggressively 'simulated' world serving to help make the rest of 'America' seem real. Lyotard, also, sees the reality of social fragmentation made more palatable by the emphasis on 'globalization'. Although their emphasis is quite different, both Baudrillard and Lyotard seem to argue for a postmodern dynamic where false oppositions are set up between an assumed 'reality' and a reproducible version of it. This reproduction – or simulacrum, or language game – then paradoxically serves as a guarantor of a 'reality' that is, in fact, only posited by the reproduction itself to give the image (Baudrillard) or the word (Lyotard) a semblance of authority and legitimacy.

Baudrillard's early work in the 1970s begins with Marx and Henri Lefebvre in order to re-examine the notion of 'everyday life'. If, for modernism, the 'everyday' was marked by a self-conscious awareness of the passage of time (T. S. Eliot's 'I measure out my life with coffee spoons'), the postmodern 'everyday' is not so much generated by subjecivity as generative *of* subjectivity. Marx talks about the self-alienation brought on by early capitalism. The worker was reduced to his function. Inner potential is ignored in favour of productivity; modes of production become the infrastructure which controls the superstructure of ideology. Baudrillard's advance is to see Marx as outdated: modes of consumption have replaced production as the dominant infrastructure. As an advertised commodity, an object's function is now not what it does or fails to do, but its relative place in the collective meaning generated by all objects. The key theme of this early work is to stop imagining the subject determines the meaning or relative worth of objects, and understand, instead, how objects and the mass-produced advertising discourse surrounding them produces an inescapable network of signification (what Lacan might call 'The Symbolic Order') which configures, and reconfigures, subjectivity.

With a bow toward Roland Barthes, Baudrillard also insists what is to be analysed is the various fields of mass-produced objects and the discourse of mass-media designed to accompany them. The subject has become a consumer, and the 'consumer' is not an autonomous entity, as the subject was once presumed to be, but a nexus point of consumer goods circulating as 'signs'. Instead of Marx's distinction of use value and exchange value, Baudrillard does away with both terms in favour of 'sign value'. While Marx's theories might continue to be relevant to the study of an earlier era of capitalism, one where modes of production were dominant, the 'sign' now operates independently of the social codes of a class system, or the dominant discourse of an institution, or the hegemony of any given political economy. Here we can see Baudrillard's debt to Saussure, but whereas Saussure posited the signifier cannot fully represent the signified, Baudrillard aligns himself with Lacan in arguing that the 'signified' itself is a myth, just as Marx's description of an earlier time where objects had 'use value' is more nostalgia on his part than economic history.

It is the visual Baudrillard privileges in the spectacle of consumption, not the apparent monetary worth of this or that commodity. A window display does not illustrate the function of the object, nor does it, in and of itself, try to persuade the consumer of its exchange value. Instead it takes its place in what Baudrillard describes as a 'calculus of signs'. The economic 'value' of the object is unimportant; it is its value in what Baudrillard terms the 'ambience' of all other consumer signs that generates value. In this sense, Baudrillard can argue capital accumulates until it becomes visual, and becomes an image taking its place in the ambience of the spectacle of consumption. Marx's emphasis on function and production, rather than the symbol and consumption, actually provides capitalism with a sort of 'alibi' where it can continue to operate, undisturbed, because of Marx's enlightenment-influenced teleology promising the eventual rise of the proletariat and the destruction of the class system. The dynamic Baudrillard uses to expose 'use value' as an invention of the economic system – not something that preceded it – is similar to Derrida's 'metaphysics of presence' where certain metaphysical assumptions are allowed to operate undetected in order to grant a given philosophy the appearance of an authoritative logic.

In *Simulations*, Baudrillard effaces not only use-value but 'nature' as well, arguing everything is cultural in the sense that everything we know as 'reality' is, in fact, a reality effect produced by the ambience of signs in the modern-day spectacle of consumption. 'Culture' is not something pre-existing consumer culture, culture is the production and consumption of signs. Thus commodity culture is not a sub-culture, but rather produces an illusion of a prior 'culture', which it then refers to to legitimate itself. In works translated in the late 1980s, Baudrillard goes on to argue if use value and exchange value represent a self-legitimating rhetorical device rather than an implicit economic history, and if value only circulates symbolically, then in what way does ideology 'reflect' reality? Or, to ask the same question in another way, where is the 'line' between the supposedly 'real' economic infrastructure of production and the supposedly ideological superstructure of religion, art, law, etc.?

In Marx, ideology is a discourse that translates the 'reality' of the system of production and the class system into the accepted 'meaning' promoted by various social institutions. But if use value and exchange value are an 'alibi' for the circulation of Symbolic value, 'reality' and 'meaning' also operate, in tandem, as a sort of alibi that allows signs to circulate in a way independent of a conjectured 'reality' and its corresponding 'meaning'. Once again, in a sort of modernization of Saussure, Baudrillard insists the circulating sign is not related to some exterior reality; its value lies in its capacity to repress ambivalence and obscure the inevitable non-resolution of meaning. In this sense, what the sign appears to refer to is, to borrow Derrida's term, 'always already' a reflection of the sign that poses, with a sort of false humility, as representing it.

In *Fatal Strategies*, Baudrillard regards data as a new form of 'nature'. It seems to legitimate representation, when, in fact, representation creates a simulacrum of a real that does not exist beyond the presumption of its existence as the basis of the representation. Baudrillard turns his attention away from things as signs producing a 'reality-effect', or a simulacrum, and looks to see how this has changed our subjective experience of social practice. He sees 'a universe emptied of event' (1990, 25) and a 'malicious curvature that puts an end to the horizon of meaning' (25). The result is 'the transpolitical' which is the passage from organic equilibria to cancerous metastases' (25). Even seeing this as a crisis is too teleological, so Baudrillard characterizes it as a catastrophe; 'things rush into it' without reference to reality, history or destiny, even though we continue to impose these markers wherever possible. Baudrillard's much publicized declaration that history is at an end is perhaps less radical than his more quiet declaration there are no longer any secrets, everything is transparent and without depth. There is no history because an 'event' is no longer possible once the relative importance of one distinguishable phenomenon is indistinguishable from another.

In what we might regard as Baudrillard's current phase, through the remainder of the 1990s, he seems to heed his own distrust of signs as conveyors of reality, and effects an aphoristic style deliberately fragmented, mixing anecdotes from his past with accounts of travel, interladen with reassertions of his earlier, more theorized positions. In looking over the body of his work thus far, one is struck by his steadfast obsession with the contemporary and the 'everyday'. In a world of every increasing information exchange and symbolic production, Baudrillard's own high-velocity style of observation seems to keep pace in a way traditional philosophical discourse could not hope to imitate.

Perhaps the greatest affinity between Lyotard and Baudrillard is their respect for irresolution and their disdain – even contempt – for conclusion. Lyotard's famous declaration 'I define postmodern as incredulity toward metanarratives' is really declaring incredulity toward any teleological progression appearing to lead to an inevitable conclusion. Knowledge itself is not conclusive, but compensatory; it 'reinforces our ability to tolerate the incommensurable' (1984, xxv). Lyotard has no interest in what is thought, only in what happens in order for a thought to be constituted. He looks over philosophy like a referee of the intellectual, studying the rules, but remaining indifferent to the outcome of any particular game. He would seem to agree with Marx that the philosopher has an obligation to change the world, but he is interested in an infrastructure far more basic and radical than the infrastructure of the modes of production: he wants to understand the rule governing modes of coherence.

Political intervention must occur at the level of the gamesmanship that produces syntax. He tries to give voice to why avant-garde artists like Duchamp and others are political revolutionaries whether they are interested in politics or not. Avant-garde art is revolutionary because it uncouples sense, and therefore does not have to try and derail it. Lyotard redefines the concept of 'action' by disregarding its physical component and evaluating instead its capacity to produce rules of comprehensibility that can compete with, and overwhelm, other rules of comprehensibility from other discourses. If Baudrillard hovers above language, seeing it as a sign system that produces a reality-effect, Lyotard delves way beneath it, seeing 'language games' in competition with one another for the ability to produce meaning at the expense of other, competing, language games. He privileges art, especially the avant-garde, because artists alone, in any medium, create in the interstitial area between language games and meaning. For this reason, they alone draw attention to limits and inconsistencies in 'reality' by drawing attention to which competing language game is dominant in any given version of common sense or political decision-making.

Unlike Baudrillard who analyses obsessively, Lyotard analyses nothing because his interest in language games commits him to a cataloguing and a critique of styles of analysis, rather than the result of this or that analysis. Lyotard also shares Baudrillard's disenchantment with Marx's enlightenment-style dialectic, though his scepticism is based on the practical experience of political journalism and an interest in the struggle for Algerian independence. If Baudrillard is concerned with the invisibly corrosive quality of the status quo and the mundane, Lyotard reserves his ire for failed radicalism, most significantly Soviet marxism as well as what he saw as the shameful failure of marxist pragmatics in Algeria. It is perhaps here he began to prefer the primal activism of the avant-garde artist over the apparently more involved political activist. Action that does not take account of how language games form intention cannot succeed as intervention.

Not surprisingly, then, Lyotard's early work, Discours, Figure and The Libidinal Economy, turned to the field of aesthetics with the same enthusiasm previously reserved for the field of politics. Aesthetic theory attempts to offer a bridge between form and content, but aesthetic practice itself – the actual production of art – defines and explores this gap between the two, seeing it as a permanent chaos at the base of any construction of truth and desire. By positing the libidinal as an 'economy', Lyotard is insisting desire is a material process, rather than an abstract or merely emotional one. He is less concerned with what desire 'is' than in how it functions. He sees desire as the energy of society, but it is an unstable energy, unpredictably connecting the psychological to the economical in a type of feeling and desire Lyotard calls an 'intensity'. Narrative, broadly defined as a poem or an advertisement, binds these moments of intensities into an apparently coherent pattern in order to exploit the power residing there.

Instead of exploring these intensities, narrative dilutes them in order to 'explain' something else – something always beside the point, since 'the point' is always the intensity that has been exploited. In saying postmodernism expresses an incredulity toward master narratives, Lyotard is directing us away from the comfort of narrative to the more important task of understanding what provides it with its interpretive, totalizing force. The libidinal economy is always about practice, and narrative about theory. But theory for Lyotard does not translate into practice – an opinion held over from his days as a political activist. It may translate into goal-directed action, as it did for Marx, but such action promotes a self-deluding myth of cause and effect which leads to an illusion of progress, and the work of understanding the unrepresentable intensities which underlie intention goes undone. In as much as we can consider Lyotard a political thinker, it is a glaring irony in his argument that his dismissal of master narratives does not permit any grounding of argument, and therefore no criteria for judging or justice.

In other words, Lyotard's abiding suspicion of rhetoric leaves us no way to judge the relative merits of arguments, thereby giving rhetoric more sway over our feelings and actions. Both Lyotard and Baudrillard disallow cause and effect. Lyotard turns to what he calls 'gaming' and Baudrillard to what he calls 'seduction'. For Baudrillard, 'a seductive connection is one that avoids the promiscuity of cause and effect' (1990b, 172). In *Just Gaming*, Lyotard points out different discourses have different rules for playing 'the game'. Even apparently similar concepts like 'justice' and 'truth' call for a different sort of 'gaming'. The fragmentation of the postmodern, then, is an inevitable result of the incommensurability of 'language games'. In a curious parallel, Baudrillard also emphasizes the dynamic of play in his concept of seduction. Rather than interpreting in terms of repression, the conscious or the unconscious, these oppositions give way to a universe that 'must be interpreted in the terms of play, challenges, duels, the strategy of appearances – that is, the terms of seduction' (1990b, 7). As in Lyotard, there is a gamesmanship, 'a seductive reversibility' which undoes the binary oppositions underlying traditional rhetorical strategies with their presumption of access to universal truth.

Beckett's remark that his work consists of 'a stain on silence' also seems to characterize the late work of Baudrillard and Lyotard. In his attempt to find a place for 'justice' in his schema of fragmentation and 'intensities', Lyotard explores the concept of 'the sublime', especially in terms of Kant's definition of it as an attempt to represent the unrepresentable. What Lyotard appreciates the most about the sublime is that it is a feeling and not a theory; or, it is a theory about a feeling, but a feeling that nonetheless exceeds all attempts to theorize it. When a phrase or a work of art evokes a feeling of the sublime, something beyond representation or its subsequent interpretation is demanding our attention. Both Edmund Burke and Kant make it clear the sublime is a paradoxical feeling, terror and delight for Burke, pleasure and pain for Kant. Lyotard's version of this paradox is that the sublime calls for an interpretation from us in such a way as to underline our inability to supply one. Likewise, it seems to announce itself as part of the representation in a manner that can be felt, but not evaluated. In as much as the sublime draws attention to irresolution and lack of integration, it would seem to be a prelude to insight, but, uniquely among feelings, it gives notice of difference in a way that makes it clear the difference is absolute.

It is at this point, in essays gathered in *The Inhuman*, that Lyotard modernizes the debate over the sublime by linking it directly to the avant-garde. We might expect Lyotard to appreciate the goals of avant-garde art because if language is gamesmanship, and the rules of the game dictate and control meaning, than art that sets out to break the rules might, in a sense, ambush the sublime by forcing unexpected ways of thinking brought on by often unwelcome flaunting of the rules of representation. If the sublime is a feeling of 'beyond', the avant-garde produces an excess that cannot be contained and converts unacknow-ledged impossibility into startling possibility. Aesthetic criteria make interpretation easier, but only by curtailing thought. Meaning is an effect of the limits of representation as policed by the rules of the game. The avant-garde is a playfulness that is prior to the rules, and therefore exceeds them. As soon as the avant-garde is aware of its own rules, it is no longer the avant-garde.

By connecting the sublime to the avant-garde, Lyotard connects philosophy to art – perhaps his greatest contribution. The avant-garde accesses the sublime in such a way that an action is called for that can lead only to questions and away from answers. And yet this is not a sneaky return to rules of cause and effect because the avant-garde break with established rules does not operate on the axis of 'success' or 'failure', but on the strictly experimental level of playfulness, a level of play outside the rules, and therefore only aware of pleasure and pain as palpable coordinates. By insisting the sublime is the only aesthetic of the avant-garde, Lyotard is able to see art as without future, as independent of the future. The teleological machine of traditional western aesthetics blows up, assuring the destruc-tion of modernism's late-Enlightenment project of totalization – a project inspired in the first place by capitalism's obsession with quantity and quantification, and therefore something to be resisted at every turn.

Baudrillard locates his later work around the issue of the subject and the object rather than language games, but there is an equally apocalyptic air to his musings. His style grows increasingly aphoristic in his attempt to further defy any illusion of accretion, accumulation or the myth of progress. As he says: 'In the last analysis, object and subject are one. We can only grasp the essence of the world if we can grasp, in all its irony, the truth of this radical equivalence' (1996a). Where Lyotard urges dismantling, Baudrillard is content to point out inevitable dissolution: 'In the past, we had objects to believe in – objects of belief. These have disappeared' (1996a, 142). With the loss of transcendental certitude, any event is much like another, and this is the basis of Baudrillard's notorious claim about 'the end of history'. What we have instead of events is information, since information always presents itself as neither more nor less important than other information.

This belief in information is no more than 'a reflex action of collective credulity' and 'we no more believe in information by divine right than serfs ever believed they were serfs by divine right, but we act as though we do' (142). So we have the impossibility of belief within a system that continues to necessitate it, despite the fact that 'behind this facade, a gigantic principle of incredulity is growing up, a principle of disaffection and the denial of any social bond' (142). It is no longer about the destruction of meaning, or even its rearrangement by the avant-garde, as Lyotard might argue, but simply its disappearance. Where Lyotard is a strategist, planning his next move, securing himself against gamesman-ship and manipulation, Baudrillard is a survivalist, eschewing the comfort of context or meaning in order to stay focused on the reality of absence and alienation at the heart of the unprecedented proliferation of information, meaning and imagery in the mass-media of modernity. The passion for illusion, whether it comes from master narratives or mythologies of accumulation, is something both Lyotard and Baudrillard frankly acknowledge, but they point out that this passion for illusion has taken refuge in our modern passion for information.

Data, for Lyotard, has become 'nature' in postmodern culture, just as the idea of 'nature' has become the alibi for the world of simulation in Baudrillard. And presiding over this nostalgia that reality is not what it once was is theory itself. Theory is a secular religion for Baudrillard. It purports to explain the universal property of things, but in fact it helps organize them so the particular appears connected to the universal. In this sense, theory operates like ceremony: 'both are produced to prevent things and concepts from touching indiscriminately, to create discrimination, and remake emptiness, to re-distinguish what has been confused' (Baudrillard 1990a, 178). Theorists who warn against theory, Lyotard and Baudrillard are master narrativists who declare the death of transcendental certitude; they are masters of reality who insist what we believe to be reality is just the effect of the magician's language act, the illusionist's image projection. The final paradox, fittingly postmodern in its self-effacing self-reflexivity, is that these two thinkers, each insisting on their own status as false prophets, have emerged as among our most valuable commentators on the perpetual 'now' of postmodernity.

Garry Leonard

Further reading and works cited

Baudrillard, J. *The Mirror of Production*. St Louis, 1975.
—. *In the Shadow of the Silent Majorities*. New York, 1983a.
—. *Simulations*. New York, 1983b.
—. *Forget Foucault*. New York, 1988a.
—. *The Ecstasy of Communication*. New York, 1988b.
—. *Fatal Strategies*. New York, 1990a.
—. *Seduction*. New York, 1990b.
—. *Cool Memories*. London, 1990c.
—. *The Perfect Crime*. New York, 1996a.
—. *The System of Objects*. London, 1996b.
Benjamin, A. (ed.) *Judging Lyotard*. London, 1992.
Carroll, D. *Paraesthetics*. London, 1987.
Kellner, D. *Jean Baudrillard*. Oxford, 1989.
Kroker, A. *The Possessed Individual*. Basingstoke, 1992.
Lyotard, J.-F. *Discours, Figure*. Paris, 1971.
—. *The Postmodern Condition*. Manchester, 1984.
—. *Just Gaming*. Manchester, 1985.
—. *The Differend*. Manchester, 1988.
—. *Duchamp's Trans/Formers*. Venice, CA, 1990.
—. *The Inhuman*. Cambridge, 1991.
—. *Libidinal Economy*. London, 1993.

37. The Social and the Cultural: Michel de Certeau (1925–1986), Pierre Bourdieu (1930–2002) and Louis Marin (1931–1992)

Considered together, Pierre Bourdieu, Michel de Certeau and Louis Marin correspond to a line of discourse which attempts, through multiple disciplines, to articulate the processes of social and cultural interaction. While it remains impossible to create a totalizing and definitive discourse which could then be read across the various and varied writings of all three of these authors, any comparison and contrast of their respective work invites a number of considerations. It must be noted from the outset, however, that the writing of each of these authors (either explicitly or implicitly) resists attempts to place its subject within singularly literary and/or theoretical enclosures. Instead, these three authors each deliver a facet of ongoing, relational discussion which reflexively posits the creation of the individual in social and cultural spheres; the production and consumption of forms of representation in those spheres; and the relation between the individual and the official discourses created by those forms of representation. It is through the efforts of each author to express and account for these social and cultural forms of representation, and the production/consumption thereof, that a reader of Bourdieu, de Certeau and Marin comes to appreciate the impact of their discourse on methods of thinking through literary theory.

Generally speaking, Bourdieu is a philosophical sociologist, de Certeau a religious historian with an interest in French psychoanalysis, and Marin is an art historian. Bourdieu and de Certeau have, at times, been credited with assistance in creating a 'French model' of socialization which amounts to a form of or an account of the social fabrication of knowledge. These two authors explore the viability of such terms as culture, and the relationship between the individuals who both compromise and compose the very concept of culture. As such, a primary polemic in their writing revolves around the role of the individual who is both exemplary and exceptional in his/her own cultural context. Marin departs from the abstracted construction of social models and is at once situated between the divergent responses of Bourdieu and de Certeau to socially organizing forms of representation.

As suggested by the variety in their critical dispositions, a significant common concern between these authors can be located in (as with many postwar theorists) their growing anxiety with regard to the received authority and autonomy of official discourses. The very nature of their writing invariably resists ambitious actions of correlation, accumulation and generalization. Bourdieu, de Certeau and Marin tend to work both within and against traditional modes of philosophical discourse and, paradoxically, represent (or theorize) the non-theorizable through the incorporative complexity of their interests. Moreover, any proper creation and consideration of their overall oeuvre must realize the potential shortcomings of such an undertaking, as well as the incomplete nature of the individual (and therefore also the cumulative) effect of their writings. Tragically, the death of both Michel de Certeau and Louis Marin (1986 and 1992) cut short not only the work of these writers, leaving many ideas underdeveloped and in want of greater attention, but also the ongoing intercommunication and exchange of ideas between these reflexively influential figures.

Of the three authors discussed, Pierre Bourdieu stands as the most widely disseminated in the English speaking world. Bourdieu's supporters and detractors alike credit Bourdieu with the expansion and realignment of the traditional barriers of philosophy, sociology, anthropology and ethnography, through both his extension of the boundaries of socio-logical questioning and his questioning of the validity of autonomous intellectual and social domains. His ongoing endeavour to create new ways of thinking through cultural phenomena, the concept of culture itself and fundamental systems of symbolic exchange contribute significantly to both marxist and structuralist philosophies. However, the content and character of the exegesis pertaining to Bourdieu and his work, as such, tend to reside in sociological, anthropological or (only more recently) philosophical applica-tions. True to the incorporative nature of Bourdieu's programme, therefore, the explication of his work as either sociological or literary, etc., significantly diminishes and misrepresents a basic characteristic of his writing. In part, the inadequacy of much of the analysis of Bourdieu can be linked to the fact that he was initially trained as a philosopher but began his career primarily as a sociologist. A subsequent explanation of this critical frustration can be traced to the rather paradoxical relationship Bourdieu entertains with his own work. Despite the seemingly contrary evidence to be found in both the traditional rigor of his intellectual training and his election to the chair of Sociology at the bastion of intellectual institutionalism, the *Collège de France*, in 1982, Bourdieu has repeatedly insisted upon the non-theoretical, anti-philosophical and anti-intellectual position of his work. Any reading of Bourdieu, insists Bourdieu, must first consider both the 'scientific' nature of his argument and the practical nature of his analytical strategy. Of primary concern in his commentary, therefore, is the necessary creation of 'a theory of practice as *practice* ... as an activity premised upon cognitive operations involving a mode of knowledge that is not that of theory, logic, or concept' (Calhoun et al. 1993, 267). Bourdieu continues, stating 'hundreds of times' that he has 'always been immersed in empirical research projects, and the theoretical instruments [he] was able to produce in the course of these endeavours were intended not for theoretical commentary and exegesis, but to be put to use in new research' (Calhoun et al. 1993, 271). It is within this notion of scientific practicality that Bourdieu negotiates his somewhat tenuous position as the intellectual anti-intellectual, and turns the critical gaze of sociology into the subject of a sociological investigation.

Although trained as a philosopher, Bourdieu began his career as a sociologist in Algeria during the late 1950s. Concurrently, his first major works, *Sociologie de L'Algérie* (1958) and *Travail et travailleurs en Algérie* (1963) are both predominantly sociological in orientation. These early moments of sociological study in Bourdieu's career influence a great deal of the anthro-philosophical disposition through the entirety of his work. The observations made of marriage strategies, family organization, conceptualizations of honour and gift giving rituals (particularly of the Kabyle), during an extremely harsh period in the history of Algeria, return throughout his writing as a means of forming the basis of Bourdieu's sustained inquiry of social practice. In Bourdieu's own words, it was 'the gap between the views of the French intellectuals about this war and how it should be brought to an end, and [his] own experiences' which became indicative of his relationship to the intellectual elite and that first prompted him to assume his anthropological-sociological-philosophical mission (Jenkins 1992, 14). Bourdieu's early work, however, failed to earn him any notable critical attention until his book *Les héritiers, les étudiants et la culture* (1964). Here, Bourdieu announces a major (but retrospectively obvious) shift in the subject of his analytical programme. In *The Inheritors* (the English title), Bourdieu focuses on the way in which the French education system (particularly universities), despite its claims toward a progressive and egalitarian meritocracy, tends to reproduce systems of privilege. Bourdieu suggests, rather scandalously, that those who succeed in the academic world are not necessarily those best suited for fulfilling the stated public goals of the academy. Instead, success and privilege tend to be delegated to those who either explicitly or intuitively understand how to demonstrate an 'unconditional respect for the fundamental principles of the established order' (Bourdieu 1988, 87). Because of the exchange of a strain of commerce, predominantly social and symbolic in value (i.e. cultural capital), privilege tends to statistically support the maintenance of privilege. In both of his most antagonistic writings concerning intellectual institutions, *The Inheritors* and *Homo Academicus* (1984), Bourdieu turns the sociologist's attention, traditionally directed toward the exterior and foreign, upon its very own social structure, thereby implicitly questioning the validity of its own sociological agenda. In other words, Bourdieu manipulates philosophical and socio-logical discourses to examine philosophy and sociology. What emerges, therefore, is an investigation into how that which is traditionally considered common sense serves to reproduce privilege simply because it disguises itself as completely obvious, orthodox and natural.

Through his unwillingness to accept the obvious as such, Bourdieu subsequently announces a secondary departure from the traditional object of philosophical contempla-tion. In Bourdieu's configuration, the miniscule practices of everyday life represent an observable and quantifiable body of information which demonstrates an underlying consistency in human behaviour. As a result, in the investigation of everyday practice, the heretofore banal becomes the sight of an unearthing of the hidden and fundamental structures of social organization. More than merely observing the manner in which these orthodox and natural dispositions perpetuate their own validity within a culture, Bourdieu attempts to unearth the organizing structural relationships which seemingly guide the basic actions of the individual within the symbolic network of a culture. As Bourdieu states, 'I can say that all my thinking started from this point: how can behaviour be regulated without being the product of obedience to set rules?' (Bourdieu 1990, 64). Bourdieu, in other words, hopes to find a middle ground, or balance, between the specifics of individual choice with the determinism of social structures.

As an integral aspect of his method for the analysis of individual practices, Bourdieu delivers (developed from Aristotle, Aquinas and, most recently, Émile Durkheim) the concept of habitus as the means through which an agent negotiates the polarity of structuralist and phenomenological models of social interaction. Bourdieu deploys the habitus in order to describe events as neither systematically predetermined (as structuralism often suggests), thereby devastating the possibility of individual agency outside the determined social order, nor completely produced within, and contingent upon, the individual. The concept of the habitus, therefore, responds to 'the dual need to conceptualize the subject's practice as such, and as having an origin that lay outside itself' (Dosse 1997, 304) How, in other words, can an agent apply learned rules without recognizing them as such? Put simply, the dual function of the habitus, in theory, facilitates the mediation of conscious and subconscious forms of decision-making.

To understand better what is suggested in the negotiative potential of the habitus it is worthwhile to note that Bourdieu himself most often provides the simple term 'disposition' as the nearest equivalent to the habitus. Disposition allows an agent to simultaneously be the source of her actions and also permits the foundation of these actions to stem from a more intuitive level. The operative mobility of habitus closely resembles, to adopt Bourdieu's analogy, the athlete who has a deep understanding or 'feel for the game'. A well-trained and skilled athlete does not need to programmatically learn the rules, in this analogy, to every conceivable contingency possible in a game situation. Likewise, the individual within a social game need not adhere to the imposition of structural social codes to be able to work toward the end of his/her social advantage within a cultural dynamic. Instead, action becomes an intuitive process where the agent actually embodies social rules. The immediate repercussion of this embodiment formulates the cultural as both within and extraneous to the individual who may therefore negotiate his/her position within that culture on varied levels of awareness. In this sense, individual 'social agents who have a feel for the game, who have embodied a host of practical schemes of perception and appreciation functioning as instruments of reality construction ... do not need to pose the objectives of their practice as ends' (Bourdieu, 1998, 80) Thus the individual demonstrates a practised understanding of social rules and structures to an extent that they arrive but are not imposed from an exterior structure. Hence the 'natural' and culturally obvious condition of social structures as the subject becomes (both literally and figuratively) the embodiment of a cultural paradigm.

Significantly, Bourdieu conceptualizes the habitus as only operating in relation to an individual field. A field, simply, is a 'structured system of social positions – occupied either by individuals or institutions – the nature of which defines the situation for their occupants' (Jenkins 1992, 85). The field both defines and is defined by what is at stake in, the currency of, social actions. Fields, however, are not always entirely autonomous but occasionally do interconnect. Because of this, the same habitus is capable of informing a tremendous variety of practices depending upon the field(s) in which it acts. While this is to say simply that a single behavioural trait is not always as appropriate in, say, the workplace as it may be at home, it is also in the nature of dominant fields to impose their logic upon those less formidable. According to Bourdieu, this explains the reason why the social organization of the factory may resemble that of the family (or vice versa) while the two remain relatively distinct social fields.

Here, it becomes worthwhile, particularly for the analysis of Bourdieu's response to literary and artistic fields, to return to the notion of cultural capital. In his book titled, *La distinction. Critique sociale du jugement* (1979), Bourdieu advances one of his most significant contributions to marxism through his re-evaluation of what is at stake in the social game. While traditional marxism posits the desire for economic gain as the primary currency and drive in class conflict, Bourdieu suggests, instead, that symbolic capital inserts a secondary dimension to the plotting of a social graph. Noting that Marx actually creates the class which also acts as his subject ('workers of the world unite'), Bourdieu demonstrates that symbolic currency, operating in the form of education, the arts and social 'taste', etc., often works counter-intuitively to marxist thought. Instead, the introduction and exchange of cultural capital allows cultural fields to isolate and dictate the fundamental basis of their existence. The world of art, for example, tends to posit economic success as the antithesis of genuine artistic achievement. In other words, the counter-economic gains its own form of value. In this sense, Bourdieu notes that the evolution of 'societies tends to make universes (which I call fields) emerge which are autonomous and have their own laws. Their fundamental laws are often tautologies' (Bourdieu 1998, 83). Thus 'the literary field is the economic world reversed; that is, the fundamental law of this specific universe ... which establishes a negative correlation between temporal (notably financial) success and properly artistic value, is the inverse of the law of economic exchange. The artistic field is a *universe of belief* (Bourdieu 1993, 164). And so, the expression 'art for art's sake' comes to represent the interior logic exclusive to the field of art. That is, the exchange of a currency non-economic in nature creates a situation in which the field of art acts as the source of its own legitimacy. It is an end of, and in, itself. An analysis of art, by Bourdieu's reasoning, is an analysis of the circumstances and contingencies which appear in a cultural interplay that allows an artist his/her artistic validity and value.

There remains, however, a slippery residue in the trace of Bourdieu's position. Bourdieu attempts to avoid a possible conundrum in both the overstated recognition of his cultural (i.e. contaminated, subjective) complicity and the scientific nature of his argument. Put most simply, Bourdieu fails in his attempt to completely break from the determinism found in structuralist models of social control. Instead, the habitus (particularly when employed as the producer of social practice – see Jenkins 1992, 77) tends to simply replace the rigid determinism found in structuralist models. While Bourdieu allows that not all social actions can be accounted for in advance, they all at least appear accounted for within the 'space of possibles' permitted by the habitus (1993, 177). Radical innovation and resistance, therefore, are an impossibility to anyone with an understanding of the habitus and field in which any resistance occurs. And so, as the concept of the habitus appears to open a radical interpretative space, it simultaneously closes down that space by insisting on the prevalence of its overwhelming dogmatic aggression and the prominence allotted for a kind of divine spectator, or symbolic master, the sociologist. It is with this in mind that some critics have charged Bourdieu as existing in a state of radical denial with his object. One must simply locate another's habitus to be able to explain the complexity of that person's behaviour. In this, the sociologist emerges as the master symbolist who, through his superior understanding of symbolic exchange, can account for the behaviour of all others while this very action must remain unrecognized and subconscious to those actually in, embodying, the habitus. Most significantly, however, in the logical conclusion of the sociologist's symbolic dominance, Bourdieu fails in his analysis to account for the action which is conceivably devoid of symbolic value. There is, simply, no action or event which becomes truly subversive or resistant to the dominating discourse. It is in response to the rigidity of this interpretative model, then, that Michel de Certeau works to create a space outside the field of cultural production.

To a certain extent, Bourdieu and de Certeau were contemporaries. As such, there is an expected exchange of ideas which permeate moments of their parallel streams of thought. In terms of their intercommunication and reflexive influence, it is difficult to understate the significance of the fact that Bourdieu's *The Logic of Practice* and de Certeau's *The Practice of Everyday Life* were originally published in the same year (1980). As with Bourdieu, de Certeau finds a rich body of information in the events of common everyday experience. Perhaps in the spirit of Bourdieu's expansionist programme, de Certeau approaches the everyday from a dramatically different direction. In most general terms, de Certeau can be seen as representative of a shift that François Dosse describes as 'the taste for history in the seventies [which] was in some sense a continuation of the interest in anthropology in the sixties' (Dosse 1997, 266). Thus de Certeau, trained as a historian, expands many of the arguments put forth by Bourdieu (as well as Michel Foucault) by staging his arguments within the context(s) of traditionally separate forms of discourse. More than merely rotating the facets of an intellectual vogue, however, this loose shift from anthropology to history announces the continued fracturing of traditionally coherent and autonomous conceptual fields. So, while Bourdieu begins to dismantle the borders of sociology, anthropology and philosophy, de Certeau not only rethinks the external boundaries of history, but also the internal coherency and cohesion of concepts like history and culture. Like Bourdieu, de Certeau does not merely limit his analytic object or aims to the field of his initial training, but instead works through a prismatic array of disciplines to redirect the momentum of, in de Certeau's instance, methods of thinking through philosophy, psychoanalysis and history.

De Certeau takes for his beginning a mixture of his own two predominant interests. Trained as both a Jesuit and a historian, de Certeau begins with early modern religious history. In addition, de Certeau sustains an interesting relation to the French reception of Freud as a founding member of Jacques Lacan's *Ecole freudienne*. De Certeau's early writing focuses most notably on Pierre Favre (a follower of Ignatius) and Jean-Joseph Surin (a seventeenth-century mystic). Not until the 'symbolic revolution' of May 1968, however, does de Certeau begin to open the interpretative spectrum of his research. The seminal *La prise de parole. Pour une nouvelle culture* (1968) announces the redirection of de Certeau's thought. This redirection is confirmed, oddly, by de Certeau's subsequent publication, *La possession de Loudun* (1970), which simultaneously returns to the compass of de Certeau's earlier writing (religious history and mysticism) but with a noted inclusion of poignant heterogeneous social, political and social dimensions. As one might expect, and in the spirit of this expanding and increasingly unclassifiable critical approach, de Certeau's conceptualization of history remains significantly resistant to absolutism. Moreover, the work of Michel de Certeau does not simply continue the programmatic repositioning of Bourdieu's thought. Instead, de Certeau suggests that the 'interpretive mastery, which Bourdieu denies both to other interpreters and to the practitioners themselves, is itself best seen as part of a strategy of intellectual bluff and counter-bluff' (Ahearne 1995, 153). In this sense, de Certeau engages this double-bluff and adopts the critical disposition of Bourdieu, applying it not only to Bourdieu, but also to the writing of history.

And so, de Certeau works toward an understanding of history as a performative act or event which cannot possibly remain uncontaminated (in a similar manner to Bourdieu's complicit and reflexive sociology) by the practices and social structures which have made the production of history possible. Noting, for example, that a 'literary' approach to history tends to treat ideas as simply that, (while the sociological interpreter tends to treat a social artefact as indicative, or a symptom, of a larger social structure), de Certeau argues that 'historians and literary critics were employing "literary" procedures to interpret those texts which in sociological terms most resembled their own – in other words those of a cultural elite' (Ahearne 1995, 19). As such, history is made, examined and sustained by a statistical minority, the cultural elite. De Certeau, in other words, sceptically approaches the role of historian and the history that he fabricates. Instead, de Certeau turns to the margins of these official narratives, stating that:

> A society is thus composed of certain foregrounded practices organizing its normative institu-
> tion and of innumerable other practices that remain 'minor' ... It is in this multifarious and
> silent 'reserve' of procedures that we should look for 'consumer' practices having the double
> characteristic, pointed out by Foucault, of being able to organize both spaces and languages,
> whether on minute or vast scale. (1984, 48)

Furthermore, the history produced by official forms of discourse tends to grossly mis-
represent the experiences of a statistical majority supposedly involved, but unaccounted
for, in the upper echelons of cultural exchange. It is in this conflict, between the masses
and the dominant classes, that de Certeau seeks out a method for the theorization of
individual practices, practices which are not represented in official discourse and are, as
such, culturally invisible. De Certeau describes these multitudinous practices as a 'silence'
which disrupts representation. It is this silence which 'indicates a need to think the other of
theory' (Colebrook 1997, 137).

De Certeau's strategy stems from dissatisfaction with both Pierre Bourdieu's and Michel
Foucault's 'use of a single principle – power or production – to account for culture'
(Colebrook 1997, 111). Bourdieu's failure to account for an event devoid of symbolic
value also fails to note, in the same manner as the official historical discourses, the silent
representations of those outside the field of cultural production. Instead, de Certeau
heralds the critical potential of the untheorized, specific, practices of the common and
everyday. De Certeau posits, for example, that 'the modern city is becoming a labyrinth of
images ... A landscape of posters and billboards organizes our reality. It is a mural
language with the repertory of its immediate objects of happiness.' In this landscape,
'commercial discourse continues to tie desire to reality without ever marrying one to the
other. It exposes communication without being able to sustain it' (de Certeau 1994, 20–
1). The fact that the representation, described by de Certeau as both bombarding and
organizing 'our reality', operates solely in a single direction, signifies a gap in the symbolic
exchange. Perhaps best noted in the fact that 'communication' and 'community' share a
common root, de Certeau's description of the city thus organizes a community, but fails to
sustain the communication needed to impose this organization. Here, the experience of
an individual in an urban environment exposes a secondary necessity if official modes of
communication and representation are 'in reality' to shape an individual's actions; that is,
they control also the reception of those modes of discourse. De Certeau argues that this is
simply not the case. Thus the simple activity of walking in the city becomes 'one way in
which the controls and rigidities of urban planning [are] dynamically rewritten' (Haslett
2000, 147). With this in mind, de Certeau then argues (in a vein more optimistic than
that allotted by Bourdieu) that the consuming subject is, in fact, the site of a 'secondary
production' (1984, xiii).

This concern with the aberrant productions of consumers shapes a particular aspect of de
Certeau's writing. To establish this heterology, de Certeau incorporates a spectrum of travel-
writing, historiography and scientific theory in order to demonstrate the way in which
western rationality is shadowed by the concept of the other. The other comes to represent a
site for the elusive alterity that de Certeau covets, but also recognizes must remain, by
definition, defiant to theorization. Significantly, de Certeau produces the notion of 'tactics'
in order to open a space of resistance by the individual consumer who works in opposition to
standard strategies. In de Certeau's conception, 'strategy' represents the manner in which
dominant social structures, rules and norms formulate themselves. De Certeau's use of the
term 'tactics', contrarily, signifies individual practices which appropriate, 'pervert, or use

those rules in opposition to the strategy'. Thus tactics represent the other to the logic of rational strategy. For the obedient subject the 'other is memory – other times which can disrupt the logic of the present. For historiography, the "other" is the past; for reason the "other" is narrative metaphor; for theology the "other" is mysticism; while for travel-writing the "other" is figured through different cultures' (Colebrook, 1997, 124, 128–9). Thus the silence posited by de Certeau simultaneously announces the need to think of the other and, by doing so, articulates the presence of the other.

De Certeau situates culture as a dynamic and fluid network of events, strategies and tactics. Rather than isolate the cultural field, therefore, de Certeau attempts to open spaces of discourse, spaces in which one can articulate the silent margins of culture, spaces in which one can theorize the untheorizable. For this reason, one of the tropes which return throughout de Certeau's writing is the observation of the manner in which individual practices tend not to mimic the official discourses of the cultural self-representation. 'This cultural activity of the non-producers of culture, an activity that is unsigned, unreadable, and unsymbolized, remains the only one possible for all those who nevertheless buy and pay for the showy products through which a productivist economy articulates itself. Marginality is becoming universal' (de Certeau 1984, xvii). Subsequently, de Certeau announces, 'we are witnessing a *multiplicity of cultural places*. It is becoming possible to maintain several kinds of cultural references' (de Certeau 1994, 66).

So, both de Certeau and Bourdieu reposition (albeit separately and with different conclusions) the potential offered in the articulation of culture. For Bourdieu the inter-pretation of an artistic field, say literature, revolves around the identification of the symbolic (or perhaps economic) currency at stake in that field. Analysis, as such, then focuses on the subtle, disguised contingency that validates the artistic endeavour. De Certeau places a greater significance on the aberrant in order to describe a field of effects produced by consumers (in the case of textual analysis, the readers of a given work) rather than uncovering the intended design (or meaning) of the product. Louis Marin, for his part, embraces modes of representation as the fundamental origins of social control. The observation, reading, of art, therefore, also constitutes a recognition and participation in its effects. In some sense, Louis Marin represents both the middle ground and an advance-ment of the streams of thought prepared by Pierre Bourdieu and Michel de Certeau. Returning to Bourdieu's aforementioned desire not to theorize but to create a concept of 'practice *as practice*', Marin can be read as only implicitly theoretical. Rather, Marin engages the performative practical response only contemplated by Bourdieu. In a more tangible manner, however, Louis Marin relates most readily to the work of Michel de Certeau in the object of his analysis, specifically art history, and his willingness to enter into a field of tactics.

In *Portrait of the King* (a reference to a seventeenth-century portrait of Louis XIV), Marin activates de Certeau's secondary production through his resistance to consumer passivity, and through his atypical form of reading history, which is devoid of many of the standard features of historical discourse. Instead, Marin's historical account remains conventionally non-historic. As noted by Tom Conley in his foreword to that text, 'scholars might balk at Marin's attempt to write a history with a minimum of events, of dates, names, or of places' (Marin 1988, xiv). In exchange, Marin allots an increasingly prominent role to the production of his specific readings, to the performance of his interpretation and the interplay of his ideas. Thus Marin prepares an archaeology of the way in which paradigms of social control have been passed through the age of Louis XIV to the modern age. Central to these paradigms of power are the arts of representation. Here, Marin studies an identical topic to that of de Certeau in his *Writing of History* (Chapters 2–4), that is the utilization of religious doctrine to organize and justify a central bureaucratic policy. Marin, however, operates from within purely aesthetic confines, and his tactics, therefore, are tactics of play and pleasure.

Marin takes as his primary subject a series of utterances, 'L'état, c'est moi,' 'Le portrait de César, c'est César' and 'Ceçi est Mon corps' ('the state, it is me,' 'the portrait of Caesar is Caesar' and 'this is my body'). Marin contemplates the reciprocity involved in the relation-ship between king and country, the representation of a king and that king, and the transfiguration of the flesh to food and text. The tautology of each of these statements echoes the self-validating fields of Bourdieu. Their legitimacy perpetuates itself precisely because they are enclosed circuits of logic. For Marin, however, there exists a larger complicity between these expressions. As the king, who embodies the state, encounters a representation of the king, which embodies the king, we, as observers, are witnesses to the transfiguration of the individual into the apparatus of the society itself. By placing these utterances into a discussion of a portrait of Louis XIV, Marin suggests that 'the 'effects' of Louis XIV's aesthetic productions are extensions of our own relations with television, magazines, the fine arts in our best museum, and other phenomena that embody the range of popular and elite culture' (Marin 1988, vii). It is thus within the effects of representations that Marin situates the individual's complicity in allowing 'representation to be perfect in its self-representation' by breathing the life into the entire affair (Marin 1988, 178).

The life that a spectator breathes into representation is a reflexive exchange, for in that representation the observer must ultimately confront himself. As Marin writes, 'I am interested in the painting as representation, but also in the irresistible pull, and stupefying effects, of what *I see in the mirror* it creates. Although what I see is intolerable, everything else seems trifling and childish in comparison' (Marin 1995, 104, emphasis added). To observe painting is, therefore, to enact the transfiguration of the self in painting. For Marin, however, there is also a spatial and textual dimension to the processes of this representation. Aware that he dramatically reshapes the quality of painting by re-representing that event in writing, Marin discusses the textual complexity inherent in the discussion of painting, the trans-figuration of painting into text, and the text which is then consumed by the reader ('this is my body'). In Marin's *Sublime Poussin*, Marin posits the act of 'reading' a painting. With regard to the interplay of the text and the image of painting, Marin states that 'put on stage as a viewer of the picture, the reader of the letter is . . . introduced onto the stage of history as a metafigurative figure (if I may use such a term) who . . . gives the viewer – that is, himself – the exact key to the true reading of all that the picture represents' (Marin 1999, 27). Again, Marin argues against any distinction between the reader of an event and the event itself.

Thus Marin contemplates another circuitous logic which permeates all forms of representation. Here, Marin returns to the theorization of the untheorizable mentioned above. How does one contemplate and represent culture that is, in itself, composed entirely of representation? In part, Pierre Bourdieu, Michel de Certeau and Louis Marin, each in his own singular fashion, offer a reflexive recognition that the performer and the performance of a culture cannot be separated. With this in mind, then, each author must operate individually (and with relative degrees of success) to open a space of discourse for the articulation of a cultural phenomenon both shared and singular. It is, simply, the representation of the self through the discourse of the social and the cultural.

Brian Niro

Further reading and works cited

Ahearne, J. Michel de Certeau. Stanford, CA, 1995.

Bourdieu, P. Sociologie de L'Algérie. Paris, 1958.

—. Travail et travailleurs en Algérie. Paris, 1963.

—. Les hériteurs, les étudiants et la culture [The Inheritors]. Chicago, 1979.

—. Distinction. Cambridge, 1984.

—. Homo Academicus. London, 1988.

—. In Other Words. Cambridge, 1990.

—. The Field of Cultural Production, ed. R. Johnson. Cambridge, 1993.

—. Practical Reason: On the Theory of Action. Stanford, CA, 1998.

— and Wacquant, L. J. D. An Invitation to Reflexive Sociology. Chicago, 1997.

Calhoun, C. et al. (eds) Bourdieu: Critical Perspectives. Chicago, 1993.

Colebrook, C. New Literary Histories. Manchester, 1997.

de Certeau, M. The Practice of Everyday Life. Berkeley, CA, 1984.

—. Heterologies. Minneapolis, MN, 1986.

—. The Writing of History. New York, 1988.

—. Culture in the Plural. Minneapolis, MN, 1994.

—. The Capture of Speech and Other Political Writings. Minneapolis, MN, 1997.

—. The Possession at Loudun. Chicago, 1999.

Dosse, F. History of Structuralism vol. 2. Minneapolis, MN, 1997.

During, S. (ed.) The Cultural Studies Reader. London, 1993.

Haslett, M. Marxist Literary and Cultural Theories. London, 2000.

Jenkins, R. Pierre Bourdieu. London, 1992.

Marin, L. Utopics. Highland Park, NJ, 1984.

—. Portrait of the King. Minneapolis, MN, 1988.

—. Food for Thought. Baltimore, MD, 1989.

—. To Destroy Painting. Chicago, 1995.

—. Sublime Poussin. Stanford, CA, 1999.

Swartz, D. Culture and Power. Chicago, 1997.

38. Gilles Deleuze (1925–1995) and Félix Guattari (1930–1992)

Both Gilles Deleuze and Félix Guattari pursued their own authorial careers, with Deleuze's work focusing on the history of philosophy and Guattari's work concerned with the institution and politics of psychoanalysis. Their individual interests intersect in their best known jointly authored works *Anti-Oedipus* (Fr. 1972), *A Thousand Plateaus* (1980), *Kafka* (1975) and *What is Philosophy?* (1991).

Deleuze and Guattari's philosophical project is best characterized through the aim of achieving immanence: no 'transcendent' (or external) object can provide a foundation for experience. Any attempt to think of some ultimate explanatory horizon or 'plane' that would account for experience would itself be an object of experience (Deleuze and Guattari

1994, 45). This affirmation of immanence and the rejection of any transcendent ground for experience leads to a theory of 'transcendental empiricism'. If empiricism is an attention to what is given or experienced, then a *transcendental* empiricism insists that there is nothing outside the given, no point from which the given could be explained or 'justified'. But Deleuze and Guattari also expand the notions of the given, perception or experience beyond its traditional (human) boundaries. We tend to think of experience as located within the mind of a perceiving subject. But to do this, they argue, would be to locate experience *within* some plane. Rather than having some 'plane of transcendence' within which experience or the given would be located, they suggest that we should see the given as having no transcendent ground or foundation. It follows, then, that if experience or the given cannot be located within mind or the subject, then we need to think of perception, experience or givenness that extends beyond the human subject. This is why, in *A Thousand Plateaus*, they theorize a 'becoming-animal', and this is also why they consider the movements of machines, particles, genes and a desire that exceeds bounded organisms. In *What is Philosophy?* they describe science as the creation of 'observers' that are neither human nor subjective (129) and they describe art as the creation of 'percepts' that are freed from acts of perceivers. The subject, for Deleuze and Guattari, is an *effect* of a more general observation and perception that exceeds humans.

Philosophy has traditionally regarded the world as a static and inert being, while the human subject is seen to be the privileged experiencer or representer of that world. The given is located within a plane, and this plane has been constructed as an 'image of thought'. Philosophy has assumed that experience is given to a pre-experiential universal subject. Indeed, in *Difference and Repetition* (1994; published in French in 1968) Deleuze argues that western thought is dominated by two prejudices: good sense and common sense. Good sense assumes that there is some general and proper object or truth to which thought must be directed. Common sense assumes that there is a proper mode of thinking which philosophy ought to recognize. Against this traditional project of recognition, Deleuze and Guattari insist that philosophy ought to extend thought beyond any of its present recognisable forms (1994, 140). Rather than have some world correctly repeated in human representation, philosophy should free thought from dogma, preconceived images and limited notions of what constitutes experience. What differentiates philosophical concepts from science is just this 'ascension' into the virtual: whereas science concerns itself with organizing states of affairs, philosophy creates concepts that are events. Unlike the extended objects of science, events are not located within a spatially and temporally delimited field; events are a 'between-time' or *un entre-temps* (Deleuze and Guattari 1994, 148). A science works practically, by taking the *virtual* whole of all that is given and limiting its point of view to an actual field of extended objects. (Think of the way in which geometry fixes the always moving experience of space into determined extended boundaries.) Philosophical concepts move in the other direction, not organizing experience into extended actualities, but expanding the point of view in order to think the virtual whole of experience. Think, for example, of how philosophical concepts express, not this or that object, but the objectivity of being in general. A philosophical concept is not directed to extended things but to an intensity: when a philosopher defines being as expression or spirit or 'eternal return' they create an event, a way of thinking or confronting the very intensity of experience.

In Deleuze's own work, and in Deleuze and Guattari's *What is Philosophy?*, this attempt to free experience from its enclosure within the image of the human subject led to a particular way of reading texts: when we read a philosopher we need to pay attention to the unique problems and questions they create (Deleuze and Guattari 1994, 139). Doing philosophy is not about correcting errors or tidying up ambiguities; it is about creating new possibilities for thinking. Nietzsche is Deleuze's exemplary philosopher in this regard, for it was Nietzsche who enabled us to think of a givenness or experience that exceeds the human subject (Deleuze 1983). For Deleuze, Nietzsche discovered a domain of pre-personal 'singularities' or forces that could not be located within any being, but were forms of positive becoming; not the becoming *of* some identity, but a becoming *from which* any identity might then be effected. There is not one single form of becoming or affirmation but irreducible and divergent modes or 'series' of becoming. Becoming can only truly be affirmed, Deleuze argues, when we embrace empiricism and begin to experience differently. If there is nothing other than becoming, then becoming cannot be located within being or the subject. Thought, therefore, is itself a mode of becoming alongside – and in confrontation with – various other becomings. Not only is thought a form of creation, it also creates or becomes in different modes. Art, for example, is the creation and becoming of affects and percepts (Deleuze and Guattari 1994, 24), while science is the creation of functions and prospects (157). Philosophy is the creation of concepts. Neither art nor philosophy nor science are representations of the real. Deleuze and Guattari reject the idea that there is a real/actual world that then has a virtual copy. Rather, the real includes the actual and the virtual. Concepts and affects are virtual events, no more lacking in reality than actual extended beings.

If we accept this positive character of the virtual then we come close to achieving immanence and transcendental empiricism: for now the actual and the virtual are affirmed within the single and 'univocal' realm of the given. And this means that we no longer separate what *is* (matter) from some higher forming power (form or mind). It is not as though there is some inert undifferentiated being that is then differentiated by mind (dualism). On the contrary, univocal being is a plurality of singularly differentiating forces; no form of difference or becoming is privileged over any other. This was the error of structuralism; it assumed that language was a differentiating power that differentiated the undifferentiated. Against this, Deleuze and Guattari argue that difference is the whole of being. There are the differences of genetic codes, viruses, plant and animal becomings, and various other 'machinic' or inhuman series of difference. Difference is *singular*; in each case difference itself is different. The difference of each work of art is different from each work of philosophy, and each work of philosophy is itself differently different: Kant differs from Hume in a way quite different from Hume's difference from Locke. This means that difference is immanent: not the differentiation *of* some grounding being or identity. Difference itself is all that is affirmed, and to *repeat* difference is to differentiate with a maximum power. Deleuze therefore draws upon Nietzsche's concept of eternal return: difference is eternal, not grounded in a beginning or end outside difference. And difference *returns*, affirming itself over and over again, not in the repetition *of* some being, but in the repetition of difference itself. To truly repeat is to maximize difference.

An affirmative philosophy tries to live up to this challenge of eternal return by creating concepts that produce the maximum difference of thinking. Deleuze and Guattari produce a whole series of concepts. A concept, they argue, does not name some pre-given being. A concept, at its most philosophical and affirmative, dislodges our categories of being. Certain concepts carry the possibility of thought to its 'nth' degree; others, however, weaken the very power of conceptuality. Nietzsche's concept of 'eternal return', for example, affirms the very force of existence: each singular moment should, over and over again, be a radical beginning. The return or recurrence is *eternal* precisely because no moment is subordinated to any other. Without beginning and without end – without an origin and without a goal – each singular moment of existence can bear its own maximum force. But if Nietzsche has created concepts that affirm the very possibility of existence, there are also concepts that are *reactive*: capable of taking the eternal becoming of life and subordinating it to some far off goal or distant origin. The concept of 'man' or the 'human', for example, is just such a concept of 'common sense'. For it is the very nature of our concepts of 'man' or the 'human' to (a) act as an explanatory ground for other concepts; (b) prescribe a good image of thought; and (c) provide a moral foundation. A philosophical concept, by contrast, disrupts recognition and foundations. The concept of eternal return challenges us to think that unbounded force from which concepts are drawn. Leibniz's concept of the 'monad' suggests that we think a world of perceptions that are located beyond the human point of view (Deleuze 1993). Spinoza's notion of 'expression' tries to articulate a univocal being that is not subordinated to anything other than its own becoming (Deleuze 1988).

But philosophy, as the creation of concepts, is not the only domain of affirmative becoming – and *thought* is not the only domain of the givenness of existence. Deleuze and Guattari's work is also concerned with the forms of thought that exceed philosophical conceptuality and forms of experience or givenness that extend beyond thinking. In *What is Philosophy?* Deleuze and Guattari define the other two domains of thought that exist alongside philosophy as art (the creation of affects and percepts) and science (as the creation of functions and prospects). Their main contribution here is the insistence on a difference *in kind* between these domains. Philosophers, for example, aren't scientists and so their task isn't that of formalizing experience into functions; this is the scientist's task. Nor is art philosophy; art isn't about meaning and concepts. Even less is art science; art is not a picturing of the world for a certain purpose. If philosophers create concepts and scientists create functions, artists create affects. It is this emphasis on creation – rather than concepts or description – in art, which leads to Deleuze and Guattari's unique way of approaching literary texts. The most well known example is their work on Kafka (Deleuze and Guattari 1986). Kafka's texts, they argue, are not signs, allegories or metaphors for something outside the text. Indeed Kafka takes all the well-known images of meaning – the law, the father, the book – and shows these images to be the outcome of becomings. Rather than read the castle as an image of passageways directed to a law that always recedes, Deleuze and Guattari argue that it is the positive proliferation of passages and paths that multiplies the events of existence well in excess of any law. Kafka, they argue, is an author of positive becomings, and not of negative law. We should read Kafka for what his texts do and how they work, and not for what they *mean*.

Deleuze and Guattari's approach towards literature and philosophy is an affirmation of their theory of territorialization, deterritorialization and reterritorialization as described in *A Thousand Plateaus*. From an infinite and univocal becoming, always in movement and infinitely divisible, certain territories or identities are formed. And once these territories are formed they can be deterritorialized. Once an image is created, for example, it can free itself from its origin and circulate widely. *Reterritorialization* occurs when the image is then re-grounded. Take for example the formation of a language. First there is a marking out of boundaries, a *territorialization* whereby sounds are organized into phonemes, or lines are formed into script. But there is a movement of *deterritorialization* whereby such sounds can circulate and function independent of any speaker or origin. A language is essentially deterritorialization, the detachment from any ground or origin through general circulation and reference. Reterritorialization occurs when this free movement is subjected, or falls back on, one of its own components as a grounding territory. The 'I' or 'subject' is produced as a sign that grounds all other signs. Once territories are created – such as the image of the subject or the image of the law – it is possible to make the mistake of interpreting such territories as the origin of creation. Traditional readings of Kafka make just this error. They take one of the points in Kafka's castle – the centre of Law – to be the grounding origin from which all other points flow. The text has been 'overcoded' – read through the image of a single signifier. In this reterritorialization, Kafka is read as a writer who laments the ways in which Law recedes from every one of its single instances. Against this, Deleuze and Guattari read Kafka as an instance of minor literature. The major code of law, the father and meaning is deterritorialized, dispersed into movements, passages, flights and wanderings. If read affirmatively we can see Kafka as a writer who shows that any law or ground is the effect of a 'machinic' production: machinic because law is the effect of a movement that is not located within any deciding subject but is the outcome of a network or 'assemblage' of movements. To read Kafka in this way is to deterritorialize the law, to show that law is not the ground of our being but the result of a series of events. Kafka's literature creates affects: the movements and wanderings through the castle, the sounds and rhythms of his writing, and the creation of animal personae. This is why Deleuze and Guattari describe desiring production as *literally* a machine: there is just the proliferation of connections and codings, without an organizing centre (organism) or function (mechanism). Against the idea of force as issuing from a law, father or territory, Deleuze and Guattari assert the creative and affirmative nature of force. Only weak forces subject themselves to a law; active forces, by contrast, are nomadic, deterritorializing and in perpetual flight, not requiring an identity to act as a ground or justification for their becoming.

This is where Deleuze and Guattari's theory of desire comes in. Desire is not the desire *of* a subject. There is just desire, as a flow of energy, and it is from this general and immanent flow that subjects *and* transcendencies are formed. This can be made clear through Deleuze and Guattari's critique of the Oedipus complex and their embrace of a more radical Freud in *Anti-Oedipus* (1983). The Oedipus complex, they argue, is the *effect* of a certain flow of desire. It is a mistake to see the Oedipus story as a way of interpreting all other stories; to do so would be to locate the Oedipal narrative *outside* (or transcendent to) desire. By contrast, Deleuze and Guattari show that the Oedipal narrative is itself a fantasy. The father/analyst imagines that all acts of desire take place as substitutions for the lacking phallus. All desire is explained according to an original object – the full presence of the phallus – which is lost and for which all other objects stand in as signs. For Deleuze and Guattari this places psychoanalysis within a long history of *reactive* or subjectivist theories. In reactivism or subjectivism we see an action or event and then set out to describe its cause or foundation. In so doing we subordinate actions to some prior acting subject. In the case of the Oedipus complex, we assume that all specific acts of desire stand in for some original and unfulfillable desire for a complete and closed origin. But if we understand the flow of desire as existing well beyond any of its subsequent formations, then we will not take one unit of desire – the phallus – as the measure of desire in general. And this is how the critiques of psychoanalysis and capitalism are conjoined. Capital takes the flow of desire and, through a single axiom, measures all flow according to quantifiable and calculable units: the value of labour and the value of property. Similarly, psychoanalysis measures all desire in relation to one of its objects, the phallus. In this manner difference is subordinated to an identifiable measure of the same. Against this restriction of desire and capital to one of its part objects, Deleuze and Guattari insist on singularities and intensities. Desire does not pursue objects in compensation for an original lost object, and societies do not interact through the exchange of a single value. Desire is connective, continually creating new objects. And politics is not just the distribution of power and property; it also concerns the investments that create interests. The micropolitics of *Anti-Oedipus* demands that we look at how capital is created as the object of modern desire, how the subject or ego is produced as the measure for experience. Politics needs to be taken back to the ways in which the flows of desire – intensities – have been reduced to recognizable and exchangeable extended units. What Deleuze and Guattari refer to as 'schizoanalysis' is just this investigation into the 'schiz' or splitting and difference that cuts into the pure flow of desire and encloses its infinite differences into finite units, such as the phallus, the ego, the family, money, labour or property.

Ostensibly, Deleuze and Guattari's two volumes of *Capitalism and Schizophrenia* (*Anti-Oedipus* and *A Thousand Plateaus*) provide a critique of psychoanalysis and Marxism. But the word critique has to be taken seriously here. Deleuze and Guattari use the radical insights of Freud and Marx to reinvigorate the orthodox ossification of psychoanalysis and marxism. What they retrieve from Freud is the positivity of desire: prior to any subject, any 'complex' or any opposition between the actual and the virtual there is just the immanent and eternally recurring flow of desire. These flows of desire produce regularities or territories or codes. The problem comes in when certain territories or codes take themselves as being outside the flow of desire. This happens for example, when one code – the story of Oedipus – regards itself as the interpreter of all other codes. Or, when one territory – the subject, bourgeois man – locates itself as the ground for all other territories.

It is through their radical marxism that their critical theory of desire gains its truly political edge. On the one hand, Deleuze and Guattari have to remain critical of any normalizing theory of marxism. They cannot locate a subject or subject group (the proletariat) as some proper foundation for emancipation. This means also that their critique of capitalism cannot proceed as demystification of ideology to reveal the truth of, or for, some grounding subject or consciousness. Indeed, their criticism of capitalism turns on a quite unique reversal. The standard opposition to capitalism is that it has turned the world into so much quantifiable exchange, such that even the human subject becomes subjected to the flow of an impersonal market. Rather than argue that the flow of exchange should be relocated within the autonomy of the human subject, Deleuze and Guattari argue that capitalism precludes a truly radical flow of desire. Capital *deterritorializes* by subjecting everything to the flow and exchange of capital, but it then effects a massive *reterritorialization* by measuring this flow through a single axiom: the units of capital. The very notion of exchange is, in capitalism, grounded in the exchange *of* some value (capital) and *for* some end (profit). At the surface capitalism presents itself as a free flow of exchange without interference, imposed system or foundation. But in actual fact capitalism has measured and restricted flow according to the units of the monetary system. Deleuze and Guattari therefore argue for a properly dialectical extension of the force of capitalism. The flow of exchange should not be restricted to the code of labour and profit (just as the flow of desire in psychoanalysis ought not to be restricted to the signifier of the phallus). When one object locates itself as the explanation of all other objects then the pure and immanent flow of desire and exchange subordinates itself to one of its productions. If, however, we see desire as positive and productive we reverse the political and metaphysical reactions – such as psychoanalysis and capitalism – that try to explain or ground desire. It's not that there is a subject *who* desires. Rather, from certain regular flows of desire, subject effects are formed. It's not that exchange solidifies into a system; the very idea of 'exchange' is the effect of systematizing all units into quantities of capital. The response of Deleuze and Guattari is not to interpret desire, or regain control of the system, but to intensify desire beyond any single interpretation and extend the flow of capital beyond the fixed units of the system.

The political project of *Anti-Oedipus* is therefore intimately tied to the philosophical project of *What is Philosophy?* Both works are united by what Deleuze and Guattari argue to be *the* ethics of philosophy: *amor fati*. Rather than posit some value or redemption beyond or outside of existence – as though this world needed to be justified by some higher goal – the task of philosophy is to joyfully affirm what is. For the most part metaphysics has failed to be affirmative, and this is because it has posited some transcendent plane (or metaphysical ground) outside existence that will give existence its meaning. (The subject, being, God, humanity: all these operate as grounds from which the becoming of existence is explained.) If we see philosophy as metaphysics – the inquiry into some ultimate Being or ground – then we locate our cause and justification beyond existence. A more radical or superior transcendentalism, by contrast, refuses to locate existence within any plane. But this also means that philosophy and politics need to be eternally affirmative. Here, Deleuze and Guattari draw on Nietzsche's philosophy of eternal return. If we accept that there are just active desires, events or flows of force and that it is *from* these events that identifiable beings are constituted, then it is a mistake or *reaction* to take one of these beings as the ground or cause of all others. Philosophy's task is, therefore, to eternally and affirmatively *activate* thought. If some of our created concepts start to look like explanatory foundations or grounding beings, then philosophers need to create new concepts. This means that we need to think philosophy as a process of radical difference and repetition. As soon as an effected identity is taken as a transcendent origin or cause, then philosophy needs to *repeat* the creative force that formed this grounding concept. For example, to truly repeat Plato's *Republic* would not be to write a commentary on the text, but to produce a philosophical event that had the same force today as the original *Republic*. This means that true repetition of an event also creates maximum difference. What philosophy repeats is not theorems, opinions and dogmas but the *force* of philosophy, creating concepts over and over again. It is when philosophy falls into recognition that it becomes metaphysical and reactive: if philosophers see themselves as providing a faithful picture of the human subject then they have belied the active and affirmative event of philosophy. Immanence, therefore, is an eternal project; as soon as one concept operates as the transcendent foundation for all other concepts, then philosophy needs to renew its creative power.

But this project of immanence and eternal return also has a political dimension, as both *Anti-Oedipus* and *A Thousand Plateaus* make clear. It is in these volumes that Deleuze and Guattari demonstrate the concrete significance of a philosophy of immanence. Their invocation of 'becoming-woman', for example, ties the philosophical project of affirmation both to a politics and to a celebration of literature. Thought becomes reactive, they argue, when one of its effects – the image of man or the subject – is then taken as an origin. Against this reactive movement Deleuze and Guattari affirm the event of virtual becoming. The virtual is not a pale copy of the real, nor can the virtual be reduced to a set of possibilities derived from the actual; the virtual itself is real. Fantasies, images, concepts are at one with a univocal realm of being. If being is univocal then no part of being – neither mind, nor matter, nor the human – can act as the privileged ground of all other beings. The problem with the concept of man is that it is a virtual production that takes itself to be the actual foundation for all other productions. The only way to move beyond the reactive concept of man, who is that *being* through which all *becoming* is measured, is to affirm becoming-woman. What is other than the *being* of man would be becoming. Becoming-woman would be the first step in thinking an affirmative becoming capable of maximizing its own difference rather than shoring up its own identity. Becoming-woman is therefore the opening of becoming: not a woman who then becomes, but a becoming that is truly other than the *being* of man. For man's becoming has always been his *own*, a becoming that is the fulfilment or extension of what he is. Becoming-woman, on the other hand – if it is to be more than just an opposition to man – would be at one with becomings beyond thought, identity, decision and the self. Becoming-woman is not the becoming *of being*; it is other than being. This becoming can only be other than the becoming of being if it is a becoming not subordinated to an end outside itself. Molecular becomings are movements of difference that have no end other than themselves; they are neither becoming towards or from identity. Molar becomings, by contrast, are grounded in a being *who becomes*. This understanding of becoming-woman enables a whole new political theory of movements. Micropolitics attends to all those movements of difference that precede and exceed the intentions and identities of subjects. This is why, for Deleuze and Guattari, 'minor' literature is always political. Minor literature frees language from a speaking subject, and shows the ways in which subjects are effects of 'collective' ways of speaking. Politics is not the affirmation or emancipation of identity; if it were so then affirmation would be in the name of some being, and affirmation would be subordinated to one of its effects. Politics is the continual deterritorialization of identity, a 'molecular' process that exposes any 'molar' law to be the outcome of desire and not the ground of desire.

If we take literature to be the expression of some human spirit then literature is subordinated to something other than itself and is located within a historical trajectory of human becoming. But if literature is *literary* then it must be a minor literature, not the continuation or expression of an already existing identity but an event of *style*. Great texts, such as those of Joyce and Kafka, can be described as minor precisely because they are written in such a way that what they say is not located within a speaking subject. Consider the first lines of 'A Painful Case' from Joyce's *Dubliners*. The story begins in the voice of uptight bourgeois moralism: 'Mr James Duffy lived in Chapelizod because he wished to live as far as possible from the city of which he was a citizen and because he found all the other suburbs of Dublin mean, modern and pretentious.' As so often in *Dubliners*, although the sentence is not actually quoted, the way of speaking is already typical of a place rather than a subject. To use the words 'mean, modern and pretentious' or to speak of 'citizens' is to show the ways in which Dublin is already a certain lexicon. The sentence is written in the 'voice' of Dublin. This is why all minor literature is directly political: not because it expresses a political message but because its mode of articulation takes voice away from the speaking subject to an anonymous or pre-personal saying. Joyce's style, for example, is less the expression of an individual subject than it is the articulation of what Deleuze and Guattari refer to as a 'collective assemblage'. Joyce's literature is minor because it takes voice and the saying beyond any meaning, law or proper ground. And the response to such a minor literature should not be its canonization but its repetition. To affirm the event of a great work of literature, for example, is not to copy, mimic or imitate; it is to create another 'great' text. But to be truly great we must repeat all the newness, difference and stylistic divergence of the precursor. True fidelity to a major text is a becoming-minor, affirming a style that does not yet exist, that is not yet recognized and is not yet the style *of* some identifiable movement. For it is in literature that style is not presented as the ornament or overlay of an otherwise coherent content; it is not that there is a sense that is then expressed *through style*. Literature is style itself, the production of affects, masks, personae and voices – a continual affirmation of a becoming that is not the becoming *of* some prior identity. This is what sets literature, when read affirmatively, against the reactive concept of the human. It is not that there is a speaking being – the human – who then deploys style. Rather, the human is an effect of a certain way of speaking. The subject – predicate structure of our sentences, for example, leads us to think of a being who then acts, a speaker who then speaks. Against this subject – predicate structure of the proposition, Deleuze and Guattari affirm forms of literature capable of enacting a grammar of becoming. Their most well-known example is that of free-indirect style. In free-indirect style – as we have seen in the example from Joyce – it is not that there are general human characters who then speak; rather, character is effected from ways of speaking.

Deleuze and Guattari also carry the question of style through to their own philosophy. Their own work, particularly *A Thousand Plateaus*, is written in a manner that demands new ways of reading, thinking and response. Composed in a series of 'plateaus', their work uses intervening voices, oscillates between the tone of a manifesto and the tone of exegesis, wanders through observations on science, literature, politics and philosophy, and concludes not with a proposition but a created concept: 'mechanosphere'. If, as they argue, thought is a response to existence and life, and if life itself is eternal response, then philosophy will be a dynamic event. *A Thousand Plateaus* is, therefore, not a series of propositions whose truth-value can be assessed by some pre-existing logic. It is the creation of a new logic and a new synthesis. The response that such a text invites is less one of interpretation than affirmation. If we ask how *A Thousand Plateaus* works, and not what it means, then we might also be compelled to think of new ways in which texts might work. In the case of *A Thousand Plateaus* its construction or 'working' is rhizomatic or nomadic: not centred around an authorial voice and subject matter but creating new voices and inventing new questions. The challenge of this work lies in the possibility of its *repetition*: to repeat the event of *A Thousand Plateaus* would not be to write and think rhizomatically, but to think (over again) one more way in which we could think and write differently.

Claire Colebrook

Further reading and works cited

Buchanan, I. *Deleuzism*. Edinburgh, 2000.
Deleuze, G. *Nietzsche and Philosophy*. London, 1983.
—. *Spinoza*. San Francisco, 1988.
—. *The Fold*. Minneapolis, MN, 1993.
—. *Difference and Repetition*. New York, 1994.
—. *Negotiations: 1972–1990*. New York, 1995.
—. *Essays: Critical and Clinical*. Minneapolis, MN, 1997.
— and Guattari, F. *Anti-Oedipus*. Minneapolis, MN, 1983.
—. *Kafka*. Minneapolis, MN, 1986a.
—. *Nomadology: The War Machine*. New York, 1986b.
—. *A Thousand Plateaus*. Minneapolis, MN, 1987.

—. *What is Philosophy?* London, 1994.
— and Parnet, C. *Dialogues*. London, 1987.
Hardt, M. *Gilles Deleuze*. Minneapolis, MN, 1993.
Massumi, B. *A User's Guide to Capitalism and Schizophrenia*. Cambridge, MA, 1992.
Stivale, C. *The Two-Fold Thought of Deleuze and Guattari*. New York, 1988.

39. Michel Foucault (1926–1984)

Michel Foucault began his academic career in the discipline of psychology, obtaining a diploma in 1952 and working in psychiatric hospitals in the early 1950s. But apart from his first book, *Mental Illness and Psychology* (1954), his work extends across the disciplines of history, philosophy, critical theory and literary and cultural studies, as well as psychology and semiotics. His early work does indicate a persistent concern of his later writings, however, in focusing on the systems of human behaviour and thought, and in seeking to identify the reasons and motivations for particular human rituals or actions. Arguably, no other theorist since Freud has had such an impact on contemporary notions of human subjectivity and agency. His influence on the arts and social sciences in general has been both pervasive and incisive, and has had a major impact on the direction of literary and cultural studies in particular.

Along with Jacques Derrida and Roland Barthes, Foucault was perhaps the most significant intellectual responsible for the emergence of poststructuralist theories, and devised several key concepts which are common currency in contemporary critical theory, such as 'discourse', 'technology', 'power', 'epistemé' and 'archaeology'. These concepts were linked for Foucault in his methods of analysing systems of practices and ideas, and tracing these systems through history. Foucault identified sets of associated practices and rituals as indicative of systems of belief and thought. The emergence in the seventeenth century of the ritual of banishing and confining 'insane' people, for example, marked a shift for Foucault in the ways in which people of that time conceived of the relationship between 'reason' and 'madness', and thus a shift in what constituted 'normal' human behaviour. Foucault's historical methods involved identifying epistemic or epochal changes from the evidence of new terminologies, new practices and new institutions. These methods were based on the notion that we could detect that certain human actions were not accidental but occurred within frameworks of repetition, so that we can trace the emergence of specific 'technologies' in a regularity of actions. The systematic confinement of the 'insane' to a specific institution constitutes one example of the 'technologies' which Foucault analyses. Similarly, his argument that modern methods of penal correction and reform could be traced to the eighteenth century was predicated on the evidence of a new type of prison as well as associated changes in the treatment and containment of those found breaking the law. For Foucault, such changes were not isolated from wider shifts in power relations in society, and usually entailed the transformation of prevailing notions of subjectivity.

Foucault called these historical methods 'archaeology', and argued that they differed substantially from 'history' as it was then commonly practised. The 'historian's history', in Foucault's terms, was constructed to seem like a neutral, unbiased narrative of events, which traced historical continuities in order to represent disparate events as parts of the same evolutionary pattern (Foucault 1977a, 152). Foucault modelled his 'archaeological' historical practice, however, on Nietzsche's genealogies, which he discusses in his essay 'Nietzsche, Genealogy, History' (1977a). According to Foucault, genealogy searches for hidden structures of regulation and association, a method of tracing etymological, psychological and ideological ancestors of modern social, cultural or political practices 'in the most unpromising places' (Foucault 1977a, 139). Genealogy was interested in ruptures as well as continuities, contradiction as well as coherence. The genealogist, moreover, is aware of the provisional nature of her/his own subject position in relation to interpretations of the past, in contrast to the historian's pretence of neutrality.

Foucault's 'archaeology' differs only slightly from Nietzsche's genealogy in placing more emphasis on the search for origins or decisive transformations. Foucault argued that there were distinct 'epistemés', or epochs, of history, and that each epistemé contained its own particular ideas of subjectivity, power and history. In practice, this meant that there was a 'well-defined regularity' to different disciplines and modes of thought. Foucault posed the possibility that very different kinds of practices – science, literature, economics, language, anthropology, medicine, history and so on – collaborated implicitly in a self-regulating system of representations. He asks us to believe that connections between disciplines, and shared assumptions between different kinds of thought, are not coincidental. 'What if empirical knowledge, at a given time and in a given culture, *did* possess a well-defined regularity? If the very possibility of recording facts, of allowing oneself to be convinced by them, of distorting them in traditions or of making purely speculative use of them, if even this was not at the mercy of chance?' (Foucault 1974, ix). The associations between different discourses and disciplines, Foucault goes on to argue, reveal not coincidence, but instead an order regulated by powerful ideological conditions.

Foucault's work identifies the points at which new collaborations of this sort emerge and become dominant. This is evident in his 'histories' or 'archaeologies'. In *Madness and Civilization*, he traces the emergence of modern categories and concepts of insanity. In *The Birth of the Clinic*, he analyses the beginnings of modern ideas of medical care and of the care for the health of the human subject. *Discipline and Punish* examined the emergence of modern modes of penal correction, punishment and containment. His last works, the three volumes on *The History of Sexuality*, continued this work by exploring the birth of modern notions of sexual identity and practice, while also marking a return to his early interests in psychology by focusing even more intensely on human subjectivity and the 'technologies of the self'. Each of these works take as their subject different discourses or 'discursive formations', by which Foucault means the powerful collaborations of texts, images, disciplines and practices which make up the prevailing knowledge of distinct areas, such as sexuality, penality or insanity.

This has been an important dimension of Foucault's work for literary and cultural studies. According to his notions of 'discursive formations', literary texts would collaborate with texts of various different kinds – medical, juridical, penal, philosophical, psychological, etc. – to form particular kinds of knowledge and understanding. This means that we can analyse literary texts for the function which they perform in relation to different kinds of knowledge. For example, we might analyse European literary texts to see to what degree and how they collaborate with other texts and images in representing Africa as a savage, uncivilized place, and thereby identify how literary texts might collude with the politics of imperialism. Equally, we might analyse how literary texts represent women in a given time, to explore the relationship between literary representations of women and practices of misogyny. This type of analysis, which treats literary texts as agents which construct and shape the ideologies and practices of a given society or culture, borrows from Foucault's arguments that the connections between different kinds of representation are indications of a powerful discursive formation.

There is a direct correlation for Foucault between the representation of a particular concept and the situation of that concept within a field of power relations. The category of 'insanity', for example, emerges as a defined and distinct object of study at the same time as it is constituted as a site of otherness and abnormality. The production of knowledge about 'insanity' leads to the formation of institutions and technologies to treat it as a condition, and, in turn, the establishment of such institutions and technologies means that there is a new power relationship between the insane and the sane. The insane are, according to this system of representations and relationships, deemed incapable of knowing or caring for themselves, and the sane are correspondingly deemed responsible for treating the insane. This is the argument of Foucault's first major work, *Madness and Civilization* (1961). He begins that book by charting the process whereby the marginalized figures of the medieval world, lepers, were replaced by those of the modern world, the insane. This process, according to Foucault, takes place initially at the level of representations, 'first, a whole literature of tales and moral fables ... [then] in farces and *soties*, the character of the Madman, the Fool, or the Simpleton assumes more and more importance. He is no longer simply a ridiculous and familiar silhouette in the wings: he stands center stage as the guardian of truth' (Foucault 1967, 14). Gradually, the modern world develops methods and practices for dealing with insanity, confining the insane to institutions which serve to police the difference between the mad who are held within the walls of the asylum, and the 'normal' who are free to live in society unaffected. There is a direct relationship between prevailing definitions of normality, and the institutional confinement of the mad, as well as the criminal and the rebel, of course. Foucault's argument suggests that modern societies spin out a dialectic of self and other in which the stability and normality of the self can only be proved by demonizing and estranging the other.

It is important to stress that Foucault's analysis of such power relations recognizes that power is not at the control of individual subjects or groups but is instead a general force which is only visible in particular events and actions. If Nietzsche claimed to be working in a God-less universe, Foucault took this further by appearing to work in a world absent of human agency either. Power operates for Foucault in a structural and systemic way, not as an instrument mastered by human subjects. Foucault defines power relations most clearly, but perhaps also most crudely, in his later works, principally in *Histoire de la sexualité: La volonté de Savoir* [The History of Sexuality, Volume 1, 1990], first published in 1976. Here, Foucault argues that in taking sexuality as an object of study, and in particular addressing the repression of sexuality in the Victorian period, we ought to look not at the individuals or even the particular laws or institutions instrumental in the censorship of sexuality. Instead, Foucault asks us to conceive of the whole discourse of sexuality and its repression becoming prominent in a particular form as a result of the emergence of certain power relations. Sexuality only becomes a prominent discourse during this time, he argues, 'because relations of power established it as a possible object; and conversely, if power was able to take it as a target, this was because techniques of knowledge and procedures of discourse were capable of investigating it' (1981, 98). This makes the relationship between power and discourse seem to be confusingly tautological, but Foucault is emphasizing the ways in which no individual, group, class or sex is responsible for deciding to repress certain aspects of sexuality. Instead, sexuality manifested itself in its particular forms and concepts in any given time because of 'a complex, strategical situation in a particular society' (Foucault 1981, 93). For Foucault, human subjectivity and agency was as much the product of particular discursive formations and power relations as sexuality, penality, insanity or any other concept, and the human belief in the individual ability to affect the society around them consciously and decisively was the effect of a system of beliefs and discourses.

Foucault's theories, like other poststructuralist ideas, are characteristically post-humanist in the sense that they ascribe very little power or responsibility to individual human agency. In a much quoted phrase in the preface to *The Order of Things*, Foucault writes 'it is comforting ... and a source of profound relief to think that man is only a recent invention, a figure not yet two centuries old, a new wrinkle in our knowledge, and that he will disappear again as soon as that knowledge has discovered a new form' (1974, xxiii). Like Barthes and Derrida, Foucault anticipates the 'death of the subject', in which 'man' is no longer the privileged locus of sovereignty and power. His antipathy towards human sovereignty is the product of a widespread belief among postwar European and American intellectuals that the events of the Second World War revealed the dark side of Enlightenment modernity. The Enlightenment ideal that humankind would evolve progressively towards greater harmony and civilization was severely undermined in the twentieth century by the wars of mass destruction. This led postwar thinkers to argue that the Enlightenment went hand in hand with dark tendencies, which included from the beginning the destructive forces of colonialism, capitalism, poverty, war and famine. These forces were not the product of individual human agency, but were instead the logical consequences of modern social and political systems. This is what Foucault shows in his 'archaeologies', that the dark forces of sexual repression, penality and insanity are not aberrations within modern society – they are not, for example, the residual traces of pre-Enlightenment civilization – but are necessary functions in the production of modern notions of normality. Social and cultural change occurs for poststructuralist thinkers through specific structures or discourses of representation, in which human actions, thoughts and practices are produced as effects. History for Foucault is not the product of human behaviour, but of structural relations.

Some critics of Foucault's thinking have argued that this notion of power relations determining human subjectivity is too gloomy. Frank Lentricchia sees Foucault's account of the archaeologies of power as 'a totalitarian narrative' with a 'depressing message' (Lentricchia, in Veeser 1989, 235). 'Power is everywhere', writes Foucault in *The History of Sexuality*, 'not because it embraces everything, but because it comes from everywhere' (1990, 93). The implication of this notion of the omnipresence of power is that there is no possibility for the emergence of effective resistance or even escape, and indeed this appears to be Foucault's legacy for new historicist critics, particularly Stephen Greenblatt, who argues that subversion only ends up serving the interests of power (Greenblatt 1981). Because power functions by justifying itself in relation to demonized others, opposition to it can only serve to reinforce its modes of operation. Power is thus believed to be ineluctable, which Lentricchia argues, leaves us apathetic and submissive. This emphasis on the omnipresence of power, however, is a feature mostly of Foucault's later work, and perhaps is unfair to his work as a whole. Jon Simons argues that Foucault is caught between two moods, one in which he is 'a prophet of entrapment who induces despair by indicating that there is no way out of our subjection', the other in which he is attracted to the notion of 'untrammelled freedom and an escape from all limitations' (Simons 1995, 3).

The latter optimism is certainly evident in *Madness and Civilization*, for example, in which Foucault reserves a special status for art as a vehicle for freedom. Art and writing, he argues in the conclusion to *Madness and Civilization*, are outside and critical of the discourse of madness. This means that art and writing are privileged as spaces outside of the operation of power. Derrida criticized Foucault's attempt to sustain the illusion of freedom or resistance in the face of a totalitarian concept of discourse as 'the most audacious and seductive aspect of his venture', and 'with all seriousness, the *maddest* aspect of his project' (Derrida 1978, 34). Foucault seemed caught between the desire to maintain a space of freedom and yet at the same time to insist that freedom was impossible within an omnipotent system of discursive formations.

He attempted to resolve this tension in his later work by defining more clearly what he meant by 'power', particularly in arguing that power was not to be understood solely as an instrument of repression or punishment. Power could also produce pleasure, he argued:

> If power were never anything but repressive, if it never did anything but to say no, do you really think one would be brought to obey it? What makes power hold good, what makes it accepted, is simply the fact that it doesn't weigh on us as a force that says no, but that it traverses and produces things, it induces pleasure, forms knowledge, produces discourse. It needs to be considered as a productive network which runs throughout the whole social body. (Foucault 1980, 119)

The force which Foucault calls power certainly produces repression, incarceration, pain and the subjugation and exclusion of marginal peoples, and maintains a vast array of technologies and weapons in its support. But it is not, Foucault argues, an external force which is imposed on us – it is in fact the name of our own repressions, inhibitions and exclusions. It is our own process of self-fashioning and self-policing, which produces our loyalty and obedience, our conformity and unconscious submission in the act of producing us. Power is the term Foucault uses to describe the repressive apparatus of the state. It is our own repressive apparatus, and as such it allows us the pleasure of our own illusions and self-images. This is the major argument of *The History of Sexuality*, in particular, which focuses more clearly than in any other of Foucault's works on the productive and positive aspects of modern discourses on sexuality.

Foucault died in 1984, but his work has had a profound impact on the theoretical foundations of modern literary and cultural studies. In the late 1970s, Foucault conducted seminars at the University of California at Berkeley, and influenced a generation of critics who defined and practised what became known as the new historicism. Critics such as Stephen Greenblatt, Louis Montrose, Catherine Gallagher and D. A. Miller have analysed literary texts from perspectives which are broadly Foucauldian. His later work has been a major influence on the methods and arguments of gender studies too, in the work of Eve Kosofsky Sedgwick and Alan Sinfield, in particular. He has also been influential to the emergence of contemporary postcolonial studies, especially in the work of Edward Said, whose pioneering study of discourses of imperialism, *Orientalism*, borrowed from Foucauldian ideas and concepts. His pervasive impact on a wide range of academic disciplines is testimony to the breadth of thought in his work, which could not be confined to one discipline in particular. Maurice Blanchot asked 'do we know who he is, since he doesn't call himself ... either a sociologist or a historian or a thinker or a metaphysician?' (Blanchot 1990, 93). It is the virtue and also perhaps the problem of Foucault's legacy that he attempted to encompass all these roles in fashioning his structural analyses of modern civilization.

John Brannigan

Further reading and works cited

Blanchot, M. 'Michel Foucault as I imagine him', in M. Foucault and M. Blanchot, Foucault/Blanchot. New York, 1990.
Derrida, J. Writing and Difference. London, 1978.
Foucault, M. Raymond Roussel. Paris, 1963.
—. Madness and Civilization. London, 1967.
—. The Archaeology of Knowledge. London, 1972.
—. The Order of Things. London, 1974.
—. The Birth of the Clinic. New York, 1975.
—. Mental Illness and Psychology. New York, 1976.
—. Language, Counter-Memory, Practice, ed. D. F. Bouchard. Ithaca, NY, 1977a.
—. Discipline and Punish. London, 1977b.
—. Power/Knowledge, ed. C. Gordon. London, 1980.
—. The History of Sexuality, Volume 2. New York, 1985.
—. The History of Sexuality, Volume 3. New York, 1986.
—. The History of Sexuality, Volume 1. London, 1990.
Greenblatt, S. 'Invisible Bullets: Renaissance Authority and its Subversion', Glyph, 8, 1981.
Lentricchia, F. 'Foucault's Legacy: A New Historicism?', in The New Historicism, ed. H. Aram Veeser. London, 1989.
McNay, L. Foucault. Cambridge, 1994.
Rabinow, P. (ed.) The Foucault Reader. London, 1986.
Said, E. Orientalism: Western Conceptions of the Orient. London, 1985.
Simons, J. Foucault and the Political. London, 1995.
Visker, R. Michel Foucault. London, 1995.

40. Jacques Derrida (1930–2004)

Jackie Derrida was born in El-Biar, near Algiers, and moved to Paris in 1949, where he studied at the Lycée Louis-le-Grand before being admitted to the École Normale Supérieur. His teachers included Jean Hyppolite and Michel Foucault, and he met fellow Algerian Louis Althusser on the first day he attended rue d'Ulm. He taught at the ENS as *maître-assistant* until 1984 when he took up the position of *directeur d'études* at the École des Hautes Études en Sciences Sociales. On the verge of publishing his first paper, he signed himself 'Jacques Derrida' and has thereafter been known by that name. Derrida's earliest scholarly work was on Edmund Husserl – his 1954 *Mémoire*, supervised by Maurice de Gandillac, *Le problème de la genèse dans la philosophie de Husserl*, was eventually published in

1990 – and a respect for the rigour of phenomenology marks all his thought, even though his originality depends on a swerve away from Husserl.

From early on, Derrida was impressed by Martin Heidegger's dialogue with and departure from phenomenology. In particular, he was influenced by Heidegger's claim that all metaphysics is at heart a metaphysics of presence. Within western philosophy, as Heidegger reads it, being is construed as presence (an object is present or presentable) or as self-presence (divine or human consciousness). With *Of Grammatology* Derrida was to argue that the border of metaphysics is divided, so that assumptions of presence overtly or covertly structure all sorts of writings, not only those we conventionally identify as philosophy. It follows that the sciences as well as the humanities answer to metaphysics. 'Philosophy can teach science that it is ultimately an element of language, that the limits of its formalization reveal its belonging to a language in which it continues to operate despite its attempts to justify itself as an exclusively "objective" or "instrumental" discourse' (Derrida 1984a, 115). This is not a wholly negative lesson, for Derrida seeks to indicate ways of refiguring our relations to ideas and the institutions that house them. His interpretations are, he insists, affirmative. An open network of words and concepts – including 'différance', 'dissemination', 'spacing' and 'trace' – was patiently established to inaugurate and advance this discourse, although, to Derrida's surprise, his work has become known by just one of the words he put to use: *deconstruction*.

In 1983, when explaining 'deconstruction' in a letter to his Japanese translator, Derrida recalled how it imposed itself on him while writing *Of Grammatology*. 'Among other things', he says, 'I wished to translate and adapt to my own ends the Heideggerian word *Destruktion* or *Abbau*' (Derrida 1991, 270). Both words designate an operation of destructuring or unbuilding, the purpose of which is to reveal how the fundamental concepts of western philosophy have been constructed, and over the years Derrida has taken pains to distance deconstruction, as he practises it, from the instrumental and mechanical overtones of both German words. The word 'deconstruction' is not used in Derrida's first major work, *Edmund Husserl's 'Origin of Geometry': An Introduction* (1962), five years before the better known *Of Grammatology*. Indeed, the interesting metaphor in the earlier text is not 'construction' but 'sedimentation'. The term is Husserl's, and it was used to suggest how a discipline such as geometry develops by researchers building on the assumptions, methods and results of those who came before. More in harmony with Husserl than in disharmony with him, Derrida writes of 'de-sedimentation', of questioning back through history to see how meanings have been formed, reformed or deformed while being transmitted through history. It is in reading the *Introduction* that we see how carefully Derrida follows phenomenology and precisely where and why he leaves it.

Husserl argues that no sharp line can be drawn between the constitution of an ideal object – Pythagoras's theorem, for example – and its historical transmission. His reason: language preserves the sense of an ideal object and allows other people to gain access to it. Derrida agrees with Husserl that language helps to compose ideal objects; however, he disagrees with him on how language establishes itself. Husserl is especially interested in writing, which he believes preserves ideal objects in an exemplary way, and it is over the status of writing that the two philosophers fundamentally differ. For Husserl, the contingency and materiality of writing, *Verkörperung*, can be bracketed, leaving only the pure possibility of embodiment, *Verleiblichung*. Yet, as Derrida argues, *Verleiblichung* and *Verkörperung* cannot be separated in language (1978, 92). An author's pure intentional act can never be protected from the dangers of contingency and catastrophe. A manuscript can always be burned, lost, quoted out of context or delivered to the wrong address. At this point it needs to be stressed that 'writing' for Derrida denotes inscription in general, not merely ideographical marks. Cinema, cybernetics, dance, music, sculpture: all are constituted by acts of inscription, even those that do not answer to voice. The presumption that writing derives from speech, and represents a fall from a natural state of unmediated presence to a speaker or listener, is named phonocentrism. It is a general state of affairs, Derrida thinks, as prevelant in the East as in the West. Logocentrism is a European response to phonocentrism; it is the systematic tendency to locate intelligibility in a self-grounding *Logos*: God, Logic, Reason, Spirit, Will, or any of the other contenders for pride of place in the western philosophical tradition.

Derrida maintains, then, that self-expression is never pure, never fully present to either author or reader, but is always bound to its material mark. Writing is therefore always and already exposed to accidents. Even geometrical figures can be cited out of context, as the lyrics of Eugène Guillevic's *Euclidiennes* charmingly testify. Note that Derrida is not merely pointing out, as an empirical fact, that unexpected events can befall a piece of writing. Rather, he is arguing that the possibility of catastrophe is a structural component of a text. This textual structure is sometimes called destinerrance, a neologism that combines 'destination' (or even 'destiny') and 'errance' (from the Latin *errare*, to wander). A text has a destination, even perhaps a unique addressee, and yet it can always go astray and find other readers to whom it will appear as though sent to them. Beguiling in its simplicity, this formulation nevertheless guides some of Derrida's most sophisticated and subtle readings. For example, consider 'Le facteur de la vérité', his study of Lacan's celebrated seminar on Poe's short story 'The Purloined Letter'. In the original story Minister D – steals a *billet doux* from the royal boudoir with the intention of blackmail, and the brilliant detective C. Auguste Dupin eventually finds the letter in a card-rack in the Minister's rooms. For Lacan, the stolen letter *means* that 'a letter always arrives at its destination'. Derrida takes this concluding remark to be an allegory of Lacan's unconscious hopes for psychoanalysis: 'The deciphering (Dupin's, the Seminar's), uncovered via a meaning (the truth), as a hermeneutic process, itself arrives at its destination' (Derrida 1987, 444). This tacit acknowledgement of the analyst's sense of truth as presence is undone by the counter-claim that 'a letter can always not arrive at its destination' (Derrida 1987, 443–4). No transcendental structure can protect a letter from being misdelivered or not being delivered at all. On the contrary, there is an irreducible possibility of error in textual transmission that is transcendentally inscribed in the text itself.

So from the very beginning of his writing life, Derrida distances himself from transcendental philosophy while rejecting empiricism as an alternative. Instead, he elaborates the meaning and pertinance of what he comes to call 'quasi transcendental' structures (Derrida 1986, 151a–162a, trans. modified). The condition of a mark's possibility to be singular is also, and at the same time, the condition of its possibility to be repeated and thereby to lose any title to absolute singularity. (Incidentally, this clarifies what Derrida means by *la trace*: a singularity erases itself in the very act of being inscribed, leaving only a trace of what has never been able to present itself as such.) In the Parisian intellectual world in which he began to publish and teach, Derrida's discovery of a third position between transcendental philosophy and empiricism meant that he had found a place or, better, a non-place from which to criticize and reformulate both phenomenology and semiology, two of the most important discourses of the time, not least of all because they were opening up new ways of reading Freud and Marx. Derrida used this position both to criticize hasty moves away from philosophy and to affirm the archive of philosophy. On the one hand, contemporary attempts to find a way beyond philosophy (Bataille, Foucault, Lacan, Levinas, Lévi-Strauss) are shown to rely on a venerable metaphysical notion of presence. And on the other hand, the great philosophers (Plato and Hegel, above all) are revealed not to be in fee to metaphysics in any simple or straightforward way. In the *Phaedrus* Plato both fears writing that is removed from its source and affirms the writing in the soul, while Hegel is 'the last philosopher of the book and the first thinker of writing' (Derrida 1976, 26).

Thus far there seems to be no very good reason to link Derrida to literature. In his first writings he appears as a philosopher writing with other philosophers in mind. Later, he will argue that he is not practising philosophy as narrowly understood but trying to find a place or non-place, which as we have seen he calls *la différance* or *la trace*, from which he can question the grounding assumptions of philosophy (Derrida 1984a, 107). It would be a mistake to think that an interest in literature and poetry derives from his years of informal association with *Tel Quel* in the late 1960s, or from his time as a visiting professor at Johns Hopkins University, where he went first in 1968, or from his sojourn at Yale University where he taught regularly for part of each year from 1975 to 1986. To be sure, at Yale he became friends with several eminent literary critics – Harold Bloom, Geoffrey Hartman, Paul de Man and J. Hillis Miller – but while de Man's work in particular would become very important to Derrida, his interest in literature precedes his years of teaching in the United States. While defending his *thèse d'état* in 1980 he reminded the jury that 'my most constant interest, coming even before my philosophical interest I should say, if this is possible, has been directed towards literature, that writing which is called literary' (Derrida 1983, 37). That latter distinction is important. Derrida is less interested in literature understood by way of aesthetic qualities, fictionality or the pleasures of form, than in the acts of inscription which literature allows and encourages. An inscription of the singular, as we have seen, introduces a trace of what cannot be presented; and in considering this trace one uncovers *aporias* – unavoidable and irreconcilable forks encountered in a path of reasoning – that introduce differences and thereby dislodge the metaphysics of presence.

Yet had Derrida spoken only of inscription and never said anything about literature or poetry, one can still imagine authors and critics being intrigued by his work, beginning with his early commentary on Husserl. The *Introduction* develops a phenomenologically exact description of the death of the author (Derrida 1978, 88), which Maurice Blanchot had proposed in a more essayistic manner in the early 1950s and which Roland Barthes was to popularize in the late 1960s. It also gives philosophical justification to the theme of misprision that Harold Bloom was to establish, with Emerson and Freud mainly in mind, in the 1970s. For Derrida argues that 'non-communication and misunderstanding' are 'the very horizon of culture and language' (Derrida 1978, 82). More generally, in its attention to the historicity of ideal objects, the *Introduction* invites us to rethink the meanings and functions of archives and literary histories. After all, the class of ideal objects includes literary texts as well as mathematical theorems. Derrida was of course well aware of that in 1957 when, with Hyppolite as his supervisor, he registered as a thesis topic, 'The ideality of the literary object' (Derrida 1983, 36).

It is no surprise then to find literature itself evoked at the very centre of the *Introduction*. A 'choice of two endeavours' (Derrida 1978, 102) is proposed there, the one associated with Husserl and the other with James Joyce. Here philosophy and literature are seen to offer competing ways of gaining access to the past. Where the Husserl of 'The Origin of

Geometry' tries to render language clear and unequivocal so that a tradition can be passed on without impediment, the Joyce of *Finnegans Wake* seeks to maximize equivocity and thereby to encode the past, in all its variety, in the languages of his text. Husserl aims for complete translatability; Joyce stymies translation in each and every sentence. To choose between these alternatives is impossible. Univocity must remain a horizon for Joyce if he is to remain intelligible, while Husserl must admit that were equivocity completely reduced and expunged from historicity no unique event would be legible. Needless to say, this contrast between Husserl and Joyce is unable to support all that Derrida has said about literature. However, we see from early on that literature is considered in terms of a discussion of philosophy, that no strict and final distinction between the two is countenanced, and that although literature, like philosophy, preserves the past, the possibility of error in transmission cannot be eliminated *a priori*. None of these thoughts supplies any firm leads about the value of Derrida's writings for literary criticism, but taken together they allow us to track him more closely as a reader of literature.

Two ways of following the question of literature in Derrida immediately present themselves. *First*, one could isolate and read his accounts of dramatists, novelists and poets. There are, as one would imagine, a number of French authors on or about whom he writes – Antonin Artaud, Charles Baudelaire, Maurice Blanchot, Gustave Flaubert, Jean Genet, Michel Leiris, Stéphane Mallarmé, Francis Ponge, Philippe Sollers and Paul Valéry – along with people who compose in languages other than his own: Paul Celan, James Joyce, Franz Kafka, Edgar Allen Poe, William Shakespeare, P. B. Shelley and Sophocles. The disparity in size between the two groups could be taken to indicate the greater influence of imaginative writing in his mother tongue, although that could well turn out to be a hasty induction. Joyce impinges on him at least as forcefully as Mallarmé, and we have no reason to suppose that Derrida has written on all the authors whose work is important to him professionally or personally. *Second*, one could seek out Derrida's general remarks on literature. Here we would quickly find ourselves entangled in discussions of literature and ethics, literature and law, literature and metaphysics, literature and politics, literature and psychoanalysis, assuming that we could isolate such pure strains to begin with. We would also find ourselves pondering distinctions between literature, poetry and *belles lettres*, and in the process reflecting on borderline cases excluded from the list of authors with which we started, writers such as Friedrich Nietzsche and Jean-Jacques Rousseau. (The pressure of other borders can be felt now and then: for instance, when Derrida comes to write on André Gide, an important figure in his adolescence, it is not until 1995 and then he writes not on his stories but on a travel narrative, *Retour de l'URSS*.) Passing to more familiar topics of literary criticism, we would discover Derrida's thoughts on autobiography and testimony, genre and the letter, literacy and orality, metaphor and catachresis, mimesis and representation, signs and translation.

To follow the question of literature in Derrida with any sensitivity one must combine the two alternatives. It is by no means easy to do so, since Derrida uses literary writings in very different ways and to very different ends. Sometimes there is very extensive discussion of a writer: in *Glas*, for instance, printed in two side-by-side columns, an entire column is devoted to Genet as well as Hegel. Even so, while the relations between literature and philosophy are discussed from time to time in each column they do not dominate the entire text. Indeed, it is hard to say whether a stretch of text on either side is commentary, criticism, interpretation or paraphrase; it involves all four while not being limited to any. At other times Derrida will evoke a writer with little or no direct acknowledgement of the text. 'Tympan' quotes a passage from Leiris's *La Règle du jeu* in the right-hand margin and, without examining it, lets it resonate with his meditations on borders and limits (Derrida 1982, x–xxix). Always, though, he is concerned with the interrelations of the singular and the general. There are no absolute singularities, he argues, or if there are they cannot be identified. Even an apparently pure singular mark can be repeated outside its original context, and although repetition leads to difference the trait of singularity will be legible in any of the repetitions.

It is this relation of uniqueness and iterability that Derrida calls *idiom*. This is not a style that one can learn, let alone perfect (in the sense that people talk of John Henry Newman as 'a great stylist'); it is 'an intersection of singularities, habitats, voices, graphism, what moves with you and what your body never leaves' (Derrida 1995, 119). No writer can discern his or her idiom, but an acute reader can identify it in another's work. A strong reading would take stock of both an idiom in a lyric, say, as well as the contexts – formal, historical, political, religious, social, and so forth – in which the poem participates. Derrida is no formalist: he insists that 'no meaning can be determined out of context, but no context permits saturation' (Derrida 1979b, 81). Nor is he committed in Arnoldian fashion to a hierarchical distinction between literature and criticism. A strong reading might itself cross a text in a singular fashion, and thereby generate its own idiom. In this way we could talk about the idiom of a critic like Samuel Johnson, S. T. Coleridge or T. S. Eliot, and to the extent that we can and do talk in just that way their critical writings can be considered literature. This is not to say that there are no distinctions whatsoever between literature and literary criticism, only that in their highest reaches they generate similar effects.

Not only does Derrida discuss the relations of the singular and the general but also he performs them by leaguing a particular text with a general question or set of questions. In 1971, while engaging with J. L. Austin's theory of speech acts, Derrida turned his attention to the status and function of signatures. As Austin conceives matters, a signature bespeaks the absence of the singular human being who has signed a document while nonetheless presuming that he or she had been present while signing. His or her proper intentions are in principle needed to be presentable for the signing to be a felicitous performative act. For Derrida, though, this 'signature effect' is underwritten by an aporia: 'the condition of possibility of those effects is simultaneously ... the condition of their impossibility, of the impossibility of their rigorous purity' (1982, 328). To sign one's name is necessarily to allow it to be contaminated by all manner of impurities. A signature can in principle, if not always in fact, be forged, cut into pieces or quoted out of context. Strictly speaking, it is neither inside nor outside a text; it traces an equivocal limit between life and death, subject and work. More surprisingly, Derrida suggests, a signature is not completed when an author appends his or her name to what has been written but when a reader, who may have been quite unforeseen by the author, receives what has been communicated in the signed text. This countersignature, as it is called, is not accidental but constitutive of a text; and those texts which are frequently countersigned, often in different ways, are precisely those whose force we experience. Inevitably, part of this force comes from the passion and insight with which the text in question is a countersignature of other texts.

Derrida's most sustained exploration of signing a work of literature is *Signsponge*, the revised text of his paper at the 1975 Cérisy colloquium on Ponge. A question immediately comes to mind. What relation is there between Derrida's general ideas about signatures and this, or any other, particular body of work? Certainly one cannot rightly speak of applying deconstruction to literature, for it 'is not a doctrine; it's not a method, nor is it a set of rules or tools; it cannot be separated from performatives, from signatures, from a given language' (1996, 217). And yet precisely because deconstruction is not a self-contained theory 'the only thing it can do is apply, to be applied, to something else' (1996, 218). One would therefore expect that when Derrida considers Ponge's signature the earlier remarks on Austin's theory of speech acts will be reset and redirected by the poems he reads. This is indeed what happens. When examining the author of *Le parti pris des choses*, Derrida shows how signification overruns nomination: a proper name such as 'Ponge' can be turned into a common noun such as 'tissu-éponge' (sponge-cloth) or 'serviette-éponge' (sponge-towel). Plainly, one would not expect to find the same thing in a discussion of Genet's signature in *Glas* or Blanchot's in *Parages*.

Even so, it is reasonable to ask why Derrida countersigns some literary texts and not others. The first thing to say, by way of preparation, is that he seems to write on literary authors for somewhat different reasons than those that ground his selection of philosophers. As we have seen, he shows that Plato and Hegel are not committed to a metaphysics of presence in a simple or straightforward way, and he reads his older contemporaries, the Foucault of *Madness and Civilisation* and the Levinas of *Totality and Infinity*, in order to indicate, among other things, that they cannot escape metaphysics as readily as they might think they can. Rousseau is chosen for close discussion in *Of Grammatology* because his age is granted an ' "exemplary" value ... between Plato's *Phaedrus* and Hegel's *Encyclopaedia*' (Derrida 1976, 97). And Husserl is inspected partly because of the rigour of the phenomenological method and partly because of his covert dependence on the metaphysics of presence. A good deal more could be said about other philosophers on whom Derrida has written, and of course one could cite seminal thinkers about whom he has said little or nothing. Perhaps given world enough and time he would write about Thomas Aquinas, David Hume or Karl Rahner in a way that would surprise even his most devoted readers.

It is sometimes said that when Derrida writes on literary works he does not seek to uncover strata of presence in the writing but rather affirms the work under consideration. This resolves his writing too readily into a duality of literature and philosophy, and attention to his texts on philosophers he admires such as *Le toucher, Jean-Luc Nancy* will show that his interest is in following a guiding thread through a complicated fabric of ideas. Literature plays no one role in his writing. At times Derrida turns to a poem or story because of its ability to unsettle the effects of a metaphysical assumption: thus in 'The Double Session' Mallarmé's 'Mimique' is inscribed in a passage of Plato's 'Phaedrus', while in 'Le facteur de la vérité', as we have seen, Poe's story 'The Purloined Letter' is read even more closely than was done in the seminar that Lacan consecrated to it. At other times a literary corpus is scrutinized without being paired with a philosophical text, although philosophical issues are never far away. Questions and themes from the long sequence 'philosophy' can, and often are, tightly folded into the shorter sequence called 'literature' where their provenance will not always be apparent. One thing that attracts Derrida to some literary texts rather than others is a critical relationship with their literariness. 'They bear within themselves, or we could also say in their literary act they put to work, a question, the same one, but each time singular and put to work otherwise: "What is literature?" or "Where does literature come from?" "What should we do with literature?" ' (1992, 41).

This helps to explain why Derrida's interest in literature converges on writing of the nineteenth and twentieth centuries. For it is there more than anywhere else that literary works tend to contest their presumed literariness. That said, we should be wary of extending the concept of literature into the indefinite past in order to make an appropriate backdrop for what critics often call, all too quickly, modernist and postmodernist writing. 'Only under the conditions of law does the work have an existence and a substance, and it becomes "literature" only at a certain period of the law that regulates problems involving property rights over works' (Derrida 1992, 215). With the development of copyright laws in Europe from the late seventeenth to the early nineteenth centuries, the meaning of the word 'literature' slowly shifts from 'polite learning' to 'imaginative writing chiefly in the drama, poetry and prose fiction'. The reference to Europe is not accidental since 'literature' is a Latin word, and 'to take account of the latinity in the modern institution of literature' would involve a consideration of 'Christendom as the Roman Church, of Roman law and the Roman concept of the State, indeed of Europe' (Derrida 2000, 21). Literature is an institution not only because it is taught in schools and universities and is regulated by positive laws but also because it is a part of what he calls globalatinization, a covert leaguing of Christianity and capitalism. Latinity is being extended across the world, mainly in and through Anglo-American speech and writing, and the institution of literature plays highly complicated roles in this process.

Enshrined in the notion of literature, as determined before the law, is what Derrida calls 'the right to say everything' (Derrida 1992, 36). The very idea of literature is coordinate with a freedom from political and religious censorship. On Derrida's reasoning, this comes to mean that literature is positively and essentially related to the modern idea of democracy or, more exactly, what in any democratic state is promised about democracy. At any given time, no state coincides perfectly with itself, and from the gap between what is promised and what it is actually performed one can always draw bypassed, repressed or unthought possibilities that can be recombined and reaffirmed. It is these unrealized possibilities, not a future state or a utopia, that constitute what Derrida calls 'a democracy to come'. Derrida himself stresses the importance of forgotten and untried possibilities in Marx and, more generally, has supported an 'open marxism' in France.

An emphasis upon the historical formation of literature, and on the political character of what is formed should not be taken as a sign that literarity has no effects in poems, stories or plays. Although Derrida rejects Husserl's 'principle of principles' because it leads to the fullness of an intuition, and hence to presence, he does not thereby abandon the protocols of phenomenology. And so, while he never posits a literary essence, he credits literarity: 'It is the correlative of an intentional relation to the text, an intentional relation which integrates in itself, as a component or an intentional layer, the more or less implicit consciousness of rules which are conventional or institutional – social, in any case' (Derrida 1992, 44). A poem by Celan, for instance, will encode a good deal of the history and institutions of poetry, and this will be legible for an attentive and well-informed reader.

Not all of Derrida's attention to literature is taken up with archives and traditions, however. He is equally concerned with imagination and invention, about which he has original things to say. In a study of Étienne Bonnot de Condillac's *Essay on the Origin of Human Knowledge*, Derrida observes that all Condillac's problems gather around the two senses of the word 'imagination': 'the reproductive imagination which retraces ... and the productive imagination which, in order to supply, adds something more' (1980, 76). For Derrida, the imagination does not work in the present. Rather, the act of writing introduces a detour which the author follows, and only after the fact is the deviation from the norm perceived and understood, by which stage something new has been added in and through the writing. This approach to the imagination is taken up later by Derrida under the less romantic rubric of invention. Strictly speaking, no invention can abide wholly within the possible, understood by way of conventions, forms and rules; it must also draw on what, from the perspective of the possible, seems quite impossible. 'The interest of deconstruction', we are told, 'is a certain experience of the impossible' (1992, 328). This should not be taken to affirm that a poem, for example, should simply flout all conventions, forms and rules, such as one is sometimes led to believe by the surrealists. On the contrary, a lyric such as Celan's 'Psalm' involves a singular negotiation of German grammar, the poetics of psalms and an understanding of negative theologies, on the one hand, and Celan's experience of the impossible, on the other.

'Nor must we forget', Derrida tells us, 'that deconstruction is itself a form of literature' (1984, 125). Certainly the writings of Jacques Derrida offer their readers a highly distinctive idiom, one that has been heard in all manner of places and with regard to all manner of topics for the last forty years. His influence can be recognized in literature and philosophy, history and politics, theology and the visual arts. If his arguments about inscription have generated controversy inside and outside the university, they have also subtly changed what is studied and how it is studied.

Kevin Hart

Further reading and works cited

Bennington, G. and Derrida, J. *Jacques Derrida*. Chicago, 1993.
Caputo, J. D. (ed.) *Deconstruction in a Nutshell*. New York, 1997.
Clark, T. *Derrida: Heidegger, Blanchot*. Cambridge, 1992.
Culler, J. *On Deconstruction*. Ithaca, NY, 1982.
Derrida, J. *Of Grammatology*. Baltimore, MD, 1976.
—. *Edmund Husserl's 'Origin of Geometry': An Introduction*, preface J. P. Leavey, Jr, ed. D. B. Allison. Stony Brook, NY, 1978.
—. 'Living On', in Harold Bloom et al., *Deconstruction and Criticism*. London, 1979a.
—. *Writing and Difference*. London, 1979b.
—. *The Archeology of the Frivolous*, intro. J. P. Leavey, Jr. Pittsburgh, 1980.
—. *Dissemination*. London, 1981.
—. *Margins of Philosophy*. Chicago, 1982.
—. 'The Time of a Thesis: Punctuations', in *Philosophy in France Today*, ed. A. Montefiore. Cambridge, 1983.
—. 'Deconstruction and the Other'. in *Dialogues with Contemporary Continental Thinkers*, ed. R. Kearney. Manchester, 1984a.
—. *Signéponge/Signsponge*. New York, 1984b.
—. *The Ear of the Other*, ed. C. V. McDonald. New York, 1985.
—. *Glas*. Lincoln, NE, 1986.
—. *The Post Card*. Chicago, 1987.
—. 'Letter to a Japanese Friend', in *A Derrida Reader*, ed. P. Kamuf. New York, 1991.
—. *Acts of Literature*, ed. D. Attridge. London, 1992.
—. *Specters of Marx*, intro. B. Magnus and S. Cullenberg. New York, 1994.
—. *Points: Interviews, 1974–1994*, ed. E. Weber. Stanford, CA, 1995.
—. '"As if I were Dead": An Interview with Jacques Derrida', in *Applying: To Derrida*, eds J. Brannigan et al. Basingstoke, 1996.
— and Blanchot, M. *The Instant of My Death/Demeure*. Stanford, CA, 2000.

Gasché, R. *The Tain of the Mirror*. Cambridge, MA, 1986.
Hart, K. *The Trespass of the Sign*. New York, 2000.
Kamuf, P. (ed.) *A Derrida Reader*. New York, 1991.
Norris, C. *Derrida*. London, 1987.
Schultz, W. R. and Fried, L. L. B. *Jacques Derrida*. New York, 1992.
Wood, D. (ed.) *Derrida*. Oxford, 1992.

41. Luce Irigaray (1930–)

Feminist philosopher, psychoanalyst, linguist, political thinker and activist, Luce Irigaray is best known for her theory of sexual difference as the horizon of political justice and the ethical paradigm of intersubjective relations. These multiple interdisciplinary affiliations and the centrality of sexual difference in her work have produced many controversies and misunderstandings, ranging from the early charges of essentialism to the more recent critiques that the privileging of sexual difference either ignores other forms of difference, such as race, class and sexuality, or reduces multiple modalities of alterity to the heterosexual model. Despite the growing body of excellent interpretations of Irigaray's thought (Whitford, Chanter, Grosz, Cornell, Butler, Deutscher), the reception of Irigaray has often been often characterized, according to Margaret Whitford, by 'a simultaneous attraction and rejection' (1991, 4) or, according to Penelope Deutscher, by 'Irigaray anxiety' (1996, 6).

To facilitate what Whitford calls critical '*engagement* with Irigaray' in place of 'the alternatives of dismissal or apotheosis' (1991, 25), I would like, first, to sketch out briefly the changing style and emphasis of Irigaray's research, and second, to map out the diverse and often seemingly antinomic connotations of sexual difference in her writings. In a 1995 interview in *Hypatia*, Irigaray describes the three 'phases' of her work on sexual difference. Even though these phases cannot be understood in a linear chronological fashion because they often coexist in her work, Irigaray identifies the first with 'a critique, you might say of the auto-monocentrism of the western subject', the second with an attempt to recover and redefine female subjectivity, and the third with an invention of 'a new model of possible relations between man and woman' (1995, 96). As she writes:

> The third phase of my work thus corresponds … to the construction of an intersubjectivity respecting sexual difference. This is something, a task, that no one has yet done, I think, something that's completely new. The second phase of my work was to define those mediations that could permit the existence of a feminine subjectivity – that is to say – another subject – and the first phase was the most critical one … It was a phase in which I showed how a single subject, traditionally the masculine subject, had constructed the world and interpreted the world according to a single perspective. (1995, 96–7)

Associated primarily with *Speculum of the Other Woman* (1974) and *This Sex Which Is Not One* (1977), the first stage of Irigaray's research diagnoses the erasure of sexual difference in the discourses of philosophy, sciences, linguistics and politics. In her critical engagement with key philosophical figures ranging from Aristotle, Plato, Descartes and

Hegel to Nietzsche, Freud, Marx, Heidegger, Levinas and Lacan, Irigaray provides the most sustained critique of the monologism and indifference of the western philosophy, which is incapable of acknowledging the sexed other otherwise than as a deficient copy, a negation, or the atrophied version of the masculine subject. Anticipating the arguments of Eve Kosofsky Sedgwick, Irigaray argues that the regime of the compulsory heterosexuality represents in fact a masculine homosocial order (what she calls 'the reign of masculine hom(m)o-sexuality'), supported by the traffic in women, on the one hand, and the prohibition of homosexual practices, on the other: 'Reigning everywhere, although prohibited in practice, hom(m)o-sexuality is played out through the bodies of women, matter, or sign, and heterosexuality has been up to now just an alibi for the smooth workings of man's relations with himself, of relations among men' (1985, 172).

In her critique of the homosocial order, Irigaray focuses not on the way femininity is represented but on the paradoxical logic of exclusion behind these representations. As she points out, 'the rejection, the exclusion of a female imaginary certainly puts woman in the position of experiencing herself only fragmentarily, in the little-structured margins of a dominant ideology, as waste, or excess, what is left of a mirror invested by the (masculine) 'subject' to reflect himself . . . (1985, 30). In particular, Irigaray contests a confinement of time to the interiority of the male subject and the corresponding association of the female body with the exteriority of the space – a set of distinctions, as her work on Aristotle and Plato shows, deeply entrenched in the western philosophical tradition. As she famously writes, in this philosophical imaginary – the imaginary characterized by the unity of form, the predominance of the visual, and 'rather too narrowly focused' on the masculine economy of sameness (1985, 28) – woman and her sex appear as the negative space, abyss, the obverse of God (1993, 7), as 'a horror of nothing to see', or as a nostalgic fantasy of the first and ultimate dwelling associated with the maternal body. What is original in this stage of Irigaray's work is the diagnosis of the numerous symptoms of this sexual indifference, which manifests itself not only in the disregard for the specificity of feminine embodiment, desires and genealogies but also in the disembodied character of linguistic analyses, in the erasure of the drama of enunciation, in the separation of the subject of knowledge from carnality and desire, in the infatuation with formalism and with it the obverse side, the crippling nostalgia for the maternal body, in the rigid separation between the immanence of flesh and the transcendence of the spirit, and, finally, in the nihilism of western culture.

In the second phase of her work, Irigaray is concerned with the recovery and the symbolic reinscription of the 'second sex'. It is important to stress that for Irigaray the work of recovery is inextricably intertwined, first, with the strategic mode of reading – what she calls 'mimicry' (*mimétisme*) – and, second, with the construction of the alternative 'mediations that could permit the existence of a feminine subjectivity' (1995, 96) such as the formation of the maternal genealogy, resymbolizing the mother/daughter relationship, the rethinking of the way space and time has been gendered, the rearticulation of the Divine, or the institution of sexuate rights. As this double emphasis on mimicry and mediation suggests, Irigaray is not concerned with the immediacy of the female experience, the affirmation of embodiment or, as some critics have argued, the regression to the pre-Oedipal period. According to Whitford, at stake here is not a recovery of the unmediated female experience, subjectivity or embodiment but a reconstruction of their linguistic and cultural conditions of possibility – that is, the formation of the alternative female imaginary and symbolic orders (1991, 42, 89–97).

The exclusion of femininity means that the female imaginary and the symbolic has to be reconstructed out of the 'remains' which the homosocial economy cannot accommodate and which historically 'have been abandoned to the feminine' (1985, 111, 116). An important first step in this reconstruction is the rhetorical strategy of mimicry. Opposed to masquerade (*la mascarade*), that is, to the unconscious identification with the feminine position in the masculine symbolic, mimicry for Irigaray is a strategic move of a deliberate yet playful repetition, which, by defamiliarizing and denaturalizing the homosocial logic, reveals the historical mechanisms of the exploitation of the feminine and thus opens up the possibility of their reinscription. As she famously writes:

> To play with mimesis is thus, for a woman, to try to recover the place of her exploitation by discourse, without allowing herself to be simply reduced to it. It means to resubmit herself – inasmuch as she is on the side of the 'perceptible', 'matter' – to 'ideas', in particular to ideas about herself, that are elaborated in/by a masculine logic, but so as to make 'visible', by an effect of playful repetition, what was supposed to remain invisible: the cover-up of a possible operation of the feminine in language. (1985, 76)

In Irigaray's later work the strategy of mimicry is supplemented with the reconstruction of the alternative structures of mediation enabling the symbolic and cultural inscription of the female subjectivity. Drawing on a variety of sources – Merleau-Ponty, Levinas, Lacan, Castoriadis – Irigaray offers an alternative paradigm illustrating the intersection between the female imaginary and the symbolic in the figure of the two sets of lips: 'Two sets of lips that, moreover, cross over each other like the arms of the cross, the prototype of the crossroads *between*. The mouth lips and the genital lips do not point in the same direction' (1993, 18). As this chiasmic structure formed by the intersection of the imaginary and the symbolic suggests, Irigaray stresses the inseparability of embodiment and speech, language and subjectivity. Another important feature of Irigaray's articulation of the female symbolic and imaginary is her emphasis on temporality, which displaces the concept of femininity from the negation of essence, expressed in the famous statement by Lacan that the Woman does not exist (1998, 72–3), to the affirmation of becoming. As I argue in 'Toward a Radical Female Imaginary: Temporality and Embodiment in Irigaray's Ethics' (*diacritics*, 1988, 61–7), the discontinuous temporality of becoming is what is at stake in the often misunderstood concept of 'the "mechanics" of fluids' obfuscated on the imaginary level by the structure of the specular image and on the symbolic level by the privilege given to closed sets and to the 'symbol of universality' (1985, 108). According to Drucilla Cornell, the temporal structure of the female imaginary in Irigaray's writings is intertwined with 'the uneraseable trace of utopianism' (1991, 169), a term which does not imply some specific goal outside culture, but, as Elizabeth Weed and Judith Butler similarly argue, a mode of reading 'something other than the already known, the already legible' (1997, 285). By refusing what Butler calls 'the conflation of the social with what is socially given' (1997, 23), Irigaray's emphasis on the futurity of the imaginary and the symbolic structures suggests that 'femininity' is irreducible to its current definitions and representations and thus open to resignification and contestation.

As the protracted debate on essentialism suggests, many readers of Irigaray have ignored not only her strategic mode of reading based on mimicry but also her twin emphasis on temporality and mediation. As a result, it has often been assumed that the reconstruction of the feminine subjectivity is based on unmediated experience or embodiment existing outside culture. According to Christine Holmlund, where Irigaray seems problematic to her readers is not in her critique of phallocentrism but in 'her visionary re-creations of an undefinable, non-unitary female identity based on difference' (1991, 296). For Mary Ann Doane such a project leads to 'a kind of ghetto politics which maintains and applauds women's exclusion from language and symbolic order' (1987, 12). In the context of such misreadings, it is important to recall that Irigaray consistently criticizes the lure of immediacy on many levels ranging from the mystification of the pre-oedipal sexuality ('extolling the pre-oedipal as a liberation from the norm of genital sexuality entails all the caprice and immaturity of desire' (1996, 27)) to intuitive knowledge of experience, from the historical empiricism to the utopian dream of the immediate community among women. Consequently, the recovery of femininity cannot be confused with 'immediate affect, with self-certainty, mimetic or recapitulative intuitive truth, with historical narrative, etc.' (1996, 62). In response to these lures, she flatly proclaims that 'there is no ... "natural immediacy"' (1996, 107). In fact, it is Irigaray who criticizes women's liberation movements based on 'the fetish' of the unmediated personal experience or on the politics of voice:

> Many women have understood ... that liberation for them was simply to say I ... then they fight among themselves to see who says 'I' the loudest: your 'I' versus my 'I' ...

> Thus, if you like, I think that the purely narrative, autobiographical 'I', or the 'I' that expresses only affect, risks being an 'I' that collapses back into a role traditionally granted to woman: an 'I' of pathos ... It seems to me important to accede to a different cultural 'I' – that is, to construct a new objectivity that corresponds not to an indifferent 'I' but to an 'I' that's sexed feminine. It is necessary to remain both objective and subjective. And to remain within a dialectic between the two. (1995, 103)

And she adds, 'I can't myself, all alone, affirm my own experience, since this is something I know only after the fact ... I can't affirm that this is always already the experience of a woman. It must be a dialectic between subjectivity and objectivity' (1995, 104).

Irigaray's emphasis on the reconstruction of the linguistic, cultural and political mediations enabling the existence of the second sex culminates in her work on citizenship and sexuate rights, such as the prohibition of the exploitation of motherhood by religious and civil power, the right of women to civil identities and to the control of their public representations, and finally the right to equal wages and equal share of economic goods. Growing out of her engagement in social liberation movements, this conception of sexuate rights advocates political and institutional changes addressing oppression of women in western democracies, for instance changes in the status of the family (in order to challenge its institutional functions of the accumulation of property and reproduction), in the structures of law and religion (since, as Irigaray insists, religion remains a civil power despite Enlightenment's secularism), and finally in the economic distribution of goods. Irigaray's notion of sexuate rights implies a notion of justice based on an equivalent exchange for both sexes in the economic and the symbolic registers. According to Drucilla Cornell, Irigaray's sexuate rights are an expression of equivalence within the larger horizon of sexual difference:

> The political struggle against *dereliction* in the name of equality of well-being involves the recognition of feminine difference in those circumstances when we are different, as in our relationship to pregnancy, while simultaneously not reinforcing the stereotypes through which patriarchy attempted to make sense of this difference ... These rights are equivalent because they allow difference to be recognized and equally valued without women having to show that they are like men for legal purposes. (1992, 293)

Irigaray's conception of sexuate rights suggests a revision of democratic citizenship in the context of sexual difference. In the late 1980s Irigaray argues for complementing the economic justice (this argument has to be considered in the context of her involvement with the Italian Communist Party) with the constitution of women's political identities as women: for the 'social justice to be possible, women must obtain a civil identity simultaneously' (1994, 63). Without a mediation between economic equality and political identity, women, according to Irigaray, are caught in a double bind between 'the minimum of social rights they can obtain ... and the psychological or physical price they have to pay for that minimum' (1991, 207). As she argues:

> Women must obtain the right to work and to earn wages, as civil persons, not as men with a few inconvenient attributes: menstrual periods, pregnancy, child rearing, etc. Women must not beg for or usurp a small place in patriarchal society by passing themselves off as half-formed men. (1994, 63)

By providing new modes of mediation between the subjective and the objective, between the private and the public, the economic and the symbolic, the inscription of sexual difference into democratic citizenship creates an alternative 'political ethics that refuses to sacrifice desire for death, power, or money' (1996, 33).

Irigaray's work on sexuate rights and citizenship overlaps with the third and the most controversial stage of her work devoted to the construction of a culture of sexual difference: 'The third phase of my work thus corresponds, as I said, to the construction of an intersubjectivity respecting sexual difference' (1995, 103). In her later works, such as *Je, Tu, Nous: Toward a Culture of Difference* (1990), *Thinking the Difference: For A Peaceful Revolution* (1989), *I Love to You: For a Sketch of a Possible Felicity in History* (1992) and *Être Deux* (1997), Irigaray makes a shift from the genealogical (mother/daughter) and horizontal (women to women sociality) relations among women to 'a new model of possible relations between man and woman' (1995, 103). In place of the single individual or collective subject, her concept of a culture of sexual difference stresses the relational model of subjectivity and utterance – the paradigm of being two (*être deux*). On the basis of sexual difference, she hopes to elaborate a culture of intersubjective relations based on respect for all forms of alterity and diversity.

In order to understand Irigaray's claim that a culture of sexual difference fosters respect for all forms of alterity, it is necessary to engage two crucial concepts in her later work: the labour of the negative and the work of 'disappropriation'. Irigaray associates sexual difference not with a positive identity but with the labour of the negative – with what she calls 'taking the negative upon oneself' (1993, 120) – which produces the internal division and self-limitation of the subject. By redefining and negotiating between the Freudian (castration and the judgement based on negation) and the Hegelian (determinate negation) concepts of negativity, Irigaray argues that the labour of self-limitation in sexual difference leads to a refusal of any identity – individual or collective – based on wholeness and unity:

> The mine of the subject is always already marked by disappropriation [*désappropriation*]: gender [*le genre*]. Being a man or a woman means not being the whole of the subject or of the community or of spirit, as well as not being entirely one's self. The famous *I is another*, the cause of which is sometimes attributed to the unconscious, can be understood in a different way. I is never simply mine in that it belongs to a gender. Therefore, I am not the whole [*je ne suis pas tout*]. (1996, 106; 1992, 166)

Consequently, if Irigaray seems to privilege sexual difference it is because this difference foregrounds disappropriation, alterity and negativity 'in the self and for the self [ce négatif en soi et pour soi], (1996, 106; 1992, 166) as a condition of desire.

Because the identification with either side of sexual divide entails the labour of self-limitation and disappropriation – that is, the acknowledgement of 'not being the whole of the subject or of the community' – sexual difference, Irigaray argues, provides a model of the non-appropriative ethical relation to the Other. Since the negative turned upon the subject no longer posits the Other as the negation or alienation of the subject, sexual difference preserves the irreducible alterity of the Other while at the same time main-taining the insistence of the subject. By stressing the ethical respect for alterity, Irigaray dissociates the labour of the negative in sexual difference from the Hegelian alienation in the master/slave dialectic: 'The asceticism of the negative thus seemed necessary to me but more out of consideration for the other and from collective good sense than as a process of consciousness that would lead to a more accomplished spirituality . . . Hegel knew nothing of the negative like that' (1996, 13). For Irigaray the Other is not a hostile freedom blocking my own, but the very source of my becoming: 'Who are thou? I am and I become thanks to this question' (1993, 74). This reformulation of the negative through sexual difference transforms, according to Irigaray, the Hegelian desire for recognition into an ethical acknowledgement of the alterity of the Other.

As Tina Chanter (1995, 190–224), Drucilla Cornell (1991, 183–6), and Krzysztof Ziarek (1999) have argued, Irigaray's interpretation of the asymmetrical sexual relation in terms of the ethical acknowledgement of the 'unavoidable alterity of the other' is influenced by both Levinas's ethics and the Heideggerian concept of nearness. Unlike the different modalities of the erasure of alterity through domination, knowledge or narcissistic love, the non-symmetrical relation to the Other interrupts the ego's narcissism by calling the subject to responsibility. As her phrase 'I love to you' suggests, Irigaray defines the ethical relation to the Other in terms of indirection and intransitivity – that is, as a an oblique 'relation without a relation' that does not reduce the Other to the order of the same or the narcissistic projection of the subject: 'I cannot completely identify you, even less identify with you . . . I recognize you goes hand in hand with: you are irreducible to me just as I am to you' (1996, 103). As a trace of an oblique address and a radical disconnection, the type of relation implied by the neologism 'I love to you' marks the exposure to the Other and, and at the same time, constitutes a barrier preventing her assimilation – an assimilation that turns love into an act of 'cultural cannibalism' (1996, 110).

By promoting ethical respect for alterity, the creation of a culture of sexual difference, Irigaray argues, 'would allow us to check the many forms that destruction takes in our world, to counteract a nihilism that merely affirms the reversal of the repetitive prolifera-tion of the status quo values – whether you call them the consumer society, the circularity of discourse . . . scientist or technical imperialism' (1993, 5). If her critics charge that this primacy given to sexual difference as the model of ethical and political relations erases other forms of difference, Irigaray responds that the acknowledgement of the irreducibility of sexual difference – of that negative that cannot be sublated into unity – makes it possible 'to respect differences everywhere: differences between the other races, differences between the generations, and so on. Because I've placed a limit on my horizon, on my power' (1995, 110). In response to the charges of heterosexism, she points out that 'it is important not to confuse sexual choice with sexual difference. For me sexual difference is a fundamental parameter of the socio-cultural order; sexual choice is secondary. Even if one chooses to remain among women, it's necessary to resolve the problem of sexual difference' (1995, 112). As Pheng Cheah and Elizabeth Grosz argue in their polemics with Butler and Cornell, Irigaray's ethical and political paradigm of sexual difference does not necessarily lead to compulsory heterosexuality: 'neither *respect for* the other sex nor *fidelity to* one's own sex necessarily implies obligatory *desire for* the other sex' (1998, 13).

Nonetheless, Irigaray's claim that the culture of sexual difference fosters respect for other differences, in particular those of race and sexual orientation, not only remains disappointingly vague and undeveloped but is sometimes undercut by her own comments that 'the problem of race is, in fact, a secondary problem ... and the same goes for other cultural diversities – religious, economic and political ones' (1996, 47). As Butler writes:

> Irigaray does not always help matters here, for she fails to follow through the metonymic link between women and these other Others, idealizing and appropriating the 'elsewhere' as the feminine ... If the feminine is not the only or primary kind of being that is excluded ... what and who is excluded in the course of Irigaray's analysis? (1993, 49)

Butler repeats here Gayatri Chakravorty Spivak's criticism that French feminism fails to address the other articulations of differences among women (1988, 150). One could only wish Irigaray paid more attention to the pertinent intersections between sexual and racial differences in her work: for instance, the critical revisions of the Hegelian master/slave dialectic by black and feminist scholars would be a productive beginning of such a project. Moreover, despite her claims to the contrary, Irigaray herself does not always distinguish carefully enough between sexual difference and sexual orientation, for instance when she refers to the couple as a model not only of sexual difference but also of the ethical relation in love.

Even this cursive survey of the different stages and emphases of Irigaray's research conveys the complexity of her theory of sexual difference. In fact, I would argue that to engage critically the limitations and the possibilities of Irigaray's work, one cannot unify sexual difference into a single concept but, rather, one has to treat it as a heterogeneous configuration consisting of diverse and often seemingly antinomic formulations. Like Derrida's 'différance' or Walter Benjamin's allegorical 'constellation', Irigaray's sexual difference keeps disseminating and subdividing its own textual inscription. In order to trace this diverse configuration, I would like to propose the following seven 'theses on the philosophy of sexual difference':

1. For Irigaray sexual difference does not yet exist. The affirmations of sexual difference cannot, therefore, correspond to the acceptance of the past and present cultural formulations of femininity and masculinity, since this would amount to the reinscription of the sexual indifference, of homosociality. Hence the emphasis in Irigaray's work is on the ongoing invention of sexual difference, on what she calls in the opening pages of *An Ethics of Sexual Difference* 'the production of a new age of though, art, poetry, and language: the creation of a new poetics' (1993, 5).

2. The possibility of such an invention conveys the irreducible futurity of sexual difference. To articulate the temporality of sexual difference, it is necessary, Irigaray argues, to change our conception of becoming from a mere 'survival' to the Nietzschean intensification of living and to disclose a future no longer 'measured by the transcendence of death but by the call to birth of the self and the other' (1993, 186). In the context of feminism, the temporal character of sexual

difference affirms, according to Drucilla Cornell, the revolutionary potential of 'the feminine to be Other than the limits imposed on her' (1991, 102). As I argue in my discussion of temporality in Irigaray's work (Ziarek 1998, 60–71), the thought of sexual difference is inseparable from, to borrow Ernesto Laclau's phrase, 'new reflections on the revolution of our time'. That is why Irigaray proclaims that 'a revolution in thought and ethics is needed if the work of sexual difference is to take place' (1993, 6).

3. Irigaray refuses to define sexual difference in positive (even if only utopian) terms but stresses instead the labour of the negative. Based on a labour of the negative and a work of 'disappropriation', Irigaray's conception of sexual difference, like Lacan's, investigates the limits of the symbolic order rather than an identification with a positive identity. Rather like Joan Copjec's emphasis on the antinomies of sexual difference (1994, 201–36), Irigaray argues that sexual difference produces the internal splitting and division of the subject.

4. Although Irigaray grants the sexual difference the status of the universal, she argues that the only meaning of this paradoxical universality is that it splits the universal into two and thus renders the ideal of the ethical totality of the polis impossible: 'The particularity of this universal is that is it divided into two' (1996, 50). By positing sexual difference as this universal 'which is not one', Irigaray argues that sexual difference not only fractures the ethical totality of the Hegelian Spirit but also contests the models of political association conceived on the basis of the collective subjectivity.

5. The dialectical formulation of sexual difference as the labour of the negative not only necessitates a rethinking of universality but also of negativity. In particular, Irigaray contests the Hegelian and the Sartrean association of immediacy and facticity with nature and the body and the work of the negative with the transcendence of the spirit, culture or concept. By rejecting this model of transcendence, she reformulates the labour of the negative as 'the *sensible transcendental*' – 'as that which confounds the opposition between immanence and transcendence' (1993, 33).

6. The labour of self-limitation in sexual difference does not sublate the Other into a new totality but enables an ethical respect for the Other. In her work, Irigaray reinterprets the absence of sexual relation in Lacan's theory as the possibility of the ethical affirmation of the irreducible alterity of the Other.

7. As mode of an ethical relation to the Other, sexual difference, according to Irigaray, has also to be inscribed in democratic citizenship in order to transform the asymmetrical ethics of Eros into collective justice and to prevent the construction of sexuality either as natural immediacy or as economic commodity. This inscription of sexual difference in democratic politics constitutes another paradox in Irigaray's thought: on the one hand, it calls for the specific institutional changes enabling the legal constitution of women's civil identities as women, but, on the other hand, it foregrounds 'the *impossible*' in the formation of all political identities, preventing in this way the reification of existing gender stereotypes into political norms. Penelope Deutscher interprets this paradox in terms of a shift from a 'politics of recognition' to a 'politics of the impossible' – to 'the politics which "recognizes" that which it actually "establishes"' (1995, 154). As Irigaray suggests in *I Love to You*, another important aspect of the politics of the 'impossible' is the

emphasis on the temporal deferral and the structural indetermination of collective identities: 'I am, therefore, a political militant of the impossible (*une militante politique de l'impossible*), which is not to say a utopian. Rather, I want what is yet to be as the only possibility of a future' (1996, 10). To be a political militant of the impossible is to engage in a continuous struggle to displace the frontiers between the possible and the impossible, between the present and the future, between the socially constructed identities and their transformation.

By foregrounding the heterogenous configuration of sexual difference in Irigaray's work, I want, on the one hand, to prevent the interpretation of any of the above statements in isolation from other competing formulations, and, on the other, to frustrate the desire for the impossible unification of her theory, which sometimes can take the form of the coherent chronological narrative with which I started this essay. It is precisely the heterogeneity of sexual difference that constitutes the openness to alterity and futurity. To end I would like to suggest that despite a certain increasing simplification of style in Irigaray's later texts, a similar heterogeneity characterizes the ethical and the aesthetic mode of her writing. Speaking of the counterpoint in her texts between speech and silence, between 'logical formalization' and aesthetic composition, Irigaray suggests that her way of writing leaves the text 'always open onto a new sense, and onto a future sense, and I would also say onto a potential "You" [*Tu*], a potential interlocutor' (1995, 102). Reading Irigaray critically, entering her writings as 'a potential interlocutor' for whom a place has been reserved from the start, means, among other things, respecting this fundamental openness of her texts.

Ewa Ziarek

Further reading and works cited

Burke, C. et al. (eds) *Engaging with Irigaray*. New York, 1994.
Butler, J. *Bodies that Matter*. New York, 1993.
—. 'Against Proper Objects', in *Feminism Meets Queer Theory*, eds E. Weed and N. Schor. Bloomington, IN, 1997.
Chanter, T. *Ethics of Eros*. New York, 1995.
Cheah, P. and Grosz, E. 'Irigaray and the Political Future of Sexual Difference', *diacritics*, 28, 1998.
Copjec, J. *Read My Desire*. Cambridge, MA, 1994.
Cornell, D. *Beyond Accommodation*. New York, 1991.
—. 'Gender, Sex, and Equivalent Rights', in *Feminists Theorize the Political*, eds J. Butler and J. Wallach Scott. New York, 1992.
Deutscher, P. 'Luce Irigaray and her "Politics of the Impossible"', in *Forms of Commitment*, ed. B. Nelson. Melbourne, 1995.
—. 'Irigaray's Anxiety'. *Radical Philosophy*, 80, 1996.
Doane, M. A. *The Desire to Desire*. Bloomington, IN, 1987.
Grosz, E. 'The Hetero and the Homo: The Sexual Ethics of Luce Irigaray', in *Engaging with Irigary*, eds Burke et al. New York, 1994.
Holmlund, C. 'The Lesbian, the Mother, and the Heterosexual Lover'. *Feminist Studies*, 17, 1991.
Irigary, L. *Speculum of the Other Woman*. Ithaca, NY, 1974.
—. *This Sex Which is Not One*. Ithaca, NY, 1985.
—. *An Ethics of Sexual Difference*. Ithaca, NY, 1993.
—. *The Irigary Reader*, ed. M. Whitford. Oxford, 1991.

—. *Thinking the Difference*. New York, 1994.

—. 'Je-Luce Irigaray: A Meeting with Luce Irigaray', *Hypatia*, 19, 1995.

—. *I Love to You*. New York, 1996.

Lacan, J. *The Seminar of Jacques Lacan Book XX*. New York, 1998.

Laclau, E. *New Reflections on the Revolution of our Time*. London, 1990.

Sedgwick, E. Kosofsky. *Between Men*. New York, 1985.

Spivak, G. Chakravorty. *In Other Worlds*. New York, 1988.

Weed, E. 'The More Things Change', in *Feminism Meets Queer Theory*, eds F. Weed and N. Schor. Bloomington IN, 1997.

Whitford, M. *Luce Irigaray*. London, 1991.

Ziarek, E. 'Toward a Radical Female Imaginary: Temporality and Embodiment in Irigaray's Ethics', *diacritics*, 28, 1998.

Ziarek, K. 'Love and the Debasement of Being', *Postmodern Culture*, 10, 1999.

—. 'Proximities', *Continental Philosophy Review* (forthcoming).

42. Christian Metz (1931–1993)

Contemporary film theory as we know it today could not have developed without Christian Metz. Initially trained in 1960s structural linguistics, Metz used research methods from the emerging 'human sciences' to pursue an understanding of cinema. His work had immense influence among scholars and students for whom the new epistemologies demanded new academic disciplines. In Paul Willemen's assessment, Metz formulated 'the most systematic account of the location of language in cinema within a semiological model' (Heath and Mellencamp 1983, 147). Much of 1970s psychoanalytic film theory responded to Metz's ideas about the cinema's 'imaginary signifier' and the various psychic processes organized by the film text. Metzian tools crafted detailed or 'close textual' analyses of popular narrative movies such as Hitchcock's *The Birds* or Welles's *Touch of Evil* (Heath 1975). And the institutionalization of film studies as a university discipline (and model of interdisciplinary inquiry) is also part of Metz's considerable legacy.

He was himself the first full-fledged film academic in France, taking the first *doctorat d'état* granted for a dissertation on cinema and holding a position as *directeur d'études* in his field at the École des Hautes Études en Sciences Sociales. Metz could certainly claim a vital legacy in postwar French film culture: in André Bazin, *Cahiers du cinéma*, the filmmaker-critics of the New Wave, and new national institutions such as the Cinematheque française and the French national film school (IDHEC). French cultural critics had long taken film seriously in journalistic criticism and aesthetic philosophy. But Metz was not concerned with explaining cinema's past, evaluating its achievements, or prescribing its future. He instead devoted himself to utterly fundamental questions about the intelligibility of movies. Was there a basic 'language system' (*langue*) of film as in verbal communication? What devices might define the user or 'subject' of film language, as do personal pronouns, time and location adverbs, and verb tenses in verbal discourse? Or did the film image differ from the verbal sign? If films made information seem so 'present', so 'obvious', so 'easy to understand', as Metz asked in *Film Language*, why were they so difficult to explain (1974a,

69)? Metz's scrupulous, tenacious approach to these issues set standards that enabled film studies to emerge in many universities in the late 1960s, and to flourish there subsequently as a theoretically sophisticated activity of considerable influence on broader academic studies of culture.

Recently, film studies has undergone several significant crises, including the introduc-tion of digital audio-visual media and the critique of 'Grand Theory' research paradigms (including the subject-position theory of Metz's *Imaginary Signifier*). While Metz is so embedded in the field that any major paradigm shift would inevitably be an occasion to review his work, the present circumstance is an unusually interesting one. This is because post-Theory researchers can value the early Metz's linguistic semiology (while nonetheless rejecting his later psychoanalytic semiotics) and make connections between Metz's 'first semiology' and recent work in film pragmatics and in film narratology (Bordwell and Carroll 1996; Buckland 1995b). The purpose of this essay is to provide a perspective on this recent reactivation of Metz by reviewing the evolution of his work and by observing its effect on current conditions of the field.

Metz was really the first 'modern' film theorist, strategically defining film studies as much by his manner of scholarly communication as by his ideas on cinematic discourse itself. Metz's essays attest to being works-in-progress, more like modern scientific papers than traditional cultural criticism. Footnotes calmly explain earlier versions' imprecisions or flaws in reasoning, and pragmatically acknowledge that ongoing research has entailed reconsideration of earlier findings (Andrew 1976, 214–15). With an overlapping pub-lication schedule for the articles, books and their translations, and with a penchant for dialog with his contemporaries (by means of international colloquia, but also through a style of writing which cites and converses with others' work), Metz became widely known in Europe, Britain and the Americas.

From the early 1960s until his death in 1993, Metz published a series of major essays on the semiology of cinema. His work first appeared in its original French in a variety of Paris-based journals including *Communications, La Linguistique, Revue d'esthetique, Cahiers du cinéma* and *Image et Son*. He was interviewed by *Cinéthique and Ca/Cinéma*, and partici-pated in international scholarly colloquia as well as film festivals such as the Mostra Internazionale del Nuovo Cinema in Pesaro, Italy. Metz long maintained a dialogue with Italian semioticians Umberto Eco, Gianfranco Bettettini and Francesco Casetti. Through these activities and through translations, Metz rapidly became internationally known.

In the 1970s, the British journal *Screen* regularly presented English translations of Metz's work, prefaced by substantial editorials. In the US, *Semiotica* and *New Literary History* published Metz's essays. Moreover, Metz systematically revised his articles and published the revisions, plus new work, in the form of book-length collections: the two-volume *Essais sur la signification au cinéma* (1968, 1972), *Langage et cinéma* (1972), *Le Signifiant imaginaire: Psychanalyse et cinéma* (1977) and *L'Énonciation impersonelle ou le site du film* (1991). Again, translations quickly followed. The principal works known to English-speaking readers are *Film Language: A Semiotics of the Cinema* (1974a), a collection of revised essays drawn from *Essais sur la signification au cinéma, Langage et cinéma* and other journal articles, and *The Imaginary Signifier: Psychoanalysis and the Cinema* (1977b), a translation of *Le Signifiant imaginaire*.

Metz's work appears to comprehend three phases. His earliest work was closely tied to structural thought. In the early 1960s, Metz was part of a vanguard semiology research group led by Algirdas Julien Greimas at the Collège de France in Paris (De Behar, in De

Behar and Block 1996, 49). By the mid-1970s, Metz had become interested in explaining the effects of the classical fiction film on the spectator. He expanded the theoretical base of his research by incorporating current psychoanalytic theory, specifically Jacques Lacan's interpretations of Freud (Easthope 79). Metz's later work dealt with enunciation in film. At the time of his death, Metz was working on a study of humour in verbal language.

The linguistic agenda

In his initial semiotic studies, Metz was chiefly concerned with providing a new *logical* account of the medium's specificity. This account would supersede the prescriptive stylistic arguments of prior film theory (namely the debate between advocates of montage and the realists) by deploying the ideas of structural linguists including Saussure, Hjelmslev, Martinet, Jakobson and Halle. Comparable to the goal of Saussurean linguistics, Metz's aim was 'to identify film's specific system of articulation, which should in turn transform film theory into an autonomous, scientific paradigm' (Buckland 1991, 205).

The view that film operated like a language had of course been important to film theory's past. Between the two world wars, for example, the Russian formalist literary theorists and the Soviet montage filmmaker-theorists proposed detailed comparisons between film and language (Bordwell 1985, 17). Their film-language analogy was more complex than the slogan favoured by silent film apologists for whom cinema was a visual Esperanto (Metz 1974a, 31–44). But the conceptual framework of film semiology would claim an even greater rigour, albeit a rigour that was straitjacketed by methodology. Metz's initial film semiotics reasoned that if film possessed features of verbal language as divulged by structural linguistics (such as a relatively autonomous system of articulation), it could be said to resemble verbal language (Buckland 1991, 200). In this Metz used Saussure somewhat opportunistically. Instead of following Saussure's notion that linguistics was a branch of semiology, Metz observed Roland Barthes's reversal of this hierarchy (which meant Metz would overly adhere to Saussurean concepts of verbal signification and look for them in film). By so 'empowering' structural linguistics, Metz had the advantage of promoting systematic, prudently scaled inquiry, but also the drawbacks of negative results. Not only would Metz decide that cinema did not have an autonomous language system or *langue*, but he would also conclude that the film medium lacked the feature of intercommunication necessary to the definition of a language.

Metz nonetheless continued to try to define the specificity of film from the epistemological position of linguistics. But instead of attempting to look for commutable paradigms at the level of the individual image, he now considered the syntagmatic relations between images as the locus of a semiology of film. Deducing eight kinds of space-time relationships between events depicted in narrative films, Metz identified eight syntactic units that, accordingly, articulated such relationships. He presented them in a hierarchic typology he called the *grande syntagmatique*, and applied the whole scheme to an individual film from the French New Wave (Metz 1974a, 92–182). The *alternating syntagm*, for example, signified events occurring in two different spaces (A-B) but simultaneously (A1-B1) or quasi-simultaneously (A1-B1-A2-B2): the heroine detects the fire and runs from the building for help (A1); the firemen are sleeping at the station (B1); smoke thickens at the burning building (A2); the snoring firemen smell smoke and wake up (B2).

Many (including Metz) acknowledged the model's several problems: some syntagms were more successfully isolated than others; all eight syntagms were derived from only one type of film form (narrative); the soundtrack was ignored. Moreover, the phenomenologist in Metz maintained a realist position on the individual image as well as on the existence of a pro-filmic world. According to Thomas Elsaesser, the *grande syntagmatique* suggested that 'filmic syntax corresponds to the rhetorical trope of *dispositio* (determined ordering of undetermined elements – in this case images) rather than to a grammar' (Buckland 1995b, 12). *Language and Cinema* eventually shows Metz's adaptation of Umberto Eco's theory of codes (Heath 1975) and Metz's followers would thus make the ensuing critical trend (textual analysis of classical Hollywood film) a demonstration of rhetorical devices comprising filmic discourse.

From linguistic to psychoanalytic semiotics

In the 1970s, propelled by poststructuralist trends, Metz incorporated Freudian/Lacanian psychoanalysis into his film semiology. In this so-called 'second semiotics', Metz exploited a broader cultural understanding of cinema as a technological, institutional and psychical machine, a conception that had been recently introduced into film theory by Jean-Louis Baudry's articles on the ideological effects of this machine or 'apparatus'. In Constance Penley's words, Baudry saw the cinema as a 'faultless technological simulation' of the psyche while Metz considered cinema more as the psyche's 'extension or prosthesis' (Penley 1989, 61). Hence, Metz's contribution to this trend in film theory is distinct in that his primary goal remained that of realizing a rigorously semiological approach to cinema as a phenomenon that was both imaginary *and* symbolic.

The four essays collected in *The Imaginary Signifier* methodically engage psychoanalytic concepts and classifications to specify (1) the part of fantasy in cinematic signification and (2) the subject implied by the cinema's high quotient of 'imaginariness'. By 'imaginary', Metz meant 'to emphasize the perceptual base of filmic signification, to stress the profoundly fictive nature of the cinematic spectacle, and – most importantly – to align film with Lacan's imaginary register, the register within which identifications are sustained' (Silverman 1983, 288). Actually, Metz invokes Lacan's mirror stage only to describe one of several ways that cinematic discourse configures the subject of the discourse. Metz also conceptualizes the production of the subject (through identification) in terms of the dream-work, the scopic drives (voyeurism, fetishism, exhibitionism), disavowal, primary and secondary processes, etc.

Nonetheless, the principal critique of Metz's psychoanalytic semiotics was aimed at the emphasis he placed on 'primary identification', or the spectator-subject's identification with his own act of vision (via the camera) in experiencing a film. Feminist film theorists took issue with the unacknowledged masculinity of Metz's transcendent and coherent subject (Rose 1980; Doane 1980). They proposed different interpretations of Freudian-Lacanian psychoanalysis and advocated its explicitly political use in gender-specific film theory and practice (Mulvey 1986). Other theorists moved to challenge Metz's reductive account of social, economic and film history (Elsaesser 1986; Nowell-Smith 1985). Still others raised objections to Metz's exclusion of avant-garde, non-narrative and other non-dominant cinematic forms (Penley 1989).

A return to language analysis

On the first page of *The Imaginary Signifier*, Metz asked what psychoanalysis could contribute to the study of cinema. His answer is that it would effect a shift from structural to 'operational' analysis of cinema. But he was not abandoning his original research agenda. 'The psychoanalytic itinerary is from the outset a semiological one, even (above all) if in comparison with a more classical semiology it shifts from attention to the *énonce* to concern for the enunciation' (Metz 1982, 3). Even as he raises the lid on his Pandora's box of the imaginary, Metz remains committed to particular *linguistic* concepts (*énonce*, the utterance; enunciation, the speech act). By then Metz had acknowledged the importance of notions of textuality and subjectivity in a theory of cinematic signification. Psychoanalysis clearly represents an extension of Metz's first semiotics (Rosen 1986, 170), rather than a radical break or a rejection of earlier work (Silverman 1983, 288).

Nonetheless, compared to *Language and Cinema*, *The Imaginary Signifier* reads as a different sort of theoretic investigation. Perhaps the psychoanalytic paradigm proves *too* adequate a basis for analogical reasoning about film, in contrast to Metz's prior experience with the logical reasoning of structural linguistics. As Charles Altman observes, the psychoanalytic paradigm's 'constitutive metaphor (the cinema apparatus equals the psychic apparatus)' confers a unity on the cinematic experience 'it would otherwise lack'. (1985, 530).

But just as Metz had concluded that a structural-linguistic definition of cinema would fail because cinema had no abstract language system or *langue*, he was similarly aware that the question of how film is understood could only be resolved partially by a psychoanalytic methodology. The latter had offered a way to acknowledge and describe the subject in cinematic discourse. But, disseminated in film studies as 'a polemical tool and didactic shorthand' (Elsaesser, in Buckland 1995b, 10), Metz's psycho-semiotics became identified with an amalgam of several other distinct theoretic concerns (apparatus theory, Louis Althusser's notion of interpellation, etc.). In the process, some of the careful discriminations of Metz's linguistic agenda were obscured, notably his definition of the subject as an immanent linguistic entity. He did not equate the subject or 'user' with the actual spectator, but others in the field did, 'adding to the confusion by attributing to this "spectator" a set of constraints and limiting conditions known as subject-positioning, which in turn were said to determine the way films were read by actual spectators' (Elsaesser, in Buckland 1995b, 13).

Towards the end of his life, Metz returned to linguistics, to the work of his teachers, Algirdas Julien Greimas and Roland Barthes, and to the enunciation theory of Emile Benveniste. In the second essay of *The Imaginary Signifier*, 'Story/Discourse: A Note on Two Voyeurisms', Metz had already used Benveniste's distinction between two kinds of utterance (*histoire* and *discours*), here to describe two scopic drives mobilized by cinema (voyeurism and exhibitionism). The merger of linguistic and psychoanalytic paradigms facilitated his thesis: the traditional narrative cinema is primarily voyeuristic and it is an instance of historic utterance. Through techniques such as continuity editing or actors' avoidance of looking directly at the camera, traditional or 'classical' cinema hides or minimizes its discursive markers, its status as speech – just as the voyeur conceals his gaze. This was just the kind of idea that would be used in 'subject-positioning' studies of film spectatorship.

Metz's agenda, though, was not the ideological criticism which developed around issues of subject-positioning. Nor did he attempt a logical or grammatical account of film enunciation. Indeed, in his last published work, *The Impersonal Enunciation, or the Site of Film*, Metz argues that films typically do not 'grammaticalize' enunciator and addressee through deictic terms like personal pronouns. Yet Metz's 'second semiotics' had convinced him of the importance of explaining subjectivity in filmic discourse, and that meant sticking with enunciation theories. This was no minor dilemma, as Warren Buckland and Jan Simons point out, because enunciation was an ambiguous concept in poststructural semiotics (in Buckland 1995b, 113). Sometimes it was construed as an instance of communication, but more often it designated something more immanent, a linguistic instance, that of an abstract subject's discursive competence). In continuing the latter line of reasoning, *The Impersonal Enunciation* was, characteristically, both scrupulous and bold. Enunciation in cinema was reflexive, Metz argued, not deictic. Instead of grammatical categories, rhetorical terms (anaphora, metalanguage) were more adequate to the task of describing a film text's metadiscursive markers–markers, that is, of enunciation.

Metz always remained concerned with film as text rather than as communication. With this last work, though, his more explicit interest in spectatorial competence suggests he may have been reconsidering a communication framework, but was unable to take its broader view of language. That recent cognitive-theoretic studies of narrative film comprehension (Bordwell 1985; Branigan 1992) and a new film semiology (Buckland 1995b) *can* surely attests to Metz's enormous and lasting influence.

Marcia Butzel

Further reading and works cited

Altman, C. F. 'Psychoanalysis and Cinema: The Imaginary Discourse', in *Movies and Methods II*, ed. B. Nichols. Berkeley, CA, 1985.
Andrew, J. D. *The Major Film Theories*. New York, 1976.
Augst, B. 'The Lure of Psychoanalysis in Film Theory', *Cinematographic Apparatus*, ed. T. Hak Kyung Cha. New York, 1980.
Bordwell, D. *Narration in the Fiction Film*. Madison, WI, 1985.
— and Carroll, N. (eds) *Post-Theory*. Madison, WI, 1996.
Branigan, E. *Narrative Comprehension and Film*. London, 1992.
Buckland, W. 'The Structural Linguistic Foundation of Film Semiology', *Language and Communication*, 11, 3, 1991.
—. 'Michel Colin and the Psychological Reality of Film Semiology', *Semiotica*, 107, 1995a.
— (ed.) *The Film Spectator: From Sign to Mind*. Amsterdam, 1995b.
Cook, P. (ed.) *The Cinema Book*. London, 1985.
De Behar and Block, L. (ed.) *Semiotica*, 112, 1996.
De Lauretis, T. *Alice Doesn't: Feminism, Semiotics, Cinema*. Bloomington, IN, 1984.
Doane, M. A. 'Misrecognition and Identity', *Cine-tracts*, 3, 3, Fall 1980.
du Pasquier, S. 'Buster Keaton's Gags', *Journal of Modern Literature*, 3, 2, April, 1973.
Easthope, A. 'Classical Film Theory and Semiotics', *The Oxford Guide to Film Studies*, eds J. Hill and P. Church Gibson. Oxford, 1998.
Elsaesser, T. 'Primary Identification and the Historical Subject: Fassbinder and Germany', in *Narrative Apparatus, Ideology*, ed. P. Rosen. New York, 1986.
Heath, S. 'Film and System', *Screen*, 16, 1, Spring 1975; 16, 2, Summer 1975.
—. *Questions of Cinema*. Bloomington, IN, 1981.
— and Mellencamp, P. (eds) *Cinema and Language*. Frederick, MD, 1983.
Marie, M. and Vernet, M. (eds) *Christian Metz et la théorie du cinéma*. Paris, 1990.
Metz, C. *Essais sur la signification au cinéma* [1968]. Paris, 1972.
—. *Film Language*. New York, 1974a.
—. *Language and Cinema*. The Hague, 1974b.

—. 'The Imaginary Signifier', *Screen*, 16, 2, Summer, 1975.

—. 'History/Discourse: Note on Two Voyeurisms', *Edinburgh 76 Magazine*, 1976.

—. *Essais semiotiques*. Paris, 1977a.

—. *The Imaginary Signifier: Psychoanalysis and Cinema*. Basingstoke, 1977b.

—. 'The Cinematic Apparatus as Social Institution: An Interview', *Discourse*, Fall, 1979.

—. *The Imaginary Signifier*. Bloomington, IN, 1982.

—. *L'Énonciation impersonelle ou le site du film*. Paris, 1991.

—. 'The Impersonal Enunciation, or the Site of Film', in *The Film Spectator: From Sign to Mind*, ed. W. Buckland. Amsterdam, 1995.

Mulvey, L. 'Visual Pleasure and Narrative Cinema', in *Narrative, Apparatus, Ideology*, ed. P. Rosen. New York, 1986.

Nichols, B. 'Style, Grammar, and the Movies', *Movies and Methods I*. Berkeley, CA, 1976.

— (ed.) *Movies and Methods II*. Berkeley, CA, 1985.

Nowell-Smith, G. 'A Note on Story/Discourse', in *Movies and Methods II*, ed. B. Nichols, Berkeley, CA, 1985.

Penley, C. *The Future of an Illusion*. Minneapolis, MN, 1989.

Rose, J. 'The Cinematic Apparatus: Problems in Current Theory', *The Cinematic Apparatus*, eds T. de Lauretis and S. Heath. New York, 1980.

Rosen, P. (ed.) *Narrative, Apparatus, Ideology*. New York, 1986.

Sandro, P. 'Signification in the Cinema', in *Movies and Methods II*, ed. B. Nichols. Berkeley, CA, 1985.

Silverman, K. *The Subject of Semiotics*. New York, 1983.

Stam, R. et al. *New Vocabularies in Film Semiotics*. London, 1992.

43. Guy Debord (1931–1994) and the Situationist International

Drawing on previous artistic and political avant-gardes, the Situationist movement emerged in the early postwar period. Its membership included writers, painters, film-makers, architects and journalists who saw art as a political intervention capable of providing both an analysis of society's ills and the means to remedy them. The Situationist International (*L'Internationale situationiste*) came into official existence in 1957. Its various small national groups – in France, Algeria, Belgium, Denmark, England, Germany, Holland, Italy, Sweden and the United States – were held loosely together by annual conferences and by the twelve issues of the underground journal *L'Internationale situationiste* that appeared between 1958 and 1969. The movement attained a brief moment of notoriety, even cult status, in the aftermath of May 1968, to which it had made significant theoretical contributions and whose revolts are marked by the Situationists' slogans and their ludic style. The Situationist focus became increasingly sociological and political over time, with members taking outspoken stands on such issues as racial conflict in the United States, the Chinese Cultural Revolution and the war in Indochina. The movement was officially dissolved in 1972. While their names, writings and art works remain virtually unknown, the Situationists had a lasting though largely unacknowledged impact on the terms of debate in French intellectual and cultural life.

Guy Debord – agitator, film-maker, writer, publisher and social critic – was born in Paris and raised in Nice, Pau and Cannes. Unassiduous at school, he spent his childhood reading – Rimbaud, Lautréamont and the Surrealists were among his favourites – and developing a passion for the cinema. In 1951, he moved back to Paris to continue his studies but immediately began to frequent intellectuals seeking to distance themselves from the Saint-Germain-des-Près crowd. Chronic alcoholism and illness made him physically and mentally fragile and would contribute to his suicide on 30 November 1994.

The Situationist movement's dominant spirit and only continuous member, Debord authored most of the articles in *L'Internationale situationiste*, publishing them either signed or anonymously. His originality, his energy and his tenacity held the movement together and account for its lasting importance. It is therefore not implausible to read the imprint of his own psychology in the movement's personality. Orphaned by his father's early death and the indifference of his mother and stepfather, and raised by an over-attentive grandmother, he became the irascible and volatile chief guru of a movement known for its tendency to engulf and then to expel its members without rhyme or reason. Very early, he manifested strong ambivalence about bourgeois values: he denounced all social institutions and disregarded civil authorities yet nevertheless completed his baccalaureate, announcing his brilliant success in the 1951 exams by sending a black-bordered note to his friends. He mocked marriage and defended sexual freedom, yet he was twice married: to Michèle Bernstein from 1954 to 1972 and to Alice Becker-Ho from 1972 to his death. He never held a regular job, insisting on the debilitating effects of paid labour. He thus remained financially dependent most of his life: first on his grandmother, then on Bernstein, who worked at menial jobs and wrote two novels in order to subsidize the Situationist group, in which she nevertheless remained a subordinate member (see Bourseiller, 1999). Further study will hopefully reveal to what extent Bernstein, Becker-Ho, and other women contributed to the elaboration of Situationist positions.

Debord rejected the concept of private property and eschewed copyrights, yet he accused his one-time friend and mentor, Henri Lefebvre, of plagiarism. Frustrated by public resistance to his analyses of the evils of consumer capitalism, he was equally ferocious in his own resistance to fame, realizing that his own positions could too easily be commodified into a fad. Without doubt, Guy Debord was a troubled individual. It is equally clear that he was a genius. He understood the role of culture in society with a prescient clarity that ultimately became so thoroughly absorbed by both mainstream and intelligentsia that his signature remains largely invisible.

Situationist ideas arose in a postwar society characterized by prosperity, material comfort and a growing emphasis on consumer goods. The invention of artificial fibres and building materials provoked an awareness of the threat to the environment posed by excessive consumption. New technologies reduced labour at work and home, turning attention toward leisure activities. At the same time, suburbs sprouted around cities which were increasingly plagued by crime, housing and transportation problems. Decolonization was a preoccupation, as was the enigma of an alienated youth generation, described by Françoise Giroud in her book, *La Nouvelle Vague; Portrait de la jeunesse* (1958). Situationists saw both prosperity and its drawbacks as signalling a crisis in civilization. As early as 1953, Ivan Chtcheglov (a.k.a. Gilles Ivain), a member of the Lettrists, declared that 'A mental disease has swept the planet: banalization. Everyone is hypnotised by production and conveniences – sewage system, elevator, bathroom, washing machine' (Knabb 1981, 2). By 1957, Debord was arguing that modern life had reduced free individuals to the status of cogs in a capitalist machine. No longer active participants, people had become hypnotized spectators of their own lives. What was needed was a revolution in everyday life (*la vie quotidienne*).

Situationists were motivated by a desire to oppose capitalism while avoiding orthodox communist (socialist realist) and surrealist (psychoanalytic) conceptions of art. The intellectual climate in which they developed their critique was already attuned to the problems of modernity. Claude Lévi-Strauss had published his work on the structures of kinship and exchange in traditional societies. Jean Baudrillard was examining the role of consumer objects in urban France, while Roland Barthes was studying its modern mythologies. Sociologists and historians of the *Annales* school were developing social science paradigms for the study of collective 'mentalities', Michel Foucault was pursuing his historical studies of discourses and material culture, and Louis Althusser had launched his neo-marxist analysis of ideology and representation. In the United States, David Reisman, Herbert Marcuse, Marshall McLuhan and Vance Packard were describing the alienated individual in relation to the communications media and the city.

The Situationist project of transforming consciousness by changing everyday life harks back to Rimbaud and Lautréamont, to be sure, but its most immediate intellectual precursor was Henri Lefebvre, whose *Critique de la vie quotidienne* (1947) was an important influence on the evolution of Debord's thinking, and the two men were for a short time close friends. Bringing a marxist perspective to the study of daily life, Lefebvre applied the concepts of alienation and mystification to leisure. Before Debord, he observed that bourgeois society has separated work from leisure; capitalism sells activities, objects and images that fail to produce relaxation, creating instead passive attitudes and artificial desires that cannot be satisfied. Before the Situationists, he decried the complicity of culture (movies, advertising, commercial eroticism) in this process.

Previous avant-gardes also influenced the early Situationist movement. At the 1951 Cannes film festival, Debord viewed an unsettling film by Isidore Isou. Entitled *Traité de Bave et d'Éternité*, the film was characterized by disconnection of sound and image, sequences composed entirely of quotations, and deliberately scratched and distorted filmstock. Arriving in Paris that autumn, Debord began to frequent Isou and his friends, who called themselves *Lettrists* to signal their interest in materialist conceptions of art. Other Lettrists were Jean-Louis and Eliane Brau, Gil Wolman and Maurice Rajsfus. Debord and Bernstein joined and then soon created a splinter group, the Lettrist International, that in turn became the founding kernel of the Situationist movement.

The Lettrists favourite strategy was to disrupt and provoke, and their carefully staged public scandals resulted in memorable notoriety. For example, they invaded the 1950 Notre Dame Easter mass in order to proclaim the death of God. A 1952 press conference with Charlie Chaplin, in Paris to promote his new film *Limelight*, was interrupted by Lettrist agitators, including Debord, distributing tracts and shouting offensive though nonsensical accusations (Bourseiller 1999, 60). Although the declared purpose of both incidents was to raise public consciousness and demystify institutions and icons, one also detects a youthful rambunctiousness reminiscent of the Dadaists. Debord retained from these experiences a conception of art as performance and direct intervention in (or assault on) spectators' complacency.

Also committed to cultural revolt and contributing to the Situationists' evolution was the *International Movement for an Imaginist Bauhaus* (MiBi), which included most notably painters Asger Jorn (from Denmark) and Giuseppe Pinot-Gallizio (Italy). These two artists had also participated in the short-lived COBRA group (short for Copenhagen-Brussels-Amsterdam) and were in communication with small groups in Germany, Holland and England, each with its own journal and agenda. These groups shared an emphasis on the material basis of cultural production and a commitment to using art to promote class struggle. Other artists who were at some point associated with the Situationists included Jôrgen Nash, Ralph Rumney and Jacqueline De Jong. Three writers were also already active at this stage of the movement's development and later made important contributions to the journal, L'Internationale situationiste, Attila Kotányi, Raoul Vaneigem and René Viénet. Along with Debord's La Société du Spectacle (1967), Vaneigem's Traité de savoir-vivre à l'usage des jeunes générations (1967) and Viénet's Enragés et situationnistes dans le mouvement des occupations (1968) played an important role in shaping and interpreting the events of May 1968.

Surrealism was also, of course, an important precursor. The first issue of L'Internationale situationiste acknowledged this debt while proclaiming the intention of applying a more resolutely materialist analysis of culture and of avoiding the recuperation to which the earlier movement had fallen victim. The Situationists remained faithful to the surrealist project of gaining access to repressed creativity, spontaneity and a sense of play. At the same time, they conceived of 'repression' in terms more political than psychoanalytical. Peter Wollen goes so far as to say that 'In many ways [the Situationist] project was that of relaunching surrealism on a new foundation, stripped of some of its elements (emphasis on the unconscious, quasi-mystical and occultist thinking, cult of irrationalism) and enhanced by others, within the framework of cultural revolution' (1989, 22).

In the summer of 1957, a meeting in Cosio d'Arroscia in Northern Italy brought together representatives of various European experimental movements. Present at the gathering were Ralph Rumney (for the London Psychogeographic Committee), Asger Jorn and Giuseppe Pinot-Gallizio, along with several fellow artists from the Italian section of MiBi: Walter Olmo, Elena Verrone and Piero Simondo. Michèle Bernstein and Guy Debord represented the French Lettrist International. On 27 July, those assembled voted the Situationist International into existence. Debord presented a theoretical document entitled 'Report on the construction of Situations and on the International Situationist Tendency's Conditions of Organization and Action' (Knabb 1981, 17–25). The essay sets out the basic premise that a complete transformation of society is imperative, and that change can be brought about by means of 'revolutionary experiments in culture'.

Debord's most sustained exposition of the strategies that must be deployed to achieve this goal is to be found in his 1967 book, The Society of the Spectacle. The volume consists of 221 numbered propositions redefining consumer capitalism and the class struggle in terms of the spectacle, Debord's term for a mode of social relations mediated by representations. As he saw it, capitalism harnesses our imagination for use by the consumer market. Our lived experience and even our desires are transformed into media images and then sold back to us in the form of consumer goods. We thus become the passive spectators or consumers rather than the creators of our lives. Spectacle has become the new religion or opiate that keeps consciousness asleep.

Debord thus moves away from Marx's focus on production toward an emphasis on consumption and leisure. Vacations and television place 'play' in a pseudo-cyclical alternation with 'work', producing only an alienating parody of life. Similarly, separating homes from work and suburbs from cities necessitates networks of automobiles, parking lots, freeways and bypass roads, resulting in a vicious circle of isolation and passivity.

Families remain isolated in their homes, where television saturates them with 'pseudo-needs'. Capitalist spectacle offers an illusion of diversity, but no real choices. This is as true of modes of production as of politicians, movie stars, self-images and soap powder. Because domination is not only economic but also spectacular, the idea of competing economic systems is illusory. Capitalism will not be overthrown by economic revolution. The proletariat will only be liberated by a revolution in consciousness.

With few exceptions (Marguerite Duras's and Alain Resnais's *Hiroshima mon amour*, for example), contemporaneous experimental fiction in cinema and novel were subjected to harsh Situationist criticism for insufficient disruption of existing values. Situationists sought instead to instigate cultural revolution by deploying anarchistic and utopian strategies that we might call genres of living art. They would break rules and wrench objects, images, phrases, the city, desires, leisure activities, human interactions and the self out of their institutionalized meanings. The practices outlined below are all modes of 'constructed situations'. Implicitly indebted to Sartre, these are defined in the first issue of *L'Internationale situationiste* as 'A moment of life concretely and deliberately constructed by the collective organization of a unitary ambience and a game of events'. Their purpose was to produce new social realities by means of (somewhat) controlled experimentation: participants begin by 'setting up, on the basis of more or less clearly recognized desires, a temporary field of activity favourable to these desires'. This leads to 'clarification of these primitive desires' and to the emergence of new desires, which will in turn reveal a 'new reality engendered by the situationist constructions' (Knabb 1921, 43–5).

The most direct of the 'revolutionary experiments in culture' invoked at the 1957 founding meeting involved subverting the market value of the art object. This could be accomplished by mass production, as in Pinot-Gallizio's 'industrial paintings', drawn on rolls of paper to be sold by the metre. The art object's value as private property could also be disrupted through the systematic practice of plagiarism. Each issue of *L'Internationale situationiste* disclaims copyright, declaring that 'All the texts published in *L'Internationale situationiste* may be freely copied, translated or adapted, even without indication as to their origin'. The cultural object as commodity emanating from a (preferably famous) signature could be abolished through *détournement* or diversion: the recycling of texts and images in new contexts. Recalling Duchamp's ready-mades, Warhol's paintings and the surrealists' playfully moustached Mona Lisa, this strategy demonstrates that art involves creating new meanings for existing material. Putting into practice Lautréamont's axiom that 'Plagiarism is necessary; civilization demands it', painter Asger Jorn systematically painted over works by others, appropriating their vision. Debord made films whose soundtrack consisted of quotations, sometimes unaccompanied by images.

Other practices redefined art as an activity without material support. Since desires have been most successfully harnessed for the uses of capital in leisure activities, this is where Situationists invest their efforts. Since they conceived their revolution in *urban* terms, the city served as their laboratory. Prefiguring studies of what was later known as 'social space', Debord and his colleagues posited that psychological states, and thus social relations among individuals, were a function of physical environment. To explore modalities of 'psycho-geography', or the affective dimension of environment, they cultivated la *dérive*, a fashionable French leisure activity defined as 'a mode of experimental behaviour linked to the conditions of urban society: a technique of transient passage through varied ambiences' (Knabb 1981, 45), the Situationist *dérive* consisted of drifting through urban landscapes and becoming attuned to the auras of locales and neighbourhoods. This made it possible to take possession of the city and overcome its alienating fragmentation, rather than mindlessly passing through to a pre-chosen destination. Recalling the surrealists' automatic writing, the *dérive* is thus a kind of automatic walking, whose goal was to bring people into affective harmony with their surroundings. This practice would eventually contribute to the creation of new cities ('unitary urbanism') adapted to human needs – for play and freedom, for example.

Concepts of play and constructed situations are keys to understanding the Situationists' role in the Events of May 1968. Situationists were influential at the earliest stages of the revolts, which began in Strasbourg in 1966, where student anarchist groups came close to resembling the 'workers' councils' the Situationists felt would be the vanguard of the revolution. These groups protested the regimentation and restrictions imposed on student life, outdated styles of teaching, and the alienated nature of student work in a bourgeois university that privileged consumer values over discovery and knowledge. Inspired by Situationists, they created scandals and provoked incidents, distributed 'detourned' comic strips and posters, and published a pamphlet ponderously entitled 'De la misère en milieu étudiant considérée sous ses aspects économique, psychologique, politique, sexuel et notamment intellectuel, et de quelques moyens pour y rémédier'. The pamphlet was written by Mustapha Khayati, a Tunisian Situationist living in Strasbourg, with Guy Debord's editorial support. The brochure ends with a paean to proletarian revolution, conceived as a celebration of unalienated time and unmediated enjoyment of life (1966, 223–5). In the fall of 1967, in the midst of protests against United States, policy in Vietnam, the 'Enragés de Nanterre'e demanded changed living conditions at the Cité universitaire, while *L'Internationale situationiste* called once again for a 'decolonization of daily life'. The liberation of creativity and imagination as forces for social change were central to the student revolts. From Berkeley to Paris, freedom of expression was an act of participatory democracy. Debord himself could be found among the 'students' occupying the Sorbonne and in ad hoc committees attempting to spread the revolts into the factories. Although the Situationists' agenda was only imperfectly understood by the student protesters, their techniques and their spirit of liberation through play were prominent in the revolts.

The first issue of the *Internationale situationiste* (1958) had been categorical: 'There is no such thing as situationism, which would mean a doctrine of interpretation of existing facts. The notion of situationism is obviously devised by antisituationists'. It had been the Situationists' intention to remain in the shadows. Virtually unknown before the Events of May, Debord was in danger of becoming a media star. Imitators and admirers multiplied, but Debord and his colleagues continued to refuse interviews and resist commodification of their positions as just another bourgeois fad. But the tide was against them. The pressure of being idolized from the outside combined with the usual internal conflicts caused the movement to disintegrate. The last issue of *L'Internationale situationiste* appeared in 1969, and the group disbanded early in 1972. It could almost be said that the movement was killed by its own success.

Debord nevertheless continued to militate by returning to his original film-making career. In 1971, he became the protégé of film agent, producer and distributor, Gérard Lebovici. Lebovici, whose sympathies were with the radical Left and the insurgents of May, had also created the publishing house 'Champ Libre', with the editorial support of writer Jorge Semprun. Lebovici agreed to publish a new edition of *La Société du spectacle* and in 1974 produced its film adaptation, a collage of archives, texts, and images, accompanied by a soundtrack of Debord reading from his book. Lebovici subsequently produced several more of Debord's films, including his autobiographical *In girum imus nocte et consumimur igni* (1977). Debord continued to write and translate revolutionary pamphlets, and Lebovici, at the head of his distribution company Artmedia, became one of the French cinema industry's most powerful figures. In March of 1984, Lebovici was assassinated for reasons and by perpetrators unknown. Although not implicated, Debord suffered a media trial by innuendo in connection with the affair. The case was never solved. Although he continued to publish books, notably his 1988 *Commentaires sur la société du spectacle*, after Lebovici's death, he withdrew his films from circulation.

The Situationist movement appeared at the intersection of many artistic and political currents, and it embodied a certain spirit of the times. Consequently, the Situationist legacy is difficult to circumscribe. Some commentators maintain that it remains most visible in a style of thinking and writing that includes, among other features, the typical rhetorical figure of the reversed genitive (as in 'Let's put an end to the spectacle of contestation and move on to the contestation of the spectacle'). Slogans of this sort were so common in public discourse, and the Situationists were so unconcerned with claiming authorship, that their influence dissolved into the larger cultural landscape. Other more significant and lasting contributions can nevertheless be discerned:

- The Situationists exerted an obvious impact on subsequent avant-gardes. For example, Greil Marcus (1989) traces Situationist influence on punk and especially on Jamie Reid, Johnny Rotten and the Sex Pistols, whose irreverent record jackets, posters and performance style recall Situationist provocations.
- The Situationists refused all orthodoxies, and Debord was consistently against totalitarianisms of all stripes. In the face of widespread infatuation with Mao among the intelligentsia, Debord was outspokenly critical of the Chinese Cultural Revolution. He also remained resolutely anti-colonialist. Situationist positions helped to legitimize a diversity of thought in a French Left dominated by the Communist Party. History and a post-Cold War perspective have retrospectively enhanced Situationist credibility.
- If May 1968 placed art closer to the centre of the political map, this is largely attributable to the Situationist movement, which a decade earlier had begun to challenge assumptions about the social functions of culture. The 1960s and 1970s saw a convergence of social and cultural theory, with the result that art was increasingly seen as political. The Chinese Cultural Revolution of course also contributed to the increasing conviction that culture was as important as economics in the political debate. If not displaced, marxist economism was enhanced by the belief that a better world could be imagined and even brought into reality by liberating art and creativity.
- Like earlier cultural figures in the tradition of social and political *engagement* that included Zola, Breton, and Sartre, Situationists signed petitions, penned manifestos and manned barricades. They also went farther than other avant-garde movements in joining revolutionary theory to artistic praxis. The notion that art itself, independent of its creator, can be militant contributed to postmodern conceptions of art as object and as process. Situationists conducted valuable experiments with forms of cultural production that remain indigestible, that resist being bought or sold, kept as an investment or displayed on coffee tables. Contemporary explorations of the aesthetics of everyday experience, of urbanism, and of performance art are indebted to Situationist precursors. The Situationists' success in deconstructing the opposition of highbrow and popular

culture, in creating collective art, and in artistic practices drawing on anthropological conceptions of festival, play, gift, waste and excess contributed to the contemporary discipline of cultural studies.

• In France, the Women's Movement became a significant social force after 1968. Although members of the Situationist International failed to alter power relations between the sexes in their own behaviour, and in fact *L'Internationale situationiste* reproduces the dominant culture's tradition of representing women as spectacle, they did establish a critique of gender roles that helped shape feminist analyses. Their emphasis on everyday life as it is determined by institutions, including marriage and the family, contributed to contemporary under-standings of the private as political. These ideas also notably influenced the cinema of Jean-Luc Godard. For example, in *Tout va bien* (1974), Godard foregrounds the inseparability of public and private spheres, complicating his representation of class with an analysis of gender relations. Here and elsewhere, Godard uses Lettrist and Situationist techniques of *détournement*, dissociation of soundtrack and image, altering the material nature of film-stock, and thematizing the material nature of film-making.

The Situationist experiment retains its vitality of the 1960s and 1970s. Now that everything from love to information and from medical care to legal protection is no longer conceived in terms of rights and responsibilities but as consumer goods, and now that education and political leadership have turned into spectacle, Situationist insights seem more pertinent than ever.

Lynn A. Higgins

Further reading and works cited

Althusser, L. *Pour Marx*. Paris, 1965.
Barthes, R. *Mythologies*. Paris, 1957.
Baudrillard, J. *Le Système des objets*. Paris, 1968.
Bourseiller, C. *Vie et Mort de Guy Debord, 1931–1994*. Paris, 1999.
Debord, G. *Oeuvres cinématographiques complètes, 1952–78*. Paris, 1978.
—. *The Society of the Spectacle* New York, 1994.
Giroud, F. *La Nouvelle Vague: Portrait de la jeunesse*. Paris, 1958.
Internationale situationiste, 1958–69. Amsterdam, 1970.
Khayati, M. *De La Misère en milieu étudiant*. Strasbourg, 1966.
Knabb, K. (ed.) *Situationis International Anthology*. Berkeley, CA, 1981.
Lefebvre, H. *Critique de la Vie Quotidienne*, 2 vols, Paris, 1958.
Lévi-Strauss, C. *Les Structures élémentaires de la parenté*. Paris, 1949.
Marcus, G. *Lipstick Traces; A Secret History of the Twentieth Century*. Cambridge, MA, 1989.
McLuhan, M. *The Medium Is the Message*. New York, 1967.
October 79, Winter 1997.
Riesman, D. et al. *The Lonely Crowd*. New Haven, CT, 1950.
Sussman, E. (ed.) *On the Passage of a Few People Through a Rather Brief Moment in Time: The Situationist International, 1957–1972*. Cambridge, MA, 1989.
Vaneigem, R. *The Revolution of Everyday Life*. London, 1983.
Viénet, R. *Enragés et situationniste S dans* le mouvement des occupations. Paris, 1968.
Wollen, P. 'Bitter Victory: The Art and Politics of the Situationist International', in *On the Passage of a Few People Through a Rather Brief Moment in Time: The Situationist International, 1957–1972*, ed. E. Sussman. Boston, 1989.

44. Umberto Eco (1932–)

Sul finire del primo secolo della nostra era, nell'Isola di Patmos, l'apostolo Giovanni ebbe una visione. Se non fu Giovanni, se non ebbe la visione e semplicemente scrisse un testo sul genere letterario 'visione' (o *Apokalypsis*, Rivelazione), poca conta. Perché quello di cui ci stiamo occupando è un testo (e il modo in cui fu letto). Ora un testo, quando è scritto, non ha più nessuno alle spalle: ha invece... migliaia di interpreti di fronte. La lettura che essi ne danno genera altri testi, che ne sono parafrasi, commento, spregiudicata utilizzazione, traduzione in altri segni, parole, immagini, persino musica.

Un testo è una sfilata di forme significanti che attendono di essere riempite (che la storia, dice Barthes, passa il tempo a riempire): i risultati di questi 'riempimenti' sono quasi sempre altri testi. Peirce avrebbe detto: gli *interpretanti* del primo testo ... [Q]uesto volume verte su alcuni 'interpretanti' del testo detto *Apocalisse* ... [I]l presente volume li ha scelti come punto di partenza e non come punto di arrivo ... [H]anno generato altri testi, di cui quello che ora si legge, su pagine azzurre e rilegato in nero, è ancora uno degli interpretanti, non l'ultimo.

[At the end of the first century of our era, on the island of Patmos, the apostle John had a vision. If it hadn't been John, or if he didn't have the vision and simply wrote a text in the literary genre, 'vision' (or Apocalypse, Revelations), no big deal. Because that which interests us is a text (and the way in which it was read). Now a text, when it is written, no longer has anyone to help it; instead, it has ... thousands of interpretations facing it. The reading these give it generates other texts, which are paraphrases of it, commentaries, open-minded uses, translations into other signs, words, images, even music.

A text is a procession of significant forms that wait to be filled (that the story, says Barthes, passes the time to fill): the results of this 'filling out' are almost always other texts. Peirce would have said, the *interpretants* of the first text ... (T)his volume is concerned with some 'interpretants' from the text called *Apocalypse* ... (T)he present volume has chosen them as the point of departure and not as a point of arrival ... (T)hey have generated other texts, of which this one you now read, on blue pages and re-bound in black, is another one of the interpretants, not the last.]

I've taken the space to cite from the first two paragraphs of Umberto Eco's introduction to the *Beato di Liébana* (1973, 23), mainly because they convey the major aspects of his work I'd like to introduce here: an attraction to multimedia and communication, a preoccupation with the subject of reading, a concern with authority, a recourse to medieval texts as well as to Charles Sanders Peirce, and finally, his narrative voice.

'traduzione in altri segni, parole, immagini, persino musica': multimedia and communication

At first, it may seem odd to cite the *Beato di Liébana* as an example of Umberto Eco's fascination with multimedial modalities, since the text he edits and comments upon stems from a medieval manuscript, hardly the latest in communication technology. Nonetheless, as his self-conscious attention to the blue pages and to the black-bound volume suggests, Eco is just as interested in the medium as in the message. Indeed, Eco's self-reflexive commentary on the *Beato*'s commentaries on the last book of the New Testament, *Revelations*, highlights the edition's reproductions of the original manuscript's striking illuminations. Likewise, at the end of the volume, attention is drawn to the interplay between medieval and modern book production itself through a facsimile copy of Eco's handwritten response to the publisher's request for a biographical statement.

Actually, this edition's self-conscious and self-reflexive attention to the medium mirrors that of the genre known as *Beatus* – after Beatus of Liébana, who composed his commentary on the Apocalypse in ca. 776. Indeed, by the late Middle Ages, vivid and elaborate illuminations had become a characteristic marker of the *Beatus*. Moreover, the term *apocalypse*, as evidenced still today in films and television series, has come to function as a dark and evocative touchstone for the visionary, for scenarios of death and destruction racing alongside the four final horsemen. Replete with such associations, both the genre and the more widely-spread term almost require articulation in diverse media.

Yet, ironically, although the apocalypse evokes and inspires creation in various media, its message is concomitantly concerned with the single event that will end all mortal communication. Medium and message rival each other in the attempt to express such inexpressibles, thereby creating the kind of paradox fomenting at the centre of mystery, of secrecy, the kind of paradox that has intrigued Eco for decades, as evidenced by two of his most popular, 'genre-bending' novels. Thus, generating the action of *The Name of the Rose* (1983) is a monk's poisoning of an Aristotelian manuscript in order to prevent others from being (in his view) destroyed by its persuasive pagan ideas, thereby mirroring the text's deadly message in its murderous medium. Likewise, *Foucault's Pendulum* (1989) narrates an occult society's sinister attempts to define and control the message conveyed by their canonical texts. Secrecy, mystery, paradox – these entice readers to decode, to gain control of, to escape, to create.

Such alluring invitations occupy Eco and prove critical to his semiotic theory. Looking at how western European readers, for example, confront interpretation historically, Eco arrives at two philosophical strains. In his terms, hermeticism transforms the world into an allegory whose codes can be cracked, while gnosticism positions the enlightened individual as able to free humanity from original error. He argues, '[b]oth together, the Hermetic and the Gnostic heritage produce the syndrome of the secret ... the initiated is someone who understands the cosmic secret' (Eco et al. 1992, 38). Importantly, the reduction of the universe into an allegory and the individual into someone who can decode it not only underscores the reader's role in the grand scheme of things, it also transforms all media, everything, into a text to be interpreted correctly.

While not accepting such interpretative constraints in their entirety, Eco probes various contexts and media, undoubtedly propelled in part by his own voracious appetite for enigmas, puzzles, and all forms of communication. Indeed, in addition to his novels and short stories, Eco has conducted semiotic analyses not only of literary texts, but also of computer culture, books *per se*, comic books, films and architecture. Likewise, Eco has participated in multimedial enterprises: he has collaborated on children's books as well as on WWW and CD-Rom projects, worked for Italian television, lectured widely, been involved in education and pedagogical projects at various levels, and written for print media, including a weekly column for a prominent Italian weekly, *L'Espresso*.

In thus focusing both theory and practice on various instances of communication, Eco conducts semiotic analyses in a quintessentially rhetorical framework. Simply defined, and along classical lines, rhetoric is the art of persuasion which makes an author's attempt to reach an audience its primary aim. And effectively complementing rhetoric's aim is semiotics' concern with signs, how they're made, how they're received, and how they communicate.

Thus, in Eco's approach, the endless possibilities of semiotics are filtered through typically rhetorical concerns, such as accounting for contexts as well as the codes that an author plays against in order to communicate with her or his audience. As Eco puts it:

> The existence of various codes and subcodes, the variety of sociocultural circumstances in which a message is emitted (where the codes of the addressee can be different from those of the sender), and the rate of initiative displayed by the addressee in making presuppositions and abductions – all result in making a message (insofar as it is received and transformed into the *content* of an *expressionn*) an empty form to which possible senses can be attributed. Moreover, what one calls 'message' is usually a *text*, that is, a network of different messages depending on different codes and working at different levels of signification. (1979, 5)

With rhetorically framed semiotic theory, Eco theorizes and practises in various media. And since his subject is often communication, Eco's theory, fiction, and forays into the public circle about the possibilities and limits of communication (as made perhaps most obvious by the secretive, the paradoxical, the mysterious).

La lettura . . . genera altri testi: reading

Although Eco's semiotic framework is rhetorical, his approach differs from that of classical instruction in so far as he minimizes the author's concern with how to cajole audiences into accepting a certain point. Instead, Eco starts from the reader's position in order to explore how readers react to texts and in the process create new ones: 'every reception of a work of art is both an *interpretation* and a *performance* of it, because in every reception the work takes on a fresh perspective for itself' (1979, 49).

It is from this reader's perspective that Eco classifies texts as *open* and *closed*, although pure forms of either type do not exist (1962, 33–5). According to Eco, closed texts, such as Superman comics or Ian Fleming's James Bond novels, attract specific audiences and elicit specific readings. In contrast, open texts, such as James Joyce's *Finnegans Wake*, attract readers who dwell on structure and don't demand a simple message. Whether open or closed, Eco argues that a text (not the author) selects or attracts its own kind of reader, which he calls its Model Reader (1979, 7–10).

This description of how the reader functions, it seems to me, draws upon the same kind of paradox impelling mystery. Readers are *selected* by a text which will either entice them into believing they understand the secret completely or lead them to generate other texts in the attempt to come to terms with its paradoxes. Although a productive approach, at times it also limits the author – audience axis a bit too snugly. For example, while replicating (perhaps) how many readers experience a text, this approach makes the author vanish from view, a marginalization that concomitantly creates slippage. Thus the text seems to transform into a completely unified, almost organic, independent entity: 'any interpretation given of a certain portion of a text can be accepted if it is confirmed by, and must be rejected if it is challenged by, another portion of the same text' (Eco et al. 1992, 65).

Perhaps given Eco's emphases and approach, the diminishing of the author in favour of the text and the location of authorial activity in the reader are inevitable, since highlighting the reader in a rhetorical framework brings interpretation, the semiotic enterprise, to the foreground. Bridging the gap and critical to Eco's approach is the context which both readers and authors share – the unhierarchically arranged, open, culturally coded knowledge and intertextual frames that Eco calls an encyclopaedia, and within which *all* interrelated properties of any given sememe, or potential text, are stored (1986, 68–84).

Eco's concept of the encyclopedia nuances while underlining the importance of contexts. It accounts for the same sign meaning different, or simply differently received, things, and suggests that reading involves a series of operations. For example, texts reveal their topics by means of isotopies, a term Eco borrows from A. J. Greimas to designate the different semantic strategies that allow a text to generate interpretative coherence (1986, 189–201). By means of isotopies, the reader is called upon to implement what Eco calls semantic disclosures. 'Semantic disclosures have a double role: they *blow up* certain properties (making them textually relevant or pertinent) and *narcotize* some others' (1979, 23). So, when readers can forecast what will occur in a narrative, they are led to do so by isotopies, which in effect narrow down the plethora of information provided by intertextual frames, the encyclopedia.

Interpretation, then, involves the ability to negotiate detail and a series of frameworks, which Eco describes as a somewhat circular process: 'the text is an object that the interpretation builds up in the course of the circular effort of validating itself on the basis of what it makes up as its result' (Eco et al. 1992, 64). Recognizing that this description in effect defines the hermeneutic circle, Eco coins a pair of terms: the intention of the text (*intentio operis*) and the intention of the reader (*intentio lectoris*). In doing so, not only is the author marginalized, the text has essentially become a sign for both author and writer: it *stands for* the author to the reader while it concomitantly *stands for* the reader to the author.

I italicized 'stands for' in the last sentence because these words form the defining marker of the sign most used in semiotic theory. As Charles Sanders Peirce defines it, 'A sign, or *representamen*, is something which stands to somebody for something in some respect or capacity.' Peirce goes on to describe the sign's *interpretant*, that sign which is created in the mind of the addressee and which stands for the *object* to be read against a *ground* (Peirce 1960, 135). It is this definition of the sign, and particularly the role of the interpretant, that fuels Eco's approach, so much so that he can identify the *Beato* as an interpretant of *Revelations*.

'Se non fu Giovanni . . .': authority

Over time, the *Beato* had become just such a sign for a certain type of commentary. Part of its credibility as a sign stemmed from Beatus' inclusion of writings by earlier canonical thinkers, such as St Augustine, who too commented on *Revelations*.

Church authorities like Augustine frequently generated commentaries on sacred texts that later themselves became authoritative and were cited to signal, among other things, a conceptual framework. Likewise, Eco cites Barthes and Peirce to situate this *Beato* in a semiotic framework. Such allusions to authority cajole the reader to play text against literary contexts. Yet, once a narrative has widely spread authority – even one as subject to multiple commentaries and interpretative problems as the Bible – ensuing reader-generated narratives tend to conform to it:

...in 1699 we see John Webb...making a different hypothesis: after the Flood, Noah and his Ark did not land on top of Mount Ararat in Armenia but instead in China. Thus the Chinese language is the purest version of Adamic Hebrew, and only the Chinese, having lived for millennia without suffering foreign invasions, preserved it in its original purity. (Eco 1998, 64)

Although inviting readers to engage in literary encyclopaedias, authority curtails the extent of that engagement. Nonetheless, unexpected uses of encyclopaedias, such as Webb's, give life to authoritative narratives, shifting mystery from the message or medium to *how* a reader reads.

'come punto di partenza e non come punto di arrivo': Recourse to Medieval Texts

Although Eco's training in medieval textual culture is most widely known through *The Name of the Rose* (1983), as his preoccupation with authority demonstrates, medieval influence on his work goes beyond his first novel. Indeed, Eco's writings are peppered with references to Dante, speculative grammar, and various medieval theologians as well as with medievally derived terms, such as *intentio operis* and *intentio lectoris*. In addition, Eco has explored and applied the scholastic thought of Thomas Aquinas, whose work he has characterized as structuralist, in *Il Problema estetico in Tommaso d'Aquino* (1970) and in his *Arte e bellezza nell'estetica medievale* (1987). Moreover, Eco relies on medieval rhetorical schemes, such as the *ars combinatoria* (the art of generating various combinations from a set of certain givens), which serves him to explain not only how encyclopedias work but also James Bond novels (1979, 155).

At the foundation of Eco's approach to and application of medieval textuality is his fascination with language. Thus *The Search for the Perfect Language* (1995) also reflects medieval preoccupation with Edenic, fallen, and redeemed language, categories that in the Middle Ages defined humanity as well as mortals' relationships to the divine (Colish 1968, 8–81; Gellrich, 1985). Further, Eco's semiotic thought is reflected in the Middle Ages' tripartite approach to language, the *trivium* or the arts of grammar, rhetoric and logic. Indeed, as already stated, Eco's work has similarities with the second art of the *trivium*, rhetoric (Baldwin 1972). Most importantly, since rhetoric only recommends and has no hard and fast rules, it has no signposts to inform users they have erred. Thus its practitioners must be able to read audiences – to read readers – while writing texts that are not delimited by subject matter or scope. Moreover, they should be able to pick out the most appropriate *topoi*, or commonplaces, in order to establish a 'meeting place' for both audience and author. In Eco's terminology, the author must know how to make effective use of shared encyclopaedias.

'è ancora uno degli interpretanti, non l'ultimo': Charles S. Peirce

Influenced by medieval foci on language, Eco's semiotic work was foreshadowed in *Opera aperta* (1976a) and *La struttura assente* (1968) and developed in two key texts, *A Theory of Semiotics* (1976b) and *Semiotics and the Philosophy of Language* (1986). Importantly, Peirce's logic-trained language and analyses percolate throughout Eco's rhetorically-framed semiotic approach, as for example seen in Eco's attention to abduction (1976a, *Theory*, 131–3) and to the theory of possible worlds (1994, 65–82).

Abduction is the process by which a conclusion is drawn from a single example, a reader-centred process that depends heavily on contexts and encyclopaedias to fill in gaps. Fitting into this process is Peirce's analysis of two kinds of object, the *dynamic object* (or the object *per se*) and the *immediate object* (or the object as represented through its sign), whereby Peirce argues that we know reality through signs and not through the actual objects themselves. Encyclopedias, however, reveal that signs have multiple meanings. Faced with the numerous possible meanings a sign can have, we can nonetheless understand texts since they are contextualized in a ground and limited by a linear process – that is, according to Eco's reading of Peirce, 'a sign establishes step by step a *habit*, a regularity of behaviour in the interpreter or user of that sign, a habit being 'a tendency . . . to behave in a similar way under similar circumstances' . . . a cosmological regularity' (1979, 192). And abduction-framed, habitually perceived immediate objects allow readers to enter fictional worlds, 'worlds' which readers furnish from encyclopedias to approximate possible scenarios that reference our 'dynamic' world.

This type of channelling of the myriad possibilities invited by an encyclopaedia is critical to Eco's semiotic theory. Rejecting the propensity of some readers to see in every text a world of infinite possibilities along with the attempt of others to find the original intent of an author, Eco argues that texts may have multiple, but not infinite, meanings. He bases this approach in Peirce's notion of unlimited semiosis, whereby each interpretant, in itself constituting a sign, can infinitely produce others. In Peirce's system, however, the inter-pretants become more and more determined, not loosely associative (1994, 38–41). In theoretical circles, Eco is probably most well known for this position, which he often sets against that of deconstructionists whom he characterizes as more or less libertine readers.

By considering sociocultural contexts in the isotopic framework of possible worlds, Eco is able to explore multiple media, place the reader at the centre of the semiotic enterprise, and bring the reader's creative abilities to the foreground. In doing so, Eco emphasizes that what we know we understand through representations that are grounded in encyclopedias.

'Ora un testo, quando è scritto, non ha più nessuno alle spalle': narrative voice

At the end of a discussion of *Un Drame bien parisien*, Eco writes:

> *Drame* is only a metatext speaking about the co-operative principle in narrativity and at the same time challenging our yearning for co-operation by gracefully punishing our pushiness. It asks us – to prove our penitence – to extrapolate from it the rules of the textual discipline it suggests.

> Which I humbly did. And so should you, and maybe further, gentle reader. (1979, 256)

Thus Eco gives this text a voice and a will, thereby figuratively transforming it into a conversational partner that does its best to elicit its Model Reader.

In this manner, Eco replicates tensions found in Plato's *Phaedrus*, a dialogue depicting Socrates conversing on the topics of love, myths, memory and language. Important here, Socrates contrasts the inferiority of written to oral language. Written language, he complains, cannot interactively respond to different readers' needs nor further the talent of memory (Plato 1993, 274e–275a). Thus, on the literal level, Plato has Socrates prefer the virtues of reasoned conversation over writing. Yet, Socrates' critique must be read with care since, most obviously, his dialogue is conveyed by Plato through writing. Indeed, by building on such ironies, Plato is able to make the dialogue 'spea[k] about the co-operative principle in narrativity and . . . challeng[e] our yearning for co-operation . . . [and] asks us . . . to extrapolate from it the rules of the textual discipline it suggests.'

Eco's often ironic tone and recording of ironies work somewhat like Plato's condemnation of writing in writing. There is truth in the message, but the medium – or in Eco's case, the narrative voice – creates a rival. As such, writing can also function both as an antidote to and as an enhancer of mystery, paradox, language, myth, and thereby create the type of dialogue with readers, perhaps Model Readers, who will contribute to the conversation with other texts.

SunHee Kim Gertz

Further reading and works cited

Baldwin, C. S. *Medieval Rhetoric and Poetic to 1400*. St Clair Shores, MI, 1972.

Barthes, R. *Elements of Semiology*. New York, 1967.

—. *A Barthes Reader*, ed. S. Sontag. New York, 1982.

Bondanella, P. *Umberto Eco and the Open Text*. Cambridge, 1997.

Bouchard, N. and Pravadelli, V. (eds) *Umberto Eco's Alternative*. New York, 1998.

Colish, M. L. *The Mirror of Language*. New Haven, CT, 1968.

Deely, J. *Introducing Semiotic*. Bloomington, IN, 1982.

Eco, U. *La struttura assente*. Milan, 1968.

—. *Il problema estetico in Tommaso d'Aquino*. Milan, 1970.

—, text and commentary, and L. Vázquez de Parga Iglesias, intro. and bibliographical entries. *Beato di Liébana: Miniature del Beato de Fernando I y Sancha (Codice B. N. Madrid Vit. 14–2)*. Parma, 1973.

—. *Opera aperta*. Milano, 1976a.

—. *A Theory of Semiotics*. Bloomington, IN, 1976b.

—. *The Role of the Reader*. Bloomington, IN, 1979.

—. *The Name of the Rose*. New York, 1983.

—. *Semiotics and the Philosophy of Language*. Bloomington, IN, 1986.

—. *Arte e bellezza nell'estetica medievale*. Milan, 1987.

—. *Foucault's Pendulum*. New York, 1989.

—. *The Limits of Interpretation*. Bloomington, IN, 1994.

—. *The Search for the Perfect Language*. Oxford, 1995.

—. *Serendipities*. New York, 1998.

— et al. *Interpretation and Overinterpretation*, ed. S. Collini. Cambridge, 1992.

Elam, K. *The Semiotics of Theatre and Drama*. London, 1980.

Gellrich, J. M. *The Idea of the Book in the Middle Ages*. Ithaca, NY, 1985.

Innis, R. E. (ed.) *Semiotics: An Introductory Anthology*. Bloomington, IN, 1985.

Jakobson, R. *On Language*, ed. L. R. Waugh. Cambridge, MA, 1990.

Peirce, C. S. *Collected Papers of Charles Sanders Peirce*, eds C. Hartshorne and P. Weiss. Cambridge, MA, 1960.

Plato. *The Symposium and The Phaedrus: Plato's Erotic Dialogues*. Albany, NY, 1993.

Scholes, R. *Semiotics and Interpretation*. New Haven, CT, 1982.

Sebeok, T. A. *Signs: An Introduction to Semiotics*. Toronto, 1994.

45. Modernities: Paul Virilio (1932–), Gianni Vattimo (1936–), Giorgio Agamben (1942–)

Modernity has been and remains a vexed term in the field of recent cultural and philosophical thinking. It is possible, for example, to conceive of a 'modernity' that has existed and developed in the West since the Renaissance, centred around specific notions of sovereignty and subjectivity; it is possible to think modernity as a more specifically 'Enlightenment' project, stemming from a set of beliefs about the inevitability of progress; it is possible to become more all-encompassing and to set a date for the invention of 'history' and the consequent destabilization of 'traditional' cultures, a date that has been set at many points between ancient Rome and the 'industrial revolution'; or it is possible to think modernity as an identifiably twentieth-century project, in which case it comes into uneasy relation with notions of the 'postmodern'.

If we were, however, to name the major terrain on which this definitional conflict has been taking place in the West over the last several decades, it would be one decisively marked by the two great figures of Nietzsche and Heidegger; the principal continental theorists of modernity return again and again to these pillars of the temple with an insistence that borders on the idolatrous, thereby neatly encapsulating the thought that modernity, whatever else it might be, is inevitably striated and fissured by its own forebears. These particular forebears, of course, could be said to be united specifically around their scepticism towards 'enlightenment' and the general forward movement of culture; we thus have within the theory of modernity a continual undertow, a movement backwards that seldom fails to invoke a past, 'pre-modern' model even as it denies the very philosophical ground on which such a fantasy construct might be produced. The theory of modernity, then, is of necessity locked into the cyclical, the circular; even as it asserts the irremediable gap, the unbridgeable difference between present and past, so the past reappears once more as the constitutive feature of its own horizon, as the essential enabling reactive force against which modernity seeks to achieve its own novel velocities.

We need to point too to a further major constituent feature of theories of modernity, inherited again from Heidegger and also from Walter Benjamin, which is the attempt to locate and deal with technology. Again we find ourselves involved here in a play of difference; we might emblematically rediscover it in Baudrillard's joyful pessimism, his exultant castigations, his hallucinated rebuttals of precisely the simulacra that he reproduces time and time again in his work; we will find it, certainly, in the work of the three thinkers to whom I shall attend in this essay: Paul Virilio, Giorgio Agamben and Gianni Vattimo. What we also find in their work is a series of breakings of the boundaries: however modernity is described, it is constantly predicated on the assumption that the old cultural and disciplinary boundaries are impossible to sustain, that what is needed is not merely new methods of approach to cope with the plethora of novelty that characterizes the contemporary West but also a demarcation of the terrain that will set radically new boundaries between disciplines: from which, as would also be the case with Deleuze and Guattari, one might approach, or at the very least gesture towards, a 'disciplinary state' within which there are no boundaries at all, a field and mode of inquiry characterized not by the dogmatic exigencies of subject and object but rather by flux and intensity, by mergings and separations, by slogans and instructions, by language in a condition of essential contortion.

Virilio, for example, is a military historian, architect, urban planner, photographer, cultural theorist, philosopher, film critic and peace strategist. In this mix of skills and disciplines one can simultaneously glimpse the outlines of the field of knowledge as it appears in the guise of modernity, a field principally characterized – and this is to become Virilio's most (paradoxically) enduring theme – by the evanescence consequent upon acceleration and speed:

> – With acceleration there is no more here and there, only the mental confusion of near and far, present and future, real and unreal – a mix of history, stories, and the hallucinatory utopia of communication technologies. (1995, 35)

Such a perspective, such a shattering of lineally conceived times and spaces, is essentially for Virilio a matter of nothing short of a revolution in information, and principally in the media, both those media apparently dedicated to information itself and those aspiring to entertainment:

> – Speed guarantees the secret and thus the value of all information. Liberating the media therefore means not only annihilating the duration of information – of the image and its path – but with these all that endures or persists. What the mass media attack in other institutions (democracy, justice, science, the arts, religion, morality, culture) is not the institutions themselves but the instinct of self-preservation that lies behind them. That is, what they still retain of bygone civilizations for whom everything was a material and spiritual preparation directed against disappearance and death, and in which communicating meant to survive, to remain. (1995, 53)

In Virilio, as we see here, there is a continuing enactment of a play between depth and surface; it is as though Freudian insights about the prevalence of the thanatic can be gestured towards, but to move too deeply into them would mean, as it were, to lose one's footing, to risk one's own critical disappearance before the flood of information, the mesmerizing flow of culture that has replaced or overturned the old boundaries. What Virilio conjures, especially in his best-known text Speed and Politics, in order to capture this new economy of sight and sound is the term 'dromology'. What is at stake here has its origins on the site of the urban revolution; the book opens with Engels' remark of 1848 that 'the first assemblies take place on the large boulevards, where Parisian life circulates with the greatest intensity' (1986, 3), and proceeds through a series of analyses of transitions and transformations in the relative speeds of life in city and countryside, paying particular attention to the military implications of various modulations of speed, from the 'time of the siege' to the era of mass mobilizations. Virilio offers an intrinsic connection between military development, urban planning and the fate of socialism, culminating in an assertion that

> today many people are discovering, somewhat late in the game, that once the 'first public transport' of the revolution has passed, socialism suddenly empties of its contents – except, perhaps, military (national defence) and police (security, incrimination, detention camps). (1986, 18)

It is difficult to say whether Virilio, a writer notable more for a certain stridency of tone than for subtlety of wit, meant to plant this ambiguity about 'public transport'; but certainly the equation thus proposed between *jouissance* and the mode of transport and communication, be it military road or suburban boulevard, would emblematize the inseparability he proposes between desire and movement, the inadequacy of any assessment of the political or sociocultural situation that fails to take into account the simple but all-important facts of access, travel, circulation and destination.

War is, for Virilio, both the enduring emblem and also the machinic driver behind these developments, which tend toward a wholly 'different' distribution of spaces, mobilities, even scales:

> ... in the modern arsenal, everything moves faster and faster; differences between one means and another fade away. A homogenising process is under way in the contemporary military structure, even inside the three arms specifications: ground, sea, and air is diminishing in the wake of an *aeronautical coalescence*, which clearly reduces the specificity of the land forces. But this homogenising movement of combat techniques and instruments of warfare is coupled to one last movement. This is, with the 'weapon-vehicle' *contraction* and the cybernetisation of the system, the volumetric reduction of military objects: *miniaturisation*. (1994a, 18)

I quote this passage as an example of how Virilio's military-historical analyses come to have a clear bearing on a contemporary phase of modernity, in this case of, to take a few re-localized instances, the 'style-cluster' of the 'urban combatant' on the streets of Brixton or Maryhill, the advent of the pseudo-militarized four-wheel-drive as vehicle/weapon of choice for drug dealers and country vets, and the advent of the WAP-mobile phone.

Speed goes hand in hand with the development and exorbitation of the simulacrum, and the representation here which has always fascinated Virilio (with all the force, we might say, of a forbidden love) is the cinema. But the submersion of the subject in an undecidable play of simulacric forces goes deeper than this and exerts greater pressure on the key issue of technologization:

> Man, fascinated with himself, constructs his double, his intelligent spectre, and entrusts the keeping of his knowledge to a reflection. We're still here in the domain of cinematic illusion, of the mirage of information precipitated on the computer screen – what is given is exactly the information but not the sensation; it is *apatheia*, this scientific impassability which makes it so that the more informed man is the more the desert of the world expands around him, the more the repetition of information (already known) upsets the stimuli of observation, overtaking them automatically, not only in memory (interior light) but first of all in the look, to the point that from now on it's the speed of light itself which limits the reading of information and the important thing in electronic-information is no longer the storage but the display. (1991a, 46)

In modernity, wherever it might be situated against an uncertain background of a perhaps already disappeared realm of 'history', there is a constant emptying out, a demonic *kenosis* that paradoxically encloses desire and replaces its object with a – ghosts on the screen, spectral urban enemies who can never be caught, the shades of absent machines, 'motor-souls' passing invisibly in the night at unimaginable speeds. We might speak here, as Virilio does in *The Lost Dimension*, of the impossible ubiquity of the distant, of that which has already been (telekinetically) 'transported' – the telecommunicative, the 'tele-labourer', the 'tele-spectator', 'tele-local' machinery that is inevitably accompanied by the equipment of 'tele-informatics' (Virilio 1991b, 73–6).

In *Open Sky* Virilio will add to this armoury, this catalogue of the disappeared, a new term from the environs of the cinema and the VDU:

> After 'anthropocentrism' and 'geocentrism', our contemporary *savants* seem now to be in the grip of a new kind of illuminism, or rather **luminocentrism**, capable of hoodwinking them about the profound nature of space and time, the old perspective of the real space of the Quattrocento once again blocking the perspective of the real time of a horizonless cosmos. (1997, 5)

But in this depiction it is surely impossible to miss the tone of nostalgia, the longing for a 'real time' to appear somehow, mysteriously, within the emptied horizon of a cosmos become indeterminately lit, objectless. Onto this scenario comes the ghost of a long-past historical desire–

> According to Epicurus, *time is the accident to end all accidents*. If this is so, then with the teletechnologies of general interactivity we are entering the age of the **accident of the present**, this overhyped remote telepresence being only ever the sudden catastrophe of the reality of the present moment that is our sole entry into duration – but also, as everyone knows since Einstein, our entry into the expanse of the real world.

> After this, the real time of telecommunications would no longer refer only to delayed time, but also to an *ultra-chronology*. Hence my repeatedly reiterated proposal to round off the chronological (before, during, after) with the **dromological** or, if you like, the **chronoscopic** (underexposed, exposed, overexposed). (1997, 14–15)

Thus we return full circle to a dromology, to a science, or perhaps better practice, of speed and relativity; and to a field that is both populated with delights (everything available at the same time, sex while shopping) and yet simultaneously the abandoned site of the concentration camps and military defences that bulk so large – in *Bunker Archeology*, for example – in Virilio's war-conditioned imagination. What has happened, we might say, is that modernity has renounced its hauntings by the past, even if it has had to run so fast in order to do so that the world through which it speeds is reduced to flickers of ambiguous colour on an empty (cinema) screen; the fear is that were the motion to stop it would be to find other spectres, spectres of the present, crowding around the opaque windows of the protected carriage, demanding global redress for their exclusion from the last redoubt.

To turn from Virilio to Giorgio Agamben is to turn from city to study, from a hyperbolic repertoire of public gestures to a medieval intricacy of recourse. The scope of Agamben's work is similarly encyclopaedic, but his reference points are to be found in philology, linguistics, medieval poetics, the psychoanalysis of objects, the psychology of infancy, political theory. *Stanzas: Word and Phantasm in Western Culture*, for example, touches on medieval *acedia*; on Eros, mourning and melancholia; on the theory of fetishism; on Marx and the mystical character of labour; on Benjamin, Baudelaire and Beau Brummell; on the logos and the phantasm; on Narcissus and Pygmalion; on Oedipus and the Sphinx; and on Saussure and Derrida. The book reflects a pure myth of the Fall: the poetic sign, according to Agamben, achieved a fullness of representation in the thirteenth century, following which came an emptying of the sign's supposed plenitude. This structure of a fall from grace runs also through *Infancy and History: Essays on the Destruction of Experience*, from which I will quote a representative passage:

> The question of experience can be approached nowadays only with an acknowledgement that it is no longer accessible to us. For just as modern man has been deprived of his biography, his

experience has likewise been expropriated ... Today, however, we know that the destruction of
experience no longer necessitates a catastrophe, and that humdrum daily life in any city will
suffice. (Agamben 1993a, 13)

In tones reminiscent of Benjamin, whom he quotes, Agamben goes on to detail the
quotidian effects of that negativity which he will elsewhere explore at a philosophical level.
None of this, he claims, constitutes 'experience' for the modern man:

> Neither reading the newspaper, with its abundance of news that is irretrievably remote from his
> life, nor sitting for minutes on end at the wheel of his car in a traffic jam. Neither the journey
> through the nether world of the subway, nor the demonstration that suddenly blocks the street.
> Neither the cloud of tear gas slowly dispersing between the buildings of the city centre, nor the
> rapid blasts of gunfire from who knows where; nor queuing up at a business counter, nor visiting
> the Land of Cockayne at the supermarket, nor those eternal moments of dumb promiscuity
> among strangers in lifts and buses. (1993a, 13–14)

Thus far we may not seem too far from Virilio, although Agamben's prose is notably less
hiatic, less hysterical, more sombre, more measured: we are in an apparently 'public' world,
albeit one from which the meaning of 'public' has drained away, one based on an
impossible, phantasmatic notion of plenitude from which we 'measure' (even if through
an unavoidable disavowal) the curiously enclosed negativities of the present.

It might well be said that, if we put this together with Virilio, what we unearth from a
difficult (bunkered) archaeology is the 'founding conundrum' of the discourse of modernity: namely, that we shall only consider modernity, in its technological fixations, its
obsessive renunciations under the guise of pleasure, to have achieved its trajectory when we
find ourselves *no longer able to write about it*; for the very act of our inscriptions inevitably
recapitulates the mnemic trace, the obliteration of which is, according to these thinkers,
modernity's destiny (and 'destiny', in its Nietzschean and Heideggerian articulations, is a
repeated textualizing master-code).

Modern poetry, according to Agamben, is 'founded not on new experience, but on an
unprecedented lack of experience' (Agamben 1993a, 41). What experience, we may fairly
ask, is it that is textually absent, and how may we know its trace? It would seem possible,
turning to *Language and Death: The Place of Negativity*, to reassign the epistemic break, for
here it is the transcendentalist discourse signalled by Hegel and Hölderlin (and Kojève's
laconic and urgent Hegel) that seems to serve to remind of the world we have lost. If the
'mute foundation' of a 'Voice' is

> the mystical foundation for our entire culture (its logic as well as its ethics, its theology as
> well as its politics, its wisdom as well as its madness) then the mystical is not something
> that can provide the foundation for another thought – attempting to think beyond the
> horizon of metaphysics, at the extreme confine of which, at the point of nihilism, we are
> still moving. The mystical is nothing but the unspeakable foundation; that is, the
> negative foundation of onto-theology. Only a liquidation of the mystical can open up
> the field to a thought (or language) that thinks (speaks) beyond the Voice and its *sigetics*;
> that dwells, that is, not on an unspeakable foundation, but in the infancy (*in-fari*) of
> man. (1991, 91)

How, though, does this critique link with modernity? In part, perhaps (and in the fuller
articulation of this analysis the Jewish roots of Agamben's thought are important) in the
figure of the modern student, whose prototype sits 'in a low-ceilinged room "in all things
like a tomb", his elbows on his knees and his head in his hands', and whose 'most extreme

exemplar is Bartleby, the scrivener who has ceased to write' (Agamben 1995, 65). Or only at the point of an extreme alteration in the concept of history, for

> History as we know it up to now has been no more than its own incessant putting off, and only at the point in which its pulsation is brought to a halt is there any hope of grasping the opportunity enclosed within it, before it gets betrayed into becoming one more historical/epochal adjournment. (1995, 88)

Or in, perhaps, the 'coming politics', the novelty of which will be *that it will no longer be a struggle for the conquest or control of the State, but a struggle between the State and the non-State (humanity), an insurmountable disjunction between whatever singularity and the State organisation'* (1993b, 85, emphasis in original). The word 'whatever' is talismanic for Agamben, signifying a collaborative refusal, at the extreme limit of state power, by critic and actant to name and thus demolish their own activity; it is, one might like to say, the inscription on the tomb of the unknown thinker; and if it also seems to stand for precisely a conventional defeat of discursive specificity, a kind of high-school signing-off without content, then this would precisely redouble its symbolic force, as well as reminding us of one of Agamben's major works, *The Man without Content*.

The Man without Content is a book about art and aesthetics which points to the absence of art, the destructive power of aesthetics. It looks, as usual in Agamben, to a prior principle of unity, in this case the *Wunderkammer* wherein the 'work of art' would be displayed and thus achieve its meaning in the context of 'natural' curiosities, monsters, bizarrely represented perversions, aberrancies of all kinds; art not as mimesis of the norm but as a marginal representation of the impossible, a curiosity at a level with *trompe d'oeuil*.

> The interruption of tradition, which is for us now a *fait accompli*, opens an era in which no link is possible between old and new, if not the infinite accumulation of the old in a sort of monstrous archive or the alienation effected by the very means that is supposed to help with the transmission of the old ... Suspended in the void between old and new, past and future, man is projected into time as into something alien that incessantly eludes him and still drags him forward, but without allowing him to find his ground in it. (Agamben 1999a, 108)

Perhaps between Virilio's deluges, his drowning speeds and the painful struggles of Benjamin's Angel of History to keep his feet before the blowing gale, we might see Agamben's subject as dragged unwillingly, as into a mire, a swamp, an image of modernity as an obliterating, obscuring force, a further cover for emptiness.

The final words to the Introduction to *Homo Sacer* leave us with the flavour of this willy-nilly tug that can obliterate our best attempts at understanding: 'This book', Agamben says,

> which was originally conceived as a response to the bloody mystification of a new planetary order, therefore had to reckon with problems – first of all that of the sacredness of life – which the author had not, in the beginning, foreseen. In the course of the undertaking. . . it became clear that one cannot . . . accept as a guarantee any of the notions that the social sciences (from jurisprudence to anthropology) thought they had defined or presupposed as evident, and that many of these notions demanded – in the urgency of catastrophe – to be revised without reserve. (1998, 12)

Perhaps what is most surprising about this statement is that any theorist of modernity could have supposed at all the possibility of accepting 'guarantees' from the deeply compromised fields of jurisprudence or anthropology; we might also want to 'reckon with' Kristeva's linkage of the sacred with the schizophrenic, and with the whole question of what it might mean for an 'author' (of modernity) to 'in the beginning' *foresee*.

However, this inscription of revision is perhaps an essential (if unforeseen) feature of the texts of modernity and requires its own recourses: if Virilio's has been to the urban space, and Agamben's to a lost cultural infancy, that of Gianni Vattimo has increasingly been to the cloister and, eventually, to the bosom of Holy Mother Church. Such a trajectory, however, can be shown to have its origins in a by now predictable scenario, namely in an encounter with Nietzsche and Heidegger. *The Adventure of Difference: Philosophy after Nietzsche and Heidegger* touches upon modernity, perhaps, only through Vattimo's dealings with issues of *Überwindung* and *Verwindung* in relation to Heidegger's pronouncements on technology, and in particular with the nature of thinking as:

> The relation between deployed technology and the possibility that thinking may be able to put itself into a position of *Andenken* cannot be direct: *andenkend* thinking is not to be identified with technological thinking, nor is it prepared for by technological thinking, in the sense of being the dialectical outcome of technological thinking. The relation between *Andenken* and technology can only be oblique. (1993, 133)

In later works, however, Vattimo has addressed the consequences of this obliquity for modernity with considerable force. In, to take a major and well-known example, *The End of Modernity* he takes up the complex of issues surrounding the contested rhetorics of 'modernity' and the 'postmodern' and speaks unequivocally of modernity as

> dominated by the idea that the history of thought is a progressive 'enlightenment' which develops through an ever more complete appropriation and reappropriation of its own 'foundations'. These are often also understood to be 'origins', so that the theoretical and practical revolutions of Western history are presented and legitimated for the most part as 'recoveries', rebirths, or returns. (1988, 2)

What becomes immediately apparent at this point is that whatever it is that Vattimo is taking to be 'modernity', it is far more closely aligned with the problematics of western 'modernism' than with the notions espoused by either Virilio or Agamben. 'Modernity', he says later in the book,

> is primarily the era in which the increased circulation of goods ... and ideas, and increased social mobility ... bring into focus the value of the new and predispose the conditions for the identification of value (the value of Being itself) with the new. (1988, 100)

Vattimo's authorities here are Simmel and Gehlen; the focus is evidently on a certain phase of material and ideological production, the mobility of which, for example, has nothing whatever to do with Virilio's hectic history of speeds, nor with Agamben's deep (if weirdly belated) mistrust of the *méconnaissances* of jurisprudence or anthropology. What Vattimo is more concerned with is a detailed interrogation of the 'modern moment': in such a moment, he notices, 'progress seems to show a tendency to dissolve itself, and with it the value of the new as well', and 'this dissolution is the event that enables us to distance ourselves from the mechanism of modernity' (Vattimo 1988, 104). What, here, would constitute 'ourselves'? It would seem that Vattimo is speaking of a historically distanced scenario, rather than one that can be reduced to the mere simulacra of tele-distance.

In accordance with such a historicist, or pragmatic, turn Vattimo provides us with at least the beginning of a way in which the thus far unspoken 'foundation' of modernity (as a westernizing imperative, as the name of global free trade, as the excuse for US neo-imperialism, as the structure underpinning the unequal 'exchange' of 'goods' – in both senses – across the world) might be brought on stage, although it is couched in a further encounter with the Heideggerian and in a re-encounter with anthropology that seems rather after the fact. He says that

> the experience of the anthropologist who wishes to reject both the (Euro- or ethnocentric) evolutionary perspective and the illusion of a possible dialogue or interplay between different cultures is itself a deeply ambiguous one ... The ideal of an anthropology which would be the locus of an authentic encounter with the other – in accordance with a model which, in an over-simplistic and optimistic fashion, would make anthropology the rightful heir to philosophy after the end of the metaphysical epoch, when the hermeneutic perspective predominates – cannot be set in opposition to the notion of anthropology as a scientific description of the constants of all cultures, a notion that has been deeply conditioned by the metaphysical idea of science and, at a practical level, by Western domination of the planet. (1988, 157)

Although this inconclusive reflection might at first glance seem marginal to the 'project of modernity' (by which I mean to designate not a historical or cultural 'fact' but the constructed object of the discourses we are here discussing), I suggest that it is 'in fact' (by an essential postcolonial logic) central, for if there is the prospect of a discourse that is obliterated by modernity, then that discourse would be one that would inspect modernity's promises from a 'different' perspective – the perspective, for example, of China, within which context the modernizing project presents itself with a totally different force.

Vattimo does not pursue these insights, but what he does do, in *The Transparent Society*, and in particular in the chapter 'Utopia, Counter-Utopia, Irony', is provide us with an essential link, on the perhaps unlikely terrain of the film *Blade Runner* and its clones, between technology and the ruin. 'Paradoxically', he says,

> the post-apocalyptic condition these works describe is in some sense a happy one; that is, at least the atomic catastrophe that weighs upon us as a constant threat is imagined to have happened already, and for the survivors this somehow amounts to a form of liberation. A sense of liberation – albeit, as ever, paradoxical – also cloaks the retreat from technology and its products within the post-apocalyptic genre. (1992, 84)

Although he does not go on to discuss it in detail, what Vattimo here touches on is both an essential dialectic of expectation and also a reappraisal of the role of the ruin – the ruins of previous philosophical 'systems', the ruins of the city, the ruins of progressive thought swamped by the vicious divisions of that form of capitalism which is conventionally referred to as 'late', as though its succession by some unimaginably different form, some unimaginable form of difference, were somehow already on the (already foreclosed) global horizon.

But perhaps it is in *Beyond Interpretation: The Meaning of Hermeneutics for Philosophy* that Vattimo most clearly shows both the promise and the defeat of the circular Heideggerian approach to the sacred – and fatal – triptych of metaphysics, modernity and technology:

> The relation of hermeneutics to modern techno-science breaks with all metaphysical and humanist associations when hermeneutics, taking science seriously as a determinant factor in the configuration of Being in modernity, grasps the essential nihilistic meaning of science which is at the same time constitutive of its own destiny. The world as a conflict of interpretations and nothing more is not an image of the world that has to be defended against the realism and positivism of science. It is modern science, heir and completion of metaphysics, that turns the world into a place where there are no (longer) facts, only interpretations. (1997, 26)

The fatal hinge here is 'destiny', the notion that in the hypostasized motion beyond all human control that characterizes the 'progress' of modernism – or perhaps of 'techno-science', whatever that might be – there remains the ineradicable shade of a transcendental meaning towards which culture continues to move, even if that destiny be one of disaster. It is at this point, I would say, that the radicalism derivable from the Nietzschean and Heideggerian models decisively reveals its 'other', the way in which such anti-metaphysical moves, such anti-technological scepticisms, can be automatically – somnambulistically – inverted to provide a further lock on the door to the future.

Modernity, to conclude, may be seen to appear in the works of Virilio, Agamben and Vattimo as a doubly constructed object, constructed first on the site of a global westernizing project and second in the complexly dialectical discourse of theorists who would seek both to espouse – or emulate – the rapidity of its motion and to halt its flow through the appropriation of technological anxieties. What gets ignored in this process is, among other things, the violence which is masked by the smooth flow of 'the modern'. The shades of Nietzsche and Heidegger (even when accompanied by a Japanese interlocutor) serve further to embed the discourse of modernity within a Eurocentric frame, from which the wider consequences of modernization – global warming, the destruction of the environment, the perpetuation of inequities in the international division of labour – are ever more permanently exiled.

In thinking about Virilio, Agamben and Vattimo, perhaps the most salient approach would be through a new (postal) geography. To what addresses are these messages sent? Through what customs points, what passport control, do they pass in their claim on a 'planetary' interpretation of technology? Perhaps even more saliently: what is accomplished by the continuing reduction of the plethora of burgeoning technologies to a single, unitary category of 'techno-science'? It might be suggested that the era in which such a concept could adequately represent such a multiplicity is long gone: Virilio's deployment of weapons science, Agamben's understanding of medieval physics, Vattimo's dealings with the techno, which serves, as it turns out, to be a prelude to a re-espousal of Catholicism – how far do these go in outstripping the complexities of techno-insertion into the heart of the disasters of the global economy, the disavowals and violences signified in the notion of a modernizing 'new world order'?

David Punter

Further reading and works cited

Agamben, G. *Language and Death*. Minneapolis, IN, 1991.
—. *Infancy and History*. London, 1993a.
—. *The Coming Community*. Minneapolis, IN, 1993b.
—. *Stanzas*. Minneapolis, IN, 1993c.
—. *Idea of Prose*. Albany, NY, 1995.
—. *Homo Sacer*. Stanford, CA, 1998.
—. *The Man without Content*. Stanford, CA, 1999a.
—. *The End of the Poem*. Stanford, CA, 1999b.
Der Derian, J. (ed.) *The Virilio Reader*. Oxford, 1998.
Derrida, J. and Vattimo, G. (eds) *Religion*. Cambridge, 1998.
Vattimo, G. *The Transparent Society*. Cambridge, 1992.
—. *The Adventure of Difference*. Cambridge, 1993.
—. *Beyond Interpretation*. Cambridge, 1997.
—. *Belief*. Cambridge, 1999.

Virlio, P. *Speed and Politics*. New York, 1986.
—. *War and Cinema*. London, 1989.
—. *The Aesthetics of Disappearance*. New York, 1991a.
—. *The Lost Dimension*. New York, 1991b.
—. *Bunker Archeology*. New York, 1994a.
—. *The Vision Machine*. Bloomington, 1994b.
—. *The Art of the Motor*. Minneapolis, IN, 1995.
—. *Open Sky*. London, 1997.
—. *The End of Modernity*. Cambridge, 1998.
—. *Polar Inertia*. London, 2000.

46. Hélène Cixous (1938–)

Hélène Cixous, critic, poet, playwright, novelist, academic innovator, has bent her work in all domains of her activity toward recognizing and exploring *sexual difference* in language and literature. She has insisted unyieldingly on *woman* – a stance that has proved as enigmatic as it is controversial. Because of it, she early came into conflict with a French feminism that had adopted a militant stance regarding the sexes as absolutely equal and interchangeable (e.g., Monique Wittig). In Anglo-American feminist and critical culture Cixous was quickly labelled an 'idealist', 'uneasy about the power of words to hold out against the power of opposition' (Schiach 1991, 33). Her peculiar way of moving back and forth among 'text, performance, unconscious, and biography' (33) has also puzzled many of her readers: but this is Cixous' way of holding out against the inevitable hierarchies that oppositions always bring in their wake. She has indeed baffled critical categories, yet this is also her point: Cixous has held out for the recognition of sexual difference and of 'woman' and made them essentially into non-negotiable demands for critical theory and literary practice with a view to impeding the rigid and false categorizations that arise with sexual opposition. For her, woman is something 'more' than her subjection to the phallic signifier, but in this more, some of her critics have labelled her an 'essentialist'. Yet, no one but Shakespeare, perhaps, has had so fluid a sense that both sexes may at once occupy one body, at least in the 'country of literature'. In an age, she says, where *inscription* has displaced the older literary forms of *representation* and *expression*, we need to acknowledge sexuality in art in order to transcend it. If she has, at times, described herself as 'a woman made of women' (in Cixous 1990, 203), at others, she paints her artistic process as a playwright by claiming that she not only can but that she must reach a way to identify herself with 'man' in order to write:

> I write as a woman . . . I can use my body to inscribe the body of a woman. But I can't do that for a man [in prose] . . . There are plenty of men in my plays. But that is because the theater is not the scene of sexual pleasure . . . in the theater it's the heart that sings. And the human heart has no sex. Sexually, I cannot identify with a male character. Yet the heart feels the same way in man's breast as in a woman's.

Cixous' reasons for her stance on sexual difference have, moreover, a sound philosophical, analytic and literary grounding that has nothing to do with 'biologism', 'essentialism' or anti-equalitarianism. They do, however, have a great deal to do with her alliance with the anti-Hegelian strain in French thinking, a position common to her fellow theorists Jacques Derrida, Michel Foucault and Jean-François Lyotard, not to mention Jacques Lacan. In standing firm for the recognition of sexual difference, Cixous has intended to strike a blow against the 'metaphysics' of opposition in which any difference tends inevitably toward becoming binarily opposed concepts where one always yields to the dominion of the other, à la Hegel. The case of sex is egregious in this respect: the domination of feminine by masculine in western culture is long-standing. An anti-Hegelian stance was, of course, also adopted by the leading male philosophers and critical theorists of Cixous' Parisian circle, but in her hands it is modified in a unique way. Cixous took it upon herself to work out, through the very language that fosters metaphysical skewing, new strategies for 'righting' the system, correcting the imbalance, and providing for what been silenced, engulfed or incorporated by its opposite to have its 'say.' That is why her first major theoretical statements take a poetic, hysterical form: as poetry is repressed by prose, a hysteric's sexual ambivalence is repressed by the prevailing order of binary sexual oppositions.

Cixous' theory often has a militant tone, but it is the tone of someone who takes language as the most serious means of combat: her 'Sorties' of 1975 (in Cixous and Clément 1988) means both 'exits' or the 'way out' and the excursive raids made by a garrison under siege to lift it. Like her fellow émigré to France, Julia Kristeva, Cixous designates the 'way out' of the impasses of contemporary culture and politics as existing in the nether side of language. Unlike Kristeva, Cixous sees human being entirely made of language, so that the raids made by the underside of language are at the same time the same as those made by what Kristeva would call 'the body' or 'the woman'. For Cixous, both body and woman are linguistic effects, but that very fact makes them capable of subverting the language that oppresses them. Where Kristeva's 'revolution in poetic language' locates a choric reserve of 'semiotic' rhythms that disrupt surface discourse but do not overthrow it, however, Cixous is determined to have the feminine rewrite and re-invent that 'surface'.

When Cixous founded the first programme of doctoral studies in Études Féminines in France at Paris VIII (Vincennes) in 1974, she had been Chair of the English Department at the University of Paris at Nanterre since 1967. Even as head of the new programme she continued to direct English doctoral studies: she was, after all, an internationally acclaimed Joyce scholar, and, at age 40, the youngest holder of the doctorat d'état in France, having published her major thesis on Joyce (The Exile of James Joyce) and written a minor thesis on Robinson Jeffers. Within the university system, the emphasis on women in Études féminines was most radical politically. Cixous has, however, claimed that, at the time, she would have greatly preferred to title the new doctoral programme 'Studies in Sexual Difference' (Calle-Gruber 1994, 211). If she was not simply after the 'study of women', what then did Cixous seemingly have in mind in pursuing the politics of feminine studies, the practices of feminine writing and the strategies of feminine reading (see Schiach 1991, 38ff.)? What did 'sexual difference' really mean to Cixous?

It meant that there are two different logical positions that can be taken within language (language being what defines human being as such) and that these go by the name of masculine and feminine. The two perspectives do not fully overlap nor do they diverge completely; they hold a common, vacuous centre – the phallic signifier – but they appropriate or resist it in different ways. In short, they specify two distinctive ways of apprehending and reflecting certain universal human predicaments.

Cixous' commitment to the problematic of difference is linked to her more or less absolute commitment to *literary* language. It is a commitment that has clearly shaped her institutional practices (she insisted on hiring mainly leading creative writers at Vincennes: Butor, Cortazar, and 'poetic' literary critics like Jean-Pierre Richard and Tzvetan Todorov to teach there). It has also deeply informed her theories of feminine writing (*écriture féminine*) and shaped her literary criticism into a uniquely poetic prose. It is crucial to note that her procedure as critic, writer and reader is to force sexual difference to the surface of writing – be it theoretical, dramatic, political, or poetic in nature – so that the writing at last comes to mirror the schism of language, the internal limit that each 'sex' poses to the other within the 'same' language. The goal is not to achieve a Hegelian *sublation*; it is, rather, to accomplish its aesthetic *sublimation* by the 'emptying of the subject' of sex: its capacity for enjoyment is unlocked, but only – and this seems to be crucial for understanding Cixous – at the literary level. She does not seem inclined to bring the programme into everyday life except where life itself has attained poetic insight.

It is thus entirely legitimate, in Cixous' critical theory, to tie literary language to the particular biography and elective theoretical alliances and affective political allegiances of its author. The theme of exile in language, for example, has often informed her theory of poetry. It has drawn her to write about poets like Osip Mandelstam (whom she pairs, unexpectedly, with Nelson Mandela on the basis of the common part-signifier in their names (Cixous 1988)), Anna Akhmatova and Tasso, playwrights like Kleist and Shakespeare, and novelists like Kafka and Joyce, whose language bears the indelible mark of an internal exile. At the same time, Cixous conscientiously admits that her critical predilection for such authors is rooted in her own sense of the linguistic exile she felt as a child of Jewish parents (one of Spanish descent whose family had lived in Morocco, the other an Austro-Hungarian who emigrated from *Mitteleuropa* in 1933) in largely French and Arab speaking Algeria.

Cixous depicts her own particular 'coming to language' as shaping her poetic as well as her critical practice. Her earliest discussion of her artistic process (*La Venue à l'Écriture*, 1977) links it to the fact that, as a child in her peculiar circumstances, she found herself opened to the heteroglossic light that different tongues shed upon each other. For her a language exists beyond languages, something like Benjamin's *reine Sprache* that is 'universal' to human being, but it is a *concrete* universal that she calls different 'countries' in language: the country of poetry, the country of theatre. This 'universal' face is always particularized by reference to her own familial biography: she looks to her father (and his premature death when she was eleven) as crucial for bending her toward poetry in her earliest reflections, but by her 1994 book, Hélène Cixous, *photos de racines* (Calle-Gruber and Cixous), Cixous also begins to track part of the history of her own poetic language to her maternal language, German, with its particular resonances and rhythms.

The authors toward whom Cixous has been drawn in her criticism, from Lispector to Joyce, are generally those who most intensely mark the dramatic rise of a repressed side of language to the surface of discourse. That this 'repressed' or deeply alienated part of language more often than not bears a feminine figure (like Molly Bloom) may account for another aspect of her focus on *woman*. Cixous sees the direct effect of poetic and literary language as having greater power than political engagement or a social choice to grant a voice to what has been unable to speak for itself. When Cixous restaged Sophocles, for example, in her opera, *Le nom d'Oedipe* (1978), she focused on Jocasta, the mother-wife that the ancient playwright all but overlooks as a dramatic presence. When she wrote her first play, *Portrait de Dora* (1976a) (a great success), she dramatized Freud's 'Case of

Hysteria' from the point of view of the analysand, young Dora, and not from that of the good doctor.

Cixous' closest theoretical ally thus seems to be Jacques Derrida (with whom she began discussing Joyce in 1962). His *Glas* influenced her take on Hegel more than a little, as did his work on the critical role of *écriture* in his 'Freud and the Scene of Writing', and his *De la grammatologie*. Cixous' political engagements, always passionate, found expression in close work with Michel Foucault, with whom she examined (and protested through a kind of guerrilla theatre) prison conditions in France. Psychoanalytically – although this is not generally recognized in Anglo-American circles – she is also linked to Jacques Lacan, to whom, of course, most critics assume she is strictly 'opposed' (Sellers 1996, 6, 47). But Cixous's resistance to oppositional thinking should already indicate that her relation to the body of Lacan's work is not simple.

Even if we wished to speak about Cixous purely as a critic (which, given the enormous corpus of her critical work, would be entirely legitimate) it would not be possible to separate her theory from her life entirely; in her theory, no clear demarcation between them is possible. Thus interjecting some of the biographical record may clarify her relation to the thought of Lacan. Lacan was interested in James Joyce, about whom he would eventually write in his seminar on *Le Sinthome*. Because of her great knowledge of Joyce, Cixous' thesis director, Jean-Jacques Mayoux, introduced her to Lacan, and she and Lacan worked together for two years, from 1963 to 1965. Her long-time partner Antoinette Fouque, a political activist in the *Mouvement des femmes* and co-founder of the publishing house, Éditions des femmes, was analysed by Lacan, creating another tie between Cixous' sensibilities and the French teacher of Freud.

In terms of theory, we can say that, like Lacan, Cixous sees human 'life' as an effect of a signifier that excises *jouissance* from reason and from a social life that is ruled by the Law (of language). From Lacan and from Freud both, Cixous learned to appreciate the degree to which language *is* the essence of human life, and that when woman's speech (or anyone else's speech, for that matter) is radically impeded, cut off by cultural limits, that life becomes the object of unleashed, irrational forces of repression as well as the return of the anguishing presence Lacan termed *jouissance*. In the place of a *vouloir-dire* (literally, a 'meaning', but also etymologically, 'a wanting-to-say'), the repressed subject produces only stifled gestures, awkward jerks inconsonant with verbal expression – the kind of verbal expression that grants masculine speakers social rewards and assures them their social place and psychological balance.

Those in command of the word can hide behind it – behind the mask that speech provides (recall Stendhal's dictum that 'words were made to hide men's thoughts'). The hysteric's unbidden gesture is, by contrast, all too visible – to the point that it becomes a 'writing' that can never stop writing itself, even and especially when all avenues of speech are cut off to it. Cixous's aim, in 'The Laugh of the Medusa' and in 'Sorties', is to read the *writing* in hysteria, to read its proto-*écriture féminine*.

In her best-known longer critical work, *The Newly Born Woman* (1975, with Catherine Clément), Cixous and Clément use quotations from Lacan to contest Freud's too narrow view of women. Lacan's own work on sexual difference, *Encore*, appeared the same year (having been offered by him as his seminar of 1972–3). Freud's view of women inspires them to bring out the most subversive feminine positions to challenge male-dominant 'rational' culture – positions that, because they threaten male dominance, have long been severely repressed. One such energetic resource is sorcery and witchcraft.

It is difficult not to read Cixous' criticism and her creative work, especially the 'history plays' she has written, without thinking of hers as an activist social stance. She has resisted the political repression of artists and, more generally, of those, like Nelson Mandela, 'whose word has not been heard for twenty six years' (1990, 196). Yet it cannot be said that her activism has a social as much as it has a literary basis. Her interest in the work of Mauss on 'the gift' and her disdain for consumerism (Schiach 1991, 20ff.) are tied less to an organized political positions than they are to her sense that masculine-based cultures and economies are deeply weakened by a failure to recognize 'the other sex', and that in every domain culture stands in strong need of supplementation not only by a feminine perspective, but by the kind of irrepressible disruption that alone allows the unspoken to be said.

In her life and work Cixous can thus be said to exemplify the comprehensiveness, scope and uniqueness that she believes 'woman' as the revenge of the repressed can bring to bear on those cultural domains traditionally foreclosed to her. But not only 'woman'. For Cixous, woman is more or less the emblem of a power, an energy in language that has been prematurely stifled by a culture of the (phallic) signifier. The hallmark of her own critical prose is its singular power to compress grand philosophical, political and psychoanalytic theories into tellingly pithy, epigrammatic formulations that communicate explosively their critical stance as much through their handling of the signifier – language, sound, rhythm, style – as through systematic exposition and, at times, bitter irony. For example, for her critiques of Freud in *La Jeune née* [*The Newly Born Woman*, 1975] and in *Le rire de la Méduse* ['The Laugh of the Medusa', 1981] Cixous consciously adopts a 'hysterical' *persona* and tone that become no small part of the criticism she launches. Her way of responding to Hegel's overbearing metaphysical oppositions is to penetrate one side by the other, and to take the most abstract metaphysical concepts and imbue them with familiar objects – especially sex and feminine *jouissance* ('Sorties', in Cixous and Clément, 1988). Cixous' critical reproaches of Hegel are worthy of Kierkegaard and made in the same spirit, but Cixous' texts could never have been written by the Danish male philosopher in the special feminine way central to Cixous' language. Nor does her prose resemble that of Kristeva, who is equally informed in linguistic and philosophical theory, but whose highly theoretical prose could never be mistaken for Cixous poetically condensed formulations.

It is important to return once more to Cixous' double insistence on *woman* and on *sexual difference*. It is a stance that distinguishes her markedly from Judith Butler who, like Cixous, is allied with Derridean deconstruction, but whose fundamental orientation remains Hegelian. Butler, too, contests the 'Hegelian' binary opposition between masculine and feminine (in which one must succumb to the other); her technique is to 'subvert' gender repressions by undermining and loosening the cultural codings of gender, detaching gender from any necessary biological or any linguistic tie to the subject. Cixous' approach sounds superficially similar, but it is really quite different, for she is committed to the struggle within language as such; to wresting the subject free from language by means of language itself. Cixous' argument with the feminist position of egalitarianism is that it is premature and may too quickly override what of 'woman' still needs to be explored, what woman may yield for the arsenal needed to combat language's insistent categorizations. Cixous does not work at the level of shifting surface *personae*, or masks, like Butler. She instead works her way through language and its laws to the surface: for Cixous, it is the moment of surfacing that counts. Liberation must be constantly re-secured through intimate linguistic struggle that takes the full measure of its opponent's force and dominance.

The critical distinction to be drawn between Cixous's adherence to the principle of sexual difference and that of Lacan is that, for Lacan, sexual difference as such is *the* response of the subject to the effect of the signifier. Cixous has, by using psychoanalytic thought 'creatively', placed herself more in the Derridean deconstructive camp than in the scientific rigour of Freudian-Lacanian thought, to which she (and Derrida) remain, of course, also indebted. For Lacan, the sexualized response to the traumatic alienation of the subject by the signifier dates from the subject's very first encounter with the signifier, with language, with the phallus coming to the rescue and organizing the disarray the signifier introduces into the subject. This encounter structures the logic of the psyche and thus of sex for each subject. For Cixous, in contrast, *writing* – the fact of inscription – voids such unconscious structuring. Writing empties out the subject and makes it available for adopting either masculine or feminine postures – or even a mix of both. This is a mixing that psychoanalysis reserves only for hysteria and to perversion. Cixous appropriates hysteria's unique writing for her dramatic art. Dramatic art sustains (and may even require) the sublimation of sex. Poetry and novel – which operate in the intimate sphere – can, however, never dispense with a sexuality, for sexuality is what defines one's subjective being.

For Cixous, 'masculine' and 'feminine' are nothing more than orientations toward language and its logic – orientations that affect the body and soul alike and are the source of sexual energy. As a creative artist, Cixous has made full use of this energy, derived from an original principle of clivage in much the same way that Hazlitt said Shakespeare did: she works her way toward the emptying out of its cultural remainders, the restrictions produced by the metaphysics of oppositional thinking, but she does so only in order to be able to inhabit other subjects that she *artfully* produces as linguistic effects. At the level of art, sexual difference is neither a given, nor an eternal opposition, but a fundamental principle of insight. In her essay, 'The Two Countries of Writing', Cixous says:

> 'I'm mostly composed of 'women' – quite by chance. I have no trace of my grandfathers except as being wiped out of life. And neither of my grandmothers had traces of grandfathers ... So I am mostly peopled with 'women.' And it's probably made me write the way I write. I might have been composed of 'men;' and I would have written differently. But then, what are 'men' or 'women' composed of? (Cixous 1990, 197)

The implication is that men and women are composed of language, of effects of the signifier, as Lacan put it.

If one were to make a global assessment of Cixous' critical stance, one would have to place it in the line of German critical romanticism, from Schlegel to Benjamin, in which the transcendence of traditional oppositions opens up the critical beauty of *Kunstprosa*. It is in this context that Cixous' theory and her politics of writing come together in what is perhaps her most interesting *Gesammtwerk* – her 'history plays'. In her collaborations with Ariane Mnouchkine at the Théâtre du Soleil in Paris – on *The Terrible but Unfinished Story of Norodom Sihanouk, King of Cambodia* (1985) and her very popular *L'Indiade* (1987) – all of Cixous' major poetic, theoretical and political practices join together to produce major literary works.

Juliet Flower MacCannell

Further reading and works cited

Calle-Gruber, M. and Cixous, H. 'Portrait de l'écriture' and 'Générique', in Hélène Cixous, photos de racines. Paris, 1994.

Cixous, H. Portrait de Dora. Paris, 1976a.

—. The Exile of James Joyce. London, 1976b.

—. 'The Laugh of the Medusa', in The Signs Reader, eds E. Abel and E. K. Abel. Chicago, 1983.

—. Le Nom d'Oedipe: Chant du corps interdit. Paris, 1978.

—. L'Indiade, ou, l'Inde de leurs rêves: et quelques écrits sur le théâtre. Paris, 1987.

—. Manne aux Mandelstams aux Mandelas. Paris, 1988.

—. 'The Two Countries of Writing: Theater and Poetical Fiction', in The Other Perspective in Gender and Culture, ed. J. Flower MacCannell. New York, 1990.

—. The Terrible but Unfinished Story of Norodom Sihanouk, King of Cambodia. Lincoln, NR, 1994.

—. Rootprints. London, 1997.

— and Clément, C. The Newly Born Woman, intro. S. Gilbert. Minneapolis, MN, 1975.

Conley, V. Andermatt. Hélène Cixous: Writing the Feminine. Lincoln, NE, 1984.

—. Hélène Cixous. Toronto, 1992.

Derrida, J. De la grammatologie. Paris, 1967.

Foucault, M. and Cixous, H. '"A propos de Marguerite Duras", par Michel Foucault et Cixous', Cahiers Renaud-Barrault, 89 (1975).

Sellers, S. Hélène Cixous. Cambridge, 1996.

Shiach, M. Hélène Cixous. London, 1991.

47. Philippe Lacoue-Labarthe (1940–) and Jean-Luc Nancy (1940–)

Philippe Lacoue-Labarthe and Jean-Luc Nancy have co-authored important commentaries on some of the decisive texts of our modernity. In 1980, they assembled a conference called 'Les Fins de l'homme: à partir du travail de Jacques Derrida' and, in December of the same year, they co-founded the 'Center for Philosophical Research on the Political', which ran until 1984 and produced two volumes of collected writings (Rejouer le politique, 1981 and Le retrait du politique, 1982). Their individual publications are not only impressively numerous (far outnumbering their co-authored work), but also impressively diverse, ranging from learned discussions of painting, poetry and music to intricate meditations on freedom and community, subjectivity and mimesis.

Most readers of Lacoue-Labarthe's and Nancy's work will attest to both its usefulness and its difficulty. For over thirty years, their writings and lectures have proved a fecund and indispensable resource for students and scholars interested in literary theory. This necessity is dictated not only by the formidable consensus of academic response (both favourable and unfavourable) to their work, but also by the highly instructive nature of the work itself. Studying a text or a question Lacoue-Labarthe and Nancy have treated without consulting what they have said is like missing a crucial lecture.

Perhaps the best testimony to their pedagogical exemplarity as readers comes from those they have submitted to close reading. One, Jacques Lacan, started a 1973 seminar by strongly urging his students to read *The Title of the Letter*. Not usually disposed to praising his commentators, Lacan continued:

> I can say, in a way, it is a question of reading, that I have never been read so well – with so much love ... We shall say, then, that this is a model of good reading, so much so that I am able to say that I regret never having obtained anything close to it from my followers. (Lacoue-Labarthe and Nancy 1992, vii)

Whether their object is Plato or Aristotle, Descartes or Kant, Schlegel or Schelling, Nietzsche or Heidegger, Blanchot or Bataille, Derrida or Girard, Lacoue-Labarthe and Nancy give us models of good reading – so good, in fact, rarely does anything else come close.

On the other hand, their texts are exceptionally difficult. I would like to dwell for a moment on this difficulty in order to accentuate the constitutive and irreducible role difficulty itself plays in their thinking. One of the first difficulties a new reader will encounter in coming to Lacoue-Labarthe and Nancy, especially one unfamiliar with continental philosophy, is the presupposition of a certain philosophical knowledge. This is itself a familiar objection lodged against 'high theory': theory's assumption that we are already well versed in the concepts, arguments and idioms of an immense and difficult philosophical tradition. It is true that Lacoue-Labarthe and Nancy undertake, for the most part, philosophical readings of (diverse) texts. Their readings mobilize various terms and concepts which are weighted with a specialized and frequently quite complicated meaning; in the movement of their commentary, in their attempt to get from one point to the next, these items are not always unpacked for the 'lay' reader. To be fair, however, Lacoue-Labarthe and Nancy never attempt to burden one with verbal jargon. They use technical-theoretical terminology only in so far as it facilitates their travel. Moreover, they frequently circle back on their language. In the manner of good teachers and translators, they take time to explicate the sense of key words or phrases, remind us of their provenance and descent, their valence and limitations. See, for example, the carefully layered, historical delineation of the term romanticism which prefaces *The Literary Absolute*; or, in their study of Lacan, the helpful explanation of the slippery materiality of the letter and of the crucial role it plays in his constitution (or de-constitution) of the subject (Lacoue-Labarthe and Nancy 1992, 27–32); or the patient tracing of Freud's axiomatic (but unfinished) theory of *identification*, a theory which both grounds and shakes his construction of sociality (Lacoue-Labarthe and Nancy 1989, 1991 and 1997, 1–31).

But there is a more fundamental, and more fundamentally difficult, philosophical presupposition at work in Lacoue-Labarthe's and Nancy's readings. This 'given' which shapes the mode of their inquiry does not involve (at least not primarily) the marshalling of a philosophical vocabulary, tone or posture. Rather, it concerns what the two call *the philosophical*. The generalized tenor of this term seeks to distinguish it from this or that philosophical system, literature, practice or tradition. In 'The "Retreat" of the Political', Lacoue-Labarthe and Nancy define the philosophical as 'a general historico-systematic structure – which, up until recently, one could have called the West – of which philosophy is each time the thematisation, the prefiguration or the anticipation, the reflection (critical or not), the contestation, etc., but which largely overflows the basically restricted field of operations of actual philosophising' (1997, 124).

I call this philosophical premise of their work difficult for several reasons. Difficult, first of all, in the sense of hard to understand and easy to misconstrue. Lacoue-Labarthe and Nancy set up shop in the work space hollowed out by Heidegger's *Destruktion* ('destructuring', 'dismantling') of western metaphysics. This project of destructuring metaphysics follows from the recognition that metaphysics is closed or finished. This critical movement – philosophy is closed, therefore we must dismantle it – would be a non sequitur if the close of philosophy were (mis)taken to mean that philosophy is simply over and out, ineffectual and irrelevant. On the contrary, as Lacoue-Labarthe and Nancy put it, ' "closure" indicates, first of all, the completion of a program ... *and* the constraint of a programming' (Lacoue-Labarthe and Nancy 1997, 125). The exigency of deconstruction emerges from the recognition of philosophy's programmatic endgame, its deathgrip on our modernity.

A related and widely spread misunderstanding which arises from Heidegger's thesis about the end of metaphysics is the notion that if we really want to end metaphysics all we need to do is stop talking about it and move on to something else. A good deal of the politically well-intentioned impatience or hostility towards 'French Heideggereanism' derives, I think, from just this commonsensical view that the endless chatter about the end of philosophy is basically disingenuous. Certainly, when Heidegger says 'Metaphysics cannot be abolished like an opinion' (1993, 67) we do not have to take him at his word; that is, he might only be expressing an opinion. But the least we can do as readers, as Lacoue-Labarthe and Nancy do with equal measures of fidelity and resistance, is to take Heidegger at his word, taking seriously the premise of metaphysics (in both turns of the genitive).

Nowhere is this difficulty more clearly inscribed than in the opening to Lacoue-Labarthe's *Heidegger, Art and Politics*. Echoing the line from Heidegger cited above, Lacoue-Labarthe writes: 'We cannot pass beyond the limit, or what Heidegger called the "closure". We are still living on philosophical ground and we cannot just go and live somewhere else' (1990, 3). Perhaps we need to read these lines in context to hear that they are not spoken in a self-satisfied tone. Terry Eagleton reminds us that for Marx social class is not just an empty metaphysical category, but a form of social alienation. It cannot simply be wished away; 'to undo this alienation you [have] to go, not around class, but somehow all the way through it and out the other side' (1990, 23). Marxists do not dwell on class in order to indulge in the identity it confers or the symbolic distinction it brings, but rather to get out of it. There is a comparable predicament in Lacoue-Labarthe's (and Nancy's) relation to the philosophical. The tone of 'we cannot just go and live somewhere else' is not only sober and severe, but is tinged with a certain anguish or melancholy, a rigorously negated desire to do just that, to 'go and live somewhere else'. The difference between being constrained by metaphysics and being constrained by class, however, is that there is no way of getting out of the former. This places the philosopher in a truly difficult situation. For Lacoue-Labarthe the difficulty of dwelling on this side of philosophy's limit gives rise to a paradoxical imperative: that we no longer desire philosophy and yet desire nothing else, 'that we let philosophy collapse within ourselves and that we open ourselves up to that diminishing, that exhaustion of philosophy, today' (1990, 5). Such a frankly conflicted relationship to philosophy's exhaustion can hardly be deciphered as a calculated recovery of philosophical discourse. Rather, it describes the obligation of a thinker who finds himself enfolded in the unending 'today' of metaphysics.

This difficult, paradoxical experience of his own philosophical orientation relates to another, more spectacular difficulty – namely, the problem of 'Heidegger'. Some chroniclers of the 'Heidegger affair' have contended that the publication of Victor Farias's book

Heidegger et le Nazisme (1987) forced 'French Heideggereans' to awaken from their dogmatic slumber and retreat into a defensive posture. Whatever the accuracy of such a claim, a few things need to be underscored in the case of Lacoue-Labarthe and Nancy. First, the dreadful correspondence between Heidegger's engagement with Nazism and certain aspects of his thought does not come as a surprise to them in 1987. On the contrary, the question of the relation between Heidegger and Nazism in particular, and philosophy and politics in general, animates their teaching and writing since at least the mid–1970s. Second, their paradoxical relationship to the philosophical can only be fully understood in this highly *political* context. For them, it is not a question of 'salvaging' Heidegger but of asking: *given* that Heidegger was the greatest thinker of his century, the one who gave us the most to think, what was it in his thinking that allowed for, or was not sufficiently vigilant to prevent, its (and his) affiliation with the very worst. Finally, taking such a critical stance towards Heidegger presupposes they do not identify what they are doing with any 'Heideggereanism' – for if such a thing exists *in* Heidegger it would be found in those moments of his thought where he abandons the ceaseless interrogation of philosophy for philosophy proper.

Years before the 'Heidegger affair' broke in France, Lacoue-Labarthe and Nancy had begun to bend their philosophical commentary in a political direction. Indeed, the 'Center for Philosophical Research on the Political' was founded in order to enable a serious philosophical questioning of politics – or rather, not politics (*la politique*), but the political (*le politique*); not an analysis of political positions, struggles and ideologies (the domain of political science), nor a reflection on the *specificity* of the political (the domain of political theory), but an inquiry about what constitutes the '*essence* of the political'. Taking their cue from Jacques Derrida's essay 'The Ends of Man', Lacoue-Labarthe and Nancy note in their opening address to the Center:

> What today appears to us necessary, and hence urgent, is rigorously to account for what we are calling the essential (and not accidental or simply historical) co-belonging of the philosophical and the political. In other words, to account for the political as a philosophical determination, and vice versa. (1997, 109)

Of these two research aims, they place special emphasis on the latter: re-examining the philosophical *as* the political. This does not mean excavating the politics of philosophy, probing philosophy's practical agendas, ideological ramifications, or political consequences. Rather, it means treating 'western' thought as essentially political from its very beginnings.

Rethinking metaphysics *politically* marks a significant and productive swerve from the path Heidegger lays down. Much of what is stirring and original in Lacoue-Labarthe's and Nancy's later, single-authored work develops out of their collective investigations of the political. But what do they mean by the political? If their understanding of the philosophical is deeply indebted to Heidegger's understanding of western metaphysics, then it follows that the political might just as well be thought under Heidegger's rubric of *der Technik* (technology or, more accurately, *technics*, on this latter translation, see, Weber 1996, 59–60). But while the political shadows (follows and retraces) the rich critical motifs which cluster around the theme of technology – including the operationalization of knowledge, the anthropological valorization of work, the globalization of techno-economies, the reduction of the public sphere to opinion management and more – it can't simply be absorbed into Heidegger's framework. Why not?

A brief detour is necessary here. For Heidegger, technology is the 'basic form of appearance in which the will to will arranges and calculates itself in the unhistorical element of the world of completed metaphysics' (1993, 74). In other words, it is merely the outward form and mundane name for some more essential metaphysical operation – namely, what he calls the *Gestell* (usually translated as 'enframing', Lacoue-Labarthe proposes 'installation' or 'erection' (1989, 64–71) and Weber 'emplacement' (1996, 71–2)). *Ge-stell* semantically umbrellas a host of terms that share the root verb *stellen*, meaning to put or to stand or to emplace. Heidegger asks us to hear in *stellen* (and this is important for grasping the tie between the essence of technology and 'the will to will' of modern metaphysics) the overtones of provocation and demand (1977, 14). Technology besets nature as a provocation, a demand to stand by as raw material and energy. This characterization of technology is often interpreted as a critique of instrumental reason. But the critical point for Heidegger is not that technology as an instrument of man winds up instrumentalizing and dehumanizing him (in fact he objects to this instrumental and anthropological conception of technology). Rather, the problem with technological production is that it forgets or ignores a more originary experience of *techne* (art, craft, know-how, knowledge). The decisive meaning of pro-duction (*poiesis*) is not provocation (*Herausfordern*), but bringing-forth (*Hervorbringen*). For Heidegger, the essence of technology is poetic production in the Greek sense of bringing-forth into presence, bringing 'hither out of concealment forth into unconcealment' (1977, 11) – production in the sense, then, of revealing, of *aletheia*. Only in light of this definition can we take full measure of the distortion technology suffers in its metaphysical and modern guises.

Lacoue-Labarthe's and Nancy's analyses of the political cannot be collapsed into Heidegger's questioning of technology because, to put this very schematically, they find something amiss both in his philosophical premise (the staging of *aletheia*) and in his characterization of technology's provocation (the dismantling of *Gestell*). In a minute, patient reading of the *stellen*-words which interlace with *Gestell* across several of Heidegger's texts, Lacoue-Labarthe detects how one of these words goes, effectively, missing: namely *Darstellung* (1989, 43–138). *Darstellung* covers several meanings – portrayal, depiction, exposition, *mise-en-scène*, representation – each of which may be referred (this is essential for Lacoue-Labarthe and Nancy) to the idea of *presenting* in the literary or fictive sense. Tracing how *Darstellung* drops, here and there, out of Heidegger's theoretical view, enables Lacoue-Labarthe to profile a kind of blind spot in his thought. This blind spot marks the formative role fiction or, as he puts it, '*fictioning*' plays in the ontological definition of being itself. For Lacoue-Labarthe, fictioning does not only play a role on the stage of metaphysics, for example, in the form of what Heidegger calls 'the poetizing essence of reason', Kantian reason's 'forming force' (*die bildende Kraft*); fictioning takes part in, or in fact 'is', the *staging* of metaphysics. It is constitutive of metaphysical programming itself. In perhaps the most important vector of his work, Lacoue-Labarthe develops this concept of the fictioning essence of philosophy (what he calls 'onto-typo-logy') in relation to the ancient question of mimesis. Another way he describes Heidegger's blind spot, then, is by pointing to an 'original' or productive mimesis (a 'mimetology') at work in his thought which, because of his Platonic depreciation of mimesis as imitation, he fails to see (1989, 297). Relatedly, Nancy observes that Heidegger's privileged concept of *aletheia* presupposes *Darstellung*. What was supposed to evade the provocations of a frontal set-up, what was supposed to take place outside the metaphysical staging of truth, cannot avoid *exhibiting* itself. Regardless of how philosophy conceives of truth, it always remains something which must be made to appear *as such*. Thus, in *The Sense of the World*, Nancy states a certain reservation in regards to Heidegger's thinking of truth: 'This reservation concerns the degree to which truth as *aletheia* ("veiling/unveiling"), like all other types of truth, continues to operate in terms of presentation, placing-in-view, exhibition, and manifestation' (1997, 16).

But why dwell on something Heidegger misses (especially since his thought enables us to see it)? For this reason: the 'missed' thing – mimesis, fictioning, fashioning, staging, manifestation, presentation, and so forth – is *the political itself*. In other words, Heidegger's disregard of philosophy's foundational fictioning goes hand in hand with his unwillingness to think the essential co-belonging of the philosophical and the political. This inattention to the 'literary' at work in the machinery of philosophy is furthermore inseparable from what Lacoue-Labarthe calls Heidegger's 'overvaluation of the philosophical' – an overvaluation most visible in his 'fundamental reduction of existence to philosophizing' (1989, 288). This is precisely why Lacoue-Labarthe and Nancy provisionally favour the term 'the philosophical' over 'metaphysics'. Heidegger's critical delimitation of metaphysics serves to shield some more authentic philosophizing (the privilege given to *questioning*, for instance) from dismantling. By (re)designating *metaphysics* as *the philosophical*, Lacoue-Labarthe and Nancy leave no margin of philosophy free from deconstruction.

In his introduction to *Retreating the Political*, Simon Sparks proposes that the literary-presentational motifs partially listed above (mimesis, fictioning, fashioning and so forth) be gathered under the heading of the *figure*. Lacoue-Labarthe's and Nancy's theoretical originality lies in their accentuation of the figurative essence of the philosophical – a figurative essence, a will-to-figure, which yokes the philosophical indissociably with the political. According to Sparks the figure is the dominant theme of both their work. Why do they place such theoretical importance on the figure? Sparks writes:

> Because, for them, metaphysics in the process of completing itself, is historically and *essentially* committed to mobilising figures in order to represent itself. Responding to the constraint of an originary programmation. . .the epoch of onto-theology, what Lacoue-Labarthe and Nancy call the epoch of philosophy 'actualising' itself as the political (and vice versa), is nothing other than the epoch of the bestowal of (the) meaning (of being, of existing) through figures.

Sparks goes on to note that this metaphysical mobilization of figures occurs 'most decisively, through the figure of man, the figure of a human *tupos* determined as the *subjectum* or as the Subject of meaning' (Lacoue-Labarthe and Nancy 1997, xxii). Following Heidegger in this respect, modern metaphysics for Lacoue-Labarthe and Nancy installs the reign of the subject. But for them this subject is above all figurative – or rather, auto-figurative, auto-fictioning.

But where is this metaphysical determination of our modernity, this will-to-figure, figured? Where in the world does it appear? It appears most spectacularly in or as *totalitarianism*. For Lacoue-Labarthe and Nancy, totalitarianism represents, adapting a phrase from Sartre, 'the unsurpassable horizon of our times' (1997, 126). By totalitarianism they refer, of course, to the recent historical examples of the phenomenon: Stalinism, Fascism and, perhaps especially, Nazism. Following the influential analyses of Hannah Arendt and Claude Lefort, they characterize totalitarianism as 'the attempt at a frenzied re-substantialization – a re-incorporation, a *re-organization* in the strongest and most differentiated sense – of the "social body"' (1997, 127).

But Lacoue-Labarthe and Nancy also use totalitarianism to index a more generalized phenomenon, one which extends the frenzy of the recent past into the unending present. This afterlife of totalitarianism is diffuse. It takes the form of the banal and unquestioned view that 'everything is political'. Unlike fascist or soviet totalitarianism, wherein the total domination of the political presented itself quite clearly as terror, today the global ubiquity of such total domination allows it to disappear from view. Total domination goes without saying. Arendt describes total domination as the attempt 'to organize the infinite plurality and differentiation of human beings as if all of humanity were just one individual' (Arendt 1973, 438). In philosophical terms, the total domination of the political denotes the completed installation of the Subject. What goes utterly unchallenged in totalitarianism is the subordination of human beings, of human singularities (but perhaps the talk of the 'human' has always given itself over to such subordination), to the self-actualizing thrust of a heroic humanity. Today this undivided reign of the will-to-figure does not present itself in the figure of a leader, nation, class, or people. Rather it appears as a sort of figurative drive without a figurehead, a headless auto-organization driven by the banal rule of what Jean-François Lyotard has called 'the logic of maximum performance' (1984, xxiv). What Arendt impeccably discerned as total domination continues unabated in the assimilation of all public and human life to the logic of maximal operativity and production. In this insidious form, the political holds total sway by its (almost) total withdrawal or retreat ('retrait').

Useful and urgent as Lacoue-Labarthe's and Nancy's philosophical diagnostic is, their work does not stop here. In addition to its descriptive sense, their catch-phrase 'le retrait du politique' carries also a prescriptive force: to retreat the political in the sense of re-treating it, treating it again, tracing it in a new way. This retreatment is, they acknowledge, an extraordinarily difficult task. It entails, first of all, trying to withdraw the political from its ubiquitous withdrawal. The ethico-political exigency of Lacoue-Labarthe's and Nancy's more recent works issues from their attempt to free the political. Freeing the political means, to put it less heroically, taking the political to its philosophical limit or breaking-point (and vice versa); looking for fissures and openings in its metaphysical foundation; unsettling the grounding of the subject and interrupting its auto-figurative impulse. How is any of this possible? For Lacoue-Labarthe and Nancy the crux of the matter lies in re-examining the borders of the subject, there where it greets or fails to greet the other (or others). In other words, 'the question of the political evokes the necessity of dwelling on what makes the social relation possible as such' (1997, 180).

Their collective research on the making of the social tie begins, of all places, with psychoanalysis. In some brilliant readings of Freud's socio-cultural texts, Lacoue-Labarthe and Nancy draw our attention to an irresolvable tension between his theoretical assertion of an identity principle at the root of all sociality and a logical unravelling of this principle set in motion by his own attempts to *account* for identity, that is give an account of identity formation (the process of 'identification') that does not presuppose the very thing it is trying to account for (identity). To abbreviate rather brusquely here, they discover at the logical origin of the Freudian subject not a simple relation to others (which would presuppose subjects coming into the social sphere fully constituted, that is, already socialized), but rather a constitutive social alterity, an original dis-connection. 'At its extreme', they write, 'the question of identity is, for Freud, the question of *the identity of a dissociation*' (1991, 39). This question is again foregrounded towards the close of 'The "Retreat" of the Political': 'The so-called question of relation remains, to our mind, *the* central question ... In a general way, one can suggest that this question intervened with the insistence of a theme ... the theme of *desertion* or *dissociation* ...' (1997, 133).

As singular and differentiated as Lacoue-Labarthe's and Nancy's own writings are, we might say that, following their collective interrogation of the political, the difficult obligation to rearticulate the social tie *as* dissociation informs both of their numerous publications. We might even say the motif of dissociated identity is something they share in common with other 'French Heideggereans' (Derrida, Levinas, Blanchot) – were it not for the fact that, as Derrida points out, their thought of dissociation ('the condition of my relation to others') marks a decisive departure from Heidegger's philosophical and political privileging of 'gathering' (*Versammlung*) (Derrida 1997, 14). In order to flesh out this idea of a constitutive dis-association – the '*rapport sans rapport*, the relationless relation' (Derrida 1997, 14) – so central to each of their concerns, I will close with a sketch of Nancy's work on 'being-in-common'.

The text of Nancy's which has received perhaps the most extensive commentary and response is 'The Inoperative Community' (see, for example, Miami Theory Collective (MTC) 1991, Blanchot 1988, and above all Agamben 1993). Towards the beginning of this essay, he notes: 'Until this day history has been thought on the basis of a lost community – one to be regained or reconstituted' (1991, 9). Nancy himself does not conceive community on this traditional humanist model of a lost or broken immanence that must be reworked and restored. Instead he steers the communitarian interrogation of community's substantive identity towards the question of community's very condition of possibility. He asks: before fashioning this or that idea of community, what does it mean to be-in-common? For Nancy, this question is, like the question of being itself, presupposed in our daily being-there in the world. Being-in-common is not a predicate added on to an essentially solitary being. Rather, being-there (*Da-sein*) is none other than being-with (*Mit-sein*). As Christopher Fynsk puts it, '*Mitsein* and *Dasein* are co-originary; Dasein must be thought in its very possibility as being-together' (Nancy 1991, xvi–xvii). Indeed, my feeling lonely or being alone depends for its possibility on a prior ontological potential – a built-in inclination – to share my existence.

Nancy accents Heidegger's relational definition of *Dasein* in order to set us thinking about being-in-common as an enabling rift or partition in our ontological fabric. But where does this being-in-common come into play? 'Community is revealed in the death of others', Nancy says (1991, 15); being-in-common bears an essential relation to death. Human finitude relates to community in both a negative and a positive way. First, the death of the other reveals to me the radical alterity of the experience, the impossibility of fusing the other into some meaningful whole, some larger corporate body. The dying of the other exposes the absolute unavailability of communal immanence. Second, the other's death touches me to acknowledge what we share in common. It is important to discern the precise nature of the pathos in this death scene. The death of the other – be it a loved one, lover, friend or some other – does not bring the inexorable truth of death 'home' to me in the sense of a specular recognition. I do not share the experience of the other's death as an intense imaginative empathy wherein I see myself in the other's place and thereby arrive at a fuller, more appreciative sense of my own. In other words, what I experience in the other's death is not myself, nor myself in the other's place, but the other as such. And in experiencing the alterity of the other at this most altered of moments, I am altered myself – that is, exposed to the alterity 'in' 'me'. In an early text entitled 'Obliteration', Lacoue-Labarthe speaks of this alterity as:

that which, in the subject, deserts (has always already deserted) the subject *itself* and which, prior to any 'self-possession' (and in a mode other than that of dispossession), is the dissolution, the defeat of the subject in the subject or *as* the subject: the (de)constitution of the subject or the 'loss' of the subject – if indeed one can think the loss of what one has never had ... (1993: 81–2)

But what is described here in terms of the subject's self-loss is also the community's gain. Nancy takes the delicate 'internal' trembling of the subject and inclines it outwards. The dissociation of the self which I feel most acutely before the other's death becomes something I *share* with the other.

Community begins with the sharing of death that takes me out of myself and positions me in the *in* of being-in-common, the *with* of being-with, and the *and* of you and I. These little words (and others like them) are the mundane linguistic particles that most adequately translate the great existential theme of death. They are place-holders for the outside where you and I are exposed to and share our finitude. Nancy says that this *and* of you and I should not be understood as a social relation that is superimposed on two subjects. Being-in-common should not be confused with intersubjectivity or the ideality of communicative exchange. The *and* must be thought as a *between* which is more originary than the social tie – so originary in fact that the *you* and the *I* can only appear with the prior emergence of the *and*. The *and* says in effect that you and I do not appear to one another – I here and you there – but rather that we co-appear or 'compear' (*com-paraît*) (Nancy 1991, 28). As a thinking oriented towards the outside, the end, the limit and the between, community resists going indoors, retreating to the familiar space of the subject who is one or the subject who contains the many. Nancy writes: 'Community...is not a common *being*; it is to be *in* common, or to be *with* each other, or to be together' (1993a, 154). Being-in-common does not take the form of a selfless fusion into a group. Rather, it emerges from the *in*, the syncatagoreme that interrupts my participation in a nominal unit at the same time that it hinges me to others. What we share in common is death – or, in a somewhat less intoxicated idiom – interruption. Without the interruption of the self by others there can be no being-*in*-common, only the abandonment of relation and the mystical hope of communion.

Perhaps the most difficult thing to grasp in Nancy's thinking of community is that our strange built-in sociality does not provide any groundwork for building a community in any identifiable sense. As Fynsk puts it, '[Being-in-common] is not something that may be produced and instituted or whose essence could be expressed in a work of any kind (including a *polis* or state): it cannot be the object or the telos of a politics' (Nancy 1991, x). Community's absolute resistance to work is indicated in the title of Nancy's texts, *La Communauté désœuvrée*. As a translation, 'The Inoperative Community' emphasizes rightly that community can't be operated or operationalized. But in this translation we miss the crucial conceptual component of work (*œuvre*). In fact, Nancy says explicitly, 'community is made or is formed by the retreat or the subtraction of something: this something ... is what I call its "work" (1991, xxxviii–ix). Nancy's usage of this word is drawn largely from the writings of Blanchot and, inevitably, the Jena romantics. These sources should alert us to the fact that the defining semantic register here is aesthetic. The work is above all the work of art. The work does not refer to any single object of art, but rather the theoretical work of art – that is, the total or absolute artwork which, thought on the model of organic achievement, becomes itself the working model for all other human projects of self-manifestation (see Lacoue-Labarthe and Nancy 1988). Nancy intends his sense of community to disrupt the work aim and working premise of communitarian thought. Thus, although the term *désœuvrée* means *idle* or *at loose ends*, it should be heard more actively. For *désœuvrement*, instead of *idleness*, which suggests the state that follows from work's absence, Fynsk proposes *unworking* (Nancy 1991, 154, n.23). *La Communauté désœuvrée* is the unworking community. But here too we must press on the translation a little to extract the sense of unworking as an active interrupting or incompleting of some process or product which aims at auto-figuration.

Nancy writes: 'community cannot arise from the domain of *work*. One does not produce it, one experiences or one is constituted by it as the experience of finitude' (1991, 31). Throughout 'The Inoperative Community' the experience of finitude is set to work against work. Not only does finitude unwork the work of community, it also opens the possibility for community as being-in-common. The exceptional difficulty in giving a theoretical account of being-in-common results from the stricture that it cannot be a work, hence cannot be the object of a representation. There is no general theoretical model that can encompass the countless singular experiences of our daily and nightly finitude. Nancy's extended discussion of experiencing the other's death would seem to privilege mortality as the determining paradigm for finitude. But death is just the limit case (as is birth) in an immense phenomenological spectrum of irreducible community experiences. One thing that all these experiences share, however, is the experience of sharing itself. Once again, Nancy does not conceptualize sharing as a selfless melding into a group or as a reciprocal exchange between two subjects. As an experience of the limit, sharing (*le partage*) partitions out my self-identity; in sharing I am exposed to my dissociation, divvied outwards. What we share at the ends of ourselves is neither some commonality nor our separate individualities, but our uncommon *singularity*. For Nancy, singularity names the irreducible particularity of this or that being, *but only in so far as that being is being-with or being-in-common*. In other words, singular beings – we, you, I – cannot appear alone. They or we must appear in common; they, we, must compear. The compearance or sharing of our singularities is so fundamental to our being-in-common, all it takes is a minimal exposure to others. Nancy gives the following example:

> Passengers in the same train compartment are simply seated next to each other in an accidental, arbitrary, and completely exterior manner. They are not linked. But they are also quite together inasmuch as they are travellers on this train, in this same space and for this same period of time. They are between the disintegration of the 'crowd' and the aggregation of the group, both extremes remaining possible, virtual, and near at any moment. (MTC 1991, 9)

Exposure to singularity: that means to be scattered together, like passengers on a train, not quite face-to-face, oscillating between the poles of group fusion and social dispersal, 'solitude and collectivity, attraction and repulsion' (MTC 1991, 9).

The example of strangers on a train illustrates perfectly the banal relation without relation – the exposition of the *with*, the *in*, the *between* and the *and* – in which singularities appear prior to the introduction of identities. However, it strikes me as a rather indifferent example of singularity as such. A better example might be found in the singular relationship of Lacoue-Labarthe *and* Nancy. In his useful introduction to the English volume of Lacoue-Labarthe's *Typography*, Derrida writes:

> What I share with Lacoue-Labarthe, we also both share, though differently, with Jean-Luc Nancy. But I hasten to reiterate that despite so many common paths and so much work done in common, between the two of them and between the three of us, the work of each remains, in its

singular proximity, absolutely different; and this, despite its fatal impurity, is the secret of the idiom. The secret: that is to say, first of all, the *separation*, the non-relation, the interruption. (Lacoue-Labarthe 1989, 6–7)

Earlier Derrida describes Lacoue-Labarthe's 'idiom' in terms of a signature rhythm, a movement of speech that 'multiplies caesuras, asides, parenthetical remarks, cautions, signs of prudence and circumspection, hesitations, warnings, parentheses, quotation marks, italics – dashes above all – or all of these at once ...' (1989, 3). Following Derrida's lead, could we not adduce Lacoue- Labarthe's and Nancy's writing *voice* or *style* as examples of a dissociative relation, a compearance? As markedly different as their voices sound, they seem to share – both writing alone and together – an interrupted or unworking style. By that I mean, in addition to the verbal gestures Derrida compiles, a seemingly endless series of sentences beginning with *on the other hand, on the contrary, more precisely, however, nevertheless* and especially *or, but, yet.* Certainly these words and phrases underscore Lacoue-Labarthe's and Nancy's prudence and circumspection as readers: their patience (but perhaps also their impatience) to get it right. And they may also be read as the mundane markers of collective authorship, rather like stage cues to signal where one voice leaves off and the other takes over. But I would propose we read the *ors* and *buts* which texture their writing as the accents of a shared dissociation – less the signs of a collective authorship than the active unworkings of the very ideas of collectivity and authorship. These endless interruptions make the experience of reading their texts difficult. But it is a difficulty that is absolutely commensurate with their ethico-political intentions – in other words, a pedagogically useful difficulty. Or, from the perspective of re-treating the political, completely useless – that is, unworkable.

Heesok Chang

Further reading and works cited

Agamben, G. *The Coming Community*. Minneapolis, MN, 1993.
Arendt, H. *The Origins of Totalitarianism*. San Diego, CA, 1973.
Blanchot, M. *The Unavowable Community*. Barrytown, NY, 1988.
Cadava, E. et al. (eds) *Who Comes After the Subject?* New York, 1991.
Derrida, J. *Deconstruction in a Nutshell*, ed. J. D. Caputo. New York, 1997.
Eagleton, T. 'Nationalism: Irony and Commitment'. *Nationalism, Colonialism, and Literature*, ed. S. Deane. Minneapolis, MN, 1990.
Farias, V. *Heidegger et le Nazisme*. Paris, 1987.
Heidegger, M. *Being and Time*. New York, 1962.
—. *The Question Concerning Technology and Other Essays*. New York, 1977.
—. 'Overcoming Metaphysics', in *The Heidegger Controversy*, ed. R. Wolin. Cambridge, MA, 1993.
Lacoue-Labarthe, P. *Typography*, ed. Christopher Fynsk. Cambridge, MA, 1989.
—. *Heidegger, Art and Politics*. Oxford, 1990.
—. *The Subject of Philosophy*, ed. Thomas Tresize. Minneapolis, MN, 1993.
—. *Musica Ficta*. Stanford, CA, 1994.
—. *Poetry as Experience*. Stanford, CA, 1999.
— and Nancy, J.-L. *The Literary Absolute*. Albany, NY, 1988.
—. 'The Unconscious Is Destructured like an Affect', *Stanford Literature Review*, 6, 2, Fall 1989.
—. 'The Nazi Myth', *Critical Inquiry*, 16, 2, Winter 1990.
—. 'From Where Is Psychoanalysis Possible?', *Stanford Literature Review*, 8, 1–2, Spring-Fall 1991.

—. *The Title of the Letter*. Albany, NY, 1992.
—. *Retreating the Political*, ed. S. Sparks. London, 1997.
Hamacher, W. 'Working Through Working', *Modernism/Modernity*, 3, 1, January 1996.
Kamuf, P. (ed.) *Paragraph*, 16, 2, 1993.
Keenan, T. *Fables of Responsibility*. Stanford, CA, 1997.
Lyotard, J.-F. *The Postmodern Condition*. Minneapolis, MN, 1984.
—. *Heidegger and 'the Jews'*. Minneapolis, MN, 1990.
Miami Theory Collective (ed.) *Community at Loose Ends*. Minneapolis, MN, 1991.
Nancy, J.-L. *The Inoperative Community*, ed. Peter Connor. Minneapolis, MN, 1991.
—. *The Birth to Presence*. Stanford, CA, 1993a.
—. *The Experience of Freedom*. Stanford, CA, 1993b.
—. *The Sense of the World*. Minneapolis, CA, 1997.
Sheppard, D. et al. *On Jean-Luc Nancy*. London, 1997.
Weber, S. *Mass Mediauras*, ed. A. Cholodenko. Stanford, CA, 1996.

48. Julia Kristeva (1941–)

Although of Bulgarian origin, Julia Kristeva has long been associated with the French poststructuralists. Arriving in Paris as a doctoral research fellow in the mid-1960s amid what Kristeva describes as the 'theoretical ebullience' surrounding the emergence of structuralism, with its rejection of philosophical humanism and its discovery of the role of language in the constitution of the conscious subject, Kristeva was immediately caught up in the intellectual fervour of the period. Under the tutelage of Lucien Goldmann and Roland Barthes and through her encounter with Philippe Sollers, her future husband and founder of the French literary journal *Tel Quel*, Kristeva came into contact with a number of structuralist and poststructuralist theorists and soon forged a path, along with Foucault, Lacan and Derrida, that diverged from the current structuralist fashion by becoming one of the leading critics of poststructuralist thought. Through her reworking of theoretical concepts borrowed from many different disciplines including structural linguistics, psychoanalysis, literary criticism, marxism, Derridean theory, and Hegelian and Heideggerian philosophy, Kristeva contributed significantly to the advancement of the poststructuralist critique not only of structuralism but also of the rationalist, humanist assumptions structuring the western philosophical and literary tradition as a whole.

That critique provides the basis for the entirety of Kristeva's project from the 1960s to the late 1990s – despite the numerous shifts in focus that occur over the years as she responds to the changes in the social and political context in which her writing takes place. Indeed, given Kristeva's sensitivity to cultural questions, it is surprising that so little attention has been paid by Anglo-American critics to her analysis of contemporary culture. Her reception in the English-speaking world has been largely confined to the questions Kristeva's work raises with regard to feminist issues, questions that have precipitated lively debates as to the usefulness of her theory for a feminist politics, but that have overshadowed any consideration of the highly politicized intellectual and social environment which initially fostered Kristeva's revolutionary project. That environment was characterized not only by the theoretical upheaval wrought by the structuralists' and poststructuralists' interrogation of traditional philosophical and literary precepts but also by the political turmoil that erupted in the 1960s, particularly in the form of the student – worker uprisings of May 1968. Although the revolt was ultimately unsuccessful, the events of May, as Kristeva's recent writings attest, pointed the way toward the possibility of a radical contestation of all forms of authority, including not only that of the state, of the family and of a repressive socio-economic system, but also on a more theoretical level of the exclusionary and ultimately oppressive notions of identity at the very foundations of western thought (Kristeva 1998b, 14–77).

The contestatory spirit that found its expression in the Parisian streets was thus closely echoed in the theoretical and literary work of the period, particularly among those literary writers and theorists associated with *Tel Quel*. Rather than becoming actively involved in the student effort to overturn an oppressive social system, the members of the *Tel Quel* group, which at this point also included Kristeva who began contributing to the journal in 1967, believed that the revolutionary struggle should take place on a more fundamental level, on the level of language itself. Claiming that communicative language is a principal vehicle in the preservation of the ideological structures that dominate western culture and revealing their growing interest in marxist theory, Kristeva and her fellow members attempted to formulate and put into practice a revolutionary materialist theory of language in an effort to work against the traditional concept of the literary text and of language itself as predominantly meaningful structures, and thus to help achieve, by indirection, a transformation of the social order and its oppressive laws as well.

Laying the theoretical groundwork for the *Tel Quel* project in her first work in French, *Séméiotiké* (1969), Kristeva begins by taking up the structural linguists' investigations of language but attempts to counter their tendency to remain within the confines of a strictly linguistic system. Claiming the scientific-positivist approach to semiotics reduces its object of study to a system of verifiable rules or laws while ignoring the productive operations within language that precede signification, Kristeva sets out to formulate an open-ended, self-critical method of analysis, one that she calls *semanalysis* which will account for the heterogeneous elements involved in the process of textual production (27–42; Moi 1986, 74–88). Kristeva's emphasis on 'textual productivity' and her attempt to uncover the multiple, pre-linguistic processes that both constitute but also undermine the unity of meaning are not only central to her own and *Tel Quel*'s critique of traditional notions of language, they are also directly related to their critique of the social order as a whole. By drawing on Marx's analysis of the relations of production within the capitalist system, Kristeva and the *Tel Quel* group conclude that western communicative language and western society are governed by a similar logic, subjected to the very same laws of exchange that structure the capitalist marketplace. For whether the reference is to the exchange of commodities or the exchange of messages, the focus in a capitalist system is always on the goods produced, on the finished and immediately consumable product that hides the processes of production. The communicability of discourse and the self-contained and unified identity of what a capitalist society produces are thus dependent on the exclusion or repression of these processes, Kristeva argues. They must be subordinated to the preservation of a cohesive and productive socio-economic system and to the integrated identity of the principal support of that system, the individual social subject (1969, 34–40).

A concept of the open text which breaks through the boundaries imposed by traditional notions of language by focusing on the process of textual production rather than on the finished product is thus what emerges in the course of Kristeva's analysis. Although its psychoanalytical implications are developed more fully in subsequent texts, Kristeva's concerns in *Séméiotiké* are primarily textual. As opposed, however, to the more formalist approach to the structural linguists who analyse language and the literary text as cut off from their social and historical context, Kristeva elaborates, through the writings of Barthes and especially those of the post-formalist Mikhail Bakhtin, a notion of the text that is not confined to the purely linguistic, written body of literary or non-literary works but that incorporates the unwritten, non-linguistic signifying practices also involved in the process of meaning formation. The text emerges as the intersection of a multiplicity of voices, all of which participate in the production of the text's meaning. Indeed, out of her reading of Bakhtinian dialogism, which sees the text in relation to other texts, or more precisely as a 'dialogue among several writings' including that of the writer, the reader and the socio-historical context, comes her influential concept of intertextuality, a notion that not only poses an important challenge to the objective status of the literary text, but that also deals a serious blow to western notions of the subject as a self-contained, integrated identity (1969, 143–73; Roudiez 1980, 64–91). For the identity of the author who 'creates' the text is called into question. As only one productive voice among many, including those of the non-linguistic social and historical forces that also shape the literary work, the author no longer stands outside the work as the sole source of its language but is drawn into the dynamics of the written text, his activity constituting but also finding itself constituted by its complex operations. The author emerges here not as the unitary subject instituted by a repressive social order but as a subject-in-process/on trial, caught up in the interweaving movement of multiple textual surfaces which at the same time construct themselves as 'the operation of [the subject's] pulverization' (1969, 15; Guberman 1996, 188–203).

Although Kristeva claims that these operations are fundamental to the structure of any text, whether it be traditional or modern, she maintains that it is only in the modern 'literary' work that its intertextual function is rendered explicit. The challenge to what Kristeva calls, following Bakhtin, the traditional monological novel, with its subordination to the Law of One (one author, one meaning, and one legitimate interpretation), does not come from within the traditional novel itself, it comes instead from a radically different text, from the polyphonic novels of Kafka or Joyce, or from the works following the examples of Mallarmé or Lautréamont 'which perceive themselves, in their very structures, as a production irreducible to representation' (1969, 41; Moi 1986, 86, trans. modified). In directing our attention away from the meaning of the text (the *phenotext*) toward the material processes of textual production (the *genotext*), the pluridimensional spaces of these avant-garde literary works form the basis for Kristeva's own revolutionary project, one that is meant to counter western society's 'reifying' logic by preventing the text's emergence as a literary object or 'product' to be consumed by a reading public (1969, 278–317; Moi 1986, 24–33, 120–3).

Whether or not Kristeva is successful in this regard has been subject to debate. For although the emphasis on 'poetic' language is not to be construed, Kristeva argues, as an hypostatization of poetry but rather as a way of describing any discourse in which the material process of its own generation is brought to light, some critics claim that Kristeva's conception does not always avoid the objectifying logic that her semiotic practice is meant to oppose. This criticism has been voiced in particularly strong terms with regard to Kristeva's well-known and much debated distinction between the semiotic and the symbolic in *Revolution in Poetic Language* (1984a) where she extends the more textual aspects of her argument by examining its intrapsychic or psychoanalytical implications. Here, marxist theory is combined with Freudian and Lacanian psychoanalysis in an effort to show that the relations of production, or the economic infrastructure uncovered by Marx, could be equated with the heterogeneous impulses within the individual unconscious that Freud discovered, impulses that have a role in the constitution of the speaking subject but that must be repressed in order for the individual to emerge as an integrated identity. As Kristeva describes the process, the individual establishes himself as an independent and conscious subject (and enters the 'symbolic' order of identity) only after cutting himself off from and repressing the instinctual drives (the 'semiotic *chora*') that lie within his prelinguistic unconscious. This occurs during the earliest 'pulsional' stages of a child's life when his first sounds, rhythms and intonations which are uttered according to the needs of the bodily impulses are repressed in order to establish the discursive function of language and the individual's identity.

The child, at this point, must be weaned from his attachment to the mother so that he may become conscious of his own existence as a distinct and separate identity. This break occurs when the child has mastered normal patterns of speech, and only then is the individual as an integrated being actually formed. Thus the symbolic, as Kristeva describes it, always refers to the logical and syntactical function of language (Roudiez 1980, 133–41). The semiotic, on the other hand, is chronologically prior to the constitution of the linguistic sign and the subject, and although Kristeva maintains that it is also necessary for the acquisition of language in that it provides the foundation out of which language and the subject develop, the integral identities of both can only be constituted after cutting themselves off from this anteriority, by repressing these prelinguisitc 'heterogeneous pulsions'. The task, then, of the revolutionary text is to reactivate these 'repressed drives', to introduce the semiotic in the form of rhythm, intonation and repetition of sounds and rhyme, which becomes the genotext, into the phenotext, so that the unity of the sign and the subject will ultimately be undermined and the differential process of generation itself will be allowed to emerge uncontaminated by its precepts (1984, 19–106; Moi 1986, 89–136).

What Kristeva's critics find objectionable here is that, despite her claim that the two modalities are interdependent and therefore inseparable, the semiotic and the symbolic are often separated by rather clear lines of demarcation. Indeed, a number of Kristeva's detractors have been highly critical of her tendency to define the semiotic and symbolic in essentialist, phallocentric terms. They claim that her view of the semiotic as the 'outside' of language, as an 'archaic, instinctual and maternal territory' that must be repressed or 'sealed off' if the symbolic order of identity is to function, reveals not simply an essentializing celebration of the semiotic's disruptive potential but also, through an uncritical acceptance of the Freudian Oedipal framework, a notion of identity that is paternally grounded, dependent upon both a rejection of the mother as 'abject' and a conception of the paternal order of the symbolic as 'exclusively *prohibitive*' (Butler 1993, 177).

Whether or not one chooses to agree with these critics – and there are many who do not – one can find in Kristeva's next major work, *Powers of Horror* (1982), a continuation of her study of the symbolic's repressive function. Tracing the logic of exclusion operating within primitive societies and throughout biblical history from Judaic monotheism to Christianity, Kristeva calls up disturbing images of the abject. These are the 'horrors' that lie just beneath the surface of civilized society and that are treated as objects of loathing – filth, bodily excretions, the instinctual drives that dwell within the unconscious – indeed, all those elements within our culture that inspire disgust and revulsion and that must be purged or cleansed and purified if the symbolic order of identity is to be instituted. The effort to contest this logic by focusing on those 'borderline practices' that disturb notions of identity, system and order can thus be viewed as a continuation of Kristeva's project to undermine a culture whose social systems are seen as totalizing and repressive. And although the revolutionary rhetoric that often characterized *Séméiotiké* and *Revolution in Poetic Language* has been considerably toned down, she sees in *Powers of Horror* the possibility for a 'great demystification of Power (religious, moral, political, and verbal)' (210) where the 'return of the repressed' in the form of abjection becomes a way to wedge a slight opening in the closures constituted by civilized society, by its 'homogenizing rhetoric' and by its systematized thinking.

If the revolutionary rhetoric appears to have been toned down in *Powers of Horror*, it all but disappears in her work of the 1980s, due in part to the repudiation by the members of *Tel Quel* of their own revolutionary project, following their disillusionment with both Soviet and Chinese marxism, and their loss of faith in the literary avant-garde's utopian objectives. It is attributable also to Kristeva's growing interest in psychoanalysis, which she came to see as a process that 'cuts through political illusions' and thus serves as 'an antidote to political discourse' (Moi 1986, 304). This re-evaluation of her position and the fact that she became a practising psychoanalyst in 1979 bring a change in perspective in Kristeva's work, leading her to focus less on the dynamic of exclusion and more on the inclusive character of the various signifying practices. In *Tales of Love*, for example, which examines western images of love as elaborated in the writings of Plato and certain Christian theologians, as well as in a wide range of literary texts, rather than positing, as she often does in her earlier work, a subjectivity constituted by a radical break with the instinctual heterogeneity of the maternal phase, Kristeva in her analysis of the narcissistic under-pinnings of love in western culture aims to show that drive-dominated narcissistic impulses continue to structure adult relationships to an other. This drive dynamic is indeed what 'feeds' the amatory identifications so essential to subjectivity, according to Kristeva, and it means that, far from repressing instinctuality, the subject in its very essence as a being for another reveals the continuation of the narcissistic economy.

In exposing, however, the problematic of the self that is implied in the narcissistic relation to the other, Kristeva stresses not so much its revolutionary potential as its capacity to support through psychoanalysis the individual's fantasies of wholeness and self-suffi-ciency. In her concern as an analyst for the 'outbreak' of psychic disorders that western society is witnessing today, Kristeva finds in psychoanalysis the possibility for a 'cure'. Recognizing that love is essential to the structuration of the self, she argues that the aim of psychoanalysis today must be to reconstitute the narcissistic relationship through the 'transference love' that inevitably arises between analyst and patient. The goal, however, is not to restore the plenitude that has supposedly been lost, but to allow the subject to construct some measure of subjectivity and thus to function, however tentatively, within the social system. The modern subject thus becomes what Kristeva calls a 'work-in-progess', constantly constructing itself as a necessarily false identity, while recognizing and indeed accepting the inauthenticity of its imaginary constructions (1987, 380–81).

While the stabilizing work of the symbolic is always provisional for Kristeva and should never be understood as a desire to reconstitute its repressive power, there is clearly a change in emphasis here that stems from changes in Kristeva's perception of the social organization and of the place that the individual subject occupies within it. Indeed, it is the very 'insufficiency' of the 'symbolic dimension' that becomes an important issue for Kristeva as she moves into the 1990s. Extending her investigations in psychoanalysis to the cultural sphere in a series of essays appearing in *Nations without Nationalism* (1993) and in *Strangers to Ourselves* (1991), Kristeva responds to a whole range of social problems that, in her view, no longer stem from an oppressive capitalist system but come instead from a society that is in a state of disarray. With the substantial flow of immigrants and the pressures of European economic competition, France, Kristeva writes, is undergoing a crisis in national identity, one that has provoked nationalist, anti-immigrant responses as well as a rise among those who take refuge in their own ethnicity. Turning once again to psychoanalysis as a possible response to growing social conflict and fragmentation, Kristeva calls for a rethinking of our concept of nationhood, for moving our perceptions of national identity beyond their 'regressive, exclusionary . . . or racial pitfalls' (1993, 59) by recognizing the difference of the foreigner 'without ostracism but also without levelling', that is without subsuming diversity under a new homogeneity. This recognition of 'otherness' is made possible, according to Kristeva, through the extension of the Freudian notion of the unconscious to the cultural sphere. As an uncanny strangeness or otherness that inhabits the human psyche, the Freudian unconscious allows for a notion of community that would no longer be assimilated to some national, ethnic or religious identity but would stem instead from a recognition of the difference and foreignness that reside at the core of every being (1991, 185–92).

Kristeva's elaboration of a new ethics of tolerance for today's emerging multinational societies thus restores to psychoanalysis its political dimension and moves her discourse to the point where, in the mid- to late-1990s, it begins to take on some of the political colourations of her work in the late 1960s and 1970s. Indeed, in a series of still untranslated works beginning with *The Sense and Non-Sense of Revolt* and continuing through *La révolte intime*, *Contre la dépression nationale* and *L'avenir d'une révolte*, one finds traces in her writing of the old revolutionary rhetoric, for not only does psychoanalysis function as a '*discours-révolte*', according to Kristeva, but it becomes once again a means of affirming the contestatory spirit of *Tel Quel* and of the generation of May 1968 (1998b, 14–53; Guberman 1996, 172). Kristeva is quick to point out, however, that her call for the revival of the revolutionary 'spirit of '68' should not be understood, as it was in the 1970s, as a simple opposition to repressive social institutions and norms. The old dialectical model of revolt, which assumes a dramatic confrontation between the law and its transgression is no longer operable in the 1990s primarily because the structures of authority against which the protestors rebelled have lost their capacity to exercise power. The disintegration of the family, the replacement of political authority with an amorphous, fluctuating global market, rapid developments in technology and the rise of the mass media with the proliferation of its mind-numbing images have not only rendered contemporary society infinitely more complex but have constituted a power vacuum that deprives individuals of a stabilizing centre. Drawing from Guy Debord's influential work, *The Society of the Spectacle*, Kristeva argues that it is indeed this 'invasion of the spectacle' that is diminishing dramatically our imaginary life. The new technologies of the image threaten to 'abolish the deepest regions of the self [*le "for intérieur"*]' (1997, 127) by transforming individuals into passive, indeed 'robotic', consumers of the products of a commercialized media.

In such a situation as this, however, where the individual suffers from a debilitating lack of constraints, the spirit of revolt is all the more necessary, according to Kristeva. For, not only did Freud's discovery of the unconscious provide the basis for an interrogation of the symbolic (an interrogation that Freud himself never explicitly developed), but his analysis of the process of psychic individuation showed to what extent revolt, whether it be the revolt against Oedipal father, so that the 'I' can come into being, or the revolt of the primal hoard in *Totem and Taboo* that founds the social pact, is an essential condition of both individual and social life. Thus, as a process that allows for the constitution of subjectivity even as it is also accompanied by the forces of dissolution and dispersion, revolt, in the Freudian sense, is seen by Kristeva as a remedy for both the public and private malaise that plagues western culture. Linked to the etymological meaning of *revolvere*, the term, as Kristeva uses it, is understood not as a transgression, as it was during her more militant phase, but as an anamnesis, a movement of 'revolt' that returns to the past, that repeats, interrogates and re-elaborates the most archaic, intimate phases of psychic development (2000, 28–9). Indeed, it is this reconstruction through psychoanalysis of the initial stages of subjectivation that allows for the reinstatement of the limits and prohibitions so essential to our condition as speaking beings and, in so doing, it both rehabilitates the individual subject and gives him 'a capacity for contestation and creation' (1998b, 41).

The rehabilitation of the subject through psychoanalysis should not, however, be understood as a return to the humanist premises of the past. For, if Kristeva's notion of re-volt involves the affirmation of prohibition and the law, it also exposes the subject to an 'unbearable conflictuality', unleashing, in the course of the patient's recounting of his narcissistic and Oedipal dramas, the pulsional forces of the semiotic and the destabilizing relation to an other as well, both of which prevent the subject from closing itself off, from becoming a fixed and unchanging identity. The analytic experience involving the free association of ideas, memories and sensations is not, then, a simple rememoration or repetition, it is also what displaces the past and allows for a 'reformulation of our psychic map' (2000, 50; trans. modified), an 'eternal return' that brings the perpetual deconstruction and renewal of the self. Such an experience has obvious political implications for Kristeva, in that the permanent questioning and restructuring of the individual psyche provides the basis for an interrogation and reshaping of the social structure as well. With its return through psychoanalysis to the archaic imaginary realm, Kristeva's concept of revolt is designed to 'save us' from this 'automation of humanity' (2000, 7), and it does so by giving voice to the heterogeneous processes that lie within the most 'intimate' reaches of the self.

In this context, then, the challenge to 'mediatic' society through an 'appeal to intimacy' can be seen, as Kristeva herself affirms, as a continuation of her earlier work (Guberman 1996, 222, 258–62). It could also be seen as a continuation of a more dialectical notion of revolt as well, one in which the subversive capabilities of a literary and artistic avant-garde come once again into play. Because of their capacity to engage in a fundamentally Proustian exploration of the 'intimacy of the senses' (*l'intimité sensible*), many of the artistic practices of the twentieth century, which include the writings of the surrealists, for example, or those of *Tel Quel* (2000, 112), or even Kristeva's own novel, *Possessions*, can bring us into contact with the very frontiers of thought or, more precisely, of the 'unthought' (*l'a-pensée*) where unconscious pulsions and sensations contest the very possibility of meaning. Returning then to the arguments voiced earlier in *Revolution in Poetic Language*, Kristeva sees the avant-garde literary text as a practice that places the subject, once again, 'in process/on trial', as a confrontation with the 'semiotic *chora*' through which the unity of identity is shattered or destroyed (*se néantise*) (1997, 20).

In walking such a fine line between two contradictory possibilities, involving a concept of revolt that allows for the rehabilitation of the subject (and thus runs the risk of reinstating the humanist or essentialist concept of subjectivity that Kristeva has always opposed) and another that calls for the permanent deconstruction of all notions of identity (and is more in conformity with the contestatory spirit of *Revolution in Poetic Language, Tel Quel* and May 1968), Kristeva's recent works will undoubtedly generate a considerable amount of debate. Kristeva's feminist critics might be appeased, however, by the fact that she has now turned to a question that she had previously ignored, to that of the feminine experience and to the influence of women writers on twentieth-century thought. Her most recent work, *Le génie feminin* (1999), devoted to the writings of Hannah Arendt, is only the beginning of a project that takes her through the texts of the psychoanalyst Melanie Klein, as well as those of the early twentieth-century author, Colette (forthcoming). In light of her earliest resistance to the 'self-enclosed category of the "feminine"' (Guberman 1996, 269), which was perceived by Kristeva as inconsistent with her persistent questioning of traditional notions of identity, Kristeva's current explorations of 'feminine genius' represent a significant departure from her earlier position. And although she still avoids any affiliation with an emancipatory, feminist movement, Kristeva affirms the opportunity women present for the 'revalorization of the sensorial experience' and for their capacity to serve as an 'antidote to technological ratiocination' (1997, 11).

Although some of Kristeva's feminist critics might still object to her continued identification of women with the sensorial or instinctual realm, it is this sensitivity to cultural questions and to the place of the subject within the social context that can be considered one of the most compelling aspects of Kristeva's work. Indeed, that sensitivity, which was evident from the very beginning during her association with *Tel Quel*, has led her to produce a body of work that is extraordinarily wide-ranging in scope. Of interest to those who specialize not only in cultural criticism and psychoanalysis but also to those with interests in philosophy, literature (including her own works of fiction), marxist theory and linguistics, her writings should be recognized for the major contributions they have made to poststructuralist thought. Their persistent interrogation of the subject and of its cultural context, their elaboration of such influential concepts as intertextuality, the semiotic and the symbolic, abjection, avant-garde aesthetics and its role in effecting social change, have clearly established Kristeva as one of the most important and provocative theoreticians writing in France today.

Joan Brandt

Further reading and works cited

Brandt, J. *Geopoetics*. Stanford, CA, 1997.
Butler, J. 'The Body Politics of Julia Kristeva', in *Ethics, Politics, and Difference in the Writings of Julia Kristeva*, ed. K. Oliver. New York, 1993.
Fletcher, J. and Benjamin, A. (eds) *Abjection, Melancholia and Love*. New York, 1990.
Fraser, N. 'The Uses of Abuses of French Discourse Theories for Feminist Politics', *Boundary 2*, 17, 2, Summer 1990.
Guberman, R. M. (ed.) *Julia Kristeva Interviews*. New York, 1996.
Jones, A. R. 'Julia Kristeva on Femininity: The Limits of a Semiotic Politics', *Feminist Review*, 18, Winter 1984.
Kristeva, J. *Powers of Horror*. New York, 1982.
—. *Revolution in Poetic Language*. New York, 1984a.
—. 'My Memory's Hyperbole', in *The Female Autograph*, ed. D. C. Stanton. Chicago, 1984b.

—. *Tales of Love*. New York, 1987.
—. *Black Sun*. New York, 1989.
—. *Strangers to Ourselves*. New York, 1991.
—. *Nations without Nationalism*. New York, 1993.
—. *New Maladies of the Soul*. New York, 1995.
—. *Sens et non-sens de la révolte*. Paris, 1996a.
—. *Time and Sense: Proust and the Experience of Literature*. New York, 1996b.
—. *La Révolte intime*. Paris, 1997.
—. *L'Avenir d'une révolte*. Paris, 1998a.
—. *Contre la dépression nationale*, ed. Philippe Petit. Paris, 1998b.
—. 'The Subject in Process', in *Tel Quel Reader*, eds P. ffrench and R.-F. Lack. New York, 1998c.
—. *Le Génie féminin*. I, II. Paris, 1999, 2000.
Lechte, J. *Julia Kristeva*. New York, 1990.
Moi, T. (ed.) *The Kristeva Reader*. New York, 1986.
Oliver, K. *Reading Kristeva*. Bloomington, IN, 1993.
Rose, J. *Sexuality in the Field of Vision*. London, 1986.
Roudiez, L. S. (ed.) *Desire in Language*. New York, 1980.
Smith, A.-M. *Julia Kristeva*. London, 1998.
Stone, J. 'The Horrors of Power: A Critique of Kristeva', in *The Politics of Theory: Proceedings of the Essex Conference on the Sociology of Literature, July 1982*, eds Francis Barker et al. Colchester, 1982.

49. Slavoj Žižek (1949–)

As recently as 1988, Slavoj Žižek was unpublished in English. Since that date, however, his position as researcher at Ljubljana's Institute for Social Studies has enabled him to produce an average of more than one monograph a year, not to speak of a number of edited collections. At the time of writing, a check of titles forthcoming reveals no fewer than five more books written or co-written or edited by Žižek. Meanwhile, a speaker giving a presentation at a scholarly conference may now find that s/he is giving the second or third Žižekian talk in a row. For sudden full-blown appearance on the intellectual scene, then, Žižek has few rivals. However, one of these few is his principal interlocutor, Jacques Lacan, who had from 1932 to 1966 published only a dissertation and a few stray articles, but then suddenly produced the 924 pages of the *Écrits* and announced as forthcoming the twenty-six volumes of his seminar for the years from 1953 to 1979.

Understand, however, that the groaning shelf of Žižek is informed as much by post-Althusserian marxism and by the whole tradition of German idealism as it is by Lacanian psychoanalysis. Žižek's books are copiously illustrated with discussions of such popular-cultural figures as Raymond Chandler, Patricia Highsmith, Alfred Hitchcock and David Lynch, and are full of asides on *Robocop*, *The Flintstones*, *Forrest Gump* and Michael Jackson. Their principal subject-matter is a rethinking of the problematic of subjectivity and ideology that first emerged in France during the 1960s and made its way into English-speaking criticism during the 1970s. The essential thesis of Žižek is that the 'last Lacan' completes and retroactively restructures a philosophical and theoretical tradition whose main figures are Kant, Hegel, Schelling, Marx, Althusser, Jameson, and Laclau and Mouffe.

In other words, Žižek would have no real quarrel with those intellectual historians for whom modern European thought is a series of French commentaries on German idealism.

By 'the last Lacan', Žižek means the Lacan of Seminars like *Encore* and essays like 'Kant with Sade'. This is the Lacan of the 'obscene shadow of the law', of the interface between the Real and the Symbolic, and of the distinction between reality and the Real, and is understood by Žižek as the last word in an intellectual tradition that reaches back beyond German idealism to Descartes, and perhaps even to Aristotle. This means that Žižek finds his favoured philosophers always more subtle, more prescient and more radical than one would ever gather from the standard histories of philosophy – in fact, one of the most frequent of Žižek's rhetorical moves is the excoriation of the typical reading, the standard reading, the doxa. Thus, in fewer than a dozen pages of *For They Know Not What They Do* (1991a), we find Žižek distancing himself from a 'commonplace opposition' (33), repudiating 'well-known textbook phrases' (33), beginning sentences with 'contrary to the usual conception' (35) and 'contrary to the usual notion' (44), and distinguishing his arguments from the 'everyday' (34) and the 'commonsensical' (44). In principle, this is laudable. Subtle and/or difficult theoretical discriminations do commonly degenerate into an easily applicable received wisdom which deprives them of the forensic value that made them worthwhile to begin with. However, the repudiation of the 'usual conception' is in Žižek a reflex so constant that it begins to seem symptomatic; at the very least, it prepares the way for an outcome in which Žižek's favourites (at first Hegel, then Kant and Descartes, then Schelling) have always-already made the points that later writers imagine they have scored against them. Thus, on the same few pages of the same book, we find first that 'The crucial aspect not to be missed is how Derrida is here thoroughly "Hegelian"' (1991a, 32), then that 'Andrzej Warminski ... falls prey to the error common among perspicacious critics of Hegel and formulates as a reproach to Hegel what is actually a basic feature of Hegel's thought' (40), and finally (à propos of Althusser) that 'Although one usually conceives the category of overdetermination as "anti-Hegelian" ..., it actually designates precisely this inherently Hegelian paradox of a totality which always comprises a particular element embodying its universal structuring principle' (45).

In other words, there's no arguing with a thoroughgoing Hegelian; this is a position that always-already anticipates (or sometimes just 'implies') anything of value that is subsequently voiced. So it is with characteristic relish that Žižek comments after quoting some paragraphs of Hegel: 'Everything is in this marvellous text: from the Foucauldian motif of disciplinary micro-practice as preceding any positive instruction to the Althusserian equation of the free subject with his subjection to the Law' (1999, 36). Žižek's enthusiasm is infectious, so that one feels almost churlish in saying that 'from the Foucauldian motif' to 'the Althusserian equation' can scarcely be described as 'everything', is in fact no great distance – Foucault was Althusser's student, and is cited by his former teacher in the first footnote to *Reading Capital*. This sense of a pre-ordained inevitability is reinforced by Žižek's other favourite formulations, the paradox (*Looking Awry* follows Jean-Claude Milner in reading those of Zeno as psychoanalytic truths), the 'nothing but' ('Lacan's whole point is that the Real is *nothing but* this impossibility of its inscription', 1989, 173) and the rhetorical question – 'Is not the supreme case of a particular feature that sustains the impossible sexual relationship the curling blonde hair in Hitchcock's *Vertigo*?' (1999, 286); 'Do we not find the ultimate example of this impossible Thing ... in the science-fiction theme of the ... Id-Machine?' (1999, 301); 'Is it not clear already in Kant that there is transcendental self-consciousness?' (1999, 304).

Žižek makes much of a concept he derives from Laclau and Mouffe, that of an antagonism fundamental to sexuation, to politics, to ideology, to society and to reality itself. Among other things, this means that his writing has its philosophical antagonists as well as its heroes. But his habit of finding a germinal version of any interesting current perspective in Hegel and Kant turns some of these into straw men. Derrida, chief representative of what Žižek calls the 'postmodern and/or deconstructionist morass' (1999, 232) is a particular problem. Turning once again to *For They Know Not What They Do*, we find that 'the slip unearthed by the hard labour of deconstructive reading is with Hegel the very fundamental and explicit thesis' (1991a, 63), that 'Hegel himself had already "deconstructed" the notion of reflection' (80), and that 'the basic premiss of the Derridean critique of Hegel ... misfires completely' (86). Readers should of course be grateful for Žižek's rubbishing of the facile 'poststructuralism' in which 'everything is language' or 'everything is discourse'. But the 'everything is' kind of statement has long been one of Derrida's favoured targets, and Žižek's repeated attempts to reinscribe Derrida as 'commonsensical' seem at best eccentric. Lacan's Hegelianism, for Derrida such a weakness, is for Žižek a key strength, so one is hardly surprised to find Žižek disdaining Derrida – yet one is still dismayed by Žižek's relegation of Derrida to the philosophical level of Stalin (1999, 133). Similarly debatable is Žižek's Foucault, who is repeatedly assigned positions which seem in fact closer to the antithesis of his arguments. All of this can perhaps be understood as an unfortunate weakness for imaginary combat – Žižek does tend to understand contemporary theory as a struggle for hegemony among Habermas and Derrida, Lacan and Foucault, Lyotard and Deleuze, and clearly sees himself as championing Lacan against these others. Žižek shares with Derrida, Deleuze, Lyotard and Badiou the wish to reassert the importance of philosophy per se, but (as befits a proponent of paradox) takes ideas most frequently from Lacan, the advocate of 'antiphilosophy'.

Žižek is in any case the thinker least likely to agree with Deleuze and Guattari that 'there is no ideology and never has been' (1987, 4). His first book in English is titled *The Sublime Object of Ideology* (1989), and as early as its second page praises Althusser for his 'thesis that the idea of the possible end of ideology is the ideological idea par excellence'. His second book, *For They Know Not What They Do* (1991a), begins similarly, with a discussion of Charles Maurras rallying the right against Dreyfus as an example of the process by which a particular ideological signification gains hegemony. In both books, Žižek is quickly arguing that reality is ideological per se: 'The fundamental level of ideology ... is not that of an illusion masking the real state of things but that of an (unconscious) fantasy structuring our social reality itself. And at this level, we are of course far from being a post-ideological society' (1989, 33). But if reality is ideological by definition, if the end of ideology can never come, how can any statement, including those of Žižek, hope to avoid complicity? One way of escaping this impasse (or at least of complicating it) is to recognize that what Žižek finds in the late Lacan is not only a reality thoroughly permeated with ideology but also something else called the Real.

In Lacan, the Real is by turns the body, birth, death, the unconscious and the pain of the symptom; it is whatever is radically resistant to symbolization, whatever cannot be integrated into our infinite (but never total) universe of signifiers and objects. The idea that the Real cannot be symbolized is the beginning of the difference between the Real and reality, since reality consists of what is symbolized. As Lacan puts it, 'reality is marked from the outset by a symbolic nihilation' (1993, 148); this is to say that the signifier constitutes reality for the subject by negating the Real in favour of objects and symbols. In related formulations, Lacan says that language covers the Real with the network of signifiers (1988a, 262), and that 'the symbolization of the real tends to be equivalent to the universe' (1988b, 322). In other words, reality is un-Real. Reality begins with symbolic opposition, with difference, but the Real is 'without fissure' (1988b, 97), without absence (1988b, 313). This is to say that the Real is an absolute horizon against and out of which reality is constructed; it is encountered as such only exceptionally, only traumatically, when symbolization fails. Death, for example, is Real, and it fully structures the reality of the obsessional, but it can never be experienced as such (Lacan 1988a, 223). The psychotic is close to the Real, but even he or she experiences not the Real itself so much as the signifier in the Real, as in paranoid symptoms that the neighbours are plotting against one or that media voices are addressed to oneself in particular.

In his most stringent formulations, Lacan speaks of the Real as something quite intractable. Not merely something difficult to symbolize, the Real is 'absolutely resistant' to symbolization – we can do nothing with or about it, can never come to terms with it. Thus the notorious dictum that 'the Real is the impossible'. At the same time, a more dialectical Lacan suggests that the Real is the event-horizon against which what we can do and know is defined; thus we will always try to come to terms with it, so that reality represents a determined if doomed attempt to symbolize the Real. There is a definitive sense in which the Real is beyond signification, so that we can never encounter it, but also a sense in which signification works to retrieve a reality from the Real, so that we can never disengage from it. This is by no means to find in Lacan a surprising warrant for returning to an 'objective' reality. As Žižek stresses, 'the Real is not a transcendent positive identity persisting somewhere beyond the symbolic order' (1989, 173). But it is to return to the idea that something defies and limits representation, and thus gives the lie to the easy formula that 'everything is language'. In fact, this traumatic Real with which we cannot come to terms is the reason that we think of any given reality as constructed and partial rather than definitive. As Žižek puts it:

> Our common everyday reality, the reality of the social universe in which we assume our usual roles of kind-hearted, decent people, turns out to be an illusion that rests on a certain 'repression', on overlooking the real of our desire. The social reality is then nothing but a fragile symbolic cobweb that can at any moment be torn aside by an intrusion of the real. (1991, 17)

For Žižek, then, the basic ideological gesture is the symbolization of the 'impossible' Real. This is to say that ideology goes all the way down, since the symbolization of the Real is basic not just to ideology but to thought as such. Why then is the formulation helpful? Because it suggests an understanding true to our experience of ideology as something mutable in practice and yet immutable in principle. Any given instance of ideology is something that, for all our theoretical sophistication, we tend to perceive as just wrong, yet ideology as such is something we recognize as stubbornly insistent in our lives and cultures.

The dialectic of reality and the Real that Žižek derives from Lacan is correlated in *The Plague of Fantasies* (1997) with the idea of a fundamental antagonism mentioned above: 'antagonism, again, is not the ultimate referent which anchors and limits the unending drift of the signifiers ... but the very force of their constant displacement' (216). By the same logic, 'class struggle means that there is no neutral metalanguage allowing us to grasp society as a given objective totality, since we always-already take sides' (216). Meanwhile, sexual difference 'skews the discursive universe, preventing us from grounding its forma- tions in "hard reality"', and 'every symbolization of sexual difference is forever unstable and displaced with regard to itself' (216). Real antagonism is to be understood not as 'the transcendent Beyond which the signifying process tries to grasp in vain' (217), but as something intrinsic to the symbolic, 'the internal stumbling block on account of which the symbolic system can never achieve its self-identity' (217).

Such phrases make clear that the Lacanian–Žižekian Real is quite different from the Kantian thing-in-itself. The main reason is that the Real is not a substance, but instead an 'abyss'. Coterminous with but never available to the Symbolic, the Real is nothing in itself, yet reality is wholly premised on it. But even though the Real is not the thing-in-itself, the distinction between it and reality is inconceivable without the example of Kant. Žižek explains the importance of German idealism as follows: 'the great breakthrough was to outline the precise contours of this pre-ontological Real which precedes and eludes the ontological constitution of reality' (1999, 54). In other words, German idealism is understood as establishing a reality essentially invulnerable to the claims of postmodernism and the tactics of deconstruction. An argument this ambitious is worth delineating in its exact sequence. According to *Tarrying With the Negative* (1993), 'Descartes was the first to introduce a crack into the ontologically consistent universe' (12). That 'crack' is the subject and by extension the whole modern problematic of subjectivity. But Žižek points out that Descartes is quick to plaster over this crack; he 'does not yet conceive of the cogito as correlative to the whole of reality' (13). In other words, Descartes is not properly an idealist, and therefore cannot be reinscribed nearly as effectively as Kant and Hegel under the sign of Lacan. The breakthrough of Kant is that his subject is 'a necessary and simultaneously impossible logical construction' (14) such that 'the inaccessibility of the I to its own "kernel of being" is what makes it an I' (14). In other words, Kant anticipates Jacques-Alain Miller's Lacanian idea of 'extimacy'; this neologism formed by analogy with 'intimacy' proposes that the core of subjectivity must be understood as something 'outside' the experience of the subject. In the simplest sense, this is a restatement of Freud's thesis that the unconscious is primary, that subjectivity is constituted and dominated by an 'otherness'. On a more sophisticated level, the idea becomes a spiralling dialectic that replaces the traditional distinction between subject and object. Thus 'the very notion of self-consciousness implies the subject's self-decenterment' (15), and 'The Kantian subject ... is this very abyss, this void of absolute negativity to whom every ... particular positive content appears as ... ultimately contingent' (27).

Kant's Lacanianism before Lacan may seem to leave little for Hegel to do. However, explains Žižek, Kant's idea of the subject contradicts his own basic principle of a distinction between the unknowable thing-in-itself (the noumenal) and the realm of experience (the phenomenal). This contradiction is for Hegel not a failing, but a clue as to what remains to be thought. The result is that 'Hegel's "absolute idealism" is nothing but the Kantian "criticism" brought to its utmost consequences' (20), so that 'the Hegelian subject ... is nothing but the very gap which separates phenomena from the Thing' (21), or 'a name for the externality of the Substance to itself' (30). The terms 'subject' and 'substance' here may be understood as replacements for the traditional subject and object, necessary to account for the capability of the subject to understand itself as one of the 'objects'. The last (or at any rate latest) word in this sequence belongs to Lacan, for whom the subject 'although nowhere actually present ... nonetheless has to be retroactively constructed, presupposed, if all other elements are to retain their consistency' (33), while the substance too 'is a mirage retroactively invoked' (36). Thus 'what we experience as "reality" discloses itself against the background of the lack ... of the mythical object whose encounter would bring about the full satisfaction of the drive' (37). 'Reality' still denotes everything we can experience and understand, but it is fully premised on the Real, which can never be experienced and understood. In other words, the idealist tradition cannot be written off as a series of delirious involutions of the hard facts of life; on the contrary, we can come to terms with the personal, critical and political questions that most concern us in the material world only by beginning with 'the split separating the accessible, symbolically structured, reality from the void of the Real' (37). It is worth noting that Kant is not unaware of the 'contradiction' in his account of subjectivity, indeed presenting it as a virtue, but it is also worth noting that Žižek elaborates an idea of 'retroactivity' as a way of legitimating a phrase like 'kernel of being', which echoes post-Kantians from Hegel to Lacan more than Kant himself.

All this perhaps begins to explain the importance to Žižek of Lacan's essay 'Kant with Sade' (1989). In that essay, Lacan reads *Philosophy in the Bedroom* alongside *The Critique of Practical Reason*, arguing that both texts urge obedience to a categorical imperative. In Kant, this is the moral law that we find within ourselves; in Sade, the subject is every bit as bound by duty, but in this case is required to do 'the bidding of the Other', to instrumentalize himself in the service of the pleasure of the Other. Where the Kantian subject is unitary, the Freudian–Lacanian–Žižekian subject is constitutively split. Thus the commanding voice of the Other, named by Freud the superego, is another case of 'extimacy', an agency that derives from 'outside' and yet seems to speak from 'inside'. Therefore the superego is not the voice of conscience but the 'obscene imperative' to enjoyment that Žižek discovers in nationalism, in racism, in popular culture and in numerous other contexts.

It is probably fair to say that Žižek's influence on criticism is still formative. Apart from figures like Joan Copjec, whose carefully argued account of Lacan's formulas of sexuation in terms of Kant's antinomies seems more persuasive than Žižek's own efforts, Žižekians tend to fasten onto one or two of Žižek's ideas, to openly imitate his rhetoric, or to proceed directly to textual analysis, frequently dealing with the same figures Žižek himself discusses. Such copycat 'applicationism' is of course typical of the first stage of the reception of any significant thinker. Not so well understood is that the writing of Žižek implies a reorientation of the whole relationship between reality and textuality. This is to say that the calculated outrage to common sense of a distinction between reality and the Real has consequences for the understanding of both the various realisms and the various anti-realisms in every field. Perhaps the most important of these is that representation becomes as much continuous as discontinuous with the everyday conception of reality – both are attempts to come to terms with the impossible Real, and both are polarized against it, since what cannot be symbolized is also what remains to be symbolized, in some cases what most needs to be symbolized. This is a way of thinking quite different from the present critical status quo, which is much better at polemicizing against traditional realist aesthetics than it is at positively rethinking reality and the real. Current criticism is nearly ritual in its quickness to assert that reality is constituted by the signifier; what ensues is typically so much preoccupied with the signifier that reality is effectively ceded to a traditional positivism and/or empiricism. In place of this binary opposition, the work of Žižek suggests a tripartite system (the 'impossible' Real, reality as an attempt to symbolize the Real, and renderings of reality such as fiction and film). In sum, we might propose that the work of any signifying or cultural practice, including those consciously conceived in opposition to realism, is to retrieve a reality from the Real. Only when this begins to sink in will we see Žižekian criticism that passes beyond imitation and/or homage.

When the ideas of Althusser and Lacan first inflected English-speaking criticism in the early 1970s, one of the routine citations of that still politicized period was Lenin on Hegel, to the effect that an intelligent materialism is closer to an intelligent idealism than to an unintelligent materialism. Though the reference has long since fallen into disuse, it remains a virtual template for the analyses of Žižek. This is to touch on the recognition factor, to suggest the extent to which Žižek rethinks an earlier and still influential problematic. Žižek is more Hegelian and (despite his fondness for semiotic rectangles) less semiological than the typical issue of *Screen* from 1975, but is nonetheless asking many of the same questions. Thus the first move of *The Sublime Object of Ideology* is to interrogate 'the sudden eclipse of the Althusserian school', which is best understood not as an intellectual defeat but as a 'theoretical amnesia' (1989, 1). Such a return was always possible insofar as 1970s theory, like so many other intellectual projects of the twentieth century, was not so much surpassed as slowly abandoned when diminishing returns began to set in – that is, when other ideas and approaches began to seem more productive. But a mere return to the thinking of the 1970s would hold little interest. So Žižek is better understood as a renovator, giving distinctly new kinds of answers to previously posed questions.

The theoretical project of the 1970s was at once the continuation of the political project of May 1968, and the beginning of the work of mourning for it. In its utopian, wish-fulfilling dimension, that project thought it possible to combine semiology, psychoanalysis, marxism and feminism into a key to all ideologies. The dream of an all-encompassing, all-purpose theory slowly dissipated, until by the mid-1980s it began to be recalled as something of an embarrassment. Žižek is by no means naive enough to think that one can reanimate an earlier theoretical moment by a effort of sheer will, but he is reminiscent of the utopianism of the earlier project in his sheer exuberance – Janet Bergstrom describes the 'high-energy Žižek-effect' as consisting of reference in the course of twenty-five pages to more than four dozen philosophers, novelists, psychoanalysts, political leaders, patients of Freud, fictional characters, films, plays, operas and developments in computer culture.

For Žižek, the personal equivalent of May 1968 must be 1989, the year of both his first English publication and the collapse of the Soviet empire. Žižek is a Slovenian who played a role in the dissident movements which helped bring down Titoist Yugoslavia, and his second book in English is based on a series of lectures given in Ljubljana in winter 1989–90. He describes the dissident movement as a 'vanishing mediator' between state socialism and the new capitalism of Eastern Europe. The vanishing mediator is a notion that Žižek finds in an essay of Fredric Jameson on Weber and applies in literally dozens of contexts. In Jameson, the vanishing mediator is an element essential to a historical and/or intellectual transition that disappears when its work is done. For Žižek, it is an element that is 'nowhere actually present and as such inaccessible to our experience, [but] nonetheless has to be retroactively reconstructed, presupposed, if all other elements are to retain their consistency' (1993, 33). Thus the two books on Schelling value their protagonist as the vanishing mediator between Kant and Marx, Kant himself 'brings to light ... a moment which has to disappear if the Cartesian res cogitans is to appear' (1993, 14). Forrest Gump is a vanishing mediator in that he unwittingly enables a whole series of events in recent American history, and the 'paradoxical relationship of subject and substance, where the subject emerges as the crack in the universal Substance, hinges on the notion of the subject as the "vanishing mediator" in the precise sense of the Freudian–Lacanian Real' (1993, 33). Like the refusal of the usual reading, the paradox and the rhetorical question, the vanishing mediator is an index of Žižek's thinking as a whole; this missing link that must be thought is close to the idea of 'the pre-synthetic Real' as 'a level that must be retroactively presupposed but can never actually be encountered' (1999, 33), and helps to sustain the Hegelian vision of that level as 'already the product, the result, of the imagination's disruptive ability' (1999, 33). With this argument that 'the mythic, inaccessible zero-level of pure multitude not yet affected/fashioned by imagination is nothing but pure imagination itself' (1999, 33), we reach the Žižekian first principle or declaration of faith.

Žižek clearly considers himself quite the card for presenting his difficult philosophical ideas in terms of popular culture; the discussion of subjectivity from Descartes to Lacan summarized above refers throughout to Ridley Scott's 1984 *Blade Runner*. At moments, however, Žižek suggests that he is as much disgusted as enthralled by popular films and fictions, and that Lacan's *jouissance* ('enjoyment') can be understood as precisely this paradox of an element in which one revels despite one's 'better' judgement. At the same time, Žižek's taste in popular culture could not be much more male-professorial – he deals mostly with hard-boiled writers of comparatively established literary value (Hammett, Chandler, Highsmith) and with film directors of auteur status (Chaplin, Hitchcock, Lynch). By the later 1990s, it is true, he does discuss New Age religious books like *The Celestine Prophecy* and mass-audience movies like *The Flintstones*, and (in one of his less persuasive analyses) proposes Mary Kay Letourneau, a 35-year-old schoolteacher who had a compulsive affair with a 14-year-old pupil, as an authentic ethical hero, since she lets us see the distinction between the ethical and the good. But this 'lower' popular culture is dealt with mostly in passing; extended and/or truly philosophical readings are reserved for Conan Doyle rather than Conan the Barbarian. Žižek is in any case just as likely to discuss Joyce and Kafka and Wagner as *Nightmare on Elm Street*. At times, this leads to outright confusion – the works of 'popular literature' listed in the index of *Looking Awry* include *Antigone*, *Un Amour de Swann* and *Finnegans Wake*, as though 'popular' meant the same thing as 'famous'.

Another negative is that Žižek is among the most repetitious of contemporary theorists. The same anecdotes, examples and arguments reappear from text to text, sometimes verbatim and sometimes at length, so much so that it is hard not to think longingly of Lacan's habit of ending the analytic session as soon as the analysand begins to repeat. By *The Ticklish Subject* (1999), Žižek at least begins to seem aware of his habit, offering a self-deprecating footnote to his nth discussion of Hegel's famous paragraph 'the human being is this night'. Yet this does not mean that whole books can be dismissed as rehashes; each of Žižek's titles offers perspectives and analyses not found elsewhere. New readers are best advised to begin at the beginning, with *The Sublime Object of Ideology* and *Looking Awry*, whose problematic is further developed some nine years later in the tour de force that is *The Plague of Fantasies*. A more purely philosophical voice begins to speak in Žižek's *For They Know Not What They Do*; that same voice, as we have seen, discusses Kant and Hegel in *Tarrying With The Negative*, and Heidegger, Alain Badiou and Judith Butler in the encompassing and brilliant *The Ticklish Subject*. Readers more interested in Žižek's Lacan are advised to begin with *Looking Awry* and the edited collection *Everything You Always Wanted to Know About Lacan (But Were Afraid To Ask Hitchcock)*, to look next at *Enjoy Your Symptom!*, and finally to consult two anthologies, *Gaze and Voice as Love Objects* and *Cogito and the Unconscious*.

Michael Walsh

Further reading and works cited

Althusser, L. and Balibar, E. *Reading Capital*. London, 1970.
Bergstrom, J. (ed.) *Endless Night*. Berkeley, CA, 1999.
Boynton, R. 'Enjoy Your Žižek', *Lingua Franca*, October 1998.
Copjec, J. 'Sex and the Euthanasia of Reason'. *Supposing the Subject*, ed. J. Copjec. London, 1994.
Deleuze, G. and Guattari, F. *A Thousand Plateaus*. Minneapolis, MN, 1987.
Eagleton, T. 'Enjoy!', *London Review of Books*, 27 November 1997.
Jameson, F. *The Ideologies of Theory. Essays 1971–1986. Volume 2*. Minneapolis, MN, 1988.
Kant, I. *Critique of Practical Reason*. Cambridge, 1997.
Lacan, J. *Ecrits*. Paris, 1966.
—. *The Four Fundamental Concepts of Psychoanalysis*. New York, 1978.
—. *The Seminar of Jacques Lacan. Book I*. New York, 1988a.
—. *The Seminar of Jacques Lacan. Book II*. New York, 1988b.
—. 'Kant with Sade', *October*, 51, 1989.
—. *The Seminar of Jacques Lacan. Book III*. New York, 1993.
—. *The Seminar of Jacques Lacan. Book XX. Encore*. New York, 1998.
Laclau, E. and Mouffe, C. *Hegemony and Socialist Strategy*. London, 1985.
Miklitsch, R. 'Going Through the Fantasy: Screening Slavoj Žižek'. *South Atlantic Quarterly*, 97, 2, Spring 1998.
Miller, J.-A. 'Extimité'. *Prose Studies*, 11, 1991.
Sade, Marquis de. *Philosophy in the Bedroom*. New York, 1966.
Žižek, S. *The Sublime Object of Ideology*. London, 1989.
—. *For They Know Not What They Do*. London, 1991a.
—. *Looking Awry*. Cambridge, MA, 1991b.
—. *Enjoy Your Symptom!* London, 1992a.
—. *Everything You Always Wanted to Know About Lacan (But Were Afraid To Ask Hitchcock)*. London, 1992b.
—. *Tarrying With the Negative*. Durham, NC, 1993.
—. *The Plague of Fantasies*. London, 1997.
— (ed.) *Cogito and the Unconscious*. Durham, NC, 1998.
—. *The Ticklish Subject*. London, 1999.
— and Salecl, R. (eds) *Gaze and Voice as Love Objects*. Durham, NC, 1996.

50. *Cahiers du Cinéma* (1951–)

When, in October of 1970, François Truffaut was asked his reasons for leaving the editorial staff of *Cahiers du cinéma*, he replied:

> It was not a disagreement. My name no longer represented the basic tenets of the magazine. When I worked on *Cahiers*, it was another era. We spoke of films only from the angle of their relative beauty. Today at *Cahiers* they do a marxist-leninist analysis of films. Readership of the magazine is limited to university graduates. As for me, I have never read a single line of Marx. (1999)

This statement, coming from a former contributor who had gone on to become a leading participant in the *Nouvelle Vague*, the film-making movement which confirmed *Cahiers du cinéma* in the forefront of French film criticism, clearly indicates the shift the magazine underwent in its first twenty years of publication. However, beginning in the mid-1970s, *Cahiers* returns to alliances with the Nouvelle Vague and a renewed respect for Hollywood, supplanting the most politically engaged phase of *Cahiers'* history. Today, *Cahiers* has come almost full circle, back to the embrace of a critical view that champions popular films of merit, while still trying to broaden filmic tastes. Young French film-makers are championed, but political and theoretical issues are addressed far less frequently. Tracing this history, this essay will look at *Cahiers* in context, examining how the various essayists who wrote for this review brought to film aesthetics a political and theoretical dimension, and how commercial viability and historical shifts affected the life of this influential journal.

The aesthetic viewpoint that gave birth to *Cahiers* and to the Nouvelle Vague is firmly grounded in a school of French film analysis which began in the 1920s. In a theoretical debate on the cinema, leading voices agreed that movies were not vulgar entertainment, but an art form. Canudo held that cinema is a separate and equal art with its own different and specific characteristics. His position was a reaction to the fact that film had so often been judged exclusively by the criteria established for other media, particularly the aesthetics of theatre and literature. But the effect was cyclical. Because it had been assumed that film did the same things as literature and theatre, the movies that were produced in France were often adaptations of works created in other media. These adaptations were often not as expressive as the originals. In other cases, critics who did not allow for the translation of forms of expression did not really understand the specificity of the film medium. As a result, many critics treated the cinema apologetically. Canudo's theory was the beginning of recognition of the validity of cinematic expression. Elie Faure's argument that cinema is a synthesis of the other six arts also added in its own way to the prestige of film and allowed him to think through the spatio-temporal specificity of film. Other theorists who contributed to the development of the Nouvelle Vague include (and this list is still incomplete) Louis Delluc, Jean Epstein, René Clair, Rudolph Arnheim, Marcel L'Herbier, Bela Balàzs and Edgar Morin. Yet the most direct antecedent of the Nouvelle Vague is the theoretical work of André Bazin, and his influence at *Cahiers* was immense.

Bazin's writings (collected in 1958 into a four-volume series called *Qu'est-ce que c'est le cinéma?*) reveal the growth of an aesthetic that concentrated on the cinema's capacity for metaphysical transcendence through realist observation. Behind Bazin's metaphysics is an effort to analyse seriously the way in which films affected him: what filmic devices, what metaphors, and what myths serve as the basis for the transcendental expression achieved. He, too, looked to American films, particularly those of Chaplin, Orson Welles and William Wyler, as the best examples of the development of cinematic language, as well as championing the causes of Jean Renoir and Eric Von Stroheim, whom he felt had not achieved adaquate critical recognition during their careers. Bazin's overwhelming influence on the young men who were to become the 'comité de redaction' of *Cahiers* and later the *Nouvelle Vague* is illustrated by Eric Rohmer:

> Everything had been said by him, we came too late. Now we are left with the difficult duty of pursuing his task; we shall not fail in this, although we are convinced that he pursued it much further than it will be possible for us to do ourselves.... (1999, 113)

In April 1950, the editor of *La Revue du cinéma* was killed in an auto accident. Doniol-Valcroze, Lo Duca and Leontyne Kiegel decided to continue the magazine, publishing articles similar to those in *La Gazette du cinéma*, an erratic broadsheet written and circulated in the Latin Quarter by Jean-Luc Godard, Eric Rohmer and Jacques Rivette. The first issue of the new magazine, *Cahiers du cinéma*, appeared in April of 1951.

Cahiers continued in the direction indicated by Bazin. It was not, however, until January of 1954 that any cohesive definition of the staff's position was enunciated. In an article titled 'Une Certaine tendence du cinéma français', François Truffaut attacked the traditional manner of French cinema and was particularly critical of the role played by screenwriters whom he found unversed in cinematic expression. He sarcastically suggested:

> Why don't we all turn to adapting literary masterpieces of which there are probably a few left . . .
> then we'll all be steeped in the 'quality tradition' up to our necks, and the French cinema with
> its daring 'psychological realism,' its 'harsh truths,' 'its 'ambiguity' will be one great morbid
> funeral ready to be heaved out of the Billancourt studios and stacked up in the cemetery so
> appropriately waiting alongside. (1999, 4)

Truffaut called instead for a 'cinéma d'auteur' in which directors would express their personal convictions in their films. *Cahiers'* models were Renoir, Cocteau. Bresson, Hitchcock, Welles, Rosselini and Hawks.

The early success of *Cahiers* might be ascribed in part to the popularity of films, especially the American films the magazine lauded, during a period when many French people still didn't own television sets. However, *Cahiers* critics and editors, Truffaut, Rohmer, Godard, Claude Chabrol and Jacques Rivette, longed to make their own films. They began experimenting in 16 mm, made shorts, and finally graduated to feature length films. By 1959, with the release of Godard's *A Bout de souffle* and Truffaut's *Les Quatre cents coups*, the same year as Alain Resnais' *Hiroshima, Mon Amour*, the Nouvelle Vague had arrived.

There was, however, another important film magazine operating in France at this time which shared few of the aesthetic convictions of the *Cahiers* group, but instead defined its approach to film as marxist-leninist: *Positif*. Many of the *Positif* critics found Bazin and the *Cahiers* staff too liberal and bourgeois in their aesthetic and metaphysical orientation. They could not understand *Cahiers'* respect for certain American directors who produced what they considered right-wing films. Gerard Gozlan, an editor of *Positif*, characterized the Bazinian influence on the *Cahiers* approach by saying,

> It is natural that right-wing critics should welcome a critical system which lies at the crossroads
> of so many traditions – bourgeois, idealist, liberal, religious, and social democrat. It is natural
> that rightwing critics should not scorn a 'dialectic' that cleverly combines the prestige of
> rationalism and the irrational powers of the image, borrowing the linguistic charms from the
> former and the guiles of faith from the latter. (1997, 132)

The difference between the marxist analysis offered by *Positif* and that which developed in *Cahiers* is emphasized by the fact that the animosity between the two groups never relented. On the contrary, *Positif*'s attacks on *Cahiers* became even more determined as *Cahiers* developed its own form of political criticism. This chasm separating the two schools is understandable in terms of the wide range of ideologies that constitute the French Left, with the Communist Party on one side and the Maoists and anarchists on the other. The 'extreme gauche' called the CP the 'left-wing pillar of order'. It is with this extreme left that the *Cahiers* group eventually aligned. Moreover, the purely aesthetic phase that *Cahiers* criticism went through had an effect on its political criticism; the manner in which films express themselves was always in the forefront of the discussion.

The full-fledged entry of *Cahiers* into the political arena cannot be explained in isolation from the politcal changes occuring in France in the mid and late 1960s. Following two wars of decolonialization, a student and young worker movement emerged. This meant that organized opposition to Gaullism was no longer the exclusive domain of the Communist Party, an anathema to the young for its pro-Soviet line and to the film-makers for its cultural deadness.

As early as 1965, Godard turned a favorable eye to this political movement among youth. In *Masculin-Féminin* the lead character Paul, and his worker friend Robert, paint slogans against American involvement in Vietnam on the side of an American diplomat's limousine. One is reminded of Michel stealing cars in *A bout de souffle*, an earlier form of the same anarchy. While Godard was in the process of becoming an increasingly politically oriented film-maker, the *Cahiers* group began to explore earlier political artistic expression. In 1964 they devoted a section to Bertolt Brecht, arguing that his theories of distanciation should help construct future film practice.

While Brecht's influence on Godard can be seen as early as *Une femme est une femme* (1961), it was never so evident as in *La Chinoise* made in 1967. Not only is one of the characters an actor who forsakes the theatre to become involved in full-time political work and then leaves that work to read Brecht door to door, there are also sequences of pure stylization – a form of filmic guerilla theatre. After Godard left *Cahiers* to devote himself to film-making, he criticized the film-making of others through his own films. He continually suggested new directions for films to take, and his influence on *Cahiers* remained great.

The scholarly studies of Christian Metz on meaning in film began to be published in *Cahiers* in 1965. Metz's investigations, along with those of Roland Barthes and others, represented the French assimilation of and expansion on Russian formalist theorists. Semiotics offered a new methodology with which to study film. The increased academic interest in the study of film corresponded to *Cahiers'* development of longer essays and dossiers on major figures in film history, which would pave the way for the purely theoretical essays that would emerge by the end of the decade. *Cahiers'* collective texts devoted to the analysis of individual films became a prototype for a film semiotics that engaged historical and ideological analysis, on John Ford's *Young Mr Lincoln* in July 1970 followed by analyses of Renoir's *La Vie est à nous*, Von Sternberg's *Morocco* and Cukor's *Sylvia Scarlet*.

The student–worker uprising of May 1968 can be seen as a turning point for the *Cahiers* staff, just as it was for many French people. The Gaullist regime proved more vulnerable than anyone had dreamed and the lines of demarcation between the right wing and the gauchists were so clearly drawn that there remained no comfortable middle ground. The aftermath of this situation for *Cahiers* was that the magazine began to be less concerned with a 'pure' aesthetic and instead pursued a new aesthetic which could be put to concrete political use.

In 1968, the emergence of *Cinéthique*, a film magazine begun by a group formerly associated with the literary review *Tel Quel*, provided a challenge to *Cahiers* just as it was beginning to formulate a political approach. *Cinéthique* had the advantage of a fresh beginning based on a dialectical materialist approach to film. Rejecting any 'cinephile' investigation of film history or any work at documentation such as interviews with film-makers or découpage, *Cinéthique* concentrated instead on a sharply drawn political critique of films. They condemned nearly all films produced up until that point in history, and supported only those films actively engaged in combating traditional bourgeois film expression. All aesthetic considerations were shunned in favour of a critique that considered only a film's ultimate usefulness in breaking down the dominant culture. *Cinéthique* went so far as to praise films for including sequences which were aesthetic failures, arguing that they served revolutionary goals by reducing marketability.

Cahiers' response, a long evaluation of the *Cinéthique* approach, appeared in issue no. 217, November 1969. *Cahiers* criticized *Cinéthique* for the vagueness of its theoretical formulations and for forcing all understanding of cinema into a scientific system which left no allowances for a practicable cinema outside of a role definied as (1) diffusing a knowledge of theoretical science and (2) exposing its own self-conscious nature.

While *Cahiers'* arguments may be seen in part as a defence of its own tradition (including its bourgeois tendencies), they must also be seen as an attempt to salvage a working aesthetic from a purely theoretical approach of negation and rejection. Whatever the internal failings of *Cinéthique's* the very existence of a cinema magazine taking such a radical position served to stimulate *Cahiers'* own theoretical growth.

Research was begun in 1969 on Russian film-makers and theorists of the 1920s, the fertile period of Soviet cinema before the heavy control of Stalinist social realism. Eisenstein's theories of montage and film language were given exhaustive attention. A fifteen part translation of Eisenstein's 'Non-indifferent Nature' was published in instalments. There was unbounded respect for his scientific analysis of the perception and interpretation of film images as a dialectical process. Dziga-Vertov was rediscovered by *Cahiers* and studied in depth.

Thus the merging of various influences, the changing politics of the country, the research into the work of the early Russian theorists, the challenge of other film magazines and the scientific study of film language combined to give *Cahiers* a decidedly different orientation and style in the last years of the 1960s and early 1970s. In April 1969 Jean Pierre Oudart's 'La Suture' brought to the semiotic focus of film studies an ideological critique of Hollywood continuity editing. Political theoretical analysis also led to a series of articles by Jean-Louis Comolli entitled 'Technique et Idéologie' and another series on 'Politique et La Lutte Idéologique de Classe'.

Comolli's articles are a reaction to Marcel Pleynet's reflections on film technique in *Cinéthique* and Jean Patrick Lebel's book, *Cinéma et Idéologie*. Arguing against Lebel's theory, which tries to distinguish between technical innovations and the use to which they are put, Comolli expands on Pleynet's suggestion that the film image is the perfected form of Renaissance perspective in art and carries with it the advanced form of that historical movement's bourgeois ideology. Comolli argues a materialist history of film would explain the impetus of film innovations. His writing reflects a wide familiarity with film and film history and his theory is made concrete by specific references to films which illustrate his points about deep focus and distortion of perspective.

Cahiers' application of theory to discussion of specific films is also represented by Jean-Pierre Oudart's article in no. 232 called 'L'Idéologie moderniste dans quelques films récents'. Examining first what he terms the 'Bressonian Model' in which a central character refuses communication, and economic and sexual relationships, in order to avoid definition as an object within the social norms, Oudart traces how that 'anti-Hollywood structure' has been treated in films such as Bernardo Bertolucci's *The Conformist* and Louis Malle's *Le Souffle au coeur*.

This intellectual, ideological turn of *Cahiers* met with sharp opposition from its old detractors, the staff of *Positif*. In their November 1970 issue, no. 122, they devoted over a third of their pages to an attack on *Cahiers* which included parenthetically *Cinéthique* and *Tel quel*. The attack called the new form of criticism practised in *Cahiers* 'unreadable, obscure and esoteric' and dismissed *Cahiers*' classification of social realism as a bourgeois art form that should be replaced by dialectical fiction. *Cahiers* responded in its January–Febuary 1971 double issue (which, incidently, was entirely devoted to Eisenstein) with a short sarcastic rebuttal. The staff believed that its own ideology, while complex, was not obscure, and provided the only possible illumination of social conditions. Although they agreed that their theories might not be accessible to everyone, they believed that the ideas would be understood by those who mattered who would then disseminate their understanding through their films.

Cahiers has consistently held up the work of Godard as an example of the most progressive use of film. *Cahiers* has been Godard's leading critical support in his efforts made in collaboration with Jean-Pierre Gorin and the Dziga-Vertov Collective, and it has devoted much space over the last year to a retrospective view of Godard's and Gorin's political films. In March 1973, they published a long position paper entitled, 'Quelles sont nos taches sur le front culturel?' ['What are our tasks on the cultural front?'] which they worked on after an open meeting with their 'comrades on the ideological front' in August 1972. *Cahiers*' cinephilic endeavours continue throughout even the most ideologically engaged period, but they find new objects to embrace such as the films of Jean-Marie Straub and Danielle Huillet, whose political expression is embedded in formal transformations of cinematic expressions and metaphorical readings of history. The *Cahiers*' appreciation of Japanese film in general gives way to attention to the films of Oshima Nagisa that take various approaches to redefining Brechtian and politically engaged cinema at a formal level.

One might trace *Cahiers*' history through changes in cover design (yellow covers with photo inserts yielding to the larger format photo covers on glossy paper, then to the plain text 'table of content' covers during the most political period which also saw circulation drop, then the revival of the larger format glossy photo covers). These changes correspond to publisher shifts and economic reorganizations. The revival of the mass circulation cinephilic film review after the glory of the theoretical period turned a near 180 degress on the political denunciation of much of the aesthetics which had built *Cahiers*' early history. The return was a gradual process, with 1978 a transitional year in which Truffaut's *La Chambre Verte* recieved accolades from Pierre Bonitzer and attention to Martin Scorsese marks an interest in new Hollywood films. During the last twenty years, *Cahiers* has repeatedly examined what it calls 'the situation of French film', while bringing critical energy to an increasingly international cinema.

Maureen Turim

Further reading and works cited

Arnaud, P. *Robert Bresson*. Paris, 1986.
Aumont, J. *Du visage au cinéma*. Paris, 1992.
Baecque, A. de. *Les Cahiers du cinéma*. Paris, 1991.
Bazin, A. *Qu'est ce que c'est le cinéma?* Paris, 1958.
— and Narboni, J. *Le cinéma français de la libération à la nouvelle vague (1945–1958)*. Paris, 1983.
Bergala, A. and Narboni, J. *Pasolini cinéaste*. Paris, 1981.

— et al. *Orson Welles*. Paris, 1986.

Bonitzer, P. *Le champ aveugle*. Paris, 1982.

—. *Décadrages*. Paris, 1985.

—. *Eric Rohmer*. Paris, 1991.

Browne, N. (ed.) *Cahiers du cinéma 1969–1972*. Cambridge, MA, 1990.

Godard, J.-L. *Godard on Godard*. New York, 1972.

—. *Godard par Godard*. Paris, 1991.

— and Bergala, A. *Godard par Godard*. Paris, 1989.

—. *Jean-Luc Godard par Jean-Luc Godard*. Paris, 1998.

Gozlan, G. 'In Praise of Andre Bazin'. *The New Wave*, ed. P. Graham. New York, 1997.

Hillier, J. (ed.) *Cahiers du cinéma, the 1950s*. Cambridge, MA, 1985.

Le Berre, C. *François Truffaut*. Paris, 1993.

Lellis, G. *Bertolt Brecht, Cahiers du cinéma and Contemporary Film Theory*. Ann Arbor, MI, 1982.

MacCabe, C. and Godard, J.-L. *Godard*. Bloomington, IN, 1980.

Magny, J. *Claude Chabrol*. Paris, 1987.

Rohmer, E. *Cahiers du cinéma: La nouvelle vague: Claude Chabrol, Jean-Luc Godard, Jacques Rivette, Eric Rohmer, François Truffaut, Petite bibliothèque des Cahiers du cinéma, 27*. Paris, 1999.

Truffaut, F. *Cahiers du cinéma: La nouvelle vague: Claude Chabrol, Jean-Luc Godard, Jacques Rivette, Eric Rohmer, François Truffaut, Petite bibliothèque des Cahiers du cinéma, 27*. Paris, 1999.

51. Critical Fictions: Experiments in Writing from *Le Nouveau Roman* to the Oulipo

Around 1955 a small number of French authors published – or began publishing – a series of works, mostly novels (later also some short stories, drama and – a typical genre of the 1960s – radio plays), which produced shock among both critics and readers. Thus the New Novel was born and the names of its (unofficial) members became rapidly (in)famous: Alain Robbe-Grillet (*Les Gommes*, 1953; *Le Voyeur*, 1955; *La Jalousie*, 1957); Claude Simon (*Le Vent*, 1957; *L'Herbe*, 1958; *La Route des Flandres*, 1960), Michel Butor (*L'Emploi du temps*, 1956; *La Modification*, 1957) and Nathalie Sarraute (*Martereau*, 1953; *Le Planétarium*, 1959), whose first book (*Tropismes*, 1939) had been published before the Second World War and whose position in the group had always been marginal, not least because she was usually published by Gallimard, the principal mainstream publishing company, instead of by Minuit, the small independent publisher whose name was inseparable with that of the New Novel. Other writers are associated with the movement: Claude Ollier (*La Mise en scène*, 1958), Marguerite Duras (*Moderato Cantabile*, 1958), Robert Pinget (*L'Inquisitoire*, 1962) and Jean Ricardou (*L'Observatoire de Cannes*, 1961), who in fact already belonged to the next literary generation, that of the *Tel Quel* group.

All the aforementioned authors, whose main spokesman was without any doubt Alain Robbe-Grillet (the first to publish a 'post factum' manifesto: *Pour un nouveau roman*, 1963), shaped a new form of writing which was initially despised by most professional critics, largely ignored by the public, enthusiastically supported by an emergent generation of literary scholars such as Roland Barthes and Gérard Genette, and very rapidly discovered and adopted by foreign academics (New Novels appear on reading lists in the US and elsewhere, and scholarly attention is paid to the movement by all the leading institutions). The new 'thing' about the New Novel (a label neither immediately used nor immediately claimed by the authors, who always emphasized their individuality) was something very relative. In France, the plea for an 'objective' literature turned away from the humanist or political message so dominantly present in the fiction of that time (e.g. in the work of Camus, Sartre, Mauriac and many other existential, marxist or Christian authors) but turned towards a more phenomenologically inspired descriptive approach of life, which indeed produced a literary earthquake the force of which can still be compared to the intrusion of Dada and surrealism in the 1920s. The frontal attack against the 'roman à thèse' and the 'Balzacian' model dramatically changed the way the dominant genre of the novel was perceived and opened it to a more writerly vision. Viewed from abroad, however, the New Novel appeared to a certain extent to be nothing more than an overtaking manoeuvre. The New Novelists themselves liked to stress the influence upon their work of great modernist examples: William Faulkner (for Claude Simon), Henry James and Ivy Compton-Burnett (for Sarraute), Franz Kafka (for Robbe-Grillet), James Joyce (for Michel Butor, though not just for him). Nevertheless, even for the foreign public more familiar with modernism in the novel, the French New Novel remained a very innovative and disquieting movement, as it explored in a radically new way the frontier of novelistic *tellability*. New Novels, indeed, focused apparently upon something that in all other types of novel had only a secondary function: objects on the one hand, description on the other. Whereas before, even in very modernist fiction, the object was always viewed in relation to the subject, and description never functioned, except as an auxiliary in plot-making, the New Novel appeared to reject the subject as well as the plot: New Novelists stopped telling, they merely described, and their descriptions were no longer part of a fictional universe ruled by the necessity of putting characters in a meaningful setting. This was at least the way the first readers judged the literary UFOs called New Novels. And although it soon became clear that there was room for the subject, political commitment and narrative, it is important to underline the very difficulties of reading created by the thorough foregrounding of aspects until then under-stressed in novelistic writing, and the apparent censorship of the basic aspects of the novel which Robbe-Grillet called outdated: character, story, diegetic setting and above all message. In its first years, the New Novel was reduced by its enemies to its lust for description and its exclusion of any recognizable story. Its defenders logically emphasized the phenomenological added value of its writing, which can be read as a testimony of the difficulties of being in an alienated society where subjects are replaced by objects. The larger dissatisfaction with the classic rules and stereotypes of the novel was also put forward, but this dissatisfaction was only coded in terms of refusal, not in terms of a change in the hierarchy between content and form. The first labels coined to come to terms with the newness of the movement revealed much of that anxiety: before being labelled New Novel, the group was called 'l'école du regard' (the school of the gaze) and 'l'école du refus' (the school of refusal).

The history of the New Novel is very complex, not only because the New Novelists never constituted a real group and because their work went through different styles and periods, but also and maybe more because no other literary movement had ever been characterized by such a merging of creative work and critical commentary (sometimes of a highly theoretical nature). The New Novel and the theory of the New Novel (either written by the New Novelists themselves or vicariously developed by their enemies as well as their defenders) could not be separated, and the relationship between creative work and critical reflection became so strong that at the point the New Novel aspired to become a kind of writing where the very distinction of fiction and theory no longer held.

During the first period of the New Novel, which ran approximately from 1955 to 1965, creative writing was clearly dominant and theory played only a secondary role. Those were the years of avoidance of traditional plot and story elements, and of insistence on realism and 'objective' style (not fortuitously, those were also the years of New Wave in Cinema and, some years later, New Realism in painting). Slowly, the New Novel started finding its own audience, and its influence in the global cultural debate was undoubtedly growing, at the price of the more radical aspects of its writing. In the mid-1960s, however, a change of tone and style occurred.

Under the influence of radical critics such as Jean Ricardou (related to *Tel Quel* in the 1960s, where he functioned as a kind of bridge between the experiments in the 'novel' and those in 'writing'), the refusal of the *classic* novel became a refusal of the novel *tout court*, whereas the critique of the traditional content and plot elements shifted towards a plea for a formally and linguistically driven type of writing where the critique of the humanist message no longer relied upon the pre-eminence of the object but on that of language (structuralist theory on language and subject now replacing the phenomenological viewpoint of the 1950s). The New Novel was seen as a verbal architecture that no longer referred to an outside world, the rules and constraints of which were completely internal to the linguistic universe. As Jean Ricardou remarked in one of his many quoted formulas: the New Novel is not 'the story of an adventure' but 'the adventure of a story', a stance by which he meant that the story was no longer the verbal reproduction of something that has been imagined (or even that has really happened), but an invention due to the play of a structure which permanently referred to its own verbal grounding. Reading a New Novel was then no longer reading a plot, but reading the way this plot and its motifs behaved as signals pointing to the underlying verbal layers of the work (a black bird crossing the white sky, for instance, was not a black bird crossing the white sky, but the trajectory of the printed words on the sheet one is reading, and so on). Man in such a context was a useless hypothesis, and the anti-humanism of the first New Novel now turned its arrows against the role and the position of the writer himself, who was considered the mere operator of the instructions launched by the play of the chosen signifiers: the text was not written by the author, but writes itself thanks to the 'productivity' (Kristeva) of the signifier; reading was not reading but writing the text, etc. This stance, which can to a certain degree be compared to the Anglo-Saxon metafiction (but with much less fiction, much less story, much less humour and much less direct dialogue between author and reader), produced a second type of New Novel, sometimes called New New Novel (a neologism rather popular around 1970, but which now has almost completely fallen into oblivion). Contrary to the phenomenological or realist New Novel, the New New Novel was characterized by a shift from the critique of the traditional novel to the more positive affirmation of pure immanent writing. This New New Novel, however, did not go as far as the experiments of *Tel Quel*, where the writing experiments were turned against language itself and explored the domain of frankly 'non-representative' writing, which could no longer be mastered by our traditional ways of thinking but instead aimed to destabilize our very thinking. The acme of this second manner was represented by the incredibly influential conference on the New Novel directed by Jean Ricardou in Cérisy (1971). This conference radicalized the movement (it is, *grosso modo*, the confirmation of the death of the New Novel and the birth of the New New Novel) and initiated its institutionalization in France, but at the same time 'cut' it from the larger audience on the one hand and from the progressive writing community on the other. A group of seven authors were constituted (Robbe-Grillet, Butor, Pinget, Ollier, Ricardou, Sarraute and Butor) and of course immediately contested (even from the inside: Butor, who stopped writing novels after Degrés, 1960, withdrew himself very soon and several authors were not willing to accept the way Ricardou tried to transform a group of authors in a real movement with a single doctrine and one single way of writing). At the same time, the public was no longer interested in the audacious and really innovative books written in this period (Claude Simon: La Bataille de Pharsale, 1969, Les corps conducteurs, 1971, Triptyque, 1973, Leçon de choses, 1975; Robbe-Grillet: La Maison de rendez-vous, 1965, Projet pour une révolution à New-York, 1970, Topologie d'une cité fantôme, 1975; Robert Pinget: Le Libera, 1967, Passacaille, 1969, Fable, 1971; Ollier; La vie sur Epsilon, 1972, Fuzzy Sets, 1975).

In the 1980s, postmodernist fiction started penetrating the French market and many authors made a 'come-back' to more classic ways of storytelling. This was the case not only for Tel Quel, but also for the (New) New Novel. After having almost disappeared from the literary scene by the end of the 1970s, some of the New Novelists suddenly turned towards a completely different type of New Novel, more in tune with the spirit of the times than all their previous works. Robbe-Grillet, Pinget, Sarraute and maybe most of all Ollier, the most productive author of this period, stopped refusing narrative pleasure, subjective stances and 'fiction-as-worldmaking', and all of them write more or less in the vein of the so-called autofiction, a new type of autobiography reusing biographical material in order to create a work of fiction, and vice versa (Robbe-Grillet: Le Miroir qui revient, 1984, Angélique ou l'enchantement, 1987; Sarraute: Enfance, 1985; Pinget: L'apocryphe, 1980, Monsieur Songe, 1982; Ollier: Une histoire illisible, 1986, Feuilleton, 1990). Simultaneously, an important shift occurred in the scholarly and critical reception of the New Novel. Lucien Dällenbach replaced Ricardou as the leading theoretician of the New Novelists (the New Novel as such was no longer an issue) and his studies on Claude Simon clearly showed that times had dramatically changed. Instead of analysing the work as a play of signifiers, Dällenbach did not hesitate to revalorize the signified (either imagined or experienced). The main themes that he underlined were the role of memory, the physical presence of the world, the function of the body, etc. (language becoming once again a tool, not an aim in itself). As a corollary, the rediscovery of the world was also the starting point of the political rereading of the New Novel, whose ideological subtext now appeared more easily at surface level. Postcolonialism made it clear that works such as those of Ollier, to take the most evident example (since many of his fictions are situated outside Western Europe), bear from their very beginnings traces of a direct political commitment. The latest books of Claude Simon, who received the Nobel Prize for Literature in 1985 in a rather hostile environment, proved, however, that the broadening of scope and reorienting towards the world and the subject do not eliminate (as is the case in the work of other New Novelists) the desire to take language seriously and to renew permanently the genre of the novel itself (Les Géorgiques, 1982, L'Acacia, 1989, Le Jardin des plantes, 1998).

The New Novel had enduringly seduced and terrified many writers and critics. Institutionally speaking, the most astonishing accomplishment was perhaps the fact that for many years the traditional novel was no longer taken seriously. Every novel with a message, a story, an author, a Weltanschauung, etc. seemed definitely too ridiculous to discuss. Only a small set of authors were strong enough to escape from this doom in the

1960s–1970s, and to create new types of writing that did not fit the canon of the New Novel. Some well known innovative authors continued inventing without being too much influenced by the New Novel. Raymond Queneau, whose first books appeared in the 1930s, is a good example of this (*Zazie dans le métro*, 1959), and also some young authors who tried to innovate in the very fields the New Novel had declared outdated: the sociological description of the world and the psychological analysis of the subject. This was exemplary in the case of Georges Perec, whose first publications were *Les Choses* (1965) and *Un homme qui dort* (1967), which were produced against the grain: the first is the sociological portrait of a young couple whose behaviour is paradigmatic for the emerging consumer society in France; the latter is the report of a psychiatric case narrated in the second person, as if to better mark the difference of this book with the New Novel that most famously launched the success of this narrative technique, Butor's *La Modification*.

Both Perec and Queneau were typical representatives of the Oulipo (Ouvroir de littérature potentielle: workshop for virtual literature), a writers' collective founded by Queneau and François Le Lionnais in 1960, and joined by Perec in 1996 (membership of the Oulipo is only by invitation, and the 'club' now has approximately twenty-five members). Contrary to the New Novel, which was mainly intent on renewing the old-fashioned mainstream genre of the literary system, the Oulipo has a completely different aim: promoting a type of writing which is both absolutely marginal (it breaks with our dominant romantic vision of the inspired writer) and universally acknowledged (in all known literatures there are to be found Oulipian authors or texts *avant-la-lettre*). This writing is the so-called 'writing-under-constraint', a constraint being defined as a rule (or a protocol, an algorithm, a set of instructions, a programme: there is no fixed terminology) the systematic application of which triggers the creative process and is (virtually) susceptible to produce a text. Starting from this very general device, which has not changed since the very foundation of the group, the assignment of the Oulipo workshops is twofold; first, to invent new formulas of writing (and, simultaneously, to list all known examples of 'pre-Oulipian' constraints); second, but without any obligation, to produce texts intended to 'illustrate' the constraints. Most of the constraints are of course strictly formal, such as the lipogram (a text written without a certain letter or without a certain number of letters) or the palindrome (a text that can be read both forwards and backwards). Others are semantic, such as the creation of gender-neutral texts (the characters being described in such a way that the reader cannot know whether they are male or female: an easy thing to do in English (perhaps), but not in French where the nouns are gendered and where adjectives and other forms also vary depending on the gender of the nouns). Often the constraints rely on ancient rhetorical figures, but the first do much more than just radicalize the latter. The major difference is that in writing under constraint these figures were not simply used locally in order to stress from time to time a given textual aspect, but used all over in order to oblige the writer to invent things he would never have thought of without the 'help' of the constraint: Perec's *La disparition*, 1969, for instance, is a 300-page novel that never uses the letter 'e', the most frequently used letter in the French alphabet (on the contrary, the hilarious sequel of this book, *Les revenentes*, 1972, only uses the one vowel censored before: e!).

During its first years, the proceedings of the Oulipo meetings remained very confidential. The authors gathered for fun, their Oulipian activities were more seen as social events of a certain literary inner circle than as a real literary project, there were hardly any publications in the traditional sense of the word, and most attention was paid to the creation and listing of constraints, the production of constrained texts hardly exceeding the creation of some small samples. But slowly, constrained book-length texts began appearing, the group organized public events (the Oulipians also gathered in Cérisy), and some members of the group used more systematically the technique of constrained writing: Georges Perec (*Alphabets*, 1976) and Jacques Roubaud ('E', 1966) in French, Harry Mathews in English, Italo Calvino in Italian, etc. But in spite of all this, the Oulipo was slow to be perceived as a real literary group or even as a real movement. This lack of recognition contrasted strangely with the fact that the group functioned well as a unit, with closely defined rules on membership and activities (the Oulipo was, among many other things, a parody of the Académie française). One of the most important elements which explains the delay in its public recognition was perhaps the fact that not every Oulipian author always writes or publishes Oulipian books (some autobiographical works by Perec, such as the much acclaimed *W ou le souvenir d'enfance*, 1975, was certainly not a 'pure' example of Oulipian writing). Since most of the members were already active at the moment they joined the group, they sometimes acquired a double identity and continued producing two types of books: constrained and not-constrained. (The fact that some of these authors were rather successful in their traditional writing explains perhaps why they consider their Oulipian excursions as nothing more than a game.) And one has to add to this that not every Oulipian text is recognizable as such. Many Oulipian texts create indeed a problem of readability, not in the sense that they are not enjoyable to read (they are often very funny, and are always open to a 'dilettante' reading in the first degree), but in the sense that the constraints used during the production of the text are no longer visible in the final result (see Queneau's metaphor of the scaffold the writer-builder has to eliminate once the text-building has been finished). As a result, the readability issue soon became of one the hottest topics in the discussions concerning Oulipian writing: if the use of constraints is never really questioned, there are those who are in favour of the disclosure of the constraints in the final text, and those who prefer to hide them in order to guarantee the enjoyment of the average reader.

Gradually, the position of the Oulipo in the literary system changed, and although there was certainly no direct relationship with the vanishing influence of the New Novel in the 1970s and the 1980s, it cannot be denied that in many aspects the Oulipo was, more than *Tel Quel*, *Change*, *TXT* or other radical groups of the 1970s, the real inheritor of what constituted the core of the New Novel: not the revolution of the novel itself (it was only after many years that the Oulipo became interested in the novel, and poetry remains still today at the heart of its production, for instance in the work of Michelle Grangaud), but the will to invent new types of writing, a programme which could no longer be realized satisfactorily either by the autofictional versions of the New Novel in the 1980s or by the emerging literary forms of the same decade, all suspected to be a little conservative or mainstream (at least from a strictly literary and formal point of view). Just as the New Novel did twenty or thirty years earlier, the Oulipo now took some very radical stances on the pre-eminent role of language in the literary production. But unlike the New Novel, and in spite of the often thoroughly formalist plays of the group, it also took some very liberating stances on the role of storytelling, on the importance of the subject and the presence of the world outside the text. When comparing the New Novel and the Oulipo in more detail, one becomes rapidly aware of two other differences. First there is the fact that the Oulipo started from a literary theory, but finished with producing fiction that can be read without the help of any theory (of course it's helpful to know more about it, but the previous knowledge of the

constraint(s) is not necessarily a condition *sine qua non*), whereas the New Novel, which
started from practice and has remained for a very long time 'allergic' to theory, has in a certain
sense fallen into the very trap of theory (at one point the fictions produced were simply
uninteresting unless one could consider them an answer to problems of literary theory).
Second, there was the fact that the Oulipo, even as a select club of often prestigious writers,
had succeeded in creating a genuine dynamism in the global field of literature: Oulipian
circles were formed throughout the whole Francophone world, the 'ateliers d'écriture' (this
very French and most of all very idiosyncratic version of creative writing courses) have
widely adopted the technique of writing under constraint and are of invaluable help in the
canonization of the group. The way to the use of constraints (instead of inspiration, or
spontaneity, or free expression) as a pedagogic tool was certainly prepared by the anti-
humanist and formalist devices of the New Novel, but was never fully exploited by the New
Novelists who put traditional literary education under attack rather than transforming it as
do the Oulipians. (Ricardou, for instance, is possibly the first, conducted many experiments
with those 'writing workshops', and was known for the rather authoritarian way in which he
controlled the participants' output.) Despite all its theories concerning the necessity of
breaking down the frontiers between authors and writers, the New Novel never managed in
practice to transform its readers into writers.

It would be an error, however, only to stress the differences between the New Novel and
the Oulipo. At the level of their theories and the works produced, the similarities were at
least as striking as the disparities. The most basic common element was probably the notion
of constraint, although the New Novelist version of the device was without any doubt less
systematic than in the case of the Oulipo (but at the level of the global construction of the
text, the great novels by Butor can easily compete with the most famous of all Oulipian
books: Perec's *La vie mode L'Emploi*, 1978). Recently, young authors and new groups have
appeared whose explicit programme is to pursue a kind of synthesis of the several achievements of the modernist innovations à la New Novel and the more playful inventions à la
Oulipo. The most interesting of these authors have gathered to the journal *Formules*
(subtitled: 'Journal of Literature under Constraint') and they continue the innovative
impulses given by the New Novel and the Oulipo, without being seduced to radicalize them,
in what has been for so many avant-garde movements of this century an iconoclastic dead
end. *Formules* and other related groups and journals are continuing the tradition of modernist
writing and thinking and may well breed the New Novelists and the Oulipians of tomorrow.

Jan Baetens

Further reading and works cited

Dällenbach, L. *Claude Simon*. Paris, 1988.
Formules. Paris, 1997–.
Higgins, L. A. *New Novel, New Wave, New Politics*. Lincoln, NE, 1996.
Mathews, H. and Brotchie, A. *The Oulipo Compendium*. London, 1998.
Oulipo. *La littérature potentielle*. Paris, 1973.
—. *Atlas de littérature potentielle*. Paris, 1981.
Ricardou, J. *Pour une théorie du nouveau roman*. Paris, 1971.
—. *Le Nouveau roman*. Paris, 1990.
Robbe-Grillet, A. *Pour un nouveau roman*. Paris, 1963.

52. *Tel Quel* (1960–1982)

As most commentators agree, *Tel Quel* has been more than a review, a journal, a simple periodical: if it fell short of creating a cultural 'revolution' or of launching a political movement, as its main contributors would have wished at the turn of the heady 1960s, it managed indeed to embody, sum up or allegorize a whole state of mind, in short to stand for what is now seen with nostalgia and fading awe as 'the age of theory'. In order to overcome endemic intolerance which can lead to sociological reductionism and systematic debunking (Niilo Kauppi), or to avoid at the other extreme a fascinated adulation ready to engage in intellectual contortions so as to justify the most staggering reversals and palinodes (Philippe Forest), it seems the best solution is to remain historical in a broad sense, to steer away from either juvenile enthusiasm or cynical disappointment. These preliminary remarks imply that *Tel Quel* continues to shock today (though not always for the same reasons), while providing one of the best introductions to the French cultural history of the 1960s and 1970s. Historicizing the review, one should neither monumentalize nor systematically deflate; one should, for instance, resist the temptation of reducing *Tel Quel* to having been a mere tool exploited by a clever and unscrupulous literary *arriviste* like Philippe Sollers. Through his identification with the periodical that he more or less dominated (he was the only founding member who always figured on its editorial board), Sollers allows a 're-reader' to perceive the review's rise to fame, its violent contradictions and slow moral collapse as historical and cultural symptoms, compromise formations that condense an entire *Zeitgeist*. Thus, to paraphrase Lacan, one could want to alliterate and speak of 'Sollers the Symptom'; however, even if Philippe Joyaux consciously strove after a Joycean identification, taking as his model a Joyce who for Lacan (then heavily influenced by *Tel Quel*) had become 'the Sinthome', and who for the whole group embodied a radical writing that would, allegedly, provide the best antidote against fascism, one might speak of the irreducible 'saintliness' of the main animator of the periodical – to the point of perversion. Even at the time of the review's latest metamorphosis, when it had finally exchanged Marx and Mao for Pope John Paul II, and replaced dialectical materialism by the mysteries of the true Church, Sollers, tired of being called the 'Pope of the avant-garde', could both announce the 'death of the avant-garde' and claim to belong to the 'avant-garde of the Pope'.

These chiasmic reversals point to the prevalence of forcefully politicized rhetorics in the editorial power games that gave a stamp to the review and lasted for two decades, from 1960 to 1982. The history of the magazine is complex in the sense that it seemed to accelerate as it reflected more and more adequately the acceleration of real history in France after the watershed constituted by May 1968. Let us then go back to the beginnings in order to try and understand how a literary review that originally appeared apolitical in the early 1960s could become ten years later the spearhead of French Maoism, and almost as suddenly, a few years later, begin denouncing Marxism as a repressive and terrorist ideology in the mid and late 1970s.

When a number of young writers united in 1957–9 with the wish to challenge the French literary scene, it was dominated by three rival formations: Sartre's defence of committed literature flirting with marxism coincided with an increased politicization brought about partly by his recent conflict with Camus; then there was what could be considered as a purely literary avant-garde with the practitioners of the *Nouveau Roman* (*New Novel*) that had gathered a number of excellent writers whose ambitions were not identical but who shared a similar dislike for ideological pronouncements: Robbe-Grillet, Nathalie Sarraute, Samuel Beckett and a few others were mainly published by the *éditions de Minuit*. Besides, the official organ of a high culture still under the shadow of Paul Valéry and André Gide was the *Nouvelle Revue Française*, a literary review then dominated by Jean Paulhan, who had imposed his rhetorical sense blended with tact and classical restraint. In a violent political context dominated by decolonization, by the dead-end of military conflicts in Vietnam and Algeria, Sartre remained the main enemy, the successful rival, solidly entrenched with his thriving review *Les Temps Modernes*; Robbe-Grillet's new novel extolled objectivity and intransitivity in the name of a scientific outlook that took objects as objects, and writing as its own medium, never a transparent glass – and it was clear that this was where the original sympathies of *Tel Quel* lay, without endorsing it completely. It was between these ideological formations that Philippe Sollers, Jean-Edern Hallier, Jean-René Huguenin and their friends learned to manoeuvre when they launched their own review in 1960, the very year Camus died. The only acknowledged writer in the group was Philippe Sollers whose first novel had attracted some attention. Sollers had published in 1958 at the age of twenty-two an elegant short autobiographical novel, *Une curieuse solitude*, that had had the distinction of being immediately praised both by François Mauriac, a Catholic and traditionalist writer, and Louis Aragon, a communist, formerly surrealist poet and novelist.

Tel Quel had chosen a different publisher than established literary institutions like Gallimard, the owner of *La Nouvelle Revue Française*, Le Seuil, known for its left-wing Catholic sympathies and its interest for the budding market for human sciences. Earlier in the 1950s, in a depressed context marked by the end of the war, Le Seuil had allowed Jean Cayrol (who was, like Sollers, from Bordeaux) to launch a literary magazine, *Ecrire*, so as to let 'young' and aspiring writers find an outlet. Many of the first contributors to *Tel Quel* had published pieces in *Ecrire* and Cayrol was initially associated with *Tel Quel*. The two main personalities who presided over the birth of the magazine were Jean-Edern Hallier and Philippe Sollers. Hallier was soon to fight with all his other partners, and to discredit himself through dubious political ventures. What had united these young talents was a close friendship with an older writer, a poet essentially, Francis Ponge, still relatively unknown at that time. Originally close to the *New Novel* school of writing, the main inflection brought about by *Tel Quel* as it started was a constant reference to the works of Ponge, whose texts have now ascended to canonical status and are generally thought to dominate French poetics after the war. Indeed, Sartre had already saluted Ponge's groundbreaking *Le Parti Pris des Choses* for its extraordinary closeness to 'things' in 1944, seeing in these minute 'descriptions' of the most banal objects the basis of a new literary 'phenomenology'. But Ponge, who always insisted upon a proud independence, was regretting his isolation (he could only get *Pour un Malherbe*, completed 1957, published in

1965). A fruitful alliance between an older and half-recognized poet and a bunch of very young and enthusiastic young men provided *Tel Quel* with its initial impetus. The very name of the review also called up another poet, Paul Valéry, who had chosen this title when he reprinted 'as such' his critical meditations just a few years before he died (Valéry 1966, 473–781). It was in fact by a more relevant reference to Nietzsche (re-read and filtered through Georges Bataille) that the review opened its first issue. Its epigraph took from Nietzsche a concept of the 'eternal return' underwriting a positive and joyous affirmation of life considered both 'as such' and as a spectacle, which bequeathed a particularly redoubtable hesitation in view of ulterior developments:

> I want the world and I want it AS IS [*Tel Quel*], I want it still, eternally, and I cry out, insatiably: encore! and not only for myself, but for the entire play and for the entire show; and not only for the entire show, but really for me, because I need the show – because the show makes me indispensable – because it needs me and I render it indispensable. (*Tel Quel*, 1, 1960, 1, cit. and trans. Kauppi 1994, 25)

If one has a look at the table of contents of the first issue, certain choices appear clearly: one finds the names of Francis Ponge twice (he opens and closes the issue, as if to insist upon a dominant role), Albert Camus is given a homage, while alongside Virginia Woolf, translated here, only Jean Cayrol and Claude Simon appear as older and recognized writers. In the second issue, Sollers publishes 'Seven propositions on Alain Robbe-Grillet', and in the following issues the names of Claude Ollier, Robert Pinget, Michel Butor, Nathalie Sarraute, Louis-René des Forêts recur. Although the links with the *New Novel* soon become looser, Jean Ricardou who enters in 1962 will soon specialize in rigorous examinations of the formal procedures of this school.

It is the original endorsement of the 'formalism' of the new novel that leads to the first departure: Jean-René Huguenin is forced to leave *Tel Quel* in June 1960, since he embraces a romanticism that radically condemns the 'technological' style of these writers. Mauriac will see in Huguenin a 'new Romantic' who remains traditionalist enough for his tastes, while Sollers and his friends opt for more and more radical departures. Indeed, Sollers's second novel, *Le Parc* – published in 1961 and soon crowned by the coveted Medicis prize – was seen as a not too slavish imitation of Robbe-Grillet. A general uproar greeted the prize, most conservative critics deploring that Sollers should dilapidate obvious literary gifts and fall under the domination of fashion, while a number of well-known writers insisted that this showed the way for a true literary avant-garde: Leiris, Gérard Genette, Louis-René des Forêts all praised the book. What is also noted with various emphasis, is the review's political neutrality at the time of violent protest against the Algerian war. Without qualifying it as a 'right-wing' review, it is clear that the early collusion between the New Novel and *Tel Quel* goes toward a refusal of political commitment. It looks as if this was the original sin that a subsequent radicalization wished to excuse.

New personalities soon were admitted to the committee: Jean-Louis Baudry, Michel Deguy (soon excluded), Marcelin Pleynet, Denis Roche, who all brought strong voices while questioning the very possibility of poetry. Pleynet, an original poet who soon embarked in a career as a successful art critic, remained Sollers's most faithful ally, while Roche played with panache the role of a 'negative poet' who declared that 'poetry is inadmissible and besides does not exist', while working as an astute literary editor at the Seuil. Soon two important critics and philosophers joined the group, Gérard Genette and Jean-Pierre Faye. Their presence contributed to the development of a serious critical outlook, especially when they were relayed by Roland Barthes who signed a number of important essays (as in no. 7, Fall 1961, or no. 16, Winter 1964). A general survey around the use and function of criticism was published in no. 14, Summer 1963, while the names of Bataille – who had just died and was a friend of Sollers – and Ezra Pound, translated and glossed by Roche, marked another type of opening to literary and philosophical experimentation. At the same time, the review was doubled by a series at the Seuil that became rapidly prestigious and issued books by Flaubert, Barthes, Boulez, Sanguinetti, Maurice and Denis Roche, and in 1965 a collection of essays by Russian formalists that became a major element in the global strategy of the review, before publishing Derrida and Kristeva.

In the mid-1960s, *Tel Quel* indeed appeared as a serious and unrivalled magazine aiming at disseminating the theory and practice of literary structuralism. Structuralism was then associated with a revised Russian Formalism, since the Parisian avant-garde had found new bearings when it perceived deep affinities with the Russian avant-garde that had been active in the 1920s. When Tzvetan Todorov presented the texts of the Russian avant-garde poets and critics, the names of Khlebnikov, Brik, Chlovski, Jakobson, Eikhenbaum were launched for the first time in French circles. Todorov, relayed by *Tel Quel*, put an end to the obscurity surrounding these authors and when Julia Kristeva arrived upon the scene just a little later, soon to be captivated by Sollers, she brought a similar expertise to the group: coming like Todorov directly from Bulgaria, she completed the formalist picture by adding new references to the semioticians of the Tartu school and to Mikhail Bakhtin, also totally unknown in France at the time. Not only is the history of the avant-garde sanctioned by reference to an older and very political movement, but also a very concrete proof was given that one could be a 'formalist' (that is, interest oneself in exploring the literariness and literality of poetic and novelistic languages) and a revolutionary at the same time. However, Kristeva did not dispel certain ambiguities, allowing some confusion to float (Medvedev and Bakhtin were not strictly distinguished at first, which created impossible mixtures between literary marxism and anti-Stalinian linguistics of heteroglossia, while Bakhtin's staunch opposition to formalism was never mentioned).

However, from *Théorie de la Littérature* – the collection of Russian formalist essays edited by Todorov in 1965 – to Julia Kristeva's *Séméiotiké* published in 1969 and taking up texts found in *Tel Quel* as early as 1967, a whole revolution had taken place in the field of literary semiotics, a revolution in which *Tel Quel* and its members played a dominant role. Moreover, when the review devoted a special issue to Antonin Artaud in 1965, it included for the first time a ground-breaking essay by a young philosopher, Jacques Derrida. Derrida's impact was immediately and deeply felt, and his name was called upon more and more frequently in the pages of the review. One can say that he introduced yet another revolution through a more philosophical questioning of the main presuppositions that underpinned structuralism. On the other hand, *Tel Quel* provided him with a tribune, a sounding board and a series of exciting invitations to engage with literary issues: the essay Derrida devoted to Mallarmé in 1969 came from a 'double session' at the informal but very successful *Tel Quel* reading groups called *Theoretical Study Groups*, while the entire essay entitled 'Dissemination' presented itself as a jumble of quotations taken from Philippe Sollers's *Nombres* (see Derrida 1991, 173–286, 289–366). Derrida had rightly identified in *Nombres* the utopia of a new 'textual novel' – soon to become the hallmark of *Tel Quel* – that is a series of resolutely 'experimental' texts half-way between poetry and prose, that did not represent anything but the very functioning of language, in the hope that by thus exhibiting its codes, cogs and wheels, the production of a new 'truth' would shatter dominant and repressive ideologies.

The best place to examine how this double revolution was achieved is the volume put together by Sollers and his friends in the Fall of 1968, entitled *Théorie d'ensemble* – a broad title that aims at creating the impression of a group similar to the surrealists, of a collective approach with a scientific slant. However, the volume highlights clearly the importance of three 'masters', Foucault, Barthes and Derrida, whose names are separated from all the other contributors to the review and whose essays appeared elsewhere. Foucault opens the volume with a reading of Robbe-Grillet whom he compares with Faye, Thibaudeau, Pleynet and Sollers. Barthes continues with a piece on *Drame*, Sollers's novel of 1965. Derrida introduces the concept of 'différance' and the unsigned introduction makes it clear that the 'general theory' should not be reduced to either formalism or structuralism. The key words that are proffered as so many new ruptures are *writing, text, the unconscious, history, work, trace, production, scene* (*Tel Quel*, 1968, 7; a good translation of the introductory presentation is to be found in ffrench and Lack, 1998, 21–4). Each of the main theoreticians convoked has brought a new contribution – taken to be a 'definitive' revelation – to the global problematics. Foucault is credited with the idea that texts are not representative but productive; Barthes has demonstrated how writing 'scans history' and decentres it; Derrida has shown that writing can no longer be inscribed within the category of truth (ffrench and Lack 1998, 22–3). Based upon this significant convergence, a fourfold programme posited the need 'to unleash a movement . . .; to elaborate concepts . . .; to unfold a history/histories . . .; to articulate a politics logically linked to a non-representational dynamics of writing . . .' (ffrench and Lack 1998, 23). The last point concerns the clear admission that the politics of the review is linked with the construction of historical materialism and dialectical materialism, and that two other important 'masters' are Lacan and Althusser. The programme indicates the need to go back to a first 'break' in history, not stopping at the avant-garde of the 1920s (defined by surrealism, formalism, structural linguistics) but rethinking the four emblematic names of Lautréamont, Mallarmé, Marx and Freud – whose main 'discoveries', put together, roughly date from the middle of the nineteenth century. If the writer's names can change from year to year or from issue to issue, for some time this provides the basic formula upon which the review will endlessly improvise. The systematic trope of *Tel Quel* becomes the linking of writers noted for their formal experiments or unorthodox and innovative writing (they may include Dante, Pound, Woolf, Céline, Joyce, Beckett, Bataille, Artaud) with the names of Marx and Freud (for a time complemented by those of Lenin and Mao). 'Theory' understood in this way hesitates between a radical philosophical questioning of literary concepts and a more etymological sense of a 'list' or 'procession' of tutelary figures ritually invoked. Quite often, the references to Althusser and Lacan function as shortcuts for what should read like 'the real thought' of Marx and Freud – Marx 'after' the epistemological break with Hegel and idealism, Freud without the biological naturalism of 'instincts' but in possession of an equation between the Unconscious and language.

The distribution of the contributors reveals a subtle hierarchy: Sollers, Pleynet and Baudry publish four pieces; Houdebine, Kristeva and Ricardou two essays; and Jean-Joseph Goux, Denis Roche, Pierre Rottenberg, Jacqueline Risset, Jean Thibaudeau, only one essay. The overall quality of these pieces is good, and they still make fascinating reading today, if one discards some tics like the recurrent claim of being 'scientific' or the use of 'production' as a generic key term. Some of the best essays are those that link close readings and theories of literature (Ricardou on Poe, Baudry on Freud, Pleynet on Sade or Sue) or those that start from their own texts to provide a key (like Pleynet and Roche about Roche's scandalous and paradoxical anti-poetry and anti-poetics).

The combination of Saussure, re-read by Derrida, of Marx, re-read by Althusser, and of Freud, re-read by Lacan, provides the fundamental trilogy that maps out the world of knowledge and literature. This eventually will lead Goux to a wholesale systematization of the theories of Lacan, Althusser and Derrida when he points out an equivalence between money in capitalism, the phallus in psychoanalysis and the master-signifier in the production and circulation of language. Such syntheses attract to the 'general Telquelian theory' the reproach of hasty assimilation founded upon mere homologies – as if the truth of a capitalism that has yielded the formula of money as the 'general equivalent' had also provided a universal key for the theorization of the avant-garde! However, the need to move beyond a purely structuralist grid forces some authors to look for other names. Thus Kristeva uses a mathematical logic inspired by the Tartu school of semiotics in Estonia, she discusses Saumjan with Chomsky and Greimas, and refers to Peirce, Hegel or Husserl.

Roland Barthes was perhaps the first major critic who publicly acknowledged the fact that *Tel Quel* had brought about a major change not only to the writing of literary theory but to the very conception of literature – the two tending to blend together more and more. One can witness how in the texts he publishes in the late 1960s, the references to Kristeva (who had been his student) become systematic and deferential. New concepts such as intertextuality, the couple genotext/phenotext, the notion of signifying practice, of 'signifiance' opposed to 'signification', the idea of an infinite productivity identified with a 'text' that is strongly delineated from the 'work' mark for Barthes a shift from a purely 'scientific' (and slightly boring) approach to systems of signs to a new problematic in which dynamism, productivity and infinity are constantly invoked. Barthes's wonderful *S/Z* (also published in the *Tel Quel* series in 1970) manages to let the two semiotics coexist side by side. Certain writers would protest, this time less in the name of traditional values than in the name of scientific rigour. Thus in a scathing attack, Jacques Roubaud and Philippe Lusson use their first-hand knowledge of mathematics and logic to demonstrate that most of the logical formulas used by Kristeva in her first book are redundant or contradictory: they either underline decoratively what has been expressed in plain language or mix up incompatible systems of formalization (Roubaud and Lusson 1969, 56–61; 1970, 31–6).

But this attack corresponds to a more troubled period linked with the many splits and struggles that marked the end of the 1960s: the break-up between Sollers and Jean-Pierre Faye, the only intellectual and writer whose stature was equal to Sollers's, in 1967 led Faye to launch the rival magazine *Change* – also published by Le Seuil! – whose very name intends to contradict *Tel Quel* and its implied acceptance of things as they are. On the other hand, a review like *Poétique* founded by three eminent former collaborators of *Tel Quel* (Genette, Todorov and Cixous) aims less at cultural critique than at prolonging a serious and more academic investigation of the theory and practice of literature. This and the often paradoxical politicization of the review – they became close allies of the French Communist Party just before May 1968, which led most *Tel Quel* members to keep their distance from a movement considered to be too enthusiastic, dadaist and playful, while the same insistence on radical breaks and dogmatic righteousness led them to become Maoist in 1971 – at a time when pre- and post-68 surrealism is denounced as idealist and Hegelian. Curiously, if the review lost its appeal for many intellectuals upset by its lack of 'seriousness' and its modishness, it increased its publication, and most special issues reached more than

20,000 copies (whereas the usual run would have been between 3,000 and 5,000 before). The fascination for China led Sollers, Kristeva and their friends to a real effort at documentation, but their fatal mistake was to take a group trip to China in the spring of 1974 (Sollers and Kristeva went with Pleynet, Barthes and Wahl) to confront their dream with reality. Even if Kristeva brought back a beautiful book about *Chinese Women*, disillusionment and dissatisfaction with the Chinese utopia was soon to creep in, and the Chinese reference was dropped. In the winter of 1976, Houdebine denounced the dead-end of language in marxism while Sollers accused Maoism of being a mere return to Stalinism (a point that had not escaped earlier observers of the cultural revolution). In spite of its often shrill insistence on the necessary link between politics and literature, the review often evinced a great political naivety, while showing amazing skills at literary tactics of self-promotion.

The year 1976 brought about a last reversal in alliances: the review suddenly opened its pages to a group of writers who called themselves 'new philosophers' and had launched a wholesale attack not just on Stalinism but on Marx, up to then sacrosanct. Marx was suddenly accused of having generated all the subsequent totalitarian deviations produced in his name. Alexander Soljenitsyn, Iossif Brodksi, Andrei Siniaski, André Glucksmann, Bernard-Henri Lévy and Maria-Antonietta Macciocchi appear as main allies in a fight that aims at exposing marxism as the worst alienation of the century. Sollers starts opening each issue with passages from his work-in-progress *Paradis*, an interesting experimental 'text' blending the oral style of the late Céline and an unpunctuated monologue similar to Molly's monologue at the end of *Ulysses*. As if he felt compelled to always espouse the latest trends, Sollers allows himself to be fascinated by the new philosophers' return to religion – either as the Jewish foundation rediscovered by Levy, or as a more 'perverse' or 'baroque' Catholicism that might have been there all the time, after all, in Lacan. The former 'enemy' constituted by the US is now rediscovered as the place of a new utopia in a special issue devoted to the USA (nos. 71–3, Fall 1977). Hoffman, Corso, Ashberry and Roth are selected among the new important influences, while Joyce – to whom many excellent special issues had been devoted – is praised for blending 'obscenity and theology' (Special Joyce issue, no. 83, Spring 1980).

However, around 1980, it became clear that the review had lost its impetus and its impact on French culture. Its main ideas had been fully taken up by academic discourse, while the denunciation of totalitarian ideology seemed more forceful among right-wing magazines. Sollers stood out as the main puppet-master of a moribund avant-garde that had lost all confidence in its master-signifiers, and when he quarrelled with François Wahl, the editor at Seuil, who objected to the publication of *Women* (1983) because it contained a transparent satire of the intellectual milieu they had frequented, with vitriolic portraits of Cixous, Lacan, Althusser, Barthes, Derrida and some famous feminist theoreticians, the review needed to be reinvented. Sollers and Pleynet moved to Gallimard (through Denoeël at first) to found *L'Infini*. Another story had begun for the Parisian avant-garde. Le Seuil, which had intelligently speculated on the rise of the 'human sciences', was to conclude with a new disaffection for high theory. Sartre, Barthes and Lacan had died, soon followed by Althusser and Foucault. In retrospect, facing the work accomplished by *Tel Quel*, it was Sollers himself who meted out both enduring praise and damning accusation. In *Women*, a writer who is a friend of 'S' or Sollers reminisces on the crucial cultural function played by *Tel Quel*. He remembers his difficulties with Boris (an alias for Jean-Edern Hallier) at the time of the foundation of the review during the Algerian war: 'When they started their little avant-garde revue ... Which is now, thanks to S'.s grim perseverance, a kind of international institution ... It has published the best work of Werth, Lutz, Fals, and many others ... Established their reputation' (Sollers 1990, 320). These transparent pseudonyms allude to Barthes, Althusser and Lacan: even if one notes some exaggeration, which after all conforms to the model of a review that indeed became an 'institution', the assessment carries weight. *Tel Quel* managed to change durably the rapport between literature and theory, while allowing a few literary and critical landmarks to be published (besides essays by Barthes and Derrida, one can think of Maurice Roche's *Compact* (1966), subsequently rediscovered by a younger and different avant-garde). On the other hand, the judgement can turn pointedly ambivalent; but here again, the strictest caviller's abuse has been anticipated: when S is asked by Boris to write a puff for his (Boris's) latest book, he replies, in a tongue-in-cheek commendation that can rebound to its originator: '... I've got a good title for an article about you: *In praise of imposture* ... In an ultrafalse world, only the height of falsehood can tell the truth about falsehood ... You get the idea'. Like most of us who 'get the idea', Boris pretends not to see the irony and just answers: 'Splendid! Write it!' (Sollers 1990, 319).

Jean-Michel Rabaté

Further reading and works cited

Barthes, R. *Writer Sollers*. Minneapolis, MN, 1987.
Benoist, J.-M. *The Structural Revolution*. London, 1978.
Derrida, J. *Writing and Difference*. Chicago, 1978.
—. *Dissemination*. Chicago, 1991.
ffrench, P. *The Time of Theory*. Oxford, 1996.
— (ed.) *From Tel Quel to L'Infini*. London, 1998.
— and Lack, R.-F. (eds) *The Tel Quel Reader*. London, 1998.
Fletcher, J. and Benjamin, A. (eds) *Abjection, Melancholia and Love*. New York, 1990.
Forest, P. *Histoire de Tel Quel*. Paris, 1995.
Goux, J.-J. *The Coiners of Language*. Norman, OK, 1994.
Kauppi, N. *The Making of an Avant-Garde*. Berlin, 1994.
Kristeva, J. *Séméiotiké: Recherches pour une Sémanalyse*. Paris, 1969.
—. *La Révolution du Language poétique*. Paris, 1974.
—. *About Chinese Women*. London, 1977.
Pleynet, M. *Painting and System*. Chicago, 1984.
Reader, K. *Intellectuals and the Left in France since 1968*. Manchester, 1993.
Roche, M. *Compact*. New York, 1988.
Roubaud, J. and Lusson, P. 'Sur la "sémiologie des paragrammes" de Julia Kristeva', *Action Poétique*, 41–2 (1969) and 45 (1970).
Roudinesco, E. *Jacques Lacan and Co.* New York, 1990.
Sollers, P. *Women*. New York, 1990.
Tel Quel. *Théorie d'Ensemble*. Paris, 1968.
Valéry, P. 'Tel Quel', in *Oeuvres vol. 2*, ed. Jean Hytier. Paris, 1966.

53. Other French Feminisms: Sarah Kofman (1934–1994), Monique Wittig (1935–), Michèle Le Doeuff (1948–)

The 'Mouvement de Libération des Femmes' (MLF), whose name was first coined by the French press and then taken up by French feminists, comprised a shifting array of women's groups that formed in the aftermath of the student and worker movement of May 1968. Almost from its inception, the movement was characterized by fierce differences of opinion, both ideological and pragmatic. Central areas of debate included whether and how to reconcile psychoanalytic and marxist/materialist analyses; the question of sexual difference and women's sexuality; whether and how lesbians and heterosexual women should work together; whether to be 'anonymous, underground, like moles' (cit. Duchen 1986, 17) as the group 'politique and psychanalyse' ('po et psych') wished, or to draw attention via spectacular and witty demonstrations, as the 'Féministes Révolutionnaires' desired; and how to understand the relation between women and language.

The three main currents in the nascent MLF were class-struggle feminism, materialist or radical feminism and psychoanalytic feminism. While marxist/materialist analyses were central to all three approaches, by 1970 many of the women in the MLF were not involved with either socialist or communist party politics; those who were belonged to the 'class-struggle' tendency in the MLF. Class-struggle feminists were active in organized leftist politics but had grown dissatisfied with their parties' stances on women; they strove to reconcile their commitments to feminism and to Leftist politics, as the slogan 'No socialism without women's liberation; no women's liberation without socialism' suggests (Duchen 1986, 27).

Materialist or radical feminists saw women as a class and sexual difference as the effect, not the cause, of women's oppression. Arguing against the idea that sex has a natural or biological essence prior to or outside of culture, they rejected as 'biologism' the notion of an innate feminine specificity or difference. Materialist feminism was closely associated with the 'Féministes Révolutionnaires,' a group that counted Christine Delphy, Colette Guillaumin, Monique Plaza and Monique Wittig among its members; these theorists saw themselves as Simone de Beauvoir's ideological heirs, and the author of *The Second Sex* was one of the founders of the group's journal, *Questions Féministes*.

Psychoanalytic feminists, who made up the third principle tendency in the MLF, drew on Freudian and Lacanian theoretical frameworks and deconstruction. Focusing their analyses on the body, unconscious processes and repression, they theorized feminine specificity and difference by first reversing the male/female hierarchy and then exploding it by calling hierarchical thinking itself into question. Psychoanalytic feminism was popularly affiliated with the group 'politique et psychanalyse'. (Originally named 'Psychanalyse and Politique', the group reversed the order of its concerns and dropped the name's capitals to reflect a shift in its priorities.) Led by analyst Antoinette Fouque, who rejected the term 'feminist' on the grounds that 'feminists are a bourgeois avant-garde that maintains, in an inverted form, the dominant values' (cit. Marks and de Courtivron 1980, 117), the group at one time or another included Hélène Cixous, Luce Irigaray and Julia Kristeva. Another current of psychoanalytic feminism was made up of practitioners of *écriture féminine*, writing grounded in the female body and shaped by women's corporeal specificity: the breasts, the womb, the labia. Writers associated with *écriture féminine* include Chantal Chawaf, Hélène Cixous, Marguerite Duras, Madeleine Gagnon, Xavière Gauthier, Claudine Herrmann and Annie Leclerc.

The fact that some practitioners of *écriture féminine*, like Leclerc, were more concerned to reverse hierarchies that devalued women than to challenge hierarchical thinking, rejecting or ignoring deconstruction, while others, like Cixous, were greatly influenced by deconstruction demonstrates the danger of oversimplifying divisions within French feminist schools of thought. Thus the three broad categories into which I have divided the MLF should not be taken to denote simple or rigid partitions; in actuality, each current comprised multiple groups whose complicated alliances and allegiances render any neat taxonomy misleading. Women frequently belonged to, or attended the meetings of groups belonging to, more than one current, demonstrating that the positions staked out were neither as exclusive nor as comprehensive as some *post hoc* summaries have suggested.

Moreover, the various currents of the MLF shared important ideas and interests. Antoinette Fouque of 'po et psych' asserted that the group's 'top priority was given to making connections between two "discourses": psychoanalytic discourse and historical materialism' (cit. Marks and de Courtivron 1980, 117). Monique Wittig, for a time the spokesperson for 'Féministes Révolutionnaires', argued that materialist feminism 'must undertake the task of defining the individual subject in materialist terms' (1992, 19), and the class-struggle feminists sought to reconcile feminism and socialism.

In spite of these shared concerns and the fact that women moved from group to group and worked simultaneously with more than one group (Duchen 1987, 14), the MLF recorded its share of conflicts. Setting themselves against all 'isms', members of 'po et psych' demonstrated on International Women's Day with signs proclaiming 'Down with feminism!' (Moi 1987, 3) and enraged the rest of the MLF in 1979 by trademarking the name 'MLF' for their publishing house, 'des femmes' and suing those who challenged their exclusive right to the name 'Mouvement de Libération des Femmes.'

A less spectacular but more enduring point of contention has been the question of sexual difference. Annie Leclerc's *Parole de Femme* (*Woman's Word*) was an early celebration of a feminine difference grounded in corporeal specificity: 'I must talk about the pleasures of my body ... only by talking about it will a new language be born, a woman's word' (cit. Duchen 1987, 60). Leclerc invoked difference to assert women's superiority over men, but other psychoanalytic feminists, influenced by deconstruction, reversed the hierarchy in order to interrogate it. Rather than simply valorizing women, they variously theorized women's exclusion from a monosexual ('hom[m]osexual') economy (Irigaray); posited femininity as a principle of disruption or excess (Kristeva); or postulated a feminine bisexuality that does not fuse masculinity and femininity (cancelling out sexual difference), but oscillates between them (Kofman).

In contrast, the materialist feminist editorial collective of *Questions Féministes* (QF) derided both celebrations of and inquiries into women's difference as 'neo-femininity', arguing that 'it is the patriarchal system which posits that we are "different" in order to justify and conceal our exploitation. It is the patriarchal system which prescribes the idea of a feminine "nature" and "essence" ' (cit. Marks and de Courtivron 1980, 214). Seeing both women and men as classes the former of which is oppressed by the latter, they had no patience with what they saw as neo-feminism's complicity with myths that serve to naturalize cultural oppression. Thus Christine Delphy, one of QF's founders, responded to Leclerc's celebration of the female body by insisting that 'it is essential to recognize that the meaning of periods, for instance, is not *given* with and by the flow of blood, but like *all* meaning, by consciousness and thus by society' (1984, 195). Rather than attending to that which is specific to femininity – that which, 'po et psych' argued, has been repressed – they sought the end of the categories of sex, man and woman, which they saw as the result of oppression. Carefully distinguishing corporeal differences from the meanings with which such differences have been invested, materialist feminists attacked the notion of sexual difference on several fronts: by arguing that to see difference as natural or essential/biological is to make it appear inevitable and unchangeable, effectively rendering feminists' struggle against oppression moot (Delphy); by insisting on an analysis of difference in its material manifestations, as a historical rather than an essential phenomenon (Delphy, Colette Guillaumin); and by contending that empirical differences grew out of and were synonymous with women's oppression (Guillaumin, Wittig).

Ideological and pragmatic differences not only divided different currents in the MLF from one another but created internal dissension, as well. The majority of the 'class struggle' groups broke up, as some members moved away from organized leftist politics while others retained close ties to party organizations. Many women left 'po et psych', disillusioned with its leader; 'anyone who could no longer accept the group's "line" had to go,' asserted Anne Tristan (cit. Moi 1987, 53). QF and 'Féministes Révolutionnaires' foundered after the publication of two articles, Monique Wittig's 'The Straight Mind' and Emmanuèle de Lesseps' 'Hétérosexualité et Féminisme' ('Heterosexuality and Feminism'). The pieces crystallized the editorial collective's differences by offering opposing answers to the question of whether heterosexuality was compatible with feminism. The ensuing debate prompted the group to separate into the radical feminists and the political (or radical) lesbians.

As the preceding account of common projects and lively disagreements attests, 'French feminism' encompasses more than the work of Cixous, Irigaray and Kristeva. These writers' dominance has tended to obscure other currents of French feminist thought by pre-empting considerations of writers whose work criticizes or differs in its focus from these three women's critical projects; their ubiquity in accounts of French feminist thought has created an incomplete picture of the range of positions taken by feminists in France (among whom I include, albeit with reservations, theorists like Cixous who have disclaimed the name 'feminist' but concern themselves with questions of sexual difference and women's oppression and/or repression). Examining the work of other feminists allows for a more comprehensive understanding of French feminisms in the last quarter of the twentieth century.

Monique Wittig (1935–)

A materialist feminist, Monique Wittig sees women as a class constituted by economic, political and social operations and forcefully negates the notion of women's essential difference, which she argues merely masks the material conditions of women's oppression. Empirical differences between the sexes, in Wittig's analysis, are the result of that oppression, growing out of the hierarchical sex classes that organize and differentiate men and women. Her writings, both literary and critical, seek to distinguish 'woman' the myth from 'women' the social products of a political and economic system based on sex class exploitation. As one of the theorists whose writing gave materialist feminism shape, Wittig helped to define its goal of abolishing sex classes, a goal which grows out of her belief that only then will women cease to be oppressed.

In addition to destroying the categories 'man' and 'woman', Wittig aims to theorize the social basis of 'so-called personal problems' without losing sight of 'the question of the subject of each singular woman – not the myth, but each one of us' (1992, 19). Materialist feminism's task, she argues, is simultaneously to renovate and to conjoin historical materialism and a theory of subjectivity. She faults marxism for effectively naturalizing sexual difference and its categories, man and woman, and thus failing to consider women as a class. At the same time, she rejects psychoanalytic models of the subject as totalizing and ahistorical, deploring a paradigm in which 'human beings are given as invariants, untouched by history and unworked by class conflicts, with identical psyches because genetically programmed' (1992, 22).

In lesbianism, Wittig argued, radical feminism found an ideal strategy; it was both a political choice and the only rational choice for those seeking to destroy a regime of sexual difference governed by the logic of a mandatory heterosexuality whose tenet was 'you-will-be-straight-or-you-will-not-be' (Wittig 1992, 28). Arguing that both lesbianism and heterosexuality were not sexualities but political regimes, Wittig concluded that choosing lesbianism was one way to work towards the destruction of the sex classes that grew out of oppression; perhaps her most famous statement is the claim that 'lesbians are not women' (1992, 32). Rather, for Wittig, lesbians are escapees from their class, existing outside of the mutually dependent categories 'man' and 'woman'. In this sense, Wittig's lesbian is reminiscent of Cixous's or Kristeva's woman, in so far as each is marked by an inability to be contained by her excess.

Language is central to Wittig's analyses, and here she again differentiates herself from psychoanalytic feminism by taking a characteristically materialist approach. Arguing that language enforces gender by requiring those who would be subjects to assume a gender, Wittig argues that our sense of ourselves as subjects depends on our position in language, which is marked by personal pronouns. Uninflected by gender (except in French's third person plural, *ils/elles*), personal pronouns nevertheless 'support the notion of gender while ... seem[ing] to fulfill another function' (1992, 79) because they require past participles and adjectives to reflect a speaker's gender. Thus, when women use language, they are simultaneously empowered and disempowered: 'no woman can say "I" without being for herself a total subject – that is, ungendered, universal, whole ... But gender ... works upon this ontological fact to annul it as far as women are concerned and corresponds to a constant attempt to strip them of the most precious thing for a human being – subjectivity' (1992, 80–1).

Wittig reads the material effects of language on subjectivity as offering opportunity as well as constraint; her fiction is both a meditation and an operation on personal pronouns, which she claimed as 'the subject matter' of her first three books (1992, 82), *The Opoponax*, *Les Guérillères* and *The Lesbian Body*. In each, she recontextualizes a different pronoun ('one', *elles* and 'I' [*j/e*], respectively) to create a textual universe from which sex classes have been banished. It is her contention that, via such experimentation, literature becomes 'a war machine' (1992, 68) capable of destroying old modes of thought and inaugurating new ones. This capacity, she asserts, is what distinguishes her formal innovations from both conventional literature with a political or social agenda and *écriture féminine*. Although her emphasis on the transformative effects of finding/making a new language is reminiscent of the claims of practitioners of *écriture féminine*, Wittig insists that the two genres against which she defines her literary experimentation remain mired in the myths and stereotypes of heterosexuality, while her work imagines a world unencumbered by sex classes. Wittig's work as a writer of fiction, political theory and social criticism can thus be seen as uniformly marked by her commitment to materialist/lesbian feminism.

Michèle Le Doeuff (1948–)

Michèle Le Doeuff interrogates philosophy's history in order to address some of the discipline's central issues. In readings of Bacon, Descartes, Husserl, Kant, More, de Beauvoir and Sartre, Le Doeuff writes about the nature of the self, the relation between philosophy and ethics, utopianism and the role women – or rather 'woman' – has played in philosophy's conception of itself. Analysing the use philosophers have made of imagery, Le Doeuff investigates a paradox: on the one hand, philosophy dismisses 'thinking in images' (1989, 2) as both incidental to philosophical texts and antithetical to philosophy's commitment to rational thought; on the other hand, philosophical texts depend upon imagery to mask the gaps and inconsistencies in their theoretical projects. In *Recherches sur l'imaginaire philosophique* (translated as *The Philosophical Imaginary*), a collection of seven loosely interrelated essays, Le Doeuff argues for a philosophical discourse that will have relinquished its commitment to the closure of complete knowledge, a discipline more open to the inevitable failure to provide full and final answers and thus less anxious to disguise its inadequacies. Her argument works by first inverting and then calling in question the hierarchical binaries image/knowledge and myth/reason. Showing how imagery which philosophical texts would dismiss as peripheral in fact 'copes with problems posed by the theoretical enterprise itself' (1989, 5), she draws on deconstructive and psychoanalytic techniques to foreground that which has been ignored or elided and insists that thought in images and 'pure' reason are inextricably intertwined.

'The ultimate implication of my conception of the philosophical imaginary', writes Le Doeuff, is that 'it is in the administration of its own legitimacy, the establishment of its own value, that philosophy is drawn into defining and designing its own myths' (1989, 170 fn.4). One myth with which Le Doeuff occupies herself is philosophy's self-proclaimed role as arbiter of knowledge across disciplines. Its claim to this position is grounded in philosophy's endeavour to construct a complete theory of knowledge, an endeavour that also produces the discipline's theoretical bind, for an epistemology that presents itself as all-encompassing will necessarily be haunted by a fear of lacunae. Philosophy's recourse to 'thinking in images', Le Doeuff argues, eases this bind by permitting a text to supplement its rational arguments with imagery that bolsters those claims it cannot otherwise support.

In Le Doeuff's analysis, women's relation to philosophy, like that of thought in images, seems extrinsic but is in fact indispensable to the discipline's self-conception. She examines this relationship in a number of articles, as well as in both *Recherches sur l'imaginaire philosophique* and *L'Étude et le rouet* (translated as *Hipparchia's Choice*), the latter of which also experiments with form, taking the shape of four 'notebooks'. Contending that an iconography of 'woman' is central to philosophy's myths, Le Doeuff asserts that one of its functions is to guarantee philosophy's explanatory status and the philosopher's position as one who knows by relegating women to a domain outside of philosophy's realm of logic. However, in discussing women's access (or lack thereof) to philosophy, Le Doeuff argues that their exclusion has not historically been a matter of simple absence, since there have always been women philosophers; while she does not deny that many women have been prohibited from practising philosophy, she focuses instead on the way in which 'permissiveness is a sly form of prohibition' (1989, 103).

Female philosophers from Heloise to Simone de Beauvoir have approached philosophy via an apprenticeship with a male teacher – an apprenticeship that, Le Doeuff argues, gave these women access only to the school of thought espoused by one teacher, rather than to the field of philosophy as a whole. The difference, she contends, is that between the amateur, whose relation is unmediated by the context of an academic institution, and the professional trained by teachers who are part of an institution. While professional students are not immune to the transference relationship Le Doeuff ascribes to amateur women philosophers, the former enjoy a different relation to philosophy as a field. But if women are not well served by their amateur status, Le Doeuff suggests that their teachers are dependent on it, for the pupils' reverence allows the masters to forget that their theoretical projects are (always, inevitably) incomplete. These students thus serve the function of non-knowers who invest philosophers with the power of those presumed to know, banishing the masters' anxiety and offering a way to negotiate the bind described above.

Le Doeuff's approach to philosophy is in some ways reminiscent of Irigaray's reading of psychoanalysis, in so far as both women use the techniques of their respective disciplines to critique those disciplines ('a practical application of philosophy is necessary in order to oust and unmask the alienating schemas which philosophy has produced' (1989, 101), writes Le Doeuff). But while both writers insist on the need to transform their fields, Le Doeuff promotes pragmatic renovation via traditional scholarly work, steering clear of Irigaray's more revolutionary interest in jamming or disrupting a system of thought (1985, 68–85). Arguing that a feminism of difference is viable only if its practitioners do not dismiss the western philosophical tradition as a masculine mode of thought, Le Doeuff instead seeks to transform philosophy from within.

Sarah Kofman (1934–1994)

Sarah Kofman, a philosopher, has published more than twenty-five books on Comte, Kant, Rousseau, Freud, Nietzsche, Marx, Derrida and Blanchot, among others. Her wide-ranging interests include aesthetics, literary criticism, philosophy, Freudian psychoanalysis and autobiography. Kofman served for more than twenty years as an editor of the *Philosophie en effet* series, along with Derrida, Jean-Luc Nancy and Philippe Lacoue-Labarthe, and deconstruction's influence on her work is manifest. Honing in on moments of contradiction, reduction or aporia, Kofman's readings seek to keep multiple meanings in play at once; her texts eschew the closure of certainty, reversing traditional hierarchies and calling hierarchy itself into question. At the same time, Kofman's critical methodology, with its attention to both the letter of the text and its silences, owes as much to psychoanalysis as to deconstruction.

Reading symptomatically, Kofman positions herself as analyst even as she resists simply diagnosing her subjects. Applying Freud's interpretive techniques to his texts, Kofman presents herself as more faithful to Freud's theories than Freud himself. She attends to what his summaries and interpretations ignore or elide, focuses on moments when Freud short-changes his own critical method, and analyses his sexual economy. The task Kofman set herself was to identify the workings of sexuality and the question of sexual difference in texts that did not always manifest the full measure of their author's convictions – 'pushing', as she put it, 'the Freudian interpretation to its limits, in the most faithful way possible' (1991, 1). In readings of philosophers ranging from Comte to Kant to Rousseau, Kofman adopts a similar strategy. Here, however, Kofman is, as one critic puts it, 'reintroducing sexuality, and thereby the question of sexual difference, in what she calls the "economy" of a thought that claims to remain pure' (Duroux 1999, 138), whereas with Freud there can never have been any question of 'a thought that claims to remain pure.'

If Kofman's debts to psychoanalysis and deconstruction are clear, the influence of feminism in her work is less readily apparent. But while she rejected the notion of a specifically feminine discourse such as *écriture féminine* and neither worked on women philosophers nor participated in the MLF, she herself believed that her status as a woman philosopher and the fact that she wrote made her a feminist. Moreover, both the attention peripheral female figures, especially mothers, receive in her work and her penchant for questioning and analysing binary oppositions such as man/woman, reason/emotion aligns her with deconstructive feminism. Like Le Doeuff, she analyses images of women in the texts of major philosophers, showing how figures of femininity stand for unreason even as such figures expose flaws in the reasoning of the texts in which they appear.

Many critics have read Kofman's second book on Freud, 1980's *The Enigma of Woman*, as a revision of Irigaray's 1974 *Speculum of the Other Woman*, also a rereading of Freud's theory of femininity. The two analyses share both a subject and a deconstructive and psychoanalytic approach to Freud's writing, but Kofman faults Irigaray for misrepresenting Freud, relying on a sloppy translation, and subordinating critical honesty to 'the cause', while maintaining that her criticism does not stem from any wish to 'save' Freud at all costs ('I am no more likely to "save" him than [Irigaray] is' (1985, 14 fn.6), she insists). Kofman's critique of Irigaray is grounded in the notion that faithfulness to the text constitutes 'the minimal intellectual honesty that consists in criticizing an author in terms of what he has said rather than what someone has managed to have him say' (1985, 14 fn.6). But while Irigaray psychoanalyses Freud's texts, Kofman goes further; here as elsewhere in her writing she rejects any rigid distinction between the text and the life, psychoanalysing the author as well as his writings. (In doing so, she parts company with Le Doeuff, who argues that 'where texts are concerned, doubtless the only tenable "psychoanalysis" is that of the reader' (1986, 173 fn.22).)

Although Kofman rejects the notion that writers' lives explain their work in any simple way, she sees an author's life as itself a kind of text and reads her subjects' biographies and their theoretical projects intertextually, deconstructing the opposition between an author's life and work. 'Isn't it an illusion to believe I have any autobiography other than that which emerges from my bibliography?' she asks (1986, 7). Kofman's own biography complicates this question, for in 1994, shortly after publishing the autobiographical *Rue Ordener, rue Labat*, which describes hiding in Paris after her father's deportation and death at Auschwitz, Kofman committed suicide at the age of 65. It seems fitting, then, that Kofman's writing both invites us to analyse her life and work intertextually and warns us against a reductive reading that would purport to 'explain' the latter via the former.

Nicole Fluhr

Further reading and works cited

Berg, E. 'The Third Woman', *diacritics*, 12, 2, Summer 1982.

Delphy, C. *Close to Home*, ed. D. Leonard. London, 1984.

Deutscher, M. (ed.) *Michèle Le Doeuff*. Amherst, MA, 2000.

Deutscher, P. and Oliver, K. (eds) *Enigmas*. Ithaca, NY, 1999.

Duchen, C. *Feminism in France*. London, 1986.

— (ed.) *French Connections*. London, 1987.

Duroux, F. 'How a Woman Philosophizes', in *Enigmas: Essays on Sarah Kofman*, eds P. Deutscher and K. Oliver. Ithaca, NY, 1999.

Gelfand, E. D. and Thorndike Hules, V. (eds) *French Feminist Criticism: Women, Language and Literature, An Annotated Bibliography*. New York, 1985.

Irigaray, L. *This Sex Which Is Not One*. Ithaca, NY, 1985.

Kofman, S. *The Enigma of Woman: Woman in Freud's Writings*. Ithaca, NY, 1985.

—. 'Apprendre aux hommes à tenir parole', interview with R. Jaccard, *Le Monde*, 27–28, April 1986.

—. *The Childhood of Art*. New York, 1988.

—. *Freud and Fiction*. Boston, 1991.

—. *Nietzsche and Metaphor*. London, 1993.

—. *Smothered Words*. Evanston, IL, 1998.

Le Doeuff, M. *The Philosophical Imaginary*. London, 1986.

—. *Hipparchia's Choice*. Oxford, 1991.

Leonard, D. and Adkins L. (eds) *Sex in Question*. London, 1996.

Marks, E. and de Courtivron, I. (eds) *New French Feminisms*. New York, 1981.

Moi, T. (ed.) *French Feminist Thought*. New York, 1987.

Wittig, M. *Les Guérrillères*. New York, 1973.

—. *The Straight Mind and Other Essays*. Boston, 1992.

— and Zeig, S. *Lesbian Peoples*. New York, 1979.

54. Psychoanalytic Literary Criticism in France

From its inception psychoanalysis has shown a keen regard for literature in whose realm it has often sought to develop its own unique positions on the unconscious motivation of both normal and pathological human behaviour. Freud also created a 'rhetoric' of the unconscious in *The Interpretation of Dreams* (1900), drawing on linguistic and stylistic devices characteristic of western literature since antiquity. Not unlike Freudian theory itself, French criticism of the past sixty years has wavered between two complementary yet also contradictory approaches: the study of depth psychology and the procedures of symptom, text or dream formation. Recent critical developments have issued from discoveries about the mechanism of broken or dismembered signification and have explored the domain of psychological as well as textual secrets.

Early French psychoanalytic criticism followed Freud's dictum: apply the growing body of psychoanalytic knowledge to art and literature. In the 1930s and 1940s, Marie Bonaparte, Charles Baudouin and René Laforgue, among others, uncovered psychosexual turmoil, unconscious fantasies and ambivalent oedipal situations in the lives of authors – such as Charles Baudelaire, Victor Hugo, Edgar Allan Poe, etc. – through their work. Thus resulted a type of literary radiography, an X-ray procedure for illuminating the psycho-pathologies supposedly underlying creative genius. Using bits of biographical information, the critic transformed the work of art into a clinical document about the author's assumed neurosis. Creation and neurosis are indeed on the same level as we see critics treating writers as so many patients on the analytical couch. The method used resembles a word-for-word translation; the manifest subject matter of the text is converted into a latent content, the latter being proposed as the unconscious equivalent of the former. Thus Laforgue equates the 'beauty of evil' in Baudelaire's poetry with the writer's unconscious pull towards his own demise. Marie Bonaparte sees Poe's dead mother behind Lady Usher and other female characters given to death. Even though reservations quickly emerged from philosophical and artistic quarters as to the cogency of applying clinical psychoanalysis to literature – in a dubious attempt to provide psychiatric accounts of writers – a significant portion of postwar criticism in France only partially escaped this bias. For example, Jean Delay, Serge Doubrovsky, Jean Laplanche, Jean-Paul Sartre, etc. continued to emphasize psycho-biographical objectives even as they sought to address ever so gingerly aesthetic, poetic and narrative features in a more inclusive approach.

Over a long career, reaching from the 1930s to the 1960s, Charles Mauron developed a characteristic method of analysis, thematic psychocriticism. He uses the Freudian principle of free association and searches for latent networks of involuntary ideas that permeate a multiplicity of texts by the same author. Mauron obtains overlapping associative clusters that have little to do with a text's apparent subject matter but are helpful in revealing latent knots of recurring signification. For example, Stéphane Mallarmé's disparate yet frequent use of 'cradle,' 'musicienne' (female musician), 'pénultième' (the feminine form of the adjective 'penultimate') throws femininity into relief as an unconscious figure or obsessive fantasy modulating throughout the poet's work. According to Mauron, the 'obsessive themes' are steps along the path of 'unconscious self-examination' or involuntary attempts at self-analysis. Mauron views the involuntary and/or unconscious forms of self-exploration in literature as the very motor of the creative process. For this reason, his criticism made strides towards combining classical psychological studies of individual writers with textual and to some extent formal analysis. In the 1960s and 1970s, other critics such as René Girard, André Green, Max Milner and Marthe Robert (in part inspired by Mauron) have examined the latent influence of leading psychoanalytic themes – the Oedipus complex, fantasies of omnipotence, castration anxiety, the uncanny, etc. – in the emergence of specific literary genres, for example tragedy, the fantastic novella in romantic literature, and the novel.

The most innovative theorists have studied the material construction of literary discourse, the circulation of signification and the mechanism of fractured, dismembered or secreted meaning. Jacques Lacan in the mid-1950s and Nicolas Abraham in the early 1960s initiated these trends. The two theorists' approaches are convergent in some respects and widely divergent in others. The common feature of their renewal of psychoanalytic criticism on an international scale derives from their keen attention to the workings of language. However, while Lacan studied the vicissitudes of subverted meaning, Abraham sought to elaborate means whereby signification can be reinstated despite its collapse.

In his 'Seminar on *The Purloined Letter*', Lacan outlines a logical structure of the unconscious in Poe's tale of the theft by the Minister and the recovery by the detective

Dupin of a compromising letter originally received and read in a public place by the Queen. According to Lacan, the letter – actually the material, written, phonic quality of language or the signifier as such and *not* meaning – stages the dynamics of desire in general. Merely circulating from hand to hand, the letter represents the characters' (and also all humans') inability to master, to fix the object of desire or meaning. Constantly travelling and thus missing from the place where it is supposed to be at any given time, the letter assumes for the characters a delusional or imaginary power of mastery that is yet inexorably undermined by the letter's very displacement of or, formulated otherwise, by the unstoppable flight of signification itself.

Lacan also reignited interest in Freud's research into the unconscious rhetoric of dreams, emphasizing the role of metaphor, metonymy, ellipsis, condensations, semantic displacements, metasemias and the overdetermination and/or juxtaposition of composite verbal elements. Under Lacan's influence a wealth of literary and cinema criticism has developed. Critics have examined the seductive, oblique, elusive, devious and/or ostentatious and flashy course of meaning(s). Roland Barthes, Shoshana Felman, Julia Kristeva and Octave Mannoni have made original contributions to the general field of Lacanian literary criticism – at times combining it with allied approaches such as deconstruction, feminism and semiotics or with more distant disciplines such as marxism. Content and meaning are strictly de-emphasized in favour of the free, even arbitrary, play of signification. Of interest are the verbal or imagistic relations that obtain between truth and error, between manifestation and latency, since, according to Lacan, the unconscious itself is structured like language. This tenet implies that repressed or unconscious desires are transmuted into a passion for the signifier, i.e. into a potentially continuous series of displacements or substitutions along verbal chains that admit of neither a definite starting or end point.

Lacan views meaning as inherently elusive (or barred) because of the structure he confers on desire. More precisely, he equates desire with the structure of language or language with the structure of desire. On account of a putatively constitutive lack (the impossibility to possess or to be the 'phallus'), desire and language function as moving supports or as sheer instruments of purveyance for the unattainable and repressed object. Just as desire never finds more than vicarious satisfaction, language too provides only movement or a procession of (empty) signifiers. In sum, Lacanian and related forms of criticism study the shifting effects of the unconscious, the destabilizing play of language and desire, as opposed to the stability of meaning, associated with the mirage of consciousness, the illusions of power or, in Lacanian terminology, the imaginary. Not surprisingly, the privileged themes or figures of Lacanian criticism are absence, blanks, movement, flight, lack, void, death, etc. These figures serve to point out the deceits of plenitude and display the tricks of the text, played upon unsuspecting and wishful subjects, be they characters, readers or writers.

In 1962 Nicolas Abraham proposed a psychoanalytic approach to the formal aspects of literature in an essay on 'Time, Rhythm, and the Unconscious'. He analysed rhythm as an alternating game of expectations, surprises, fulfilments and disappointments, showing how and why rhythmic incidents constantly enter into or break from patterns. The creation and undoing of temporal patterns correspond to various emotional happenings, such as a narrow escape, an abrupt awakening, a nightmare, the hallucinogenic lulling of a daydream or the creeping imposition of an inexorable reality, etc. On this level of analysis Abraham deliberately disregards semantic content, viewing poems very nearly as musical pieces. He later examines the shifts of rhythmic patterning in relation to the subject matter of the poem at hand. The harmonies and especially the disharmonies between the two realms yield up the unconscious dimension of the text. Though chiefly concerned with poetry, Abraham clearly suggests that studying the dynamic layering, interplay, clashing and/or meshing of expected and unexpected (semantic, prosodic, stylistic, narrative, etc.) features can illuminate all forms of literature.

Abraham introduced the idea of the textual unconscious alongside the contention that each text is strictly speaking a symptom of itself only. In so doing, he outlines several interpretative principles. Literary texts stage fictive conflicts to which they bring solutions or with respect to which they indicate why resolutions are precluded. Literary works give no insight into the psychology of their real authors; instead texts posit a fictive entity (called the 'induced author') as the agent of their creation. Not unlike humans, each and every text is unique: the conflicts, resolutions or impossibilities the text symbolizes are nowhere else to be found. The insistence on singularity places Abraham and his frequent collaborator Maria Torok at odds with the generalizing tendencies of Freudian and some post-Freudian theory; they eschew universal structures, such as the Oedipus complex, castration anxiety, the death drive, etc., viewing them as so many symptomatic modes of expressing as yet undiscovered or undisclosed individual conflicts and traumas.

Given this stance, Abraham and Torok, and later Rand and Torok, have reconsidered the validity of Freud's analyses of literature. Most notably in 'The Phantom of Hamlet or the Sixth Act', Abraham has questioned the Freudian explanation of Prince Hamlet's behaviour (his delay in avenging his father's murder) in terms of his allegedly unresolved Oedipus complex and his unconscious approval of his father's assassin. Abraham claims that the Oedipus complex removes the play's specificity. Hamlet's indecision is the result of events that are literally beyond the Prince's reach because they happened to someone else. Conflicts or a repressed wish of his own do not beset Hamlet; he is unwittingly tormented by the shameful and secret crime of murder his father took to the grave. Interpreting Hamlet's contradictory actions in terms of the haunting influence of someone else's secrets, Abraham places cross-generational group psychology and the disturbing effect of concealed historical events in the forefront of psychoanalysis.

In their work on personal, familial and historical secrets, Abraham and Torok posit the existence of verbal mechanisms whose objective seems to be to disarray, even to destroy the expressive or representational power of language. Appearing under various names (de-signification, anti-metaphor, anti-semantics, cryptonymy, etc.), this psychic aphasia leads to obstructions that prevent linguistic entities from being joined with their potential sources of signification. Abraham and Torok's characteristic method aims at overcoming the resistance to meaning by converting obstacles into guides to understanding. Their theory of readability thus takes full account of the disintegration of meaning, yet only as a preliminary stage in the attempt to recover new forms of coherence even when the very possibility of coherence would appear to be denied.

Nicholas T. Rand

Further reading and works cited

Abraham, N. 'Time, Rhythm, and the Unconscious'. *Rhythms*. Stanford, CA, 1995.
— and Torok, M. *The Shell and the Kernel*, ed. T. Rand. Chicago, 1994.
— and Torok, M. *The Wolf Man's Magic Word*. Minneapolis, MN, 1986.

Anzieu, D. *Le Corps de l'oeuvre*. Paris, 1981.

Barthes, R. *S/Z*. London, 1975.

Baudouin, C. *Psychanalyse de Victor Hugo*. Paris, 1943.

Bellemin-Noël, J. *Vers l'inconscient du texte*. Paris, 1979.

—. *Interlignes: Essais de textanalyse*. Lille, 1988.

Bonaparte, M. *Edgar Poe, Etude psychanalytique*. Paris, 1953.

Bowie, M. *Lacan*. Cambridge, 1991.

Delay, J. *La Jeunesse de Gide*. Paris, 1956/57.

Doubrovsky, S. *La Place de la Madeleine*. Paris, 1974.

—. *Speech and Language in Psychoanalysis*. New York. 1984.

Felman, S. *Writing and Madness*. Ithaca, NY, 1985.

Girard, R. *Mensonge romantique et vérité romanesque*. Paris, 1969.

Green, A. *Un oeil en trop*. Paris, 1979.

Kristeva, J. *Powers of Horror*. New York, 1982.

—. *Sens et non-sens de la révolte*. Paris, 1996.

Lacan, J. 'Seminar on *The Purloined Letter*', *Yale French Studies*, 48, 1972.

Laforgue, R. *L'Echec de Baudelaire*. Geneva, 1964.

Laplanche, J. *Hölderlin et la question du père*. Paris, 1961.

Mannoni, O. *Clefs pour l'imaginaire*. Paris, 1969.

Mauron, C. *Des métaphores obsédantes au mythe personnel*. Paris, 1963.

Milner, M. *On est prié de fermer les yeux*. Paris, 1991.

Rand, N. 'Family Romance or Family History? Psychoanalysis and Dramatic Invention in Nicolas Abraham's *The Phantom of Hamlet*', *diacritics*, 18, 4, Winter 1988.

—. '*The Sandman* Looks at *The Uncanny*', *Speculations After Freud*, eds S. Shamdasani and M. Münchow. London, 1994.

— and Torok, M. *Questions for Freud*. Cambridge, MA, 1997.

Rashkin, E. 'Tools for a New Psychoanalytic Literary Criticism: The Work of Abraham and Torok', *diacritics*, 18, 4, Winter 1988.

Robert, M. *Roman des origines, origines du roman*. Paris, 1972.

Sartre, J.-P. *L'Idiot de la famille*. Paris, 1970/72.

Contributors

Warren Montag, Occidental College
Jacques Lezra, University of Wisconsin-Madison
Véronique M. Fóti, Pennsylvania State University
Robert C. Holub, University of California, Berkeley
Elizabeth Constable, University of California, Davis
Juliet Flower MacCannell, University of California, Irvine
Kenneth Womack, Pennsylvania State University, Altoona
Claire Colebrook, University of Edinburgh
Ullrich Michael Haase, Manchester Metropolitan University
Alison Ross, Monash University
Amir Ahmadi, University of Sydney
Jan Baetens, Katholieke universiteit, Leuven
Mitchell R. Lewis, Oklahoma University
William Flesch, Brandeis University
Stephen Shapiro, University of Warwick
Jeremy Tambling, Hong Kong University
Luke Ferretter, Wolfson College, Cambridge
Kenneth Surin, Duke University
R. Brandon Kershner, University of Florida
Arkady Plotnitsky, Purdue University
Loren Kruger, University of Chicago
Jean-Michel Rabaté, University of Pennsylvania
Mark Currie, Anglia Polytechnic University
Kevin Hart, University of Notre Dame
Karen Green, Monash University
Boris Wiseman, Durham University
Alain-Michel Rocheleau, University of British Columbia
Martin McQuillan, Leeds University
Nick Mansfield, University of Melbourne
Dirk de Geest, Katholieke universiteit, Leuven
Jeremy Lane, University of Sussex
Garry Leonard, University of Toronto
Brian Niro, De Paul University
John Brannigan, University College, Dublin

Ewa Ziarek, Notre Dame University
Marcia Butzel, Clark University
Lynn A. Higgins, Dartmouth College
SunHee Kim Gertz, Clark University
David Punter, Bristol University
Heesok Chang, Vassar College
Joan Brandt, Claremont Colleges
Michael Walsh, University of Hartford
Maureen Turim, University of Florida
Nicole Fluhr, University of Michigan
Nicholas T. Rand, University of Wisconsin-Madison

Index